QUEEN
VICTORIA

QUEEN VICTORIA

A Portrait

Giles St. Aubyn

ATHENEUM

NEW YORK 1992

Maxwell Macmillan International
New York Oxford Singapore Sydney

Copyright © 1991 by Giles St. Aubyn
First American edition 1992

Atheneum
Macmillan Publishing Company
866 Third Avenue
New York, NY 10022

Macmillan Publishing Company is part of the Maxwell
Communication Group of Companies.

Library of Congress Cataloging-in-Publication Data

Aubyn, Giles St.
    Queen Victoria : a personal portrait / Giles St. Aubyn.
        p.   cm.
    Includes bibliographical references and index.
    ISBN 0-689-12141-5
    1. Victoria, Queen of Great Britain, 1819–1901.   2.
Great Britain—History—Victoria, 1837–1901.   3. Great
Britain—Kings and rulers—Biography.   I. Title.
DA554.A918   1991   91-29123   CIP
941.081'092—dc20
[B]

Macmillan books are available at special discounts for bulk
purchases for sales promotions, premiums, fund-raising,
or educational use. For details, contact:

Special Sales Director
Macmillan Publishing Company
866 Third Avenue
New York, NY 10022

10 9 8 7 6 5 4 3 2 1

Printed in the United States of America

This Portrait
of the
Most famous of Queen Regnants
is dedicated to
Sir Martin Gilliat,
for thirty-five years Private Secretary
to H.M. Queen Elizabeth, The Queen Mother,
the greatest of Queen Consorts.

Contents

Preface

I T HAS long been my ambition to write about Queen Victoria. My interest began some thirty years ago while I was working on a book about *The Royal George*, her first cousin, the Duke of Cambridge. The more I became immersed in the Royal Archives the more I began to realise that the Queen was far more fascinating than the subject of my research. Some fifteen years later my curiosity was rekindled when I wrote a life of her son: *Edward VII Prince and King*. For some time, however, I hesitated to tackle the Queen: partly deterred by the immensity of the task, and partly disheartened by the strength of the competition. My first instinct was to focus attention on the Queen as an author, or her religious views, or her relationships with her children. In the end, however, I was persuaded by my publisher to contemplate a full blown life, encompassing the topics to which I had first been drawn. The past five years have served to confirm how right I was to be awed by the magnitude of the task, but they have also convinced me that Greville was right when he spoke of the Queen as possessing "the most interesting mind and character in the world".

Any serious effort to study Queen Victoria can hardly avoid a genealogical mare's-nest: hence the tables provided below (pages xi to xvii). The problem is not made easier by the tendency of the royal family to christen their children Albert, Frederick and Ernest. There are at least eight "Victorias" mentioned in the text. The family solved the problem of distinguishing between them by using nicknames. The Princess Royal became "Vicky" and her second daughter "Moretta". Readers who find themselves lost in a maze of diminutives are referred to the index for rescue. Equally, should they lose their chronological bearings, it may help them to turn to page 611 for help. Seeing that a massive bibliography would have required a second volume, I have had to be content with a list of books actually cited (see 633) and a guide to further reading. (see 623)

I am deeply indebted to Her Majesty the Queen for graciously permitting me to republish material subject to copyright, and for allowing me to reproduce pictures and photographs in the Royal Collection.

This book would never have been written without Christopher Sinclair-Stevenson, whose idea it was, and whose generous encouragement saved me from despair. It is becoming increasingly rare to find publishers who not only value books but see their authors as friends. I am also exceedingly grateful to Richard Ollard. Not only has he saved me from several foolish blunders, but has helped with constructive criticism. He is not, of course, responsible for such errors as remain, or for my failure to make the most of his advice. I am also indebted to Michael Mellish for wading through the manuscript and pointing out a number of infelicities. Elizabeth Murray has smoothed my path by prompt and effective research, as has Susan Rose-Smith in her work on the book's illustrations. I have also been fortunate in having the index prepared by Douglas Matthews, and I feel spoiled to have had so expert a team to see the book through the press. Finally I would like to pay a special tribute to Belinda Allies, who has somehow contrived to turn illegible drafts into faultless typescripts. Her cheerful efficiency, and willingness to work when most of the world is asleep, has helped to deprive authorship of many of its cares.

Cornwall Lodge,   Giles St Aubyn
Cambridge Park,   1991
St Peter Port,
Guernsey.

Table i

Queen Victoria's Maternal Relations
(simplified)

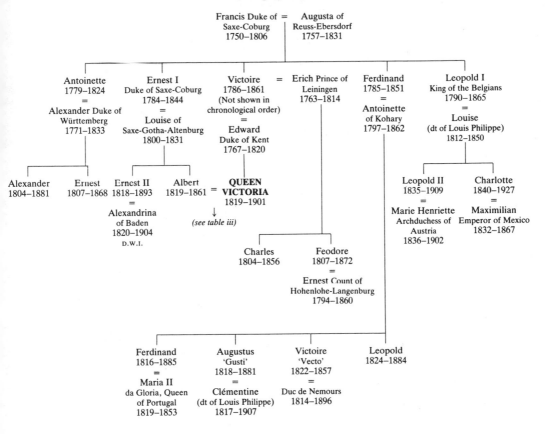

Francis Duke of = Augusta of
Saxe-Coburg | Reuss-Ebersdorf
1750–1806 | 1757–1831

Antoinette
1779–1824
=
Alexander Duke of
Württemberg
1771–1833

Ernest I
Duke of Saxe-Coburg
1784–1844
=
Louise of
Saxe-Gotha-Altenburg
1800–1831

Victoire =
1786–1861
(Not shown in
chronological order)
=
Edward
Duke of Kent
1767–1820

Erich Prince of
Leiningen
1763–1814

Ferdinand
1785–1851
=
Antoinette
of Kohary
1797–1862

Leopold I
King of the Belgians
1790–1865
=
Louise
(dt of Louis Philippe)
1812–1850

Alexander
1804–1881

Ernest
1807–1868

Ernest II
1818–1893
=
Alexandrina
of Baden
1820–1904
D.W.I.

Albert
1819–1861

QUEEN
VICTORIA
1819–1901
↓
(see table iii)

Charles
1804–1856

Feodore
1807–1872
=
Ernest Count of
Hohenlohe-Langenburg
1794–1860

Leopold II
1835–1909
=
Marie Henriette
Archduchess of
Austria
1836–1902

Charlotte
1840–1927
=
Maximilian
Emperor of Mexico
1832–1867

Ferdinand
1816–1885
=
Maria II
da Gloria, Queen
of Portugal
1819–1853

Augustus
'Gusti'
1818–1881
=
Clémentine
(dt of Louis Philippe)
1817–1907

Victoire
'Vecto'
1822–1857
=
Duc de Nemours
1814–1896

Leopold
1824–1884

KEY
dt = daughter
D.W.I. = Died without issue

Table ii

Queen Victoria's Paternal Relations
(simplified)

George III = Charlotte
1738–1820 of Mecklenburg-Strelitz
1744–1818

George IV	William IV	Edward	Ernest	Adolphus	Mary	Sophia
1762–1830	1765–1837	Duke of Kent	Duke of Cumberland	Duke of	1776–1857	1777–1848
=	=	1767–1820	King of Hanover	Cambridge	=	
Caroline of	Adelaide of	=	1771–1851	1774–1850	William	
Brunswick	Saxe-Meiningen	Victoire of	=	=	Duke of Gloucester	
1768–1821	1792–1849	Saxe-Coburg	Frederica of	Augusta of	1776–1834	
	D.W.I.	1786–1861	Mecklenburg-Strelitz	Hesse-Cassel	D.W.I.	
		(see table i)	1778–1841	1797–1889		

Charlotte		QUEEN	George V	George	Augusta	Mary Adelaide
1796–1817		VICTORIA	King of Hanover	Duke of	1822–1916	1833–1897
=		1819–1901	1819–1878	Cambridge	=	=
Leopold of		=	=	1819–1904	Frederick Duke of	Francis Duke of
Saxe-Coburg		Albert Prince of	Mary of		Mecklenburg-Strelitz	Teck
1790–1865		Saxe-Coburg	Saxe-Altenburg		1819–1904	1837–1900
(see table i)		1819–1861	1818–1907		↓	↓
		(see table i)	↓			
		↓				
		(see table iii)				Mary
						1867–1953
						=
						George V
						1865–1936
						(see table iii)

Queen Victoria's Children
And Grandchildren
(simplified)

*Female haemophilia carriers †Male haemophiliac

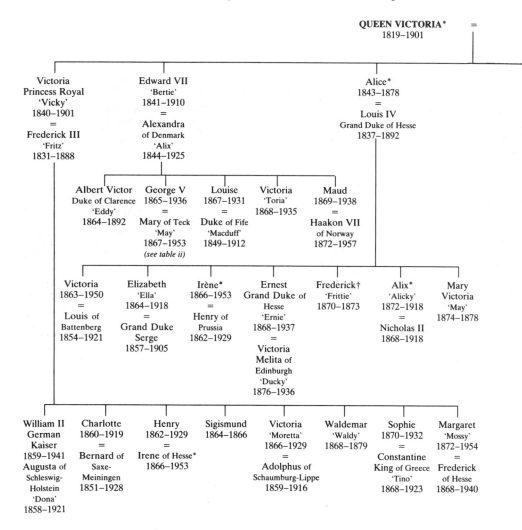

Table iii

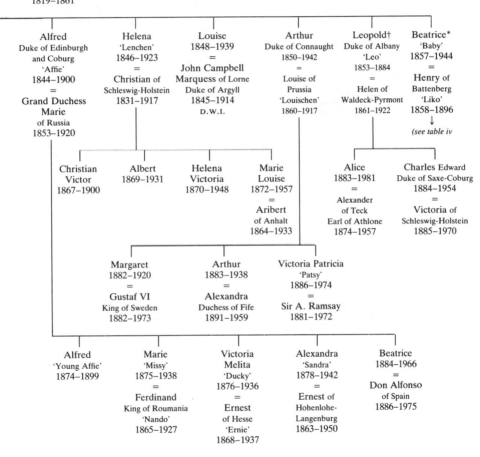

Prince Albert
of Saxe-Coburg
1819–1861

Alfred
Duke of Edinburgh
and Coburg
'Affie'
1844–1900
=
Grand Duchess
Marie
of Russia
1853–1920

Helena
'Lenchen'
1846–1923
=
Christian of
Schleswig-Holstein
1831–1917

Louise
1848–1939
=
John Campbell
Marquess of Lorne
Duke of Argyll
1845–1914
D.W.I.

Arthur
Duke of Connaught
1850–1942
=
Louise of
Prussia
'Louischen'
1860–1917

Leopold†
Duke of Albany
'Leo'
1853–1884
=
Helen of
Waldeck-Pyrmont
1861–1922

Beatrice*
'Baby'
1857–1944
=
Henry of
Battenberg
'Liko'
1858–1896
↓
(see table iv

Christian
Victor
1867–1900

Albert
1869–1931

Helena
Victoria
1870–1948

Marie
Louise
1872–1957
=
Aribert
of Anhalt
1864–1933

Alice
1883–1981
=
Alexander
of Teck
Earl of Athlone
1874–1957

Charles Edward
Duke of Saxe-Coburg
1884–1954
=
Victoria of
Schleswig-Holstein
1885–1970

Margaret
1882–1920
=
Gustaf VI
King of Sweden
1882–1973

Arthur
1883–1938
=
Alexandra
Duchess of Fife
1891–1959

Victoria Patricia
'Patsy'
1886–1974
=
Sir A. Ramsay
1881–1972

Alfred
'Young Affie'
1874–1899

Marie
'Missy'
1875–1938
=
Ferdinand
King of Roumania
'Nando'
1865–1927

Victoria
Melita
'Ducky'
1876–1936
=
Ernest
of Hesse
'Ernie'
1868–1937

Alexandra
'Sandra'
1878–1942
=
Ernest of
Hohenlohe-
Langenburg
1863–1950

Beatrice
1884–1966
=
Don Alfonso
of Spain
1886–1975

Table iv

The Hesse And Battenberg (Mountbatten) Family
(simplified)

*Female haemophilia carrier. †Male haemophiliac

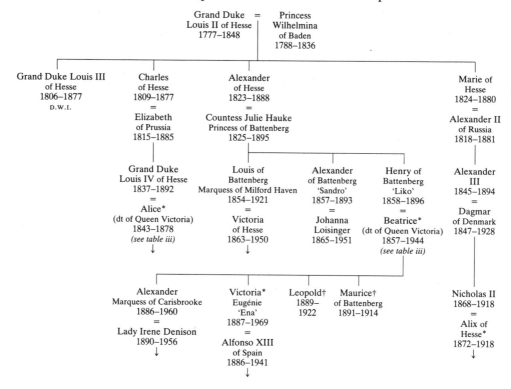

Grand Duke = Princess
Louis II of Hesse | Wilhelmina
1777–1848 | of Baden
1788–1836

Grand Duke Louis III
of Hesse
1806–1877
D.W.I.

Charles
of Hesse
1809–1877
=
Elizabeth
of Prussia
1815–1885

Alexander
of Hesse
1823–1888
=
Countess Julie Hauke
Princess of Battenberg
1825–1895

Marie of
Hesse
1824–1880
=
Alexander II
of Russia
1818–1881

Grand Duke
Louis IV of Hesse
1837–1892
=
Alice*
(dt of Queen Victoria)
1843–1878
(see table iii)
↓

Louis of
Battenberg
Marquess of Milford Haven
1854–1921
=
Victoria
of Hesse
1863–1950
↓

Alexander
of Battenberg
'Sandro'
1857–1893
=
Johanna
Loisinger
1865–1951

Henry of
Battenberg
'Liko'
1858–1896
=
Beatrice*
(dt of Queen Victoria)
1857–1944
(see table iii)

Alexander
III
1845–1894
=
Dagmar
of Denmark
1847–1928

Alexander
Marquess of Carisbrooke
1886–1960
=
Lady Irene Denison
1890–1956
↓

Victoria*
Eugénie
'Ena'
1887–1969
=
Alfonso XIII
of Spain
1886–1941
↓

Leopold†
1889–
1922

Maurice†
of Battenberg
1891–1914

Nicholas II
1868–1918
=
Alix of
Hesse*
1872–1918
↓

Illustration Acknowledgements

Dickins: 32a; Reproduced by gracious permission of Her Majesty The Queen: 2b, 3a, 3b, 4a, 4b, 4c, 5a, 5b, 5c, 6b, 7a, 9a, 10a, 10b, 11a, 11b, 12b, 12c, 12d, 13a, 14c, 14d, 15a, 15b, 16a, 16b, 17a, 17b, 17c, 17d, 18a, 18b, 18c, 18d, 19a, 21a, 22a, 23a, 24, 25b, 26, 28b, 29b, 31a; The Hulton-Deutsch Collection: 1a, 1b, 6a, 14a, 14b, 28a, 29a; Illustrated London News: 21b; Museum of London: 9b, 27a, 27b; National Portrait Gallery: 2a, 7b, 8a, 8b, 12a, 20a, 20b, 20c, 22b, 23b, 25a, 30b; Popperfoto: 13b, 20d, 30a; Eddie Ryle-Hodges: 32b; Topham: 31b, 32c; Wolverhampton Public Libraries: 19b. Special thanks are due to Frances Dimond for her help.

1

"Heiress Presumptive"
1819–1837

WHEN Queen Victoria ascended the throne in 1837 she was an unknown schoolgirl of eighteen: when she died in 1901 she was the most famous person on earth. Yet surprisingly few of those who mourned her passing knew what she was like. The copy-book Sovereign of pious propaganda bore little resemblance to the endearing but flawed mortal who governed half the world. Indeed her true likeness has been as much distorted by idolatry as by malice. This book attempts to portray the Queen as she actually was, not as icons and caricatures have depicted her.

If Princess Victoria had been the child of obscure parents, her forceful and intriguing character would have left its mark on those who came across her. But what made her unique was the fact that she was Queen. Almost everything she did, thought, or said, proceeded from her sense of royal vocation. Indeed she was only brought into the world because her father, the Duke of Kent, deemed it his duty to ensure the survival of the House of Hanover which in 1817 appeared to be threatened with extinction. The Princess's birth was the happy outcome of the panic which ensued.

George III has been lavishly abused for a catalogue of short-comings, but nobody has seen fit to reproach him for mismanaging the succession. No other British Sovereign ever produced so many potential heirs. In 1817 he had twelve surviving children: seven sons and five daughters, the youngest of whom was forty. He was credited, moreover, with fifty-seven grandchildren: fifty-six of them bastards, and the Prince of Wales's daughter, Princess Charlotte. Unhappily the Princess died that November, after forty-eight hours' labour during which she gave birth to a stillborn son. The calamity was attributed to Sir Richard Croft's treatment, a responsibility he acknowledged by blowing out his brains. French doctors, it was said, left their patients to die while English doctors killed them.

The death of Princess Charlotte persuaded her uncles to look around for brides, particularly as their eldest brother, George, Prince of Wales, who since 1811 had been acting as Prince Regent, was evidently more anxious to divorce his wife, Caroline, than to venture once more on the hazards of matrimony. Most eager of all in his search for a bride was Edward, Duke of Kent, the King's fourth son, who seemed to believe that Providence had decreed that he should preserve the dynasty.

The Duke of Kent is a somewhat shadowy figure, possibly because there were some in high places who thought it best to forget him. He was born in 1767 and brought up with his brothers and sisters at Kew. Neither his mother nor father showed him much affection and his childhood was harsh and cheerless. Early in life he plunged into debt: determined to live like a King's son without possessing the means to do so. It never occurred to him that his misfortune owed more to his own grotesque extravagance than to the King's meanness, the parsimony of Parliament, or the malignity of fate.

The Duke spent much of his early life in the army where he soon became known as a merciless martinet. He had no misgivings about sentencing a man to a hundred lashes for leaving a button undone. In 1803 his military career was brought to an end when he was recalled home from Gibraltar. It is true that he had been sent there to restore the lax discipline of the garrison, but not with such "bestial severity" as to provoke a mutiny. Wherever he went, he antagonised those under him by his disproportionate emphasis on the minutiae of his profession. His only redeeming feature as a soldier was unflinching courage on the battlefield.

The Duke appears to have been more amiable off the parade ground. Princess Charlotte regarded him as her "favourite and beloved uncle". Apart from the Prince Regent, he was the most intelligent member of the family. He was a voluble conversationalist, a gifted mimic, and an eloquent speaker. Unlike his brothers, his private life was austere. He got up early in the morning, ate sparingly, detested drunkenness, and disapproved of gambling. According to Bishop Fisher, his former tutor, nothing would induce him to tell a lie. On one occasion, when Edward was still a boy, a clock which his father cherished was found shattered on the floor. The King was furious and ordered an immediate investigation. When the Prince was asked whether he could throw any light on the mystery, he calmly replied "I did it", adding for good measure that he had broken it "on purpose".

Like most of George III's sons the Duke rejoiced in supporting His Majesty's Opposition. Almost all his political associates were either Whigs or Radicals, and included Robert Owen. Cynics alleged that he looked to them for support in his attempts to persuade the Government to pay his debts: a view of the matter to which he lent some credence by borrowing money from the "Father of Socialism". His religion was even more advanced than his politics, and from time to time he went so far as to attend dissenting services. The Archbishop of Canterbury, Manners Sutton, was so distressed that he ventured to remind him of the precept: "He that is not with us is against us". History repeated itself during Queen Victoria's reign, for successive Archbishops were dismayed by her fondness for the Kirk, and regarded her fidelity to Anglicanism with grave suspicion. The Duke agreed with Wilberforce that Christianity must be "practical", and accordingly lent his name to over fifty charities, such as "The Literary Fund for Distressed Authors", "The Bible Society" and the Westminster Infirmary. He was an energetic patron of the societies he espoused, eagerly presiding over meetings, chairing committees, making admirable after-dinner speeches, and donating his creditors' money to worthy causes. So tireless was he in promoting "every object of benevolence" that he was given the Freedom of the City of London in 1816. But not everyone was impressed by his liberality. When Princess Lieven, the Russian Ambassador's wife, learned of his death, she told her lover, Metternich, "No-one in England will mourn the Duke. He was false, hard and greedy. His so-called good qualities were only for show". It would be easier to dismiss this callous obituary as mere pique were it not for the corroboratory testimony of Edward's own sisters who called him "Joseph Surface", after the arch-hypocrite in Sheridan's *School for Scandal*.

By 1816 the Duke's financial problems had become so pressing that he decided to put the English Channel between himself and his creditors. The Duke's exile was less wretched than it might otherwise have been because he shared it with Madame Julie de St Laurent, whom he met in 1790 during the early days of the French Revolution.

Their ensuing liaison surpassed many marriages in constancy and affection. Wherever the Duke went, "Edward's French Lady" followed. She was an ideal soldier's "wife", pretty, vivacious, and trustworthy. Not least of her talents was her ability to provide the Duke with the comforts of home life in unpropitious surroundings. Had her father been a Prince rather than a civil engineer from Franche-Comté, she might well have become the Duchess of Kent. Inevitably, the Duke's liaison was frowned upon by the Court of Queen Victoria, but at least he was loyal to Julie for over a quarter of a century, and his ménage achieved a sedateness which verged on respectability.

When news of the death of Princess Charlotte reached the Duke, he was deeply disturbed by it, and Madame de St Laurent swooned on reading an ill-judged paragraph in the "Morning Chronicle" which spoke of the Prince's duty to marry. So troubled was he, that he decided to confide in his old friend Thomas Creevey. He might just as well have unburdened himself to the Town Crier. Creevey was so astonished by H.R.H.'s candour that he made a careful note of the conversation. The Duke declared that his niece's death made it necessary for him to marry, "if the crown was to be kept in the family". God only knows, he said, "the sacrifice it will be. . . . It is now seven-and-twenty years that Madame St Laurent and I have lived together. We are of the same age, and have been in all climates and all difficulties together; and you may well imagine, Mr Creevey, the pang it will occasion me to part with her." Nevertheless the Duke proclaimed himself willing to sacrifice his happiness for the sake of his country, provided, of course, the necessary funds were forthcoming. It was clear from the precision of the details which followed that he had given the matter much thought. He maintained that the Duke of York's Marriage Settlement of twenty-five thousand pounds a year was an appropriate precedent for his own annuity. Furthermore, he expected the Government to discharge his debts, especially considering what the nation owed him. Finally, after his long and intimate association with Madame St Laurent, he insisted that she should be provided with servants and a carriage.

The Duke, as events were to show, mistook the public mood. When the Government put forward proposals to increase the Civil List, the House of Commons rejected its recommendations. The Duke of Wellington was not in the least surprised by this seemingly churlish vote. "The Princes are the damnedest mill-stone about the necks of any Government that can be imagined. They have insulted, *personally* insulted – two-thirds of the gentlemen of England, and how can it be wondered at that they take their revenge upon them when they get them in the House of Commons?" Eventually the Royal Dukes were grudgingly voted an extra six thousand pounds a year: a totally inadequate sum to redeem the Duke of Kent's finances. It was like trying to revive a starving whale by offering it a sprat.

The Duke's list of possible brides was a short one, given the necessity of confining it to Protestant Princesses. Strangely enough it was his niece, Charlotte, who drew his attention to the lady he eventually married: Victoire, Dowager Princess of Leiningen, the youngest daughter of Francis, Duke of Saxe-Coburg. In 1814 Charlotte had fallen in love with Victoire's handsome brother, Leopold, but the Prince Regent refused to consider the match, believing Coburg to be an insignificant German Duchy, and Leopold an impoverished adventurer. Charlotte, who was kept a virtual prisoner, persuaded the Duke of Kent to act as a private post office. Long afterwards, Leopold told Queen Victoria that her "poor father" had been the "chief promoter" of his marriage. "Our correspondence from 1814 to 1816 was entirely carried on through his kind intervention." At length, in 1816, the Prince Regent grudgingly consented to accept Leopold as his son-in-law. During the wedding, Charlotte, who had a mischievous sense of humour, laughed aloud when her husband endowed her with "all his worldly goods".

Leopold's marriage was only the first of a series of judicious alliances which soon gave Coburg an importance altogether disproportionate to its size, and led Bismarck to describe it as the "stud farm of Europe". If Prussia's main industry was war, Coburg's was matrimony. It was no accident that the "Almanach de Gotha" was published in "the domain of a family with so strong and conscious a feeling for the dynastic". The second Anglo-Coburg match was partly of Charlotte's making. Anxious to repay the Duke of Kent's kindness in promoting her own happiness, she persuaded him that her widowed sister-in-law would make him an ideal wife. Thus encouraged, the Duke set out for Amorbach, in the autumn of 1816, to make the Princess's acquaintance.

When the Duke first met Victoire, she was only thirty, and although too plump to be considered beautiful, she had lively brown eyes, a fresh complexion, and knew how to dress to advantage.

Brought up a strict Lutheran, she retained her childhood faith to the end of her days. One thing her religion taught her was the transcendent value of truth. Napoleon once considered her as a possible successor to Josephine before she married Prince Emich Charles of Leiningen. At the time, she was barely seventeen, and he was a crusty widower of forty. The Leiningens lost their hereditary possessions in the early days of the French Wars, but were compensated by being given the Principality of Amorbach, south of Frankfurt-on-Main, which was little more than a sleepy village with a dilapidated palace on its outskirts. Prince Emich possessed an uncertain temper, aggravated by gout, and spent much of his time brooding over the wrongs his family had suffered. The only redeeming feature of Victoire's ill-starred marriage was her son, Charles, born in 1804, and her daughter, Feodore, born in 1807. In 1814, soon after Napoleon was sent to Elba, her husband died, and Victoire became Regent. Like all Coburgs, she possessed a strong sense of loyalty to her family and was ruthless in safe-guarding the interests of her children. For most of her life she had to battle against adversity and the struggle left its scars. If she was sometimes awkward or intransigent, she mellowed as she grew older. Her devoted Lady-in-Waiting, Lady Augusta Bruce, described her in old age as "so pure, so good, so childlike, so wise, so unselfish".

The Duke's visit to Amorbach lasted only two days, but he came away convinced that there was no more graceful or sympathetic Princess in Germany. Without further ado, he sent Victoire a rambling letter proposing marriage. He told her that he had been so enraptured by her charms that nothing would give him greater happiness than to make her his wife. Not surprisingly, after so brief an encounter, his offer was declined, but he was delighted to learn from Prince Leopold that he had made an agreeable impression. Refusing to regard his rejection as anything more than a customary hazard of courtship, he laid siege to the Princess, who finally succumbed. Certainly her sister-in-law's death gave added dynastic importance to marrying the Duke. But it is easy to understand why she hesitated so long. Her first experience of marriage was such as to emphasise its risks, and she was troubled over her son's future in Amorbach. At least as Regent she was the largest fish in a small but inviting pond.

Poor Madame St Laurent choked back her grief and retired with becoming dignity to live with her sister in Paris. Meanwhile, on

May 29th, 1818, Edward and Victoire were married with Lutheran rites in the "Hall of the Giants" at Coburg. The Duke looked magnificent in his Field Marshal's uniform and Victoire glowed with pride as she joined him at the altar. It hardly appeared necessary for her mother, the Dowager Duchess Augusta, to pray that her daughter's second marriage should prove happier than her first. There seemed no cloud on the horizon, particularly as the Duke had managed to borrow £3000 to meet immediate expenses. To make absolutely certain that no question should ever arise over the legitimacy of his union, he was married again on July 13th with Anglican rites. The ceremony took place in the drawing room of Kew Palace. It was especially remarkable for being a double wedding, his brother, the Duke of Clarence, being married at the same time to Princess Adelaide of Saxe Meiningen. As George III was blind and insane he was unable to attend, but Queen Charlotte, mortally ill as she was, insisted upon being present. The service was printed in English, with a German translation opposite for the benefit of the brides. For the first time Victoire gave her name as "Victoria", to make it sound less foreign. After the ceremony, the Kents drove off to Claremont, on the outskirts of Esher, the house where Princess Charlotte had died, and which Leopold now lent them for their honeymoon.

The Duke of Kent was calculating by nature, and it was hardly to be expected that his "arranged" marriage would deepen into love. Yet on New Year's Eve, 1818, he wrote Victoria a charming note, which clearly came from his heart. He would, he told her, have preferred to have written in verse, but being "an old soldier who has not this talent", was forced to resort to prose. She was, he said, his "guardian angel", and he would ever remember the year that was passing as one of blessing and joy. He enclosed a little almanack, describing it as coming "from your very deeply attached husband, for whom you represent all happiness and all consolation". In 1861, soon after the death of the Duchess of Kent, Queen Victoria discovered amongst her mother's possessions some dusty old letters and notebooks, and was taken aback to learn "how very, very much she and my beloved father *loved* each other. *Such* love and affection! I hardly knew it was to *that extent*." It seems that what began as a self-interested intrigue ended in an idyll.

Coutts' loan was soon squandered, and the Duke decided to economise by wintering in Amorbach. His plans for retrenchment suffered something of a setback when he imported an army of workmen to decorate the Palace, modernise the plumbing and enlarge the stables. In November, it became clear that the Duchess was going to have a child. The Duke was almost beside himself with delight, and wrote to the Prince Regent to give him the news, announcing at the same time that he hoped to set out for England early in April "to enable the child to be born at home". He felt sure, he said, that he could rely on his brother's goodness of heart to help him to make the journey. First and foremost he needed "pecuniary assistance", but he also wanted a yacht to convey the Duchess from Calais to Dover, and the loan for some months of the apartment at Kensington Palace formerly used by Princess Caroline, the Prince's estranged wife. Several weeks later, the Duke received an ungracious reply, professing that money was not to be found, and reminding him that the Duchess of Clarence proposed to have her baby in Hanover. If, nevertheless, he persisted in coming, he "must not expect to meet with a cordial reception". The Duke, who seldom took no for an answer, refused to be discouraged, particularly as he had long been convinced that "the Crown will come to me and my children", and hence that his heir should be born on English soil. Joseph Hume, one of his radical associates, told him that it was his duty to the country to bring the Duchess home for her confinement. "The time may come," he argued, "when legitimacy may be challenged, and challenged with effect, from the circumstance of the birth taking place on foreign soil." Early in the New Year, generous well-wishers raised £15,000 to enable the Kents to travel back to England. When the Regent learned that his brother had been "induced" to return, he relented so far as to send the *Royal Sovereign* to Calais, and to consent to the loan of the Kensington Palace apartments; but he made no secret of the fact that he thought it rash to require the Duchess to undertake the journey in the eighth month of her pregnancy.

The Kents set out from Amorbach on March 26th, 1819. The very next day the Duchess of Clarence gave birth to a daughter, who lived just long enough to be christened "Charlotte". There can seldom have been an odder cavalcade, the Duke himself driving the Duchess in a cane phaeton. Apart from the fact that he had instigated the journey, he could not have shown more concern for her comfort. The Princess Feodore, with her governess, Louise Lehzen, followed behind in a landau. Several other carts and carriages made up the procession, carrying the Duchess' obstetrician, Fraulein Siebold, her lady-in-waiting, Baroness de Späth, and assorted courtiers, cooks, servants, trunks and silver. It was just such a convoy as highwaymen dream of meeting. Most days they travelled twenty- five miles, stopping the night at flea-ridden inns. On the evening of April 24th, they were safely ensconced in Kensington Palace. Their apartments had been unoccupied since 1814. In spite of evidence of neglect, for instance the windows let in rain, the Kents were delighted with their new home, temporary as it was. Hardly twenty-four hours had passed before the Duke began ordering new curtains, wallpaper, carpets, chandeliers, looking-glasses and furniture. Carpenters were set to work to construct a library with "book cases in fifty-two parts", and, most important of all, one of the rooms on the north side of the building was transformed into a nursery. Kensington in 1819 was still a rural retreat, with enchanting views over the Park and surrounding fields. The Kents' principal reception rooms opened onto their own private garden. Although London was so close, it seemed a thousand miles away, and nothing more discordant than the chatter of birds and an occasional dog barking disturbed the peace of the Palace.

At 4.15 in the morning of Monday, May 24th, five days before the anniversary of her wedding, the Duchess gave birth to "a pretty little princess as plump as a partridge". Her husband insisted upon remaining at her bedside throughout her labour, while the Duke of Wellington, Archbishop Manners Sutton, and other Privy Councillors, waited in an adjoining room. It was their duty to ensure that the royal child was indeed that of the Duchess and not some supposititious infant smuggled into her bed. That evening the Duke wrote to his mother-in-law, Augusta, Dowager Duchess of Coburg, to tell her that Victoria had given birth to a girl, who was "truly a model of strength and beauty", and that mother and child were doing "marvellously well". The Duke was not in the least disconcerted by having a female heir. "I am decidedly of opinion," he declared, "that the decrees of Providence are at all times wisest and best." The Salic Law did not apply in Britain, although it did in Hanover, and consequently his daughter was legally in line for the crown. "Take care of her," he would say, "for she will one day be Queen of England."

In May, 1819, Princess Victoria was fifth in line of succession. First came her uncle, the Prince Regent, who succeeded George III in 1820. When his wife Caroline died the following year it was thought he might remarry, but his mistress, Lady Conyngham, was careful to ensure that he looked no further than her for consolation. Next in line was the Duke of York who died without issue in 1827. The most serious threat to Victoria's chances came from her uncle William, Duke of Clarence, the third of the seven royal brothers. Before he married, he lived with the actress, Mrs Jordan, and their family of ten FitzClarences augured well for his union with Princess Adelaide. In fact, the Duchess bore him two daughters: Charlotte, who only lived for a few hours, and Elizabeth who was born in December 1820, six weeks premature and "disturbingly small". Three months later she was buried in the Royal vault at Windsor having died of a fit. Poor Adelaide, who adored children, seemed fated to be denied them. As late as 1835 she was thought to be pregnant but the rumour turned out to be false. Until his dying day, William IV denied Victoria the title of "heir apparent". It was, after all, conceivable that even after his death his wife might produce a child and deprive his niece of the crown. So long as William had no heir, the Duke of Kent was fourth in line and Victoria fifth. His three younger brothers, all of whom had married and all of whom had children, were forced to yield precedence to his daughter by the law of primogeniture.

The story goes that in 1879 Queen Victoria's claim to the throne was almost overturned when the Historical Manuscripts Commission discovered an old black box amongst the Duke of Buccleuch's papers at Dalkeith, which was found to contain a contract proving that Charles II had married Lucy Walters. In effect, the document meant that the Duke was rightful King of England. Fortunately, when he was shown the deed, he threw it on the fire, remarking as he did so, "That might cause a lot of trouble".

The Prince Regent took it upon himself as acting Head of the Family to decide the date of his niece's christening. The Kents were given three days' notice that the service was to take place in the Cupola room at Kensington Palace on the afternoon of June 24th. The ceremony was to be private, only a few members of the family were to be invited, and nobody was to appear in uniform. In short, nothing was to be done to mark the occasion as special. The Prince Regent consented to be a godfather, as did the Tsar of Russia, Alexander I. The Duke of Kent's sister, Augusta, was one godmother, and the Dowager Duchess of Coburg the other. The Kents sent the Regent a list of names they had chosen for their daughter. In the event, an unseemly dispute broke out at the most sacred moment of the service. The Archbishop asked the Prince Regent to name the child, and was told to baptise her "Alexandrina". The Duke then proposed she should also be called "Elizabeth". His brother shook his head. "Charlotte" had previously been ruled out so he tried "Augusta", but that too was brushed aside. "Then what name would he suggest?" "Give her the mother's name," said the Prince, "but it cannot precede that of the Emperor". The infant was accordingly baptised "Alexandrina Victoria", much to the indignation of her parents. At first, the Princess was generally called "Drina", but as she grew older she came to be known as "Victoria".

The Prince Regent, although supposedly "The first Gentleman in Europe", by virtue of "the inimitable grace of his bow and the dazzling quality of his waistcoats", was, in reality "the first bounder in Europe, vain as a peacock, false to his friends and remorseless to those who had offended him". For instance, he never forgave the Duke of Kent for the sympathy he had shown for the Princess of Wales. For years he had turned a deaf ear to Edward's appeals for help, and nothing would have given him more pleasure than to banish him to Amorbach. Squabbling amongst themselves was one of the principal recreations of George III's sons. In August 1819 the Kents took their daughter with them to a military review. The Prince Regent, incensed at the sight of the innocent usurper, loudly demanded to know "What business has that infant here?" Later the same month, he publicly turned his back on the Duke but was gracious enough to exchange a few words with the Duchess.

The Kents decided to winter in Devonshire, nominally to help the Duchess recruit her strength, in fact to avoid the expense of living in London. The Duke rented a modest house for his family some hundred and fifty yards from the sea at Sidmouth. It was called "Woolbrook Cottage", and was built in a style that owed much to Strawberry Hill. Rich as it was in Gothic romance it possessed few other amenities. The family reached Sidmouth on Christmas Day, only to discover that the Devonshire "Riviera" was more like the North Pole. On January 12th, 1820, the Duke went to bed with a high fever which failed to respond to blisters, leeches and bleeding. Soon his condition became so grave that the Duchess sent for her brother Leopold. By the same post, the Prince Regent was told that the Duke was dangerously ill. He at once wrote back expressing "anxious solicitude", much to his brother's delight. Prince Leopold, accompanied by Dr Stockmar, his loyal friend and counsellor, reached Sidmouth on January 22nd. Stockmar took one look at the invalid, and warned the Duchess that "human help could no longer avail". That afternoon, the Duke summoned up strength to read and sign a will, appointing his wife sole guardian of his daughter, and bequeathing his assets in trust for their joint enjoyment. He died the next day, holding his wife's hand and imploring her not to forget him.

Princess Victoria was only eight months old when her father died, so her memory of him was necessarily second-hand. Most of her information was inspired by the amiable principle of not speaking ill of the dead. Brought up to obey the fifth commandment, she did her best to honour her parents. Sometimes she spoke of her "beloved father" as if she could recall him. But even before Greville's Diary was published in 1874, with its contemptuous portrayal of the Duke, rumours seem to have reached her of his frailties. When people remarked how much she resembled him, "she would claim with a tightening of the lips to have inherited 'more from my dear mother'". They shared, however, a number of traits, amongst which were truthfulness, courage, exceptional powers of observation, and a love of order and punctuality. But it is probably wiser to note such similarities than to assign them to heredity. Indeed, some of her traits, for example her thrift, are probably best understood as reactions against her father's infirmities.

Three things the Princess may confidently be said to have inherited from the Duke: her claim to the throne, her solitary upbringing in a one parent family, and a mountain of unpaid bills. Part of her later life was occupied in searching for surrogate fathers to compensate for her loss. As her formative years were spent mostly among women, she tended to yearn for male protection and guidance. Throughout her reign, "the stupidest man's opinion" carried more weight with her "than the cleverest woman's". Outwardly, she appeared resolute and majestic, but at the core of her being she seldom felt really secure. "I am a person," she once acknowledged, "who has to cling to someone in order to find peace and comfort." Her first Prime Minister, Lord Melbourne, gave her precisely what she sought, a feeling of "confidence and security". Her longing to put down roots, her love of familiar landmarks, her dislike of change, her disposition to lean upon people she trusted, were instincts she clearly derived from her insecure childhood. Indeed, a description of it reads more like an extract from a probation officer's casebook than the life of a Princess.

Loneliness was one of the greatest misfortunes of Victoria's life, gloriously relieved during her supremely happy marriage. As a girl, she was deprived of her father's reassuring presence and the companionship of other children. As a Queen, she was "so alone on that terrible height", as Tennyson called it, as to discourage intimacy. Worst of all, Prince Albert's early death left her solitary and crushed. "God knows," she wrote despairingly in 1865, "how much I want to be taken care of." Many years later, she told Archbishop Benson how in her "sad, lonely position" she needed, above all, "loving and sympathetic help and someone to lean on". Thus spoke the fatherless child as well as the widowed Queen.

The Duke of Kent's death left his wife at the mercy of a family who had shown her nothing but hostility. The Prince Regent, in particular, regarded her with the "greatest animosity", and was evidently anxious to get rid of her. It is hardly surprising therefore that the Duchess's first instinct was to leave the country. In the end, Prince Leopold managed to persuade her that she should settle in England and devote herself to bringing up her daughter. When she returned to Kensington Palace on January 29th, she heard that George III was dead. The new King resolutely refused to help her in any way and seemed to believe that it was an indictable offence to give birth to an heir to the throne. When the Prime Minister, Lord Liverpool, proposed to make some provision for the Duchess and her daughter, George IV said he "would be damned if he consented", and that it was Prince Leopold's duty to support them. The King, in common with many of his subjects, resented the £50,000 annuity which Parliament had settled on his son-in-law, and was only too eager to make him responsible for the Duchess and his niece. Eventually, it was agreed that he would make his sister an allowance of £3,000 to supplement her Parliamentary grant of £6,000. Helpful as this was, her income remained insufficient to meet the expenses of the most frugal royal household. Partly on grounds of economy, and partly because she wished to distance herself from her husband's relations, the Duchess of Kent increasingly withdrew into the small circle of German ladies who made up her court at Kensington. The Duke of Clarence encouraged his wife, Adelaide, to do what she could to comfort her compatriot, but this was the only kindness shown her by her late husband's relations.

The Princess's early upbringing was decidedly imprudent, but then love is often as foolish as it is blind. In 1872, Queen Victoria wrote a brief account of her earliest recollections, in which she acknowledged that she had been "very much indulged by everyone and set pretty well all at defiance". The brightest moments of her "otherwise rather melancholy childhood", were spent under her "beloved" uncle's roof at Claremont, where she was recklessly pampered by "dear old Louise", Princess Charlotte's "devoted Dresser and friend". She was no less spoiled at Kensington, where the Baroness de Späth, and Mrs Brock, the Princess's nurse, "worshipped the little fatherless child" with a fervour approaching idolatry. Before Victoria was a year old, the Duchess ruefully noted that she was beginning "to show symptoms of wanting to get her own little way". The last thing that such a self-willed young lady needed was to be pampered and overindulged.

In 1824 Mrs Brock retired, and Fräulein Lehzen replaced her as Drina's governess. Louise Lehzen was the daughter of a Lutheran Pastor in Hanover. She was intelligent, serious minded, humourless and highly strung. Nobody could call her beautiful, but at thirty-five she remained presentable, although some people thought her manners uncouth and her origins rather too humble. Her practice of chewing caraway seeds was deplored as ill-bred. Stockmar believed that the habit could be explained by her need to disguise her addiction to alcohol. The Duke appointed her in 1819 to look after Feodore, planning, in due course, to put her in charge of Victoria. She naturally came with the highest recommendations, and Greville, who once sat next to her at dinner, thought her "a clever agreeable woman".

Lehzen soon found herself engaged in a battle royal with the most "passionate and naughty child" she had ever met. The Princess hated lessons and "baffled every attempt" to teach her her letters. The difficulty of persuading this stubborn, self-willed infant to apply her mind to her books was aggravated by the fact that she flew into violent rages whenever she felt thwarted. In one of these nursery tantrums she seized a pair of scissors and hurled them at her governess. On another occasion, her piano teacher told her that she must practise like everyone else, whereupon she banged down the lid of the piano, shouting, "There! There is no *must* about it". Throughout her life she struggled without much success to master her quick temper, a trait she may well have derived from her Hanoverian blood. But there was one important respect in which she could always be relied upon: undeviating truthfulness. "As a child," she claimed, "I never told a falsehood, though I knew I would be punished." Later in life, she was justifiably proud of her reputation for "fearless straight forwardness", and nothing would have delighted her more than to learn that Lord Melbourne described her as "the honestest person I have ever known".

When occasion demanded Lehzen could be very firm, but preferred to appeal to affection rather than fear. "I adored her," said the Queen in retrospect, "though I was greatly in awe of her." Lehzen was quick to appreciate that her pupil was exceptionally warm-hearted, and both soon became devoted to one another. Never once during the thirteen years she was employed as governess did she leave her charge. The Dowager Duchess of Coburg, who visited Kensington in 1826, described Lehzen as Drina's "great love", while Drina herself spoke of her as "precious Lehzen", "the best and truest of friends". Lehzen led a very solitary existence, entirely cut off from her German relations, and most of the time a prisoner in the Palace. Hence her devotion to her pupil in some degree satisfied her own need for companionship and love. Their life together was not all lessons, for Lehzen helped the Princess to play as well as to learn. Together they clothed an impressive array of dolls, dressing them as characters from opera or history. In 1890 the collection was publicly exhibited, and the Queen wrote by way of explanation "That she was quite devoted to dolls and played with them till she was fourteen". Being an only child, who "except for occasional visits of other children lived always *alone*, without companions", she turned for friends to a make-believe world.

It would be almost impossible to exaggerate the strength of German influences on the young Princess, who had hardly a drop of English blood in her veins. It is necessary to go back to the seventeenth century to trace her British ancestry. The Electress, Sophia, George I's mother, was James I's granddaughter, and Victoria's great, great, great, great grandmother. Her grandparents, on both sides of her family, were Germans. Her grandfather, George III, much as he might "glory in the name Briton", was a Hanoverian, and Queen Charlotte was a Princess of Mecklenburg-Strelitz. Her mother's father was Francis, Duke of Coburg, who married Augusta, Princess of Reuss. Between 1714 and 1901 all Britain's Hanoverian Sovereigns were married to German consorts. Victoria herself married her Coburg cousin, and six of their nine children chose German brides. It should, of course, be emphasised that the Germany to which she was proud to belong was not the united militaristic, aggressive Fatherland of Bismarck, William II and Hitler; but a country consisting of some forty kingdoms or principalities which posed no sort of threat to Britain: indeed had been our ally against Napoleon. Greville and others grumbled about her "inveterate predilection for everything German" but as she herself explained, it was "that country from which *everyone* nearest and dearest to the Queen has come and to which she is bound by every possible tie". In 1917, towards the end of the First World War, George V repudiated the German titles of his family, saying that he would be damned if he was an alien, although no amount of whitewash could conceal his genealogy, or make him more of an Englishman than the Kaiser.

Princess Victoria was not only born a German, but she spent the first eighteen years of her life in an enclosed German community. Her mother, Baroness Späth, Lehzen, her half-sister, Feodore, uncle Leopold, were all Germans, and most of their visitors were Coburgs. The nearest thing to a resident Englishman at Kensington was the Duchess of Kent's Comptroller, Captain Conroy, and he, in fact, was Irish. When Leopold persuaded his sister to remain in England after her husband's death, he did so because he believed that her daughter might one day be Queen, and hence should be brought up in England, by Englishmen, to be English. In fact, only the first of these conditions was ever fully met, although the Duchess did insist that English should be the Princess's first language. In 1840 Agnes Strickland brought out a book about Queen Victoria to commemorate her wedding. Knowing that the Duchess spoke English very badly, she rashly described the Princess as "lisping in the teutonic accents of the Duchess's dear Fatherland". "Not true," wrote the Queen in the margin of her copy, "Never spoke German till '39. Not allowed." Nevertheless, according to Eleanor Stanley, one of her early Maids of Honour, the Queen spoke with a "decidedly foreign accent", which the Aga Khan described as a "mixture of Scotch and German", spiced with "the German conversational trick of interjecting 'so' – pronounced 'tzo' – into her remarks".

Life at Kensington was simple and sometimes Spartan. In 1875 the Queen told Disraeli about her privations as a child. "I never had a room to myself; I never had a sofa, nor an easy chair; and there was not a single carpet that was not threadbare." The food at the Palace was so frugal that the Princess "determined that if she ever came to the throne she would never have mutton for dinner; such was the surfeit of that article at the Duchess of Kent's table." Only on rare occasions, and as a "great treat", was she allowed to have tea. Such austerities were primarily enforced on principle but partly to economise. However much she grumbled at the time, she later described it as a "great blessing and advantage to have lived in such very simple and restricted circumstances", and she attributed her "humble tastes" and dislike of "great Palaces" to her plain upbringing. But nothing ever reconciled her to the stifling regime of Kensington, surrounded as she was by middle-aged women, and "immured within our old Palace". The experience left her curiously aloof from the ways of everyday life. She once casually mentioned in the course of conversation that she thought that a railway ticket was a thin sheet of paper. Possibly the worst feature of the life she led was that it forced her to lavish her "violent affection" on Lehzen, her dolls and her dogs.

Rigorous as was the Princess's life, she could not be altogether protected from flattery and obsequiousness, and it could hardly have escaped the notice of such an observant young lady that the life of Kensington revolved around her. Long before she was told of her probable destiny, she already knew that there was something singular about her. Few children, if any, could remain wholly impervious to being addressed as "Ma'am", or "Your Royal Highness", from infancy, to bowing and curtseying, to the deference of servants, to admiration and applause. It was a considerable tribute to her character that she contrived to remain humble in spite of so much praise. But the constant anxiety shown to meet her slightest wishes, conditioned her to believe that she possessed a divine right to order her life to suit herself. In short, she succumbed to the endemic disease of royalty: egotism. How could she be persuaded to believe that the world was not her oyster when all the available evidence suggested that it was? Greville was over severe when he described her as "hardhearted, selfish and self-willed", but it is true that she never succeeded in subjugating the "spoiled child" within her.

In 1827, with the appointment of the Reverend George Davys as her "Principal Master", Victoria's education became more formal and intensive. Meanwhile Lehzen continued to supervise the Princess's daily life, and so successful was she in teaching her perfect manners that Carlyle remarked, "It is impossible to imagine a politer little woman". An obituary of the Queen referred to her courtesy as

reminiscent of a bygone age, presumably forgetting that she had
learned how to behave in the reign of George IV. Her mother and
Lehzen also taught her the finer points of deportment. Her grandmother, the Dowager Duchess Augusta, described her at the age of
six as "poised and graceful". But nothing was left to chance, and a
sprig of holly was often tied under her chin to make her hold up her
head. Eventually her harsh training reaped an ample reward. Nobody
who saw the grace of her low sweeping curtsey ever forgot its majesty. "She moves with great ease, grace and lightness" wrote Lady
Wolseley in 1885. "She swims and floats." Her success in overcom-
ing the fact that "we are rather small for a Queen", was principally
due to her "genius for movement".

Davys devised a weekly timetable to accommodate an impressive
range of subjects. He was personally responsible for teaching the
Princess history, geography, Latin and religion, while experts in
other fields gave her lessons in handwriting, English, poetry, French,
German, drawing, music and dancing. It is true that she never mastered Latin, which she learned from a book written for Etonians, but
in other respects her progress was commendable. She pronounced
French with "exquisite precision" and soon became fluent in German. Her soprano singing was pure and true – Mendelssohn was
later to congratulate her upon it – and her painting and drawing
showed verve and an eye for detail. In fact, she was a talented young
lady and much better educated than most boys of her age: partly
because of the distinction of those who instructed her, partly because
she possessed an astonishing memory, and partly because she was
not restricted to the classical curriculum beloved of the public
schools. She was no bluestocking, indeed highly educated women
alarmed her, but she rejoiced in a lively intelligence, intense curiosity,
and a clarity of understanding and expression made all the sharper
by her seeing issues either in black or white. Her down to earth
common sense, her intuitive insight, and her hatred of shams could
not but make her formidable.

Davys believed that his most important task was to make the Princess a devout Christian. It needed no gift of prophecy to foresee that
the demure little girl he taught her Catechism might one day become
the "Supreme Governor" of the Church of England. The Duchess,
who tended to lose her way in the Prayer Book, gave Davys the sole
charge of her daughter's Anglican education. She had chosen him
because of his Evangelical background, authenticated by his author-

ship of several improving tracts. Before coming to Kensington, where he resided for ten years, he was a Fellow of Christ's College, Cambridge, and Vicar of Willoughby-on-the-Wolds, a remote Lincolnshire parish. George III had brought up his children as strong Churchmen, a tradition from which the Duke of Kent strayed. Neither the Duchess, nor Lehzen, both pious Lutherans, nor even Davys, who was known for his Low Church views, was greatly concerned with the subtleties of Anglicanism. "You know," the Queen told Gladstone, "I am not much of an Episcopalian." "No Ma'am," he replied resignedly, "I know that well."

Davys was scrupulous in trying to avoid indoctrinating his pupil with the specific tenets of the Evangelical faith. Instead, he encouraged her to take a liberal view of the varieties of religious experience. But although he succeeded in persuading her to be tolerant of other creeds, he made her too zealous a Protestant to sympathise with the Catholic revival in the Church. The Princess grew up at the height of the Evangelical Movement, and consequently many of her religious views were coloured by its teaching, however careful Davys might have been to shield her from its impact. Her deep attachment to the Bible, her open preference for plain services, her earnest interest in sermons, provided they were short, her pathological suspicion of clericalism, and her conviction that Christianity should be practical, all bore the trademark of Davys's brand of religion. In common with most other girls at that time, she was brought up to believe that it was frivolous to read novels, even those of Sir Walter Scott whose poetry enchanted her. "Mamma admonished me for reading light books", she later told Lord Melbourne. More characteristic still of Evangelical piety was the meticulous record she kept in her diary of the use she made of God's precious gift of Time. She turned to her journal as a substitute for Confession, abhorrent as she would have found the suggestion.

Davys became very attached to his pupil, who showed some reserve in returning his affection. Sometimes the strain of teaching was too much for him and he was abrupt and ill-tempered. In due course, however, she rewarded him for his devotion by persuading Lord Melbourne to make him Bishop of Peterborough: "the dead see" as the wits called it. When he died in 1864, surrounded by prints of the Queen and her children, The Times paid him a curiously ambivalent tribute. "His ambition through life was rather to be good than great. Higher praise it is impossible to bestow."

The man who most profoundly influenced the life of the young Princess was Captain John Conroy, her mother's Comptroller. Conroy belonged to an Anglo-Irish family. In 1803, when he was seventeen, he purchased a commission in the Royal Artillery, but although he remained on "active service" until 1815, he contrived to avoid the perils of campaigning. In 1808 he married Elizabeth Fisher, a niece of the Duke of Kent's old tutor, Bishop Fisher of Salisbury. He was well over six foot tall and imposing rather than handsome. What he lacked in good looks he made up for by charm. Shrewd, overbearing and quick tempered, he pursued his selfish ends with ruthless ambition. The Duke of Kent chose Conroy as his Military Equerry in 1817. On the Duke's death he offered his services to the Duchess, who found his help "invaluable". "I don't know what I should do without him," she said. "His energy and capability are wonderful." Soon the Conroys, with their daughters, Jane and Victoire, took up residence at Kensington, where the Captain made the acquaintance of Princess Sophia, one of the King's younger sisters, and a neighbour in the Palace. So successfully did he ingratiate himself, that she appointed him her Comptroller. In 1827 he persuaded Princess Sophia to request the King to make him a Knight Commander of Hanover. George IV, who was devoted to his sister, not only did as she asked, but for good measure made Lehzen a Hanoverian baroness.

When Conroy transferred to the Duchess's Household during the sad days at Sidmouth, he was under no illusions about his immediate prospects. For the time being he was prepared to accept the role of an underpaid major domo, but only because he looked to the future. His eventual ambition was nothing less than to make himself master of England by means of the influence he was determined to exert on the child who would one day be Queen. Slowly and patiently over many years he planned to subordinate her will to his own. More immediately, there was the distinct possibility that both George IV and his brother the Duke of Clarence would die before Princess Victoria reached eighteen, the royal age of majority. Under such circumstances, it seemed almost certain that the Duchess of Kent would be asked to act as Regent, with Conroy, of course, to advise her. Then, at last, he would reap the reward of long years of intrigue. But before he became the power behind the throne, wielding its authority to serve his own ends, he had first to assert his mastery over the Duchess. Hence for eighteen years he waged a ceaseless campaign within the Palace to destroy all influences other than his own.

Nothing could be more apt than Conroy's official title "Comptroller" to the Duchess of Kent, because that was what he became. She was, in fact, easy prey: a lonely and bewildered foreigner, ignorant of business, and cold-shouldered by most of her late husband's family. Naturally diffident and self-doubting, she yearned for reassurance and advice. Above all, like her daughter after her, she depended on male guidance, and hence was peculiarly vulnerable to efforts to impose on her. To begin with she looked to her brother for help, but soon rejected his "black views" in favour of Conroy's optimism, preferring the comforts of a fool's paradise to the stark realities of life. Sir John's plan of campaign was precisely that which Lehzen pursued with her pupil, to exploit the Duchess of Kent's affectionate nature. Unlike her former husbands, he was her own age, and his Irish charm and soldierly bearing sufficed to win her heart. Whatever the world might say – and it was vociferous on the subject – they were probably guilty of nothing more than an innocent flirtation. But Regency gossips refused to believe that it was possible for a man and a woman to live under the same roof without committing adultery. That arbiter of manners, the Duke of Wellington, assumed that the Duchess and Conroy must be lovers. There are several good reasons, however, for suggesting that he was wrong. The Queen, whose behaviour towards Sir John was often cited as proof of her mother's guilt, emphatically denied it, insisting that the Duchess's piety and Conroy's devotion to his wife combined to show the absurdity of the charge. Moreover, the Duchess was far too fond of Elizabeth Conroy to risk destroying her marriage. Nor would she have been willing to give George IV such a splendid excuse to take Victoria from her. Finally, the Duchess would hardly have insisted upon her daughter sleeping in her bedroom if she was in the middle of an affair.

In 1830 the Duchess of Clarence decided to warn her sister-in-law that she was allowing Sir John to manage her life to an extent of which she seemed unaware. She began by remarking that it had been noticed in the family "that you are cutting yourself off more and more from them. This they attribute to Conroy, whether rightly or wrongly I cannot judge; they believe that he tries to remove everything which might obstruct his influence, so that he may exercise his power *alone*, and alone, too, one day reap the fruits of his influence.

He cannot be blamed for cherishing dreams of future greatness . . . but everyone recognises these aspirations, towards which his every action is directed." It was quite wrong that he should be allowed to forbid access to Kensington "to all but his family, who in any case are not of so high a rank that they *alone* should be the entourage and the companions of the future Queen of England." Adelaide's warning was not made any more palatable by its shrewd presentation of Conroy's hidden motives. The battle royal which broke out between Clarence House and Kensington owed much to Conroy's smouldering resentment, and William's anger with the Duchess over the insolent answer she foolishly sent his wife.

In 1840 Prince Charles of Leiningen, Victoria's half-brother, dictated a long memorandum containing "A Complete History of the Policy pursued at Kensington under Sir John Conroy's guidance". At first the Prince found Conroy "extremely charming", and believed that his only concern was to help the Duchess. On several occasions he spoke of his plans "to give the Princess Victoria an upbringing which would enable her in the future to be equal to her position" and "to win her so high a place in the hearts of her future subjects" that she would one day become the most popular Queen who ever ascended the throne. But he was also concerned "to assure a pleasant and honourable future for the Duchess of Kent". The various means which Conroy devised to realise these objectives came to be known as the "Kensington System". Just as Wotan surrounded Brünhilde with a ring of magic fire, so Conroy barred access to the Palace to any who posed the faintest threat to the Duchess's authority.

In some respects, Sir John followed the old Hanoverian tradition of establishing a rival Court to the King's, except that the "Conroyal Family" at Kensington was more like an enclosed order than a Royal Household. Fate seemed to favour Conroy's plans by removing two likely obstacles. In 1828 Princess Feodore married Prince Ernest of Hohenlohe-Langenburg, thereby escaping "some years of imprisonment" under her mother's roof, but leaving her half-sister, to whom she was devoted, without a companion and ally. Then in 1831 Prince Leopold accepted the Crown of Belgium and departed for Brussels. The only remaining sources of resistance were Späth and Lehzen. Somehow Sir John prevailed upon the Duchess to dismiss her Lady-in-Waiting, after a quarter of a century of loyal service, simply because she expressed her doubts about the "Kensington System".

But even he could not get rid of Lehzen who was known to possess the King's support.

Conroy preached to the converted when he urged the Duchess to rebuff the English Royal Family, although he made an exception of Princess Sophia, who acted as his "spy" at Court and supported the "Kensington System". Never one to leave anything to chance, Sir John terrified the Duchess by telling her that the King, "who was as great a despot as ever lived, was always talking of taking her child from her". Although this particular risk was removed when George IV died in June 1830, his successor, William IV, was almost as hostile and threatening. But the greatest danger of all, according to Conroy, came from Ernest, Duke of Cumberland, the fifth of George III's seven sons, a Prince who was said to have ravished his sister and murdered his valet. His forbidding appearance, made more repulsive by a fearful scar, honourably won in battle, helped cast him as a villain. The Duke was an arch-reactionary, a born mischief-maker, and singularly ungracious. It was even suggested that he intended to poison his niece in a bid to secure the throne. Years later, the Queen dismissed the notion that her uncle had threatened her life as "Sir John's invention" and "utterly false", but at least at the time her mother remained convinced that there was a "Cumberland Plot". Consequently the most stringent precautions were taken to preserve the Princess from poison or attack. Sir John and the Duchess agreed that she must never be left alone by night or day. When she went to bed, Lehzen remained on guard until the Duchess retired. Sir Walter Scott, who was invited to dine at Kensington, noticed how closely the Princess was guarded, and concluded that such "isolation and seclusion" was hardly "the best training ground for a life destined to be spent among an almost infinite diversity of people". The poignant paradox of her childhood existence was that although she was often acutely lonely she never was left alone.

Sir John was exceedingly skilful in exploiting the Duchess' obsessive dislike of her English relations, and argued, with telling effect, that the future Queen should be kept away from her uncles. The Duchess, of course, was easily persuaded to place the Court in quarantine, and ensure that the Princess was kept in the dark about her father's relations: hence the intense curiosity she displayed when discussing them with Lord Melbourne. In 1836 she told the King of the Belgians that "from my earliest years the name of *Uncle, alone,* meant no other but you!" That she could brush aside her father's brothers so lightly shows the success of the "Kensington System".

The Princess was naturally sociable and revelled in music, dancing and laughter. But, thanks to Conroy, she was seldom allowed to meet boys of her own age. "I am very fond of pleasant society," she once complained, "and I long sadly for some gaiety." Her journal shows how susceptible she was to the charms of good-looking young men. In June 1833, when she was barely fourteen, her two Württemberg cousins, Alexander and Ernest, "sons of Mamma's sister, my Aunt Antoinette", paid a visit to Kensington. "They are both *extremely* tall," she noted, "Alexander is *very* handsome, and Ernest has a *very kind* expression. They are both EXTREMELY *amiable* ." The feverish excitement with which she described the visits of Coburg cousins shows how she longed for male companionship. It was a cruel twist of fate that the only "friend" of her own age she was encouraged to see was Victoire Conroy, particularly as the more she came to detest Sir John the less she liked his daughter. She first appeared in the Princess's journal as "Poor Victoire", and then became "Miss Conroy": the absence of a qualifying adjective being far more eloquent than the customary gush of endearments.

The blame for the Princess's dull and unhappy youth belongs mainly to Sir John, to a lesser extent to the Duchess for her complicity in his plans, and to some degree to the fact that her father's early death left her an only child. The Kensington System was Conroy's inspiration. It was he who cut her off from her English relations, he who insisted upon her being guarded day and night from largely imaginary dangers, and he who deprived her of youthful companions apart from his own daughter. So far from attempting to sugar the pill, he teased her for being as mean as Queen Charlotte, and told her how much she resembled the Duke of Gloucester, her least prepossessing uncle. Possibly he treated all young people in a similar fashion, or perhaps he believed he could bully her into submission. So strongly did she object to the way he treated her that she complained to her half-brother, Prince Charles, of the "personal affronts" to which Sir John subjected her. The Duke of Wellington even went so far as to attribute her "hatred" of Conroy "to her having witnessed some familiarities" between the Duchess and her Comptroller.

It is curious that so skilled an intriguer as Conroy should have been so inept in handling the future Queen, the keystone of his strategy. He appears to have been blind to the obvious fact that she was bound to resent his "slights and incivilities", not to mention his ill-judged witticisms. Had he been wiser, he would have devoted less time to cultivating the Duchess and more to ingratiating himself with her daughter. Her response to his hectoring manner and crude attempts to coerce her was merely to be more stubborn. Little did he seem to appreciate that he had joined battle with one of the most resolute characters in Europe. So alarmed was the Duchess by her daughter's hostility to Conroy, that she sought help from Baron Stockmar, Leopold's *éminence grise* and the Coburg's family guru. "Your Royal Highness", he replied, "must not forget that the Princess must have known from her earliest youth that she is a Princess. Wherever she looked in the house, she encountered Sir John as the sole regulator of the whole machine." Consequently, as she grew up, she became increasingly resentful of "what must have looked to her as an exercise of undue control over herself".

The most damaging feature of the Conroy era was that it estranged Victoria from the Duchess. In 1861, looking back at her childhood, the Queen told her eldest daughter that she had been almost "at enmity" with her mother, upon whose sanction the Kensington System depended. Inevitably, some of the hostility the Princess felt for Sir John was bound to include his employer. When describing her blighted youth to Lord Melbourne, she repeatedly used the plural pronoun "they" to describe her persecutors, thus making it clear that she saw the Duchess as Conroy's willing dupe.

Until Victoria was nearly eleven it was thought best to shield her from the knowledge that she was likely to become Queen, but on March 11th 1830 she finally learned the truth when Lehzen tucked an up-to-date genealogical table into her history book. "I never saw that before" she said on discovering the insertion. "It was not thought necessary that you should," replied Lehzen. For some moments she examined her family tree and then remarked, "I see I am nearer the throne than I thought". The Queen later recollected "I cried much on learning it and ever deplored this contingency". According to Lehzen, when the Princess discovered what her destiny might be, she promised "I will be good": a version of events the Queen apparently endorsed by allowing Martin to make use of it in his *Life of the Prince Consort*. Nevertheless, when Mrs Alaric Grant, one of her Ladies-in-Waiting, asked whether the story was true, she denied it emphatically. "Of course not! How could I say such a thing?" Once the Princess had fully grasped where she stood in the line of succession, Lehzen pointed out that Aunt Adelaide was still young and might have children. "If that was so," Victoria answered, "I should never feel disappointed, for I know by the love Aunt Adelaide bears me, how fond she is of children." The more the Princess came to terms with the full implications of the most important discovery of her life, the more she became aware of the nature of Conroy's ambition.

On June 27th, 1830, the second day of William IV's reign, the Duchess sent the Prime Minister, the Duke of Wellington, a letter, written in Conroy's hand but signed in her own, proposing that she should be treated as Dowager Princess of Wales and given an income appropriate to the role. Furthermore, she asked to be recognised as her daughter's sole guardian, and, should the need ever arise, Princess Regent. The Duke was astonished by the effrontery of these proposals and advised her to wait until Parliament raised the matter. In July, the House of Commons debated what should be done if the King died before his niece came of age. Normally, the next heir, in this instance the Duke of Cumberland, would be seen as possessing the best claim to be Regent. But hardly anyone in the House was anxious to appoint one of the most detested men in England. Eventually an excuse was found to exclude him. Because the Salic Law prevailed in Hanover, Princess Victoria was debarred from the succession, and consequently the Duke would succeed William IV as King of that country. Clearly it was unthinkable that an alien sovereign should govern England, and therefore the best suited person to become Regent was "the illustrious Princess, the Mother of Her Royal Highness the Princess Victoria". When news reached Kensington in November that an Act of Parliament had been passed appointing the Duchess of Kent sole Regent for her daughter, Conroy rejoiced to see his dream come true, and the Duchess declared that it was the first happy day she had known for ten years.

William IV and Queen Adelaide were both very fond of their niece and wanted to introduce her to Court life. The King was an eccentric, peppery, good-natured old sailor, while the Queen, who was twenty-eight years younger than her husband, had beautiful manners, a generous heart and a natural piety. But, unfortunately, Conroy was determined to prevent either of them lavishing affection on Victoria. Nobody, if he could help it, other than the Duchess and her Comptroller, should be allowed to influence the Heir Presumptive. The Queen, who had loved her niece from infancy, was especially grieved to see so little of her. The very first letter Victoria ever received was written by her Aunt Adelaide in 1821.

Relations between the Court and Kensington deteriorated fast in the first months of the reign. The King and Queen were violent Tories, bitterly opposed to the passing of a Reform Bill, and were consequently furious with the Duchess of Kent for patronising the Whigs. But what angered the King most was the way she treated his children by Mrs Jordan. Queen Adelaide welcomed them as part of the family, but the Duchess refused to acknowledge their very existence. Even when she met them under the King's roof at Windsor she did her best to ignore them. Like so many disagreeable acts it was done on the loftiest principle. As she explained to the Duchess of Northumberland, "I never did, neither will I ever, associate Victoria in any way with the illegitimate members of the Royal family. Did I not keep this line, how would it be possible to teach Victoria the difference between vice and virtue?" The Duchess's rigorous morality somehow fell short of her neighbour, Princess Sophia, and her illegitimate son, Captain Garth.

Many disputes between the Duchess and the King took place without Victoria knowing, but she could not but be involved in the great Coronation row. It began when her mother refused to answer a series of enquiries sent to her by Lord Howe, Queen Adelaide's Chamberlain. Eventually the King, infuriated by her obstruction, affixed his own signature to one of Lord Howe's letters, to show it was written on his authority. Even the Duchess dared not ignore so clear a royal command. There then followed a furious exchange on the question of precedence: an ever fertile source of umbrage. When the Duchess learned that her daughter had been assigned a place in the procession behind her royal uncles, she immediately argued that Victoria, as Heir Presumptive, should come next after the King. Nothing, however, would persuade him to alter the arrangement, not even the fact that he was clearly in the wrong. The Duchess, rather than give in on a matter so near to her heart, announced that the fatigue of the ceremony would prove too much for a girl of twelve, and that consequently she and her daughter would be unable to attend. The Princess wept copiously when she learned of her mother's decision. "Nothing could console me," she wrote later, "not even my dolls."

From an early age, experience taught the Princess the wisdom of keeping her own counsel. But when she felt free to let her opinions be

known, it at once became clear how much she resented her mother's
disputes with the King. On one occasion the Duchess suggested that
her uncle was jealous of her and did not really love her. But the
Princess had a mind of her own, and turned a deaf ear to all attempts
to undermine her loyalty. In 1835, after she had grudgingly been
permitted to spend a night at Windsor, she noted in her diary: "I
was very much pleased there, as both my Uncle and Aunt are *so very
kind* to me." Much later, in a footnote to Martin's *Life of the Prince
Consort*, she spoke of her "affectionate gratitude" to William IV for
his "kindness to herself, and his wish that she should be duly prepared for the duties to which she was so clearly called". But the most
telling evidence that Victoria secretly took the King's part in his
quarrels with her mother may be seen in the way she behaved on
becoming Queen. Her "attentions and cordiality" to her Aunt Adelaide, and "her bounty and civility to the King's children", showed
where her sentiments had been in the late King's reign. Actions spoke
louder than words.

In 1834, the Duchess of Kent appointed Lady Flora Hastings, a
gaunt, sharp-tongued spinster, as an extra Lady-in-Waiting and companion for her daughter. This apparently innocent move was part of
a larger plan to destroy Lehzen's influence. Lady Flora became a
devoted disciple of Conroy, but made no headway with the Princess,
who saw through Sir John's plan, and who never took kindly to
people forced upon her. There followed a second campaign to get
rid of Lehzen by treating her with such "incredible harshness" that
she would send in her resignation. But the Baroness stood her
ground and refused to be intimidated. The King was furious when he
heard what was going on, and showed what he thought by ordering
Conroy out of the Chapel Royal at Victoria's confirmation: to the
dismay of the Duchess and the secret delight of her daughter. After
the service, the Duchess handed her daughter a letter in which she
said that she must in future treat Lehzen in a more formal and dignified manner to mark the new era in her life. She also hinted that her
maternal authority would continue until the Princess was twenty-
one, although she knew perfectly well that the royal age of majority
was eighteen.

In the struggle for power which was waged at Kensington, there
was only one person to whom the Princess could turn. Her uncle
Leopold was in Belgium, and her half-sister, Feodore, in Germany.
Späth had been dismissed, and Lady Flora was plainly an enemy

agent. That left the intrepid Lehzen, without whose shrewd advice, force of character, and influence at Court the Princess could not have prevailed against Conroy and her mother. Again and again she acknowledges in her journal how much she owed to Lehzen's unfailing support. "I never can sufficiently repay her," she wrote in 1835, "for all she has *borne* and done for me. She is the most affectionate, devoted, attached and disinterested friend that I have, and I love her most *dearly*." By 1838 she felt so estranged from the Duchess that she actually described the Baroness as "my ANGELIC dearest mother *Lehzen*, who I do so love!"

A principal feature of Victoria's character was her sense of insecurity. This was no imaginary phobia, but rooted in the realities of her childhood, during which she had never known the protection of a father, and was necessarily forced to distrust her mother: the one person, above all others, with whom she should have felt safe. Moreover, she could hardly avoid a sense of vulnerability when faced by Conroy's attempts to destroy her independence. She felt threatened because she was threatened. Sometimes she dealt with this feeling by confronting it head on, battling against it with the full force of her resolute personality. At other times she sought protection in the strength of those whom she trusted. "I am so helpless," she wrote in 1864, "so clinging". These contradictory reactions flowed from the same source: her feeling of defencelessness. It was typical of her that she reacted in opposite ways, never quite sure whether to seek "a strong arm to help and lean on", or to depend upon self-reliance. To dominate, or to be dominated, that was the question.

The Duchess, advised by Conroy, decided that the Princess's education should extend beyond mere book-learning to travel: partly so that she might become acquainted with her future Kingdom, and partly to enable her prospective subjects to see her. Between 1832 and 1835 a series of English tours was planned. Sometimes the royal party stayed in hotels, like the "Old Bell" on Barnby Moor, which the Princess thought "extremely clean and pretty", or the "Beaumaris Arms", where she lodged for several days. More often, she and her mother were guests of eminent political families, staying at Eaton Hall, Alton Towers, Belvoir, Chatsworth, or "*dear*" Plas Newydd. A small library of books was packed into the Duchess's coach to ensure that not a moment was wasted.

The day before Victoria set out on the first of her educational tours, her mother gave her a small leather-back notebook in which to write an account of the journey. The diary opens with a brief record of its origin. "This book Mamma gave me, that I might write the journal of my journey to Wales in it. Victoria, Kensington Palace, July 31st, 1832." From then onwards, until January 14th 1901, eight days before her death, she faithfully filled a further one hundred and twenty-one volumes, with only two gaps: one during an illness in 1835, and the other following Prince Albert's death in 1861. Such was her dedication to her task that she forced herself some years later to supply a detailed description of her husband's last hours. Few things illustrate her inflexible self-discipline better than the way she sat down every night to record how she spent her time, and her character shines through every page of her journal. Her massive integrity, her stubborn common sense, her quick, observant eye, her passionate enthusiasms, her royal memory, her naive simplicity, are all disclosed in her vivid, staccato style. Part of her purpose in keeping a diary was to forestall the Recording Angel by acknowledging her shortcomings, and numerous entries speak of her earnest resolve to mend her ways.

The very first entry of all in Victoria's journal shows her obsession with time. "Wednesday, August 1st. 1832. We left Kensington Palace at 6 minutes past 7 and went through the Lower-field gate to the right. We went on and turned to the left by the new road to Regent's Park. The road and scenery is beautiful. 20 minutes to 9. We have just changed horses at Barnet, a very pretty little town. 5 minutes past half past 9. We have just changed horses at St Albans. The situation is very pretty and there is a beautiful old abbey there. . . ."

Queen Victoria appointed her youngest daughter, Beatrice, to act as her literary executor, who unfortunately decided that her mother's journals were too revealing for other eyes than her own. She consequently copied out suitable passages from the diaries into a series of blue notebooks, burning the original manuscripts as she went along, much to the distress of King George V and Queen Mary, who were powerless to prevent this ill-judged act of vandalism. Even the extracts which survived were often severely mutilated. According to Roger Fulford, if her journal "could ever have been published in full we should possess a revelation of human character which would rank with the great diarists – with Pepys, with Fanny Burney or with Parson Woodforde".

The Tour of North Wales in 1832 began and concluded with visits to a number of English towns and country houses. The Princess was accompanied by her mother, Lehzen, Sir John and Lady Conroy, and the inevitable Victoire. On the second day of the journey they passed through Birmingham, which had recently played a major part in the triumph of the Reform Bill, and now clamorously welcomed the widow of their late champion, the Duke of Kent. The warmth of her reception was naturally interpreted as an oblique censure of the King, who had strenuously supported the opponents of reform. Conroy, to whom disloyalty was second nature, was quick to emphasise that the sympathies of Kensington had long been pledged to the Whigs.

The Princess was astonished and dismayed by the squalor of the Midlands. "We just passed through a town," she recorded on August 2nd, "where all coal mines are and you see the fire glimmer at a distance in the engines in many places. The men, women, children, country and houses are all black. . . . The Country is very desolate every where; there are coals about, and the grass is quite blasted and black. I just now see an extraordinary building flaming with fire. The Country continues black, engines flaming, coals, in abundance, every where, smoking and burning coal heaps, intermingled with wretched huts and carts and little ragged children." Her compassionate nature was always stirred by the desolate and downtrodden, but the "Two Nations" of rich and poor lived such separate existences, and her own life was so peculiarly sheltered, that she hardly ever encountered "Darkest England". Like many of her contemporaries she learned more about the horrors of industrialism in the novels of Dickens and George Eliot than from observing them first hand. Once she became Queen, most politicians preferred her not to know how deprived her subjects were. It was invincible ignorance not lack of sympathy which encouraged her to turn a blind eye to the evils of her reign.

The journey to Wales was punctuated by a number of ceremonies which greatly annoyed William IV. Everywhere flags and banners greeted the royal party, the streets were strewn with flowers, arches were built, speeches were made, addresses exchanged, salutes fired, and at the Menai Bridge an unaccompanied male voice choir sang "God Save the King". Lord Anglesey, the first Marquis, who lost his leg at Waterloo, lent the Duchess Plas Newydd. On the return journey, the party stayed at Chatsworth, where one evening after dinner the Princess was introduced to what became two of her

favourite diversions: charades and tableaux vivants. "At about 10",
she wrote in her diary on Saturday October 20th 1832, "the charade
began in 3 syllables and 4 scenes. The first act was a scene out of
'Blue-beard'; Lady Caroline Lascelles and Miss F. Cavendish acting
the ladies, and Count Karoly as Bluebeard, with Lord Newburgh
and Mr Lascelles as their friends. The next act was a scene carrying
offerings to Father Nile. . . . The third act was a scene of 'Tom
Thumb'; Lord Morpeth as Tom Thumb, and Lord Newburgh as the
nurse. The fourth act was a scene out of 'Kenilworth' (which was
the word). . . . When it was over, which was at quarter to 12, I went
to bed."

Before returning home the Duchess descended on Oxford, a city
her daughter later dismissed as "monkish". The fact that the University conferred an honorary Doctorate of Civil Law on Conroy hardly
commended its wisdom to her. During a visit to the Bodleian Library
she was shown "Queen Elizabeth's Latin exercise book when she
was my age. (13)." On Friday, November 9th, the royal carriages
finally clattered to a halt before the grand entrance of Kensington
Palace. The Duchess was delighted with the success of the expedition
which was generally hailed as a triumph, except by the King, who
regarded her "royal Progress" as a "disgusting" affront.

In July the following year, the Princess set out on a tour of the
South of England, accompanied for the first few days by her Württemberg cousins, and, of course, by her mother, Lehzen and the
Conroys. So excited was she that she woke up at four thirty on the
morning of their departure. The party left Kensington at seven in
a cavalcade of carriages, reaching Portsmouth by four. They then
embarked on the "Dear little 'Emerald'" and crossed the Solent to
Cowes. By seven o'clock they reached Norris Castle, which they
had previously visited in 1831, and which once more became their
base for exploring the Isle of Wight. Meanwhile the Conroy family
took up residence nearby at Osborne Lodge.

Victoria was greatly distressed by the departure of Ernest and
Alexander, although both were a good deal older than she was. "At
about a quarter to 8 we walked down our pier with them and there
took leave of them, which made us both VERY UNHAPPY. We
saw them get into the barge, and watched them sailing away for
some time on the beach. They were so amiable and pleasant to
have in the house; they were *always satisfied, always good humoured*;
Alexander took such care of me in getting out of the boat, and rode

next to me; so did Ernest . . . we shall miss them at *breakfast*, at *luncheon*, at *dinner, riding, sailing, driving, walking*, in *fact everywhere*."

While staying at Norris Castle, the Princess visited Nelson's Flag-ship, *Victory*. "We saw the spot where Nelson fell, and which is covered up with a brazen plate and his motto is inscribed on it, 'Every Englishman is expected to do his duty'. We went down as low as the tanks, and there tested the water which had been in there for two years, and which was excellent. We also saw the place where Nelson died. The whole ship is remarkable for its neatness and order. We tasted some of the men's beef and potatoes, which were excellent, and likewise some grog. . . . We both wished so much that *dear* Alexander and *dear* Ernest had been there, I think it would have amused them."

After leaving the Isle of Wight, the Duchess cruised along the south coast of England on board the *Emerald*, despite being "*dread-fully* sick". On August 2nd they anchored off Plymouth, and the next day Victoria presented new colours to the 89th Regiment (The Royal Irish Fusiliers) then stationed at Devonport. The Duchess told the assembled troops that her daughter's study of English history had inspired her with martial ardour. This was no mere flight of oratory, for she never faltered in her devotion to the Army. After all, as she often boasted, she was "a soldier's daughter".

The last of the Duchess's "Progresses" was planned for September 1835. It began inauspiciously when the Princess protested that she felt too unwell to travel, adding for good measure that she wanted no part in a journey of which the King disapproved. Later, she told Lord Melbourne that Conroy had "made her mother do all the things she ought not", and was responsible for making her "go that tour about the country receiving addresses, which she, Victoria, very much disliked, and did all she could to prevent. She said 'I knew it was improper, and very disagreeable to my Uncle, who always behaved very kindly to me, but it was all Sir John's influence, and what could I do?'" On September 2nd, the day before they set out for York, the Duchess handed her daughter a long letter in which she rehearsed her reasons for insisting upon going. Naturally, she wrote, she felt "disappointed and grieved" that Victoria felt so averse to travelling, but, nevertheless, she must try to recognise "that it is of the greatest consequence that you should be seen, that you should know your country, and be acquainted with, and be known by all classes. If the King was another man, and if he *really* loved you", he would welcome the tour. "Can you be dead to the calls your position demands? Impossible! Reflect – before it is too late. . . . Turn your thoughts and views to your future station, its duties, and the claims that exist on you."

From the moment the Princess started her tour of the North and East of England she felt unwell, and complained of tiredness, back pains and headaches. When she reached York, after a week's travelling, Lehzen thought she was "so markedly unwell, in body and soul, that it seemed almost a marvel she did not succumb there". During the rest of the tour she lost her appetite, and was so "greatly fatigued" that she nearly fell asleep over dinner at Holkham. When she returned home on September 25th she wrote in her diary: "I was much tired by the long journeys and the great crowds we had to encounter. We cannot travel like other people, quietly and pleasantly, but we go through towns and crowds and when one arrives at any nobleman's seat, one must instantly dress for dinner and consequently I could never rest properly". Considering Victoria's exceptional vitality, the Duchess proved curiously insensitive to her unwonted lassitude.

During their stay in the North, the royal party were guests of the Archbishop of York, Edward Vernon Harcourt, a "most sumptuous prelate", who was born in 1757 in the reign of George II, and who died ninety years later after falling off a bridge into a pond. "Well Dixon," he said to his chaplain on that melancholy occasion, "I think we've frightened the frogs." One of the supposed highlights of the Princess's visit was a performance of *The Messiah* in the Minster. But although, as she acknowledged, the Oratorio "is considered very fine", she personally found it "heavy and tiresome". She was "not at all fond of Handel's music, I like the present Italian school such as Rossini, Bellini, Donizetti, etc. *much better*". Already, by the age of sixteen, the Princess had become a most decided critic, possessing a mind of her own, and the audacity to defy received opinions.

On the return journey, which despite the Princess's reservations proved something of a triumph, the Duchess stopped at Stamford to receive an Address. Greville, who had just watched his horse lose the St Leger, attended the ceremony. "They arrived from Belvoir," he wrote describing the scene, "at three o'clock in a heavy rain. . . . When they had lunched, and the Mayor and his Brethren had got dry, she received the Address, which was read by Exeter as Recorder. It talked of the Princess as 'destined to mount the throne of these

realms'. Conroy handed the answer, just as the Prime Minister does
to the King."

The royal travellers returned to Kensington on September 25th,
and, after only three days' rest, set off once more for an autumn
holiday at Ramsgate, where the Duchess had taken a small house
overlooking the sea. A principal purpose of this visit was to join her
brother, the King of the Belgians, who was booked for a week at
the Albion Hotel. Both she and her daughter were particularly eager
to meet Leopold's new wife, Princess Louise, the eldest daughter of
Louis Philippe, King of the French, whom he had married in 1832,
partly to conciliate his Catholic subjects, partly to secure Belgium
from French aggression, and partly to provide for the succession.

Ever since Leopold left England in 1831, he had taken great care
to keep in touch with his niece, and a stream of admonitory letters
flowed between Brussels and Kensington. Like most Coburgs, he
rejoiced in a "firm grasp of the obvious", hence the necessity of
discarding tons of ore to yield a nugget of wisdom. But the Princess
was uncritical, and welcomed tokens of her uncle's affection. He also
kept closely in touch with Lehzen, who sent him reports on her
pupil's progress, and the latest news of the power struggle at Kensington. Leopold, a born intriguer, who greatly preferred to work
behind the scenes than to court the limelight, regarded his influence
over the future Queen of England as a major political asset.

The letter Leopold sent Victoria on her thirteenth birthday offered
her a characteristic piece of advice. "By the dispensation of Providence", he told her, "you are destined to fill a most eminent station;
to fill it *well* must now become your study". While nobody would
be disposed to deny the truth of this maxim, it seems improbable
that it had escaped the Princess's notice. The letter concluded more
promisingly, by assuring her that whenever she felt "in want of
support or advice", she could always "call on him with perfect confidence", assured "of the sincere attachment and affection with which
I shall ever be, my dearest Love, your faithful and devoted Friend
and Uncle, Leopold. R." On her fourteenth birthday she received a
further "sermon", this time concerned with a favourite theme: the
importance of being earnest. "You are now fourteen years old," he
told her, "a period when the delightful pastimes of childhood must
be mixed with thoughts appertaining already to a matured part of
your life." So highly did the King rate seriousness amongst virtues,
that he once reprimanded Louise with the words: "Pas de plaisanter-

ies, Madame". In his next letter, Leopold advised his niece to regard
history as the most important of her studies because of the light it
threw on "human-kind's ways". Later he sent her Sully's Memoirs
to encourage her interest in the past, recommending her to consult
Lehzen about which passages should be omitted, seeing that the
work had not been "written exclusively for young ladies".

Victoria was thrilled to meet her uncle Leopold at Ramsgate, after
a separation of "4 years and 2 months". Twice during his visit she
contrived to talk to him privately about the difficulties of life at
Kensington, Conroy's presumption, and the antagonism between
her mother and the King. "He gave me very valuable and important
advice", she wrote in her journal on Sunday, October 4th. "We
talked over many important and serious matters. I look up to him
as a Father, with complete confidence, love and affection. He is the
best and kindest adviser I have. He has always treated me as his child
and I love him most dearly for it." In an effort to relieve the boredom
and monotony of his niece's life, he promised to send her a letter
every Friday, and to persuade Louise to write each Tuesday.

The early pages of Victoria's journal are rich in tribute to her
uncle's wisdom. "He is *so* clever, *so* like my real father, as I have
none, and he is so kind and good to me." "To hear dear Uncle speak
on any subject," she noted a few days later, "is like reading a highly
instructive book; his conversation is so enlightened and clear. He is
universally admitted to be one of the finest politicians now extant."
Nobody else could have governed Belgium "so beautifully", and he
was a model for other sovereigns. "*That* country owes *all* its prosperity, happiness, everything to dearest Uncle Leopold; it was in a
sad state when Uncle arrived, and by his great prudence, sagacity,
and extreme cleverness, Belgium is now one of the most flourishing
Kingdoms in Europe." The Princess showed a pathetic devotion to
her uncle in whom she reposed unstinting trust. "You know, I
think," she once told him, "that *no* creature on earth *loved* you *more*
dearly, or has a higher sense of admiration for you, than I have.
Independent of all you have done – which I never, never can be
grateful enough for – my love for you exceeds all that words can
express."

Victoria soon came to love her "Aunt Louise" almost as much as
she did King Leopold. The Queen, who was only seven years older
than her niece, combined gaiety, charm and vivacity: qualities
frowned on by her husband and in short supply at Kensington. After

only a few days together at Ramsgate, the Princess thought Louise "quite delightful" and already loved her "*most dearly*". In particular, she admired the young Queen's beauty, and sought her advice about clothes. Consequently, Louise told her maid to arrange the Princess's hair in side curls, and when she returned to Brussels sent her two boxes of Paris dresses and bonnets. Soon after Victoria succeeded to the Throne, the King and Queen of Belgium paid her another visit. "I cannot say *how* I shall miss my dearest Aunt Louise", wrote the Queen on the day of her departure. "She combines with *great* cleverness and learning, so much merriment, and has all the liveliness and fun of a girl of 16, with all the *sense* and *deep* thought of one of 30. . . . She is so *lovely*, so graceful, she has such an angelic expression in her clear eyes; and she dresses *so well*, morning and evening." By 1846 the Queen's regard for her aunt was such that she told King Leopold "She is the dearest friend, after my beloved Albert, I have."

Even during her uncle's visit, Victoria still felt unwell, but it was not until after she saw him off from Dover that she finally collapsed. She became so ill that she was confined to her room for five weeks, and between October 7th and October 31st was too weak to keep up her journal. None of her doctors seemed to know precisely what was wrong with her. Dr Clark, the Duchess of Kent's physician, spoke of "bilious" fever, but diagnosis was never his strongest point. She herself believed that she had caught typhoid, while others suggested that she was suffering from blood poisoning provoked by septic tonsils. It is possible that her disorder was in some degree psychosomatic, a consequence of the traumas of adolescence and the stresses of life at Kensington. The bewildering variety of her symptoms, which ranged from back pains, stiffness and poor circulation, to lack of appetite and loss of hair, would seem to support this view. The Duchess, however, remained unconcerned, and even scolded Lehzen for exaggerating the Princess's condition, while Sir John referred dismissively to "childish whims". Not until Victoria became delirious was her mother convinced that something was seriously wrong. By the New Year the patient had recovered, thanks to Lehzen's devoted nursing and the strength of her constitution.

Conroy, with the Duchess's tacit approval, determined to browbeat the Princess into submission while she was too ill to resist him. But try as he did to force her to make him her secretary, she resolutely refused. Even when he thrust a pencil into her hand and ordered her to sign a document appointing him to the post, he failed to make her yield. "I resisted in spite of my illness," she later told Lord Melbourne with a pardonable note of pride.

There can be little doubt that Victoria was born stubborn, nor that the unhappy experiences of her childhood served to strengthen her will, generating "in the very core of her nature a vein of iron". No wonder that when she became Queen, Greville remarked on her "peremptory disposition", for she had been trained in a hard school. "If Sir John could not defeat her, worn down as she was by the tour and the ravages of typhoid, what chance had Ministers like Sir Robert Peel and Gladstone?" Sometimes her stubbornness was a fault, but at others it verged on heroism. When Balfour visited her during "Black Week", in the early days of the Boer War, she detected a note of defeatism in his remarks. "Please understand," she told him, "that there is no one depressed in this house; we are not interested in the possibilities of defeat; they do not exist." In her opinion, it was the duty of a Sovereign to be decisive and determined, and not to be guilty of Hamlet's penchant for "pottering".

Queen Victoria, despite rumours to the contrary, possessed a tremendous capacity for being amused, and retained into old age a childlike enjoyment of simple pleasures. When she spent a Spring holiday at Grasse in 1891 she relished "everything as if she were seventeen instead of seventy-two", and laughed "heartily at the extremely comic account of her arrival in the local paper". It would therefore be wrong to suppose that her childhood was not without moments of joy. She spent many enchanting evenings in the theatre, watching, wide-eyed, operas, ballets and plays. But, above all, she delighted in the visits of her relations, such as that paid in March 1836 by her mother's younger brother, Ferdinand, and his two sons.

Duke Ferdinand of Coburg, while serving in the Austrian cavalry, married Princess Antoinette, the fabulously rich and beautiful daughter of Prince Kohary of Hungary. His eldest son, Ferdinand, had been married by proxy the month before to Maria da Gloria, Queen of Portugal, and was travelling to Lisbon via England to meet his bride. The Prince, who was only nineteen, was tall and good looking, but "spoke through his nose in a slow funny way", and shook hands, in the German fashion. The Duke's younger son, Augustus, whom Victoria described as a "dear boy", possessed of a "sweet expression and kind smile", was a year older than she was. William IV, who did not much care for the Coburgs, graciously invited the Duchess, her brother, her daughter, and her two nephews to stay at

Windsor for a dinner and dance given in honour of the Prince Consort of Portugal.

The Coburg Princes reached Windsor on March 17th, still suffering from the ill effects of a boisterous Channel crossing, and were instantly plunged into a round of festivities, including a State Banquet and Ball. Before going to bed that night, Princess Victoria confided her first impressions of her cousins to her journal. Ferdinand, she wrote, "has a very slight figure, rather fair hair, beautiful dark brown eyes, a fine nose, and a very sweet mouth. . . . He is very good looking I think. It is impossible to see or know him without loving him." Augustus, she thought, was as tall as his brother, had "very fair hair, small blue eyes, a very pretty nose and likewise a very pretty mouth". Clearly little escaped the Princess's searching eyes and sharp observation: especially where handsome young men were concerned. During dinner, the Princess sat between the King and her cousin George, son of her Uncle Adolphus, Duke of Cambridge. Prince Ferdinand sat opposite her. The State Ball was held in the Waterloo Chamber. "I danced 3 quadrilles; 1st with dear Ferdinand, then with George Cambridge, and lastly with dear Augustus. During the evening dear Ferdinand came and sat near me and talked so dearly and sensibly. I *do* so love him. Dear Augustus also sat near me and talked with me and he is also a dear good young man, and is very handsome. I am so fond too of my Uncle Ferdinand. I stayed up till One. I was much amused and pleased." Within twenty-four hours of their first meeting, the Princess not only came to love her cousin Ferdinand "more and more", but to appreciate how sensible, unsophisticated, and "truly good" he was.

On March 19th the Duchess and her relations returned to Kensington Palace for a grand dinner and dance. The Princess sat between "dear Ferdinand and dear Augustus, two delightful neighbours. It was a most merry and happy dinner, the merriest we have had for a *long long* time." Even the spectre of Conroy at the feast failed to dash her spirits. "When Ferdinand is not in company, he is most funny and childishly merry, which I delight in. . . . We laughed a great deal together." Two days later there was another party at Kensington, this time a fancy dress ball. Before supper had even begun, the Princess had danced seven quadrilles. Only the thought that Ferdinand was due to depart on March 27th – a fortnight before the Duke and Augustus – made her feel wretched. If only her cousins would never leave her how happy she would be. When the time came for the Prince to sail to Portugal, they embraced before parting, tears streaming down their cheeks.

The Princess's grief at the departure of "dear, dear Ferdinand" was alleviated by her growing recognition of his brother's charms. Eventually, he too had to go, leaving her "lonely and unhappy" and missing him "dreadfully". Because the Princess was starved of young companions, she tended to lose her heart to every young man she met, but these schoolgirl enthusiasms proved to be passing whims. She was in love with dancing, and parties, rather than this Prince or that. When Augustus had gone, and silence reigned in the Palace, she found her old routine more depressing than ever, and longed for the sound of laughter and a glimpse of her charming cousins. "It seems like a dream," she wrote, "that all our joy, happiness and gaiety should thus suddenly be over". She turned to uncle Leopold for consolation who told her that there could be no hope of lasting happiness this side of the grave. She had asked for bread and was given a stone.

Prince Ferdinand's visit was followed in May by that of Ernest, Duke of Coburg, the Duchess's eldest brother, and his two sons. The Duke was a dissolute, debt-ridden roué, whose Court was notorious for its profligacy. In 1817 he married Princess Louise, the only child of Duke Augustus of Saxe-Gotha-Altenburg, who was then just sixteen, and half his own age. He was partly attracted to her by the knowledge that she would one day inherit her father's possessions, and partly because of her beauty. Her intelligence, her sense of fun, and her high spirits, added to her enchantment. Her eldest son, Ernest, was born in 1818, and her second son, Albert, a year later, on August 26th. Ernest was the image of his father and followed in his footsteps, while Albert took after Louise, who made no secret of her preference for him. He was born and brought up at Rosenau, a sham gothic castle some four miles out of the town of Coburg, nestling on a foothill of the Thuringian mountains in the midst of forests and meadows. The river Itz flowed through its grounds, and only the music of a waterfall tumbling into a grotto could be heard in this haven of peace. In 1822, provoked by her husband's infidelity, Louise began a liaison of her own with a young Lieutenant, Baron Alexander von Hanstein. The Duke demanded a separation, and in September 1824 the Duchess left Coburg, never to see her sons again. Two years later she was divorced, and immediately married Von Hanstein. Their happiness, however, proved short-lived as in 1831 she was found to be suffering from cancer, and before the year was out died suddenly of a haemorrhage. Shortly afterwards, Ernest married his niece, Princess Marie of Württemberg, his sister Antoinette's daughter. They were not particularly happy together, although Marie seemed willing to disregard her husband's endless debauchery.

Because Albert was totally unlike the Duke, or his own elder brother, it was often alleged that he must have been born out of wedlock. Even the omniscient Stockmar admitted that he could not explain the extraordinary difference between such close relations. Some people claimed that Albert looked Jewish, and consequently deduced that he was the son of the Court Chamberlain, Baron von Meyern. Others suggested that Leopold was his father, seeing that he had spent much of the winter of 1818 in Coburg. It was even rumoured that Lord Melbourne had refused to agree to Queen Victoria marrying her first cousin until he discovered that Albert was illegitimate. Not only is there no evidence to support such theories, but there are cogent reasons for rejecting them. Throughout the time of the Duke's marriage, his mother, the Dowager Duchess Augusta, constantly wrote to the Duchess of Kent, yet never so much as hinted at a rift until after the birth of her grandsons. Furthermore, had Louise taken a lover in 1818, the Duke's lawyers would have seized on him to blacken her reputation, but, in fact, the only name mentioned in his Divorce Petition was that of Baron von Hanstein, whom she first met when Albert was four years old. Finally, throughout her married life, Louise exchanged the most candid and intimate letters with her old friend Augusta von Studnitz, from whom no secrets were hid. Yet not until 1821 did she ever speak ill of her husband. The old maxim is false: there can be smoke without fire.

The very special value which Victoria and Albert attached to family life, was clearly the consequence of their both having lost a parent in early childhood. Although Albert was only five when his mother left him, he never forgot her. One of his first presents to Queen Victoria was a pin which Louise had given him. In 1848 the Queen set her seal of approval on her mother-in-law, divorced as she was, by naming her daughter after her. It is said that the Prince inherited his mother's fair hair and blue eyes, and those who knew them both were struck by their resemblance. Stockmar furthermore claimed that they shared the same intelligence and the same approach to human foibles. For the rest of his life the Prince bore the scars of his bereaved childhood. Just as his cousin Victoria grew up surrounded by women, his boyhood was spent among men, and as a result he felt bashful in female company. Sometimes he was so overpowered by shyness that he would hide from strangers and refuse to speak a word. On one shameful occasion, at a children's fancy dress ball, he ran screaming from his partner.

When he was four years old, Prince Albert was committed to the care of a tutor, Herr Christoph Florschütz, a young graduate from Munich, whom Stockmar recommended. "The Rath", as the Princes called him, was an admirable choice, being exceptionally widely read, a fluent linguist, and also well versed in science. Moreover, he possessed the rare ability to inspire his pupils with his own regard for scholarship. For fifteen years Florschütz became the dominant influence in Albert's life, his guide, philosopher, and friend. So much did the Prince love him that some people feared that his passion was too ardent. No wonder he often told the Queen that his boyhood years were the happiest of his life. He adored "the Rath", was inseparable from his brother, and even contrived to be fond of his father, who punctuated neglect with spasmodic bursts of oppression. Prince Albert spent most of his youth at Rosenau, relishing country pursuits and the study of nature. He was never particularly strong and throughout his life had difficulty in digesting, especially when suffering from stress. At such moments he gave way to fits of Coburg melancholia and "wished himself out of this world". By the time he first visited England he was remarkably well informed and a skilful musician and artist.

The Duke of Coburg's visit in 1836 was supposedly intended to celebrate Victoria's seventeenth birthday, but in reality was undertaken to pave the way for her marriage to Prince Albert. From the moment of Albert's birth, the Dowager Duchess Augusta toyed with the idea of a marriage between her grandchildren. "The little fellow," she told the Duchess of Kent in 1821, is the "pendant" to his English cousin. Stockmar was strongly in favour of the plan, partly because he greatly admired the British Constitution, partly because the future Queen of England was the most illustrious prize that Coburg could ever win, and partly because "in the whole Almanach de Gotha there is not a single Prince of riper years to whom we could entrust the dear Child without incurring the gravest risk". On May 1st 1836, King Leopold wrote secretly to Lehzen, instructing her to convey the gist of his letter to his niece, and claiming that they were "the only two people" who "cared about her for her own sake". An "immediate alliance" between the Princess and her cousin "was out of the question", as the Prince was only sixteen. "But the Princess might perhaps do well, for the sake of composure and peace of mind", to make a choice for the future "and firmly anchor herself to it". If Victoria was left in no doubt about the purpose of the visit, neither was Albert, who had known since the age of three where his destiny lay.

The most serious problem confronting the Coburgs was the fact that William IV disliked them so much. The King's chosen candidate for Victoria's hand was Prince Alexander of Orange, the younger son of the King of the Netherlands. In April 1836, not only did he invite the Dutch Royal Family to visit him, but did all in his power to prevent Duke Ernest coming. Leopold was furious when he learned of these proceedings, particularly as the King of the Netherlands was his "bitter enemy", and complained to his niece: "I never heard or saw anything like it, and I hope it will a little rouse your spirit." Fortunately, she was able to set his mind at rest when she sent him a letter describing the party the King and Queen gave at St James's for the Princes of Orange. "The boys," she wrote, "are both very plain, and have a mixture of Kalmuck and Dutch in their faces, moreover they look heavy, dull and frightened and are not at all prepossessing. So much for the *Oranges* dear Uncle."

The Duke of Coburg and his two sons reached Kensington at a quarter past two on Wednesday, May 18th. The Princess described Ernest as having "dark hair, and fine dark eyes and eyebrows, but the nose and mouth are not good; he has a most kind, honest and intelligent expression in his countenance and has a very good figure". But her journal gave pride of place to his younger brother. "Albert, who is just as tall as Ernest but stouter, is extremely handsome; his hair is about the same colour as mine; his eyes are large and blue, and he has a beautiful nose and a very sweet mouth with fine teeth; but the charm of his countenance is his expression . . . full of goodness and sweetness, and very clever and intelligent." In 1864 the Queen recalled that "the Prince was at that time (1836) much shorter than his brother, already very handsome, but very stout, which he entirely grew out of afterwards." Seeing that when they met Albert was worn out by his journey, and suffering from the aftereffects of seasickness, her first impression was surprisingly favourable. "They are both very amiable," she reported to King Leopold, who was eager to hear her verdict, "and extremely merry, just as young people should be."

Princess Victoria thought that her cousins were as gifted as they were affable. "They both draw very well, particularly Albert, and both are exceedingly fond of music." Sometimes she sat between them on a sofa, looking at prints and water colours, and often they played duets together on the piano, or sang arias from operas. "The more I see of them," she concluded, within three days of first meeting them, "the more I am delighted with them, and the more I love them. They are so natural, so kind, so *very* good and so well instructed and informed; they are so well bred, so truly merry, (always a high commendation in her eyes) and quite like children and yet very grown up in their manners, and conversation." Those who knew Ernest in his disreputable old age would have had difficulty in recognising him from this glowing tribute. When the Duchess took her nephews to a service in St Paul's, the Princess never forgot how "intently" Albert followed the sermon.

The Princes were only allowed rare moments of relaxation from a punishing round of entertainments. Their programme of visits, dinners and balls, was almost as arduous as an assault course. But Victoria's vitality and stamina was match for any challenge, and she was perfectly happy to dance the night away while those about her wilted with fatigue. On May 20th, the Duchess took her guests to a levée at St James's Palace, which was followed by an interminable dinner, and a concert which kept the Princes on their feet until two the following morning. Next evening they were obliged to attend the King's "official birthday" celebrations, consisting of a Drawing-Room for nearly four thousand guests, another great banquet, and yet more music. May 22nd was a Sunday, and observed as a day of rest. But on Monday, the Duchess gave a dinner at Kensington Palace in the Duke of Coburg's honour. As soon as the meal was over, Prince Albert retired to bed, explaining he felt unwell. By May 24th he appeared to have recovered sufficiently to attend Victoria's seventeenth Birthday Ball, held at St James's Palace. But he still was "very poorly", and after a couple of dances "turned as pale as ashes" and hastily took his leave. On May 30th, the Duchess gave a dance to which she magnanimously invited the Prince of Orange and his sons. Presumably she felt sufficiently assured of Albert's success to risk a possible rival. The Duke of Wellington came for part of the evening, and the band of the Grenadier Guards provided the music. Victoria hardly missed a dance. Gaiety and late hours suited her every bit as much as they demoralised her cousin. "All this dissipation," she reassured uncle Leopold, "does me a great deal of good."

The Duchess thoughtfully organised a number of visits to the opera, knowing that her nephews were "exceedingly fond of music". They both were enchanted by Donizetti's "Marino Faliero", and both were in "perfect ecstasies" over Bellini's "I Puritani". During these performances, the Princess made a remarkable discovery, upon which she commented in her diary: that she "liked the Opera twice as much" when she was accompanied by her "*dearest, most beloved cousins*" as when she went with her mother or the Conroys.

Prince Albert's feelings about his visit to England fell short of rapture. He told his stepmother, in a letter written from Kensington, that he missed "good Florschütz", that neither late hours nor the English climate suited him, and that he "had many hard battles to fight against sleepiness". Nor did he show that ardour for Victoria which his family hoped to see. "Dear Aunt is very kind to us," he remarked, "and our cousin is very amiable." The Prince was an early riser, but, by the same token, hated staying up late. As a boy he was ready for bed soon after nine, and quite often fell asleep over dinner, or curled up behind a curtain dead to the world. Even in later years he tired easily and found it a struggle to keep awake. General Grey, who published an account of Prince Albert's early years in 1867, candidly acknowledged that "he never took kindly to great dinners, balls, or the common evening amusements of the fashionable world". He only endured them out of his stern sense of duty, without "pleasure or enjoyment". The Queen, under whose "direction" the work was written, added the following footnote: "Yet nothing, at the same time, could exceed the kind attention he paid to everyone – frequently standing the whole evening that no one might be neglected".

Albert's visit, for all its trials, proved an undoubted success. The King, who had resolutely opposed it, was generous enough to admit that the Prince had impressed him favourably, and that he was one of the most handsome young men he had ever come across: precisely what Napoleon said on first meeting King Leopold. But, of course, what really mattered was what the Princess thought. On June 10th, the day her relations left, she cried "very bitterly" at the prospect of being separated from her "*dearest*, beloved Cousins". Fond as she was of Ferdinand and Augustus, she loved "Ernest and Albert *more than them*, oh yes, MUCH *more*". They were both so "*very, very merry and gay and happy*" and Albert was wonderfully witty at breakfast, and played so funnily with her King Charles spaniel, "Dash". But for all that, he was "the most reflecting of the two", and talked so cleverly about "serious and instructive things". Just as the Duke of Coburg was leaving, she gave him a letter for King Leopold, with whom he was going to stay on his way home. In it, she thanked her "beloved Uncle" for the promise of "great happiness" he had given her "in the person of dear Albert", who possessed "every quality that could be desired" to render her "perfectly happy". She concluded by begging Leopold "to take care of the health of one now *so dear* to me", and to take him under his "*special protection*".

At no time did the Duchess, her daughter, or her nephew allude to the real purpose of the visit, and nothing was said about further meetings. The Queen told Lord Melbourne in 1839 that no "understanding" had ever been discussed, let alone reached. A year after her marriage, Prince Albert wrote a memorandum describing their first meeting. He, too, was adamant that "not a word in allusion to the future passed between them", although they "were very much pleased with each other".

If the Princess's letters and journal are taken at face value, they seem to suggest she had fallen in love with Prince Albert, but only three months before she had sung the praises of Ferdinand and Augustus with almost equal fervour. The fact that Prince Albert's second visit was delayed for three years hardly suggests her raging impatience to see him. As for her letters to uncle Leopold they were clearly intended to please. When she finally lost her heart to the Prince in 1839, the lyrical language which flowed from her pen showed her earlier efforts were froth.

One of the greatest joys of the Princess's childhood were evenings spent at the theatre. Her sketch books and journals are full of vivid glimpses of the happy hours she spent at Covent Garden and Drury Lane. Momentarily, when the lights went down, she forgot her lonely, humdrum existence, as she sat bolt upright on the edge of a gilt chair waiting for the curtain to rise and her dreams to begin. For her, the royal box was a "magic casement" through which she could watch a world she would otherwise never know. The first play she ever saw was "Charles XII", performed at Drury Lane in 1828. She was only nine at the time but she never forgot it. Ballet, which in the early nineteenth century was still an embellishment of opera rather than an independent art, particularly intrigued her. One of her earliest heroines was the great Ballerina, Marie Taglioni, whom she watched dance *La Sylphide*, quite "beautifully". But the Princess's theatrical tastes were principally formed by opera. During the Summer Season at the King's Theatre, soon to be renamed "Her Majesty's", it was possible to hear some of the finest singers in Europe. Of these, Giulia Grisi, who made her London début in 1834, was the Princess's favourite. She first saw Grisi in Donizetti's "Anna Bolena" and thought her "a most beautiful singer and actress". On returning that night from the opera, she wrote in her journal in large capitals "I was VERY MUCH AMUSED INDEED". But greatly as she admired her idol, she acknowledged her short-comings. "It is a great pity," she wrote, that "she now wears her front hair so much lower than she did. It is no improvement to her appearance, though, (do what she may) *spoil* her face she *never* can, it is too lovely for that." Once, she spotted that Grisi had made a mistake in her role in "I Puritani". Normally, when she sang the Polacca, she was supposed to appear as a bride attired in white satin, but on this particular evening she forgot to make the change. Nothing escaped those wide open blue eyes or that penetrating stare.

The Duchess of Kent, knowing how devoted her daughter was to Grisi, persuaded her to sing in a concert she planned to give for Victoria's sixteenth birthday. The Princess was delighted to find that Grisi was just as beautiful off stage as on it, and that she spoke in the most "ladylike and unaffected" manner. The concert concluded with the great quartet from "I Puritani" "A te o Caro!", sung by Grisi, Rubini, Tanburini and Lablache. "This ended the *most delightful concert* I *ever heard*. Aunt Sophia, who had *never* heard any of these singers before, was delighted; but no one could be *more enchanted* than *I* was. I shall never forget it. . . . I stayed up till 20 minutes past 1. I was MOST EXCEEDINGLY delighted."

So struck was the Princess by Luigi Lablache, the finest bass-baritone of his day, that she begged her mother to let him give her singing lessons. These were arranged in 1836 and continued on and off for twenty years. Lablache, who was half Irish and half Italian, possessed the charm of both nationalities, and regaled his pupil with such a rich fund of stories that his lessons became the high point of her week, and greatly enlarged her knowledge of operas and their production. Soon she became so fond of her "dear Master" that she pined for him to return from his tours abroad. "I shall count the weeks and months eagerly till next April," she wrote in her diary on August 10th 1836, "when I shall resume my delightful lessons with him."

The Princess was almost as fond of going to plays as she was of listening to operas. She never saw the great Edmund Kean, probably because of his fondness for the bottle, but she often watched performances by William Macready and Charles Kemble. Kemble, she thought, had once been "a very fine actor", but now his manner was stilted and unnatural, and she preferred truth and sincerity to affectation. When she saw him take a leading part in "The Separation", an indifferent tragedy in five acts, she complained that he whined too much, drawled his words in a "slow, peculiar manner", and made "terrible faces" which spoiled his countenance. So stage-struck did she become that most of her precious collection of dolls portrayed characters from drama, but more important still, she made good use of the lessons she learned from actors to further her own calling. Nature had not endowed her with a regal presence, and she knew very well she was short, plump and plain. But, nevertheless, she radiated majesty and stole the limelight from more glamorous rivals. In so far as it is possible to analyse the secret of her artistry, it seems to have consisted of an unfailing sense of theatre, an exquisite grace of movement, and the gift of faultless timing: partly, no doubt, learned from watching Marie Taglioni float across the stage with matchless poise and elegance. During the early years of her reign she was a loyal patron of the drama, and sought to make acting respectable by honouring such leaders of the profession as were not disqualified by the depravity of their lives.

The constant squabbles which plagued relations between the Court and Kensington came to a head in the summer of 1836. Greville learned all the details from a privileged eye witness, Adolphus Fitz-Clarence, the King's natural son. Queen Victoria was horrified when his diary was published in 1874, and denounced it as "a dreadful and really scandalous book". She particularly resented his "disloyal disposition" towards George IV and William IV, "whose hospitality he had enjoyed" as Clerk to the Council. Nevertheless, she acknowledged that he generally spoke with authority, and that his description of the "unfortunate Dinner in '36", was essentially true.

William, who did his best to placate his fractious sister-in-law, invited her to Windsor in the summer of 1836 to celebrate the Queen's birthday on August 13th, and his own eight days later. The Duchess, whose talent for giving offence amounted to genius, replied that she preferred to spend her own birthday on August 17th at Claremont, but that she would be happy to join the King on August 20th. Nothing was so calculated to infuriate William as disrespect for Adelaide, but nevertheless he contrived to keep his temper and said nothing.

On August 20th the King prorogued Parliament and afterwards paid a surprise visit to Kensington, in the certain knowledge that the Duchess had preceded him to Windsor. A quick tour of the building disclosed the fact that she had appropriated seventeen rooms which he had positively forbidden her to occupy. In 1832 she had requested Sir Jeffry Wyatville to prepare a scheme for enlarging her apartments, but William refused to consider his proposals and wrote on his plans "the King says 'no'". The Duchess, however, refused to be discouraged, and when Dr Clark suggested that Princess Victoria should move to a more salubrious part of the Palace, she adopted his recommendations without reference to His Majesty. The Princess, not realising she was an usurper, was delighted with the move, for her new quarters commanded splendid views of Kensington, and were a great deal lighter and more spacious than those she had just left.

The King returned to Windsor at about ten o'clock that evening, and joined his guests in the Drawing-room. The very first person he spoke to was his niece. Taking her by both hands he expressed his pleasure at seeing her and his regret that they met so seldom. Then, turning to the Duchess of Kent, he protested in loud and angry tones that "a most unwarrantable liberty had been taken with one of his Palaces; that he had just come from Kensington, where he found apartments had been taken possession of not only without his consent but contrary to his commands, and that he neither understood nor would endure conduct so disrespectful to him." This bitter harangue "proved to be only the muttering of the storm which was to break the next day".

Although the Birthday Dinner on Sunday, August 21st, was supposedly "private", over a hundred guests were invited. The Duchess of Kent was placed next to the King, and Victoria sat opposite. At the end of the meal a toast was drunk to "His Majesty's health and long life". But the King, instead of graciously replying, delivered a furious tirade during which he expressed the hope that his life would be spared for nine months longer until his niece came of age, thereby averting the threat of a Regency. "I should then have the satisfaction of leaving the royal authority to the personal exercise of that Young Lady (pointing to the Princess), the Heiress presumptive of the Crown, and not in the hands of a person now near me, who is surrounded by evil advisers and who is herself incompetent to act with propriety in the station in which She would be placed. I have no hesitation in saying that I have been insulted – grossly and continually insulted – by that person, but I am determined to endure no longer a course of behaviour so disrespectful to me. Amongst many other things I have particularly to complain of the manner in which that Young Lady has been kept away from my Court; she has been repeatedly kept from my drawing-rooms, at which She ought always to have been present, but I am fully resolved that this shall not happen again. I would have her know that I am King, and that I am determined to make my authority respected, and for the future I shall insist and command that the Princess do upon all occasions appear at my Court, as it is her duty to do." While the King excitedly gave rein to his pent up fury, the Queen was visibly distressed, Victoria burst into tears, and her mother sat motionless while the storm raged around her. But once the guests had left the table, the Duchess ordered her carriage. It was only with great difficulty that she was prevailed upon to stay the night at Windsor and avoid a flagrant scandal.

Greville expressed the view, held by most Englishmen, that "Such a gross and public insult, offered to her at his own table", was inexcusable "from a man to a woman, from a Host to his guest, and to the last degree unbecoming to the station they both of them fill." The King's peppery temper explained but could not excuse "this awful philippic". The Duke of Wellington's comment was characteristically succinct: "Very awkward by God!" Neither the King nor the Duchess showed the faintest sign of contrition. The very next evening, presumably on purpose, she kept him waiting for dinner, and so exasperated did he become that he proclaimed to all within hearing "That woman is a nuisance."

The King's speech, like most rash acts, proved totally counterproductive. Far from persuading the Duchess to spend more time at Court, it convinced her of the wisdom of staying away. The Princess never forgot the horror of that evening. Some twenty years later she told her eldest daughter how she remembered always being "on pins and needles, with the whole family hardly on speaking terms. I (a mere child) between two fires – trying to be civil and then scolded at home! Oh! it was dreadful, and that has given me such a horror of Windsor, which I can't get over . . .". Later still, Queen Victoria told her granddaughter, Victoria of Hesse, that she detested the "Tapestry Room" in the Lancaster Tower at Windsor, because she remembered being "terribly scolded" in it by the Duchess, who accused her of "making up to William IV" after he had grossly insulted her.

During the last month of her uncle's reign, Victoria found herself caught up in a series of melodramas almost as improbable as the plots of her favourite operas. On May 18th, 1837, William IV instructed the Lord Chamberlain, Lord Conyngham, to present himself at Kensington next morning with a letter for the Princess. Both the Duchess and Sir John attempted to intercept it, but Lord Conyngham insisted upon handing it to her personally, producing as his authority a note in the King's hand commanding him to do so. The letter informed the Princess that the moment she came of age, William intended to ask Parliament to vote her an annual income of ten thousand pounds a year: a sum sufficient to build a Man-of-War. It went on to authorise her to set up a separate Establishment of her own, should she wish to do so, and to appoint a Keeper of her Privy Purse. Nothing could have been better calculated to drive Conroy to frenzy, for the King's proposals struck the Kensington System a mortal blow. Instead of the Princess being subject to his will, she had been offered a chance of freedom. In six days' time, if William had his way, Sir John's dreams would be shattered. There would be no Regency, no prospect that he would one day rule England, no hope of Victoire becoming a Lady-in-Waiting. That evening, the Princess decided to dine alone so oppressive was the atmosphere at the Palace. Meanwhile, her mother and Conroy desperately sought ways to thwart the King.

The next day, May 20th, a series of letters passed between Kensington and South Street, Lord Melbourne's residence. The Duchess fired the first salvo by asking the Prime Minister what part his Government had played in the King's recent offer. Melbourne replied by pointing out that "every proposition submitted by the Crown to Parliament" was dependent on previous advice from "His Majesty's Confidential Servants, and for that advice they are necessarily responsible". This impeccable constitutional lecture provoked an indignant response. The Duchess reproached the Prime Minister for supporting a plan which was contrary to the wishes of her child, who, "of her own free will", had told the King that she wished "to be left as heretofore with her mother". No sooner had William read his niece's reply, than he saw at once it was suspect. "Victoria," he insisted, "has not written that letter": a verdict confirmed by her diary entry for May 20th. "Wrote a letter to the King, which Mamma had previously written for me." Some years later, when the Prince Consort was helping the Queen to sort out her papers, he came across the Duchess's draft, which now bears the following note in his hand: "Written by the Duchess of Kent on Sir John Conroy's advice". Between them, they obliged the Princess to refer to her "youth and inexperience", and to express the wish that the income she had been promised "should be given to my dear mother for my use." At first the Princess refused to copy the draft letter. Then she attempted to amend it. Finally, she begged to be allowed to consult Lord Melbourne before sending it. But in the end she succumbed to remorseless pressure. It was the only time during her struggle for independence that she yielded to duress. That evening she dictated a memorandum to Lehzen in which she made clear that she had been forced to write as she did against her will.

May 24th, 1837, Victoria's eighteenth birthday, was a sombre day for Conroy, for it put an end to his hopes for a Regency. Moreover, the King's life was clearly ebbing, and it could not be more than a few weeks before his niece succeeded to the Throne. Sir John had no illusions about his prospect in the new reign. Having tormented and insulted the Princess for many years, he could hardly expect anything from her other than revenge. The future, once so rich in promise, now looked dark and menacing. He had not spent twenty years in the Duchess's Household merely to end his days as her Equerry. However, Conroy was not the man to surrender without a fight, and towards the end of May he flung all his reserves into a last desperate assault, with the abandon of one who has little to lose and a world to win. Over and over again he had been repulsed by a mere slip of a girl, but now that time was rapidly running out he decided to make a final bid for victory. Part of his strategy was to revive the project which met with failure at Ramsgate: to force the Princess to make him her private secretary. He also toyed with an updated version of his Regency plan, whereby Victoria was to be browbeaten into inviting her mother to act on her behalf, regardless of the fact that she had come of age.

The battle waged at Kensington was not unlike that between David and Goliath in that the odds were weighted heavily against the eventual victor. Conroy began with the enormous advantage that he possessed the powerful if misguided support of the Duchess of Kent, whom Creevey described as "the most restless, persevering troublesome devil possible". He could also depend on the help of Princess Sophia, Lady Flora Hastings, and Victoria's half-brother, Prince Charles of Leiningen, whom the Duchess had summoned from Amorbach in February. Prince Charles was a wild young man, self-willed, idle, mischievous and debauched. He boasted that his philosophy was that "life is for enjoyment", and nobody could accuse him of not sticking to his principle. The Duchess knew she could rely on her son for support as he looked to her for help to discharge his debts. Seeing she paid the piper, she insisted on calling the tune. Soon after Charles arrived on the scene, Lehzen wrote secretly to King Leopold to assure him that Victoria was "fully aware of the wickedness of the Prince of Leiningen and his friend Sir John". Stockmar already had reached the same conclusion, and warned the King of the Belgians that his young nephew shared "the same madness, the same perversity, the same clinging to straws" as characterised Conroy.

The Princess fought a stubborn and courageous rearguard with only one ally, the ever steadfast Lehzen. There could hardly have been more triumphant proof of her capacity to govern than the resolute way in which she refused to be battered into submission. As the King's life ebbed away, hardly an hour passed without the Duchess or Sir John harassing the Princess. But neither their threats nor their entreaties persuaded her to yield. King Leopold, although he had heard the distant rumble of gunfire, was so "completely in the dark" over the "battles and difficulties" with which his niece contended, that he requested Stockmar to sort things out. The Baron reached Kensington on May 25th only to discover that the Duchess was so bewitched by Conroy that it was impossible to trust her. The moment he saw that intrigues were afoot to "entrap" the "future Sovereign", he decided to do what he could to rescue the Princess.

Stockmar kept closely in touch with King Leopold and sent him detailed accounts of his conversations with the leading actors in the drama. The Princess, he reported, was calm but resolute, and gave the impression of being "extremely jealous of what she considers to be her rights", and consequently refused "to do anything which would put Conroy into a situation to be able to entrench upon them. Her affection and esteem for her mother seem likewise to have suffered by Mamma having tamely allowed Conroy to insult the Princess in her presence." In later letters Stockmar described succeeding scenes in the tragi-comedy played out at Kensington. "O'Hum (Sir John Conroy) continues the system of intimidation with the genius of a madman, and the Duchess carries out all that she is instructed to do with admirable docility. . . . The Princess continues to refuse firmly to give her Mamma her promise that she will make O'Hum her confidential adviser." Almost the most distressing feature of the whole unhappy affair was the Princess's discovery that her mother had plotted behind her back to rob her of her birthright.

On June 15th, as the bulletins about the King's health grew increasingly gloomy, the Duchess turned to Lord Liverpool in the hope of recruiting him as an ally. He was an old family friend, indeed one of the few Tories of her acquaintance, and a half-brother of the late Prime Minister. His daughter, Lady Catherine Jenkinson, a Lady-in-Waiting to the Duchess, was one of Victoria's few friends. So momentous was his visit that he wrote an authoritative account of it while it still remained fresh in his memory. He first saw Conroy, who tried to convince him that the Princess was totally unfit to succeed to the Throne. All the old arguments were rehearsed about her frivolous tastes and retarded development. But happily Sir John had a proposal which would overcome the problem: if he were appointed the Princess's private secretary he could supervise her so closely as to prevent her making mistakes. Lord Liverpool, in common with most other politicians of the day, had long felt grave misgivings about the growth of the King's Secretariat. He was therefore horrified by the notion that the royal prerogative should be effectively exercised by a nominee of the Crown. Few principles were as sacred to the Constitution as that of ministerial responsibility, and Liverpool curtly dismissed Conroy's suggestion. There must be *"no private secretary"*, he told him firmly.

After his contretemps with Sir John, Lord Liverpool saw the Princess. She particularly requested that nobody else should be present at the interview. In order to make the best possible use of the discussion, she came with a carefully prepared agenda, and Lord

Liverpool was greatly impressed by her businesslike approach. Could this purposeful young lady he saw before him be the same backward and frivolous girl whom Conroy had just described? He strongly advised her to send for Lord Melbourne the moment she succeeded and to put herself in his hands: which was precisely what King Leopold told her to do. It would be a great mistake, he said, to appoint a private secretary, and it was out of the question that she should have Sir John Conroy forced upon her as Keeper of the Privy Purse after the "slights and incivilities" she had suffered from him. He concluded by telling her that he thoroughly approved of the firm way in which she had handled her mother, and that she was absolutely right to refuse to commit herself by making any promises. One conversation with the Princess was enough to persuade him that she was being terrorised and maligned.

In 1854 Lord Granville told Charles Greville a story he learned from Stockmar. According to the Baron, the Duchess and Conroy in the summer of 1837 "plotted to get a Regency established for a couple of years on the pretext of the Queen's youth and inexperience, and to force her to give a promise in writing that she would make Sir John her private secretary". On June 16th, when all their efforts had failed and the King's life hung by a thread, Sir John urged the Duchess to shut the Princess up "and keep her under duress till she had extorted this engagement from her". Prince Charles claimed in a memorandum of 1840, written primarily to clear his name, that he overheard Conroy tell the Duchess "If Princess Victoria will not listen to reason *she must be coerced.*" Apparently this dastardly suggestion shocked him so deeply that he warned his mother to have nothing to do with it. Presumably he saw the game was up and preferred to join the winning side before it was too late. Greville attributed the failure of the plan to the "spirit of the daughter" and the "timidity of the mother".

The King, like Charles II before him, was an "unconscionable time dying". At a levée he held on May 18th, he was obliged to receive his guests seated. Six days later he was unable to be present at the ball he gave for his niece's eighteenth birthday. By the middle of June it became clear that he could not recover. "It may *all be over* at *any moment*," Victoria told King Leopold on the sixteenth, "and yet *may* last a few days. . . . Since Wednesday (June 14th) all my lessons are stopped, as the news may arrive very suddenly". King Leopold, who was as profuse with advice as he was niggardly with money, wrote back to tell her precisely what she should do on becoming Queen. "The moment you get official communication of it, you will entrust Lord Melbourne with the office of retaining the present Administration. . . . I have already – if you would read it over – written to you some months ago on the subject of the necessity of maintaining the influence of conservative principles, and of protecting the Church. You will do well to keep both objects in view." Leopold ended his letter by saying that he had decided not to come over immediately, in case people fancied "I thought of ruling the realm for *purposes of my own*," but as soon as she wanted him he would willingly "come in a moment". On June 17th William asked his doctors "to tinker him up" so that he could celebrate the anniversary of Waterloo next day. By the evening of June 19th the Queen was told that the King's end was near; and Prince Ernest of Hohenlohe, Feodore's husband and a cousin of Queen Adelaide, was sent to Kensington to warn the Princess. The news came as no surprise, but, nevertheless, distressed her, and she "turned very pale" and "burst into tears". Prince Ernest, she wrote in her journal, "brought her a kind message from the poor Queen, and also one from the poor old King". According to Lord Holland, one of Melbourne's Ministers, "the King on his deathbed found means to convey a message to her, unknown to her mother, advising her . . . to continue Lord Melbourne and his colleagues and to signify that intention to them without loss of time."

At twelve minutes past two on the morning of Tuesday June 20th, William IV died, piously muttering "The Church! The Church!" Shortly afterwards, a carriage, which had been waiting in the Lower Ward at Windsor, set off for Kensington. Crowded into it were Dr Howley, the Archbishop of Canterbury, Lord Conyngham, the Lord Chamberlain, and Sir Henry Halford, the late King's doctor, who had been with him when he died. Shortly before six they reached the Palace gates and had some difficulty in persuading the porter to let them pass. Like most officials, he was governed by precedent, and never before had been confronted by the Archbishop of Canterbury at such an unholy hour. Some minutes later, the Duchess proved almost equally reluctant to wake her daughter, until Lord Conyngham told her that they came to see "The Queen" on State business. That night, Queen Victoria wrote an account of her accession which marked a crucial milestone in her journal. Hitherto, the Duchess had studied every entry, but from now on it was closed to her inspection. "I was awoke at 6 o'clock by Mamma," runs the entry for June 20th, "who told me that the Archbishop of Canterbury and Lord Conyngham were here, and wished to see me. I got out of bed and went into my sitting-room (only in my dressing-gown), and *alone*, and saw them. Lord Conyngham then acquainted me that my poor Uncle, the King, was no more, and had expired at 12 minutes past 2 this morning, and consequently that I am *Queen*. . . . Since it has pleased Providence to place me in this station, I shall do my utmost to fulfil my duty towards my country; I am very young and perhaps in many, though not in all things, inexperienced, but I am sure, that very few have more real good will and more real desire to do what is fit and right than I have." The Silver Candlestick, which Victoria held during the first audience of her reign, was later presented to Balliol by Conroy's eldest son, then a Fellow of the College. How his father acquired this signal memento history does not relate, but one thing is certain: the Queen would never have given it to him.

Queen Victoria, looking back on her early life, was disposed to complain of her miserable childhood. "I never was happy" she insisted, "until I was eighteen." This conviction remained with her for the next sixty years. A few days before her eightieth birthday, she paid a visit to Kensington Palace, which had just been renovated. Lord Esher, who had supervised the work, showed her round. As she was wheeled slowly from room to room, she told him about her life there half a century before. Her power of recall astonished him, but when she claimed that "She had no happy recollections of her youth except her dogs", memory played her false. In fact, as her journals plainly show, she was often "very much amused". It was, however, certainly true that her "Kensington life for the last six or seven years had been one of great misery and oppression." In 1858, she told her eldest daughter, that she "had led a very unhappy life as a child – had no scope for my very violent feelings of affection – had no brothers and sisters to live with – never had a father – from my unfortunate circumstances was not on a comfortable or at all intimate or confidential footing with my mother – much as I love her now – and did not know what a happy domestic life was!"

The Queen had been hurt for life by her troubled childhood. As Prince Albert told Florschütz, "Wrong upbringing" has warped her "naturally fine character". Stockmar expressed the same idea in a slightly different way. The Princess, he said, had been forced for many years to exercise a degree of restraint which was hardly natural in a girl of her age, and the effort had taken its toll on her nerves. The Queen herself endorsed this diagnosis and told Lord Melbourne that "worry and torment" had stopped her growing. In the first few weeks of her reign, she severed almost all the ties which bound her to her childhood. If she could not forget the past she could, at least, ignore it. After she left Kensington in July 1837 she did not go back for thirty years.

The effects of adversity on Queen Victoria were not all damaging. On the contrary it served to strengthen her naturally formidable character. She once said that the hard school through which she had passed probably did her good by helping to form her mind, and somehow she never lost, despite her trials, "the strong, generous, childlike, simple nature which those who knew her best loved most truly". Conroy helped her to shed some naive illusions, but did not entirely destroy her innocence. Misfortune became for her an anvil on which to forge the finest steel. She was born with a "very inflexible disposition", but, at least, her resolute will prevented her being crushed by the weight of the Kensington System.

Nobody can hope to understand the Queen without recognising that her nature abounded in contradictions, and it can only be misleading to seek rational explanations for what was essentially illogical. It has even been hinted that her confusion of mind was a feminine disorder, but such perilous judgements are best left to the verdict of the reader. The facts, however, are clear enough. At one and the same moment the Queen vociferously urged her Ministers to teach the Tsar a sharp lesson, and deplored the senseless waste of life which doing so entailed. She was equally ready to exhort the Queen of Prussia to give her son his freedom, while stubbornly refusing to permit the Prince of Wales to be trusted with State Papers. In 1863, to take a final example, she complained how she dreaded the thought of leaving Windsor, where "the last happy and sad days of my marriage were spent", and to which she was bound by "sacred ties". Yet not long afterwards, in stark defiance of this sentiment, she wrote to her daughter, Vicky, from Balmoral, deploring the prospect of returning to that "dungeon Windsor", with its gloomy apartments and unwholesome climate. The Queen not only simultaneously held incompatible beliefs, but rooted "in the very depth of her being" were "lodged contrary qualities which might have caused another personality to split into fragments". Indeed, the temperamental storms to which she was only too prone were the outward signs of such inner conflicts.

The Queen's reaction to the quarrels and plots which made her childhood wretched was characteristically paradoxical. On the one hand she craved help and support. On the other, necessity forced her to stand on her own feet. The consequence was that she became exceptionally self-sufficient but still yearned to be cosseted, and there always remained within this most dominant of women an infant crying out for succour. "Nature and circumstances combined to make the eighteen-year-old girl who ascended the Throne of England in June 1837 an extraordinary and paradoxical mixture: blending a child's simplicity and a child's uninhibited violence of feeling with the self-command of a mature woman and the unhesitating authority of a born monarch."

It was hardly necessary for King Leopold to warn his niece not to lose sight of the experience she had gained living amongst intriguers. The Kensington System had taught her to be suspicious and distrustful, and the lesson was such that she was unlikely to forget it. But, by the same token, as she herself remarked, "I have, alas! seen so much of bad hearts and dishonest and *double* minds, that I know how to value and appreciate *real worth*". Her own behaviour was so straightforward that she naturally expected the same openness in others. Her association with Conroy taught her three things: that power corrupts, that she needed to be constantly on her guard against those who tried to coerce her, and that to survive the wiles of a wicked world required reticence and discretion.

Surrounded as she was by malice and intrigue, the Queen was obliged to practise an art abhorrent to her nature: dissimulation. Circumstances forced her "to be precociously self-controlled, precociously prudent, and precociously secretive". Merely to survive, she had little choice but "to live on outwardly submissive and affectionate terms with people she distrusted and disliked". The skills she acquired in concealing her feelings were an admirable training for a political career, but they crossed the grain of her candid nature, and set up the tensions which Stockmar believed took a heavy toll on her nerves. Such was her control of her features that she trained herself to assume a fixed, impassive look, "curiously at variance with the intensely emotional nature that lay beneath". Lord Melbourne was so astonished by the Queen's discretion that he thought it "almost unnatural in one so young".

King George IV and his brothers established a tradition of reckless overspending: none more so than the Duke of Kent, whose debts his daughter discharged as soon as it lay in her power to do so. The Royal Dukes never fully grasped the necessary connection between expenditure and income. Even the prudent Leopold owed eighty thousand pounds when elected King of the Belgians. Queen Victoria, however, broke the mould and became the first solvent sovereign of the century: partly because as a child she was trained to know the value of money, partly because her mother's "poverty" forced frugality on her, and partly because her father's misfortunes warned her against improvidence. Miss Harriet Martineau, a prolific writer on political economy, was loud in the Queen's praise, but her children and grandchildren tended to be more sceptical. Others were touched or amused by her economies, of which she was often the principal victim. When she set out for London for her Golden Jubilee, she decided to wear her second-best hat, bought from a Windsor draper. It is hard to imagine what kind of occasion she had in mind for wearing her smartest headdress.

Even when the Queen was an old woman she remained agonisingly shy, mostly because as a child she was given so few opportunities of "rubbing shoulders on equal terms with other people". As Sir Walter Scott foresaw, it would have been hard to devise a more inappropriate training for a future sovereign than a life of planned seclusion. In 1867, after the Queen had been nearly thirty years "in harness", she confessed "I am terribly shy and nervous and *always was so*". When Samuel Wilberforce paid homage to her on becoming Bishop of Oxford, he noticed that as "she held my hand in hers, her hands trembled greatly". Her efforts to hide her nervousness were often misunderstood. For instance, her stiff and distant manner was seen as a sign of disdain, whereas, in fact, it proceeded from embarrassment. Those who knew her well noticed a number of little tricks by which she betrayed her anguish, such as a faint shrug of the shoulders, and a "curious nervous laugh". Towards the end of her reign, when the Queen had become so venerable as to inspire her subjects with an awe verging on terror, people were amazed to be introduced to "an amiable field-mouse", who greeted them with a bashful smile, and radiated benevolence. Instead of a scowling matriarch they beheld a timid schoolgirl. The first time Theodore Martin met her, to discuss the possibility of writing the Life of the Prince Consort, he was taken aback by her "nervousness almost amounting to shyness . . . so little to be expected in a Sovereign". If she felt shy at eighty, she was distraught at eighteen, especially when she was required to go everywhere first, in front of her uncles, having previously been brought up "very humbly at Kensington Palace", and knowing so little about the life of the Court.

Soon after the Queen's accession, she admitted to Lord Melbourne that she was painfully short of small-talk and tended to feel gauche. His advice was simple enough. The more time one spent thinking what to say, the more silent one became. It was better, therefore, to say something, however foolish or commonplace, than to remain floundering for words. The Queen was always eager to excuse awkwardness or timidity in others, admitting with her nervous laugh that she had long suffered from a "stupid feeling of shyness". Ill-prepared as she was by her solitary childhood to shine in the society of which she became the head, she did, at least, know something of the wicked ways of the world.

2

A Party Queen
1837–1839

Sir Robert Peel predicted in 1830 that Monarchy had become so unpopular in Britain that only a miracle could save it. Two years later, at the height of the battle to pass the Reform Bill, King William himself protested that he felt the crown "tottering" on his head. The lowest ebb, in fact, was reached during the reign of George IV. Greville, who knew him well, described him as "a mixture of narrow-mindedness, selfishness, truckling, blustering, and duplicity, with no object but self, his own ease, and the gratification of his own fancies and prejudices". These shortcomings were combined with a number of "contemptible" vices of the most "atrocious" kind. In short, "a more cowardly, selfish, unfeeling dog does not exist". *The Times* obituary of George IV was unusually candid. "The truth is," it declared savagely, "there never was an individual less regretted by his fellow creatures than this deceased King." William IV was a good deal more popular than his brother. Nevertheless, he was rumoured to be "cracked". At his best, he radiated a boisterous geniality, but at his worst he was ill-tempered and partisan. Before Queen Victoria came to the throne it was occupied successively "by an imbecile (George III), a profligate (George IV), and a buffoon (William IV)". As for the rest of the royal family, "the three kingdoms cannot furnish such a brood – rogues, blackguards, fools and whores".

Queen Victoria's accession saved the country from being ruled by the Duke of Cumberland, the eldest surviving son of George III, and probably the most hated man in England. He did, however, inherit the throne of Hanover, where the Salic Law debarred his niece. The

62

Whigs, who had long enjoyed the open support of the Duke and Duchess of Kent, naturally hoped that their daughter would prove as devoted to their cause. Regardless of party politics, the whole country delighted in welcoming the new Queen, whose innocence compared so favourably with the sordid lives of her uncles. It now appeared that the age of chivalry had been dormant rather than dead. "The nasty old men," wrote Lytton Strachey, "debauched and selfish, pigheaded and ridiculous . . . had all vanished like the snows of winter, and here at last, crowned and radiant, was the spring." The optimism with which the Queen's reign began was not, of course, based on knowledge of her character. Certainly nobody as yet suspected, what Sir John Conroy had learned to his cost, that this slip of a girl was a great deal more formidable than first impressions suggested.

The Queen's early popularity could hardly have been avoided. Naturally, in contrast with George IV, she appeared to be almost perfect. But she could not hope to sustain her reputation on the strength of an odious comparison. She came to the throne at an exceptionally testing moment. "Poor little Queen!" wrote Carlyle in 1838, "She is at an age at which a girl can hardly be trusted to choose a bonnet for herself; yet a task is laid upon her from which an archangel might shrink." Monarchy was on trial throughout Europe and its prospects looked bleak. The growing pains of the Industrial Revolution were never more agonising. Mass unemployment, degrading poverty, and even starvation, threatened the working class, at a time when the gulf between rich and poor had widened menacingly. Not only did the Queen succeed to a country threatened with revolution, but to an Empire in decline. Canada was in rebellion, India was governed by a private company, and, sixty years before, her own grandfather had driven his subjects in America to repudiate their allegiance. The first Colonial Empire was in terminal disarray and the second was yet to be born. Despite the rapture which greeted the new reign, it seemed more likely to start with a "winter of discontent" than the coming of spring.

The Queen's appearance in 1837 was not particularly imposing, and even her youth was a transient asset. In repose, she could only be called plain. Estimates of her height differ, but she was less than five feet tall, and most of her subjects towered above her. Creevey, who saw her at Brighton in October 1837, thought her "a homely little being". Her majestic presence owed everything to artistry and nothing to nature. The Dowager Duchess of Coburg believed that she looked like the Duke of Kent, while others thought she resembled her grandfather, George III. Certainly her bulging, blue eyes and receding chin were distinctly Hanoverian. The first time Lady Paget saw her she was at once struck by her "commanding look", but she also noticed that when she spoke her eyes were "kind and gentle". Sometimes the Queen's features became fixed in a piercing stare, and nobody caught in that Gorgon-like gaze could encounter it undismayed. On the other hand, she possessed "the sweetest and most enchanting smile" in the world. Charitable people spoke of her "high colour", or "rosy" complexion, while others referred to her red face or her red nose. Her voice, according to Ellen Terry, was "like a silver stream flowing over golden stones". Bernard Shaw, the least obsequious of critics, heard the speech the Queen made in her old age at the opening of the Imperial Institute, and was enchanted by her "beautiful voice", "first rate delivery", and marvellous clarity. "There is not an actress on the English stage who could have done it better."

Andrew Stevenson, the Minister Plenipotentiary of the United States of America at the Court of St James's, was invited to dine at Buckingham Palace in the first weeks of the new reign. His wife, Sarah, sat directly opposite the Queen, and thus was given "a fair opportunity of getting her face by heart". "It is one of very sweet expression," she wrote to her family in Virginia, "though not handsome. . . . Poor young thing! Whilst I gazed upon her innocent and happy face my heart offered up a prayer for her future happiness and prosperity. She looked so young, so innocent and good, I sighed to think of the time when that fair brow would be wrinkled with care, that light heart oppressed with sorrows, and the joyous laugh be heard no more." In a later letter, Mrs Stevenson compared the Queen's voice with the song of a Virginian nightingale, which dwelt "upon the memory like a spell after the sound had passed away. It is sweet yet soft; powerful yet melodious". Sarah, finding herself in the midst of a "royal magnificence" which reminded her of the enchanted castles of the Arabian Nights, was suddenly struck by the thought that people might say "look at that wild American, how she is staring at everything!" So, with "Indian-like caution", she "cast furtive glances around" and tried to bear herself as if such surroundings were part of her everyday life. The Queen's size, she wrote, "is below the middle, but her figure is finely proportioned, and a little embonpoint. Her bust, like most English women's, is very good; hands and feet are small and very pretty. Her face, though not beautiful, has a look of spirituality, so bright and yet so tranquil that one feels involuntarily impressed with an idea that a good and pure spirit dwells within. . . . Her eyes are blue, large, and full; her mouth, which is her worst feature, is generally a little open; her teeth small and short, and she shows her gums when she laughs, which is rather disfiguring". In January, 1840, the Stevensons were invited to stay at Windsor, which gave Sarah a further opportunity to study Her Majesty at close quarters. "Her laugh," she wrote, "is to me particularly delightful, it is so full of girlish glee and gladness, while her countenance beams with such an expression of innocence and sweetness, so blended with dignity and majesty of the Queen, that it would be impossible for a person ignorant of her high destinies not to be struck and impressed by her manners and appearance."

June 20th 1837 was as important an anniversary for the Queen as was July 4th 1776 for the American people, for that was the day on which she achieved independence. Five times in her journal account of the first few hours of her reign she stressed that she acted "alone": once underlined, and once in capital letters. Over breakfast that morning, she talked to "good faithful Stockmar", who presumably advised her what to say to the Prime Minister when she met him an hour later. At half past eight she wrote to give her uncle Leopold "the melancholy news" that William IV had expired soon after two a.m. She signed the letter for the first time: "Ever my beloved Uncle, your devoted and attached Niece, *Victoria*, R." At nine o'clock, she saw Lord Melbourne, "of *COURSE quite ALONE* as I shall *always* do all my Ministers". Much as her mother would have liked to have chaperoned her on such occasions, she was rigorously excluded. Indeed, she hardly so much as glimpsed her daughter between waking her at six and saying good night to her at ten thirty. The Queen had clearly prepared for this moment because she told Lord Melbourne that it had long been her intention "to retain him and the rest of the present Ministry at the head of affairs, and that it could not be in better hands than his". Lord Melbourne then read her a draft of the declaration he had prepared for her to read at the meeting of the Privy Council to be held at eleven, which she thought "very fine". In it she said that she had been brought up from infancy to "respect and to love the Constitution of her native country", and that she intended to protect the rights of her subjects and to safeguard religious liberty.

The Queen's first audience sufficed to convince her that she liked and trusted her Prime Minister, whom she found "very straight-forward, honest, clever and good". She always prided herself on possessing "a tolerable quick and correct appreciation of character". Mary Ponsonby, the wife of her greatest private secretary, believed that she was "scarcely ever wrong" in her assessment of people, and Archbishop Benson was equally struck by her "sagacity" in discerning "their ruling motives", and the way she was quietly amused by their foibles.

Before attending the Privy Council meeting, the Queen wrote an affectionate letter of condolence to her aunt, which she addressed to "Her Majesty the Queen, Windsor Castle". Somebody, probably Lehzen, pointed out that she should have written "Her Majesty, the Queen Dowager". "I am quite aware," she replied, "of Her Majesty's altered status, but I would rather not be the first person to remind her of it." At eleven o'clock, Lord Melbourne returned for a further audience, and half an hour later she went down stairs to meet her Privy Council in the Red Saloon at Kensington Palace. She was dressed in deep mourning, and entered the room "quite alone". Lord Rosebery, the last Liberal Prime Minister of her reign, was told by his father that the Queen looked "perfectly composed and dignified" as she confronted that venerable gathering, "though a red spot on either cheek showed her mental agitation". Seated on one of her mother's dining room chairs, she read the speech which Lord Melbourne had prepared for her, in which she began by saying that she was only too deeply aware of the "awful responsibility" imposed upon her, "so suddenly" and at so early a period of her life. After her Privy Councillors had all been sworn in, the ceremony was over. Her dignity and self-possession amazed all who saw her, but on leaving the improvised Council Chamber "she forgot that it was a glass door through which she had retired, and the moment it closed upon her she rubbed her hands and skipped off with a step as light and girlish as tho' she had just escaped from her school mistress". The Queen wrote that evening that she had not been "at all nervous", and that she was gratified to learn that people were "satisfied" with what she had done and how she had done it. The word "satisfied" hardly describes the impression the Queen made. Several Councillors, including the Prime Minister, who it must be acknowledged was easily moved to tears, wept copiously. The Duke of Wellington declared that "if She had been his own daughter he could not have desired to see her perform her part better".

Immediately after the Council Meeting, the Queen saw the Prime Minister, the Archbishop of Canterbury, Lord Albemarle (The Master of the Horse), Lord John Russell (The Home Secretary), and Baron Stockmar. That evening she dined upstairs "alone", and after another talk with Stockmar had a "very important and a very *comfortable* conversation" with Lord Melbourne: the fourth of the day. He left at about ten, and Stockmar saw her again. Finally, she "went downstairs and said good night to Mamma etc. My *dear* Lehzen will *ALWAYS* remain with me as my friend but will take no situation about me, and I think she is right".

The Queen consulted Stockmar on the day of her accession even before the Prime Minister. Her unbounded confidence in him was not shared by her subjects, although those who knew him best admired his dexterity. "He is one of the cleverest fellows I ever saw", said Lord Melbourne, and Palmerston praised him for being uniquely disinterested. But, for all that, his position was deeply resented. In 1838, the Speaker of the House of Commons went so far as to threaten to call the attention of Parliament to the unconstitutional nature of Stockmar's position, but was eventually persuaded to drop the matter by Lord Melbourne who assured him that he knew and approved of the Baron's activities.

If the Queen gained an adviser in Stockmar, she lost one in Conroy, whom she banished from her Court. Unhappily, by doing so, she appeared to confirm rumours about his conduct with her mother. "How could such a thing be believed?" she asked indignantly. No sooner had William IV died than Conroy cornered Stockmar and told him that he had come to the conclusion that "retirement would be the best course for him to take". He had therefore prepared a memorandum in which he specified the rewards he deemed appropriate to his services. Provided these proposals were met, he would send in his resignation. Stockmar showed Conroy's paper to the Queen who told him to consult Lord Melbourne on the matter. The Baron urged Melbourne to meet Conroy's demands because of the mischief he would otherwise make. Sir John had for many years persuaded the Duchess of "the *immensity* of his *service* and sacrifice", and his memo consisted of improbable variations on that theme. He had served the Duke and Duchess, he said, for over eighteen years, without a moment's respite, and at great cost to himself. Not only had he turned down military promotion so as to devote himself exclusively to his royal Mistress, but he had lost a fortune in her service. "My reward for the *past*" he therefore argued, "should be – a peerage, the red ribbon (viz. the Grand Cross of the Bath) and a pension of three thousand a year from the Privy Purse".

Lord Melbourne regarded Conroy's demands as outrageous. "This is really too bad!" he exclaimed indignantly, "Have you ever heard such impudence?" Reluctantly he offered Sir John the pension, exorbitant as it was, and a baronetcy. But Conroy insisted that he deserved a peerage, and that nothing less would induce him to retire. Stockmar begged Melbourne to yield to this monstrous demand for the sake of peace at the Palace. On June 26th, Melbourne compromised and offered Sir John an Irish peerage should a vacancy arise while he remained Prime Minister. "This promise," he said, "is made with the knowledge, assent, and approbation" of the Queen.

Both partners of this unsavoury bargain soon accused the other of playing false. Conroy accepted Melbourne's offer of June 26th, but failed to resign from the Duchess's Household. When Stockmar asked for an explanation, Sir John replied that he was "not bound to fulfil the engagement upon his part before the Queen had fulfilled *all* she had promised on hers". When an Irish vacancy eventually arose, Peel was Prime Minister and refused to offer it to Conroy on the ground that Lord Melbourne was no longer in office. The Conroy family felt so aggrieved by this "betrayal" that they took the unusual step of deploring it in marble. Sir John's monument at Arborfield accuses the Queen of treachery, in that he died a baronet, in spite of her "promise under the hand of her Prime Minister to create him a peer of Ireland". Lord Melbourne got the worst of all possible worlds by trying to be too clever. He intended to buy off Conroy in instalments, but ended up paying him an enormous pension without actually getting rid of him. Moreover, so far from making peace, Sir John renewed his intrigues in a "spirit of feminine revenge". Lord Liverpool told Stockmar that he was well aware of "Lord M's careless way of doing things", but he had not expected him to be so completely duped by Conroy who still retained "unlimited means" of conspiring against the Queen. Nevertheless, there was nothing Sir John could do to undermine Lehzen's influence. "In the recesses of the Palace her mysterious figure was at once invisible and omnipresent. When the Queen's Ministers came in at one door, the

Baroness went out by the other, when they retired she immediately returned." No one it seemed could ever destroy her ascendancy over her pupil.

The Queen decided to move to Buckingham Palace in the middle of July, only to be told that it could not possibly be made habitable at such short notice. But excuses fell on deaf ears, and she wrote instructions in her own hand to say that she proposed to move on July 13th and expected the necessary work to be finished. Panic ensued, an army of workmen was hired, and the Queen took possession of her "Palace at Pimlico" on the very day she appointed. Buckingham House had originally been bought by George III, and was rebuilt by George IV with the help of John Nash. William IV so disliked it that he lived at St James's Palace, with the result that Queen Victoria was the first Sovereign to occupy it. She left "Kensington with mingled feelings". It was, after all, her birthplace, associated with happy memories of visits from "many dear relations", and "pleasant balls and *delicious* concerts". On the other hand, it conjured up "painful and disagreeable scenes" which had made her childhood wretched. Soon after completing the move, she gave orders for a door to be constructed opening out of her bedroom into Lehzen's room next door. Never before having slept alone she was frightened by the dark. The Duchess, meanwhile, was banished to the furthest extremity of the Palace, and soon began grumbling that her apartments were too small.

When William IV died, the Duchess of Kent's position was almost as dramatically transformed as that of her daughter. While the Queen succeeded to power and independence, her mother lost every shred of influence she had hitherto possessed. For eighteen years, she complained to Princess Lieven, "Victoria had been the sole object of her life, her thoughts and hopes", but now she had nothing left to live for. The public, of course, knew little of these tensions. Creevey, for instance, declared that he had never seen "a more pretty or natural devotion" than that of the Queen to the Duchess. In so saying, he failed to discern the powerful undercurrents of dissension which bubbled beneath the surface. Lady Cowper was more perceptive when she noticed that although the Queen behaved "with great kindness and attention to her mother", she was nevertheless "not fond of her", and kept her "at arm's length in the new Palace". While the Duchess thought her daughter so ungrateful that she gave her a copy of "King Lear" for her nineteenth birthday, the Queen was convinced that her mother had ill-treated her for many years past.

There could be little hope of reconciliation while Sir John bullied the Duchess into pleading his cause at Court. Her repeated attempts to persuade the Queen to relent ensured that the wound was never left to heal. The Queen's journal bears witness to her exasperation with her mother's importunity. In August 1837, after the Duchess had made yet one more attempt to plead on Sir John's behalf, the Queen expressed her surprise that she had been asked to receive him at Court, considering "his conduct towards me for some years past, and still more so after the unaccountable manner in which he behaved towards me, a short time before I came to the Throne". Under these circumstances, she thought that the Duchess should have been "amply satisfied" by the baronetcy and pension bestowed on her Comptroller. But the Duchess was not satisfied, and returned to the fray like a punch-drunk prize fighter. "For the sake of your Mother" she pleaded, make peace with Sir John and his family.

The Duchess not only "plagued" her daughter about Conroy, but expected her to pay off her debts of some £70,000. Lord Melbourne believed such demands were preposterous, and told the Queen that he thought it deplorable that she should be "subjected to so much annoyance and importunity from a quarter in which your Majesty ought only to find assistance and affection." Lord Melbourne persuaded Parliament to increase the Duchess's grant by £8,000 a year, but this neither resolved her financial problems nor diminished further demands. The Queen commented on one such claim in her journal, on January 15th, 1838. "Got *such* a letter from Mamma, oh! oh! *such* a letter." Melbourne suggested that he should be left to answer the Duchess formally, but she was not to be circumvented. "My appeal was to *you* as my child," she wrote back, "not to the Queen."

Until Parliament met in November to settle the Civil List, the Queen had to ask for a loan from Messrs. Coutts to meet her immediate expenses. Eventually she was voted an annuity of £385,000: a sum which was never altered during her reign of sixty-three years. Her other sources of revenue, the Duchies of Lancaster and Cornwall, produced between them a sum of £27,000. Admittedly the Queen had vast expenses to meet, but she remained an exceedingly rich woman, much as she tried to deny it. One of the first uses she made of her sizeable Privy Purse was to pay off her father's debts. The Queen had an excellent head for business, and detested financial disorder and waste. Curiously enough, the Duchess brought up her daughter to be as provident an economist as Peel or Gladstone. It was only when she came to apply her admirable precepts to her own finances that she ceased to carry conviction.

The Duchess's status was another bone of contention. "For some confused reason of her own," she wrote to the Speaker of the House of Commons demanding the rank and precedence of Queen Mother. The proposal was referred back to Queen Victoria who rejected it out of hand. "It would do my mother no good," she explained, and would probably "offend my aunts". Because the Duchess, urged on by Conroy, was eager to pick quarrels, the Queen did her best to keep her at arm's length. Nevertheless, she would burst in un-announced, spoiling for a row. On one occasion, so the Queen informed Lord Melbourne, she was forced "to remind her *who* I was". "Quite right," said Lord M, "disagreeable but necessary." Such were the strains of life in the Palace that Princess Lieven wrote: "Je doute que la mère et la fille habitent longtemps sous le même toit."

It never occurred to the Duchess to attribute her loss of influence to her own behaviour. Instead, she preferred to blame Lehzen and Lord Melbourne for usurping her natural rights. Not being one to keep grievances to herself, it soon became known in court circles how deeply injured she felt. She only remained at Buckingham Palace to keep up appearances, and to avoid the expense of a separate establishment. The Queen, for her part, convinced herself that her mother had never been fond of her. When the Duchess died in 1861 and the Queen went through her papers, she was chastened to learn of the depth of her mother's devotion. "Her love for *me*," she confided to King Leopold, "is *too* touching. I have found little books with the accounts of my babyhood and they show *such* unbounded tenderness." But in 1837 the Duchess showed few such signs of affection, and relieved her frustration by scolding her daughter for going to the theatre too often, or eating and drinking too much. Conroy, meanwhile, sedulously stirred up mischief by accusing the Queen of breaking her mother's heart.

Lord Melbourne took the Queen's part in her battles with her mother, and was almost too generous with his sympathy. He had not forgiven the Duchess for deceiving him over her daughter's wish for a Regency, and he was exasperated by her incessant requests for favours. At one moment she was on her knees beseeching him for help, and in the next she was treating him like a troublesome footman. The Queen and Lord Melbourne discussed the Duchess with such startling candour as to infringe the fifth commandment. "Talked of my dislike of Mamma," wrote the Queen in her journal. "Lord M said she was a liar and a hypocrite." It is inconceivable that he would have said any such thing unless he felt sure it would be endorsed. On another occasion, he remarked "I never saw so foolish a woman", which the Queen noted was "very true, and we both laughed". But peacemaking came as naturally to Lord Melbourne as did caustic comments, and he knew how important it was to preserve the Queen's reputation. He therefore urged her to treat the Duchess with patience and civility. It often appeared, however, "as if he were more anxious to exacerbate the relationship than to heal it, so vigorously did he take the Queen's part and encourage her into intransigence". More than once, the Duchess held out an olive branch which Lord M declined to accept, justifying his rebuff on the ground that he doubted her sincerity. Indeed, he was much to blame for providing the Queen with "new nourishment for the animosity she now felt justified in indulging". It seems that his love of gossip, his dislike of the Duchess, and his eagerness to show sympathy, blinded him to the fact that he was preaching conciliation but waging war.

Lord Melbourne was something of an enigma. At first sight, he seemed the most fortunate of men, but fate struck him a number of cruel blows, hence his air of melancholy. He was born in 1779 and christened William. His father, Peniston Lamb, the first Lord Melbourne, came from a family of lawyers who had enriched themselves by timely marriages and dubious dealings in property. Peniston certainly did not achieve greatness but had it thrust upon him. Soon after he came of age he was bought a seat in Parliament, and eventually earned a peerage for his generous support of the Whigs. In 1769 he married Elizabeth Milbanke, who came from an old Yorkshire family. She was outstandingly beautiful, highly intelligent, and extremely ambitious. She soon became known as a great hostess and her parties at Melbourne House had few rivals. Neither she nor her husband took their marriage vows seriously, and only one of their six children was assuredly a Lamb. William's father was reputedly Lord Egremont, and it was said that his brother, George, was the Prince Regent's son. William was sent to Eton and then to Trinity College, Cambridge. On leaving the University he studied for the

Bar, sharing a house in Chesterfield Street with Beau Brummell, his Eton contemporary, and the greatest of Regency bucks.

In 1805 William made a disastrous marriage to Lady Caroline Ponsonby. He first set eyes on her when she was only fourteen, and was instantly bewitched. "Caro" proved impossible: she was brilliant and enchanting but so wild that even her own family concluded that she was mad. In 1811 she fell violently in love with Lord Byron who was willing enough to seduce her but not to return her passion. After two years, he grew weary of her tantrums and her insistence upon monopolising him. Besides, both of them were so fond of talking about themselves that neither much relished the other's conversation. The affair came to a dramatic climax at one of Lady Heathcote's balls, when Caroline seized a knife intending to murder Byron and afterwards kill herself. Only with some difficulty was she prevented from carrying out her design. Eventually William found the strain of living with her intolerable, and sent her to live with his father at Brocket, the family house in Hertfordshire. When he learned she was seriously ill in 1828, he hurried back from Ireland to be by her bedside, and remained with her till she died. Nobody could have been more long-suffering towards a wayward wife who had made his life wretched. Throughout their turbulent marriage he showed nothing but compassion and forgiveness. He loved her from the first, and when she died he was overwhelmed by grief. They had only one child, a son, Augustus, who was born in 1807 and died in 1836. It soon became evident that the boy was mentally retarded and suffered from violent fits. It seemed as if Providence had decreed that the last drop of bitterness should be drained from Melbourne's marriage. Nobody was more intrigued by this sad history than Queen Victoria. "The Duchess of Sutherland," she wrote in her journal on January 1st, 1838, "spoke to me last night about Lady Caroline Lamb, Lord Melbourne's wife. . . . The strangest person that ever lived, really half crazy, and quite so when she died; she was not good-looking, but very clever, and could be very amusing. She teased that excellent Lord Melbourne in every way, dreadfully, and quite embittered his life. . . . He was the kindest of husbands to her, and bore it most admirably; any other man would have separated from such a wife."

Melbourne did not belong to the old Whig aristocracy whose ancestors had brought about the Glorious Revolution of 1688, but came from a family which rose to eminence later. As a young man he was put up for Brooks's by Charles James Fox, the Whig leader, and entered Parliament in 1806 as Member for Leominster. In 1827 he became Irish Secretary under Canning. The fact that he was willing to serve under a Tory Prime Minister showed his lofty disdain for party distinctions. In 1829 he succeeded his father and went to the House of Lords. The following year the Whigs returned to power and Melbourne drifted nonchalantly to the top, serving Lord Grey as Home Secretary for four years, and succeeding him as Prime Minister in 1835: a post he retained until 1841, apart from a brief interval of a hundred days (December 1834 – April 1835) when Peel temporarily replaced him.

Twice Lord Melbourne was dragged into court and twice found innocent. The first case was brought by Lord Branden in 1829 and was very properly dismissed for lack of credible evidence. The second case was that of George Norton, a brute of a husband, who in 1836 sought to divorce his wife, Caroline Sheridan, a granddaughter of the great playwright. It is highly improbable that she and Melbourne were lovers – certainly the court found no evidence of their guilt – but he greatly enjoyed her company and visited her so often as to set tongues wagging. Although he was cleared of both charges, "a disquieting whiff of the Regency" still hung about him. The Queen, however, was not in the least bit disturbed, and often questioned him about the beautiful Sheridan sisters. Indeed, to please him, she even received Mrs Norton.

Lord Melbourne was fifty-eight when he became the Queen's Prime Minister and was forty years older than she was. Naturally he had lost the dazzling good looks of youth but he still was "exceedingly handsome". His musical voice and joyous laugh were a pleasure to listen to, and his conversation was "honest, blunt and amusing". The Queen found his startling candour irresistible, and was equally taken by his shrewdness and insouciance. Even his melancholy moods she thought rather romantic. Melbourne loved to pose as an indolent dilettante, whereas, in fact his happy-go-lucky air concealed a seriousness of purpose which would have delighted Dr Arnold. Sydney Smith, who was equally disposed to disguise earnestness with flippancy, was the first to see through the pretence. "Our Viscount," he wrote, "is somewhat of an impostor. . . . I am sorry to hurt any man's feelings and to brush away the magnificent fabric of levity and gaiety he has reared, but I accuse our Minister of honesty and diligence."

In many respects Melbourne and Disraeli were the most unlike of all the Queen's Prime Ministers. But some things they shared in common: they were both her special favourites, they both exercised enormous influence on her political outlook, they both were especially dependent on the companionship of women, and they both came to office at a time of their life when they had never felt so lonely. Much as Lord M enjoyed talking "broad" in the Subscription Room at Brooks's, he was happier still sprawled at full length on a sofa indulging in gossip with Mrs Norton.

Throughout his life Melbourne remained a voracious reader, indiscriminately devouring memoirs, histories and theology. He became almost as conversant with the Church Fathers as were Newman and Pusey. Wherever he went he was surrounded by books, even his bed was piled high with them. Were it not for the fact that he was obviously a man of the world, he could easily have been mistaken for a professor. His vast fund of miscellaneous knowledge poured out in his conversation, but he carried his learning so lightly that it never became tedious. No man was less censorious than Lord M, who took the world as he found it. He regarded the whims of mankind as rather diverting. Others might choose to rebuke evil but he preferred to mock it.

Melbourne's political instincts were basically conservative, which was something of an anomaly in the leader of the popular party. He conceived that the role of government was to leave things alone, and deeply suspected philanthropic meddling. "Try to do no good, and then you won't get into any scrapes." Change and reform he saw as necessary evils, but he greatly preferred what was "tranquil and stable". Grudgingly he supported Lord Grey's Reform Bill in 1832, not because he approved of it but because he saw it as inevitable. In fact, he privately confessed that he thought its proposals nonsense. Between 1834 and 1841 "he was only half identified in opinion and sympathy with the party to which he belonged" and which he supposedly led. Indeed for most of the seven years he was Prime Minister, he "was secretly the enemy of the measures which his own Government originated".

The Queen, at first, was totally lost in what for her was the unknown world of politics. Several years later, Lord Melbourne told Prince Albert that when he first began to advise the Queen he was taken aback by her innocence of statecraft. Fortunately, she was the first to admit her inexperience, and looked to Lord Melbourne to guide her through a mysterious, male preserve. Apart from her tutor, Davys, he was the first Englishman she ever got to know well. Seeing she was still at a highly impressionable age, and ignorant of her duties, she was bound to be deeply influenced by her first Prime Minister. Soon, however, her fondness for Lord Melbourne increased her dependence upon him. The death of her father, and her unhappy relations with her mother, led her to long for an ideal parent. For a time she saw her uncle Leopold as a surrogate father, in spite of the fact that he visited her so seldom, but the moment she got to know Lord Melbourne well, she transferred the role to him. In May 1839, when she was terrified the Commons might force him to resign, she begged him "ever to be a father to one who never wanted support more than she does now". "I feel so *safe*" she wrote in her journal, when he "is with me". It was such a wonderful change to deal with someone who was always straight-forward and honest. Conroy had forced her to guard her tongue; an affront to her open nature. But now she felt free to say whatever she liked and was even prepared to discuss such intimate matters as her problems with her mother. "As for the confidence of the Crown," she once wrote, "God knows! No *Minister*, no *friend* EVER possessed it so entirely as this truly excellent Lord Melbourne possesses mine!" In her mind's eye she conceived of herself as a "poor helpless girl" buffeted about by the storms of life, desperately clinging to Lord Melbourne for protection. On Christmas Day 1839 she took Communion in St George's Chapel, Windsor. "Lord Melbourne was there, the one whom I look up to as a father, and I was glad he took it with me."

The Queen's passion for Lord Melbourne cannot be wholly explained in terms of paternal affection. Her solitary upbringing had retarded her development and in 1837 her emotions were still those of a schoolgirl. What she really desired was a hero to worship and Melbourne fitted the bill. Almost everything about her tended to be rather larger than life so fervent were her feelings. "Her enjoyments were more rapturous than the average girl's, her sentimentality more unbridled, her interest in detail more inexhaustible, her partisanship more violent, her innocence more dewy." On January 9th, 1838, after she had barely known him for six months, she confessed in her journal "I am very sorry to lose him even for one night". It is hardly surprising therefore that her extravagant devotion to Lord Melbourne was sometimes mistaken for a grander passion. People saw how her eyes followed him round a room and were quick to draw the wrong conclusion.

Not long after Queen Victoria's marriage she discussed her school-girl infatuation for Lord Melbourne with her husband. "Albert," she admitted, "thinks I worked myself up to what really became at last quite foolish." She herself was inclined to attribute her "unbounded affection and admiration for Lord Melbourne" to two things: her need for someone to cling to, and her natural warmth of feeling. Greville went even further. Writing some seventy years before Freud revolutionised Psychology, he described the Queen's feelings for Lord M as "*sexual* though she does not know it". Be that as it may, it was perfectly understandable that she should associate her "good old Primus" with her newly won freedom. For eighteen years she had been confined, repressed and restricted. Then suddenly, over-night, she became her own mistress and her lightest whims were law. Nobody could have withstood the intoxication of such a moment. Nor is it surprising that she bestowed her imprisoned love on the man who had helped to unlock the door of her dungeon. During the early years of her reign, her journal was largely devoted to Lord Melbourne's sayings and doings, so obsessed was she by her hero. Indeed, it is arguable that his best contemporary portrait comes from the pen of the Queen, who observed so sharply, recalled so faithfully, and wrote so vividly. If ever a man comes back to life, Lord Melbourne does so in the pages of this schoolgirl Boswell. She made no attempt whatever to hide her affection from him. For instance, she once told him "I am sure none of your friends are as fond of you as I am". She even sometimes exposed the depth of her feelings by admitting to jealousy. Once, when Melbourne dined at Holland House, she wrote in her journal "I WISH he dined with me!" On another occasion she plucked up courage to tell him that Lady Holland, who was then nearly seventy, was not half as fond of him as she was.

If the Queen saw Lord M as a substitute father, he looked on her as a surrogate daughter. When they first met, he had never felt so lonely. His son, Augustus, had died the year before, and nothing had reconciled him to the loss of Caro. "In spite of all," he once remarked, "she was more to me than anyone ever was, or ever will be." In some ways he was almost as warm-hearted as the Queen. Greville described him in 1837 as "a man with capacity for loving without having anything in the world to love". But Nature abhors a vacuum, and in a matter of months he had found in his youthful sovereign an outlet for his affections. She possessed, like Caro and Mrs Norton, just those qualities he had always found most attractive: charm, vitality, and outstanding honesty. The ageing sceptic had stumbled on the antidote to melancholia: the magic of the Queen, "the last love of his life". So infectious were her sudden enthusiasms, her enchanting smile, her uninhibited laugh, her engaging innocence, her sense of fun, that he found her joyous response to life irresistible. Moreover, the better he came to know her, the more he admired her understanding, common sense and good feeling. All were agreed that he handled her impeccably, mingling candour with solicitude. For all his apparent cynicism, he was at heart a romantic, with a poetic sense of the majesty of history. His role was half that of a statesman and half of a parent: natural, easygoing, compassionate, always respectful, never obsequious. He loved the Queen as a child but he treated her as a Sovereign. Nothing gave him greater pleasure than to initiate her in her duties and to hand on his experience, but almost as important was the intensity of his affection which satisfied both their needs: his to love, and hers to be loved.

Melbourne's friends were astounded to learn that their former companion, one of the most sophisticated of men, who had enchanted Society with his wit and erudition, and whose youth had been wasted carousing with the Prince Regent, now spent his days at Windsor and Buckingham Palace making decorous conversation to a schoolgirl. "Never," said Greville, "was such a revolution seen in anybody's occupations and habits." If the Queen had stepped from the schoolroom to the throne, Lord Melbourne had quit Devonshire House for the nursery. The born-again Melbourne, who in his un-regenerate days had loved to sprawl on sofas, or put his feet up on a fender, now sat bolt upright on a gilt chair, apparently relishing the "wearisome inanities of the royal circle", and carefully guarding his tongue to prevent the escape of one of those oaths with which his remarks were customarily spiced. In fact these restraints, which were after all self-imposed, proved much less irksome than most of his friends imagined. His very familiarity with London Society had bred a certain contempt, and the life of the Court at least was refresh-ingly novel. Just like a sated gourmet, who tires of the rarest deli-cacies, his appetite was revived by bread-and-butter pudding.

The world at large was not unduly disturbed to learn that the Queen and her First Minister had become so fond of each other.

There were jokes, of course, but few were ill natured. "The relationship was too obviously and too charmingly innocent for people to want to be malicious about it." But not everyone thought their intimacy prudent. The Duchess of Kent particularly resented Lord Melbourne's influence, which she saw as supplanting her own. "Take care," she warned, on one occasion, hoping to make mischief, "that Lord Melbourne is not King." When the Queen discussed her mama's objection with Lord M he told her that the Duke of Wellington had said "that if he was me he would establish himself in the Palace", to which the Queen replied that she wished he would. Lord Shaftesbury, the great philanthropist, whose wife Minny was Lord Melbourne's niece, shared the Duchess's misgivings, but, nevertheless, understood why the Queen had become so infatuated. "This intimacy," he wrote, "is natural, very natural. The constraint and reserve under which she had lived", combined to invest the first person she could trust and speak to openly "with many attractions which few youthful minds could resist", especially when he was "a singularly engaging man" upon whom "sixty years of age sit as pleasantly . . . as thirty-five on any other".

The Queen's day followed a rigid pattern. She was called at eight o'clock and devoted the morning to work. At eleven, Lord Melbourne joined her to discuss the day's business. After luncheon the Court went out riding, generally at a gallop: the Queen accompanied by an equerry on her right and the Prime Minister on her left. The rest of the afternoon was devoted to music, painting, or romping with children. Dinner was served at eight. Lord M invariably sat on her left and monopolised her attention. After the ladies retired for coffee, the gentlemen were left to their port and brandy. The Queen so disliked this "horrid custom" that she summoned them to the Drawing Room within minutes of her departure. It was alleged that this was one of the few matters on which she and Lord M did not see eye to eye. Her Majesty then made a circle of her guests, addressing a few remarks to each. These "short uneasy colloquies" proved up-hill work, as she was shy of strangers, and never acquired the art of fluent small-talk. The evening concluded with the Duchess of Kent playing a hand of Whist, occasionally nodding off over the cards, while Lord Melbourne talked to the Queen, often turning the pages of a volume of engravings and commenting on its contents. During the course of the day, she spent some six hours with her Prime Minister: "an hour in the morning, two on horseback, one at dinner, and two in the evening". She was perhaps more fortunate than she appreciated in being served by a man who possessed no family ties and was willing to spend so much of his time at Court. For most of her reign she was ground down by her duties, but when Melbourne was there to shoulder the burden she had very few worries and plenty of leisure.

The role of private secretary to the Sovereign was no more recognised by the Constitution than that of Prime Minister or Prince Consort. Nevertheless, George III, George IV, and William IV all employed personal secretaries. Soon after she came to the throne the Queen asked Stockmar to accept the post, but he was "wholly *averse* to such an appointment being made". Lord Grey, the former Whig Prime Minister, insisted that she was entitled to appoint whomever she pleased, "a negro if she likes", but agreed with the Baron that it would be most unwise to appoint a foreigner. Parliament invariably objected to servants of the Crown whom it could not hold accountable for their actions. Although Stockmar declined to take any formal position, he was willing to act as a go-between, and nothing could stop him from giving advice. Lord Melbourne was strongly opposed on "constitutional grounds" to the Queen appointing a private secretary. In 1812 he had publicly opposed the Prince Regent's appointment of Colonel McMahon to the post, and more recently had told Sir John Conroy that he was unwilling to risk "the peculiar functions of the Chief Magistrate" ever being usurped. Recognising, however, that the Queen needed help, he offered his own services. It was the only time in history that the role of Prime Minister and private secretary have ever been combined.

The enduring importance for Queen Victoria of her first Prime Minister was that he taught her her profession. When she came to the throne she was necessarily ignorant of government, and so turned to him for instruction. Nobody was better qualified to give it. "He has such *stores* of knowledge;" she wrote, "such a wonderful memory; he knows about everybody and everything; *who* they were, and *what* they did; and he imparts all his knowledge in such a *kind* and agreeable manner." Lord Aberdeen told Princess Lieven that no minister "since the days of Protector Somerset, ever was placed in such a situation as that which is occupied by Melbourne. He had a young and inexperienced infant in his hands, whose whole conduct and opinions must necessarily be in complete subservience to his views." Aberdeen was undoubtedly right to regard the Queen as eager to learn, and susceptible to the influence of a man of whom she was fond, but seems to have overlooked her independent spirit.

There were few qualities the Queen valued more than honesty and candour, and she was therefore delighted to find that Melbourne "never scrupled to declare boldly and frankly his real opinions, strange as they sometimes sounded, and unpalatable as they often were". It is part of the destiny of Kings and Queens to live in an "atmosphere of flattery and deceit". But Lord M was determined that Queen Victoria should be told the truth and face reality. At all costs he wished to prevent her retreating into a fools' paradise and being lured to her doom like the Bourbons. He proved an inspired teacher, who knew how to make lessons palatable by spicing them with anecdotes. Sometimes he told her about recent history, part of which he had made. Sometimes he gave her character sketches of the statesmen of the day, and sometimes he ventured on politics and philosophy. Besides his role of political tutor, he also became her social guide, and helped her to understand the customs, cliques and factions of the aristocracy. Recognising, as he did, that the Queen possessed a generous measure of youthful bigotry, and that her categorical love of truth encouraged her to be tactless, he did what he could to preach the virtue of tolerance. "If people are made to do what they dislike," he once told her, "you must allow a little ill humour." Nobody makes friends by being censorious. "If you want to influence a person you must not begin by reprimanding him." When the Queen said she disliked Lord Lyndhurst because he was a bad man, Lord Melbourne told her that she had placed him in a category embracing most of mankind.

The Queen found Lord M's companionship an intoxicating novelty. He was not only a scintillating talker but a sympathetic listener. When there was "disagreeable business" to discuss, he proved "the best-hearted, kindest and most feeling man in the world". Both greatly enjoyed their endless conversations, "I being seated on a sofa, and he in an armchair near or close to me," with Islay, her Scotch terrier, stretched out at her feet. She could have listened for ever to his stories told "in such an amusing way". The early volumes of the Queen's journal put Lord Melbourne in the centre of the stage. There we see him "talking, joking, gossiping, instructing, clarifying, helping, reassuring, encouraging, enlivening, a brilliant, droll individual mind forming that of a simple ingenuous

young woman forty years his junior". In spite of all the distractions
of her life, the Queen forced herself to sit down late at night to note
the events of the day in meticulous detail: especially those which
concerned her Prime Minister. When it came to recording his conversation she did so with a fidelity of recall made possible by her absorb-
ent memory. She was a born reporter and left a vivid account of her
hero. "Her untiring interest in life and her taste for detail made her
notice so much; while her literalness, her candour and her careful
accuracy stopped her from colouring or altering what she noticed."
Not even the size of his appetite escaped her. "He has eaten three
chops and a grouse for breakfast," she noted disapprovingly. What
makes the Queen's journal so compelling is its incongruous mixture
of innocent zest and shrewd discernment.

Lord Melbourne's conversations with the Queen covered a bewildering range of topics, extending from man-eating in New Zealand
to the shortcomings of Eton's Montem celebrations, which the
Queen remarked "generally ended in the boys being sick and drunk".
The discussion about cannibalism was suggested by their looking at
a recently published book of engravings of *The People and Country
of the Island of New Zealand.* Lord M said on opening it, "'These are
a fine race, but they eat men, and they say it is almost impossible to
break them of it.' Lady Mulgrave observed that she thought they
only eat their enemies; Lord Melbourne said, 'I fancy they eat them
pretty promiscuously.' Lord Melbourne was in excellent spirits, and
very funny in his remarks about the different drawings". Later he
had the Court in fits of laughter when he told them the story of an
old woman who was ill, "and they asked her what she would like
to have; and she said, 'I think I could eat a little piece of the small
bone of a boy's head.'"

Sometimes the talk turned to books. In 1839 the Queen read *Oliver
Twist* and was deeply moved by its descriptions of "squalid vice"
and its "accounts of starvation in the Workhouses". Like most of
the governing class, she learned more about poverty in the pages of
novels than from confronting it first hand. When she persuaded Lord
Melbourne to read it he complained of its "low debasing style" and
its background of "Workhouses, and Coffin-makers, and Pick-
pockets". The Queen strenuously defended the book, but Melbourne
remained unmoved. "I don't *like* those things," he said, "I wish
to avoid them in *reality*, and therefore I don't wish to see them
represented." He quoted Goethe as saying that "one ought never to

see anything disagreeable; he wouldn't look upon the dead. . . . It's a bad, depraved, vicious taste".

Much of Melbourne's conversation arose from the business of the day, and often was little more than a discreetly disguised lesson. For example, in September 1838 he received a long despatch from Lord Durham, then Governor General of British North America. "Before he read it, he said that I must know that Canada originally belonged to the French and was only ceded to the English in 1760, when it was taken in an expedition under Wolfe; 'A very daring enterprise', he said. Canada then was entirely French, and the British only came afterwards; they divided it into Upper and Lower Canada, and allowed the French to keep their particular rights and Institutions; and in a little while gave the country Executive and Legislative Assemblies like England. Lord Melbourne explained this very clearly (and much better than I have done). He then read me Durham's Despatch, with that fine, soft voice of his, and with so much expression, so that it is needless to say I was much interested by it."

By common consent Lord M was conceded a freedom of expression denied to ordinary mortals. Even the Queen allowed him the licence of a court jester. He was not a philosopher in the strictest sense, but was temperamentally sceptical, and impatient of talk of human perfectibility. He viewed mankind with an aristocratic aloofness tinged with irony. When the conversation once turned to the divinely inspired disclosures supposedly vouchsafed to some of Irving's disciples, he drily remarked that those who received such revelations would be well advised to make sure from what quarter they came. Sometimes, one suspects, the Queen gravely reported Lord Melbourne's ironic remarks without recognising that they were not to be taken literally. For all his apparent flippancy, he could not have been more serious in his attempts to instruct the Queen: a fact which she intuitively recognised when she spoke of his wisdom and good sense. Talking to him, she said, "does me a *world* of good; and his conversations always *improve* one greatly". Beneath the froth on the surface, a wholesome brew lay concealed.

Lord Melbourne believed that the best political education must include the study of history, and he agreed with Cicero that to remain ignorant of the past is to be for ever a child. His historical judgements tended to be contentious. Once, when discussing the Tudors, he justified Henry VIII's ill-treatment of his wives by saying "Those women bothered him so", and that Catherine of Aragon was a "sad, groaning, moaning woman". There seemed to be no end to the fund of stories with which he amused the Queen. One evening at Windsor, she asked him about Cambacérès, Napoleon's second Consul under the Constitution of 1799, whose portrait she had found in a volume of engravings. The Consul, Lord M told her, was a great gourmand, who resented the General's practice of conducting meetings which kept him from his dinner. "One day, Napoleon saw him writing a note, and insisted on seeing it; it was to his cook: 'Sauvez les rôtis; les entremets sont perdus.'" The Queen was especially intrigued by Lord M's reminiscences of recent history, and never tired of his stories about George III, the Royal Dukes, Mrs Fitzherbert, Pitt, Fox and the Hollands. Pitt, he once told her, from personal observation, was "a tall, thin man with a red face who drank amazingly".

The Duchess of Kent had taken enormous care to shield the Queen from her father's relations, which only excited her appetite for Lord Melbourne's reminiscences. The more he told her about her Hanoverian ancestors, the more she began to feel part of the family, although he made no attempt to mitigate their foibles. It was only when the discussion turned to her father that he erred on the side of charity, and left her with the impression that the Duke was the most gifted and agreeable of the royal brothers. "Spoke of George IV," the Queen wrote in her journal in September 1838. "It is so interesting to talk with Lord M on *all* subjects, and he knew George IV *so* well, that it's peculiarly curious. He said George IV seemed to be a Whig before he came to the throne, but that 'he did it from opposition and not from principle. His principles all along were the contrary'." Whenever he took offence at the Church, he used to say, "By God, my Uncle the Duke of Cumberland was right when he told me, the people you must be apprehensive of, are those black-legged gentlemen".

The Queen was particularly eager to hear Lord Melbourne's recollections of Byron: a sensitive subject to broach in view of his wife's distressing passion for him. But somehow she contrived to edge the conversation in the desired direction and to elicit the following description of Lord M's erstwhile rival. "He was extremely handsome; had dark hair, was very lame and limped very much; I asked if the expression of his countenance was agreeable; he said not; 'he had a sarcastic, sardonic expression; a contemptuous expression.' I asked if he was not agreeable; he said 'He could be excessively so';

'he had a pretty smile'; 'treacherous beyond conception'." Lord Melbourne added "he dazzled everybody, and deceived them; for he could tell his story very well".

Naturally enough Lord Melbourne enjoyed talking about himself, a common enough human frailty, but even so found it hard to quench the Queen's curiosity. She loved to discuss his friends and relations, his school days at Eton, his life at Cambridge, and anything else to do with him. Above all, she was inquisitive about "Caro", but knew that the subject was too delicate to broach. Her journal shows the extent of her appetite for details about her hero. Lord M told me, she solemnly recorded, that until he was seventeen "he wore his hair long, as all boys then did; (*how* handsome he must have looked); but that 'it was always dirty'; a boy, he said, can't comb his long hair as a girl can, and that it got matted, so that no comb would go through; he only cut it just before he left Eton. I asked him if his hair was always so dark. He said, 'It was about the colour of your Majesty's hair, I should say, when I was a child'." The Queen clearly had never been taught that it was considered ill-mannered to pass personal remarks, for she often reproached the Prime Minister for absenting himself from church. He tried to excuse himself on the ground that he feared "hearing something very extraordinary", but the Queen remained unconvinced.

In playful mood the Queen was distinctly coquettish. When Lord Melbourne insisted that his house in South Street, Mayfair, "wouldn't hold any one else" but himself, she asked pointedly, "No one else?" "No one else," he replied, "not by any means", which made them "both laugh very much". The Queen further noted that the rent on South Street was a thousand pounds a year, and that he paid seventy pounds a year for his coal. On one occasion she took Lord M to task for falling asleep in public, particularly as he snored. "'That proclaims it too much', he said, in which I *quite* agreed."

One of the most admirable of Melbourne's characteristics was his good-natured acceptance of criticism. It was typical of him that he repeated to the Queen what the Duke of Wellington had said to Lord Clarendon about him. "I like Lord Melbourne and think he's the best Minister the Queen can have, and he has given her very good advice I've no doubt; but I am afraid he jokes too much with her, and makes her treat things too lightly, which are very serious." The Queen's instinct was to reject the stricture, but Lord M insisted that there was some truth in it. Most of his jokes were certainly harmless enough. When the Queen was presented with a new brand of Assam tea, she decided to try it out on Melbourne. It came with a printed paper which he read out "so funnily". Amongst other things, the document quoted the opinion of a Dr Lun Qua, "which name put him into paroxysms of laughter, from which he couldn't recover for some time, and did one good to hear". But whatever they chose to discuss, whether it was Lord M's "new olive green velvet waistcoat", or the advantage of employing Dissenters as gardeners ("They don't go to the races, they don't hunt, and don't engage in any expensive amusements") there was a carefree, idyllic charm to their conversation. So much so, that few people remained unmoved by the sight of the Prime Minister's palpable devotion to his sovereign, or by the way the Queen gazed up at him with adoring eyes like one of Landseer's spaniels.

Melbourne left Lord Palmerston, the Foreign Secretary, to initiate the Queen into the mysteries of the Foreign Office. Palmerston in 1837 had been a member of successive governments for all but two of the past twenty-nine years. From 1808 to 1828 he served under the Tories, but finally resigned from the Duke of Wellington's Ministry which he found too reactionary for his liking. In 1830, after two years in the wilderness, Lord Grey appointed him Foreign Secretary. For the next thirty-five years Palmerston dominated Britain's foreign policy. At the start of the new reign he was in high favour at Court. Anybody of whom Lord Melbourne approved possessed an important recommendation, and the Queen thought him "clever", "amusing", and "agreeable". Naturally, she then knew nothing of his scandalous private life which led *The Times* to refer to him as "Cupid". The Foreign Secretary was always the first to volunteer to be Minister in Residence because he was deeply in love with Melbourne's sister, the widowed Lady Cowper, who was one of the Queen's favourite ladies-in-waiting.

In the first two years of her reign, Palmerston taught the Queen virtually all that she needed to know about protocol: the correct mode of addressing European Sovereigns, the regulations governing foreign orders, and the proper procedures to follow when ambassadors presented their credentials. But he did not confine his instruction to the niceties of etiquette. Once he spent three hours explaining the historical background to the political problems of Greece, and he also carefully briefed her about Russia, France, Belgium, Portugal, Spain, Mexico and Canada. Many of the Queen's later opinions may be traced back to the influence of her first Foreign Secretary. At the time of the Boer War she addressed Lord Roberts in tones learned from Lord Palmerston. The extent to which he helped form the Queen's mind is often overlooked because of their subsequent disputes. In fact, much as she grew to deplore his high-handed ways of conducting foreign policy, and his impudent disregard for the prerogatives of the Crown, she, nevertheless, endorsed his basic ambition: to exalt Britain's interests over those of all other countries, and to make her respected and feared to the ends of the earth. The foreign and imperial policy of her beloved Lord Beaconsfield was the logical corollary of that pursued by Palmerston.

From the first the Queen rejoiced in her new way of life and could hardly conceal her excitement. "Her occupations, her pleasures, her business, her Court", presented her with "an unceasing round of gratifications", and she entered "into the magnificent novelties of her position with the zest and curiosity of a child". Never before had she basked in the sunshine of success, approval and affection. She even relished the duller parts of her work. Ten days after she came to the throne, she remarked in her journal that she had "a *very great* deal to do", such as dealing with countless communications from her ministers, and getting "so many papers to sign *every* day". But so far from complaining, she actually professed to "*delight* in this work". Few things gave her more pleasure than being able to entertain, and she particularly enjoyed showing visitors round Windsor or Buckingham Palace, still hardly able to realise the vastness of her possessions. According to Lady Cowper, "she says that sometimes when she wakes of a morning she is quite afraid that it should be all a dream. (Is this not so natural?) She enjoys her happiness so much." In October 1837, the Queen described the previous few months as "the pleasantest summer I *EVER* passed in *my life*."

Hardly a discordant note was sounded in the chorus of admiration which greeted the Queen in the first year of her reign. Lord Melbourne, who was not one "to be easily captivated or dazzled by any superficial accomplishments", spoke of her in ever more glowing terms. Mrs Stevenson told her sisters in Virginia that everybody was running about "mad with loyalty to the young Queen. Even the Americans here are infected. In all societies nothing is talked about but her beauty, her wisdom, her gentleness, and self-possession. A thousand anecdotes are related to her goodness, and the wonderful address with which she manages everybody and everything".

Creevey, who was no sycophant, went so far as to claim that the "dear little Queen" was "in every respect perfection", and he quoted Palmerston as saying "that any Ministers who had to deal with her would soon find that she was no ordinary person".

At first, the Queen felt so unsure of herself that she told Lord M that there were times when she feared that she was unfit to wear the crown, but gradually she became a little too self-assertive. It was, of course, almost impossible not to become headstrong when everyone treated her lightest whims with deference. The symptoms of her growing self-confidence were not always agreeable. When she attended a ball, given in her honour by her aunt, the Duchess of Cambridge, she was extremely indignant with her for not greeting her at the door. Lord Melbourne soon discovered that one of his more important duties was to restrain her impetuosity: a task he performed with greater zeal than success. "She might listen to him and love him; but once she had made up her mind to do something, she did it – whether he wanted her to or not." Sometimes he was overheard telling her: "For God's sake don't do that, Ma'am". Once the Genie was out of the bottle no one could coax it back.

During the early months of her reign the Queen received a constant flow of advice from the King of the Belgians. "My Beloved Child," he wrote in answer to her letter announcing her accession to the throne, "May I have the *happiness of being able to be of use to you.*" He went on to advise her to seize every opportunity to stress that she had been born and brought up in England. He ended with the rather ominous request that "Before you decide on anything important I should be glad if you would consult with me." The Queen immediately wrote back thanking him for his "kind and useful letter", and assuring him that his advice was always of "the *greatest importance*" to her. But she gave him to understand that she did not propose to surrender her judgement to him. For all the oblique delicacy of her hint, its import was unmistakable. "Before I go further," she wrote, "let me pause to tell you how fortunate I am to have at the head of the Government a man like Lord Melbourne. . . . The more I see him, the more confidence I have in him. . . . He is of the greatest use to me both politically and privately."

The Queen showed her wisdom not only in occasional displays of independence, but also in generally taking her uncle's advice, which came after all from a shrewd and experienced King. On June 27th, for example, he warned her how dangerous it could be to come to instant decisions. "Whenever a question is of some importance," he suggested, "it should not be decided on the day when it is submitted to you. Whenever it is not an urgent one, I make it a rule not to let any question be forced upon my *immediate* decision; it is really not doing oneself justice *de décider des questions sur le ponce.* . . . The best mode for you will be, that each Minister should bring his box with him, and when he submits to you the papers, *explain them to you.* Then you will keep the papers, either to think yourself upon it or to consult somebody, and either return them the next time you see the Minister to whom they belong, or send them to him. Good habits formed *now* may for ever afterwards be kept up." An entry in Greville's diary in August 1837, show that the Queen took her uncle's suggestions seriously. "When applications are made to Her Majesty, she seldom or never gives an immediate answer, but says she will consider it, and it is supposed that she does this because she consults Melbourne about everything, and waits to have her answers suggested by him. He says, however, that such is her habit even with him, and that when he talks to her upon any subject upon which an opinion is expected from her, she tells him she will think it over, and let him know her sentiments the next day."

Leopold, like Stockmar, was wedded to lofty generalisations, but sometimes his counsel could hardly have been more specific. For example, in July, he warned the Queen to be wary of Princess Lieven, whom he suspected of matchmaking. The best rule he told her was "*never to permit* people to speak on subjects concerning yourself or your affairs without your having yourself desired them to do so. The moment a person behaves improperly on this subject, change the conversation". This excellent proposal was instantly put into practice. "J'ai vu la Reine deux fois," the Princess told Lord Aberdeen, "Elle est d'une extrême réserve dans son discours. On croit que la prudence est une de ses premières qualités." She said much the same to Greville when she told him that she found H.M. "Very civil and gracious, but timid and embarrassed" and talking of "nothing but common places". Greville, with his customary discernment, concluded that the Queen "had probably been told that the Princess was an 'intrigante' and was afraid of committing herself."

One of the Queen's most appealing virtues was her extravagant gratitude for relatively trifling services. She wrote such an appreciative letter to her uncle for his warning about Princess Lieven that he described it as being "amongst *so many kind letters, almost the kindest*

I yet received from your dear hands. My happiness and my greatest pride will always be, to be *a tender and devoted father to you, my beloved child*, and to watch over you and stand by you with *heart* and *soul as long* as the heart which *loves* you so sincerely will beat." The King's letter is not only interesting as proof of his affection for his niece, but also as evidence that the Queen's partiality for underlining derived from her uncle's example.

As the Queen grew in self-confidence, she almost ceased to consult her uncle, who, nevertheless, maintained a ceaseless flow of suggestions. Eventually she became somewhat restive under "that most cruel of all afflictions – good advice". After all, her Prime Minister, who was always at hand, was the obvious person to whom she should turn. Stockmar warned the King that Lehzen was poisoning the Queen's mind against him, probably because she foresaw that his promotion of Albert's marriage was a threat to her own position. By December 1837 Leopold recognised that his niece was cooling towards him. "My dearest child," he said in reply to a distinctly peevish letter, "You were *somewhat irritable* when you wrote to me." The fact was that the Queen was dragging her feet over the question of her marriage, partly because she relished her newly won independence, and partly because she disliked being reminded of her obligation to Albert. Moreover, as Stockmar told King Leopold, she suspected him of intending to rule her through his influence over her husband. Conroy's attempts to dominate her had left her with an exaggerated fear of efforts to manipulate her. For almost a year, Albert was scarcely mentioned again, and was not even asked to her Coronation.

In June 1838 King Leopold made a serious tactical error when he sought his niece's support on Belgium's behalf. The independence of his country, he told her, had "always been an object of importance to England". The fact that in 1914 Britain went to war to defend Belgium's territorial integrity would seem to endorse this view. But the Queen was quick to recognise that her uncle's advice was self-interested. "All I want from your kind Majesty," he wrote, "is that you will *occasionally* express to your Ministers, and particularly to good Lord Melbourne, that, as far as is *compatible* with the interests of *your own* dominions, you do *not* wish that your Government should take the *lead* in such measures as might in a short time bring destruction on this country, as well as that of your uncle and his family." Unfortunately, the Queen regarded his letter as an unwarrantable attempt to dictate her foreign policy. Naturally, she replied, nothing would ever diminish her affection for her uncle, nor would alter "the ancient and hereditary policy of this country with respect to Belgium". But having said this, she went on to commend the sanctity of treaties in a way which offered him precious little comfort.

Five months later, King Leopold issued a second appeal in more peremptory terms, in which he complained of Lord Palmerston's unfairness, and warned of the "serious consequences which may affect more or less everybody" if Belgium was ill-treated. The tone of this letter was most injudicious, as attempts to browbeat the Queen almost always rebounded. "You must not, dear uncle," she replied on December 5th, "think that it is from want of interest that I, in general, abstain from touching upon these matters in my letters to you; but I am fearful, if I were to do so, to change our present delightful and familiar correspondence into a formal and stiff discussion upon political matters, which would not be agreeable to either of us, and which I should deeply regret." The King accepted the hint, and his next letter made no mention whatever of politics but was confined to reminiscences of Brighton in the days of the Prince Regent. The Queen showed a remarkable maturity for a girl of nineteen in frustrating her uncle's efforts to influence her.

Often a note of asperity crept into the Queen's letters which vanished the moment she met her correspondent. When Leopold visited her in the summer of 1838, he could hardly have been greeted more warmly. The Queen recorded his arrival at Windsor on August 28th with all her former ecstasy. "At 7 o'clock arrived my *dearest most beloved* Uncle Leopold, and my *dearest most beloved* Aunt Louise. . . . It is an inexpressible *happiness* and joy to me, to have these dearest beloved relations with me and in *my own* house." At dinner that evening she sat between her "dear Uncle" and her "good Lord Melbourne" whom she described as "delightful neighbours". Leopold had the good sense to express his approval of Lord M, which made the Queen very happy, "as I am so fond of Lord Melbourne, and he *has been* and is *such a kind friend* to me. Uncle and he perfectly agree in Politics too". One evening the Queen and her Aunt Louise played a game of chess together, in which she was eagerly assisted by her Prime Minister, her Foreign Secretary and her Lord Chamberlain. But as they offered conflicting advice, "I got quite beat, and Aunt Louise triumphed over my Council of Ministers". The match was further confused by the fact that there were four Queens present: two on the board and two playing each other.

The King's visit came to an end on September 18th, and Lord M was "touched to tears" by the leave-taking. The Queen, who always detested partings, was equally dejected. When the King returned to Belgium he found a letter from his niece thanking him for all "his *very* great kindness", and expressing her "*great, great grief*" at his departure: "God knows *how sad, how forlorn* I feel".

The Queen's relations with King Leopold further improved in 1839 when she asked Prince Albert to marry her. One of the principal points at issue between them had been her reluctance to make up her mind on this very question. But once she had fallen in love, she could not thank her Uncle enough for all he had done to promote the match. "Next to her husband," she once claimed, she loved the King and Queen of the Belgians "best in the world". Leopold and Louise became such frequent visitors that the rooms they occupied at Buckingham Palace are known to this day as the "Belgian Suite".

Few people knew better than Lord Melbourne how seriously the Monarchy had been damaged since the death of George III. He therefore decided to exploit the Queen's youth to revive the Crown's reputation. Clearly the Coronation provided an unique opportunity to awaken the loyalty of her subjects, and Melbourne persuaded Parliament that no expense should be spared to make it as splendid as possible. It was eventually agreed that the ceremony should be held on June 28th, 1838, and that the Queen should drive to the Abbey in full state for the first time since 1760. The festivities included a fair in Hyde Park, mass bands, fireworks, and the consumption of such torrents of gin and beer as to appal the growing temperance movement. However, so far from there being an orgy, the crowds lining the streets were exceptionally well behaved, although London went "raving mad" about what promised to be one of the greatest spectacles the city had ever seen. The American Legation was besieged by requests for tickets for the Abbey, and huge sums were paid for windows along the route. Greville said of London on the eve of the Coronation, "it is as if the population had been on a sudden quintupled; the uproar, the confusion, the crowd, the noise, are indescribable. . . . The town all mob, thronging, bustling, gaping, and gazing at everything, at anything, or at nothing; the Park one vast encampment, with banners floating on the tops of tents". Almost every hour excursion trains discharged hundreds of passengers to swell the crowds in the capital. Greville found the incessant noise "uncommonly tiresome", and disliked being jostled in the streets, but, nevertheless, felt bound to admit that "The great merit of this Coronation is, that so much has been done for the people: to amuse and interest *them* seems to have been the principal object". For the first time in history Members of the House of Commons were invited to the service in the Abbey, in deference, no doubt, to the spirit of Democracy.

The Queen only slept fitfully on the morning of the Coronation, and was woken at four o'clock by the sound of guns in the Park. Such was the noise of the crowds near the Palace that she could not get back to sleep. At seven she got up and looked out of the window at the hordes of troops and spectators swarming over Green Park. At ten, her procession set out for the Abbey, following a route almost as circuitous as that of Chesterton's "rolling English drunkard": up Constitution Hill, along Piccadilly, down St James's Street, across Trafalgar Square, and thence via Whitehall to the Abbey. The houses along the road were crammed with people and even their roofs were covered in spectators. The visual effect was that of a bed of flowers. Long before she set out from Buckingham Palace, the congregation awaited her in the Abbey. France's representative, Marshal Soult, arrived in a carriage even more magnificent than the Queen's State Coach. Mrs Stevenson described it as being "of cobalt blue, trimmed with bands of pure silver and gold". Nobody seems to have told her that it had once belonged to Le Grand Condé, the victor of Rocroi (1643), one of Louis XIV's greatest generals. The morning of June 28th began overcast, but by nine the clouds cleared and the rest of the day remained fine. Throughout the journey from Buckingham Palace to Westminster, which lasted an hour and a half, the Queen bowed and smiled to her loving subjects. Never before had she seen such crowds, and she thought "their good humour and excessive loyalty beyond everything". "I really cannot say *how* proud I feel to be Queen of *such a Nation*."

When the Queen caught her first sight of the interior of the Abbey, "she paused, as if for breath, and clasped her hands. The orchestra broke out into the most tremendous crash of music and everyone literally gasped for breath". The scene she beheld was of unsurpassed magnificence. The Abbey was hung with gold and crimson awnings, and the floors were covered with oriental rugs. The Archbishop wore a "remarkably handsome" cope, which dated from the time of

James I. The most opulent sight of all was the Austrian Minister, Prince Esterhazy, who was covered in jewels from head to heels. When the sun caught him, he turned into a dazzling rainbow of light. But nothing detracted from the diminutive figure of the Queen, as she slowly processed down the whole length of the Abbey, preceded by Lord Melbourne carrying the Sword of State, and followed by eight train-bearers. Disraeli told his sister, Sarah, that Lord M "looked very awkward and uncouth, with his coronet cocked over his nose, his robes under his feet, and holding the great Sword of State like a butcher". It should, however, be pointed out that he felt so ill that he dosed himself with brandy and laudanum to give him strength for the ceremony. Moreover, as the Queen remarked in her journal, he found the huge sword "excessively heavy".

During the early part of the service the Queen promised on the Bible to maintain "The Protestant Reformed Religion established by Law": the very oath which had persuaded George III to refuse his assent to Catholic Emancipation. She took her promise equally solemnly, and later reminded Gladstone that having sworn to preserve the Church of England "inviolably", she could never consent to its disestablishment. Before the actual moment of crowning, the Queen withdrew into St Edward's Chapel to put on a supertunica of gold and to take off her circlet of diamonds. After a few moments, she returned bareheaded and was led to St Edward's Chair. As Archbishop Howley placed the Crown on her head, the Peers and Peeresses put on their coronets. At this "most beautiful and impressive moment", she glanced towards Lord Melbourne, who gave her "*such a kind*" and "fatherly look". There followed the homage of the Bishops, Royal Dukes, and Peers. When Melbourne knelt and kissed the Queen's hand, he gave it an affectionate squeeze, whereupon "I grasped his with all my heart, at which he looked up with his eyes filled with tears and seemed much touched".

Twice during the course of the five hour service the congregation burst out in applause: first when Marshal Soult, Britain's old enemy, passed down the aisle, and secondly when the Duke of Wellington paid homage. Soon afterwards, the Queen caught Lehzen's eye and gave her a loving smile. Then she received Communion from the Archbishop, and withdrew once more to St Edward's Chapel, where the altar was covered with sandwiches and bottles. Few things could have demonstrated more clearly just how necessary was the emphasis of the Oxford Movement on reverent Churchmanship. Lord

Melbourne took the opportunity to refresh himself with a glass of wine, while the Queen removed the Crown for a few minutes. At last, the final procession was formed, and "loaded" with the Orb in her left hand, and the Sceptre in her right, she proceeded through the Abbey amidst fervent cheering.

Only the Queen and some of the officiating clergy realised how many mistakes had marred the proceedings. Nobody had rehearsed her in the ceremonies which took place, and, worse still, nobody had explained their spiritual significance. Nothing she wrote in her journal describing the service suggests that she grasped its inner meaning. She saw it as a momentous, historic event, not as a sacrament. The Dean of Westminster, Dr John Ireland, who had conducted the Coronations of George IV and William IV, was too infirm to supervise Queen Victoria's. Consequently, he delegated his duties to his Sub-Dean, The Reverend Lord John Thynne, who admitted to Greville "that nobody knew what was to be except the Archbishop and himself". In fact, Howley made at least three serious mistakes and was less in command of events than Thynne suggested.

The Queen never once lost her presence of mind despite the bungling of the clergy. Disraeli told Sarah that "the Queen looked very well, and performed her part with great grace and completeness, which cannot in general be said of the other performers; they were always in doubt as to what came next, and you saw the want of rehearsal". At one moment the Queen whispered to the Sub-Dean: "Pray tell me what I am to do, for they (the Bishops) don't know." Dr Maltby, Bishop of Durham, was, in H.M.'s phrase, "remarkably maladroit and never could tell me what was to take place". At entirely the wrong moment he suddenly thrust the Orb into her hand, which so surprised her that she asked Thynne what she was meant to do with it. "Your Majesty," he replied, "is to carry it, if you please, in your hand." "Am I?" she asked resignedly, "It is very heavy." Later, when she had withdrawn to St Edward's Chapel, "The Archbishop came in and *ought* to have delivered the Orb to me, but I had already got it, and he (as usual) was *so* confused and puzzled and knew nothing, and went away". The most painful mistake of all came when the Archbishop placed the ruby ring on the wrong finger, and used so much force to get it on that the Queen could scarcely conceal her agony. It took almost half an hour at the end of the service to ease it off with the help of iced water. The final mistake was made by the Bishop of Bath and Wells, who accidentally turned over two pages at once, and then told the Queen that the ceremony was over. Lord Melbourne, always in search of the easy solution, asked "What does it signify?" but the Sub-Dean insisted that the service should be properly concluded.

The Queen re-entered her State Coach at a quarter past four, wearing the Crown, and carrying the Orb and Sceptre. She returned home by the same route she had taken earlier that day. The crowds, if anything, were even greater, and touched her deeply by their "enthusiasm, affection and loyalty". Eventually she reached Buckingham Palace some eight and a half hours after she had left it that morning. Gathering up her train, she ran upstairs to her room, changed out of her robes, and gave her spaniel, Dash, a bath. That evening, she officiated at a State Banquet, and then watched the firework display in Green Park until after midnight. It is hardly surprising she felt a "little" exhausted. "You may depend upon it," said Lord M, "that you are more tired than you think you are."

During the course of the evening, Melbourne congratulated the Queen on "this most brilliant day", which "had gone off so well". "You did it beautifully," he said, "every part of it, with so much taste; it is a thing you can't give a person advice upon; it must be left to a person." The Queen confessed that it gave her "great and real pleasure" to receive such a compliment from her "kind impartial friend". The French Ambassador, Count Sebastiani, told her that thirty-four years before he had been present at Napoleon's Coronation, at which Pius VII officiated, but although he had been deeply impressed by the ceremony, it was not so imposing as that he had just witnessed.

Not until the Golden Jubilee, almost half a century later, was the Queen ever as popular as in the summer of 1838. Within a year of her Coronation she had dissipated the enormous good will with which her people had welcomed her. So much so, that she was hissed at Ascot and warned to steer clear of London. This drastic reversal of public affection arose from a tragic misunderstanding over the Duchess of Kent's lady-in-waiting, Lady Flora Hastings. In 1839 Lady Flora was a spinster of thirty-two, who combined chilling piety with malicious wit. The Queen disliked her from the moment they first met in 1834, mostly because she supported the "Kensington System", and threatened to oust Lehzen. When she moved with the Duchess to Buckingham Palace, the Queen referred to her as "that odious Lady Flora", and as a "spy of J.C." Sir John always prided himself on being a great man with the ladies, and in the winter of 1838 there was a good deal of lighthearted banter when the pair travelled together in the same post-chaise on their way back from Scotland. Because Queen Victoria's hatred of Conroy verged on the pathological, she accused Lady Flora of guilt by association, and believed the worst of both of them.

Lady Flora spent the Christmas of 1838 with her mother, the Dowager Marchioness of Hastings, at Loudoun Castle in Scotland. Throughout the festivities she suffered from violent pains in the stomach. For a time, she attributed her discomfort to turkey and plum pudding. But the pains persisted, and when she came back into waiting on January 10th, she consulted the Queen's doctor, Sir James Clark. Sir James saw her several times during the month, but never once examined her undressed. The simple remedies he prescribed, such as a diet of rhubarb, do not suggest that he thought her symptoms serious. On January 12th, the Queen and Lehzen noticed that Lady Flora had grown decidedly plump, and discussed the obvious explanation for this change. By early February, conjecture had hardened into certainty. "We (the Queen and Lehzen) have no doubt that she is – to use plain words – *with child*!! Clark cannot deny the suspicion." Not satisfied with this leap in the dark, the Queen jumped to the further conclusion that "the horrid cause of all this is the monster and devil incarnate", Sir John Conroy. Once the Queen was persuaded of anything it was difficult enough to dislodge the idea from her mind, but no power on earth could dispose of this fanciful hypothesis, which coincided so aptly with her view of Sir John's character. The belief that he had seduced Lady Flora struck her with all the force of a proven fact, although there was not a shred of evidence to support it. Lady Flora regarded the charges against her as part of a "horrible conspiracy" to discredit Sir John and the Duchess. By an unhappy chance she had become caught in the crossfire of a vendetta. The Duchess told the Dowager Marchioness that the attack on her daughter's honour "was levelled at me through your innocent child".

Towards the end of January 1839, Lady Tavistock, one of the Queen's senior Ladies of the Bedchamber, came into waiting. No sooner had she arrived at Buckingham Palace than she found the place in turmoil. The existence of two courts under one roof was bound to generate gossip, but not the intensity of recrimination which now rampaged through the Household. Several of the

Queen's ladies begged Lady Tavistock "to protect their purity" from "contamination". She proved rather a curious choice as an arbiter of propriety seeing that she later became Landseer's mistress, but she agreed to approach Lord Melbourne and raise the matter with him. The Queen noted in her journal on February 2nd that the interview took place with "Lehzen's concurrence". The matter, of course, should have been resolved by a conference between the Queen and her mother, but this was rejected on the ground that they were not on "good terms". After hearing what Lady Tavistock had to say, Melbourne sent for Sir James Clark, who seems to have shown no scruples about his Hippocratic oath. Sir James told Lord M that he felt reasonably sure that Lady Flora was pregnant, but that the wisest thing to do was to wait and see: advice which precisely squared with Melbourne's instinct. "If you remain quite quiet," he assured the Queen, "you'll get through it very well." This policy, however, possessed two vital defects: it was impossible to achieve, and it enabled rumours to spread without being contradicted.

Lady Portman, the next senior Lady of the Bedchamber after Lady Tavistock, came into waiting early in February only to find that everybody in the Palace seemed anxious to share their wild surmises with her. Probably prompted from on high, she asked Sir James to inform Lady Flora of the suspicions her figure aroused. This awkward assignment was made a great deal easier when Lehzen proposed that Clark should approach the problem by saying: "You must be secretly married". Accordingly, on February 16th, Sir James put this suggestion to his patient who indignantly repudiated it. The next day, Lady Portman informed the Duchess of Kent of Clark's "strong suspicion", and said that Lady Flora must leave the Palace until she had cleared her name by consenting to be medically examined. Shortly afterwards, the Queen discussed the matter with her mother for the first time, and noted she was "horror struck": not, as the Queen supposed, because of Lady Flora's "guilt", but because of the callous ineptitude with which the affair had been handled.

Naturally, Lady Flora's family demanded to know the source of the slander. Lord M told her brother, Lord Hastings, that the charge originated with the "Ladies of the Court". The Duchess of Kent held the widely shared opinion that Lehzen was to blame as her aversion to Lady Flora was notorious. The Speaker of the House of Commons assured Melbourne that the Baroness was "the snake in the grass", and that the Queen had behaved like a "heartless child". But subsequently Lady Portman informed Lord Hastings that Lehzen had not been responsible for the accusations which had led her to urge Sir James to confront his sister. The persistent refusal of the Women of the Bedchamber to name the culprit, despite unrelenting pressure, led to the theory that they must be shielding the Queen. Whether or not she master-minded the campaign, three things are certain. First, she was convinced in her own mind of Lady Flora's guilt. Second, she was one of the first, if not the first, to remark on her changed appearance. Third, she was desperately anxious to exploit the supposed scandal to force Sir John to resign.

Initially, Lady Flora refused to submit to any examination, but after it became clear that there was no other way out, she reluctantly consented. It took place on Sunday, February 17th, in the presence of Lady Portman. Sir James was assisted by Sir Charles Clarke, a specialist in women's diseases. They agreed that Lady Flora was still a virgin, and issued a signed statement to the effect that they had examined her "with a view to determine the existence, or non-existence, of pregnancy", and that in their opinion, "although there is an enlargement of the stomach, there are no grounds for suspicion that pregnancy does exist, or ever has existed". Later, Lady Flora told her uncle that she had the satisfaction of possessing a certificate signed by her accuser, Sir James Clark, stating "as strongly as language can state it", that she was not, and never had been, pregnant. When the Duchess of Kent learned that Lady Flora had been proved innocent, she instantly dismissed Sir James for the part he had played in encouraging false accusations. Meanwhile, the Queen, on learning the doctors' verdict, asked Lady Portman to convey her deepest regrets to Lady Flora for all she had suffered, and an offer to see her as soon as she wished. When the two women met, the Queen was greatly distressed to see Lady Flora looking so ill. She at once took her hand, kissed her warmly, and assured her with tears in her eyes how much she regretted all that had passed. Lady Flora agreed to forgive, if not to forget, but was courageous enough to observe that she had been "treated as if guilty without a trial", and that never before had a member of her family been so maltreated by their sovereign. Momentarily it seemed as if the sordid drama had ended in reconciliation, whereas, in fact, the curtain had only fallen on the first act of the tragedy.

The public took up Lady Flora's cause with the enthusiasm with which it had earlier upheld Queen Caroline in her quarrels with

George IV. It saw her, in Lord Holland's phrase, as the innocent victim "of prudery, tittle-tattle, and folly". The Tories equally rallied to her support, for there were few more stalwart Conservatives than her family. Nor were they slow to seize the opportunity of belabouring the Whig Queen and her Whig Prime Minister. Scenting the chance of political victory, the last thing they wanted was peace in the Palace. During the first week in March, all London was engrossed in the story. So many rumours flew about that it was hard to tell fact from fiction, but enough was known to establish conclusively that the Court had behaved outrageously. Greville, whose sensitive nostrils were quick to detect the faintest whiff of scandal, was overpowered by the stench. "The Court," he noted on March 2nd, "is plunged in shame and mortification. . . . While the whole proceeding is looked upon by Society at large as to the last degree disgusting and disgraceful." Such things might be commonplace in the servants' hall, but were "unheard of in good Society". Not, of course, that adultery was unknown in aristocratic circles, but well-bred people observed the eleventh commandment.

On Monday, February 18th, Sir James Clark and his colleague, Sir Charles, told Lord Melbourne confidentially that the certificate they had signed could well prove misleading. Sir Charles emphasised that although they had found no evidence of pregnancy, the strangest things were known to have happened, and they might be shown to be wrong. Lord Melbourne at once told the Queen of the doctors' second thoughts, and she passed on the information to her mother in an incoherent note. "Sir Charles Clarke," she wrote, "has said that though she (Lady Flora) is a virgin, still that it (viz. a pregnancy) might be possible and one could not tell if such things could not happen. There was an enlargement in the womb like a child." Both Melbourne and the Queen seized avidly on the chance that they had all along been right. It was for this reason that they decided to regard Lady Flora's certificate of virginity as a worthless scrap of paper. Even when everyone else at Court could see she was gravely ill, the Queen airily dismissed her disorder as nothing more than a "bilious attack".

Sir John Conroy's ambition in life was to plague the Queen, and he viewed the prospect of peace with consternation. The Duke of Wellington was convinced that Sir John was the "grand mover" behind most of the mischief at work in the Royal Households, and seized every opportunity to stir up trouble. Towards the end of

February, Sir John urged newspapers hostile to the Government to make the most of the scandal. Furthermore, he encouraged the Duchess of Kent and Lady Flora to revive the quarrel by demanding to be indemnified. The Hastings family needed little encouragement from Conroy to seek redress, for they were proud, hot-tempered and quick to take offence, particularly when their honour was maligned. Soon after her interview with the Queen, Lady Flora wrote an account of her sufferings to her brother, Lord Hastings. So incensed was he to hear how she had been treated, that he set off for London breathing fire and slaughter. Lord Melbourne tried to calm him by blaming the unhappy affair on the "tittle-tattle" of the Ladies, and suggesting that he should consult the Duke of Wellington, to whom everyone turned in perplexity. The Duke told him that the wisest thing to do would be to hush up the whole affair, both in the interest of his sister and his Sovereign. On February 28th, Lord Hastings was granted an audience with the Queen, during which he hoped to discover "the originator of the slander, and to bring him or her to punishment", but he came away empty-handed and was forced to turn elsewhere. After pestering Lord Portman to tell him who was the culprit, he learned it was not the Baroness. But who it was Lady Portman refused to disclose.

The Dowager Marchioness was as tenacious as her son in demanding reparation. On March 7th she wrote the Queen an eight-page letter calling upon her to punish those responsible for circulating "atrocious calumnies and unblushing falsehoods" about her daughter in the very presence of Her Majesty. Above all, she appealed to her to reject such slanders by repudiating their authors. Lord Melbourne, replying on the Queen's behalf, said that the allowance which Her Majesty was anxious to make "for the natural feelings of a mother upon such an occasion, tended to diminish that surprise which could not be otherwise than excited by the tone and substance of your Ladyship's letter". On March 10th, Lady Hastings wrote a peremptory note to the Prime Minister demanding that the Queen should follow the Duchess's example and dismiss Sir James Clark "as a mark of public justice". Lord M considered that this was going too far, and told her that her suggestion was "so unprecedented and objectionable" that he could do nothing more than acknowledge it. When Lord Hastings read his reply, he was barely restrained from challenging him to a duel.

Demands for Sir James's blood were more easily made than

satisfied. Throughout the proceedings, he had either acted on instructions, or with the Queen's consent. Obviously he was responsible for his diagnosis, but it is hardly a crime to make a mistake. Lord Melbourne feared that if Sir James was dismissed he would be tempted to justify his conduct by embarrassing revelations. It must also be said that one of the Queen's greatest virtues was her support of those in adversity. Clark's practice had suffered disastrously because of his treatment of Lady Flora, and he could not hope to survive without royal favour.

On March 8th, Lady Flora wrote to her uncle, Captain Hamilton Fitzgerald, who was then living in Brussels, saying that he had no doubt heard the gossip with which London was ringing, so she thought it best he should hear the truth from her. She explained that she had become the victim of a "diabolical conspiracy" to ruin the Duchess of Kent, which she attributed to a "certain foreign Lady whose hatred to the Duchess is no secret". Throughout the whole sordid business H.R.H. had stood by her "most gallantly, and I love her better than ever. She is the most generous-hearted woman possible". Flora spared the Queen, but nevertheless alleged that she had only apologised half-heartedly for the humiliating charges blazoned about the Court. On March 25th, *The Examiner* published *A Narrative of the Principal Facts*, which was written by Captain Fitzgerald, who justified publication on the grounds that his niece's reputation was still being blackened in spite of her proven innocence. Lord Hastings had done everything in his power to redeem the family honour without the slightest avail. Indeed, it had even hinted that he had no spirit for the fight and wanted the matter hushed up. Under these circumstances, Captain Fitzgerald saw no alternative but to seek justice from the public. The Tory press took up the hue and cry, and lambasted Lord Melbourne, Baroness Lehzen, and, to some extent, the Queen. When the Dowager published her correspondence with the Prime Minister in the *Morning Post*, the Queen was furious and wanted to hang the Editor "and the whole Hastings family". Lord M had to deploy a battery of arguments to prevent her from writing to the newspapers herself. The trouble was that she was so absorbed by the threat to her own reputation, that she failed to recognise that unless the Hastings family spoke out publicly, their silence would be interpreted as guilt. Having tried and failed to achieve redress privately, they had only two choices left: surrender or exposure. Greville regarded the whole affair as "a horrible, disgraceful and mischievous mess" and was particularly shocked "by the moral insensibility which is exhibited by the original wrong-doers, who cannot see the enormity of their own behaviour".

Because of its temerity in appealing to public opinion, the Hastings family found itself in the dock. It had broken the first rule of polite society by refusing to wash its dirty linen in private. The Queen blamed Lady Flora for the press campaign, and ostracised her once more: a fact which was duly reported in the papers. In her journal, she referred to her as "that wretched Lady Flo" or that "*nasty* woman". One of the most deplorable consequences of the whole shabby affair was that it further alienated the Queen from her mother. The Duchess's loyal support of the wronged family appeared in her daughter's eyes a species of treason. Discussing the matter with Lord M, she complained of harbouring an "Enemy in the house", and of her "growing dislike for Mamma". Early in April, the Duchess refused to accompany the Queen to Drury Lane because Lady Tavistock was in waiting. The audience, guessing the reason for her absence, shouted belligerently at the Royal Box, "Where's your mother?"

For some time Lady Flora bravely appeared in public, hoping thereby to stifle rumours, but early in June was confined to her room suffering from bouts of nausea. When the Queen mentioned this to Melbourne, he gave "a significant laugh". Next, her hair began to fall out and she took to wearing a bonnet. On June 16th the Duchess warned her daughter that Flora was mortally ill, and two days later the doctors told her that their patient could only last for a week. Accordingly, on June 27th, the Queen paid the stricken woman a final visit, with nobody else present. Her journal describes how she "found poor Lady Flora stretched on a couch looking as thin as anybody can be who is still alive; literally a skeleton, but the body very much swollen like a person who is with child; a searching look in her eyes, rather like a person who is dying; her voice like usual, a good deal of strength in her hands; she was friendly, said she was very comfortable, and was very grateful for all I had done for her; and that she was glad to see me look well. I said to her, I hoped to see her again when she was better – upon which she grasped my hand as if to say 'I shall not see you again'". The Queen was profoundly upset by this interview and kept repeating "Poor Lady Flora! Poor Lady Flora!" Day after day, the Duchess spent long hours sitting by Flora's bedside, holding her hand, and doing her best to soothe her. On July 4th the patient became unconscious, and the Queen put off a dinner party she had planned to give that evening. The following morning Lehzen broke the news that Flora had died shortly after two. Gossip pursued the dead woman beyond the grave and rumours were put about that she had accidentally poisoned herself while trying to procure an abortion. Her friends more charitably claimed she had died of a broken heart.

Two days before Lady Flora died she made her family promise that they would insist on a post mortem so as to dispel any doubts of her innocence. The examination was conducted by Sir Benjamin Brodie, the most eminent surgeon in England, with the help of four colleagues. Their unanimous verdict was that the patient had died of a tumour of the liver, which explained the distension of the stomach. They concluded their statement by reporting categorically that "the uterus and its appendages presented the usual appearances of the healthy virgin state".

Lady Flora was buried in the family vault at Loudoun. The first stage of her last journey to Scotland began on July 10th at four o'clock in the morning, when her body was taken from Buckingham Palace to St Catherine's Wharf. This unusually early hour was chosen in the hope of avoiding protests. The streets, in fact, were lined with silent crowds as the cortège passed down the Mall, guarded by police. The Hastings family followed immediately behind the hearse, next came the empty carriages of the Queen, Queen Adelaide, and the Duchess of Kent, and finally a long procession of mourners paying their last respects. One man shook his fist at the Queen's coachman and shouted defiantly: "What's the use of her gilded trumpery after she has killed her?" Others vented their protest by jeering and throwing stones.

From the moment the public first learned of Lady Flora's ill-treatment it was quick to express its disgust. On March 25th Greville noted that "Nobody cares for the Queen . . . and loyalty is a dead letter". Three weeks later, he wrote of the "incredible harm" the whole affair had done, by casting "dreadful odium" on the Court, and by playing "the devil with the Queen's popularity". The news of Lady Flora's death, and the report of the post mortem, provoked further violent storms, and the Queen hardly dared to open the *Morning Post* such was its "virulence and indecency". Hitherto, she had basked in adulation and applause, and had yet to learn to "meet with Triumph and Disaster, and treat those two impostors just the same". Melbourne practised, but preached in vain, the detachment which shrugs off calumny.

The Queen was not only taunted in the newspapers but personally insulted. When she was seen in London, few men bothered to raise their hats, and she was hissed while riding in Rotten Row. During Ascot Week there were shouts of "Mrs Melbourne", as she drove down the course; and the Duchess of Montrose and Lady Sarah Ingestre, "two foolish, vulgar women", joined in ill-mannered abuse. Later, the Duchess tried to excuse herself by insisting that her protest was directed at the Prime Minister. Be that as it may, the Queen maintained that the culprits deserved to be "flogged". Sir Charles Napier, a gallant veteran of the Peninsular War, attended a dinner at Nottingham and found that he was the only person prepared to respond to the loyal toast. Eventually, the Queen recovered much of her popularity, but appeared to have learned little. Only four years later, she accused Lady Augusta Somerset of being with child, and her cousin, Prince George of Cambridge, of supposedly being the father. As Greville remarked, "It is really incredible that after the Flora Hastings affair and the deplorable catastrophe in which it ended, the Queen should not have shrunk instinctively from anything like another scandal". The Somersets loyally accepted her half-hearted apology, and the matter was hushed up, but it was a serious flaw in her character that she reached such assured conclusions on such insubstantial evidence.

It was generally believed at the time that Sir James Clark was largely to blame for the Lady Flora scandal. Lady Holland, for example, maintained that "the doctor seems chiefly to blame" because "like most modern medicos" he was too "inclined to meddle with the private concerns of patients", and Lord Melbourne told the Queen that most of the trouble came "from Clark's mistake in not seeing it was a disease". Soon after Lady Flora died, a Dr John Fisher published a pamphlet entitled *The Court Doctor Dissected*. It began by examining a considerable number of illnesses in which symptoms resembling pregnancy were exhibited, and went on to argue that Sir James had been seriously negligent in failing to consider the possibility that his patient was suffering from one of these diseases. Lord Hastings corroborated Fisher's thesis by publishing a detailed list of Clark's initial prescriptions, which showed he had badly misjudged Lady Flora's true condition. Both Sir James, and his colleague Sir Charles, made a further grave mistake when they added a confidential gloss to their first published report. They should either have kept their reservations to themselves, or have listed them in their bulletin. The Queen was so sorry for "poor Clark" that she persuaded Prince Albert to make him his honorary Physician. It proved a disastrous choice, amounting to a death sentence.

Lord Melbourne, the Queen's official adviser, was obviously greatly to blame for failing to scotch the scandal. His negligence was the more astonishing seeing that he was an experienced man of the world, who normally handled delicate situations with unsurpassed discretion. But in this instance he lost his touch, and appears to have sacrificed his judgement to that of an excited young lady of nineteen. As Greville was quick to point out, the justification of his "extraordinary domiciliation in the Palace" was that it supposedly enabled him to prevent just such a mischief. The Queen was too generous and devoted to Lord M to blame him for giving her such lamentable advice, but there can be no question that his ineptitude contributed to the tragedy. Moreover, he failed in his clear duty to persuade her that one of the principal glories of the English legal system is that it presumes innocence not guilt. Indeed, he compounded this error by augmenting the Queen's suspicions rather than dispelling them. Conscious as he was of the need to safeguard Her Majesty's reputation, he unwittingly prompted her to sanction a gross miscarriage of justice which all but destroyed her good name.

When Mrs Stevenson wrote home at the end of July describing "the sad affair of Lady Flora Hastings", she told her family that everyone seemed to infer that "the blame must be with the Queen". Some people tried to defend her by arguing that her mistakes arose from her youth and innocence. But, in fact, when Lord Esher in 1904 unearthed the documents in the Royal Archives relating to Lady Flora, King Edward was "astonished" by his mother's precocious knowledge. Indeed, she seemed to know more than Sir James about female physiology. From the first, she should have refused to countenance scurrilous gossip. Instead, she repeated it, acted upon it, and some even said originated it. Only sheer obstinacy prevented her from making an adequate apology when Lady Flora was proved innocent. She remained intransigent to the end, and refused to express remorse. But despite her defiant façade she could not conceal her misgivings. She had sleepless nights haunted by bad dreams, and became peevish, listless, and irritable. On one occasion, her nerves were so stretched that she even snapped at Lord Melbourne.

In May 1839, the Queen faced the prospect of losing the services of her "dear and excellent Lord Melbourne", and being forced to accept a Tory Prime Minister. The threat arose over a rebellion of planters in Jamaica who resented Britain's attempt to free their slaves. Lord Melbourne reacted by drafting a bill to suspend the Island's constitution and hand over power to the Governor and a Council. At two o'clock in the morning on May 7th, the measure was passed by three hundred and four votes to two hundred and ninety-nine. The Queen described this narrow victory in her journal by saying "we had only a majority of five": her choice of pronoun showing how entirely she identified herself with the Whigs. Lord M and his colleagues agreed that they had lost so much support that they had "no alternative but to resign".. In announcing this decision to the Queen, Melbourne assured her that it gave him the deepest pain "to quit the services of a mistress who had treated him with such unvarying kindness and unlimited confidence". At the best of times Lord M's resignation would have grieved her, but coming as it did in the middle of the Hastings crisis, it left her totally devastated. She could hardly expect to turn to a Tory Prime Minister for help or sympathy in what had become a party political struggle. "ALL, ALL" her happiness was now at stake, and she saw herself as "a poor helpless girl" clinging desperately to Lord Melbourne for protection. When he came to the Palace to discuss what she needed to do to replace his administration, it took her some minutes to muster up courage to face so sad an interview. The moment they met, she "held his hand for a little while, unable to leave go", and entreated him not to forsake her. "He gave me such a look of kindness, pity, and affection, and could hardly utter for tears, 'Oh! no', in such a touching voice."

Later the same day, Tuesday, May 7th, Lord M presented the Queen with a memorandum listing what he thought she should do. The gist of his advice was that she should send for the Duke of Wellington and invite him to form a government. She pressed Melbourne to come back later, but he said that in view of his resignation it would not be right to do so. He promised, however, to visit her next morning before her audience with the Duke. The Queen was so grieved by this parting that she was unable to "touch a morsel of food" that evening. Lord M was equally dejected and wrote to say that nothing had ever given him more pain than to be forced to tell her that he could not return to see her. But unfortunately "it was absolutely necessary not to give occasion to any jealousy or suspicion".

Lord M, as promised, visited the Queen shortly before noon on Wednesday, May 8th. He warned her that the Duke had grown so deaf that she must make sure that he understood what she said. He also told her that she must try to get over her antipathy to Peel. The Queen saw the Duke in the Yellow Closet at Buckingham Palace. She started by saying that she imagined he knew why she had sent for him, and went on to tell him that Lord Melbourne's Ministry had enjoyed her unreserved confidence. However, as the Duke's party "had been instrumental in removing them", she looked to him to form the next government. The Duke declined the honour, arguing that "he had no power whatever in the House of Commons", and that he was "so deaf and old" that he was no longer fit for the post. That being so, he advised her to send for Sir Robert Peel, whom he described as "a man of honour and integrity". The Queen concluded the audience by telling the Duke that she regarded Lord Melbourne as "a parent", to whom she was greatly indebted, and that she therefore proposed to go on seeing him "as a friend" although he was out of office. The Duke said he perfectly understood and raised no objection to her consorting with his foremost political enemy. It was characteristic of her open nature that she should have gone out of her way to stress her unusual decision. The moment the Duke left, she sent Peel a hurried note asking him to come to the Palace as soon as possible.

Throughout much of the Queen's reign British politics was dominated by a land-owning oligarchy. But Parliamentary reform in 1832, combined with the relentless pressure of those enriched by the Industrial Revolution, gradually eroded the traditional ascendancy of the gentry and aristocracy. Peel's father, the first baronet, acquired a vast fortune by mechanising the cotton industry in Lancashire, and was a typical representative of the class made rich by manufacturing. His son, Robert, was a contemporary of Byron's at Harrow, and achieved a double first at Christ Church. Throughout its history, the English aristocracy has assimilated newcomers, while at the same time sneering at the presumption of those who have made themselves rich. Peel's shyness, his lack of small-talk and his awkward manners were a consequence of his feeling that he would always remain an outsider. In 1809, his father bought him an Irish "pocket borough" and launched him into politics. Soon he became recognised as a pre-eminent Home Secretary and a brilliant Leader of the House of Commons. Towards the end of 1834, he became Prime Minister of a minority Conservative Government which contrived to survive for a hundred days. Unfortunately, the Queen who had hardly ever met him, took a "great dislike" to him. In her eyes, he was guilty of the unforgivable sin of being a Tory. When she wrote to Lord Melbourne on May 9th to describe her attempts to form a new government, she spoke of herself as being "amongst enemies". Anybody, of course, who threatened to usurp Melbourne's place could hardly expect to commend himself to his Sovereign. Greville believed that the Queen's aversion to Peel derived from his humble background. Harrow and Christ Church had done their best, but he still betrayed his Staffordshire origins. "I was never so struck as yesterday by the vulgarity of Peel," he noted in his journal. "In all his ways, his dress, his manner, he looks more like a dapper shopkeeper than a Prime Minister. He eats voraciously, and cuts cream jellies with his knife. . . . And yet he has genius and taste, and his thoughts are not vulgar."

Peel arrived at the Palace immediately after luncheon and his audience lasted an hour. The Queen repeated what she had told the Duke earlier about her deep regard for Lord Melbourne and her intention of going on seeing him. Peel, speaking from experience, referred to the problems of sustaining a minority Government, and expressed the hope that Her Majesty would be willing to make some changes in her Household to mark her confidence in the new ministry. Nothing, of course, would be done without her "knowledge or approbation". The Queen afterwards told Melbourne that she had remained "collected, civil and high" throughout the interview, and that Peel had been "embarrassed and put out". He is "such a cold, odd man", she complained, and his stiff ways and stilted conversation were so "dreadfully different" from Lord M's "frank, open, natural" manner. The truth of the matter was that Peel possessed few of the social graces needed to overcome the implacable prejudices of his Sovereign. Neither he nor Gladstone ever recognised that the most effective way to enlist the Queen's good will was to treat her first and foremost as a woman. Both men regarded the Crown with profound reverence, but were tempted to treat its wearer more as a principle than a person: a singularly inept way to handle so warm-blooded a human being as Queen Victoria.

There was a good deal that Peel left unsaid when he mentioned

the possibility of changes in the Royal Household. The previous
Government had surrounded the Queen with their own near
relations, and her Household was therefore blatantly partisan. His
supporters were especially anxious to replace six of Her Majesty's
twenty-five Ladies. The first was the Duchess of Sutherland, the
Mistress of the Robes, and a sister of the Irish Secretary, Lord Morpeth. The second was Lady Burlington, another of Morpeth's sisters.
The third was Lady Normanby, Principal Lady of the Bedchamber,
and the wife of the Secretary at War. The fourth was Miss Spring
Rice whose father was Melbourne's Chancellor of the Exchequer.
Finally, there was an understandable agitation to get rid of Lady
Tavistock, Lord John Russell's sister-in-law, and Lady Portman,
whose father was a prominent Whig. Peel was not only under
pressure to purge the Court of political opponents, but to purify its
morals. Lord Conyngham, the Lord Chamberlain, and Lord
Uxbridge, his successor, both installed mistresses in the Palace. It
would have been far better had the Queen's Ladies directed their
malice against the depravity of their Lordships, and spared the innocent Lady Flora. Peel was particularly anxious that Lord Ashley
(later Lord Shaftesbury), a great Evangelical, should join the Royal
Household to raise its moral tone. Ashley at first refused, believing
his vocation lay amidst slums and factories, but finally relented when
Sir Robert told him that it was imperative to surround the Queen
with high-minded companions, seeing that "the welfare of millions
of human beings" depended upon her "moral and religious
character".

Negotiations over the formation of a new government began to
founder over the relatively trivial problem of the Queen's Ladies.
Lord Melbourne advised her to tell Peel, if he persisted in his proposals, that he was making demands "which no minister before had
ever pressed upon a Sovereign. If this is put to him by your Majesty,
Lord Melbourne does not see how he can resist it". But he was
careful to add that if Peel remained adamant, "it will not do to refuse
and to put off the negotiation upon it". The Queen promised to
follow Lord M's advice "in every respect", but in summarising it in
her journal she omitted to mention this last crucial proviso. She was
far too agitated by the prospect of losing her beloved Prime Minister
to deal with the problem rationally. Just how powerfully her
emotions were engaged was shown by the fervour with which she
resisted Peel.

1a (right) Princess Victoria aged 6

1b (below) the young Queen *c*1844

2a Edward[
Duke of
Kent. 181[

2b Victori[
Duchess o[
Kent. 183[

3a Queen Victoria's Coronation. June 28th 1838

3b The Queen and Lord Melbourne riding at Windsor.
1838

4a The Queen's Marriage. February 10th 1840

4b Prince Albert.
1843

4c Queen Victoria.
1843

5a The Queen and Prince Albert.
26th July 1859

5b Queen Victoria, after a Drawing
room [levée] at Buckingham Palace
May 11th 1854

5c Ball Room Buckingham Palace. 1856

6a Leopold King of the Belgians. 1857

6b Leopold's wife, Queen Louise

7a Baron Stockmar. 1847

7b Sir John Conroy. 1836

8a Lord Melbourne.
1836

8b Sir Robert Peel.
1838

9a Prince Albert. The Queen's favourite
portrait by Thorburn. [See 130]

9b Stereoscopic photograph of the opening of the Great Exhibition.
1851

10a Queen Victoria's handwriting.
1857

10b The Council room at Osborne. 1861

11a Prince Arthur and Prince Alfred (right).
Osborne 6th September 1854

11b The Royal Family. A Watercolour by Queen Victoria. 1850

12a Queen Victoria with Victoria, Princess Royal, *c* 1844–5

12b Prince of Wales. May 1868

12c The Princess Royal's Wedding Photograph 1858. [See 271]

12d Alice, Princess Louis of Hesse, *c* 1874-5

13a Louis Philippe at Windsor. 1844

13b Napoleon III with the Empress
Eugénie and Prince Imperial

14a The Dowager Lady Lyttelton

14b George Anson

14c Dean Gerald Wellesley.
1877

14d Sir Henry Ponsonby.
1889

15a The Blue Room at Windsor where Prince Albert died

15b The Mausoleum at Frogmore

16a The Four Seasons: A royal tableau. 1854
*(Left to right) Princess Alice as Spring, Prince Arthur and the Princess Royal
as Summer, Princess Helena as the spirit of Empress Helena, Prince Alfred
as Autumn, Princess Louise and the Prince of Wales as Winter.*

16b Prince Leopold at Cannes. 1862

The Queen saw Sir Robert again at one o'clock on Thursday, May 9th, and the moment he left wrote Melbourne a note describing Peel's "infamous" demands. He "insisted", she alleged, "on my giving up my Ladies, to which I replied that I never would consent, and I never saw a man so frightened. . . . The Queen of England will not submit to such trickery. Keep yourself in readiness for you may soon be wanted". Later that day, she summoned Melbourne to the Palace and gave him a fuller account of the interview. The moment Sir Robert touched on the question of the Household, she told him that she had no intention whatever of giving up her Ladies. Did that mean, he asked, that she planned to retain them all? "'*All*', I said." "The Mistress of the Robes and the Ladies of the Bedchamber?" The Queen repeated "All." He then pointed out that many of her Ladies were wives of his opponents, to which she replied that she never discussed politics with them. Then, remembering Lord Melbourne's advice, she added for good measure "it had never been done before". Peel patiently explained that he was not proposing that she should replace "*all* the Bedchamber women and *all* the Maids of Honour". But the Queen was not open to reason, and insisted upon her "right" to choose her Household. Faced by such intransigence, Peel said that he must consult the Duke and suspend all further proceedings.

At 2.30 p.m., Peel and the Duke presented themselves at the Palace, only to be told by the Queen that "her *ladies* were *entirely* her own affair, and not the Ministers'". In the course of further consultations, she asked the Duke whether "Sir Robert was so weak that *even* the Ladies must be of his opinion?" Greville was dumbfounded to learn that she had defied Wellington so brazenly. "There is something which shocks one's sense of fitness and propriety in the spectacle of this mere baby of a Queen setting herself in opposition to this great man, invested with all the authority of his experience and sagacity, of his profound loyalty, his devoted patriotism, and to whom her Predecessors had ever been accustomed to look up with unlimited confidence as their surest and wisest Councillor in all times of difficulty and danger." Nevertheless, it was impossible not to admire her amazing strength of purpose in successfully frustrating two of the most redoubtable Statesmen in Europe. She had succeeded, where Napoleon had failed, in thwarting the hero of a hundred fights. Peel, after ruefully consulting his colleagues, returned to the Palace at 5 p.m. to tell the Queen that they had unanimously agreed that unless she was prepared to make some gesture of confidence in them he could not form a Government. She replied that she preferred to "do nothing in a hurry" and would give him her final answer later that evening, or early the following morning, but she warned him not to expect her to change her mind. In thus playing for time, she was following King Leopold's advice and giving herself the chance to consult Lord Melbourne.

The Queen had more reasons for behaving as she did than those she gave. In her more fanciful moments she envisaged Peel conspiring with Conroy and Lady Flora to send Lehzen back to Hanover. Throughout her life, she detested change: a trait which became obsessional after the death of the Prince Consort. Instinctively, she clung to familiar places, familiar people, and familiar routines, and resented disruptive forces like death, marriage and politics. Her tireless odyssey in search of "safe havens", was prompted by her sense of insecurity. The Tories, by driving Melbourne to resign, and reviling Lehzen, and trying to deprive her of her Ladies, constituted the same sort of threat as had confronted her at Kensington. "They wished to treat me like a girl," she wrote imperiously, "but I will show them that I am Queen of England." Finally, she hoped that by being totally uncooperative she might yet retain Lord Melbourne as Prime Minister.

Not long after Peel's last visit on May 9th, the Queen sent for her "dear and excellent Lord Melbourne", and told him about the discussions that had taken place that day. Lord M, as always, put in a good word for his rival, and begged her not to be influenced "by any faultiness of manner" she observed in Sir Robert, "the most cautious and reserved of mankind". Later, he told her that she must remember that Peel was "not accustomed to talk to Kings; it's not like me; I've been brought up with Kings and Princes. I know the whole Family, and know exactly what to say to them; now he has not that ease, and probably you were not at your ease". Lord M, nevertheless, assured the Queen that she could not have acted otherwise than she did, and that he entirely approved of her conduct. Before leaving, he promised to summon his colleagues at once to review events.

Lord Melbourne's ministers were almost all in favour of rallying round their Sovereign. Lord John Russell quoted her saying that she had stood by them, and that she now trusted that they would stand by her. Sir John Hobhouse, distinctly the worse for drink, heroically proclaimed that he would rather cut off his hand than recommend surrender. Only Morpeth and Howick were not swept away by this tidal wave of loyalty, and suggested that somebody ought to discover precisely what Peel had proposed. After several hours of discussion, Melbourne wrote the Queen a note at one o'clock in the morning of May 10th, enclosing a draft of the answer he proposed she should send Peel. She immediately copied it out, without altering one word. "The Queen," the letter read, "having considered the proposal made to her yesterday by Sir Robert Peel, to remove the Ladies of her Bedchamber, cannot consent to adopt a course which she conceives to be contrary to usage, and which is repugnant to her feelings."

The proceedings of this midnight Cabal were highly irregular. It was an astonishing policy for former Ministers of the Crown to advise her Majesty on any subject, let alone to urge her to sabotage Peel's efforts to carry out her commission to form a Government. Melbourne, however, had chivalrously promised the Queen he would not desert her, and that mattered more to him than consti-tutional niceties. All the same, he had an uneasy suspicion that the course he was following might damage the reputation of the Crown and the longer term interests of his party.

By midday on Friday, the Queen received Peel's answer to her letter, "humbly returning into Your Majesty's hands the important trust which Your Majesty had been graciously pleased to commit to him". At one-thirty, she saw Melbourne who agreed to resume office. It was an immense relief, she told him, to get out of "the hands of people who would have sacrificed every personal feeling and instinct of the Queen's to their own bad party purposes". That evening, she gave a ball to the Tsarevich (later Alexander II), who was paying a state visit. The Duke and Peel, she noted in her journal, looked "very much put out", while her own people were in wonder-ful spirits. "I left the Ball-room at ¼ to 3, much pleased, as my mind felt happy".

Lord Melbourne's advice to the Queen, and his briefing of his colleagues, was based on a misapprehension. She had led him to understand that Sir Robert had required her to give up all her Ladies. But, in fact, as she noted in her journal, "He did not mean *all* the Bedchamber women and *all* the Maids of Honour", but only those of her Ladies who were closely related to Melbourne's ministers: less than a third of their number. At her meeting with Melbourne on May 10th, she showed him Sir Robert's letter of resignation. Mel-bourne read it with ever-increasing dismay, and "started" with surprise when it became clear that Peel had only sought "to make some changes" in her Household. "I must submit this to the Cabinet," he told her, feeling the ground crumbling under his feet. The Queen impatiently brushed his misgivings aside, insisting that "some or all was the same". In so saying, she refused to distinguish between a legitimate request and an exorbitant demand. That the Cabinet had been misled was largely its own fault. It should have listened to Howick's and Morpeth's advice and "have sifted the matter to the bottom." The Queen, of course, was far too honest to intend to deceive her ministers. The trouble was that she was so overwrought that she hardly stopped to consider what Peel was saying.

When it dawned on Melbourne that his entire strategy had been based on a false assumption, he naturally got cold feet, but the Queen inspired him with fresh courage by telling him that nothing would ever persuade her to yield, or to send for Peel again. "You are for standing out then?" he asked, to which she replied, "Certainly." Although the Cabinet on May 11th debated the matter for over four hours, the fact remained that they had little choice but to stand by their decision. When Melbourne saw the Queen that evening, he pulled out a paper from his pocket saying, "This is what you have probably never seen, and which is only done on great occasions, a Cabinet Minute." He then proceeded to read it out aloud, and was almost overcome when it spoke of her ministers' loyalty to the Crown. So was the Queen, who grasped his hand in both of hers, "with real feelings of the deepest gratitude".

The "Bedchamber Crisis" was of the Queen's own making and showed an extraordinary growth in her self-reliance. Greville condemned her for being imperious, arrogant and headstrong, but he blamed her ministers too for "upholding and abetting her". The public, however, applauded her pluck in standing up for her rights, and admired "the vein of iron" which ran through her character. When she drove to the Chapel Royal on Sunday, May 12th, she was greeted by shouts of "Bravo!" and "The Queen for ever!" Two days later, she wrote triumphantly to King Leopold to tell him how firmly she had resisted attacks on her Household, which had come from the very people "who pride themselves upon upholding the prerogative". It was a measure of the violence of her partisanship that she drove both parties to reverse their roles: the Whigs to uphold the privileges of the Crown, and the Tories to assail them. "I acted quite alone," she informed her uncle, "but I have been, and shall be, supported by my country," and "my Government have nobly stood by me."

Stockmar, from Coburg, blamed Melbourne for allowing the Queen to demonstrate her hostility to the Tories. "The late events in England distress me. How could they let the Queen make such mistakes, to the injury of the Monarchy?" That "a great Ministerial combination" could be overturned by "the caprice of a girl of nineteen", was bound to revive proposals to limit the royal prerogative. One unfortunate outcome of her victory was that it encouraged her to regard the government of the day as *her* Government, and to reproach the opposition for disloyalty. The jubilation of the Tories at the prospect of office was turned into bitter resentment when Peel was forced to resign.

Most Victorians were so steeped in the Whig view of history that they managed to persuade themselves that the Revolution of 1688 had rendered the Crown impotent. In reality, reports of its demise were exaggerated, as was shown by Dunning's resolution in 1780, which protested that its "influence has increased, is increasing, and ought to be diminished". The widespread conviction that royal power was dead owed more to wishful thinking than a close regard for evidence. Anson, in his *Law and Custom of the Constitution*, published in 1886, proclaimed that the Queen "invariably accepted the decision of the Country, as shown by a general election or a vote in the House of Commons". In fact, she did no such thing, and on various occasions defied both Parliament and the electorate. After all, to look no further afield than the events of 1839, she retained Melbourne in office despite the fact that he had forfeited the confidence of Parliament: although admittedly this was the last time that she imposed a government upon the Country for no better reason than that she personally found it congenial. In retrospect, she acknowledged that she had been "activated by strong feelings of partisanship" in her early dealings with Peel. In 1854, Lord John Russell plucked up courage to ask her from whom she had taken advice during her negotiations with Sir Robert. "It was entirely my own foolishness," she replied with characteristic candour.

Towards the end of her reign, the Queen told Henry Ponsonby that Lord Melbourne was an "excellent man, but too much of a party man and made me a party Queen. He admitted this himself afterwards". Once, she even informed Lord M that she thought the royal family should always support the Whigs. Stockmar was horrified to hear her talking in such terms, and held the Prime Minister responsible for her "pernicious" political bias. "She has made herself the Queen of a party," wrote Greville disapprovingly, "and is at no pains to disguise her hatred of everything in the shape of a Tory." There was nothing new, of course, in royal partisanship. George III personally canvassed Windsor on behalf of its Tory candidate. During one election, the King burst into a milliner's shop in the High Street, chanting "No Keppel. No Keppel". (Admiral Keppel was the Whig contestant.) Then, in the hope of clinching the argument, he added, "The Queen wants a new gown. The Queen wants a new gown".

Both Queen Victoria's parents cultivated eminent Whigs. Lord John Russell, Lord Palmerston, and Lord Durham, were often invited to Kensington. The Queen remained loyal to this tradition, and Croker informed the King of Hanover in 1839 that invitations to Buckingham Palace were based on "a very exclusive principle, no Tories being invited who could on any pretence be kept out". During the election of 1841, the Queen visited several of the great Whig houses: the Duke of Bedford at Woburn, Lord Cowper (Melbourne's nephew) at Panshanger, the Duke of Devonshire at Chatsworth, and the Prime Minister at Brocket. Naturally, this royal patronage was as repugnant to the Tories as it was agreeable to the Whigs. "I do so like our dear little Queen," wrote Emily Eden, "for starting off forthwith on that tour of Whig visits: so like her." As the Government bragged about the Queen's support, the fact that the Tories won was seen as a snub. So well known was her dislike of the opposition, that when Lord Seymour asked an Etonian whether the boys saw much of Her Majesty, he replied "Oh! no, she considers us a nest of Tories". The Queen recorded this anecdote in her journal without appearing to recognise how seriously the Crown was compromised when even a schoolboy knew she supported the Whigs.

By 1839, Tories no longer seemed to "care one straw for the Crown, its dignity, or its authority". When a radical speaker launched a violent attack on the Queen at a Conservative dinner at Canterbury, his remarks were received with unconcealed delight. Some Tories were so embittered by being deprived of office that they seemed prepared to cross the frontiers of treason, and the extravagance of the language in which they denounced the Queen only increased her antagonism towards them. Greville thought Peel was much to be pitied for finding himself the leader of "so unruly and unprincipled a faction", which in theory maintained its admiration for Monarchy, but in practice was willing "to roll the crown in the dirt".

Lord Melbourne knew very well that his days of power were numbered, in spite of his restoration to office in May 1839. He consequently did everything he could to reconcile the Queen to a Tory Government, "and to make her understand that she must not involve the whole party in the reproach which justly attached to a few foolish or mischievous zealots". In particular, he seized every opportunity to put in a good word for Peel. For example, he told her in July 1839 that he had recently been talking to Palmerston, who had predicted that she would like "Peel better when she knew him", because he was much the best of his party and was "a very fair man". He also assured her that Peel never spoke of her except in the highest terms, and that she could never hope to influence the opposition while she treated them as enemies. "Flies," he observed, "are caught with honey, not with vinegar." But nothing he said could persuade her to change her mind.

The suffering caused by the Industrial Revolution was reaching its climax when the Queen came to the throne. So much so, that the first decade of her reign became known as the "Hungry Forties". Nothing would have been easier for Lord Melbourne than to have appealed to her warm, compassionate nature, and to have enlisted her support against poverty and disease. She was incapable of seeing human misery without being deeply moved. When she was a girl of sixteen, a family of gypsies, named Cooper, encamped near Claremont, where she and her mother were spending Christmas. "I trust in Heaven," she noted in her journal, "that the day may come when I may do something for these poor people." Throughout her reign, she was spared the sight of the sordid conditions in which most of her subjects lived. Such slums as she saw were draped with flags and bunting and lined with cheering crowds. But on the few occasions when she was brought face to face with squalor, she was shocked by what she saw. In 1852, she described the Black Country as "like another world. In the midst of so much wealth, there seems to be nothing but ruin. As far as the eye can reach, one sees nothing but chimneys, flaming furnaces, with wretched cottages around them. . . . Add to this a thick and black atmosphere and you have but a faint impression of the life which a 3rd of a million of my poor subjects are forced to lead. It makes me sad!"

Lord Melbourne, so far from encouraging her sympathy for suffering, deadened her social conscience. Never was a more splendid opportunity so carelessly discarded. He knew that the Queen hung on his lightest word, and that her political opinions were a blank sheet of paper on which he could easily have inscribed a summary of the Beatitudes. But he chose to infect her with his own cynical pessimism about the efficacy of reform, and his own shortsighted optimism about working-class conditions. He taught her, by example, that the simplest way of disposing of a problem was to ignore it, and encouraged her to disregard mass protests as the work of reckless agitators. Nothing he did diminished her compassion for individual suffering, and she continued to feel, in her own phrase, "intensely for the sorrows and anxieties of others". But he did persuade her to be sceptical of philanthropy and to despair of legislation as a remedy for distress.

It would obviously be unjust to reproach Lord Melbourne for accepting conventional wisdom, or for failing to act as a latter-day John the Baptist to Sidney and Beatrice Webb. The principles of laisser faire were so widely accepted in early Victorian England that most people thought that poverty was part of the plan of creation: God made men "high or lowly and ordered their estate". What sense could there be in trying to eradicate it, especially as Christ Himself had proclaimed "The poor ye have always with you"? Furthermore, the iron laws of political economy provided consoling arguments for doing nothing. In fact, the Tories, inspired by their tradition of paternalism, were better disposed to social legislation than the "party of reform". It was no accident that Lord Shaftesbury was a Conservative. Lord Melbourne, however, went further than his colleagues in resisting change, and insisting that the road to Hell was paved with good intentions. The working class never forgot that he was the Home Secretary who instigated the proceedings at Dorchester Assizes against the "Tolpuddle Martyrs".

The extent to which Lord Melbourne indoctrinated the Queen may be seen in the pages of her journal, in which she recorded his conversation with evident approval. He told her, for example, that Sir Walter Scott was right when he said: "Why bother with the poor? Leave them alone." Later, he assured her that Ashley's attempts to improve the conditions of children in mines and factories were useless and unnecessary, adding, for good measure, that work kept them out of mischief. "Inter-meddling," so he said, actually "produces crime", and he thought it most improbable that education "would ever do any good".

The sole purpose of government he informed her was "to prevent and punish crime and to preserve contracts": a classic definition of Whig orthodoxy. In 1836, after Lehzen had taught her about Irish history, the Queen wrote in her diary: "How ill treated that poor country and nation has been". But only two years later, under Melbourne's sardonic influence, she treated its tragic problems as a joke. "What happened," she asked, "to Irish tenants after their landlords evicted them?" "They become *absorbed* somehow or other," he replied, which "made them all laugh amazingly". It was precisely such flippant remarks which led Wellington to complain that Lord Melbourne encouraged the Queen to take serious matters too lightly.

Lord Ashley, although married to Melbourne's niece, was savagely critical of his influence over the Queen. He recognised Lord M's "sincere and even ardent affection" for her, but accused him of not possessing the "courage to act and advise her according to her real interests. He will be, if not checked, her political and moral destroyer. His society and conversation are pernicious to a young mind. I have seen this much of late – his sentiments and manner blunt the moral sense and lower the standards of judgement and feeling". Lord Melbourne's past life, his "reckless language", and his cynical outlook, were a "perpetual source of poison to her mind".

The Queen was too generous and forgiving to blame Melbourne for giving her bad advice. Nor did she reproach him when he mismanaged legislation made necessary by her marriage. His faults, however, were not without compensation. The very levity, with which he was often reproached, was his way of responding to human frailty. He was flippant about his fellow politicians because he thought them absurd. The Queen had grown up at a time when Evangelicals had elevated "Seriousness" into what Matthew Arnold called a "capital virtue". It seems improbable that she risked her immortal soul by occasionally joining in Melbourne's carefree laughter. Nobody was better qualified to introduce her to the workings of Parliament and the Cabinet, the niceties of the Constitution, and the day-to-day business of the Sovereign. Merely by listening to his conversation, she acquired a sophistication and knowledge of the world which Lehzen could never have taught her.

Three weeks before Lady Flora died, the Duke of Wellington somehow persuaded Conroy to retire. Just how he contrived to do so remains a mystery, although he himself ascribed his success to his use of "plenty of butter". For some years Sir John and his family settled in

Rome, where he remained in constant correspondence with the Duchess. He was succeeded by Colonel George Couper, who had previously served on Lord Durham's staff in Canada. It was laid down before he joined the Household that he was not to concern himself with the Duchess's accounts prior to his appointment. In fact, it would hardly have been possible for him to have done so as they were kept under lock and key in the library of Clarence House, to which the Duchess had moved in the autumn of 1840. After living abroad for a few years, the Conroys returned to England to live in considerable style at Arborfield Hall, a few miles from Reading. Sir John never wearied of pestering successive Prime Ministers for his Irish peerage, but failed to convince them that he had merited the honour.

In 1850 the Duchess at last gave Couper the keys to the boxes containing Conroy's accounts. On February 16th, he handed her a detailed report which he warned would "greatly shock" her. His memo provided distressing proof that H.R.H. had been ruthlessly defrauded, and that some £60,000 had vanished under Sir John's "stewardship". For instance, her brother, Prince Leopold, gave her £16,000 which was never paid into her bank. It also transpired that Sir John had pocketed huge sums of money belonging to Princess Sophia. Her executors calculated when she died in 1848 that she was worth about £400,000, but all they could find was a balance of £1,600, and a few shares in the Great Western Railway. When Conroy was earlier asked how he had managed to buy an estate in Montgomeryshire, he claimed that the money was a gift from the Princess, but whether she ever knew just how generous she had been remains exceedingly doubtful.

Conroy died suddenly of a heart attack in 1854, and the Duchess was "painfully affected" on learning the news. By then, she had long since been reconciled with her daughter – Sir John's departure having cleared the way – and the letters they exchanged on this sensitive subject did credit to them both. "I quite understand," wrote the Queen, "your feelings on the occasion of Sir John Conroy's death. . . . I will not speak of the *past* and of the many sufferings he entailed on us by creating divisions between you and me which could never have existed otherwise, they are buried with him. For his poor wife and children I am truly sorry. *They are now free* from the *ban* which kept them from appearing before me." The Duchess replied by blaming herself. "I shall not try and excuse the many errors that unfortunate man committed, but it would be very unjust if I allowed all the blame to be thrown on him. I am in justice bound to accuse myself. . . . I erred in believing *blindly*, in *acting without reflexion.* . . . God be praised that those terrible times are gone by and that only death can separate me from you My beloved Victoria." Sir John proved no more capable of handling his own affairs than those of his royal mistress, and died more or less insolvent. His wife and children were forced to depend on the Duchess for support, and, after her death, the Queen.

The initial elation with which the Queen began her reign ended in disillusion. After two happy years of marriage to Prince Albert, she happened to come across her journal entry for March 22nd, 1839, in which she asserted that "*No Minister* EVER possessed . . . the confidence of the Crown . . . so entirely as this truly excellent Lord Melbourne possesses mine". This now struck her as being so extravagant that she added the following note: "Reading this again, I cannot forbear remarking what an artificial sort of happiness *mine* was *then*, and what a blessing it is I have now in my beloved husband *real* and solid happiness. . . . It could not have lasted long, as it was then, for after all, kind and excellent as Lord M is, and kind as he was to me, it was but in Society that I had amusement, and I was only living on that superficial resource, which I *then fancied* was happiness! Thank God! for *me* and others, this is changed, and I *know what* REAL happiness is. V.R." More than twenty years later, in a memorandum she wrote about her engagement to Prince Albert, she recalled once more the early days of her reign. "A worse school for a young girl, or one more detrimental to all natural feelings, cannot well be imagined, than the position of a Queen at eighteen, without experience and without a husband to guide and support her."

In 1869, when Theodore Martin was sorting through a mountain of material to write his five-volume life of the Prince Consort, the Queen sent him a note explaining why she had burned so much of her correspondence. Her letters, she told him, "between 1837 and 1840 are not pleasing, and are, indeed, rather painful to herself. It was the least sensible and satisfactory time in her whole life, and she must therefore destroy a great many. That life of constant amusement, flattery, excitement, and mere politics had a bad effect on her naturally simple and serious nature. But all changed in 1840." It was largely because of her growing disenchantment with the shallow delights of the Court that her thoughts began to turn to the "solid joys and lasting pleasures" of marriage.

3

A Struggle of Wills
1839–1842

L ONG before Queen Victoria's own thoughts turned to marriage, there can hardly have been a royal family in Europe who had not reviewed her prospects for her. There was, after all, no greater prize for a prince in search of a bride. Even before she came to the throne, William IV and Queen Adelaide had ventured to find her a husband. Their first candidate, Prince Alexander of the Netherlands, had been rejected out of hand. Next, they proposed an alliance with her cousin, Prince George of Cumberland, in whom she was said to show a "tender interest", largely because he had lost his sight as a boy. The obvious benefit of the plan, the preservation of the union of Hanover with England, was offset by two massive disadvantages: fear of hereditary blindness in the next generation, and the prospect of uncle Ernest as a father-in-law. The King's third candidate was her cousin, Prince George of Cambridge.

Soon after the Queen's accession, tongues began to wag when it was noticed how often she chose Prince George as her partner. The fact that she was merely complying with protocol did little to stem the gossip. Prince Albert himself seems to have thought that the Duchess of Kent had "taken George Cambridge under her wing" as part of the "crosscurrents of cabal and intrigue" which "ran in every direction". In June 1838, the Queen noted in her journal, "Spoke of George who I said I did not like – thought he had nothing to say for himself and was particularly stiff with me; but that I believed his parents teased him about me, and that Ma got into the Duke and Duchess's favour by saying she would promote a match between us." The fact of the matter was that Prince George had resolved from an early age to avoid an arranged marriage. Soon after the Queen's engagement was announced, she noticed a complete change in his behaviour, and concluded that he was "evidently happy" to be clear of her. Unused to being spurned, she told Lord Melbourne that her cousin was an "odious boy" whom "she never could have thought of taking – ugly and disagreeable as he was". Seeing that most people thought him a young Adonis, it is clear that her judgement owed much to pique. Later, however, she changed her mind and came to regard him with "great affection". Sir Henry Ponsonby noticed that before a Drawing Room, "when she came into the ante-room where the royalties were assembled, she would single him out for a word of conversation before turning round and proceeding to the Throne Room".

A number of Princes cherished dreams of marrying Queen Victoria, amongst them Prince Christian of Schleswig-Holstein, later to become King Christian IX of Denmark, and father-in-law to the Prince of Wales. In 1837, King Frederick VI sent him to congratulate the Queen on her accession, and the following year to represent him at her Coronation. But there was to be no Danish conquest until 1863, when his daughter, Princess Alexandra, won all English hearts. The Queen's first formal offer of marriage came from Prince Adalbert of Prussia, when she was only seventeen, but it never got further than the Duchess of Kent. Two years later, Louis Philippe sent his second son, the Duc de Nemours, to attend the Coronation, forlornly hoping he might capture her fancy. They got on admirably, and she thought him "delightful", but there the matter ended. When the Grand Duke Alexander visited England in 1839, he set her heart aflutter, but she could hardly contemplate a future Tsar of Russia. Naturally, rumours were rife about her attachment to various eligible noblemen, but, in fact, as she told Lord Melbourne, she "*couldn't* and wouldn't like to marry a subject". Gossip especially fastened on William Cowper, Lord M's nephew, and Lord Alfred Paget. Ever since 1832, when Lord Anglesey put Plas Newydd at her mother's disposal, the Queen had remained devoted to his family. Indeed, so many of them had been given offices in her Household that Windsor became known as the "Paget House Club". Lord Alfred was her favourite Equerry, especially as he was splendidly good-looking. Soon after her accession, the Queen reviewed her troops in Windsor Park, and noted out of the corner of her eye that he "looked remarkably handsome in his uniform of the Blues". So devoted was he to her that he wore her portrait on a chain hung round his neck. Remote as the prospect was, Princess Lieven told Lord Grey that she was sure that the Queen intended to marry Lord Melbourne. Presumably those who shouted "Mrs Melbourne" as she drove down the course at Ascot, believed that the ceremony had already taken place. In truth, such talk was nothing but conjecture, for she was helplessly undecided. The problem was not so much whom to choose, for in later years she repeatedly told Prince Albert that she had never considered anyone other than him, but when to take the plunge. She once even went so far as to tell Lord Melbourne that "at present *my* feeling was quite against ever marrying".

The strain of the Queen's battles with the Tories played havoc with her nerves, and little remained of that "first fine careless rapture" with which she began her reign. By the autumn of 1839 she was peevish and on edge. When Greville congratulated Lord Melbourne on his skill in keeping the Queen straight, he replied with a hint of desperation, "By God, I am at it morning, noon and night!" She even began to complain that she found her duties boring. "You lead rather an unnatural life for a young person," Lord M explained consolingly. "It is the life of a man." But, nevertheless, there was no escaping her lot. "You have drawn that ticket."

Lord Melbourne, who hitherto could do nothing wrong, began to feel the Queen's displeasure. She had "been a good deal annoyed", she told him, by his failing to inform her about changes at the Home Office. Not for the first time, she found herself "the last person to hear what is settled and done in her own name". On several occasions she reproached him for neglecting her. Once, when he failed to attend a State Banquet, she told him that "she was a good deal vexed at his not coming as she had begged him herself to do so. . . . The Queen *insists* upon his coming to dinner tomorrow". She even scolded him for such assorted crimes as falling asleep in her Drawing Room, overeating, and lapsing into reveries. Such complaints were relatively rare, but the barometer no longer seemed to be stuck at "Fine". "I fear I was sadly cross with Lord Melbourne," she confessed in her journal. "It is shameful. . . . I cannot think what possessed me for I love the dear, excellent man." The fact that he proved "so amiable and forgiving" merely sharpened her remorse.

In 1866, when General Grey was preparing his book on *The Early Years of the Prince Consort*, the Queen told him how much she deplored having taken so long to make up her mind to marry. She could only explain her dithering by pointing out that "the sudden change from the secluded life at Kensington to the independence of her position as Queen Regnant", had "put all ideas of marriage out of her mind, which she now much regrets". Two things converged to remind her of Albert. First, she had a number of visits from her other German cousins in the summer of 1839, which revived "her liking to live with young people". Second, it slowly began to dawn on her that she would no longer have to live with her mother provided she found a husband.

From the moment she came to the throne, the Queen ceased corresponding with Prince Albert. Just how far she had put him out of her mind may be seen from her journal. On August 26th, 1837, she wrote: "To-day is my *dearest* Cousin Albert's 18th birthday; and I pray heaven to pour its choicest blessings on his beloved head." But for the next two years she ignored the anniversary: an amazing oversight for one so fond of red letter days. When King Leopold ventured to raise the question of their future she told him that she was far too young to marry, that the Prince needed experience of the world, and that "his mastery of the English language was still very imperfect". In her mind's eye, she still visualised her cousin as a plump, ungainly youth of sixteen, who nodded off while the night was yet young, and appeared to take several days to recover from mal de mer. Being herself exceptionally robust, she was disposed to dismiss the suffering of others with sceptical intolerance.

For some time the Queen hesitated to discuss the possibility of marriage even with Lord Melbourne, although she admitted it was "too silly of me to be frightened in talking to him". However, on April 18th, 1839, she "mustered up courage" to tell him that her "Uncle's great wish – was – that I should marry my Cousin, Albert". Lord M, assuming the role of devil's advocate, put forward a number of objections. What would happen, he asked, if the Prince was to side with the Duchess against her? Was it wise to marry her own first cousin? Had she fully considered how unpopular the Coburgs were in Europe? "The Russians," he said, "hate them." But the problem remained, as the Queen was quick to point out, that there were no other feasible candidates. Together they went through a list of prospective princes, but "not one", she said, "would do". Melbourne then warned her that foreigners were unpopular in England, but she countered by pointing out that "marrying a subject was making yourself so much their equal, and brought you so in contact with the whole family". Anyway, she concluded, there was no need to reach a final decision "for 3 or 4 years", and, indeed, she "dreaded the thought of marrying". The trouble was, she confessed, that she had grown so used to having her own way that "it was 10 to 1 that I shouldn't agree with anybody".

The Queen was resolved to avoid an "arranged marriage". Much as she loved her country, and ready as she was "to do what was for its good", when it came to a choice of husband her "own liking was one of the principal things". She knew that Lord M had reservations about her becoming engaged to Albert. He once told her that her mother was a good specimen of the Coburgs, and warned her that Germans smoked excessively and never washed their faces. For all that, he was willing to concede that "a great deal depended upon what sort of a person he was", and raised no objection to King Leopold's proposal that Ernest and Albert should visit Windsor that autumn. It was the Queen, not her Prime Minister, who began to drag her feet, and to complain that the prospect was "disagreeable". She told Lord M in July that she had "no great wish to see Albert as the whole subject was an odious one, and one which I hated to decide about". She assured him, however, that there "was no engagement", although "the young man was aware that there was the possibility of such a union". Melbourne took the view that there could be no harm in her "just seeing her cousins". As for marriage, he proclaimed categorically, "It is *not* NECESSARY".

On July 15th, 1839, the Queen requested King Leopold to "acquaint Uncle Ernest, that if I should like Albert, I can make *no final promise this year*, for, at the *very earliest*, any such event could not take place till *two or three years hence*." She went on to point out that, in spite of many favourable reports on the Prince she might not "have the *feeling* for him which is requisite to ensure happiness. I *may* like him as a friend, and as a *cousin*, and as a *brother*, but not *more*; and should this be the case (which is not likely), I am *very* anxious that it should be understood that I am *not* guilty of any breach of promise, for I *never gave any*". Her letter ended with two important questions. Was Albert "aware of the wish of his *Father* and *you* relative to *me*?" Was he aware that there was "*no engagement* between us?" In 1866, when the Queen discussed her marriage with General Grey, she told him that she could never forgive herself for having proposed "to keep the Prince waiting for probably three or four years, at the risk of ruining all his prospects for life, until she might feel inclined to marry!"

Ever Since Prince Albert first met the Queen in 1836, King Leopold and Stockmar had been training him for the role of a future Prince Consort. After leaving England, he and Ernest studied in Brussels. Next, in the spring of 1837, they took up residence in Bonn "in search of more wisdom". The prevailing atmosphere of both cities was liberal and democratic. Bonn, in particular, encouraged freedom of thought in the belief that the task of a university was to pose challenging questions rather than offer dogmatic answers. During his eighteen months there, Prince Albert became convinced that it would eventually prove possible to discover scientific laws governing human behaviour. What the nineteenth century needed was a sociological Newton. His philosophical outlook derived from the confident rationalism of the Enlightenment. Napoleon III, who recognised that Albert was one of nature's pedagogues, paid him a barbed compliment. Seldom, he said, had he met anyone as learned as the Prince or as dedicated to disseminating knowledge. Walter Bagehot, a fervent admirer, was none the less forced to admit that he never acquired "the knack of dropping seed without appearing to sow it". Englishmen tend to prefer those who carry their learning lightly, but the Prince flaunted his brazenly. Certainly his children believed him to be omniscient. When the celebrated conjurer, John Henry Anderson, "the wizard of the North", was invited to give a command performance at Balmoral, the Prince of Wales was overheard saying: "Papa knows how all these trick are done."

Baron Borselager, one of Albert's undergraduate contemporaries, remembered him as the perfect student, who never missed a single lecture, and who started working at five o'clock in the morning, just as his riotous fellow students were thinking of going to bed. In short, he was "the best and most obedient pupil" that Bonn had ever had. One of the ironies of his career was that his carefully fostered virtues were regarded as reprehensible. Students were supposed to sow wild oats, not to immerse themselves in Quetelet before breakfast.

Albert, a typical child of the Enlightenment, believed passionately in the education of mankind, human perfectibility, and intellectual freedom. But for all his advanced opinions, his views on royalty were those of the Middle Ages. His progressive ideology was not so compelling that it drove him to cross the frontier of self-interest. In common with most liberals, he tended to overestimate the potential of Reason: a disposition he handed on to his eldest daughter, who once assured Prince Hohenlohe that the greatest of all political forces was the intelligence of the people. She was not amused when he suggested that an even greater power was human stupidity.

In October 1838 Prince Albert set off on a Grand Tour of Italy, accompanied by Baron Stockmar. Part of the Baron's brief was to initiate the Prince in those fashionable accomplishments he tended to despise. During a long stay in Florence, Albert began his studies at six in the morning, then visited galleries and churches, and after a simple luncheon, washed down with water, went for long walks in the surrounding country. Except when he was obliged to endure an evening "entertainment", he retired for the night soon after nine. Stockmar was unable to fault the Prince's passion for artistic treasures, but reproached him for his "backwardness in paying attention to the ladies". The Prince assured him that, if only to please the Queen, he would make strenuous efforts to become an "elegant man of the world", and to master the art of "trifling chatter on trivial subjects". He proved as good as his word. "I have lately thrown myself into the whirl of Society," he told his friend, Prince von Löwenstein, "I have danced, dined, supped, paid compliments, chattered in French and English, and exhausted every conceivable phrase about the weather . . . You know my passion for this sort of thing, and must therefore admire my strength of character, in that I have never excused myself, never returned home until five in the morning, in a word that I have fairly drained the carnival cup to the dregs."

The Prince reached Rome in time for Holy Week, an experience which did nothing to diminish his confidence in Luther. Such services as he attended he thought "absurd" and savouring of "idolatory". During his visit, he was granted an audience by Pope Gregory XVI. "The old gentleman was very kind and civil," the Prince told his father. "I remained with him nearly half an hour shut up in a small room." Their conversation, conducted in Italian, was mainly concerned with Egyptian influence on Greek and Roman art. Albert, with all the audacity of a youth of nineteen, saw fit to challenge the Pope's claim that the Greeks were indebted to the Etruscans. Never for one moment did it strike him as incongruous that the doctrine of Coburg Infallibility should be blazoned from the Vatican. From Rome, the Prince and Stockmar travelled south to Naples, and then slowly wended their way back home in order to celebrate Ernest's coming of age.

Throughout the Italian tour, Stockmar reported back to the Queen giving details of the journey. He told her the Prince bore "a striking resemblance to his late mother. . . . He has the same intellectual quickness and adroitness, the same cleverness, the same desire to appear good-natured and amiable to others". But "in the matter of 'les belles Manières' there is much to desire". It was hardly surprising, said the Baron, that the Prince lacked social graces, seeing that he had "been deprived of the intercourse and supervision of a mother". According to Stockmar, the Prince was relaxed and lighthearted in the company of those he knew well, even indulging "a childlike pleasure in jokes". But in "larger circles", or in the presence of strangers, "he appeared formal, measured, and reserved, and, as many thought, cold and stiff".

In August 1839 the Queen's uncle Ferdinand paid her a visit at Windsor. King Leopold was largely responsible for the invitation, which he hoped would revive her feelings for the Coburgs. The Queen was enchanted by her cousins Leopold, Augustus and Victoire, whom she described as "*Dear dear* young people". She loved their private family jokes and their use of nicknames. Their visit brought home to her how much she had missed by being an only child, and she joined in their affectionate chaff with all the enthusiasm of a Trappist monk released from his vow of silence. She was in despair when they finally set sail from Woolwich. "We were *so* intimate, *so* united, *so* happy" she wrote.

King Leopold's plan had worked triumphantly, for she could hardly have been in a more receptive mood to welcome her cousins Albert and Ernest. Just as in 1836, the Channel crossing proved stormy, and at one moment their paddle steamer was almost dashed to pieces on the cliffs of Dover. Needless to say both Princes were desperately seasick, and looked pale and shaken when they reached Windsor on the evening of Thursday, October 10th. The instant the Queen set eyes on them, she noticed how much they had changed. "It was with some emotion that I beheld Albert – who is *beautiful*." Next day, she described him as "quite charming, and so excessively handsome, such beautiful blue eyes, an exquisite nose and such a pretty mouth". Two days after his arrival, the Queen told Leopold that "Albert's *beauty* is *most striking* and he is so amiable and unaffected – in short very *fascinating*; he is excessively admired here". The worst his detractors could find to say was that he reminded them of an Italian tenor. But to the Queen, who never did things by halves, he seemed to personify chivalry and romance. Her favourite portrait of him was painted by Thorburn in 1843, in which he was represented as a knight in full armour. That was how she saw him, a mixture of Tristan, Siegfried, and Sir Galahad: an entirely appropriate subject for Tennyson's preface to his "Idylls of the King". The Queen, on the third day of her cousins' visit, told Lord Melbourne that she was now the first "to own the advantage of beauty", in spite of her previous comments to the contrary.

On Friday, the Queen held a small informal dance and watched Albert gallop and waltz with growing admiration. As she chatted to Lord Melbourne, her eyes followed her cousin round the room, admiring his "broad shoulders" and "fine waist". Never had she enjoyed anything more sublime than the delicious moments when he took her in his arms and danced with her "so beautifully". Next morning, the Court went out riding in Windsor Park, with Lord Melbourne and Albert on either side of her. Throughout their "heavenly time together at Windsor", the cousins conversed in German. That afternoon, while the Queen was writing to uncle Leopold, she heard Ernest and Albert playing Haydn symphonies on the piano in the room beneath her. How foolish she had been to insist on that tour of Italy when there appeared to be no accomplishment he lacked.

The next day, October 13th, was Sunday, so the Queen drove to St George's Chapel with "Mamma and my beloved cousins". "Dearest Albert sat near me, who enjoyed the music excessively and thought it quite beautiful". After luncheon, the Queen had a long, confidential talk with Lord Melbourne, to whom she confessed that she had changed her mind about marrying. Lord M told her that he thought Albert "a very fine young man and very good looking". A "delightful evening" followed, during which Ernest played chess, while the Queen and Albert sat on a sofa looking at drawings by Domenichino, with Eos, the Prince's greyhound, yawning at their feet. Finally, before parting for the night, they played two games of "Tactics", and two of "Fox and Geese".

When the Queen saw Lord Melbourne the following afternoon, she told him her cousins had gone out shooting. Then, "After a little pause I said to Lord M, that I had made up my mind (about marrying dearest Albert)." "I am very glad of it," he replied gallantly. "I think it is a very good thing, and you'll be much more comfortable; for a woman cannot stand alone for long, in whatever situation she is." They agreed it was time that she told Albert of her feelings, and they laughed to think of this strange reversal of roles. Next, they discussed the Prince's future status. Both thought he should be appointed a Field Marshal and given the title of "Royal Highness", but the Queen was opposed to making him a Duke. When Lord Melbourne rose to go, she took his hand and thanked him for being "*so* kind" and "*so fatherly*" about her decision to marry. But grateful as she was, she only partly recognised how selfless he had been in encouraging her to take a step which must put an end to his happiness. Their intimate friendship, the principal joy of his life, could hardly survive her marriage. That evening, when the cousins said "Good night", Albert gave the Queen's hand an affectionate parting squeeze. Was this, she wondered, a signal to let her know that she would not propose in vain?

Shortly before luncheon on Tuesday, October 15th, the Queen sent for Albert who had been out riding. After a few moments' conversation, she said that she imagined he was aware why she had invited him to Windsor, and that it would make her "too happy" if he consented to marry her. "We embraced each other over and over again, and he was *so* kind, *so* affectionate; Oh! to *feel* I was, and am, loved by *such* an Angel as Albert was *too great delight to* describe! he is *perfection*; perfection in every way – in beauty – in everything. I told him I was quite unworthy of him and kissed his dear hand." Albert, for his part, was "carried away" by the Queen's "joyous openness of manner", and assured her that nothing would make him happier than to share his life with hers. From that moment, she resolved to do everything in her power to mitigate what she saw as his "great sacrifice". So tumultuous were her feelings that they almost defied description. The best she could do in her journal was to admit that she could not find words to express how much she adored him. They decided that the engagement should be kept secret for the time being, except from a few very privileged people. Both of them wrote letters breaking the news to the Duke of Coburg, uncle Leopold, and Stockmar, and both let the other read what they had written. That evening, the Prince appeared at dinner for the first time in the dark blue Windsor uniform with its red facing and cuffs, and the Queen could barely conceal her admiration. However rigorously she might curb her tongue, her eyes betrayed her secret. Just before she retired for the night, she was handed a note from Albert. It was addressed to his "Dearest greatly beloved Victoria". "How is it," he asked, "that I have deserved so much love, so much affection?

I cannot get used to the reality of all I see and hear, and have to believe that Heaven has sent me an angel whose brightness shall illumine my life." The letter was signed "In body and soul ever your slave, your loyal, ALBERT". The Queen, "overcome with joy, gratitude and happiness", burst into tears.

Nobody was more delighted to learn of the engagement than King Leopold. Writing on October 15th, his niece told him that "the last few days have passed like a dream to me, and I am so much bewildered by it all that I hardly know how to write; but I *do* feel *very*, *very* happy". She begged her uncle to keep the news to himself because "*strict* secrecy" was necessary before Parliament met. "I think you might tell Louise of it, but none of her family." Leopold replied that her news made him feel like "Old Zacharias – 'Now lettest Thou Thy servant depart in peace'!" Knowing Albert as he did, he felt confident that he possessed "the very qualities and dispositions which are indispensable for your happiness, and *which will suit your own character, temper, and mode of life.*" In the meantime, she could depend upon him to say nothing to the Duchess, Charles or Feodore.

The Queen finally broke the news to her mother on November 10th. "I sent for Mamma," she wrote that night in her journal, and said "I was going to tell her something which I was sure would please her, namely that I had chosen Albert to be my future husband; she took me in her arms and cried, and said, though I had not asked her, still that she gave her blessing to it, and seemed delighted." The Queen then sent for Albert, whom the Duchess embraced, "and said it made her so happy, that she was *as* anxious for his happiness as for mine . . .". Pleased as she was that her daughter had chosen to marry a Coburg, she made no attempt to conceal her indignation that she was almost the last person to learn of the engagement, and that even the servants at Windsor knew of it before she did. Moreover, she dragged her feet over leaving Buckingham Palace, and alleged that her daughter was turning her out of her house. But the Queen remained adamant that the Duchess must set up a separate Establishment, and nothing could persuade her that a resident mother-in-law would help to promote her marriage. Despite these difficulties, Prince Albert handled his aunt with exceptional tact, and even the Queen's asperity towards her was mellowed by her happiness. The Prince, from the first, was determined to act as a peace-maker. A week after he left England, he wrote to the Duchess to tell her how deeply gratified he was by the sympathy she had shown him. "You wish me," he said, "to give you something I have worn. I send you the ring which you gave me at Kensington on Victoria's birthday. From that time it has never left my finger. . . . It has your name upon it: but the name is Victoria's too and I beg you to wear it in remembrance of her and of myself. . . ." He signed the letter "Your devoted nephew, Albert."

The Queen's engagement was officially announced on November 23rd. The news was received in Coburg with rejoicing, as well it might be. Never before in the history of a dynasty renowned for judicious marriages had there been such a dazzling match. But in England a wealth of objections were raised against the proposed alliance. One satirist crudely accused the Prince of marrying for money.

> "He comes the bridegroom of Victoria's choice,
> The nominee of Lehzen's voice;
> He comes to take 'for better or for worse'
> England's fat Queen and England's fatter purse."

Many predicted dire genetic disasters from the union of such close relations. Several years after Prince Albert's death, a scatterbrained guest at Osborne stunned the company by denouncing the marriage of cousins. His harangue was cut short by the Queen. "You must remember," she said, "We are cousins." The Dukes of Sussex and Cambridge showed little enthusiasm for the match, largely because they saw Coburg as a contemptible little Duchy whose entire population was less than that of Bristol. The decades following the overthrow of Napoleon were the most chauvinistic in Britain's history, and Melbourne proved right in believing that the majority of Englishmen would deplore the Queen being married to a foreigner. Prejudice feeds on ignorance, but those who knew Prince Albert best endorsed the Queen's choice. Lady Cowper, for instance, met him at Windsor in the first week of November, and thought him "a very charming young man, very well mannered, and handsome, and gay, and said to be very well informed and sensible, so that I don't think she can find a better person to marry".

The Queen later chaperoned her daughters so strictly, that it is interesting to note that she spent a great many hours alone with Albert in her blue sitting-room at Windsor: particularly after Ernest retired to bed with "jaundice", a euphemism for syphilis. Sometimes she worked in a desultory way signing papers and warrants, but more often they sat together on a sofa planning their future, while the Queen gazed fondly into "those lovely, lovely blue eyes". "Oh! dear uncle," she wrote to King Leopold, "I do feel so happy! I do so adore Albert! he is quite an angel, and so very, very kind to me." Never had she known such bliss as when he clasped her "tenderly in his arms, and kissed her again and again, calling her 'vortrefflichste'" (incomparable). The Prince was so overwhelmed by the intensity of her devotion, that he turned in bewilderment to Stockmar. The food and climate of England were strange enough, and neither suited him, but what puzzled him most of all was to find himself "the object of so much affection". By November 14th, Ernest had recovered enough for the Princes to take their leave. Only the year before the Great Western Railway had completed a line between Slough and Paddington, so they travelled by train for the first time in their lives. The Channel, as usual, was rough and stormy. By the time they reached Calais they all felt "fearfully ill", but Prince Albert assured the Queen that her image had filled his soul. "Even in my dreams I never imagined that I should find so much love on earth."

When Prince Albert wrote to his friends and relations announcing his engagement, he struck a decidedly melancholy note. For instance, he told his stepmother that the "skies above me will not always be blue and unclouded. Still, life, wherever one is, has its storms". More often than not, he spoke of marriage as something of an ordeal. Nevertheless, it was consoling to think that he would be able to use his position for "promoting the good of so many". The portrait he gave of his bride was strangely detached and negative. "She is really most good and amiable," he wrote, "and I am quite sure heaven has not given me into evil hands." In none of his letters did he ever mention love, except to describe the Queen's feelings for him. The most he felt able to say to his old friend Prince Löwenstein was that "Victoria possesses all the qualities which make a home happy, and seems to be attached to me with her whole heart. My future lot is high and brilliant, but also plentifully strewed with thorns". This was hardly the language which Browning chose to describe Elizabeth Barrett.

Because the Prince was reserved and undemonstrative, it would be wrong to conclude that he did not possess a heart. Certainly he lacked the Queen's "passionate nature, but equally certainly he loved her deeply and truly". Several of the letters he wrote her on returning to Coburg, halting and reticent as they were, gave fitful expression to the fervent feelings he found so hard to articulate. In one he promised her "unchanging love and devotion", in another he imagined her in her "little blue sitting-room feeling rather lonely; we were so happy sitting together there on the little sofa. How I would like to be there by magic to cheer your loneliness". "Your dear picture," he added, "stands on my table in front of me, and I can hardly take my eyes off it." Later he told her how much he rejoiced in her "dear, dear loving letters", the "intimate outpouring" of her warm and tender heart, which he read over and over again "to see in your own words what I love to see – that you love me. I have no words to express my feelings about you, however much I try to look for them". When he sent her a bracelet for Christmas, he begged her "to think not of the object but of the feelings of love and attachment it dedicates to you". It pained him to think how "cold and stiff" his letters must seem compared with hers, but, nevertheless, he trusted she recognised that only the thought that he existed for her gave value to his life. The closest he ever got to baring his heart was in a letter he wrote her at the end of November, expressing his wish "to walk through the whole of my life with its joys and its storms, with you at my side! Where love is, there is happiness. Love of you fills my heart."

On Saturday, November 23rd, shortly after luncheon, the Queen formally announced her decision to marry at a special meeting of the Privy Council. The ceremony, which she later described to Prince Albert as "rather an awful moment", was held at Buckingham Palace. The Duke of Wellington, who was amongst those present, was still recovering from a stroke, and "looked very old, very feeble, and decrepit". The Queen was so nervous that her hand trembled visibly, but she none the less read her speech "in a clear, sonorous, sweet-toned voice". She told Lord Melbourne that her courage had been sustained by Ross's miniature of Prince Albert which dangled from her bracelet. The Duchess of Gloucester asked her the day before the ceremony whether she felt nervous. "She said, 'Yes; but I did a much more nervous thing a little while ago.' 'What was that?' 'I proposed to Prince Albert'."

The first serious dispute between Prince Albert and the Queen was conducted by correspondence over the question of his Household. The high-handed way in which she ignored his opinions augured ill for the future. She seemed, from the first, to assume that it was the Prince's duty to submit his will to hers, and to trust her to know what was best for him. The instant he showed a glimmer of independence, she reminded him that he was dealing with the Queen. Towards the end of November, she wrote to tell him that "young Mr Anson", Lord Melbourne's private secretary, had expressed the wish to join his Household. Seeing that he was "an excellent young man, very modest, very honest, very steady, and very well informed", she greatly favoured the plan. Prince Albert, understandably enough, resented the way in which important decisions were being taken out of his hands, but confined his objections to matters of principle. Household appointments, he argued, "should be chosen from both sides – the same number of Whigs and Tories". His insistence that the Crown should always remain above Party was in stark contrast to previous practice including that of the Queen. He owed the idea, as so much else, to Stockmar. "You always said," he reminded the Baron in 1844, "that if Monarchy was to rise in popularity it could only be by the Sovereign leading an exemplary life, and keeping quite aloof from and above party."

Prince Albert saw the proposal that Anson should join his Household as a Whig plot to enslave him, and stuck "to his principle of not identifying himself with a party". Lord Melbourne, however, rejected the doctrine as "nonsense", arguing that it was the Sovereign's duty to support the party in power, not to pursue an independent policy. There was the grave risk that the Crown, in its efforts to be "above" party, might, in effect, obstruct an elected government. Moreover, Lord M, believing that almost all foreign royal families were die-hards, feared that the Prince would gravitate to the Tories if left to his own devices. Consequently, he encouraged the Queen to persist in thwarting Albert. "As to your wish about your gentlemen," she wrote on December 8th, "I must tell you quite honestly that it will not do. You may entirely rely upon me that the people who will be about you will be absolutely pleasant people, of high standing and good character." She was equally dismissive of an "ungracious letter" from King Leopold written on Albert's behalf. The King had begged Melbourne to "speak out to the Queen" in an attempt to persuade her to take a *"correct view"* of her duties as a wife, and to recognise that it was just as much in her interest as the Prince's that they should "make common cause and live well together". She proved, however, in no mood to heed unwelcome appeals, and accused the King of being "nettled" because she no longer depended on his advice. "Dear uncle," she told Albert, "is given to believe that he must rule the roast (sic) everywhere", but "that is not a necessity". She ended her letter with an astonishing piece of news. "The *second*, as you always call Palmerston, is to be married in the next few days to Lady Cowper, the sister of my Premier (Primus). . . . They are both of them above fifty, and I think they are quite right so to act, because Palmerston . . . is quite alone in the world, and *Lady C* is a very clever woman, and *much* attached to him; still, I feel sure it will make you smile."

The Prince refused to give up the struggle without a further fight. Experience had taught him, he said, only to bestow his trust upon those of whom he had personal knowledge. Apart from the fact that he had seen Anson dancing a Quadrille, he knew nothing whatever about him. Besides, he would inevitably be regarded as a partisan Whig if he made the Prime Minister's secretary his principal adviser. The Queen, however, remained intransigent, in spite of the fact that the matter touched him so nearly. On December 18th, he tried for the last time to persuade her to change her mind. "I am leaving home," he wrote, "with all its old associations, all my bosom friends, and going to a country in which everything is new and strange to me – men, language, customs, modes of life, position. Except yourself, I have no one to confide in. And is it not even to be conceded to me that the two or three persons, who are to have the charge of my private affairs, shall be persons who already command my confidence?" When Lord Melbourne advised the Queen to yield, she was too stubborn to do so. "It is, as you rightly suppose," she told the Prince, "my greatest, my most anxious wish to do everything most agreeable to you, but I must differ with you respecting Mr Anson. . . . I am distressed to tell you what I fear you do not like, but it is necessary, my dearest, most excellent Albert. . . . I only do it as I know it is for your own good." The Prince was tempted to carry on the struggle, but Stockmar advised him that further resistance was useless. A couple of days after Christmas, the Queen told King Leopold, "I have just heard from Albert, who, I am glad to say, consents to *my* choosing his people; so *one essential* point is gained." It was greatly to the credit both of Anson and the Prince that they became the firmest friends, but the struggle had shown just how hard it was going to be for the Queen and Albert to act as "one soul and one will".

Early in 1840 Parliament considered two bills arising from the Queen's marriage. So ineptly did Lord Melbourne handle the legislation that he seems to have been possessed by an unconscious urge to subvert it. Between January 22nd and 27th there were three debates on Prince Albert's annuity. Ever since George II became King in 1727, it had become customary to grant the Sovereign's Consort £50,000 a year. But when Lord John Russell, following over a century of precedents, proposed a similar annuity for Prince Albert, he fell into an ambush. Colonel Sibthorp, an ultra Tory and champion of lost causes, moved an amendment reducing the sum to £30,000. His motion won the day with a majority of over a hundred: partly because of massive Whig abstentions, and partly because most Radicals voted against the Government. The Queen, ignoring the extent to which this defeat had been brought about by Melbourne's own supporters, blamed it on the Tories. Lady Clarendon, whose husband was Lord Privy Seal, dined with her on the night of Sibthorp's triumph. "The Queen took the news very well," she recalled, "though she certainly was much annoyed at the large majority. . . . When she heard that Sir Robert Peel had spoken against the £50,000 she said to George (Lord Clarendon) 'Sir Robert Peel spoke against it! It is too bad; I shall never forgive him'."

The Second Bill to receive a rough handling concerned the Prince's precedence. If the Queen could have had her own way, the Prince would have been recognised as "King Consort", with precedence over all other members of the royal family. She repeatedly told Lord Melbourne that "he ought to have the title of King", and that her power was hardly worth having if she "couldn't even give him the rank he ought to have." But Lord M maintained that to make the Prince "King" required an Act of Parliament, as had been shown in 1689 when William was recognised as joint Sovereign with Mary. Moreover, no arrangements made in England could be enforced abroad. When the Queen visited Prussia in 1845 she was furious to find that her husband was obliged to yield precedence to an Austrian Archduke, on the ground that his rank was only that of the younger son of the late Duke of Coburg. The Queen conceived of herself as possessing a life tenancy to the Crown, and saw it as her primary duty to hand it on intact. Sometimes, she protected her privileges so jealously that she reacted to purely imaginary threats. It was, therefore, natural that she should interpret attempts to challenge Prince Albert's status as attacks on the royal prerogative: hence her furious indignation with the Tories for disregarding her wishes.

King Leopold tried to persuade the Queen that she ought to make Albert a duke, so that his "foreignership should disappear as much as possible". He told her that experience had taught him how wrong he had been to decline the Dukedom of Kendal in 1816. But the Queen remained unconvinced, and told him firmly that "the *whole Cabinet* agree with me in being *strongly* of the opinion that Albert should *not* be a Peer: the English are very jealous at the idea of Albert having any political power or meddling with affairs". In fact, her principal reason for opposing the suggestion was that she craved for a more imposing title. Nor did the Prince himself show much enthusiasm for the plan, as he regarded a Duke of Saxony as "much higher" than a "Duke of Kent or York". Besides, he saw no reason to rush the decision as it only needed a stroke of the Queen's pen to make him a peer whenever she chose.

The Queen was slow to abandon the idea of Albert becoming King, and one evening, at Windsor, cast a fly at Melbourne, reminding him that Philip II had been given that title on marrying Mary Tudor. When Lord M refused to rise to the bait, she told him that Princess Charlotte had "always said she would make Uncle King if she came to the Throne". But Melbourne stuck to his guns, and is supposed to have said, "For God's sake, Ma'am, let us hear no more of it." The fact was that the best way to resolve the issue was to follow the most recent precedent, that of the last Prince Consort, Queen Anne's husband, Prince George of Denmark: a comparison which always irritated the Queen as she thought him so "stupid and insignificant". Lord M's trump card was the argument that those who made Kings had an equal right to depose them, and that nothing should be done to encourage such pretensions. The Queen reluctantly agreed to drop the idea, at least for the time being, provided the Prince was given precedence over her "English" relations. "There'll be no difficulty about that," said Lord M soothingly.

On January 27th, 1840, the day when Sibthorp carried his amendment in the Commons, the Lords debated a "Naturalization Bill" which made the Prince a British subject. One of its clauses declared "that the Prince for his life, was to take precedence in rank after Her Majesty, in Parliament and elsewhere, as Her Majesty may think fit and proper, any law to the contrary, notwithstanding". Wellington objected to the way in which this controversial issue had been smuggled into a Bill on Nationality, and Lord Brougham maintained that the power to decide the Prince's rank was vested in Parliament not the Crown. Lord Melbourne, belatedly recognising that the opposition had grown peevish, was anxious to let the matter drop, but the Queen insisted "he must fight it out", in spite of the risk of defeat. Indeed, she became so "violent and eager" that she feared she had "vexed" him by her "pertinacity". Next day, she asked him whether he thought she was growing obstinate. "'Rather', he replied, mildly and kindly."

The King of Hanover, who retained his English title of Duke of Cumberland, refused to agree that "the old Princes of the family of Brunswick" should yield precedence to a "paper Royal Highness". Nor was he slow to seize other opportunities to make himself disagreeable. For instance, he refused to allow the Duchess of Kent to occupy his apartments in St James's Palace, and he prepared to lay claim to the Crown Jewels of Hanover which his ancestors had bought with English money. The Queen found it hard to decide which she hated most, that "old wretch", the King of Hanover, or those "abominable, infamous Tories". So distraught did she become, that she struck out at Lord M, who was, in truth, very largely to blame for mishandling the whole affair. The matter was finally resolved, following a suggestion of Greville's, by the use of the royal prerogative. On March 5th, Letters Patent were issued granting the Prince precedence, after the Queen, on all occasions, other than in Parliament and the Privy Council: a proviso made necessary by a Statute of Henry VIII which regulated these bodies.

The Queen's marriage took place at much the same moment as the controversy aroused by the Oxford Movement was reaching its climax. The country was in the throes of one of its fits of Protestant hysteria, recalling the worst days of the Popish Plot or the Gordon Riots. It was widely believed that both Church and State were riddled with papal agents, and even the royal family itself was not above suspicion. On November 27th, 1839, the Queen warned Prince Albert that the Tories were "making a great disturbance" about him being "*a Papist*", because "the words '*a Protestant Prince*' had not been put in the Declaration". Seeing that the Prince's Protestant credentials were his principal recommendation, it was clearly an error of judgement to pass them over in silence. Stockmar believed that the King of Hanover was to blame for encouraging Tory qualms, his hatred of the Pope being such as to disturb his peace of mind. In 1829 he had denounced Catholic Emancipation as "one of the most outrageous measures ever proposed in Parliament", and had been rewarded for this outburst by being made Grand Master of the Orange Lodges throughout the United Kingdom. If ever a man was qualified to sniff out Papists it was the Queen's uncle Ernest. Many Tories, while remaining sceptical of the Prince's supposed inclination, saw the omission in the Declaration as a convenient stick with which to beat the Government, and Wellington succeeded in carrying an amendment inserting the word "Protestant" in Parliament's congratulatory address. In the course of his speech, he accused the Ministers of intentional negligence, claiming that they had avoided the issue of the Prince's religion for fear of antagonising their Irish supporters.

The Prince, at the Queen's request, sent her a brief history of his family, in which he claimed that Luther owed his life to the protection of one of his ancestors (Frederick of Saxony). During the sixteenth and seventeenth centuries, the Coburgs lost almost all their possessions because they refused to betray their Protestant faith. For three hundred years, following Luther's excommunication, not a single Coburg married a Catholic Princess. Nothing, therefore, could be more ludicrous than to accuse so staunch a Lutheran as Prince Albert of sympathy for Rome. As final proof of his Protestant credentials, he sent the Queen a copy of the Confession of Faith he made at his Confirmation in 1835, which left no doubt where his sympathy lay.

The Queen grew "quite frantic" with the Tories for making political capital out of her marriage. Her first entry in the new volume of her journal for 1840 began with a brief but heartfelt litany: "From the Tories good Lord deliver us!" Three weeks later, she told Prince Albert that "the Whigs are the only safe and loyal people. . . . It is a curious sight to see those, who as Tories, used to pique themselves upon their exclusive loyalty, doing everything to degrade their young Sovereign in the eyes of the people". It never seems to have occurred to her that she was entirely to blame for poisoning their allegiance. The fact that her nerves were overwrought as her Wedding Day approached hardly justified the unrestrained way in which she indulged her emotions. So agitated did she become, that she told Lord Melbourne that she would never "look at the Duke again". "Don't be angry," he said, in an effort to calm her; but, as she later noted, "I was quite furious and raged away". She described Peel in her journal as a "low hypocrite" and a "nasty wretch". Never, as long as she lived, would she forgive his supporters who had acted from "personal spite". "Poor, dear Albert," she added, "how cruelly they are ill-treating that dearest Angel! Monsters! You Tories shall be punished. Revenge! Revenge!" She did not have long to wait to hit back at the "wicked, foolish old Duke". "I won't have that old Rebel" she said, when she saw his name on a list of her wedding guests. Lord Melbourne begged her to think again on the ground that the Duke's "age, station and position" could not be overlooked. In the course of the altercation, she protested, "It is MY marriage and I will only have those who can sympathise with me." Lord M then suggested that the Duke, his followers, and even the country at large, would be gravely offended by her refusal to ask him. But the Queen was incorrigible and told him that that was precisely what she intended. "What *does* she owe them? Nothing but hate." In the end, she yielded to Melbourne's urgent pleading, but only because he managed to convince her that she risked a national scandal.

There were almost as many problems over the Queen's brides-maids as her guests. Lord Melbourne was dumbfounded by Prince Albert's proposal that it was necessary to consider their parents' reputation. It was one thing, he argued, to demand references for stableboys and housemaids, but another for persons of quality. His view in the end prevailed, although Albert continued to struggle against such laxity. In 1852 he lectured Lord Derby, who was twenty years his senior, on the duties of Prime Ministers. These, so he claimed, included the responsibility of being "Keeper of the King's Conscience". He must therefore never forget that the Queen insisted that the "moral character" of the Court must be beyond reproach.

On New Year's Eve of 1839, the Queen and Lord M discussed Prince Albert's principle that he should be surrounded by people of "good character". In the course of their conversation Lord Melbourne told her that Lady William Russell had said that "the Prince's character is such as is highly approved of at a German University, but which would be subject to some ridicule at ours". The Queen replied it "was too shocking" that morality should be ridiculed in Universities, and went on to tease Lord M for not liking "Albert so much as he would if he wasn't so strict. 'Oh! no, I highly respect it,' said Lord M. I then talked of A's saying I ought to be severe about people. 'Then you'll be liable to make every sort of mistake. In this country all should go by law and precedent,' said Lord M, 'and not by what you hear.'" The Queen, it appears, took this precept to heart. When Palmerston showed her a libellous letter he had been sent, she told him she made it her "invariable rule never to take upon herself the office of sitting in judgement upon accusations or reports against private character. No person therefore can have any reason to suppose that she will by marked neglect or manner appear to pronounce a verdict upon matters in which she is not the proper Court of Appeal." In so far as she managed to convince herself that she lived by this admirable maxim, she must have forgotten her treatment of Lady Flora.

Lord Melbourne told Greville in 1841 that the Prince was chiefly responsible for excluding people from Court, as he "was extremely strait-laced and a great stickler for morality. Whereas she was rather the other way and did not much care about such niceties of moral choice". When Greville met Wellington the next day, he agreed with Lord M "that it was the Prince who insisted upon spotless character, the Queen not caring a straw about it". Sometimes, she even went so far as to warn the Prince that it was "not right" to find fault too readily.

Before the Prince left Coburg, he wrote to the Queen on the subject of their honeymoon, which he urged her to make as long as possible. In the course of his letter, he reminded her of the usual custom in England "for newly married people to stay up to four or six weeks away from the town and society". His suggestion was loftily brushed aside. "You forget, my dearest love," he was told, "that I am the Sovereign, and that business can stop and wait for nothing. Parliament is sitting, and something occurs almost every day, for which I may be required, and it is quite impossible for me to be absent from London; therefore two or three days is already a long time to be absent. I am never easy a moment, if I am not on the spot, and see and hear what is going on, and everybody . . . says I must come out after the second day, as I must be surrounded by my Court. This is also my own wish in every way." Later on in her reign, when Gladstone implored her to leave Balmoral to deal with a change of government, she claimed that she found it essential for her health to remain in Scotland. But then consistency was never her strongest point.

Prince Albert set out from Coburg for his wedding on January 28th, 1840. He was escorted by Lord Torrington and Colonel Grey, whom the Queen had sent to present him with the Garter and to accompany him back to England. The royal party, which included the Prince's father and brother, travelled in eight carriages, three of which had been sent from London. They were followed for much of the journey by a bitter north-east wind through country covered in snow. When they stopped for the night at Aix-la-Chapelle, Prince Albert discovered from a newspaper that Parliament had cut his annuity almost by half. The family stayed for a few days in Brussels as guests of the King, who wrote to warn Queen Victoria that Albert was "rather exasperated about various things, and pretty full of grievances". The Prince, who at the best of times fell prey to melancholia, appeared more like a doomed man being led to his execution than a bridegroom meeting his bride. Three things especially contributed to his despair: the pain of separation from his beloved Coburg, concern over evident hostility to his marriage, and the daunting battle he had on his hands to master his stubborn wife. When it came to taming his Katharina he lacked Petruchio's stamina.

The party embarked at Calais on February 6th in the packet ship *Ariel*. Inevitably, the wind blew half a gale, and the crossing took over five hours. The Prince and his brother Ernest clung despairingly to a companionway, while their father lay prostrate on a bunk. When they eventually reached Dover, looking the "colour of wax candles", Albert summoned up strength to acknowledge the cheers of the huge crowds lining the harbour wall. Next morning, he wrote to tell the Queen that he had landed in England after a "terrible crossing. . . . I never remember having suffered so long or so violently, Papa and Ernest too were in a miserable condition. However, our reception was very satisfactory. Thousands were standing on the quay, and greeted us with loud and continuous cheering."

The Prince was escorted to London by the Eleventh Light Dragoons, renamed "Prince Albert's Own Hussars" in honour of the occasion. They were commanded by Lord Cardigan, who fourteen years later led the Light Brigade "into the Valley of Death" at Balaclava. After a brief stay at Canterbury, the royal party finally drove through the gates of Buckingham Palace on the afternoon of February 8th. The Prince's jet black greyhound, Eos, had been sent ahead to herald their arrival.

The Queen, like the Prince, approached marriage hesitantly. Shortly before he landed, she had an angry row with her mother, who was showing increasing reluctance to set up a separate establishment. So heated was their dispute that the Duchess refused to have dinner with her daughter. The nearer the great day approached, the more the Queen betrayed her agitation: a symptom not wholly unknown amongst brides-to-be. Dr Clark, who specialised in inept diagnosis, maintained she had caught measles. In fact, she was suffering from nothing more deadly than pre-marital nerves. Greville reported her as saying that marrying was "a very hazardous experiment", and what "a dreadful thing it would be" if the Prince tried to thwart her. Her craving for power, he concluded, was "stronger than love". But all her misgivings vanished when the Prince's carriage clattered into the courtyard at Buckingham Palace and she ran down to greet him. One glimpse of his "*dear* dear face" sufficed to dispel her doubts.

The Queen got up at a quarter to nine on the morning of her wedding, Monday, February 10th, 1840. After breakfast, usurping the prerogative of the bridegroom, Lehzen gave her "a dear little ring", and helped dress her hair with a wreath of orange flowers. Both Lord Melbourne and her mother tried to persuade her to follow the English custom of not seeing the Prince until they met in church, but she swept such objections aside as "foolish nonsense". Shortly after midday, Albert set off for the Chapel Royal, wearing the uniform of a Field Marshal and the Order of the Garter. As he processed down the aisle, escorted by his father and brother, the organ thundered "See the Conquering Hero Comes", the gentlemen in the Congregation clapped politely, and their wives waved their handkerchiefs. The Queen's guests were almost all Whigs, apart from the Duke of Wellington, who owed his invitation to Lord Melbourne's intercession; Lord Liverpool to whom she had turned for help in 1837; and Lord Ashley, who was married to Melbourne's niece. "Nothing could be more improper and foolish," complained "grumpy" Greville, than to turn her wedding into "a mere Whig party". While Albert sat waiting for his Bride to arrive, his eyes caught Stockmar's black, gaunt figure sitting near the chancel.

The Queen set out from Buckingham Palace at 12.30 dressed in a white satin gown, flounced with Honiton lace, and wearing the sapphire brooch which Albert had given her. The celebrated "Queen's Weather", which graced the Jubilee summer of 1887, was so far from being in evidence that she drove to the Chapel Royal through "torrents of rain and violent gusts of wind": but then February is not the most propitious month for a wedding. The crowds in the Park refused to let the downpour damp their spirits, and cheered their heads off as the Bride passed down the Mall. The Queen was led to the altar by Lord Melbourne, once more carrying the Sword of State before her, and looking especially splendid in a new full dress coat, the making of which he told her was "like building a seventy-four gun ship". Two days before the Wedding he made her "laugh excessively" by telling her that he expected it "to be the thing most observed".

It was generally believed that the Queen was totally composed, but those who were close enough noticed that the orange flowers in her wreath were shaking as if caught in a breeze. Moreover, instead of her usual high colour, she was as pale as her satin dress. So skilled had she become in concealing her agitation, that she made her responses with bell-like clarity, and her promise to "obey" the Prince was heard throughout the Chapel. When he, with equal distinctness, promised to love and to cherish her, "she turned her sweet and innocent looks upon him with an expression that brought tears into every eye that saw it". The core of the Service remained essentially simple, despite the pomp of a royal wedding. She especially liked the way in which the Archbishop asked her: "Victoria, wilt thou have this man to thy wedded husband?" Solemn moments like this, she thought, "OUGHT to make an everlasting impression on everyone who promises at the Altar to *keep* what he or she promises."

The Queen and the Prince finally reached Windsor before seven. She was so worn out by the stress of the past week and the wedding day itself, that she "could eat nothing and was delighted to lie down on the sofa. But, ill or not, I NEVER NEVER spent such an evening!!! My DEAREST DEAREST DEAR Albert sat on a footstool by my side, and his excessive love and affection gave me feelings of heavenly love and happiness, I never could have *hoped* to have felt before! He clasped me in his arms, and we kissed each other again and again! His beauty, his sweetness and gentleness – really how can I ever be thankful enough to have such a *Husband*! . . . To be called by names of tenderness, I have never yet heard used to me before – was bliss beyond belief! Oh! This was the happiest day of my life! May God help me to do my duty as I ought and be worthy of such blessings!" From the very first moments of her marriage, she discovered that it offered her a "foretaste of Heaven". Early next morning she scribbled Lord Melbourne a hasty note to tell him "how *very, very* happy" she felt. "She never thought she could be so loved as she is by *dearest, dear* Albert. . . . The kind and paternal interest Lord Melbourne has ever taken in the Queen makes her sure he will be happy to hear this. The Queen cannot finish without saying to Ld Melbourne most sincerely, God Bless You!" Lord M could hardly have failed to be touched by her thoughtfulness in writing to him on the first day of her honeymoon, but he must also have recognised the valedictory tone of her letter.

When Greville was told that the Queen was up and about at 8.30 on the first morning of her honeymoon, he complained to Lady Palmerston that so short a wedding night was "not the way to provide us with a Prince of Wales". But as things turned out his fears proved groundless. The Queen's first child was born nine months later, to be followed by eight more over the next sixteen years. Indeed, if there was any cause to grumble it arose over the cost of providing for such a brood. On their second evening together at Windsor, the Queen invited eight guests to dinner for "a very delightful, merry, nice little party". Albert obligingly played the piano and sang a few arias, but he would have been happier spending the evening alone with his bride of twenty-four hours. The fact that she pined for company so soon arose from her fondness for dancing and desire to show off her husband. Whatever the Prince may have thought, it in no way diminished her passionate feelings for him. "*His* love and gentleness is beyond everything," she wrote in her journal, "and to kiss that dear soft cheek, to press my lips to his, is heavenly bliss. . . . Oh! was ever woman so blessed as I am!" On the morning of February 11th, she snatched a few moments to write to her uncle Leopold and tell him that she was "the happiest, happiest Being that ever existed. Really I do not think it *possible* for anyone in the world to be *happier*. He is an Angel, and his kindness and affection for me is really touching. To look in those dear eyes, and that dear sunny face, is enough to make me adore him."

On Wednesday, February 12th, the Queen sent a message to Lord Alfred Paget instructing him to arrange a dance at Windsor that very evening. Lady Palmerston declared that she was very "much vexed" to hear of such proceedings. Was nobody brave enough to tell the Queen how to behave, or did she refuse to listen? That night she danced so late that when she finally retired she found Albert fast asleep on the sofa of their bedroom, "looking quite beautiful". During their last evening at Windsor there was more dancing and more head-shaking. Next morning, they returned to Buckingham Palace after a honeymoon of three "*very very* happy days".

The Queen told King Leopold within hours of her wedding that her "greatest delight" would be to make her husband happy. Yet hardly was the ink dry than she invited hordes of guests to Windsor, knowing perfectly well that Albert disliked meeting strangers, and had hoped to withdraw from Society for the first few weeks of his marriage. It was behaviour such as this which led her godson, Arthur Ponsonby, to describe her as thoughtless and inconsiderate. Part of her trouble arose from the fact that as Queen she became *so* accustomed to having her own way that she lost the habit of thinking of other people. Every profession has its occupational hazard, and that of sovereigns is to take themselves at their subjects' valuation. Those who are treated as if the world revolves round them tend to become self-centred. Greville may have been right to describe the Queen as "a spoiled child, only intent upon the gratification of her own social predilections", but he failed to recognise the unique temptations to which she was subjected. After all, her merest whims were regarded as royal commands, and people fell over themselves in their eagerness to please her.

Just how selfish the Queen could sometimes be, was shown in the design of the *Victoria and Albert*, launched three years after her marriage. Everything in the ship was sacrificed to her comfort. Even her hand-picked officers were packed two to a berth, measuring about five feet by seven. When it was pointed out to her that the crew's quarters were totally inadequate, she preferred to condemn them to a gilded gaol than risk possible inconvenience. The obsequious deference with which her demands were met only made her more unreasonable. The whole affair revealed with shaming clarity how accustomed she was to please herself without counting the cost to others.

It might be supposed that an engagement of five days and a honeymoon of three was a recipe for disaster, but the Queen had fallen so passionately in love that nothing could deter her. The Prince, however, felt ill at ease in the presence of violent emotion, and sometimes was almost overwhelmed by the turbulence of her feelings. From the first, her letters were "sprinkled thick with raptures". One of the surest ways of winning her approval was to praise the Prince in her presence: a fact which Disraeli was later to put to good use. In 1841, she told her "dearest" uncle, Leopold, that it would gladden his heart to know "*how* happy, how blessed I feel and how proud" in possessing such a husband. Two years later, she described the Prince, "*without* vanity or flattery or *blindness*", as "the *most perfect* being in existence. . . . I doubt whether anybody *ever* did love or respect another as I do my dear Angel!"

There was really no need for the Queen to tell the world how supremely happy she was, for her feelings were plain to see. Lady Lyttelton, then one of Her Majesty's Ladies, remarked how touching it was to see the Queen and Prince together: "not a look, not a tone of hers but expresses the most respectful confiding affection. It is the most perfect wife's manner one can imagine." For the first time in her life she could enjoy the delights of "unguarded" conversation, free from the galling restraints to which she had hitherto been subjected. For one so naturally "frank and fearless", the need for constant discretion proved singularly vexatious. Mrs Stevenson, who dined at Buckingham Palace a few weeks after the wedding, thought the Queen "more joyous and happy" than she had ever seen her before. At dinner, Prince Albert sat on his wife's left, and the two spent most of the evening talking together and roaring with laughter.

The longer the Queen was married the more convinced she became that Prince Albert was unique and that nobody could stand comparison with him. Long before his Memorial was built in Hyde Park, his wife had already placed him on a pedestal. "I never admit any other wife can be as happy as I am," she once told her eldest daughter, Vicky, "for I maintain Papa is unlike anyone who lives or ever lived and will live." In her letter to thank King Leopold for his good wishes on the Prince's twenty-ninth birthday, she said that it reminded her that "a purer, more perfect being than my beloved Albert, the Creator could *not* have sent into this world". Understandably, she felt unworthy of "one so great and perfect". When Vicky, writing from Prussia in 1858, asked her to kiss "beloved Papa's hand", she replied she would really prefer "to fall at his feet". "What a pride it is for me," she added, "to be his wife."

In the first few months of the Queen's marriage, she was more swayed by her husband's "striking beauty" than his intellectual gifts. But the better she came to know him the more she learned to admire his "wonderful mind", his "large views" and his "extreme lucidity". The Prince's "greatness", she told Stockmar, after the triumph of the Great Exhibition in 1851, was combined "with abnegation of self, with humility, with great courage – with such kindness too, and goodness, and such a love of his fellow-creatures. And then there is always such a desire to do everything without *shining* himself. But he does shine and every word that falls from his lips is listened to with attention." To begin with, old habits die hard and she clung to her independence: despite her promise to "obey". But as she increasingly grew to recognise how wise her husband was, she came to rely on his guidance and support and to submit her will to his. In 1848, an anxious year for Monarchy, she told King Leopold that she could "*not* exist" without Albert, and that she would "sink under the troubles and annoyances and dégoûts of my *very* difficult position, were it not for *his* assistance, protection, guidance, and comfort". Ten years later, she told Vicky just how much she owed to "dearest Papa", whom she described as "my father, my protector, my guide and adviser in all and everything, my mother (I might almost say) as well as my husband". So dependent did she become, that she chose to refer to him as her "dearest half" and her "all in all". The insecure child who yearned for a father's protection found in the Prince a parent as well as a husband.

Melbourne foresaw that the crucial problem of the Queen's marriage would be to reconcile "the authority of a sovereign with the duty of a wife". In so far as she contrived to solve the dilemma, she did so with characteristic ambivalence. On the one hand, she thought that her husband should be given the title of King, and scathingly denounced the "subordinate part played by the very stupid and insignificant husband of Queen Anne". But on the other, she told Prince Albert, in no uncertain terms, that "the English are very jealous of any foreigner interfering in the government of this country." Much as she adored him, she remained exceedingly jealous of her rights, and for the first months of her marriage performed her duties as if he did not exist. She would not even permit him to play a part in the management of the Household which she left in Lehzen's hands. When Martin agreed to write *The Life of the Prince Consort*, the Queen was anxious for him to remain silent about his rows with the Baroness. In deference to her wishes, he discreetly observed that Lehzen's devotion to Her Majesty blinded her to the fact "that her former influence, must in the course of things, give way before that of a husband".

Unfortunately, the Queen's wishes and those of the Prince were not always easy to harmonise. Whenever they spent an evening alone together she hoped to forget affairs of state, while he longed to discuss them. Throughout her reign she was intensely reluctant to share her political duties, although the Prince eventually proved an exception to the rule. After his death in 1861, she never ceased to complain of relentless overwork, but nothing could persuade her to delegate any part of it, especially to her heir.

The Queen, according to Stockmar, had started on the wrong principle in excluding the Prince from her working life, and was making a great mistake in rejecting her natural adviser. King Leopold agreed, and urged his niece to show more trust in her husband. Lord Melbourne added his voice to this appeal, but at the same time warned Anson that "in his [Prince Albert's] position we want no activity". In other words, the Prince was welcome to talk as much as he liked provided he never did anything. But Albert was not prepared to remain a cipher, and persisted in staking a claim to a share in his wife's duties. Gradually, the Queen began to relent. By 1841, he had been given a key to Cabinet boxes, and was being sent dispatches by the Foreign Office. The moment, of course, she began to have children, the more she was forced to rely on him, and the more she learned to recognise how useful he could be. After ten years of marriage, she reached the conclusion that a Queen Regnant was "a reversal of the right order of things". At one moment she saw herself nestling in the strong arms of her husband, a clinging, submissive wife cowering for protection. At the next, she was Boadicea hurling defiance at the Roman legions. Whichever role held the stage, the other was always lurking in the wings. One of the strangest paradoxes of her baffling nature was her conflicting desire to dominate and to be dominated.

It took almost two years for the Queen to commit herself totally to political partnership with her husband: a process completed by Melbourne's electoral defeat in 1841, which left the way open to Albert to replace him. Lord M himself encouraged the Queen to put her trust in the Prince. On September 4th, the day after his resignation, he told her that he had "formed the highest opinion of H.R.H.'s judgement, temper and discretion", and that he could not "but feel a great consolation and security in the reflection that he leaves Your Majesty in a situation in which Your Majesty has the inestimable advantage of such advice and assistance". "I am glad to hear Lord M say this," the Queen wrote in her journal. "Perhaps this may be a good lesson to me." Before the year was out, she had come to identify her opinions so closely with those of the Prince that she began to use the royal "we" in preference to the first person singular: a marriage of minds which marked the end of a rough journey. The Queen, at first, had regarded her husband's role as that of a political eunuch. Then she began to see him as her co-partner, always at hand to help and advise her. Finally, as love turned to

worship, she proclaimed him her "Lord and Master". Four days
after his death, she told her eldest daughter that she had come to lean
on him "for all and everything". Without Papa, she wrote, "I did
nothing, moved not a finger, arranged not a print or photograph".
Two things contributed to the Prince's eventual supremacy: the
Queen's appetite for submission to a dominant male, and the self-
evident advantage of leaving things in his hands.

Prince Albert was almost the perfect private secretary: industrious,
methodical, well-informed, and always at hand. He first showed just
how useful he could be in the autumn of 1840, at the time of the
birth of the Princess Royal. On November 21st, the very day she
was born, the Prince represented the Queen at a Privy Council meeting. The following month, Anson described him as "in fact, tho'
not in name, Her Majesty's Private Secretary". Both at Windsor and
Buckingham Palace their writing tables were placed side by side to
help them to work together. Many years later, when the Prince's
political role was under attack, Stockmar came to his rescue. The
Queen, he argued, could choose no better private secretary "than
her husband, the father of the heir to the throne, and the Regent
appointed by law in the event of a minority". He recalled that Lord
Grey, a former Prime Minister, had told him in 1837, that should
Her Majesty "marry a Prince of ability", he would "be her most
natural and safest" adviser; and he pointed out that it would be totally
unreasonable to require the Queen "to depose her husband from the
position he is entitled to as such, and place him in one *which must be
fatal to the intimate confidentiality of the married state*".

In 1840, the Prince had been underemployed, but by 1843 his
problem was overwork. By then, politicians of all parties had come
to recognise him as the Queen's closest adviser, and although his
position was never formally defined, it was generally agreed that his
working partnership with his wife was of value to the Crown. His
skills and disposition were those of a natural bureaucrat, and he
ensured that the business side of Monarchy was administered more
efficiently than most Government departments. The Prince, with the
help of his own secretarial staff, brought order out of chaos. Never
before, and never again, was the Queen so effectively briefed. In
particular, he prepared drafts of her official correspondence, and it
does not require an especially sensitive ear to detect his stilted prose
in the pages of her letters. When he died in 1861, he left hundreds
of splendidly bound volumes in the Royal Archives, containing

meticulous records of important conversations, beautifully neat copies in his own hand of confidential letters, and a fine collection of newspaper cuttings, carefully indexed and underlined in ink. "They are gospel now," said the Queen when she could not consult him in person. The hope that one day this "treasure of political knowledge" would be handed down to the Prince of Wales had largely inspired his colossal undertaking.

In many respects, the Queen and Prince were better informed than their official advisers, particularly through their correspondence with the crowned heads of Europe, most of whom were in some way related. However indignant ministers like Palmerston might feel at being cold-shouldered, the fact remained that the majority of monarchs believed in an impassable gulf between rulers and ruled, and saw themselves as members of an exclusive freemasonry transcending national frontiers. Fritz Ponsonby maintained that the Queen "firmly believed that not only Kings and Queens, but even Princes, were on a higher plane than the rest of the human race". On the other hand, she repeatedly insisted that her eldest grandson should not be brought up to believe that he was "of different flesh and blood to the poor".

On June 4th, 1841, Lord Melbourne's Government was defeated on a vote of "no confidence" by a majority of one, and decided to go to the country. The Tories gained some fifty seats in the ensuing election and Peel returned to power. During the course of the election Prince Albert was horrified to learn that Lehzen had spent £15,000 of the Queen's money on trying to help the Whigs, but Lord Melbourne nonchalantly waved his objections aside on the grounds that it was nothing to the amount which George III had lavished on the Tories. The Prince, however, was right to be concerned, for the Queen risked alienating the Crown's natural supporters, much as James II had done in the seventeenth century. Inevitably Peel and his colleagues were deeply disturbed by Lehzen's political bias. In July, Lord Ashley warned Anson that "They dreaded her violence and imtemperance" and "felt that she used her influence against them by misrepresentation and false reports, and thereby unfairly prejudiced the Queen's mind". Anson, with masterly understatement, replied that "the Prince was quite alive to the danger".

The Queen described taking leave of Lord Melbourne as the saddest event of her life, but did not indulge in passionate outbursts of grief as in 1839. Such tears as she shed were mainly nostalgic, for this time she had her husband to console her. On August 30th she saw Lord Melbourne for the last time as Prime Minister. After dinner that evening, they stood together "in the starlight" on the terrace at Windsor talking over old times, and he told her, "For four years I have seen you daily and liked it better every day". Shortly afterwards, he assured her in a letter that he would ever consider his period of service to her as "the proudest as well as the happiest part of his life".

The Queen soon realised that the mere fact that Melbourne had resigned need not deter her from seeking his guidance, or regarding him as a "*very* useful and valuable friend out of office". It is true that she took the initiative in continuing their correspondence, indeed scolded him for failing to answer her promptly, but he ought to have told her candidly from the beginning that it was not the role of the Leader of the Opposition to proffer advice to the Crown. The trouble was that he allowed his affection for her to overcome his scruples. For several months after his resignation they exchanged two or three letters a week, and he even occasionally went so far as to urge her to thwart some of Peel's appointments. When Stockmar eventually learned what was going on, he produced a memorandum pointing out that "As long as the secret communication exists between Her Majesty and Lord Melbourne", Sir Robert's ground "must remain cut away from under his feet. . . . If I was standing in his [Melbourne's] shoes, I would show the Queen, of my own accord, and upon constitutional grounds *too*, that a continued correspondence of that sort must be fraught with imminent danger". Prince Albert instructed the wretched Anson to read the Baron's letter to Lord M, who was so provoked by its strictures that he paced up and down in a frenzy of agitation, muttering "God eternally damn it!" When he eventually calmed down, he described Stockmar's paper as "a most decided opinion indeed, an apple-pie opinion". Some weeks after Anson's abortive interview, Peel told Stockmar that if he ever discovered that the Queen was seeking political advice from anyone other than himself, he would instantly resign. It seems improbable that this timely hint was sheer coincidence, especially as rumours were circulating in London about Lord M's correspondence. Stockmar was so alarmed, that he decided to tackle Lord Melbourne in person, armed with this fresh ammunition. When the two men met, the Baron repeated Sir Robert's threat to resign, and furthermore told Lord M that his friend Mrs Norton was dining out on stories gleaned from the Queen's letters. Before leaving, he delivered a barely veiled threat that either the correspondence must cease, or Her Majesty would have to be warned of this betrayal. His parting shot found its mark, and Lord Melbourne's letters dwindled to a trickle.

The placid transfer of power in 1841 was largely the work of Prince Albert, who was anxious to save the Crown from a second Bedchamber Crisis. The principal obstacle in the way of conciliation remained the Queen. When Lord Melbourne warned her that his Government faced defeat, she told him that nothing would induce her "to send for that bad man Peel who behaved so wickedly". A couple of months before the Whigs resigned, Peel and Anson held a series of secret discussions on the vexed issue of Household changes. The initiative came from the Prince who persuaded the Queen and Lord M of the need for negotiations. The matter was eventually resolved by the proposal that Her Majesty would "procure the resignation of any Ladies whom Sir Robert might object to". This ingenious compromise neatly side-stepped the principle which had previously caused so much trouble: Peel's right to dismiss Whig Ladies-in-Waiting, and the Queen's right to retain them.

On September 3rd, the Queen held a Council at Claremont at which her former Ministers surrendered their Seals and her new Ministers were given them. Greville, as Clerk of the Council, watched the Queen closely during "a day of severe trial", and felt "the greatest admiration" for the way in which she "preserved complete self-possession, composure and dignity . . . remarkable in so young a woman". Although "she looked much flushed, and her heart was evidently brim full", she contrived to control her emotions. "Though no courtier, and not disposed to be particularly indulgent to her, I did feel a strong mixture of pity and admiration at such a display of firmness. . . . Peel told me that she had behaved perfectly to him. . . . He was more than satisfied; he was charmed by her". The Queen's courtesy to Peel was a triumph for Prince Albert, who had long struggled to persuade her that she had committed herself too blatantly to the Whigs. It was especially fortunate that she chose to behave so graciously, as the new Ministry contained seven past or future Prime Ministers and five prospective Viceroys. The very next day, Greville dined at Stafford House, where Lord Melbourne took him aside and asked him: "Have you any means of speaking to *these Chaps*? (the Tory Ministers) There are one or two things," which "Peel ought to be told, and I wish you would tell him. Don't let him suffer any appointment he is going to make to be talked about, and don't let her hear it through anybody but himself; and whenever he does anything, or has anything to propose, let him explain to her clearly his reasons. . . . She likes to have them explained to her elementarily, not at length and in detail, but shortly and clearly, neither does she like long audiences. . . . These things he should attend to, and they will make matters go on more smoothly". Earlier, Melbourne sent another message to Peel, this time using Anson as his intermediary, in which he warned him not to "irritate" Her Majesty, "by talking solemnly *at* her about religion" as she particularly disliked what she termed "a *Sunday* Face".

Even before he resigned, Melbourne's health was beginning to fail. "Nothing," reported Anson to the Queen, "can exceed his imprudence in living, and after an unwholesome dinner and much more wine than he ought to drink, he generally goes to bed *before* nine o'clock." Alternatively, he would be seen in Brooks's talking to himself, "a sad chronicle of decaying faculties and declining spirits". He missed the Queen even more than he expected. When they did occasionally meet, he was so delighted to see her, that he later felt it necessary to apologise for his "high spirits". In 1846, during a dinner at Windsor, attended by several Ministers, he denounced the repeal of the Corn Laws as "a damned dishonest act", and "the greatest piece of villainy he had ever heard of". The Queen immediately changed the subject, but there was no avoiding the fact that the old man was becoming an embarrassment. Two years later, he died what Lord Shaftesbury described as "the death of an animal", refusing the consolations of religion. The Queen received the news with unruffled composure. "Our poor old friend Melbourne died on the 24th," (November) she informed King Leopold. "I sincerely regret him, for he was truly attached to me, and though not a firm Minister, he was a noble, kindhearted, generous being." The fact was that by 1848 she had become so absorbed by Albert that Melbourne was little more than a ghost from her past. Having basked so long in the blazing heat of the sun, she hardly noticed the moon sinking out of sight.

The better Prince Albert came to know Peel, the more he grew to admire him. The feeling was happily mutual, and Sir Robert appointed the Prince as Chairman of a Royal Commission on the Fine Arts. It is true that H.R.H.'s fellow Commissioners were somewhat taken aback by his opening remarks, in which he elaborated on the need to divide their task into "categories", but they were soon won over by his tireless industry and massive knowledge. The Prince, as a token of ripening friendship, presented the Prime Minister with a copy of the *Nibelungenlied*, describing himself in his letter as "always, my dearest Sir Robert, yours very truly, Albert". Part of the secret of their partnership was that they shared the same tastes and temperament. Both were naturally shy, stiff and formal, both were only completely at ease with their families, both were connoisseurs of the arts, and both dedicated themselves with the same earnestness to the welfare of working people. When Peel died after falling from his horse, the Queen referred to "poor dear Albert" feeling "Sir Robert's loss *dreadfully*", as he had almost become a "second father" to him.

The rapidity with which the Queen forgave Peel for being a Tory was quite remarkable. The more they saw of each other, the more relaxed they became. After only six months in office, Peel felt justified in describing his "relations with Her Majesty" as "most satisfactory. The Queen has acted towards me not merely . . . with perfect fidelity and honour but with great kindness and consideration". By February 1843, the Queen had become so convinced of Sir Robert's outstanding merits that she spoke of him in a letter to uncle Leopold as "a great statesman . . . who thinks but little of his party and never of himself." That November, she paid a visit to Drayton Manor, his country house in Staffordshire, thus publicly proclaiming her confidence in him. Of the ten Prime Ministers of her reign, only Lord Melbourne, Lord Beaconsfield and Lord Salisbury were similarly honoured. Her drastic conversion owed much to her recognition of the fact that Peel was the most liberal of Conservatives, so much so that some of his own "supporters" denounced him as a traitor.

Before the Tories returned to power the Queen had almost succeeded in alienating half the country by her evident distaste for them. But as soon as it became clear that Sir Robert could count on her support, she won back their dwindling loyalty. Indeed, by bestowing her favour on successive Governments of opposite persuasions, she appeared to be acting with that judicious impartiality which Albert kept telling her was the proper stance of the Crown. One of the earliest signs of the new era of good will was that the Queen dropped her ill-judged vendetta with Wellington, who by November 1841 had been transformed into "the best friend we

have". The one consistent principle uniting these apparently contradictory changes was that they had all been advocated by the Prince,
whose friendship with Peel was just as important as that of the
Queen with Melbourne. Their partnership helped "set the tone of
mid-Victorian England: sound administration, strong government,
and free trade". When Sir Robert was finally forced to resign in
1846, amidst the jeers of Protectionists, he was consoled to know
that he still retained the confidence of his Sovereign. Happily two of
his pupils became his political heirs and carried on his work: Prince
Albert and Gladstone.

The Duchess of Bedford, one of the Ladies of the Bedchamber
whom Peel had hoped to remove, told Greville in February 1840
that she got the impression that the Queen was "excessively in love"
with the Prince, but that he "was not a bit in love with her. All the
Courtiers point with admiration to their walking together arm in
arm in the garden, but the Duchess does not think it is mutual, and
he gives her the impression of not being happy." Lytton Strachey,
in his Life of Queen Victoria, took the Duchess at her word, and
concluded that Albert "was not in love". In so saying, he chose to
ignore an impressive mass of evidence. Lady Palmerston, for
example, maintained that it was "quite impossible for any two people
to be more happy". It is true, of course, as Albert himself acknowledged, that he was not of "a demonstrative nature". Nevertheless, he
did sometimes find words with which to describe his devotion. In
1844, writing to Stockmar, he spoke of the Queen as "the treasure
on which my whole existence rests. The relation in which we stand
to one another leaves nothing to desire. It is an union of heart and
soul." Those were hardly the words of a man who "was not in
love". Even when they were separated for a night, he would send her
a brief note. "You will be feeling somewhat lonely and forsaken," he
wrote in 1851, "among the two and a half million of human beings
in London; and I too feel the want of only one person to give a world
of life to everything around me. I hope to fall into the arms of this
one person by 7.30 tomorrow evening, and remain till then, your
faithful and loving A." The Queen herself again and again bore
witness to his fervour. As she told Lord Melbourne on the first
morning of her marriage, "she never thought she could be so loved"
as she was by her "*dearest*, dear Albert".

Towards the end of March 1840 the Queen was distressed to discover she was pregnant, and described the news in her journal as

"the ONLY thing I dread". She had hoped for "a year of happy enjoyment" with her husband, "but . . . I was in for it at once – and furious I was". When Albert told his brother a year later that he was expecting an increase in his family, he added ruefully, "Victoria is not very happy about it". The Queen, looking back on the first two years of her marriage, described them as "utterly spoiled by this occupation! I could enjoy nothing – not travel about or go about with dear Papa . . ." She constantly complained of "the trials which we poor women must go through", while acknowledging that it could not "be otherwise as God had willed it so". Whenever her daughters or granddaughters announced that they were pregnant, she described their "unhappy condition" as "horrid news", and spoke gloomily of the "shadow side" (die schattenseite) of marriage. Child-bearing, she warned her daughter Vicky, was not only dangerous and agonising, but "a complete violence to all one's feelings of propriety (which God knows receive a shock enough in marriage alone)". When her youngest daughter, Beatrice, married Prince Henry of Battenberg, the Queen remarked that "no girl could go to the altar if she knew all", and that there was "something very dreadful in the thought of the sort of trap she is being led into".

The Queen was "sorely" tried by having to bear "aches, and sufferings and miseries and plagues" "nine times over for eight months". During her pregnancies she complained of being "pinned down – one's wings clipped – in fact at the best only half oneself. . . ." What especially stuck in her throat was the fact that "the poor woman is bodily and morally the husband's slave". Even Albert, that most perfect of men, was not totally exempt from "despising our poor degraded sex – for what else is it, as we poor creatures are born for man's pleasure and amusement". A few weeks before the birth of her first grandchild, she said that she hoped that Fritz, Vicky's husband, was duly shocked by his wife's sufferings, "for those very selfish men would not bear for a minute what we poor slaves have to endure". The Queen, like other egotists, was peculiarly sensitive to selfishness in others, and never ceased to deplore the male role in marriage. Indeed, there was almost a maso-chistic relish in the way she referred to women's "degradation". Could it be that her constant complaints of "slavery" were actually inspired by a hidden craving for bondage?

In most matters the Queen was an unabashed Romantic, but her views on childbearing were of the earth, earthy. When Vicky spoke of her pride in "giving life to an immortal soul" (in fact the Kaiser, William II), the Queen replied that in such moments she felt much more "like a cow or a dog . . . when our poor nature becomes so very animal and unecstatic". She maintained, furthermore, that wives who were "always enceinte" were "quite disgusting": a remarkable rebuke to come from a mother of nine. "Papa," she said, was shocked "at that sort of thing", which was "more like a rabbit or guinea-pig than anything else". One reason why the Queen so disliked pregnancy was that she suffered severely from depression both before and after childbirth. Consequently, the first decade of her marriage, during which she had four daughters and three sons, was an era of storm and stress. On one occasion, she became hysterical because Albert complained that she had allowed her attention to wander while they catalogued prints together. "This miserable trifle" led to a distressing scene, the backwash of which was felt for twenty-four hours. Sometimes, if she became too passionate, the Prince would retreat to his room to give her time to calm down, only to find her following him "to renew the dispute and to have it *all* out". In better moments, she recognised how impossible she could be, and once even begged Stockmar to persuade Albert to ignore the stupid and hurtful things she said in the throes of passion. The trouble was that pregnancies left her so "wretched", "low" and "depressed", that she could not summon up strength to master her wayward moods. For all her proclaimed dislike of childbearing, she astonished Vicky in 1863 by saying that after Beatrice was born she had longed for a tenth baby.

The Queen was three months pregnant when she faced the first of seven attempts on her life. At six o'clock in the evening of June 10th 1840, she set out with the Prince from Buckingham Palace to visit her mother, who had moved to Belgrave Square a couple of months before. As their open droshky drove down Constitution Hill, she was momentarily stunned by a loud explosion which brought the horses to a halt. "My God!" shouted Albert excitedly, "don't be alarmed!" In fact, of the two, she remained the more self-possessed, and laughed at his agitation. The Prince, who was seated on her right, then noticed a little man holding a pistol in each hand and looking absurdly "theatrical". Before he had time to fire a second time, Albert pushed the Queen down so that the bullet flew over her head. Later, she told Lord Normanby, the Home Secretary, that she saw her assailant taking aim which "was not at all pleasant". Almost immediately, a crowd surrounded the gunman shouting "Kill him! Kill him!" The royal pair ordered the postilions to drive on so that they might reassure the Duchess that they had come to no harm. On their return journey they were followed back to the Palace by an ever growing escort of carriages and riders, eager to show their relief that a "half-crazy potboy" had failed in his attempt to change the course of history. Few things were better calculated to arouse the dormant loyalty of Englishmen than an attempt on the Queen's life, which, had it proved successful, would have placed the King of Hanover on the throne. When some days later the Queen attended an opera, she was greeted with wild enthusiasm, hats and handkerchiefs were waved, and cheering delayed the performance for several minutes.

The assassin turned out to be a sullen youth named Edward Oxford. Lord Melbourne described him as "an impudent, horrid little vermin of a man". It was said that the pistols he used bore the monogram E.R. (Ernestus Rex) and that a number of letters posted in Hanover were discovered among his belongings. Stockmar refused to credit such rumours on the ground that the King would never have countenanced so ungentlemanly an act, nor would he have been so careless with incriminating evidence. Oxford was committed to Newgate charged with treason, of which he was eventually found "guilty but insane". After languishing for twenty-seven years in a criminal lunatic asylum, he was released on condition that he emigrated. Neither Lord Normanby nor Prince Albert believed that Oxford was in the least bit mad, while Lehzen insisted that he deserved to be hanged. As for the plea of insanity, she remarked cogently: "Dere was too much of de method in his madness." Whatever differences there might be over the justice of the sentence, it was universally agreed that the Queen had shown exemplary courage. "It is fortunate," said Lady Lansdowne, "that she has her Grandfather's (George III) nerves." In fact, she had rather a timid disposition, but an iron will: hence her ability to appear calm while inwardly deeply agitated. For all her outward composure, she was much shaken by this first attempt to kill her, especially when Albert showed her the pistols "which might have finished me off". Nevertheless, she refused to make use of the green parasol, lined with chain mail, provided for her protection.

During the next decade, four further attempts were made on the Queen's life, quite apart from a number of threats which happily came to nothing. One man told the Privy Council that he planned to tear the Queen to pieces, and another, found hiding in the Palace, confessed that he "had come there with the sole purpose of killing Her Majesty". The second attempt to shoot her came in 1842, and was made by "a little swarthy, ill-looking rascal", called John Francis, the son of a stage carpenter at Covent Garden. On Sunday, May 29th, as the Queen and Prince drove home from the Chapel Royal, Albert noticed a man point a pistol at their carriage which apparently misfired. The matter was kept extremely quiet and only those immediately concerned with the Queen's safety were let into the secret. That evening, the Prince discussed the affair with Sir Robert Peel as they paced up and down the garden of Buckingham Palace. Albert described how he had seen "a man of the age from twenty-six to thirty, with a shabby hat and of dirty appearance, stretch out his hand and snap a small pistol at the carriage window" from a distance of three or four feet. He distinctly heard the hammer strike and noted that the culprit's expression was that of an idiot. But as nobody else had seen a thing, he began to distrust the evidence of his eyes. Many hours later, a boy named Pearse, who spoke with a strong stammer, reported that he had seen a man level a pistol at the royal carriage, and heard him exclaim "Fool that I was not to fire".

Next day, the Queen resolved to go for a drive in the hope of provoking a second attempt. She far preferred "to run the immediate risk", than to have the threat hanging over her. Greville described the decision as "very brave but imprudent". Before setting out, the coachman was ordered to drive rather faster than usual, and the Equerries to ride as close to the carriage as possible. The Queen's Lady-in-Waiting, Lady Portman, was left behind, much to her indignation, and was very shamefaced when she learned of the danger she had been spared. Both the Queen and the Prince felt certain that their would-be assassin would be "skulking about the Palace", and police in plain clothes lurked behind every tree. "You may imagine," wrote Albert to his father, "our minds were not very easy." It was a superb summer afternoon, and the sun smiled so brightly that it was difficult not to believe that all was right with the world. At four o'clock the Queen set off on her dangerous expedition, but Francis was not to be seen. Her instinct, however, proved sound, and on the return journey a shot was fired not far from the spot which Oxford had earlier chosen. Once more a plea of insanity was advanced, and once more the Queen remained sceptical. "He was *not* the *least* mad," she insisted, "but very cunning." During his trial, Francis assumed an air of insolent nonchalance, and was even so rash as to try to make fun of the Judge. But when on June 17th he was condemned to death as a traitor, he "fell swooning into the turnkey's arms". The sentence was later commuted to transportation for life because there was reason to doubt that his pistol had been loaded.

Lord Melbourne told the Queen that Francis had displayed "a depravity and a malice as unintelligible as it is atrocious". But the Prince attributed "the proneness of the people to committ (sic) attempts upon the person of the Sovereign" to "the increase of demo-cratical and republican notions and the licentiousness of the Press". Liberal as he was, he drew a line at condoning attacks on royalty. He was also inclined to suspect the sinister influence of uncle Ernest working behind the scenes. When Oxford heard that a second attempt had been made on Her Majesty's life, he told a warder, "If I had been hanged there would have been no more shooting at the Queen".

Francis was reprieved on July 1st, and two days afterwards the Queen was shot at once more on her way to the Chapel Royal. Her would-be assassin was a diminutive hunchback named John Bean. It later transpired that his pistol was loaded with paper and tobacco. A boy called Dassett tore the weapon from Bean's hand, but the crowd, in the mistaken belief that the whole thing was a joke, shouted "Give him back his pistol". In the confusion, Dassett was arrested, and it took some time to establish that he was innocent. Bean meanwhile had disappeared, but was found and seized before the day was out. The Queen only learned what had happened after returning to the Palace, but this third attempt on her life confirmed her view that the law should be changed to avoid recourse to cumbersome charges of treason. The moment Peel heard the news he hurried to London to see the Prince to discuss preventative measures. When he saw the Queen, he burst into tears at the thought of the risks she faced. Nine days later, a bill was passed making attempts on the Queen's life "high misdemeanours", punishable by transportation, imprison-ment, or whipping. There was reason to doubt whether Bean had intended to kill, and even the Prince admitted that to have executed him would have been a "judicial murder". Fortunately for him, he was sentenced under the new legislation to eighteen months in gaol. Some years later, in May 1849, a mad Irishman, named Hamilton, borrowed a pistol from his landlady and fired at the Queen as she was driving in Hyde Park. Lord Shaftesbury noted in his journal that evening, "The profligate George IV passed through a life of selfishness and sin without a single *proved* attempt to take it. This mild and virtuous young woman has, four times already, been exposed to imminent peril." Although Hamilton's gun was not actually loaded, he was transported for seven years.

The last attack made on the Queen in Prince Albert's lifetime took place on June 27th 1850, while she was visiting her uncle Adolphus a few weeks before his death. As her carriage squeezed through the narrow gateway to Cambridge House in Piccadilly, a man stepped from the crowd and struck her with his walking stick. The force of the blow was abated by the brim of her hat, but it momentarily knocked her unconscious. This time her assailant was a youth of "good" family, named Robert Pate, who had recently retired from the 10th Hussars. He was immediately seized by the crowd and his own days seemed numbered. The Queen, in the hope of restoring order, staggered to her feet and shouted to make herself heard, "I am not hurt". In fact, she was badly shaken, her forehead was bruised and her eye swollen. That evening she was supposed to be going to the opera, and it was suggested to her that she ought to remain at home. "If I do not go," she objected, "it will be thought I am seriously hurt." "But you are hurt Ma'am." "Very well, then everyone shall see how little I mind it." When she appeared in the royal box, the performance stopped and the audience cheered wildly for five minutes. Pate was manifestly deranged and was given the same sentence as Hamilton. Some time afterwards the Queen told Gathorne Hardy that she bore the scar of Pate's attack for the next ten years. Of all the attempts on her life, this was the one she minded most. "It is very hard and very horrid," she wrote, "that I, a woman . . . should be exposed to insults of this kind, and be unable to go out quietly for a drive. . . . For a man to strike *any woman* is most brutal."

Oxford's attempt to shoot the Queen in June 1840, served to remind Parliament that she was not immortal and might well die in childbirth. Statistically the risk of her doing so was far greater than that of assassination. Lord Melbourne, having learned from bitter experience to consult the Opposition, requested Stockmar to agree with Wellington and Peel on a bill to appoint Prince Albert "Regent" in the event of the Queen being survived by their child. The only person to object was her uncle, the Duke of Sussex, who argued in favour of a "Council of Regency", in which he intended to play a prominent part. But the Duke of Wellington insisted that "It could and ought to be nobody but the Prince". Melbourne assured the Queen that the fact that the Bill became law without further opposition was proof of the Prince's standing in the country. Albert described the measure in a letter to his father as "an affair of the greatest importance to me". For the first time since his marriage, he had been officially recognised as possessing political status.

Throughout the Queen's confinement, "the Prince's care and devotion were quite beyond expression". He refused to leave the Palace, and spent hours in her darkened room, writing letters for her, or reading to keep her amused. Nobody else was allowed to lift her from her bed to her sofa, and whenever she wanted him he came as quick as he could with "a sweet smile on his face". His care, she said, was "like that of a mother, nor could there be a kinder, wiser, or more judicious nurse". Most English husbands at the time steered well clear of childbeds, leaving their wives to the mercy of Mrs Gamp. Early in the morning of November 21st, the Queen woke up feeling "very uncomfortable", although her baby was not expected for a fortnight. She woke Albert with some difficulty, who sent for Sir James Clark and Dr Locock. At two that afternoon, after ten hours' labour, "a perfect little child was born, but alas a girl and not a boy, as we both had so hoped and wished for. We were, I am afraid, sadly disappointed". Only three people were actually present at the birth: Dr Locock, the Queen's obstetrician, the Prince, and Mrs Lilly, the royal nurse, who had previously worked for the Duchess of Sutherland. As required by law on such occasions, a number of ministers and other dignitaries were present in an adjoining room to ensure that a suppositious infant was not smuggled into the bedroom as allegedly happened in 1688. Lord Erroll, the Lord Steward of the Household, saw the Queen plainly through the open door connecting the two rooms. When the child was born he heard Locock exclaim: "Oh, Madam, it is a Princess." "Never mind," she replied, "the next time it will be a Prince." After a few moments, the naked baby was placed on a table for the Councillors to inspect. King Leopold, in congratulating his niece on the birth of her daughter, expressed the hope that she was only the first of "une belle et nombreuse famille". "I think dearest Uncle," the Queen replied, in a tone of pained reproach, "you cannot *really* wish me to be the Mamma 'd'une *nombreuse* famille', for I think you will see with me the great inconvenience a *large* family would be to us all, and particularly to the country, independent of the hardship and inconvenience to myself; men never think, at least seldom think, what a hard task it is for us women to go through this *very often*."

The Princess was christened on February 10th, 1841, the first anniversary of "our dear marriage day". She was given the names Victoria Adelaide Mary Louisa, or "Vicky" for short. The Dowager Queen, the Duchess of Kent and King Leopold of the Belgians acted as godparents, while the Duke of Wellington stood proxy for Albert's father. It was a measure of the Prince's growing influence that the Queen should invite the Duke to assume such a role. Throughout the ceremony Vicky crowed with delight at the glittering uniforms around her, savouring every moment of her earliest public appearance. It was clear to all who saw her that she was a lively, attractive, intelligent child. The Prince described her as behaving throughout the proceedings "with great propriety, and like a Christian".

On November 9th, 1841, less than a year after Vicky's birth, the Queen redeemed her promise: "Next time it will be a boy". The child was again premature, and Peel's invitation to dine at the Palace that evening had to be hurriedly cancelled. In retrospect, the Queen said she "suffered far the most severely" over the Prince of Wales's confinement than those of her other children. "I don't know what I should have done," she wrote in her journal, "but for the great comfort and support my beloved Albert was to me." Never before had a Queen Regnant given birth to an heir. The official bulletin announced: "The Queen was safely delivered of a Prince this morning at 48 minutes after 10 o'clock. Her Majesty and the infant Prince are going on well." She insisted on the insertion of the word "infant" so as to avoid confusion with her husband.

The Queen decided to name her son Albert after his father and Edward after his grandfather, and resolved the problem of having two Albert's in the family by calling the boy "Bertie". Lord Melbourne cautiously ventured to remonstrate. He acknowledged that Albert was "an old Saxon name", but it had virtually fallen out of use. On the other hand, Edward was "a good English appellation and had a certain degree of popularity attached to it from ancient recollections". The Queen, however, was not to be persuaded for she longed for her son to share his father's name and to follow in his footsteps. The former task was easily accomplished but the latter proved insuperable. "You will understand," she told King Leopold, "*how* fervent my prayers and I am sure *everybody's* must be, to see him resemble his angelic dearest Father in *every, every* respect, both in body and mind." Prince Albert raised no objection to the Queen's ambition. It was not for him to challenge the wisdom of turning the Prince of Wales into "Albert Junior". The child was christened in St George's Chapel, Windsor on January 25th 1842, amidst complaints that the guests were almost all German. Prince Albert, believing that Prussia was England's natural ally, invited its King, Frederick William IV, to be one of his son's godparents. The ceremony was performed with Jordan water in the font in which Charles I had been christened. The Queen proudly informed uncle Leopold that "*little* Albert (what a pleasure that he has that *dearest* name!) behaved so well". When she opened Parliament on February 3rd, she spoke of her son's birth as completing the measure of her "domestic happiness".

The Queen was too honest and independent to pretend to emotions she did not feel, and stoutly refused to idolise her offspring. "I have no tendre for them," she said with her customary candour, "till they have become a little human; an ugly baby is a very nasty object – and the prettiest is frightful when undressed – till about four months; in short as long as they have their big body and little limbs and that terrible frog-like action." Prince Albert regarded children, especially his own, through a haze of sentimentality, but the Queen's view of them bordered on the disdainful. "I don't dislike babies," she once observed, "though I think very young ones are rather disgusting." Above all, she hated their inordinate worship, and discussions about "their animal existence". The Duchess of Kent, an ardent disciple of Rousseau, nourished her children at "Nature's font": the Duke's discreet phrase. But the Queen regarded breast-feeding with "insurmountable disgust", and constantly reproached her daughters and grand-daughters for "making cows of themselves". The fact that she resorted so often to the adjective "disgusting" in describing the mysteries of creation, would seem to imply that the Almighty was guilty of indecency.

Most of the early quarrels between the Queen and her husband can be traced to the malice of Lehzen. The Queen never forgot how much she owed the Baroness in her battles against Sir John, and allowed this ancient debt to colour her judgement. "Victoria," the Prince told Stockmar, "takes everything about the Baroness so much

to heart" that she "feels she ought to be her champion". Because the
Queen regarded "her governess as an oracle", she allowed her to
reign supreme over much of her private life. Lehzen was given sole
charge of the Queen's personal correspondence, acted as Super-
intendent of the Royal Households, and controlled the Privy Purse.
Naturally, the Prince saw her as an usurper, and they could not but
come to blows the moment he claimed his rights. Convinced that
the Queen's feelings for Lehzen owed more to fear than affection,
he maintained "she would *really* be happier without her".

Lehzen was well aware that her influence and authority over the
Queen were threatened by Prince Albert, and she therefore possessed
a vested interest in doing her best to discredit him. Anson warned
Lord Melbourne that the Baroness was always "pointing out and
exaggerating every little fault of the Prince, constantly misrep-
resenting him, constantly trying to undermine him in the Queen's
affections and making herself appear a martyr". In her eyes the Prince
was a mere boy who presumed to dispossess her. When the Prince
attempted to order her out of the Palace, she openly defied him, on
the ground that nobody, other than Her Majesty, had "the power
to turn her out of the Queen's house". She even went so far as to
persuade the Queen that the Prince had no right to accompany her
when she drove in state to Parliament. Lord Melbourne, however,
insisted she was wrong, and cited the precedent of "that infernal
George of Denmark" to prove his point.

It was not long before the Prince felt the same obsessional hatred
for Lehzen as she had always shown him. There seemed no limit to
her sinister intrigues. Nothing was too bad to believe about her, and
he assured Stockmar that "all the disagreeableness I suffer comes
from one and the same person, and that is precisely the person whom
Victoria chooses for her friend and confidante". He was even disposed to blame the Baroness for the Queen's faults, while assigning
her virtues to her own sweet nature. His letters home showed how
deeply he resented the rival he chose to call the "Yellow Lady": an
unkind reference to the fact that Lehzen suffered from jaundice. But
then charity was the last sentiment he was disposed to show to "a
crazy, stupid intriguer, obsessed with the lust for power, who
regarded herself as a Demi-God".

Some three months after his wedding, Prince Albert complained
to one of his student friends, "I am only the husband and not the
master in my house". Considering how deeply he resented his life

of decorative inconsequence, he was hesitant to the point of cowardice in his efforts to assert himself. Instead of declaring open war on
Lehzen, he preferred the more tortuous strategy of attrition. Like
some Teutonic Hamlet he trembled on the verge of actions and then
drew back in the hope that a better chance might arise. In an effort
to justify what Anson called his "constitutional timidity", he told
Lord Melbourne that "his good feeling and affection for the Queen
prevented him from pressing what he knew would be painful, and
what could not be carried out without an exciting scene". Whenever
he tried to reason with her on matters which touched her nearly, she
refused to hear him out, and flew into a passion. In the summer of
1840 he achieved an important victory in his struggle to become
master of his household. He had from the first deplored the profligacy and venality of the ubiquitous Pagets, who were Lehzen's allies
at Court. Lord Alfred Paget was such a favourite with her that she
jokingly called him her "son". The Prince was finally goaded to fury
with the family when he heard Lord Alfred proclaim at the top
of his voice that "Foreigners are inferior and Germans are dregs".
Enlisting Lord Melbourne's help, he persuaded the Queen to clear
out the whole clan: a brilliantly timed "master-stroke" seeing that
Lehzen was suffering from jaundice. Their summary despatch put
an end to a dissolute era in the history of the Court, which thereafter
became as impeccable as a Lambeth Conference.

When despair eventually drove the Prince to make a stand over
Lehzen, he found he had set a match to a keg of gunpowder. The
Queen's tempestuous nature, combined with her habit of "heaping
up large stores of combustibles", proved dangerously explosive.
In calmer moments, she was the first to admit she was "too
passionate" and "too fervent", and was filled with remorse when
she yelled at her dressers, or lost her temper with Albert. Repeated
resolutions to curb her "irascible temper" were scattered throughout her journal like confetti at a wedding. The very number of
such entries show how dissatisfied she was by her lack of self-
control. Her opening observation on New Year's Day, 1881, read:
"How sadly deficient I am, and how over-sensitive and irritable,
and how uncontrollable my temper is when annoyed and hurt".
Although she never forgot Albert telling her "your great task in
life is to control your feelings", try as she would, her emotions
got the better of her.

The Prince, who was usually so deft in managing his wife, proved curiously inept in dealing with her tantrums, and often was desperately hurt by the cruel things she said. Introspection could teach him nothing about her sudden violent outbursts. His own temperament was so logical and restrained that he was mystified by her passions: hence his attempts to calm the storm by resort to pen and paper. As a child of the Enlightenment, Albert possessed abundant faith in the efficacy of reason, and believed that the problems of the world were best resolved by writing memoranda. But the Queen was peculiarly unresponsive to pages of closely reasoned arguments, categorising the causes of her distress and proving by incontestable logic that her husband was right and she was wrong. What the Queen sought, consciously or unconsciously, was to purge the emotions seething within her. She yearned for love and sympathy, to be folded in Albert's arms and smothered in kisses. She asked for a cuddle and he gave her a treatise. But nothing could change his nature. "To me," he once said, "a long closely connected train of reasoning is like a beautiful strain of music", and he never felt wholly at ease with a problem until he had traced it back to First Principles. Lady Ponsonby maintained that his metaphysical cast of mind irritated most Englishmen, who greatly preferred a pragmatic approach to abstract speculations.

According to Stockmar, Albert was fatally inhibited in his efforts to assert himself by his "perpetual terror of bringing on the hereditary malady". George III had supposedly died insane and his fate haunted his children and grandchildren. The Prince was consequently "completely cowed" by the dread of over-exciting the Queen. He once told Lord Clarendon that he felt obliged to guard her mental health as "a cat watches at a mousehole". But whatever he did to placate his wife tended to turn out wrong. If he answered her back he further opened the wound. If he remained silent he was accused of having no feelings. If he sought refuge in his room the Queen tracked him down and refused to give up the struggle. After one particularly violent squabble he locked himself in his study in the vain hope of breaking off the argument. Some moments later there was an imperious knock on the door. "Who is there?" he asked. "The Queen of England" came the reply. After a long pause, she banged again demanding instant admission. Once more the Prince enquired who it was, and once more she told him, "The Queen". Never before had that majestic title met with so little response. At last, contrite and weary, she gave a gentle tap. For the third time

Albert enquired who was there. "Your wife" she said humbly, and the door was unlocked.

The bitterest row of the Queen's married life concerned the royal nursery and took place a couple of months after the Prince of Wales was born. The two events were closely connected as she was suffering from a severe bout of postnatal depression. Later, she told King Leopold that after Bertie's birth "my poor nerves were so battered that I suffered a whole year from it". In the autumn of 1841, Vicky began to lose weight and to have problems with her digestion. Lady Lyttelton believed she was "over watched" and "over doctored", and that the asses' milk she was ordered was far too rich. But Albert tended to blame Lehzen's interference, and even the Queen admitted that her "poor old governess would meddle". The children's head nurse was a Mrs Southey, a distant relation of the Poet Laureate, whose heart was not in her work. She loved to live in a hothouse and kept the nursery at far too high a temperature. Whenever the Prince visited his children he found her gossiping with Lehzen in front of a roaring fire. Not only had he misgivings about the Baroness and Mrs Southey, but he also suspected Sir James Clark of pocketing a commission on the medicines he supplied.

Early in January 1842 the Queen and Prince were staying at Claremont when Stockmar summoned them back to London because Vicky was seriously ill. On January 16th, a Sunday of all days, they had a furious row over the nursery regime, Lehzen's meddling, and Sir James Clark's treatment. The Queen, in the heat of the moment, accused Albert of trying to drive her out of the nursery, and even went so far as to say that he could murder the child if he wished. Never before had he felt so wounded by the insults she hurled at him, nor more determined to stand his ground, if only for Vicky's sake. Recognising that she had gone too far, the Queen begged Stockmar to help to restore peace. She hoped, she said in a contrite note, to master her passionate nature. "I knew," she confessed, *before* I married that this would be a trouble." In particular, she implored the Baron to tell Albert not to believe "the stupid things I say (when I am in a passion) like being miserable I ever married and so forth", and insisted that she had never for one moment allowed Lehzen to come between her and her "dearest Angel". But the Prince was so overwrought that he sent her a terrible note. "Dr Clark," he said, "has mismanaged the child and poisoned her with calomel, and you have starved her. I shall have nothing

more to do with it; take the child away and do as you like and if she
dies you will have it on your conscience."

Although Stockmar was anxious to be of service to the Queen, he
took the Prince's side. "The nursery," he said in a fit of exasperation,
"gives me more trouble than the government of a Kingdom." On
the whole he agreed with Albert in distrusting Sir James's treatment,
and he recognised perfectly clearly that there would never be lasting
peace while Lehzen remained in the Palace. He therefore decided to
give the Queen a virtual ultimatum: she must either insist on the
Baroness retiring or he would himself withdraw from her Court. At
the same time he solemnly warned Lehzen that the English would
never forgive her for coming between the Prince and his wife.
Stunned by Stockmar's plain speaking, and disarmed by her love for
Albert, the Queen capitulated. In the last resort, obstinate as she was,
she could see the need for concessions. In 1891, when Princess May,
later Queen Mary, was first engaged, the Queen warned her that
marriage "should not be looked upon lightly or as *all roses*. The trials
in life in fact *begin* with marriage, and no one should forget that it is
only by mutually giving way to one another, and by mutual respect
and confidence as well as love – that true happiness can be obtained."
Two years later, she returned to the same theme in a letter to her
granddaughter, Princess Victoria of Hesse. "So many girls," she
said, "think to marry is *merely* to be independent and amuse
oneself – whereas it is the very *reverse* of independence – 2 wills
have to be *made* to act together and it is *only* by *mutual* agreement
and *mutual yielding* to one another that a happy marriage can be
arrived at." She omitted to mention how slow she had been to
learn this salutary lesson, or the bitter price she had paid to acquire
such wisdom.

For most of her life the Queen was obliged to keep strict control
of her feelings, as she lived in a goldfish bowl, surrounded by prying
eyes. Only in relatively rare moments could she do or say what she
liked. The best chance of all she ever had to unwind was when she
and Albert found time to be alone. All the pent-up feelings, which
as Queen she was forced to repress, came pouring forth in the privacy
of her family. In the later years of her marriage, when so much of
the Prince's time was absorbed by public business, she almost appears
to have welcomed occasional tiffs as a means of attracting attention.
It would, however, be totally wrong to suppose that sporadic royal
rows, dramatic as they might be, were signs of a deep rift. On the

contrary, the Queen's marriage was one of the great romances of the nineteenth century.

In September 1842, Lehzen was finally prevailed upon to retire to live with her sister in Bückenburg near Hanover. Early in the morning of September 30th she quietly slipped away to avoid the ordeal of a formal farewell. Few things in her life became her more than her manner of departing. Although the Queen had come to accept that it was "for our and her best", she was none the less greatly distressed to lose her old governess. But soon the pain of separation was diminished by her growing awareness of the mischief Lehzen had wrought. "I blame myself for my blindness," she wrote in her journal. "I shudder to think what my beloved Albert had to go through. . . . It makes my blood boil." It became clear to all in the Palace that a new era had begun with the departure of the Baroness.

The Queen did her best to ensure that Lehzen retired in comfort by presenting her with a carriage and an exceptionally generous pension. But unfortunately her sister died soon after she joined her, and she found herself living alone. Day after day, she sat in her dreary sitting room, surrounded by portraits of her illustrious pupil, poignant reminders of her former glory. She detested her solitary life and craved for a good gossip. So eager was she for companionship, that she kept a box of the finest Havana cigars to lure her friends to visit her. For several years the Queen wrote once a week, and then later once a month, but they only met twice in twenty-eight years. The first time was in Gotha in 1845, and the second time at Rheinhardsbrunn in 1862, a year after Albert's death. "Saw my poor Lehzen," she wrote on the latter occasion, "she is grown so old, we were both much moved." The Baroness died in 1870 during the Franco-Prussian War, just in time to see Hanover overrun by the Prussians. "My poor dear old Lehzen is gone to her rest," the Queen informed Vicky, "within less than a month of her 86th birthday! I owed her much and she adored me! Even when she was quite wandering she spoke of me." Indeed, it was said that her last word was "Victoria".

The Queen paid Lehzen a splendid tribute when she wrote of her death in her journal. "She was an admirable governess, and I adored her, though I also feared her." For thirteen years she "devoted her life to me, with the most wonderful self-abnegation, never ever taking one day's leave!" With typical candour the Queen admitted that Lehzen "got to be rather trying", but with equally typical generosity she attributed her mischief-making to her "mistaken idea of duty and affection". In 1873, the Queen assured Theodore Martin that Lehzen had never been influenced by "personal ambition", but had got it into her head "that *no one* but herself was able to take care of the Queen". Admittedly, she had behaved very badly to the Prince, but only because of a misplaced sense of devotion. Moreover, "the Queen owed her so much, that she did *not* wish her faults to be brought forward (as they are *quite forgotten now*)". Indeed, she very much hoped that Mr Martin would see his way to praising "her merits and faithfulness". Queen Victoria's passionate loyalty was one of her foremost virtues: probably learned from her mother, and certainly passed on to her children, especially her two eldest. When the rest of the world turned against her friends, nothing persuaded her to join the hue and cry. Her trust once given was never withdrawn, whatever the provocation: hence her almost perverse allegiance to Lehzen.

In April 1842 the Prince was able to take the nursery in hand, and to implement a proposal of Lord Melbourne to replace Mrs Southey by a lady of high rank, hopefully possessing sufficient status to keep the servants in order. Accordingly, Lady Lyttelton was appointed as "Governess" to the Royal Family. She was an old-fashioned Whig, tolerant, well-read, and devoted to children. She was born Sarah Spencer, her mother was a Lucan, and one of her earliest recollections was being taught mathematics at Althorp by Edward Gibbon. Her husband died in 1837, leaving her five children but not much money, so she was delighted the following year to become one of the Ladies of the Bedchamber. Her only drawback in the Queen's eyes was that she was known to hold "Pusey" views: betrayed by her practice of receiving communion with reprehensible regularity. Worse still, her brother, George Spencer, had gone over to Rome, become a Priest, and was known as "Father Ignatius". His occasional visits to the Palace in full canonicals were fraught with terror for his sister.

Another important result of Lehzen's retirement was that Albert at last made peace between the Duchess and her daughter. Even Conroy's departure in 1839 had not put an end to their feud. When the Queen looked back on the early years of her reign, she blamed the Baroness for being "so foolish – not to say more –" as "to confound her very right opposition to Sir John, with my love and affection for my dearest Mama". It drove her "wild" to think that she had consequently missed "a mother's friendship . . . when a girl *most* needs it". "But thank God!" she wrote in 1861, "that is all passed *long, long* ago, and she (the Duchess of Kent) had forgotten it, and only thought of the last very happy years." The Prince was the ideal peace-maker, as he had always been fond of his aunt since they first met in 1836. If the Queen felt deprived of a father's loving care, Albert was equally starved of maternal affection, and looked to the Duchess to satisfy his longing. She was, moreover, the one person at Court, other than Stockmar, with whom he could talk about Coburg. Nobody appreciated better than the Prince how cruelly relegated she had felt since her daughter came to the throne, and how much she longed to be noticed. From the first, he went out of his way to show her every attention, and to humour her "with a species of good-natured banter exactly suited to her warm heart and simple nature".

The Coburgs were well known for their strong family feeling, indeed it was almost the only resource which enabled the Duchy to flourish. Albert was consequently deeply distressed to see his wife and her mother so often at odds, and made it his mission to end the bitter acrimony which had scarred the Queen's youth. So successful was he, that she eventually found that "Every succeeding year seemed to draw beloved Mama nearer and nearer to me". In fact, they shared a great deal in common: their love of home life, their affection for children, their devotion to Germany, and their preoccupation with births, betrothals, weddings and funerals. The moment they ceased to live under the same roof, there were fewer occasions for friction, and absence played a salutary part in making their hearts grow fonder. The Queen's aunt, Princess Augusta, died in the autumn of 1840, freeing two residences for the Duchess: Clarence House in St James's and Frogmore Lodge at Windsor. Living as she now did within walking distance of the Court, hardly a day passed without her lunching or dining with her daughter. One thing which helped the Queen to become more charitable towards her mother was that she was beginning to learn for herself that bringing up children was not without its problems.

The Duchess adored the young and proved an exemplary grandmother: indeed, after the death of Albert's father in 1844, she was the only grandparent the royal children possessed. As her family multiplied, the Queen increasingly felt the need for her mother's help and advice. Part of the secret of the Duchess's success was that she "kept so much youthful feeling about her", and was always "so dear, kind and merry". It seemed difficult to believe that the benevolent old lady peacefully ensconced with her embroidery in the garden at Frogmore had once been a belligerent dragon breathing fire and slaughter. Time, of course, had mellowed her, but more important still was the fact that the causes for which she had fought had long since been won. Once her battles were over the Duchess could live in peace in that spirit of magnanimity which was one of her foremost virtues. The testimony of her Ladies-in-Waiting, who knew her best, bore witness to "the dearest old lady that ever existed". Lady Augusta Bruce ran out of superlatives in her effort to portray the "Beloved one", with her "beaming face", her "unselfish" character, her "childlike" simplicity, her wisdom, goodness and purity.

The Prince, from the earliest days of his marriage, set out to mould the Queen in his own image. Anson spoke of him "systematically" going over her education and "reforming her mind". In a memo he wrote in 1843, he described the Prince's progress as "quite wonderful", especially in widening her horizons, and revising her views of the role of the Crown. "It is you," the Queen once told him gratefully, "who have entirely formed me." The Coburgs were cursed with melancholia, and hilarity withered under their gaze. Many who knew the Queen well thought that Albert was much to blame for repressing her natural gaiety and exuberance.

A remarkable instance of the Queen's re-education may be seen in her views on happiness. The Prince detested late hours, and the "pleasures" of Society: both of which the Queen craved. The grime and smoke of London made him long for the "fine fresh air" of Windsor. "Now I am free," he would say on reaching the country, "now I can breathe." Before her marriage, the Queen told Palmerston, "I am like Lord M. I like London." But by January 1841, she insisted that "the solid pleasures of a peaceful, quiet, yet merry life in the country, with my inestimable husband and friend, my all in all, are far more durable than the amusements of London, though we don't despise or dislike them sometimes". Lady Lyttelton was quietly amused by the Queen's conversion to rural pursuits. On one occasion, as they were walking together in Windsor Park, she said "quite gravely and low, half shy, 'That, Lady Lyttelton, is a tulip tree'." Only a few months before she could not have told "an elm from an oak". The Queen's "Leaves" from her Highland Journals published many years later, showed a concern for nature which bore Prince Albert's unmistakable imprint. It was clear by the end of 1842 that "the old firm of Victoria, Melbourne and Lehzen was finally dissolved: from henceforth it was to be Victoria and Albert".

4

"Beloved Albert"

1843–1851

Prince albert had long recognised that the organisation of the Household was confused, corrupt and extravagant; but only after Lehzen's retirement was it possible to reform it. Huge sums of money were lost by embezzlement or wasted on specious charity. During the first three months of 1840 over twenty-four thousand dinners were served below stairs at Buckingham Palace, mostly to "guests" whom the Queen never met. Meanwhile the fires in the kitchen at Windsor were like Nebuchadnezzar's "burning fiery furnace", roasting twenty joints a day for an army of scroungers. The most frustrating feature of the whole system was that it provided the royal pair with lamentably poor service at a ludicrously high cost, its principal beneficiaries being the parasites who preyed on it. Both the Prince and Stockmar thought its deficiencies outrageous, and itched to replace it with something a great deal more logical. Like Bentham and Mill they required the most venerable institutions to justify their utility at the bar of Reason.

As early as January 1841 Stockmar produced a mammoth memorandum on the "State of the Royal Household; written with a view to amend the present scheme". It described the remarkable division of responsibility between the Lord Chamberlain, the Lord Steward, and the Master of the Horse, all of whom only held office for the lifetime of a government. Between 1830 and 1841 there had been six Lord Stewards. The Household suffered from two further defects apart from discontinuity: there was no co-ordinating machinery, and no clear definition of who was supposed to do what. Whether the Lord Chamberlain or the Lord Steward was responsible for the kitchens was an unresolved mystery. None of the principal officers of the Household actually resided at Court, and their duties were mostly delegated "to servants of very inferior rank". Stockmar illustrated just how cumbersome the administrative machinery had become by describing the procedures necessary for repairing a broken pane of glass in a scullery cupboard. "A requisition is prepared and signed by the Chief Cook, it is then countersigned by the Clerk of the Kitchen, then it is taken to be signed by the Master of the Household, thence it is taken to the Lord Chamberlain's Office, where it is authorised, and then laid before the Clerk of the Works . . . and consequently many a window and cupboard have remained broken for months."

The most frustrating of all Crown agencies was the Office of Woods and Forests, responsible, among other things, for the external repair of royal palaces. The "Circumlocution Office" moved with the speed of a bullet compared with the pace of this dilatory department. The only thing which aroused them from their torpor was if harassed officials, driven to desperation, ordered repairs on their own initiative. When the Queen bought Osborne in 1845, she rejoiced in possessing a property of her own, "free from the Woods and Forests and other charming departments, which really are the plague of one's life". Just how obstructive they could be was shown over the vexed issue of sweeping royal chimneys. The Queen, as Patron of the Society to Prevent the Use of Climbing Boys, forbade their use in any of her residences. Nevertheless, in spite of her instructions, and in defiance of two recent acts of Parliament, children were still employed to sweep her chimneys at Windsor. The Lord Chamberlain, Lord De la Warr, turned a deaf ear to repeated complaints, but eventually Lady Lyttelton's brother, Lord Spencer, prevailed on "Woods and Forests" to investigate the charges. Their Surveyor, Edward Blore, reported that some of the more ancient chimneys in the Castle could not be swept by machines. They were therefore left with two choices: either not to light fires in the rooms to which they belonged, or to continue employing climbing boys "in those flues which cannot be swept otherwise". Neither royal commands nor Acts of Parliament prevailed on Blore to change his ways.

The management of the Household Staff was a masterpiece of confusion. The Lord Chamberlain was responsible for housemaids, the Master of the Horse for footmen, and the Lord Steward for cooks

and porters. Stockmar regarded this arbitrary division as a stimulus
to indiscipline. "If smoking, drinking, and other irregularities, occur
in the dormitories, where footmen, etc. sleep ten and twelve in each
room, no one can help it." At Buckingham Palace, where over two
thirds of the servants were "without a master in the house", it was
left to them to decide when to start or stop working. Prince Albert,
who followed up Stockmar's Report with enquiries of his own,
found an item in the accounts amounting to thirty-five shillings a
week – enough to pay the wages of four housemaids – for "Red
Room Wine". Further enquiries revealed that the charge dated back
to the reign of George III when a room in the Castle had been
temporarily assigned to the garrison with an allowance of five shillings a day to supply claret for the officers.

A fortnight after the birth of the Princess Royal, a curious incident
occurred which showed how seriously the negligence of officials
threatened the Queen's safety. In December, 1840, a youth of seventeen, of "most repulsive appearance", was discovered under a sofa
next door to Her Majesty's bedroom. It turned out that he had
often visited the Palace, that he had overheard conversations, helped
himself to "soups and eatables", and even sat on the Throne. "The
Boy Jones", as the newspapers dubbed him, was sent to a House of
Correction. The moment he was released, he returned to the Palace,
climbed over the garden wall, was re-arrested and sent back to
prison. Eventually, after declining a tempting offer from a music
hall, he was shipped off to sea in the *Warspite*, and was last heard of
in 1844 having been nearly drowned off Tunis. The enterprising
young man, whom Punch described as a "genius", and the Court
christened "In-I-go Jones", had exposed for all to see how lax was
the Queen's security.

The rigours of life at Buckingham Palace were more evident than
its luxuries. Doors jammed, chimneys smoked, windows were
broken, bells did not work, and, most serious of all, "noxious effluvia" pervaded the building. When a new lavatory was installed above
the Queen's apartments, its waste discharged on the roof outside her
dressing-room. The drains at Windsor were the subject of constant
lamentation from the Lord Chamberlain to the Commissioner of
Woods and Forests. In 1848, for example, he complained of the
numerous cesspools still in use, which often became "so exceedingly
offensive as to render many parts of the Castle almost uninhabit-
able". Dr Lyon Playfair, who sat on the Commission of 1844 to

investigate working class housing, claimed that the sanitation in royal residences was worse than in most of the slums he visited. In spite of gross over-staffing, the Queen's visitors were often left "helpless and unassisted", to find their own quarters. The "Boy Jones" found his way around far better than most of Her Majesty's guests. In 1844, François Guizot, the French Prime Minister, spent almost an hour searching for his room. The Maze at Hampton Court was simplicity itself when compared with the layout of Windsor. At last he saw what he thought was his bedroom door and opened it without knocking, only to discover that he had burst into the Queen's dressing-room while she was having her hair brushed. She, if anything, suffered more than her guests from the shortcomings of the system. On one occasion, she complained that her dining room was freezing, and asked Stockmar to speak to Sir Frederick Watson, then Master of the Household. Sir Frederick denied that it was "properly speaking" his fault, as the Lord Steward was responsible for seeing that fires were laid, and the Lord Chamberlain for having them lit.

Stockmar suggested that the simplest way to reform the Household, while retaining a semblance of its traditional structure, would be to persuade the great Officers of State to delegate their duties to "the Master of the Household". It should then be possible for a single official to co-ordinate work and to substitute order for chaos. Between 1843 and 1845, Prince Albert waged a fervent campaign against waste and inefficiency. Some of his economies were as unpopular as they were overdue. He contrived, for example, to save £25,000 a year by reducing over-manning, but those discharged were slow to recognise the merits of his schemes. Jasper Judge, a radical journalist, exploited the grievances of former royal servants and did what he could to discredit H.R.H. Even so stalwart a courtier as Arthur Ellis was dismayed to discover the lengths to which savings were taken, and deplored such "thrifty dodges" as supplying the lavatories at Windsor with "NEWSPAPER". Justified as he was in supposing that frugality can be taken to excess, it would be wrong to assume that waste is some kind of virtue. The Prince at the time was still very young, and disposed to be brusque in tackling hallowed abuses, but the Archangel Gabriel himself could not have dismantled so ancient a system of spoils without provoking resentment. Unfortunately, the entire Household, from the Lord Chamberlain down to the meanest bootboy, were partners in malpractices, and hence disposed to accuse Prince Albert of treating the richest Empire in the world like an indigent German Duchy.

Peel foresaw the problems the Prince was likely to meet. "It is no easy matter," he warned, "to apply REASON to the constitution of the Royal Household. Ancient usages are half the essence of royalty in England." But Sir Robert's advice was not wholly impartial, as he feared that reforms might put strains on the Exchequer. In fact, so far from costing the Government money, the Prince achieved such enormous savings that the Queen was able to purchase Osborne without recourse to the House of Commons. Indeed, his administrative reforms, including those of the Windsor estates and the Duchy of Cornwall, were so profitable, that he put an end to the constant bickering over money which had poisoned relations between Parliament and the Crown.

Seven of the Queen's nine children were born during the first ten years of her marriage. Most of her time, consequently, in the eighteen-forties, was spent on childbearing and the nursery. Her third child, Alice, was born on April 23rd, 1843, with relatively little trouble; Prince Albert, as usual, being kindness and goodness itself. The following year, on August 6th, she gave birth to a second son, Prince Alfred, Duke of Edinburgh, known to the family as "Affie". Long before his conception, his destiny had been settled. In 1839, the Queen told Prince Albert that "in case Ernest (Albert's brother) should die without children . . . your second son, if you had one, should reside at Coburg". "The little one", was therefore to be brought up "to love the small dear country to which he belongs in every respect, as does his Papa". The Queen's third daughter, Helena, was born on May 25th, 1846, at the height of the Corn Law struggle. She turned out to be the least temperamental of the family, and was a regular tomboy who settled disputes with her brothers by punching them on the nose. "Lenchen", as she was called, shared her father's love of machinery, and would emerge from the bowels of the *Victoria and Albert* covered in grease. The Queen grieved that she was so indifferent to her appearance, especially as nature had not been over-prodigal. The next child, another girl, was born on March 18th, 1848, when all Europe was threatened with revolution, and the Queen could hear an angry mob shouting in the Mall. She was named Louise, after Albert's mother, and was the most beautiful of the sisters. The Queen's third son, the Duke of Connaught, was born on May 1st, 1850, Wellington's eighty-first birthday. Because of this happy chance, it was decided to call him "Arthur", and to invite the old hero to be his godfather. From the first, the Prince was resolved to join the army. "Arta," he said firmly, "is going to be a soldier." When Wellington died in 1852 the royal family was plunged into deep mourning, and Prince Arthur expressed his personal sense of loss by telling everyone that the Duke of "Wellikon" was "little Arta's Godpapa". The boy was always the Queen's favourite son, and unlike his other brother seldom gave her trouble.

Prince Albert's father, Ernest I, died suddenly at the end of January 1844. In recent years his relations with his son had come under strain, mainly because of his debts. "Always money, money, money" wrote the Prince, after receiving one more demand for help. But now that the Duke was dead, such wrangles were forgotten, and Albert recalled the miserable old reprobate through a mist of filial piety. "Here we sit together," he wrote to Stockmar, "poor Mamma, Victoria, and myself, and weep with a great cold public around us, insensible as stone. . . . The parent stem has been levelled by the storm, and the branches, which are scattered all over the world, must now strike separate roots for themselves." It is difficult to see why the honest burghers of Windsor were supposed to grieve over a wanton German Prince only known to them for debauchery.

The Queen, who barely knew her father-in-law, rivalled the Prince in the frenzy of her despair. "God has heavily afflicted us," she told uncle Leopold, "we feel crushed, overwhelmed, bowed down by the loss of one who was so deservedly loved, I may say adored, by his children and family; I loved him and looked on him as my own father; his like we shall *not see again*. . . . I have never known real *grief* till now, and it has made a lasting impression on me." The extravagance of her anguish seems almost incomprehensible, but Lady Lyttelton was probably right in thinking it was "all on the Prince's account". The best way to alleviate his suffering was to share it with him. The Queen reacted to death with what seemed a morbid obsession. "One loves to cling to one's grief," she remarked in a moment of self-revelation. Because she spent most of her life in a battle for self-control, she relished this chance to indulge her emotions shamelessly: hence the gusto with which she observed the rituals of death.

Prince Albert left for Germany on March 28th to help his brother, now Ernest II, to sort out the late Duke's affairs. Soon after her marriage, the Queen proclaimed that nothing would separate her from her husband, "even if he was to go to the North Pole". But, in fact, he was forced to go to Coburg alone to prevent his mission becoming a State Visit. "I have *never* been separated from him even for *one* night," she said, and the thought of his having to leave her was "quite dreadful". Before the Prince sailed from Dover, he scribbled a hurried note to the Queen. "My own dear darling," he said, "I have been here about an hour, and regret the lost time which I might have spent with you. Poor child! you will, while I write, be getting ready for luncheon, and you will find a place vacant where I sat yesterday. In your heart, however, I hope my place will not be vacant. I at least have you on board with me in spirit. I reiterate my entreaty 'Bear up!' and do not give way to low spirits. . . . You are even now half a day nearer to seeing me again; by the time you get this letter you will be a whole one – thirteen more, and I am again within your arms." On April 11th, Albert described their re-union in his journal. "I arrived at six o'clock in the evening at Windsor. *Great joy.*"

None of the Queen's residences was well adapted to the needs of her growing family, least of all Buckingham Palace, which had been bought in 1762 by George III for his wife, Charlotte. In 1821, George IV decided to make the "Queen's House" his principal residence, and commissioned Nash to transform it. When the King died before the work was finished, William IV instructed Edward Blore to complete the alterations and make the building habitable. Blore's reputation had been won by designing Abbotsford for Sir Walter Scott, and he was happier working in a gothic style than in the grand classical manner. The Queen wrote to Peel in February 1845 to complain of the state of the Palace and its "total want of accommodation for our own little family (then consisting of two sons and two daughters) which is fast growing up". The Prince reinforced her strictures by describing it as "a disgrace to the Sovereign and the Nation". But whenever he raised the matter with Peel, Sir Robert put on his "wooden face", and respectfully pointed out that the country was in recession. In the end, he agreed to set up a Royal Commission to prepare plans and estimates, and Blore was invited to write a report to help it in its discussions. When Sir Robert resigned in June 1846, he generously told his successor, Lord John Russell, to blame him for expenditure on the Palace, on the ground "that it had all been settled when he came into office".

Blore insisted that there was no room in the Palace for the Queen's growing family apart from an attic intended as servants' quarters, that the State Apartments were wholly inadequate, and that the kitchens and sanitation had been condemned by Dr Playfair. Nor was there any practical way of providing additional accommodation within the existing structure. Nash's design consisted of an open quadrangle, approached down the Mall through a Marble Arch. Blore now suggested that this courtyard should be closed with an east wing, and that a separate extension should be built on the southern side of the Palace to house kitchens and a Ballroom. He calculated that the plan would cost £150,000, part of which could be met from the sale of the Brighton Pavilion. In the event, this figure proved unrealistic. The cost of moving Marble Arch to its present site at the north end of Park Lane alone exceeded ten thousand pounds. Parliament, ignoring a number of radical protests, decided to go ahead, and the contract was given to Thomas Cubitt. The Palace was ready for the royal family by 1850, except for the Ballroom, which was finally finished in 1856. Many of the rooms in the new east front were decorated with chandeliers, fire-places, and furniture saved from the Brighton Pavilion. The Chinese style had completely gone out of fashion, but Prince Albert had the good taste to recognise its merit and to rescue George IV's treasures. It was Blore's inspiration to construct the famous balcony in the centre of his façade.

In October 1843, during the Queen's usual morning walk in the garden of Buckingham Palace, she discussed the possibility with Albert "of buying a place of our own". Her new found desire to withdraw from social life into the privacy of the home was one of the first fruits of the Prince's influence. Even as early as 1844, she told King Leopold "God knows *how willingly* I would *always* live with my beloved Albert and our children in the quiet and retirement of private life, and not be the constant object of observation". Fourteen years later, she told Princess Augusta of Prussia: "Every year I feel less and less desire for the so-called 'worldly pleasures', and if it were not my duty to give receptions and banquets, I should like to retire to the country with my husband and children". After Prince Albert's death, the Queen's longing for seclusion became so obsessive as to threaten the very survival of the Crown. One of her reasons for wanting a place of her own was her fear that the Court might spoil and corrupt her children. Nobody believed more devoutly than she did in the words which she sang with such heartfelt emotion:

"Mid pleasures and palaces though we may roam,
Be it ever so humble, there's no place like home."

The Queen possessed in a marked degree the urge to be "snug"
and "cosy": an ideal she summed up in a favourite German word
"Gemütlich".

The Prince had his own reason for wanting a place of their own:
his wish to be free of the stifling embrace of government departments, and hence to have scope to indulge his taste for building,
designing, and gardening. None of the residences at their disposal
met their requirements. George IV had made Brighton so fashionable
that by 1840 his Pavilion was hemmed in by houses. The Queen
complained that she only glimpsed "a morsel of sea" from one of
her sitting room windows. When she and the Prince took a stroll
along the beach, they were besieged by a crowd, some of whom had
the effrontery to peer under her bonnet to see for themselves the face
on the new penny stamp. "We are more disgusted with Brighton
than ever," she told Peel in 1845. "WE were mobbed this morning
at our walk in a too disagreeable way." Besides, the Pavilion itself
was a bizarre extravaganza, suited, no doubt, to the exotic taste of
the Prince Regent, but not to the needs of a family. Windsor, of
course, was beautiful and historic, but it was more of a palace than
a home.

The Queen had happy memories of holidays in the Isle of Wight
in 1831 and 1833, when she had stayed for several weeks at Norris
Castle, on the outskirts of East Cowes. She and the Prince visited
the Island in the summer of 1843, and both were delighted by it. In
a sense it was pleasantly remote, and yet now that it had become
possible to travel to Portsmouth by railway, and to cross the Solent
by steamer, it was less than a three-hour journey from London.
When they visited Norris Castle, the Queen expressed her regret
that she had failed to buy it. The Prince asked her why she had not
done so, and she told him "very simply" that at the time of its sale
"she had not then money enough". Later that same year, Peel heard
that Lady Isabella Blatchford had decided to sell Osborne. The estate
amounted to some eight hundred acres and immediately adjoined
Norris Castle. It was large enough to offer total privacy, and the
house commanded magnificent views of the Solent.

Lady Isabella proved rather an awkward vendor, but eventually a
sale was agreed for £26,000, and a further £20,000 was paid to Win-

chester College for additional farmland. Osborne was admirably suited to the Queen's needs. The climate was healthy, if a trifle relaxing, there was an excellent water supply and the soil and drainage were good. Its principal drawback was that ministers sometimes needed to travel all day for an audience lasting ten minutes. In 1869, Gladstone spoke for his colleagues when he described "Osborne during the session" as "the great enemy".

The Prince persuaded the Queen to employ Thomas Cubitt to refurbish the old house, a three-storey, Georgian building. Cubitt, who made his name by developing Pimlico and Belgravia, was not a qualified architect but a practical master-builder. Such was his command of every branch of his trade that he won the ungrudging respect of his workmen. Soon the Queen came to regard him as a personal friend, and "an honest, kind, good man". It was his practice to do all his own work and dispense with sub-contractors. Much of the material for Osborne was prefabricated in his factory at Thames Bank. In April 1845 he produced a survey of the existing house in which he argued that it would be better to pull it down and start afresh.

The Prince and Cubitt collaborated closely on the plans for a new building. The view from Osborne reminded Albert of Naples, hence the Italianate style of the house. Its most prominent feature, its twin campaniles, comprising the Clock Tower and Flag Tower, was entirely his idea. The core of the building was the "Pavilion", for the use of the Queen and her family, attached to which was a guest wing, including apartments for the Duchess of Kent and a Household wing. Various cottages nearby were assigned to members of the Court for whom there was no room in the main house. The Queen had always admired the grand staircase at Claremont, so Cubitt copied it for her in the Pavilion, and Albert arranged for Dyce's painting of "Neptune entrusting command of the sea to Britannia" to hang above it. The Prince, like Cubitt, was a great innovator, and embodied a number of novel ideas in constructing the new house. The Drawing Room and the Billiard Room were built on an open plan in the shape of an "L", and the Dining Room was connected to the Drawing Room by wide opening doors. The shutters in all the principal reception rooms were lined with looking-glass, and when closed in the evening not only reflected the light from the chandeliers but helped to create an illusion of space. Even the billiard table, with its curious slate legs, was made to Albert's design. Other innovations included a system of fireproofing and soundproofing using cockleshells, the extensive employment of "plate" glass, a warm air heating system, the substitution of iron girders for wood, and a stucco facing of the exterior brickwork etched to look like stone. Most of the rooms were unusually light and bright with their large windows and cheerful chintzes. Throughout the house and grounds might be seen the letters V and A, ingeniously intertwined, the outward sign of their inward union of heart. As far as the interior of the house was concerned, the Prince sought advice from Ludwig Grüner, an art expert from Dresden, who scoured Europe for paintings on his behalf. But it was entirely the Queen's inspiration to give him a work of Winterhalter for his thirty-third birthday, which hung opposite their desks in her Sitting-room. It was entitled "Florinda" and portrayed a bevy of voluptuous nudes cavorting in a garden.

The transformation of the grounds was almost as drastic as the rebuilding of the house. The estate eventually extended to over two thousand acres: six hundred of which consisted of coastline and farms. The Prince had a genius for gardening on the grand scale, and a recondite knowledge of trees and shrubs. Like the great Lancelot Brown he was quick to recognise the "capability" of a landscape. But his vision was also intensely practical, and he spent as much time on drainage and irrigation as planning the avenue of cedars which led to the main entrance of the house. One of his most exceptional achievements was to make his farms pay: a fact which his critics regarded as proof that he never would learn to behave like a gentleman. Each of the royal children was given a garden plot and his or her initialled tools. The boys, under their father's supervision, built a model fort nearby, and Prince Arthur never tired of "War Games". In 1853 Prince Albert imported a prefabricated wooden building, which soon became known as the "Swiss Cottage". Part of the purpose of this life-size Dolls' House was educational, as it was hoped it would teach the girls domestic science. Sometimes the Queen and Prince would be invited to tea and given home-made cakes. If the Revolution came, Vicky and Alice would at least be able to cook.

In 1844 the Royal Family spent their first holiday in the old house at Osborne, which the Queen described as her "dear little home". Two years later they moved into the new Pavilion. Lucy Kerr, a young Maid of Honour, celebrated the occasion by throwing an old shoe into the house to bring them good luck. The Prince preferred to mark the moment in a more devout manner, and recited part of Luther's paraphrase of the hundred and twenty-first psalm:

> "God bless our going out, nor less
> Our coming in and make them sure."

His own private prayer was that he should be able to re-create for his children something of the magic of his own boyhood in Coburg.

The Queen, from the first, was enchanted by Osborne, the more so because it was "all our *very* own". "How happy we are here!" she wrote in her journal in July 1849. "And never do I enjoy myself more, or more peacefully, than when I can be so much with my beloved Albert and follow him everywhere." They would breakfast together in the summer-house, then go for a ride, or play with the children, or sketch in the grounds. When they walked in the woods, Albert would whistle to the nightingales "in their own peculiar long note", and always evoked a response. In a footnote to *The Early Years of the Prince Consort*, the Queen remarked that she could not hear the nightingale's song "without fancying she hears him, and without the deepest, saddest emotion". Part of the reason she felt so happy at Osborne was that Albert loved it so much. "It does my heart good," she wrote, to see how he "enjoys it all; and is so full of admiration for the place, and of all the plans and improvements he means to carry out. He is hardly to be kept at home for a moment." After dining alone, they would often go out onto the terrace, designed like that at the Rosenau, and gaze at the glimmering lights of Gosport and Portsmouth, and the shadowy forms of warships off Spithead. Last thing at night, they would stand together on the balcony outside their rooms, listening to the fountains below, the bell chiming from the Clock Tower, and the melancholy roar of the sea as it washed up the beach.

Even before the new house was finished, the Queen told Lord Melbourne how delighted she and the Prince were "with *our new* and really delightful home". It would be impossible, she wrote, "to imagine a prettier spot – valleys and woods which would be beautiful anywhere; but all this near the sea (the woods grow into the sea) is quite perfection; we have a charming beach quite to ourselves. The sea was so blue and calm that the Prince said it was like Naples. And then we can walk about anywhere by ourselves without being followed and mobbed, which Lord Melbourne will easily understand is delightful". Most, if not all, of the other rulers of Europe hardly knew what it was to withdraw from the public eye. King Leopold described himself as "walking round and round like a tame bear" in a menagerie. But the Queen and Prince pioneered a new style of life for royalty in which for part of the year they could live in the privacy of their own home, free from much of the protocol of a Court. Never before had she found such "peaceful enjoyment" as at "dear Osborne – the deep blue sea, myriads of brilliant flowers – the perfume of orange blossoms, magnolias, honeysuckles – roses etc. of all descriptions on the terrace, the quiet and retirement all make it a perfect paradise".

To this very day, the Queen's private apartments in the Pavilion remain precisely as she left them, "a veritable fly in amber". Few nineteenth-century buildings have exercised a greater influence on architectural style. Miniature Osbornes proliferated all over Britain, and even the silhouette of the Smithsonian Institution at Washington resembles that of the Queen's "Marine Residence". More important still was the way it came to symbolise the bourgeois ideal of the family home, admittedly on an unusually grand scale. If the Brighton Pavilion reflected the exotic decadence of the late Georgian era, Osborne exhibited the sober respectability of Victorian England, but tinged with something of that aura of romance which crowned the late King's Folly.

The Queen was so delighted by possessing a home of her own that she decided to buy another in the Highlands. In the eighteenth century the English regarded Scotland as barbarous and forbidding. Travellers pulled down the blinds of their carriages to shut out the view of "horrid crags". When Dr Johnson toured the Hebrides with Boswell he never ceased to complain of its primitive people and barren scenery. But the Romantic Movement changed all that. Such writers as Rousseau and Wordsworth worshipped Nature: the wilder it was, the more they yearned to commune with it. After the final defeat of the Jacobites in 1745 it became safe, and eventually fashionable, to travel in the Highlands. No one did more than Sir Walter Scott to encourage Englishmen to cherish his native land. In 1822 he even succeeded in persuading George IV to visit Edinburgh: the first King to cross the border since the days of Charles I. Queen Victoria, as a girl, learned much of her history from Scott, and looked on her northern kingdom with ever growing affection. Few things fascinated her more than her "unfortunate ancestress", Mary Queen of Scots, from whom, she said, she was proud to be descended. It does not seem to have occurred to her that her Stuart blood had become decidedly thin in the course of two centuries.

The earliest of the Queen's visits to Scotland took place in the autumn of 1842. She made the journey to Edinburgh by sea, embarking at Woolwich on the *Royal George*, the ship which had ferried her mother from Calais to Dover in 1819. During the voyage she re-read much of Scott. For the first part of the visit she stayed with the Duke of Buccleuch at Dalkeith, and then travelled north to Taymouth Castle as the guest of Lord Breadalbane. Both she and the Prince were deeply impressed by everything they saw, which included Edinburgh, Perth, Loch Leven, Scone, Stirling and Linlithgow. What particularly commended the country to Prince Albert was the way it resembled Coburg. The woods at Birnam he thought were "very like Thüringen", Perth reminded him of Basle, and he assured the Queen that many Highlanders looked distinctly "like Germans".

The Queen paid Scotland a second visit in 1844, this time sailing to Dundee in the *Victoria and Albert* for a summer holiday at Blair Atholl. Their hosts, Lord and Lady Glenlyon, later the sixth Duke and Duchess of Atholl, moved into their Factor's house, and put themselves to enormous expense to make their visitors comfortable. A new bridge was built to improve the approach to the Castle, and new carpets and furniture adorned the royal apartments. The Queen at once fell in love with the beauty of her surroundings. "I can only say," she noted in her journal on June 9th, "that the scenery is lovely, grand, romantic, and a great peace and wildness pervades all, which is sublime." One of her Ladies-in-Waiting, Lady Charlotte Canning, described her as being "quite delighted" with Blair Atholl, and the Prince as being "in ecstasies". One Sunday, the Queen paid her first visit to a kirk, which Albert told her "was very like what he was used to in Germany". Lady Charlotte, however, frowned on the expedition, and thought that they ought to have patronised "the poor little episcopal congregation". Towards the close of their visit, the Queen and Prince set off to climb the hill of Tulloch, "attended only by Lord Glenlyon's excellent servant, Sandy McAra, in his highland dress". When they reached the top, "Blair itself and the houses in the village looked like little toys from the great height we were on. It was quite romantic. Here we were with only this

Highlander behind us holding the ponies – not a house, not a creature near us, but the pretty Highland sheep with their horns and black faces, – up at the top of Tulloch, surrounded by beautiful mountains". It was, in the Queen's words, "the most delightful, most romantic ride and walk I ever had". Her enjoyment of Scotland was much enhanced by the fact that her husband was manifestly in such high spirits.

Sometimes, after dinner at Blair Atholl, while the gentlemen lingered over the port, the Queen would knock on the door of Lady Charlotte's bedroom and invite herself in for a gossip. On such occasions she was always "in very high spirits" and "full of jokes and fun". There could be no doubt that both she and the Prince had fallen in love with Scotland. On the journey home, she told Lord Aberdeen that she had found the Highlanders "such a chivalrous, fine, active people", and that she was charmed by the wildness and solitude of their country. No sooner had she returned to Windsor than she confessed to her uncle Leopold, "I cannot reconcile myself to be *here* again, and pine for my *dear* Highlands, the hills, the pure air, the quiet, the retirement, the liberty – *all* – more than is right".

Fond as the Queen had become of Scotland, it was three years before she was able to visit it again. This time she was accompanied, among others, by her half-brother, Prince Charles, her two eldest children, and Sir James Clark. After a stormy cruise up the west coast, she landed at Fort William, and stayed for a few weeks at Ardverikie, a fishing lodge belonging to Lord Abercorn on the south shore of Loch Laggan. It was so remote that it could only be reached by water. Landseer, an old friend of the family, had decorated its bare whitewashed walls with a magnificent series of frescos, amongst which was the original of "The Monarch of the Glen". Unfortunately, the lodge was burned to the ground in 1873, and only a few antlers remained of this temple to Pan. The Abercorns, like the Glenlyons, moved out to a neighbouring farm to make room for the royal party. It rained almost without ceasing, but nothing damped the Queen's ardour for the Highlands, nor her love for the solitude of Ardverikie, with its majestic views over the loch to the mountains beyond occasionally glimpsed through the mist. When she returned to Windsor she and the Prince decided to search for a Scottish estate of their own.

During the Queen's visit to Ardverikie, Sir James Clark's son, John, was recuperating from a serious illness as the guest of Sir

Robert Gordon at Balmoral. The two places were only forty-five miles apart, but their climates were totally different. As the rain poured down in torrents over Loch Laggan, young John was basking in sunshine. Investigation revealed that the district round Balmoral was one of the driest in Scotland, rain clouds tending to break over the mountains to the west before they reached Deeside. Indeed, it was precisely because Ardverikie was so wet that Balmoral remained dry. Sir James held strong views on the way in which climate influenced health, and argued that heat was debilitating and fresh air salubrious. He therefore encouraged the Queen to look for a property somewhere east of Braemar, maintaining that the climate would suit her constitution. Then, suddenly, in October 1847, fate intervened, when Sir Robert dropped dead over the breakfast table, and his brother, Lord Aberdeen, inherited what remained of the lease of Balmoral, the freehold of which belonged to the Fife estates. Before the year was out, the Queen had purchased the unexpired portion of the lease, although she had never set eyes on the property. She and the Prince made up their minds on the strength of Sir James's recommendations, and some hastily commissioned water colours painted by James Giles.

In 1848, "The Year of Revolutions", the Queen set sail for Aberdeen to inspect her new property. She arrived at Balmoral at a quarter to three on Friday, September 8th. Immediately after a late luncheon, she and the Prince climbed to the top of Craig Gowan, a hill to the south of the Castle. "To the left," she wrote in her journal, "you look towards the beautiful hills surrounding Loch-na-Gar, and to the right, towards Ballater, to the glen along which the Dee winds, with beautiful wooded hills, which remind us very much of the Thüringerwald. It was so calm, and so solitary, it did one good as one gazed around; and the pure mountain air was most refreshing. All seemed to breathe freedom and peace, and to make one forget the world and its sad turmoils." Sir James was proved right in his belief that the "glorious clear but icy cold air" would act like champagne on the Queen's spirits. Days of unbroken sunshine, and the "delightfully dry soil", combined to make her feel better at Balmoral than anywhere else on earth. Prince Albert was equally suited by its climate and rejoiced in their "mountain solitude, where one rarely sees a human face" and where "the wild deer come creeping stealthily round the house". One visit was more than enough to convince them that Balmoral possessed precisely what they sought: peace, seclusion, space, and a wild, romantic landscape in which to escape the stresses of royal existence. "It was wonderful" said the Queen, "not seeing a single human being, nor hearing a sound excepting that of the wind, or the call of the blackcock or grouse." When Albert's brother, Ernest, visited Balmoral, he remarked in his usual deflating way that he failed to see the slightest resemblance between the Forest of Ballochbuie and the woodlands of Thuringia.

Among Scotland's many charms, the Queen was delighted by its people, whom she thought "so simple and straight forward". Never did she feel safer than when surrounded by loyal and rugged Highlanders. The better she came to know them, the more she learned to recognise "their high breeding, intelligence, and wonderful warmness of heart". Her journal constantly spoke of their splendid physique, their independence of spirit, and generous hospitality. It was so refreshing to meet people who were unfailingly courteous, yet never obsequious. The Queen was so downright herself that she always responded to those who spoke their minds.

During the autumn of 1848 the Prince developed ambitious plans not only to purchase the freehold of Balmoral from the Fife Trustees, but the neighbouring estates of Birkhall and Abergeldie belonging to the Gordons, and the Forest of Ballochbuie which was owned by the Farquharsons. There was no problem over Birkhall which was bought outright by the Duchy of Cornwall on the Prince of Wales's behalf. The Gordons, however, were reluctant to sell Abergeldie, although they eventually agreed on a forty-year lease which they subsequently renewed. In June 1852, after protracted negotiations, the freehold of Balmoral was finally bought, in Prince Albert's name, for thirty thousand guineas. But it was not until 1878, seventeen years after his death, that the Queen acquired the Farquharsons' forest, and realised Albert's dream.

During the Queen's second visit to Balmoral in 1849, she and her family learned to dance Highland reels, and the Prince began studying Gaelic out of a massive dictionary. To show just how Scottish they had become, they took to wearing kilts, and Albert designed a special "Balmoral tartan", still worn by the royal family. It at once became obvious that the Castle was far too small to accommodate the Court and Household, and Ministers were astonished to be granted audience with Her Majesty while she sat on the edge of their beds. Even her own quarters were so cramped that the billiard table occupied most of the drawing-room. Only by constantly moving could the Queen and her mother avoid being struck by a cue. But nothing could be done to enlarge the building while it remained on a temporary lease. Happily the problems of overcrowding were to some extent mitigated by the fact that the royal couple spent so much time out of doors exploring their new domain.

Far away as Balmoral was, the Queen found an even remoter retreat at Alt-na-Giuthasach, consisting of two joined cottages above the shore of Loch Muich. She and the Prince stayed there for the first time at the end of August, and loved every minute of their visit to this solitary outpost. Their quarters consisted of six rooms, "delightfully papered, the ceilings as well as the walls, and very nicely furnished". They saw themselves as camping in the wilderness, in spite of the support of a lady-in-waiting, eight assorted servants, and at least four ghillies. During the day they would take out a rowing boat and fish for trout in the loch, or scramble along the shore to find a suitable place to sketch, or climb one of the neighbouring hills and picnic on its summit. Only the incessant attention of midges reminded them that they were on earth and not in heaven. In the evening their dinner was served by three footmen, and afterwards they would play a hand or two of whist, take a last stroll round the garden, and retire for the night to be lulled to sleep by the sound of the fir trees rustling in the wind.

Few things gave the Queen such exquisite pleasure as pretending to live an ordinary life. From the Petit Trianon to Alt-na-Giuthasach was but one step. Some of her happiest moments were spent alone with Albert relishing the solitude of her Highland retreat. Nowhere else could she feel so far from the madding crowd. She was not alone in chafing against being confined in a golden cage. During Napoleon III's visit to Windsor in 1855, they discussed "the want of liberty attaching to our positions", and he told her that the Empress "felt this much, and called the Tuileries 'une belle prison'". A few months later the Queen echoed this phrase in a letter to Princess Augusta of Prussia, in which she described Windsor, in contrast to Balmoral, as "so stiff, formal and full of etiquette, even somewhat like a prison". Again, in 1858, she told Vicky "How can you call Windsor 'dear' I cannot understand. It is prison-like, large and gloomy – and for me so dull after Balmoral too, it is like jumping from day into night". The Queen never succeeded in tearing herself away from the Highlands without "actual *red eyes*", but it was a comfort to her that as the railway crept northwards it only took twelve hours to reach them. In September 1849 she was able to travel by train from Perth via Crewe, instead of going by sea.

In 1852, shortly after the Fife Trustees finally agreed to sell the freehold of Balmoral, the Queen was left £250,000 by John Camden Nield, of Five, Cheyne Walk. Enquiries revealed that he had spent his life in indescribable squalor rather than spend a farthing on his welfare. Stockmar, on learning the news, wished him a "joyful resurrection", and the Queen had a window put up in his memory. At first, she thought that it was some sort of joke, as she had always been warned that one could not get something for nothing, but when she discovered that Nield had no dependants, she gladly accepted his legacy. Nowhere in his will did he explain what had inspired his generosity, and the Queen took the view that he knew she "would not waste it". The money could hardly have come at a better moment as it paid for rebuilding Balmoral. On September 23rd, 1853, the Queen laid the foundation stone of the new Castle. Prince Albert once more was its principal begetter, with the help of William Smith, an Aberdeen builder and architect. In spite of a fire, which destroyed the workmen's barracks, and a series of strikes which Albert described as "now quite the fashion", the royal family moved into the new building in 1855, although most of the Household remained in the old Castle while their quarters were being finished.

Prince Albert's creation was a bewildering hotchpotch of architectural styles. Parts were reminiscent of the early French Renaissance, parts hinting at the Scottish Baronial manner, the Clock Tower was clearly inspired by Rosenau, and a Flemish influence could also be discerned. When Lady Augusta Bruce first set eyes on it, she spoke of "a certain absence of harmony of the whole", which was a polite way of suggesting it was a mongrel of a building. The Prince, in fact, was particularly anxious that the new Castle should fit in with its surroundings, and to that end built it from granite quarried on the estate which was so rich in quartz and mica that it sparkled in the sun. Distance lent it an unostentatious majesty, while closer at hand it looked more of a hunting lodge than a palace. The Queen proudly proclaimed that Balmoral, even more than Osborne, was "my dearest Albert's own creation, own work, own building, own laying out. . . . The impress of his dear hand has been stamped everywhere".

Lord Clarendon, the Foreign Secretary, did not share Her Majesty's enthusiasm for her Highland home when he visited it in

1856. What he most disliked was an outbreak of "tartanitis" which had seemingly infected the wallpaper, curtains and carpets. As for thistles, he told his wife, they "are in such abundance that they would rejoice the heart of a donkey if they happened to *look like* his favourite repast, which they don't". Much of the criticism directed at Balmoral was unjust, most of it coming from disgruntled ministers. There was, in fact, a good deal to be said for its decoration. At a time when contemporary houses were characterised by a pious gloom, it was cheerful, light and airy. Instead of mahogany, the woodwork was maple, pine or birch, and at least the Royal Stuart tartan was more convivial than chocolate brown and dark green. Moreover, the principal windows of the Castle were large enough to let in a great deal of light and to provide enchanting views of the gardens and hills beyond. Clarendon might secretly scoff, but the Queen regarded Balmoral as "charming, the rooms delightful, the furniture, papers, everything perfection": a verdict endorsed by the vast number of her subjects who eagerly copied its style.

When Count Moltke visited Balmoral in 1855, he told his wife "It is hard to believe that the most powerful monarch in the world can leave all court life so much behind. It is just plain family life here. . . . Only one Minister is present, no door-keepers, no army of flunkeys. . . . Nobody would guess that the Court of one of the most powerful states resides here, and that from these mountains the fate of the world is determined". But others were less complimentary. "I never saw anything more uncomfortable and that I coveted less", was Lady Dalhousie's verdict. A common complaint, voiced by a Maid of Honour, was that nine pipers marching round the dinner table "nearly blew our heads off".

Few guests survived the "bracing" climate of Balmoral without being chilled to the marrow. On the coldest evenings, when snow lay on the hills, the Queen insisted on keeping windows wide open. Lord Clarendon claimed that his toes were bitten by frost as he sat at dinner, and described the drawing-room fire as consisting "of two little sticks which hissed at the man who attempted to light them; and the Queen, thinking, I suppose, that they meant to burn, had a large screen placed between the royal nose and the unignited wood". So notorious was her antipathy to heat, that when the Ponsonbys were warned that she was on her way to visit them, they removed their drawing-room fire in a bucket of water. On one occasion there was a fierce discussion over dinner between the Queen and her youngest daughter, "as to whether if you were condemned to one or the other you would rather live at the Equator or the North Pole. Princess Beatrice was for the Equator but the Queen fierce for the North Pole". The rooms and corridors of royal residencies provided convincing testimony to her preference. Even Tsar Nicholas II described Balmoral as colder than the wastes of Siberia, and Lady Ponsonby always maintained that the only place she could ever keep warm was in bed.

The Queen's attitude to the English climate was more of a medical phenomenon than an affectation. Even as a girl of seventeen, she described July as "quite dreadful for me, *who love cold*, and am always poorly and stupefied in hot weather", and she was frequently heard to deplore "the sweltering clime of the realm she rules". It was her practice to have thermometers hung in the rooms she used most often, to ensure, as far as was possible, that they never exceeded 56 degrees Fahrenheit. Whenever the temperature rose too high, she surrounded herself with buckets of ice. At Osborne she was apt to play what Clarendon called "the royal game of summer". Although her guests were shivering with cold, she was heard to express misgivings "whether it is not too hot to drive to Freshwater". On one particularly chilly evening, Princess Beatrice put the drawing-room thermometer outside the window until her mother came down to dinner. The Queen was surprised to find that it read so low, but, accepting the verdict of science, had all the windows closed. So impervious was she to cold, that she even kept Albert short of coal, particularly during the freezing Crimean winters when she insisted that it was the duty of the royal family to set a good example. The Prince, whose health was at best fragile, ordered a fur-lined coat to wear indoors, and when he was so frozen that he could hardly hold a pen he would warm his fingers over the flame of his reading lamp.

The Queen's attitude to climate was encouraged by Clark and Stockmar. The Baron, a pioneer of fresh air and cleanliness, found her a willing convert. Sir James shared his enthusiasm and carried on his good work. When she heard that Prince Arthur thought Scotland so chilly in November that he ordered a fire in his bedroom, she insisted on his extinguishing it with a wash basin full of water.

The Queen and Prince became Scottish landowners at the time of the notorious "Highland Clearances", and were resolved to set an example of how estates should be run. Accordingly, the Queen's Factor, Dr Robertson, was encouraged to do all in his power for the welfare of her tenants, and "to elevate their moral and social condition". Over the years Balmoral was transformed: cottages were rebuilt, schools provided, and an excellent library opened. When the Queen published *Leaves from the Journal of Our Life in the Highlands*, the proceeds were mostly devoted to educational bursaries. Everywhere, roads were built, ditches drained, fields fenced, trees planted, and land reclaimed. Such was Prince Albert's reforming zeal that in less than ten years there was no finer estate in Scotland.

Greville was one of the Queen's first guests at Balmoral when he attended a Council in 1849 "to order a prayer for relief against the cholera". In spite of the length of the journey, he was "glad to have made the expedition", as it enabled him to see "the Queen and Prince in their Highland retreat, where they certainly appear to great advantage". He was hugely impressed by their simple style of life, which he described as being "not merely like private gentlefolks but like very small gentlefolks". A solitary policeman was deemed sufficient to guard the royal family and "to keep off impertinent intruders". But what he found most surprising of all was the casual way in which the Queen "goes about alone, walks into the cottages, and sits down and chats with the old women".

The published "Leaves" from the Queen's journal are full of what Florence Nightingale called "poor-peopling". For example, her entry for Saturday, September 26th, 1857, describes how she set off with Vicky and Alice on a round of visits, beginning at Mrs Farquharson's shop to purchase appropriate gifts. Kitty Kear, an old lady of eighty-six welcomed them "with a great air of dignity", but continued to work at her spinning while chatting to her guests. When the Queen presented her with a warm petticoat, she burst out in a spontaneous litany: "May the Lord ever attend ye and yours, here and hereafter, and may the Lord be a guide to ye, and keep ye from harm". Often the Queen found it necessary to explain who she was, as without the royal regalia she might easily have been mistaken for a daughter of the Manse. Indeed, people found it almost impossible to believe that this homely little woman was Victoria Regina. On taking leave of Kitty, who was "very talkative", she called on old Mrs Grant and gave her a dress and handkerchief. "You're too kind to me," she said gratefully, "ye give me more every year." The Queen particularly warmed to the straight-forward way in which Mrs Grant told her, "I always say just what I think, not what is fut (fit)."

None of the families whom the Queen visited felt they were being patronised, as she was far too simple and humble at heart to be other than perfectly natural. "She has nae pride," said one old woman, "for she enters a' the houses of the poor, and should it happen to be meal time when she visits them, she always partakes of a small quantity of their homely fare", and she thought nothing "o' making purchases in the shape of butter and eggs, and taking it home herself". When she heard that a child called Sandy Rattray had been drowned in a burn, she did what she could to comfort the heart-broken parents. "We went in, and on a table in the kitchen covered with a sheet, which they lifted up, lay the poor sweet innocent 'bairnie', only three years old, a fine plump child. . . . Then the poor mother came in, calm and quiet, though she cried a little at first when I took her hand and said how much I felt for her, and how dreadful it was. She checked herself, and said, with that great resignation and trust which it is so edifying to witness, and which you see so strongly here, 'We must try to bear it; we must trust to the Almighty'." The Queen particularly liked to attend baptisms and funeral services held in the cottages on her estate: forms of worship she thought "most appropriate, touching and impressive". When her former Head Keeper, Grant, was dying in 1879, she visited him almost daily, and was present at the funeral service at his house. So completely did she come to identify herself with her Highland neighbours, that she preferred their company to that of the haut monde.

During the course of her reign, the Queen spent seven years at Balmoral, and covered a hundred thousand miles travelling to and fro. In 1871 she told Vicky that on "one of the last walks I took with darling Papa he said to me, 'England does not know what she owes to Scotland'. She is the brightest jewel in my crown." Nowhere else in her Kingdom could she find such a "combination of wood and mountain, and river", such "glorious surroundings" and "heavenly air", or such solitude from the frivolities of the wicked world. She was passionately fond of mountains, and echoed Byron's craving to return to them.

> "England! Thy beauties are tame and domestic
> To one who has roved o'er the mountains afar:
> Oh for the crags that are wild and majestic,
> The steep, frowning glories of dark Loch na Garr!"

It became obvious to those who knew the Queen and Prince that they were "never happier than when in the Highlands". Lord Clarendon thought the Queen "quite a different person" north of the Border, and Mary Ponsonby maintained that she was never "so completely charming, so easy to satisfy, so warmly genial, as when she was driving and sketching and drinking tea on the remote Aberdeenshire moors". Sir Charles Lyell, the great geologist, noticed that Prince Albert's "hauteur" vanished at Balmoral and "his nature expanded".

When the time approached for the Queen to leave Balmoral, she was like a child being forced to return to school, hoping that she "might be snowed up and unable to move". She dreaded the change of climate, and described Windsor in October as "extremely enervating", and so "hot" that she could scarcely drag herself about. Her letters to Vicky were full of the "heartache" she suffered each year at the "bitter thought" of returning to "tame, dull, formal England", after the "enchanting life of liberty" at Balmoral. The Queen was never one for halfhearted enthusiasms, and her loves and hatreds were larger than life. In 1849, when she returned to Osborne after her second visit to Balmoral, Lady Lyttelton could not resist smiling at her characteristic fervour for "Scotch air, Scotch people, Scotch hills, Scotch rivers, Scotch words", all of which she thought "far preferable to those of any other nation".

The Celtic character had an irresistible charm for her. When she heard of Napier's appointment as British Ambassador to Prussia, she described him as possessing the "great merit" of being "a true Scotchman". She particularly admired the Highlander's natural dignity and self-possession. "They are never vulgar, never take liberties, are so intelligent, modest, and well bred." Many of her most amusing stories, told in a broad Scotch accent, derived from the homely wisdom of the "dear people" at Balmoral. "It is so soothing and refreshing," she told Vicky in 1859, "when one is in such an isolated position as we are, to be able to talk freely to those below you, and to find such open independence, and such affection for you." When Charles Kingsley told her that English peasants "had not a grain of poetry in their nature whereas the Scotch are full of it", she noted "how true that is and this is what gives them such a charm and makes the Highlanders so highbred. One does require that to lift us above the heavy clay which clogs our souls".

★

Whatever may be thought of the Queen and Prince as parents, such mistakes as they made proceeded from good intentions, and they had nothing so close to their hearts as the training of their children. The Queen was determined that Albert's paternal authority would never be undermined by his secondary role as her Consort. If she could not make him King, at least she could see that his word was law in his family. It soon became clear that Vicky was very clever. By the time she was three, her father proudly boasted that she could speak French, German and English with "great fluency and choice of phrase". Her voice was absurdly like the Queen's, as indeed was her appearance. Both parents delighted in introducing her to visitors and watching them become spellbound. While Bertie was markedly "anti-studious" and looked with distaste on his lessons, Vicky read Gibbon avidly, studied chemistry as if her life depended on it, and devoured books on political economy as if they were chocolate éclairs. She was better educated at ten than most people twice her age. If Prince Albert had bought her off a shelf, she was just such a child as he would choose. Alice was less precocious, but shared Vicky's talent for music and drawing, and was exceptionally considerate. One of Lady Lyttelton's more testing problems was that all three children were prone to fly into tantrums. They were not their mother's offspring for nothing. The Prince recommended a good whipping, but "Laddle" (Lady Lyttelton) hesitated on the ground that she could not feel sure that children recognised punishment as the consequence of their naughtiness.

The Queen regarded it as of the first importance that her family "should be brought up as simply, and in as domestic a way as possible". It was, she told Vicky in 1874, "an immense advantage not to have 'been born under the purple', which was my case . . . and dear Papa's. We strove to counteract it in every way with all of you." Family meals were kept unappetisingly plain to prevent anyone getting ideas above their station. When Mary Jones, a new recruit to the royal staff, saw a tray of boiled beef and semolina pudding being carried up to the nursery, she said she "never would have believed it if she had not seen it for herself". The Queen was just as frugal when it came to matters of dress, and clothes were carefully preserved in mothballs and handed on to the younger children. Lady Lyttelton was repeatedly instructed to rebuke the faintest hint of pride in any of her charges. "The bane of the present day," the Queen declared, "is pride, vulgar, unchristian pride in high and low."

The revolutions of 1848 made a lasting impression on Queen Victoria. As Buckingham Palace filled with royal refugees from most European capitals, she was powerfully reminded "that we are before God all alike and that in the twinkling of an eye – the highest may find themselves at the feet of the poorest and lowest". On July 11th, having deplored the triumphs of Republicanism, she told King Leopold, "I always say to myself, 'Let them (the royal children) grow up fit for *whatever station* they may be placed in – *high or low*'. This one never thought before, but I *do* always now". So successful was she in keeping her children humble, that when Prince Arthur was promised an invitation to a play, he expressed the fear that the company concerned would not know where to address the ticket.

Stockmar persuaded the Queen that the only safe way to bring up her children was to keep them in moral quarantine, surrounded by those whom she knew to be "good and pure". As was only to be expected, the policy proved a disaster. Brought up to drink from unsullied springs they had no resistance to tainted water. So effectively were they preserved from the contamination of the Court that most of the Queen's ladies-in-waiting hardly knew what they looked like. When eventually a few reluctant Etonians were trundled up the hill to meet the Prince of Wales, Prince Albert never let them out of his sight "less they should throw bread pellets at each other or talk lewdly". One of this privileged group, Charles Carrington, remembered being "frightened to death" by the Prince's presence, and the sense of relief he felt after making his bow and scurrying back to his Tutor's. In addition to formal instruction in the schoolroom, Prince Albert would take his children on country rambles and tell them about wild flowers, and shells and fossils. Alternatively, the Queen would declare an impromptu holiday, much to the dismay of Stockmar and Lady Lyttelton, and the whole family would embark in the *Fairy* and set sail down the Solent, or take to the hills round Balmoral, only to stumble miraculously on a pile of picnic baskets apparently dropped from Heaven.

In prosperous nineteenth-century households children lived separate lives from their parents: first in the nursery, and later at boarding schools. The Queen and Prince, however, decided to keep their family at home and to live on the closest terms with them. Not for them the atmosphere of distrust which had poisoned the Queen's childhood. Soon, both royal parents came to regard the nursery as a haven in which to escape from the harassing world. Never before

had the Queen known what it was to join in the fun of a family, and
she felt "so happy and blessed" to be able to do so. "Come along
my chicks," she would say, as she gathered them under her wing
for a walk in the garden. "I am coming more and more convinced,"
she declared in 1856, "that the only true happiness in this world is
to be found in the domestic circle." When she saw what she called
"our tribe" going out for a walk with their father, she felt sure that
no other "Royal Ménage" was "equal to ours", nor, of course, was
"*any* one to be compared to *my dearest* Angel."

It was not in Prince Albert's nature to relax, but he never felt more
at ease than with his family. Indeed, he was almost too much at
home in the nursery and inadvertently sat in Lady Lyttelton's chair.
Vicky was so outraged that she shouted indignantly: "Papa! don't
sit there, get up! It is Laddle's chair. Give Laddle her chair!" Whenever he got the chance, he loved to play hide and seek, or fly kites,
or chase butterflies, or turn somersaults in a haystack. "He is so kind
to them," wrote the Queen adoringly, "and romps with them so
delightfully." On one occasion, he helped the Prince of Wales to
build a house "with Pezzessy's wooden bricks, to finish which he
had to stand on a chair and reach above his head. Such a fall it made!
He enjoyed it much the most." "What a joyous childhood we had,"
Alice later told her mother. "No other children were so happy; and
so spoiled with all the enjoyments and comforts children can wish
for."

It has widely been taken for granted that the Queen played a
prominent part in shaping Victorian values. But, in fact, her religious
opinions were highly eccentric and owed almost nothing to
nineteenth-century fashions. She was indifferent, if not hostile, to the
Evangelical and Tractarian Movements, which revitalised English
religion in the early part of the century, and her sympathy for the
Broad Church was not very widely shared. Nor could it be said that
she owed much to any distinctly Anglican tradition, as her opinions
were principally based on her faith in God and belief in a world to
come. Even her views on the Trinity were unorthodox, and her
Christology so reductionist as to verge on Unitarianism. Just how
unusual the Queen's beliefs were, a few examples will show. In 1841
she invited King Frederick William IV of Prussia to become one of
Bertie's godfathers, and imperiously swept aside the cogent objection
that he did not belong to the Church of England. Both she and the
Prince shared a common dislike of the Chapel Royal and St George's,

Windsor. In particular, she resented the inordinate length of their services, the precise duration of which she noted in her journal with appropriate exclamation marks. Dean Hobart of Windsor thought nothing of preaching for over an hour and a half. In 1843 private Chapels were consecrated at Buckingham Palace and Windsor to enable the royal family to worship more expeditiously. Naturally the fact that she thought it necessary to withdraw from public services was seen as proof of hostility to the Establishment.

Victorians of almost all religious persuasions, more especially Evangelicals, were obsessed by the prospect of everlasting damnation. Morality, it was commonly supposed, was only sustained by the terrors of Hell. But the Queen regarded such doctrines as "absurd" and "unutterably horrible and revolting". It was, she argued, a travesty of Christ's teaching to wish eternal damnation on anyone, and she was particularly insistent that her children should be spared what she saw as a slander on God. However angry she might get with them, she never resorted to threats of hell-fire. In a memo she wrote in 1844 she laid down the principle that she wanted her family to be brought up with a sense of reverence for the Almighty, whom they should be encouraged to regard with "devotion and love" not "fear and trembling". One Sunday, the Minister at Balmoral preached a sermon on Satan, and was rash enough afterwards to ask Princess Louise whether Her Majesty had liked it. The Princess replied that she had not so far discussed it, but that she thought it unlikely that her Mother would have approved of it as she did not altogether believe in the Devil. "Puir body" said the Minister consolingly as he contemplated the enormity of such scepticism.

Few people were more strenuously opposed to the Victorian Sunday than the Queen and Prince. "I am not at all an admirer or approver of our very dull Sundays," she told Vicky in 1859, "for I think the absence of innocent amusement for the poor people, a misfortune and an encouragement of vice." In so saying, she echoed the sentiments of her ancestor, James I, in his *Book of Sports*. She had no real objection to Sunday travelling, and wholeheartedly supported the opening of Galleries and Museums on the only free day the working class had in the week. When a bill was introduced in the House of Commons to make it illegal for bands to play in Parks except on weekdays, she told the Prime Minister that she could not "sufficiently express her regret at the incomprehensible blindness and mistaken piety of the so-called 'Evangelical Saints'", and she pointed out that bands had played on the terrace at Windsor "from time immemorial". During Napoleon III's visit to Osborne in 1857 she did not hesitate to arrange "a little dance in a tent" in spite of its being the Sabbath. As for the children, it was to be a "happy play day", devoted to "recreation and amusement", provided they went to church in the morning. Later in life, she raised no objections when her granddaughters asked to play tennis, but was most indignant to learn that an over-zealous tutor had required Prince Arthur to attend two services on the sacred day, and issued a stern decree that it must never occur again.

So strong were the Queen's Protestant instincts that she was inclined towards anti-clericalism. Such clerical friends as she possessed were mostly tainted with heresy, such as Charles Kingsley, Arthur Stanley, and Dr Mcleod. "Her own growing inclination" she told Gladstone in 1872, was "for the simplest form of service". Moreover, as the Anglican Church increasingly veered to Rome, the more she regarded the Kirk as "the real and true stronghold of Protestantism".

Prince Albert's religion was even less orthodox than his wife's, although rather more closely worked out. In many respects he was a conventional Lutheran: fearing the Pope, distrusting the clergy, and fiercely intolerant of bigotry. He had learned at Bonn to understand Christianity in terms of historical development, not as a once-for-all revelation of truth, and he therefore believed that it would only remain credible if constantly re-interpreted. So broad was his faith that he was perfectly happy to admit that "'many roads lead to Heaven' and not only the one in which we happen to believe". Although some regarded his latitudinarian views as proof of infidelity – so much so that he was widely credited with being the anonymous author of *The Vestiges of Creation* – he was, in reality, as Florschütz perceived, "instinctively devout".

From the first, the Prince antagonised most Anglicans by being too outspoken, and Anson tried to persuade him not to keep saying that the Church was in need of a second reformation more drastic than the first. Prince Albert encouraged the Queen to regard Christianity as little more than a call to moral action. Religion, he told her, was chiefly concerned with leading a virtuous life and setting a good example. There was no need to trouble one's head about the niceties of theology, provided one heeded the Ten Commandments and did one's duty. Few things showed more clearly how little the Queen understood the sacramental life of the Church than the efforts she made to persuade the Prince of Wales to follow his parents' example and only attend Communion twice a year. Presumably she was unaware of the Prayer Book injunction "That every Parishioner shall communicate at the least three times in the year, of which Easter to be one".

Naturally the religious instruction of the royal family reflected their parents' views. No particular stress was to be placed on the supernatural aspects of Christianity, "but rather upon the pure and comprehensive morality which it teaches". Above all, they were taught to be tolerant. "I remember so well," Vicky told her mother in 1873, "when we were little children thinking it very grand to abuse Catholics; and I recollect you saying you could not bear that and thought it very wrong, and that you had seen so much vulgar prejudice and foolish violence against the Catholics in former days that you had felt shocked and hurt by it."

Princess Augusta of Prussia strongly disapproved of the way the Queen and the Prince brought up their children, and was convinced that the English princesses were little better than atheists. As for the Prince of Wales it would be impossible to pretend that he was a spectacular advertisement for his parents' moral training. The Queen was not always successful in practising what she preached, and seems to have found it easier to tolerate totally different faiths than comparatively minor variants of her own. She spoke, for example, a good deal more scathingly of the Tractarians than she ever did of Islam. It was one of the strangest paradoxes of her nature that she felt greater sympathy for those who denied the incarnation of Christ, than for Christians like Pusey and Keble who worshipped Him too extravagantly. She was even distressed by what she chose to regard as Lady Lyttelton's "High Church" ways, and a crisis blew up over the question whether the children should kneel when they said their prayers. Prince Albert referred caustically to this "peculiar feature of English religiosity", but "Laddle" insisted that it would be "highly irreverent" to assume any other posture. In the end, he agreed that as the children were being brought up as Anglicans, their "prejudices must be those of the English Church".

Like most women, the Queen found it impossible to "fill the role of wife and mother with equal intensity", and made little secret of the fact that her husband came first in her affections. In 1857, when

the Prince attended the wedding of Archduke Ferdinand to King
Leopold's daughter, Charlotte, the Queen told her uncle that "*ALL*
the numerous children are as *nothing* to me when *he is away*; it seems
as if the whole life of the house and home were gone . . .". She was
even more candid to Princess Augusta, to whom she confessed that
she "found no especial pleasure or compensation" in the company
of her children, and that "only very exceptionally" did she find
"intimate intercourse with them either agreeable or easy". It was
true, of course, that Albert meant more to her than anyone else on
earth, but it is hardly possible, in the light of the way she poured
out her soul to Vicky, to accept her assertion uncritically.

During the Queen's lifetime, the public was nurtured on the theory
that nothing ever ruffled her domestic harmony: a myth which
blandly ignored the inevitable ups and downs of family life. In fact,
her children fell in and out of favour, and were left in no doubt of
the error of their ways. Moreover, particularly as they grew older
and married, they often took opposite sides in European disputes.
But, generally speaking, they remained happy and affectionate,
although sometimes, of course, their relations came under strain:
especially as they were all forthright characters. Some people thought
that the Queen was over strict, but she herself said that she loved
her children "*far* too dearly *ever* to wish to see them indulged or
spoilt". In so saying she could plausibly claim the support of the
wisdom of Solomon. When Greville met Lady Lyttelton at Althorp
in 1853, she told him that the Queen was very fond of her children,
"but severe in her manner, and a strict disciplinarian". Even Prince
Albert ventured to suggest that she was mistaken in supposing "that
the function of a mother is to be always correcting, scolding" and
ordering children about. The Prince of Wales in later life told Lady
Augusta Bruce that "we were perhaps a little too much spoken to
or at".

Prince Albert passionately believed in rational education, and
eagerly sought advice from Stockmar. Their position, he warned
the Queen and Prince, was more difficult "than that of any other
parents in the kingdom". It would have been infinitely more con-
ducive to their peace of mind had they heeded Lord Melbourne's
advice: "Be not over solicitous about education. It may be able to
do much, but it does not do so much as is expected from it. It may
mould and direct character, but it rarely alters it." Many of the
Queen's letters suggested that "children are a terrible anxiety and

that the sorrow they cause is far greater than the pleasure they give".
It was not so much physical ills she dreaded for them as "moral".
"The responsibility for these little lent souls is great and indeed none
can take it lightly who feels how important a parent's duty is."

Prince Arthur was always the Queen's favourite son. In 1860 she
told Major Elphinstone, the boy's "Governor", that she had "adored
our little Arthur from the day of his birth". But unhappily there were
times when she regarded the Prince of Wales with "unconquerable
aversion", and she once described Prince Alfred as being "reserved,
touchy, vague and wilful". On the whole, she got on better with
her daughters than her sons. In some moods she insisted that "the
only true happiness in the world" was that of the family circle, but
she was equally capable of deploring the worry children caused and
denouncing their ingratitude. For all that, she was naturally fond of
them, and felt "dreadful" when her nursery was finally broken up.

For many Englishmen the eighteen forties were the most wretched
years of their lives, but for the Queen they were gloriously happy.
In 1843, for example, she remarked in her journal that she had
enjoyed herself so much in London that she regretted having to leave
it, and then, remembering herself, added: "But *where* am I not happy
now?" During a conversation with Her Majesty, Lady Lyttelton let
slip the expression "as happy as a Queen". "Don't correct yourself
Lady Lyttelton," came the instant response, "a Queen *is* a very happy
woman." Just how much she had grown to depend on the Prince
was shown by her dread of the briefest separation. Even after she
had been married for fourteen years, she was greatly distressed not
to be able to accompany him on his visit to Napoleon III in September, 1854. "I confess I am really upset," she wrote to Princess
Augusta, "at the thought of being so long without him." The separation to which she referred lasted for four days.

The Queen was often criticised for her thoughtlessness in removing courtiers from their families, although it was plainly an
occupational hazard. In a sense, one might as well blame the Board
of Admiralty for parting sailors from their wives. "Her Majesty
thinks nothing," protested Greville, "of taking her Ladies from their
husbands for a month together". According to Arthur Ponsonby,
his father, Sir Henry, "never ceased to resent" being separated from
his wife "for weeks and months, year after year". But Sir Henry's
daughter, Magdalen, in her Memoir of her mother, tells a different
story. Not only does she speak of her father's absences from home

as "necessitated" by the exigencies of the Court, but she describes Lady Ponsonby as "receiving frequent invitations to stay at Osborne and Balmoral".

Few previous Sovereigns ever travelled as much as Queen Victoria, whose reign coincided with the greatest revolution in transport the world has ever seen. She travelled by train for the first time on June 13th, 1842, on the Great Western line from Slough to Paddington. Compared with going by road she found the journey "free from dust and crowd and heat", and was "quite charmed by it". Instead of being rattled to pieces, and surrounded by mobs the moment she stopped, she was able to proceed smoothly, speedily and in privacy. She was always nervous of accidents, particularly after one of her doctors was killed when his train was derailed between Wimbledon and Malden, and she gave orders that the royal train was never to go faster than forty miles an hour. Nevertheless, she immediately recognised that a new era had dawned of comfortable, long-distance travel. It would hardly have been possible for her to have spent so much time in the Highlands had it not been for the railway to Aberdeen. When she first read chapter three of Macaulay's History, in which he compared mid-nineteenth-century England with that of the Stuarts, she warmly endorsed his boisterous panegyric of the wonders of modern transport.

In 1842 Queen Victoria suggested that the Navy should provide her with a ship. Prince Albert, at best a hesitant yachtsman, nonetheless took an interest in its design. The *Victoria and Albert*, a twin-masted paddle steamer of some thousand tons, was launched on April 23rd, 1843, the day on which Princess Alice was born. Its first Captain was Lord Adolphus FitzClarence, one of the late King's natural sons. In August, the royal couple joined it for a "marine excursion" down the south coast. The Queen's cabins were "delightfully cool and sweet", but the "smell and heat" in the Household's quarters were "enough to knock one down". Lady Canning complained that after a few days at sea "our dinners grow very bad for wherever we go the shops are shut, and nothing can be had. We have milk from the cow on board, and a sheep was given to the Queen at Portland, but she has taken an affection for it and it is not to be killed as long as she is on board." During the cruise, the Queen came close to provoking a mutiny. On a very hot day, when the sun beat down relentlessly, Charlotte Canning discovered a delightfully shady spot "in a dirty, undignified part of the vessel", close to the cowshed. After she had been there for some time, the Queen decided to join her. Shortly afterwards, Lord Adolphus "perceived a commotion among the men who had just finished their supper. He asked what was the matter; the answer: 'Please, my Lord, the grog tub's jammed.' 'What do you mean?' 'Please, my Lord, Her Majesty's right afore it.' The Queen saw something was wanted and volunteered to move, so it was got out and she sent for some to taste."

In August, 1845, the Queen decided to visit Coburg, her mother's and husband's native land. At Bonn, she was introduced to a number of senior members of the University, "Many of whom had taught my beloved Albert, and spoke with pleasure and pride of my all in all". She also went over the house where the Prince had lived as a student. On their way to Coburg, they travelled up the Rhine, were guests of Frederick William IV, and met Metternich, who was "very amiable", but "laid down the law very much". The Queen was something of an innocent abroad, and was duly astonished by foreign ways. She noted, for instance, that "to hear the people speak German, and to see German soldiers etc. seemed to me so singular". She was utterly overwhelmed by her first sight of the Rhine and insisted on sitting all day in the bow of the steamer which carried her upstream. When the royal party finally reached the Ducal Palace at Coburg, "the staircase was full of cousins", and amongst those gathered to greet her were King Leopold, Queen Louise, and the Duchess of Kent.

During their visit to Coburg, the Queen and Prince slept in the very room at the Rosenau in which Albert had been born. "How happy, how joyful we were," she noted on August 20th, to awake "at the dear Rosenau, my Albert's birthplace, the place he most loves. . . . He was so happy to be here with me. It is like a beautiful dream." Before breakfast, on the first morning of their stay, they explored the attic rooms where Albert and Ernest had spent their youth, and the Queen was intrigued to see that the wallpaper was full of holes from their fencing. The view from the windows reminded her of Blair Atholl. "The same fir wood, only spruce and silver firs – the same wild plants." Somehow, she experienced an indescribable feeling "as if my childhood also had been spent here", and she always thereafter regarded the Rosenau as being her "second home".

During her month's absence the British press berated the Queen for her sentimental journey. *Punch*, which had only been started four years before, scathingly denounced her for unveiling a statue to "an

old, stone-deaf musician, named Beethoven". Certainly, one incident during the visit deserved to be harshly criticised. On August
30th, Ernest II arranged a shooting party in the neighbourhood of
the Rosenau. It took place in the middle of a forest which "reminded
us of Windsor". A pavilion had been erected in the centre of a clearing, from which the ladies could watch the sport, and the gentlemen
take aim. The area was surrounded by a canvas wall, and formed a
kind of corral into which some fifty stags and hinds were driven.
For over two hours the guns blazed away, and the ground was
covered with dead or dying deer. Meanwhile a band played jaunty
martial music to celebrate the gala. The day's "butchery", made
more piteous by the fact that some of the Duke's guests were deplor-
ably bad shots, was hardly a fitting spectacle to set before a Queen;
particularly one who preferred to go hungry than sentence a sheep
to death. When reports of this "brutal and stupid massacre" reached
England, indignation was "universal", and the Queen was blamed
for countenancing the carnage. *The Times* published a lurid account
of dying deer being dragged towards the pavilion so that huntsmen
might slit their throats. *Punch* resorted to doggerel.

> "The Queen sat in her easy chair, and look'd as
>   sweet as honey;
> The Prince was shooting at the deer, in weather
>   bright and sunny;
> The bands were playing Polkas, dress'd in green and
>   golden clothes;
> The Nobles cut the poor deers' throats, and that is all
>   'Punch' knows!"

The fact that the Queen spent a month in Germany before having
ever set foot in Ireland, did not escape comment. Not until August
3rd, 1849, did she disembark at Cove, after a "not very pleasant
voyage" on board the *Victoria and Albert*. During the next ten days
the Queen, Prince Albert, and their four eldest children, visited
Cork, Dublin and Belfast. Everywhere they went they were met
by enthusiastic demonstrations from a people who earlier had been
devastated by famine, and who only the year before had threatened
revolution. Immediately on landing, the Queen re-named Cove
"Queenstown", "in honour of it being the first spot on which I set

foot upon Irish ground". The most "wonderful and striking scene" of the entire visit was the procession from Dublin Station to Phoenix Park. The route was lined with "such masses of human beings, so enthusiastic, so excited, yet such perfect order maintained; then the number of troops, the different bands stationed at certain distances, the waving of hats and handkerchiefs, the bursts of welcome which rent the air, – all made it a never-to-be-forgotten scene; when one reflected how lately the country had been in open revolt and under martial law". As the royal yacht set sail for home, the Queen and Prince stood silhouetted on the paddlebox, "amidst the cheers of thousands and thousands, and salutes from all the ships".

Even Greville was obliged to concede that the Queen had scored a triumph, particularly after Lord Lansdowne assured him that nothing could have surpassed the success of her visit "in every respect; every circumstance favourable, no drawbacks or mistakes, all persons and parties pleased". Prince Albert wrote to Peel from Balmoral to tell him about their "splendid reception", which far surpassed what Sir Robert had told them to expect. "I hear" said the Prince, "that the Irish themselves . . . take pride in the mode in which they expressed their attachment to the throne. . . ." In an earlier letter, he informed his brother, Ernest, that the visit had proved "a real triumph", and had shown "that the country in our kingdom which was considered to be unhealthy (at least as regards loyalty) is as healthy as all the other places". Never again was Monarchy to reach the same peak of popularity in Ireland as in the summer of 1849. But unfortunately the Queen failed to exploit her success, and only returned three times in the remaining fifty-two years of her reign. On each occasion she met with surprising warmth, but her long absences naturally took their toll on the country's loyalty. For one glorious moment it had almost seemed as if her presence could restore harmony to a strife-torn country, but any hope that Ireland might sink its differences with England, or accept a common allegiance to the Crown, could hardly survive the neglect of half a century. It was not her fault that she could not perform miracles, but she might, at least, have tried.

Some time before the Queen actually visited Ireland she played a prominent part in supporting Peel's efforts to solve its intractable problems. In the summer of 1844, when it seemed probable that the Ministers would be forced to resign, she was almost as inconsolable as she had been in 1839 at the prospect of losing Lord Melbourne, and she told King Leopold that it would be a "great calamity" for

Europe if Peel was driven out of office. Nothing, she thought, was more disgraceful or unprincipled than the reckless way in which Disraeli attacked his leader. Not until years later was she prepared to excuse his behaviour by pointing out that he was then "very young, bitterly disappointed, and probably urged on by others". At the time, she could hardly find words to express her indignation at "the handful of foolish *half* 'Puseyite' half 'Young England' people" who attempted to bring down the Government.

Probably nowhere in the world did the clergy possess more influence than in Ireland: hence Peel's decision in 1845 to increase the Government's grant to the Roman Catholic Seminary at Maynooth. The greater their authority the more desirable it was to see they were well educated. His gesture of good will was attacked from all quarters. Presbyterians and Non-conformists protested that the Papists were being granted favours denied to Protestant Dissenters, and Anglicans claimed that the Church was being undermined. What was the point of the Establishment if it did not secure exclusive rights? Gladstone, with bewildering rectitude, appeared to recognise the merits of the proposal, but, nevertheless, resigned because of the views he had once expressed in his book on *Church and State*. The Queen, however, warmly encouraged Peel to persevere with the Bill, in spite of the risk of splitting his party in two. Protestant as she was, she "blushed" for her religion, which showed itself "so void of all right feeling, and so wanting in charity towards wise and enlightened concessions".

Eventually Peel carried the Maynooth Bill in the teeth of a hundred Tory dissidents, but it proved a pyrrhic victory as it helped to break-up his party. The Queen, who had been taught by Prince Albert to regard political detachment as a proof of statesmanship, applauded Sir Robert for preferring the interests of his country to those of his supporters. When she told King Leopold about the battle for the Bill, she referred to it as "one of the greatest measures ever proposed", and spoke of the "manly and noble way" in which Peel had fought against "wicked and blind passions". Her fellow Protestants, she said, had behaved "shockingly", and disgraced the nation by their "narrow-mindedness". So anxious was she to mark her sense of the importance of Peel's reform that she offered him the Garter, a proposal he gratefully declined on the ground that "he sprang from the people, and was essentially of the people". His heart, he assured her, was not set upon honours, and the confidence that Her Majesty had reposed in him was sufficient reward for his services. So far from being offended by his refusal, the Queen regarded it as proof of his integrity.

The failure of the Irish potato crop in 1845 and the ensuing "Great Hunger" finally persuaded Peel to introduce free trade in corn, regardless of the fact that the party he led was committed to protection. The Queen supported Sir Robert, and said that she trusted that none of his colleagues would "prevent him from doing what it is right to do". On January 27th 1846 Prince Albert was present in the Commons when Peel announced his intention to modify the Corn Laws. Lord George Bentinck, who led the Tory revolt against Peel's "apostasy", accused H.R.H. of devious behaviour. "If," he suggested, "so humble an individual as myself might be permitted to whisper a word in the ear of that illustrious and royal personage, who, as he stands nearest, so is he justly dearest to Her who sits upon the throne, I would take leave to say that I cannot but think he listened to ill advice when, on the first night of this great discussion, he allowed himself to be seduced by the first Minister of the Crown, to come down to this House to usher in, to give éclat, and, as it were, by reflection from the Queen, to give the semblance of a personal sanction of Her Majesty to a measure, which, be it for good or evil, a great majority of the landed aristocracy of England, of Scotland, and of Ireland, imagine fraught with deep injury, if not ruin, to them. . . ." The Queen was exceedingly displeased by Bentinck's outspoken criticism. What right, she demanded, had "gentlemen who did nothing but hunt all day", and drink "claret and port all night", to pronounce on such questions? The Prince never again ventured to attend a debate, although he and the Queen kept a watchful eye on the Commons. When they read Disraeli's attacks on his erstwhile leader, they looked wistfully in the direction of the Tower. The more desperate the struggle became, the more the Queen urged Peel to stand his ground, assuring him that "what was so just and wise" must ultimately "succeed".

The very day when the Bill to repeal the Corn Laws finally passed in the Lords, the Tory rebels won their revenge by bringing down the Government. They did so by voting with the Whigs against the second reading of a Coercion Bill for Ireland. Peel's letter of resignation reached the Queen while she was playing with her children on the beach at Osborne. She was greatly distressed, but accepted the blow philosophically. Politics now took "second place" to her "happy and blessed" family life. On July 1st, she wrote to Sir Robert "expressing her *deep* concern at losing his services, which she regrets as much for the country as for herself and the Prince". She spoke of him as "a kind and true friend", whom she would always regard with "the greatest esteem". The open support she gave to the anti-Corn Law campaign antagonised the landed gentry. By the same token, it helped to identify her with the middle class, who hoped that cheap food would help to keep down wages. Whatever else the Bill achieved, one thing is certain: the Tories were fatally divided between those, like Gladstone and Aberdeen, who still remained loyal to Peel; and those like Disraeli and Bentinck, who transferred their allegiance to Stanley. For the next twenty years Britain was governed by a series of coalitions.

Queen Victoria's political development followed the traditional route from left to right. She began her reign as a Whig like her mother and father. Next, she became a disciple of Peel, under Prince Albert's influence: a shift of allegiance made easier by the fact that his policies were so liberal. Finally, she succumbed to Disraeli's spell and became a Tory Imperialist, although to the end of her days she chose to describe herself as "liberal" in a non-party sense of the term. Her political odyssey took precisely the opposite direction to that of Gladstone, who began his career as "the rising hope of those stern and unbending Tories", became an ardent Peelite, and then drifted ever more to the left.

Peel's successor was Lord John Russell, who after winning a general election in 1847 remained Prime Minister until 1852. Lord John, the third son of the sixth Duke of Bedford, was a quintessential Whig, whose ancestors played a prominent part in deposing James II. He was a frail, dishevelled little man, who only weighed eight stone, and was, if anything, smaller than the Queen. He also resembled her in being exceedingly obstinate. Possessing, as he did, "a strong, narrow character, fortified by unhesitating self-confidence which was the inheritance of every member of the august house of Russell", there was nothing he was not prepared to undertake. "He would perform the operation for the stone – build St Peter's – or assume, with or without ten minutes' notice, the command of the Channel Fleet: and no one would discover by his manner that the patient had died, the Church tumbled down and the Channel Fleet had been knocked to atoms." The Queen thought Russell was far too partisan and far too weak in asserting his authority. Moreover, she found him lacking in charm and deficient in social graces. "He would be better company," she once said, "if he had a third subject; for he was interested in nothing except the Constitution of 1688 and himself." Without being positively insolent, he contrived to convey a patrician disdain for the flummery of the Court.

The Queen took a very much loftier view of her sacred office than that of her Prime Minister. She maintained, for example, that Hallam's *Constitutional History* was "too Republican" in that he claimed that the source of the Sovereign's power derived solely from the people. Lord Esher maintained that she saw her royal authority as deriving directly from God, and Lady Ponsonby spoke of her sense of divine mission. At the height of the Chartist threat in 1848, she told Lord John that "Revolutions are always bad for the Country", and caused "untold misery to the people". The interests of society were best served by "Obedience to the laws and to the Sovereign", which, in fact, was "obedience to a higher Power, divinely instituted for the good of the people". It was precisely such language which persuaded Edward Russell in the seventeenth century to invite William of Orange to become King. Stockmar was partly to blame for persuading the Queen to exaggerate her powers. Her position, he once told her, was that "of a permanent Premier who takes rank above the temporary head of the Cabinet", who "is and can be nothing else but the Chief of the Party then in power". He further encouraged her to believe that the rights of the Crown were continually being "menaced". The Whigs, he said, were mostly "unconscious Republicans who stand in the same relation to the Throne as the wolf does to the lamb". As for the Tories, they failed to live up to their principles, and proved themselves maladroit in defence of the Crown. Ever since 1830 the notion had gained ground "that the King, in the view of the law, is nothing but a mandarin figure, which has to nod its head in assent, or shake it in denial, as the Minister pleases". Under these circumstances, "No opportunity should be let slip of vindicating the legitimate position of the Crown". Stockmar's interpretation of British history was derived too much from books and was largely a caricature. But, above all, it was scarcely language to use to the Queen who was only too anxious to fight for her rights: real or imagined.

The long struggle for power between Parliament and the Crown which began in the reign of Elizabeth had not finally been resolved in 1688, and continued in muted form in the nineteenth century.

There were still vestigial prerogatives, especially relating to the
Army, which came under constant attack. Naturally the Queen had
a vested interest in preserving her royal powers, and was "determined to hand on to her successors, unimpaired and undiminished,
all the rights and privileges she had acquired at her accession".
Throughout her reign she fought an heroic battle in defence of her
rights. In 1874 she told W.E. Forster, then Minister for Education,
that "No one can be more *truly* liberal at heart than the Queen is,
but she also thinks, that the great *principles* of the *Constitution* of this
great country ought to be maintained and preserved and that too many
alterations and changes should be avoided". "There never was a
sovereign," Disraeli once told his constituents, "more jealous, or
more wisely jealous of the prerogatives which the Constitution has
allotted to her, because she believes that they are for the welfare of
her people." But not everyone joined in this chorus of praise, and
Lord Shaftesbury went so far as to call her "our most *unconstitutional*
Queen".

In practice, the question whether or not the Queen conducted
herself constitutionally was largely academic, partly because her prerogatives were imprecisely defined, and partly because what actually
mattered was what she could get away with. The Victorians persuaded themselves that the Revolution of 1688 had virtually put an
end to royal power, regardless of Dunning's famous motion in 1780
that "The power of the Crown has increased, is increasing, and ought
to be diminished". Almost all nineteenth-century constitutional text
books implied that the Queen was a cipher. Anson in his *Law and
Custom of the Constitution*, published in 1886, described her as
invariably accepting "the decision of the country, as shown by a
general election or a vote in the House of Commons". Nothing, in
fact, could be further from the truth, and Gladstone must have smiled
ruefully at such nonsense. Had Anson forgotten that in 1839 she had
insisted upon retaining the services of Lord Melbourne in the teeth
of a Commons majority? His portrait of Queen Victoria owed more
to wishful thinking than to his flesh and blood Sovereign. That he
could write as he did without being contradicted was a tribute to the
loyalty of the Establishment.

Those who encountered the Queen in her more imperious moods
would have found it hard to believe that she harboured misgivings
about her role in the State. Yet she repeatedly pointed out the
anomaly of the Sovereign being a woman. In 1852 she told King

Leopold, "Albert grows daily fonder and fonder of politics and business, and is so wonderfully *fit* for both – such perspicacity and such *courage* – and I grow daily to dislike them both more and more . . . *We women*, if we *are* to be *good* women, *feminine* and *amiable* and *domestic*, are *not fitted to reign*, at least it is contre gré".

There could be few more compelling arguments for feminism than the Queen's outstanding capacity for business, in spite of her own belief that a woman's place was primarily in the home. But nothing could persuade her that campaigns for women's rights were not "dangerous, and unchristian and unnatural". In 1870 she told Gladstone, "The Queen is a woman herself and knows what an anomaly her own position is . . . let women be what God intended; a helpmate for a man – but with totally different duties and vocations". Such was her horror at the "mad, wicked folly of 'women's rights'" that she urged Sir Theodore Martin to write an article denouncing efforts to promote them. "It is a subject," she told him, "which makes the Queen so furious that she cannot contain herself." As if to prove her point, she went on to remark that Lady Amberley – Bertrand Russell's mother and a pioneer of feminism – "ought to get a *good* whipping". The Queen, in common with most of her contemporaries, regarded it as self-evident that "God created men and women different – then let them remain each in their own position". If women were encouraged to "unsex" themselves, they risked becoming "the most hateful, heartless, and disgusting of human beings". In so saying, she presumably had Lady Macbeth in mind as a fearful warning of where feminism might lead. When a committee was set up in 1887 to establish the "Jubilee Institute for Nurses", she insisted that some of its members must be men, as "a group of women is most useless". It is difficult to account for the intensity of the Queen's disdain for feminism. Possibly her admiration for Prince Albert, and her deference to his opinions, persuaded her to regard their marriage as conforming to an ideal, which God had decreed as a model for all mankind and which women like Lady Amberley overlooked at their peril.

During the five years of Peel's Ministry, Prince Albert's role as "the Queen's chief counsellor, secretary, and sole confidant, although never formally defined, became understood and accepted" by his colleagues. The ever-increasing strain on the Queen of looking after their children necessarily made her turn more and more to the Prince to carry out her duties. She did so with Peel's full approval, partly because of his high opinion of Albert's grasp and ability. In 1843, shortly after the birth of Princess Alice, the Prince stood in for the Queen at a number of levées, only to be denounced for usurping her prerogative. The Duke and Duchess of Cambridge registered their protest by absenting themselves from Court, much to their niece's fury.

Albert, like Stockmar, was perfectly content to work behind the scenes and let others reap the glory. So much so that the Queen noted in her journal: "He always lets me get the credit for his excellent ideas". Lord John Russell and Lord Lansdowne, when they returned to power, were greatly struck by the change they found in the Prince's position. "Formerly the Queen received her Ministers alone; with her alone they communicated, though of course Albert knew everything; but now the Q and Prince were together, received Lord L and J.R. together, and both of them always said *we* – '*we* think, or wish, to do so and so; what had *we* better do, etc.' He is become so identified with her that they are one person, and as he likes and she dislikes business, it is obvious that while she has the title he is really discharging the functions of the Sovereign." After a few months' experience in office, Lord John described Prince Albert as "an informal but potent member of all Cabinets". Just as Lord Brougham feared, the country had fallen into the hands of "Queen Albertine".

In the spring of 1850, the Duke of Wellington, then almost eighty-two, suggested that it was time for him to resign as Commander-in-Chief, and the Queen invited him to Windsor to discuss his proposal that Prince Albert might succeed him. The Duke told her that "it was of the utmost importance to the stability of the Throne and Constitution, that the command of the Army should remain in the hands of the Sovereign, and not fall into those of the House of Commons". This was precisely her own view, and she never forgot what he said. Prince Albert admitted that it was a tempting offer for a young man, but that he would be "sorry to undertake any duty" which would necessarily absorb so much of his time as to interfere with his "general usefulness to the Queen", who, "as a lady was not able at all times to perform the many duties imposed upon her".

Prince Albert, whose invariable instinct was to work out his thoughts on paper, seized this "peculiarly apt" moment to put his views in writing, and on April 6th sent the Duke a long letter explaining his reasons for declining to succeed him. "I have come to the conclusion," he wrote, "that my decision ought entirely and solely to be guided by the consideration whether it would interfere with or assist my position of consort of the Sovereign." It was his duty, he said, as the Queen's husband, "to sink his *own individual* existence in that of his wife – that he should aim at no power by himself or for himself – should shun all contention – assume no separate responsibility before the public, but make his position entirely part of hers. . . . As the natural head of her family, super-intendent of her household, manager of her private affairs, sole *confidential* adviser in politics, and only assistant in her communications with the officers of the Government, he is, besides, the husband of the Queen, the tutor of the royal children, the private secretary of the sovereign, and her permanent minister." Given this formidable catalogue of responsibilities, he must regretfully "discard the tempting idea of being placed in command of the British Army".

There were times when Prince Albert suspected that nobody other than himself troubled to consider "what really is the position of the husband of a Queen Regnant". In 1854 he reminded Stockmar that when he first came to England he had been met "by this want of knowledge and unwillingness to give a thought to the position of this luckless personage. Peel cut down my income, Wellington refused me my rank, the Royal Family cried out against the Foreign interloper, the Whigs in office were only inclined to concede to me just as much space as I could stand upon. The Constitution is silent as to the Consort of the Queen; – even Blackstone ignores him, and yet there he was, and not to be done without." If somebody wished to pay him a compliment at a public meeting they extolled his "wise abstinence from interfering in political matters", as if the most useful thing he could possibly do was nothing at all: an extraordinary tribute to so obsessive a worker! In reality, of course, he exercised a far greater political influence than any previous Prince Consort. But there was a serious flaw in the way in which he perceived his role as the Queen's "permanent minister", for while ministers are "responsible" to Parliament, he was answerable only to his wife.

Nineteenth-century politicians were remarkably adept at ignoring pressing problems, such as the revolutionary transformation in the way of life of the working people of England. In less than fifty years, a predominantly rural population, principally earning a living from farming, was turned into an overwhelmingly urban society employed in mines and factories. It was the greatest change in man's mode of existence since he ceased to be nomadic. Such momentous events could not be accomplished painlessly. Towards the end of Queen Victoria's reign Governments began to accept responsibility for the welfare of the poor, but earlier on, the philosophy of laisser faire was made an excuse for doing nothing. Even an establishment figure like Greville glimpsed the awful truth that "the whole fabric of this gorgeous society" rested on a "rotten foundation . . . of misery and distress", depending, as it did, "upon thousands of human beings reduced to the lowest stage of moral and physical degradation, with no more of the necessities of life than serve to keep body and soul together". "Is it possible," he asked, "for any country to be considered in a healthy condition . . . when the extremes prevail of the most unbounded luxury and enjoyment and the most dreadful privation and suffering?"

Prince Albert was a good deal more anxious about the hardships of working people than most Ministers, and the Queen shared his concern. In March, 1848, both Claremont and Buckingham Palace were crowded with royal refugees. The Queen and Prince listened open-mouthed to the terrifying tales these fugitives told of narrow escapes from bestial mobs, of red flags fluttering over their palaces, and of how they had taken ship to England with just enough money to pay their passage. The nursery filled up with distant cousins, dressed in Vicky and Bertie's clothes; and inevitably everyone asked themselves the question: "Could the same thing happen in 'England's green and pleasant land'?"

Ever since the repeal of the Corn Laws, working class agitation concentrated on petitioning Parliament for effective representation. The movement began in 1839 with what became known as the "People's Charter", which demanded that working men should be given a vote. At first, the Chartists proposed to rely solely on "moral force", but later such leaders as Fergus O'Connor advocated violence. Encouraged by the proclamation of the French Republic in 1848, the Chartists planned a monster meeting for April 10th, to be held at Kennington Common, the present site of the Oval. The idea was to hold a great open-air rally, and then to march to the House of Commons with a copy of the Charter endorsed by millions of signatories. Like most protest movements, it attracted an assortment of mischief-makers. So alarmed did the Government become, that it put the Duke of Wellington in command of a considerable force with which to defend the capital. Charles Greville and Louis Bonaparte were among the special constables enrolled to keep the peace. Some nine thousand troops were concealed at strategic points, and four batteries of artillery were carefully positioned to rake the Thames bridges. Several great noblemen summoned their farmhands from the country to defend their London mansions. The Queen, who had just given birth to Princess Louise, succumbed to a temporary bout of post-natal depression. Prince Albert found her in floods of tears, pathetically demanding what was to become of her fortnight-old baby? Soon afterwards, having recovered her self-command, she assured King Leopold: "I was never calmer and quieter and less nervous. *Great* events make me quiet and calm; it is only trifles that irritate my nerves." The Queen, who was not ordinarily one to turn her back on danger, nevertheless agreed to take a holiday at Osborne, and on April 8th the royal family set off for the Isle of Wight.

The great procession to Kennington started at ten in the morning, and six carthorses were required to drag the waggon containing the Chartist petition. This precious burden was accompanied by some fifteen to twenty thousand people, and hardly a dog barked as they marched through the streets. After a number of speeches at Kennington, the procession started off once more towards Westminster amidst such a deluge of rain as to dampen the ardour of the most zealous revolutionary. Soon after midday, Mr Mayne, the Commissioner of Police for the Metropolis, told O'Connor that the procession must not cross the river, but that the petition might be conveyed to the House of Commons in two or three cabs. By 2 p.m. the Government was able to telegraph to the Queen that the Chartists had dispersed peacefully, and that "no disturbance of any kind had taken place and not a soldier had been seen". Next day she told King Leopold that "Thank God! the Chartist Meeting and Procession had turned out a complete failure; the loyalty of the people at large has been very striking, and their indignation at their peace being interfered with by such wanton and worthless men – immense". It was characteristic of her that she was so obsessed by the threat of Chartism that she refused to take its grievances seriously. "The few bad men," Macaulay wrote in the concluding paragraph of his *History of England*, "who longed for licence and plunder have not had the courage to confront for one moment the strength of a loyal nation, rallied in firm array round a parental throne . . .". That was the language the Queen liked to hear, and precisely her own reading of events.

Nine days after the Kennington meeting the Queen invited Lord Ashley to Osborne. "We have sent for you," she explained, "to have your opinion on what we should do in view of the state of affairs to show our interest in the working class." Like Guizot, who thought that England had been saved from revolution by the Evangelical revival, she recognised the part which religion had played in preserving law and order. "Had some talk with Lord Ashley," she wrote in her journal on April 19th, "about the state of the working classes in which he takes such an interest. He said there existed the best disposition among them all, they only needed some comforts and some improvements to render their dwellings more healthy. No Charter was wished for, only sympathy and kind feeling. . . ." The timing of Ashley's visit was, as the Queen said, determined by recent events, but it would be wrong to suppose that her interest in his work was solely inspired by her instinct for self-preservation. When in June 1842 he made a powerful speech denouncing the working conditions of children employed down coal mines, Prince Albert wrote to tell him that he had been "horror stricken by the statements which you have brought before the Country", and he prayed that "God's blessing" would support him in his "arduous and glorious task . . . I have no doubt that the whole country must be with you – at all events, I can assure you the Queen is, whom your statements have filled with the deepest sympathy".

On the morning of April 20th 1848, the Prince and Ashley took a long walk in the grounds of Osborne and discussed "the state of the nation". The Prince, Ashley said, should put himself "at the head of all social movements in art and science, and especially of those movements as they bear upon the poor, and thus show the interest felt by Royalty in the happiness of the Kingdom". It was agreed, as a start, that Ashley would accompany H.R.H. on a visit to slum tenements in the vicinity of the Strand, and then take the chair at a meeting of the "Labourer's Friend Society", soon to become known as "The Society for Improving the Condition of the Labouring Classes". Russell raised every sort of objection to the plan, but the Prince insisted that it was essential for him to demonstrate publicly that the royal family was anxious about the welfare of working people, and "ready to co-operate for the amelioration of their condition". Only if he seized every possible opportunity to express concern and sympathy would the great majority of the Queen's subjects recognise how deeply she felt for them.

On May 18th, Prince Albert paid his planned visit to the slums and was so enthusiastically received that a disgruntled Socialist complained: "If the Prince goes on like this he'll upset our apple-cart". So much for Russell's perspicacity! Afterwards, he took the chair at the meeting in Exeter Hall, and delivered a speech which the Queen had helped him rehearse. In it, he stressed the need for self-help and declared that those who were fortunate enough to "enjoy station, wealth, and education" had a peculiar duty to support philanthropic schemes to improve the lot of the labouring classes. Not satisfied with a few grandiloquent platitudes, he bombarded the Prime Minister with a mass of facts and figures in the vain hope of stirring him into action. "I think the Government," he told him, "is bound to do what it can to help the working class over the present moment of distress." Prince Albert disclaimed any wish "to follow Louis Blanc in his system of *organisation du travail*" (state-sponsored employment), but he hardly thought it appropriate to reduce government contracts, when "the number of workmen of all trades out of employment is *very* large". Nor did he think it right to discharge several hundred workmen at Westminster Palace simply to placate a clamour for economy. "Surely this is not the moment for the tax-payers to economise upon the working classes!" The Prince's enemies were inclined to dismiss his proposals as dangerously radical, but, in fact, his political philosophy owed more to benevolent paternalism than Louis Blanc. Besides, as he once remarked, "If caring for those who could not care for themselves was socialism he was all for it".

Florshütz recalled that even as a boy Prince Albert was moved by an "eager desire to do good and assist others", and Lady Ponsonby spoke of the way he was deeply pained "by the misery of other people's lives". Both he and the Queen were swept along by the tide of evangelical "good works" and "practical Christianity". Throughout his public career he waged war on poverty, malnutrition and bad housing; and was especially concerned to improve the recreation of working people, who "had most of the toil, and least of the enjoyments of this world". Nobody with a plan for a Mechanics' Institute, a Reading-room, a Public Library, a Working Man's Club, a Park, or a "Coffee Palace", sought his help in vain. But, above all, he believed that good housing was essential to health and happiness, and spent much of his time on improving artisans' dwellings. In 1851 he designed two model houses for the use of working men's families, and built them outside the Crystal Palace as part of the Great Exhibition. Nor was he slow to practise what he preached. Many of the cottages he built on the royal estates survive to this day as memorials to his tireless zeal for reform. Sir Edwin Chadwick maintained that "if all the cottage property in the United Kingdom", was kept "in the same condition as that of Her Majesty and the Prince Consort", the death-rate would be reduced by "nearly one-half".

Naturally the Queen was deeply influenced by Prince Albert's charitable ideas, but the moment demand for change became too vociferous she tended to take fright. So long as reforms were advocated sedately she did not object to discreet tinkering, but the moment she thought that society was threatened she went over to the Establishment. At the time of the "Great Hunger", for instance, she deeply sympathised with the privations of her Irish subjects, and urged Peel to abolish the duty on corn to mitigate their suffering. But in 1848, when the first mutterings of revolution were heard across the Channel, she became so alarmed by the "insubordination of the poor", that she refused to acknowledge their grievances. Nevertheless, she felt keenly for distress on her own doorstep, and in 1865 told a friend: "more than ever do I long to lead a private life tending the poor and sick". Arthur Helps, in his preface to the published *Leaves from the Journal of Our Life in the Highlands*, proclaimed that nobody wished more ardently than Her Majesty, for a "gradual blending together of all classes – caused by a full community of interests, a constant interchange of good offices, and a kindly respect felt and expressed by each class to all its brethren in the great brotherhood that forms a nation". When she learned of Dickens's death in 1870, she noted that "He had a large, loving mind and the strongest sympathy with the poorest classes. He felt sure that a better feeling, and much greater union of classes would take place in time. And I pray earnestly it may." Genuine as her concern undoubtedly was, she tended to visualise a somewhat one-sided contract, in which the rich retained the blessings of prosperity while the poor good-naturedly acquiesced in their meagre stake in the spoils.

The Queen shared Prince Albert's concern for housing, recognising, as he did, the vital part of the home in family life. Slow, as she usually was, to contemplate state intervention, she was willing to make an exception of slum clearance. On one occasion she consulted an East-End clergyman about the horrors of overcrowding, who told her that sometimes as many as seven people shared a single bed. "Had I been one of them," she replied, "I would have slept on the floor." The Queen's children were taught to share her concern for the working class. The Prince of Wales played a prominent part in a Royal Commission on Housing and Alice devoted her life to charitable works. Amongst other things, she accompanied Octavia Hill in her forays into the slums, and translated her book *On the Homes of the London Poor* into German.

The Queen showed more concern for her subjects than many of her Prime Ministers. In 1866 she wrote to George Peabody, the great American philanthropist, to thank him for the "more than princely munificence by which he sought to relieve the wants of the poorer class of her subjects residing in London", and to mark her feeling "by asking him to accept a miniature portrait of herself". He replied with an equally generous tribute, saying how greatly he valued the "appro-bation of the Queen of England, whose whole life had shown that her exalted station had in no degree diminished her sympathy with the humblest of her subjects". The Queen's compassion, like everything else about her, rang as true as a bell. When Gladstone died, Harriet Phipps asked her if she intended to write to Mrs Gladstone. "No," she said, "I did not like the man. How can I say I am sorry when I am not?" It was typical of her to refuse to profess what she did not believe, but it was equally characteristic that she eventually found a form of words to express her condolences. Her sympathy for widows came straight from a stricken heart and she shared their suffering and sorrow.

The most celebrated of Prince Albert's schemes to promote the welfare of working people was the Great Exhibition of 1851. The Queen was convinced that it was entirely her husband's brainchild. Be that as it may, he was largely responsible for its enormous success. He broached the idea with Peel in the summer of 1849, and from that moment on collaborated with Henry Cole to make his dream come true. Cole was a man of explosive energy and organising genius. When matters began to flag the Prince would say, "We must have steam, send for Cole". Among his many achievements were the establishment of the Public Record Office, the inauguration of the penny post with Roland Hill, and publishing the first Christmas Card. In the early Victorian age, before the establishment of a mass-ive state bureaucracy, it was possible for entrepreneurs to achieve miracles with minimal resources.

Prince Albert believed it was "England's mission . . . to put herself at the head of the diffusion of civilisation and the attainment of liberty". On March 21st, 1850, he told an audience at the Mansion House that he foresaw a favourable prospect for "the Unity of Mankind", made possible by railways, telegraphs, and ocean-going steamships. It was his prayer, he said, that the Exhibition would play a part in bringing the nations together in brotherly love. In fact, the decade proved one of "blood and iron". Between 1853 and 1871 a succession of wars shattered Cobden's dreams and showed that free trade was no guarantee of peace. One of the Prince's more modest aims was to help working people appreciate beauty wherever it might be found, and "soar to a nobler fuller life . . . on the strong wings of art and science". The ordinary family from Fulham, who pushed through the turnstiles of the Crystal Palace, might suppose they were going to enjoy a happy day's outing amidst a carnival of wonders. But that was not what Prince Albert had in mind. It was term-time, not a holiday, and there were lessons to be learned. The royal pedagogue, spurning "bread and circuses", preferred the lecture-room to a mammoth fairground.

Early in 1850 a Royal Commission was set up with Prince Albert as its chairman. Most of the work was done by the Prince, Cole and Lord Granville, but among its members were Gladstone, Peel, Lord John Russell, Playfair, Sir Charles Lyell, Dilke and Cobden. No decision had been reached by July on a suitable building to house it. At the very last moment, Joseph Paxton, the Duke of Devonshire's gardener, submitted a plan for a gigantic conservatory. It proved to be one of the most innovative buildings of the nineteenth century, infinitely superior to its competitors, and more of a work of art than most of the exhibits. Not only was it light, strong and visually exciting, but it was simple to dismantle and erect. Ruskin described it contemptuously as a "cucumber frame between two chimneys", but the Prince had the sense to recognise a masterpiece. The fact that Paxton possessed no qualifications provoked a storm of protest, but he put up the building within a matter of months in spite of being told that it could not be done. Few things were more remarkable than its manner of construction from prefabricated sections. But then everything about it was novel: the way it was built, the materials used, its enormous size. When finished, it covered sixteen acres of ground, was three times the length of St Paul's Cathedral, contained some 4,500 tons of iron, and almost 300,000 panes of glass, not to mention twenty-four miles of guttering. The Queen was greatly intrigued by the self-taught genius responsible for its design. On one of her numerous visits to the "Crystal Palace", she was amused to hear the Duke of Devonshire's awe-struck tribute: "Fancy one's gardener having done all this". Nor could she refrain from smiling when Paxton got into difficulty with his aitches and began telling her about "hextinct hanimals".

The Crystal Palace contained fourteen thousand displays brought together from every part of the world. The Prince, with his instinct for reducing everything into categories, divided the exhibits into four parts: raw materials (such as the Koh-i-noor diamond), mechanical inventions, manufactures, and works of art. The emphasis throughout was on modernity, indeed part of the point of the Exhibition was to glorify the inventive genius of the age. The diversity of exhibits was both dazzling and bizarre, and the most incongruous of objects might be found in close proximity. Visitors gazed in wonder at powerful steam locomotives, a garden seat hewn out of coal which eventually found its way to Osborne, a stuffed frog holding an umbrella, the three elm trees which Paxton promised not to cut down, and crates of champagne made from fermented rhubarb. It was little wonder that Kingsley dissolved in tears as he surveyed this weird miscellany.

The moment that plans for the Exhibition were announced, a furious hue and cry was raised. *The Times* objected to its being sited in Hyde Park, which it predicted would be turned into a "bivouac of all the vagabonds of London". Sir George Airy, the Astronomer Royal, prophesied that Paxton's building would collapse. Colonel Sibthorp denounced the whole idea as "the greatest imposition ever attempted to be palmed upon the people of this country", and he warned those in the vicinity of the Park to lock up their spoons and daughters. It was alleged that the glass roof would be shattered to pieces by hailstones, and that the exhibits would be obscured by mounds of guano dropped by resident sparrows. No disaster which human ingenuity could conceive appeared improbable to its critics. The Queen sprang to the Prince's defence like an injured lioness at bay, and blamed "soi-disant fashionables", and over-zealous "Protectionists", for spreading "absurd reports of every kind". She was, of course, right in supposing that the Exhibition was likely to be objectionable to Peel's Tory opponents, as they regarded it as a spectacular advertisement for Free Trade.

Prince Albert's patience was sorely tried by incessant opposition, most of which was ludicrous. "Just at present," he wrote in April 1851, "I am more dead than alive from overwork. The opponents of the Exhibition work with might and main to throw all the old women into panic, and to drive myself crazy. The strangers, they give out, are certain to commence a thorough revolution here, to murder Victoria, and myself, and to proclaim the Red Republic in England; the plague is certain to ensue from the confluence of such vast multitudes, and to swallow up those whom the increased price of everything has not already swept away. For all this I am to be responsible. . . ." It is curious how few people appear to have foreseen the actual outcome: a resounding triumph. Even the problem of the sparrows was overcome on the Duke of Wellington's advice: "Try sparrow-hawks Ma'am".

The Queen invited Crown Prince William of Prussia, his wife Augusta, and their son Fritz, to visit the Exhibition. At the last moment, the King of Hanover, more from malice than solicitude, tried to prevent them going, by writing to William's brother, King Frederick William IV, to say that he heard that the Ministers, as well as Prince Albert himself, were "beginning to jibber with anxiety over this rubbishy Exhibition". If they wanted to know the true state of affairs they should read Lord Lyndhurst's speech to the House of Lords in which he exposed "the infamies, plots and menées of the excommunicated of all lands, who are now in London". He concluded his letter by saying, "I am not easily given to panicking, but I confess to you that I would not like anyone belonging to me exposed to the imminent perils of these times. Letters from London tell me that the Ministers will not allow the Queen and the great originator of this folly, Prince Albert, to be in London while the Exhibition is on, and I wonder at William's wishing to go there with his son".

The King of Prussia, thoroughly alarmed by the King of Hanover's letter, wrote to Prince Albert suggesting that it would probably be wisest to postpone his brother's visit. Wearily, the Prince replied that there was not the slightest reason to anticipate risings or "murderous attacks", and he dismissed rumours that the Court had decided to leave London as one of "many inventions concocted by the enemies of our artistic and cultural venture to frighten the public". In his efforts to disabuse the King of his ill-founded fears, the Prince resorted to the argument ad absurdum. "Mathematicians have calculated that the Crystal Palace will blow down in the first strong gale; engineers – that the galleries would crash in and destroy the visitors; political economists have prophesied a scarcity of food in London owing to the vast concourse of people; doctors – that owing to so many races coming in contact with each other, the Black Death of the Middle Ages would make its appearance, as it did after the Crusades; moralists – that England would be infected by all the scourges of the civilised and uncivilised world; theologians – that this second Tower of Babel would draw upon it the vengeance of an offended God." Prince Albert won the day, and the Prussian princes were able to see for themselves how right he had been to scorn the Jeremiahs.

So thoroughly did the Queen identify herself with her husband's great project, that she often accompanied him to the building site in Hyde Park to see how work was progressing. In all, she visited the Exhibition some forty times. "Poor Albert," she thought, was "terribly fagged" by a constant bombardment of questions, which he took with unfailing good humour. "Great as is his triumph, glorious as is his name, he never says a word about it; but labours to the last, feeling quietly satisfied in the country's glory."

Even on the morning of May 1st, the great opening day, much remained to be done, and half an hour before the royal party arrived, Lord Granville was seen with a broom in his hand clearing the dais of rubbish. As far as the Queen was concerned it was one of the most thrilling days of her life. "The great event has taken place," she wrote excitedly, and turned out be "a complete and beautiful triumph – a glorious and touching sight, one which I shall ever be proud of for my beloved Albert and my Country. . . . Yes! it is a day which makes my heart swell with pride and glory and thankfulness!" She set off in state from Buckingham Palace at 11.30 in a shower of rain. Both Hyde Park and Green Park "were one densely crowded mass of human beings in the highest good humour and most enthusiastic". Just as she approached the Crystal Palace "the sun shone and gleamed upon the gigantic edifice, upon which the flags of all the Nations were floating". That very morning, as if in anticipation of the moment, Thackeray published a "May Day Ode".

> "As though 'twere by a wizard's rod
> A blazing arch of lucid glass
> Leaps like a fountain from the grass
> To meet the sun."

The Queen's carriage drew up at the entrance to the Exhibition facing Rotten Row. As she entered the building to a flourish of trumpets, she glimpsed a mass of "waving palms, flowers, statues" and "myriads of people filling the galleries and seats around". It took a few moments to form the royal procession, and then Albert led her slowly down the central aisle, "having Vicky at his hand, and Bertie holding mine". The effect was "magical, – so vast, so glorious, so touching". The Queen was more or less oblivious to the "tremendous cheers", the choir of six hundred voices, and the orchestra consisting of two hundred instruments. Her thoughts were focused on the "author of this 'Peace-Festival' which united the industry of all nations of the earth. . . . It was and is a day to live for ever. God bless my dearest Albert, God bless my dearest Country, which has shown itself so great today! One felt so grateful to the great God, who seemed to pervade all and to bless all!" The ceremony, she said, was "a thousand times superior" to the Coronation. When she finally left the building, a group of French visitors shouted "Vive la Reine!" Out of the corner of her eye she noticed Lord Anglesey and the Duke of Wellington walking arm in arm. It was the Duke's eighty-second birthday, and Prince Arthur's first.

On returning to Buckingham Palace, the Queen and Prince went out onto the balcony to acknowledge the cheers of the crowds below: the first occasion on which the royal family ever appeared at that celebrated window. The Queen could hardly contain her pride in her husband, whose name was now "immortalised", and whose success had confounded his critics. What astonished her Prussian guests, who accompanied her to the opening, was the behaviour of the crowds. Not a flower was picked, nor one drunk arrested. But what impressed them most, was the loyalty of Englishmen to the Crown. Only three years before, Prince William had fled from Berlin with an angry mob at his heels, and the King of Hanover had led him to anticipate the same reception in London. Instead, he had been driven through miles of cheering crowds anxious to show their allegiance.

The Queen so greatly enjoyed her frequent visits to the Exhibition that she was eager to share its delights with others. She arranged, for example, for John Grant, the head ghillie at Balmoral, to travel to London to savour its wonders. "It was quite a pleasure," she noted, "to see his honest weather beaten face again, as quiet, demure, and plain spoken as usual, in spite of all the novelties around him."

The Queen paid her last visit to the Exhibition on October 14th, the day before it closed. The canvas, she found, was very dirty, the curtains faded, and other things "very much soiled, still the effect is fresh and new as ever, and most beautiful." As she left the building, feeling very melancholy, she caught a glimpse of Mary Kerynack who had walked all the way from Cornwall to see the Crystal Palace.

The Exhibition proved a fabulous success and attracted over six million visitors in five and a half months. Every day, crowded excursion trains steamed into London with fresh hordes of pilgrims. How far it succeeded in fulfilling the Prince's aim of "elevating" the public mind it is impossible to tell; but very few Englishmen left the Crystal Palace without a feeling of relief that "in spite of all temptations to belong to other nations" they were subjects of the Queen. The Exhibition also drove home with spectacular force how rich in resources the British Empire was. "The awe inspiring majesty of the Crystal Palace in 1851 was the first step along the road of imperialist expansion – from Rotten Row to Majuba Hill, Omdurman and Mafeking." Thackeray, in his May Day Ode, described the Queen of "innumerable realms" bidding "the sons of all the earth" bow down before her. This somewhat fanciful conceit sounded a note which Kipling later struck with cruder stridency.

The Prince persuaded his fellow commissioners and the Government of the day to use the profits of the Exhibition to purchase some thirty acres of land in Kensington Gore and make the area a centre of art and science. He visualised four types of Institutions, corresponding to his four categories of exhibits: raw materials, machinery, manufactures and the arts. The land was purchased in December 1852, with the help of a grant from the Exchequer, and eventually a number of Colleges and Museums arose on the site, including Imperial College, the Royal College of Music, the Royal College of Science, the Royal School of Mines, the Natural History Museum, the Science Museum, the Victoria and Albert Museum, and the Albert Hall. The Crystal Palace itself was bought by the London, Brighton and South Coast Railway for £70,000 and re-erected at Sydenham. In 1936, the year of the abdication of King Edward VIII, this splendid memorial to his great grandfather was burned to the ground, and such was its funeral pyre that the flames which consumed it lit up the sky of London.

The enormous amount of work which the Exhibition involved seriously damaged Prince Albert's health. He drove himself so hard that he literally made himself sick with worry. By day, he toiled prodigiously, writing letters, giving interviews, chairing committees, drafting memoranda, presiding over public meetings, making speeches, visiting and inspecting. The Queen became anxious as the strain began to tell, and warned Stockmar that the Prince's sleep was "again as bad as ever", and that he looked "very ill of an evening". It was suggested that he should take a brief holiday "for the sake of his health", but he had become so indispensable that Lord Granville assured Grey that "the whole thing would fall to pieces" without him.

Throughout the months that the Crystal Palace remained open, the Queen's mind was a turmoil of pleasure, pride and triumph. The letter she sent King Leopold describing its opening would seem to justify Lytton Strachey's belief that her happiness was "delirious". She described May 1st as "the *greatest* day in our history", which witnessed the "*most* beautiful and *imposing* and *touching* spectacle ever seen". The whole "*great* conception" was Albert's own, and nobody else could have surmounted the obstacles strewn in his path. Only by his "rare qualities of mind and heart", his "self-denial", his "constant wish to work for others", had the miracle been performed. Obviously the Queen was a partial witness, but even Lord John Russell maintained that the Prince had won "imperishable fame" by the grandeur of his conception, and the "zeal, invention and talent" displayed in its execution. Gratified by this generous tribute, the Queen told Russell that it made her immensely happy to "see her beloved husband's name for ever immortalised by the conception of the greatest triumph of peace which the world has ever produced. . . . She feels grateful to Providence to have permitted her to be united to so great, so noble, so excellent a Prince. . . ."

Unfortunately for Albert, just as the work on the Exhibition began, George Anson dropped dead at his wife's feet. "The blow," he told Stockmar, "is painful and the loss immense." The Queen was so upset that "she sobbed and cried all the afternoon". "To see my poor dear Albert's deep distress," she wrote in her journal, "made me wretched, for he loved and valued Anson who was almost the only intimate friend he had in this country, and he mourns for him as a brother." Colonel Grey, a son of the Prime Minister who carried the 1832 Reform Bill, took over as the Prince's private secretary, and Colonel Phipps as treasurer.

In 1850, the royal couple were once more plunged into mourning for the death of Peel. On the afternoon of June 29th, Sir Robert took his customary ride in Hyde Park. After writing his name in the visitor's book at Buckingham Palace, he rode up Constitution Hill in the direction of Apsley House. Suddenly, his horse began to plunge and kick, threw him to the ground and stumbled on top of him. The occupant of a passing carriage immediately put it at his disposal, and he was driven home to his house in Whitehall Gardens. His suffering was so intense that the medical men were unable to make a thorough investigation, but they suspected that a broken rib had penetrated his lung. The bay mare, which was largely to blame for the accident, had been bought for him at Tattersall's a couple of months before, and it later came out that its owner had only sold it because of its bad habits. Throughout that evening, a succession of eminent visitors called to learn the latest news, including Prince Albert, the Duke of Wellington, and Prince George of Cambridge, whose own father was dying. On July 2nd Peel slipped into unconsciousness and the end came shortly before midnight.

Next morning, the road outside Whitehall Gardens was crowded with working people who had come to pay their last respects to the man who gave them cheap bread. The Queen was equally eager to express her "extreme admiration" for Sir Robert, and to pay tribute to his "unbounded *loyalty*, *courage*, patriotism, and high-mindedness". He possessed, furthermore, three qualities which she particularly valued: firm leadership, disdain for party politics, and a certain aloofness from fashionable Society. She only regretted that he had "been *kept down* to *old* Tory principles, for which his mind was too enlightened". The day after he died, Baron Bunsen, Prussia's Plenipotentiary to the Court at St James's, found the Queen "in a constant flood of tears", having "lost not merely a friend but a father". In the last years of her reign, she told Boyd Carpenter, the Bishop of Ripon, that of all her Prime Ministers "the two who held highest place in her mind were Sir Robert Peel and Salisbury". Prince Albert naturally felt Peel's loss "dreadfully", as they shared so much in common and had worked so closely together. Sir Robert had been the first person to make use of the Prince's talents, having recognised him "as one of the most extraordinary young men he had ever met". The Duchess of Kent was abroad at the time of Peel's death, and it fell to her nephew to tell her the sad news. "Since you left us," he wrote, "blow after blow has fallen upon us. . . . And now death has snatched from us Peel, the best of men, our truest friend, the strongest bulwark of the throne, the greatest statesman of his time! You know the whole extent of our loss; and such a frightful death!"

In the autumn of 1852 the Queen and Prince were staying at Alt-na-Giuthasach when they received a report of the death of the Duke of Wellington. For some unknown reason the Queen declined to believe the news, regardless of the fact that the Duke was eighty-two and had suffered more than one stroke. Soon after breakfast on September 16th the royal party set off on an expedition to the Dhu Loch, "one of the severest, wildest spots imaginable". They rode or walked for three or four hours, and then settled down to a picnic luncheon high above Loch Muich. Soon after they had finished, the Queen was handed a packet of letters including one from the Prime Minister, Lord Derby, and another from Lord Charles Wellesley, which contained "confirmation of the fatal news: that *England's*, or rather *Britain's* pride, her glory, her hero, the greatest statesman she ever had produced, was no more! Sad day! Great and irreparable national loss!"

The Queen was consoled by the thought that the Duke had "gone out like a lamp", while "still in the possession of his great mind, and without a long illness. One cannot think of this country without 'The Duke', – our Immortal hero!" Next day, she wrote to King Leopold to tell him that England had lost "the GREATEST man this country ever produced, and the most *devoted* and *loyal* subject, and the staunchest supporter the Crown ever had. He was to us a true, kind friend and most valuable adviser. To think that all this is gone; that this great and Immortal man belongs now to History, and no longer to the present, is a truth which we cannot realise."

The funeral took place on November 18th, amidst an "Empire's lamentation". The streets were lined with dense masses of mourners, many of whom had stood much of the night in the rain. The Queen watched the procession pass down the Mall. As regiment after regiment passed slowly beneath her, their bands playing the Dead March in "Saul" on muffled drums, her eyes were so full of tears that she could hardly make out the great bronze funeral car which carried the mortal remains of the Duke. But what moved her most of all was the sight of his "poor charger", with its master's boots hanging reversed over its saddle. Seldom has there been such a torrent of tributes as followed Wellington to the grave.

The rulers of Europe in the nineteenth century virtually belonged to a single royal family. By the end of her reign, Queen Victoria had become the "Grandmother of Europe", and counted the sovereigns of Belgium, Bulgaria, Denmark, Germany, Greece, Holland, Portugal, Roumania, Russia and Spain among her relations. Naturally therefore she tended to take a more personal interest in foreign affairs than other aspects of Government. Throughout her reign she conducted a prodigious correspondence with an array of uncles, aunts, cousins, daughters, sons-in-law and grandchildren, by means of which she obtained the latest inside information. After she had entertained Napoleon III at Osborne in 1857, Palmerston congratulated her on the success of the Emperor's visit, and remarked that Prince Albert had been in a position to "say many things we cannot." "Very naturally," she replied, surprised that her Prime Minister should have bothered to comment on such a self-evident truth. Who but the Queen could have rebuked her grandson, the Kaiser William II, for speaking ill of Lord Salisbury? Writing to "Dear William" from Balmoral in 1899, she said she was *greatly astonished* by the tone of his comments on her Prime Minister, which she could "only attribute to a temporary irritation", as she did not think he "would otherwise have written in such a manner", and she doubted "whether any Sovereign ever wrote in such terms to another Sovereign, and that Sovereign his own Grandmother".

Until the destruction of the Russian, German and Austrian Empires at the end of the First World War, the rulers of most European States played a prominent role in their country's foreign policy. The Kaiser once boasted to his uncle, Edward VII, that the country "*must* follow me even if I have to 'face the musik'" (sic). Ministers, like Lord Clarendon, thought that the Queen and Prince Albert held "absurdly high notions" of her prerogatives. "They labour," he said, "under the curious mistake that the Foreign Office is their peculiar department and that they have a right to control, if not to direct, the foreign policy of England." This jaundiced but recognisable parody of their views tended to overlook the Queen's undoubted right to be kept fully informed, to be consulted on all matters of consequence, and to be given an opportunity to influence decisions. None of her Ministers challenged these rights in principle, although Palmerston often flouted them in practice.

In her old age, the Queen's experience and prestige were such that successive Governments were increasingly inclined to leave her a wide discretion. Her matriarchal pre-eminence, and her formidable strength of character, could hardly have been diminished by minis-

terial fiat, and nothing a Foreign Secretary could do could stop her
influencing her daughter, the Empress of Germany, or her granddaughter the Tsarina of Russia. Nineteenth-century diplomacy was
mostly conducted in secret, often at family gatherings, and Britain
could hardly compel other countries to act more democratically.
Given the unrivalled awe in which the Queen was held, particularly
in the later years of her reign, Ministers had little alternative but to
concede her the status her fellow Sovereigns accorded her.

Peel's Foreign Secretary, Lord Aberdeen, was so cautious and conciliatory that Palmerston accused him of betraying Britain's interests
in his pursuit of peace. The policies, however, of the Queen and
Prince precisely coincided with those of the Tory Government.
Everybody agreed that the time was ripe to improve relations with
France after several centuries of conflict, and the Queen decided to
visit Louis Philippe. For some time the King's daughter, Queen
Louise of Belgium, had been urging her to meet her father, and the
initiative for this "summit meeting" came from Buckingham Palace
not Downing Street. Many years before, Louis Philippe had become
a close friend of the Duke of Kent, when as Duc d'Orleans he had
fled from France to Canada, and called on his old acquaintance,
Madame Julie de St Laurent. The Duke generously lent him two
hundred pounds, which he could ill afford, and which Louis returned
to the Duchess soon after he was invited to become King of the
French.

In September 1843 the Queen and Prince set sail in the *Victoria and
Albert* to visit King Louis Philippe and Queen Amélie at the Château
d'Eu in Normandy. Although it was supposedly only a family visit,
Aberdeen, and Guizot, the French Prime Minister, were in attendance. It was the first state visit the Queen had paid in her new yacht,
the first time she had set foot in Europe, and the first official visit of
a British Sovereign to France since Henry VIII met Francis I on the
Field of the Cloth of Gold. Among those invited to Eu were two of
the King's daughters: Louise, Queen of the Belgians; and Clémentine, who was married to Prince Augustus, Queen Victoria's and
Prince Albert's first cousin, a son of Duke Ferdinand of Coburg.

The *Victoria and Albert* arrived at Tréport at six in the evening
of September 2nd, and Louis Philippe, effusive and genial as ever,
clambered aboard to welcome his English guests. Soon afterwards,
the royal party was rowed ashore in a state barge, originally made
for Napoleon, with "the Royal Standards of France and England

floating side by side over the Sovereigns of the two Countries". Throughout their stay, the weather was perfect, and Louis Philippe went to endless trouble to entertain his visitors, even sending to England for beer and cheese which he fancied would be to their taste. The Queen enormously enjoyed her five days at Eu, and felt "quite at home" with "this admirable and truly amiable family", whom she described in her journal as "so kind and so delightful, so united that it does one's heart good to see it". The "Citizen King", having lived much of his life in poverty and exile, had learned to live simply. The bourgeois style of the Orleanist Monarchy especially appealed to the Queen who felt at her ease in a circle of persons with whom she could be "on terms of equality and familiarity". For once, she could relax and enjoy herself unrestrainedly. "I feel so gay and happy with these dear people," she wrote on the third day of her visit.

One morning the Queen concealed herself behind a curtain and sketched some French soldiers parading outside her window. On another occasion, she showed Queen Amélie "miniatures of Puss (Vicky) and the Boy (Bertie) which she admired extremely". Twice they went out for picnics in the neighbourhood which were so carefully contrived as to seem almost accidental. The King even arranged for an orchestra from Paris to play to them after dinner. Unfortunately the concert nearly ended in disaster during a solo played on the French horn. Charlotte Canning described the scene in her diary. "In the evening there was an instrumental concert and some solo playing on violoncello, and pianoforte, and on the French horn by a man who had made great discoveries in the power of that instrument – he is able to sound chords 2 or 3 notes at once – somehow it was not pretty and the sounds had the power of making everybody laugh. The Duc de Montpensier had the giggles and it caught from one person to another till all were in tears and the poor performer's sounds became stranger and stranger. I kept grave very long indeed but my lips shook and some very deep notes vanquished me at last. I was very sorry for the poor man, but his back was partly turned and I hope he did not find out, and between each spasm every good natured person called out 'C'est étonnant! Merveilleux!'"

French observers were surprised to find the Queen so gay and vivacious. Whenever they saw her she seemed to be smiling or laughing. Lady Canning described her at Eu as being "as amused as a child could be". She retained her simple sense of fun to the very end of her life. In 1900 she confessed that her visit to Ireland was "*not*

entirely to please the Irish but because I expect to enjoy myself".
Some two years earlier, Marie Mallet noted in her diary: "I have
nearly finished reading Marian Crawford's 'Corleone' to the Queen
and she has been much thrilled by the story as if she were a girl of
eighteen! It is quite a treat to read to anyone so keen and I have
enjoyed it immensely". It is true that the death of Prince Albert
plunged her into protracted mourning, but even during this melancholy period her old high spirits would often surface; and all her life
she possessed, in Princess Helena's phrase, "a wonderful capacity for
enjoying things".

There were no official discussions during the Queen's visit to Eu,
but Louis Philippe repeatedly told her how fond he had been of her
father and how pleased he was by her visit. It was his dearest wish
to become "closely allied with the English, which would be the
means of preventing war in Europe". More importantly, he told
Lord Aberdeen that he would never allow one of his sons to marry
into the Spanish royal family. The English visit was a triumph for
the Orleanists as for the past thirteen years they had been treated
"as though they were lepers, by all Europe. . . ." The Queen was
exceedingly sad to leave Eu. "At last the *mauvais* moment arrived,"
she wrote in her journal, "and we were obliged to take leave, and
with very great regret." Before they left, bundles of Gobelins tapestries and crates of Sèvres china were packed into the hold of the
royal yacht. "Adieu, Adieu!" shouted the King of the French as the
Victoria and Albert slipped anchor. The Prince later told Stockmar
that "the old King" had been "in the third heaven of rapture, and
the whole family received us with a heartiness, I might say affection
which was quite touching". The visit had given the Queen a taste
for travelling, and within less than a week she crossed the Channel
again to stay with her uncle in Belgium.

In June 1844, the Tsar of Russia, Nicholas I, made a sudden descent
on England. Nobody knew he was coming until two days before he
landed, and the Queen, who gave birth to Alfred in August, disliked
being seen in so late a stage of pregnancy. Nevertheless, she regarded
the Tsar's arrival as "a great compliment", and was much struck by
his "magnificent" bearing and handsome profile. He never really
explained the purpose of his visit, but possibly hoped to detach
England from her growing entente with France. The Queen
described Nicholas as looking unhappy, which she attributed to his
being weighed down by his "immense power and position", and she

could hardly believe that she was not dreaming when he joined the family at their informal breakfast, or when she took a stroll in the grounds of Frogmore "with *this* greatest of all earthly potentates", just as if he had been her half-brother, Charles, or any of her relations. During his stay, Nicholas attended a hastily devised military review, spent a day at Ascot, and was taken to an opera at Covent Garden. In the evenings, a series of banquets was held in his honour in the Waterloo Chamber, conducted, so he said, "on the noblest scale of any court he had seen". This compliment was the more gratifying coming from one accustomed to the splendours of St Petersburg.

The Queen respected the Tsar's "fixed principles of *duty* which *nothing* on earth will make him change", but "clever I do not think him". She came to the conclusion that his education had been sadly neglected, and that his interests were confined to politics, the army, and the pursuit of the opposite sex. She informed her uncle Leopold that Nicholas' "admiration for beauty is very great", and added slyly, he "put me much in mind of you when he drove out with us, looking out for pretty people". But for all his limitations, he won her heart by the lavish praise he bestowed upon her "Angel". "C'est impossible," he declared, "de voir un plus joli garçon; il a l'air si noble et si bon." When he finally took his leave, he told her that he parted with "les sentiments du plus profond dévouement à votre Majesté, et à celui (taking Albert's hand) qui a été comme un frère pour moi". It was music to the Queen's ears to hear the "Tsar of all the Russias" acknowledge the Prince as a "brother", especially after the slights he had been obliged to endure as the younger son of a minor German duke.

Three months after the Tsar's visit, Louis Philippe sailed into Portsmouth. During his stay he visited Twickenham, where he had lived during part of his exile, and the Queen invested him with the Order of the Garter. For the first time the phrase "Entente Cordiale" was used to describe the growing understanding between former enemies. In September 1845 the Queen and Prince paid a second visit to Eu on their way home from Coburg, and the King sent for the Opéra Comique from Paris to help to entertain them. But this time he ventured to mingle business with pleasure and raised the vexed issue of the Queen of Spain's marriage.

When King Ferdinand VII of Spain died in 1832 he left two daughters: his successor, Queen Isabella, born in 1830; and the Infanta,

Louisa Fernanda, born two years later. Until Isabella came of age, her mother, Queen Christina, acted as Regent. The question of finding a husband for Queen Isabella was one which affected the balance of power of Europe. In the eighteenth century the War of the Spanish Succession had been fought over just such an issue. The Treaty of Utrecht of 1713 provided that the Crowns of France and Spain were never again to be united: a principle confirmed by the Quadruple Alliance of 1834, signed by France, Spain, Portugal and Britain. Nevertheless, Louis Philippe secretly nurtured a plan to marry Queen Isabella to her cousin, Francisco, Duke of Cadiz, and her sister, Louisa Fernanda, to his youngest son, the Duc de Montpensier. The advantage of this scheme was that Francisco was reputed to be impotent, in which case Isabella's eventual successor would be a grandchild of Louis Philippe. In short, the King of the French hoped to abolish the Pyrenees as a national frontier and accomplish a feat which had even eluded Napoleon. Queen Victoria was deeply shocked by the proposal. Moreover, she had a candidate of her own, her first cousin, Prince Leopold, the son of her Uncle Ferdinand, and brother of the Prince Consort of Portugal. Understandably, France was as alarmed by the spread of Coburg influence in the Peninsula as were the English by the threat of Orleanist domination.

During the Queen's second visit to Eu an informal conference was held on board the *Victoria and Albert* to discuss the Spanish Marriages, with Guizot and Aberdeen in attendance. The Queen eventually agreed to withdraw support for Prince Leopold, in return for the French King's promise to abandon the claim of the Duc de Montpensier to the hand of the Infanta. She carefully noted the terms of this agreement in her journal on the evening it was reached. "The King told Lord Aberdeen as well as me, he would never hear of Montpensier's marriage with the Infanta of Spain (which they are in a great fright about in England), until it was no longer a political question, *which would be, when the Queen is married, and has children.*" Louis Philippe repeated this assurance to Lord Aberdeen when they later discussed the matter. He openly acknowledged that "he had thought of the Infanta for the Duc de Montpensier; but in order that there should be no cause for jealousy or uneasiness in England, he had resolved not to proceed with the match". The royal couples parted in the confident conviction that the "Entente Cordiale" was already yielding fruit.

Soon after Lord Palmerston returned to the Foreign Office in 1846, he sent a despatch to Sir Henry Bulwer, the British Minister in Madrid, in which he mentioned Prince Leopold as a possible candidate for Queen Isabella's hand. In the context of the note he merely listed the Prince as one of many known claimants. A copy of this despatch was sent to the French Ambassador in London as the "civilest way" of conveying the Government's views. The moment Louis Philippe learned of Palmerston's reference to Leopold, he alleged that the Foreign Secretary had broken the Eu agreement. Grasping this slender pretext to renege on his promises, he sent Palmerston's despatch to Queen Christina, drawing her attention to its violent denunciation of her Government, offering her France's military support in return for her consent to a double marriage between Isabella and the Duke of Cadiz, and Louisa and his son. These negotiations were conducted behind Britain's back, and the Queen was unspeakably shocked by Louis Philippe's duplicity. Nor did Guizot placate her ruffled feelings by representing his treachery as a triumph. The blatant violation of the King's pledges, and the secrecy with which he stabbed England in the back, destroyed the Entente. The marriages were solemnised on October 10th, and three days later the Queen told King Leopold that he could not "represent too strongly" to his father-in-law, her "indignation and sorrow at what had been done". In less than three years Isabella rid herself of her contemptible husband, having somehow contrived to be with child. Queen Victoria – so far from being shocked – thought it "a very good thing", and predicted that "no one will be inclined to cavil as to who was the *real father* considering her very peculiar and distressing marriage – for which *she* poor young creature is in no wise to blame. . . ." Louis Philippe's "triumph" proved short-lived as his government was fatally weakened by losing Britain's support. In 1848 he was driven from his throne and was forced to leave France by the "same door as he had come in": a revolution. Before the year was out, he and his family, including the Infanta, were fugitives at Claremont, which Queen Victoria had magnanimously put at his disposal. So generously did she support the refugees that the Government warned her against antagonising the new rulers of France.

Palmerston first became Foreign Secretary in 1830, a post he held for ten years under Lord Grey and Melbourne. When he returned once more to the Foreign Office in 1846 he was sixty-two and possessed unrivalled experience of diplomacy. During his long years in power, he combined an assertive faith in Britain's right to impose its will on foreigners, with a dogged confidence in his own opinions, and an enthusiasm for popular liberty which he first learned from Canning. Much as he detested tyranny, he was ruthlessly autocratic in running his department. Greville described him as exercising "an absolute despotism at the Foreign Office without the slightest control on the part of his colleagues". Having served under Perceval ten years before the Queen was born, he was notoriously disinclined to submit despatches to the correction of a young lady half his age.

The Queen was richly endowed with "Palmerstonian" instincts and it therefore at first sight seems strange that they quarrelled so fiercely. Many of their disputes arose from Palmerston's truculent practice of issuing instructions to the Chancelleries of Europe without bothering to notify her. The Queen, who at the best of times was jealous of her prerogatives, was driven to distraction when the first she heard of a change in foreign policy was from one of her relations. In 1848, Lady Palmerston, who understood her Sovereign a good deal better than did her husband, reproached him for contradicting Her Majesty "too boldly. You fancy she will hear reason, when in fact all you say only proves to her that you are determined to act on the line she disapproves, and which she still thinks is wrong. . . . You always think you can convince people by arguments, and she has no reflection or sense to feel the force of them."

Above all, it was Prince Albert's influence which prevented the Queen adopting Palmerston's views, many of which might otherwise have appealed to her. In 1883 she sent Lord Granville, then Gladstone's Foreign Secretary, a confidential note in which she said she had no doubt that he felt "as Lord Palmerston did; who with all his many faults, had the honour and power of his country strongly at heart". Prince Albert, however, persuaded her to regard Palmerston's relentless attempts to impose his will upon smaller countries as totally reprehensible. Brought up in a Duchy no larger than many Englishmen's estates, he possessed the instincts of the underdog; whereas the Queen, left to her own devices, was happy enough to be Mistress of half the world. Not until many years after her husband's death was she able to rejoice in her imperial title and Britain's unrivalled ascendancy among nations.

Between 1846 and 1851 Palmerston won virtually all his skirmishes with the royal couple, but finally lost the war. He was helped in his struggle with the Court by his enormous popularity, before which Prime Ministers quailed. Some people even suggested that the Queen regarded it as his principal offence. Moreover, in the last resort, he could always fall back on the ultimate right of governments to impose their will on the Crown. So for five years the Queen and Prince's remonstrances broke over him like "spent spray against a granite cliff".

Much of the animosity between the Queen and Palmerston arose from her dislike of his breezy manner, his tendency to play to the crowd, and his fondness for dallying with the press. Prince Albert, especially, believed that foreign policy was best conducted in private, preferably between Sovereigns, in a dispassionate, rational fashion, and he deplored Palmerston's preference for imprudent public speeches and popular agitations. The struggle between the Queen and her Minister – "Pilgerstein" as she derisively called him – was bitter and protracted. The Prince watched aghast while the Foreign Secretary pursued his policies of intuitive pragmatism and slapdash decision-making. It almost seemed that he took a frivolous pleasure in flirting with danger. It was said of him that it added savour to his cigar to smoke it in a powder-magazine. Albert, whose own approach to problems was intensely earnest, cautious, and logical, found Pilgerstein's behaviour utterly bewildering. On one occasion, the Foreign Secretary went so far as to tell him that "he was a German, and did not understand British interests". The Queen, who tended to regard the most tentative criticism of her husband as tantamount to blasphemy, never forgave the disdain with which Palmerston treated his views.

Divergences of policy played a prominent part in the feuds between Palmerston and the Court. In 1792, while only a boy, he accompanied his father on a Grand Tour of the Continent, and never forgot being forced to flee from Paris when the mob stormed the Tuileries. This traumatic experience was largely responsible for his conviction that the stability of Europe could best be secured by replacing despotic governments with liberal constitutions based on the British model. His apparent indifference to the rights of ruling sovereigns deeply shocked the Queen, especially as so many were her relations. While he was obsessed with remedying misgovernment, she was concerned with the rights of ruling dynasties. Moreover, she was quick to recognise that it was totally inconsistent to suppress "sedition" in Ireland, and to employ troops against the Chartists, while at the same time rebuking foreign governments for using force to put down insurrections.

There were hardly any subjects in the middle of the nineteenth century upon which the Court and Foreign Office agreed. The Queen and Prince favoured German unification under Frederick William IV, but Palmerston regarded the King of Prussia as a dithering reactionary, and preferred to see the country disunited. The royal pair smiled indulgently on the Habsburgs, while Palmerston was an enthusiastic supporter of the Risorgimento, and anxious to see the Austrians driven from Italy. The Queen inclined to Prussia's claim over the Duchies of Schleswig and Holstein, but the Foreign Secretary championed that of Denmark. Meanwhile, behind the scenes, Stockmar encouraged her to believe that Palmerston was out of his mind, and that she owed it to the country to assert the Crown's "right" to supervise foreign policy.

The Queen's attitude to Palmerston changed three times in less than twenty years. In the early days of her reign he was something of a favourite as he was "always so gay and amusing". Apart from Lord Melbourne, no one did more to initiate her into the intricacies of protocol. When the Whigs resigned in 1839 she told him how much she deplored "losing his valuable services, which he has performed in so admirable a manner and which have so greatly promoted the honour and welfare of this Country in its relations with foreign powers, which will ever be gratefully remembered; as also Lord Palmerston's readiness at all times to serve the Queen". But when he returned to office in 1846, he found her a changed person, principally owing to the influence of Prince Albert. What concerned him most was her evident resolve to assert what Stockmar described as "the right of supervision and control belonging to the Crown in foreign politics". When she first came to the Throne she had been reasonably acquiescent; but now she was captious and defiant. However, in 1855 she changed her mind once more when the nation turned to Palmerston during the Crimean War as "the pilot to weather the storm". So quick was she to recognise his qualities as a leader, that Clarendon described him as having "put off the old man" and become "a babe of grace".

Russell repeatedly found himself in the unenviable position of being an "umpire between Windsor and Broadlands". Often he was almost as exasperated with his troublesome colleague as she was, but he could not afford to antagonise the most popular of his ministers. Buffeted between the Court and the Foreign Office, he tried to persuade Palmerston to be more deferential and conciliatory, and the

Queen not to risk a showdown. The most frequent of her complaints concerned lack of information. As early as 1841, in the last days of Melbourne's Ministry, she told Palmerston that she feared "there must be some mistake about sending the despatches, as she has not received one box for the last five days, and she fears that if they delay sending them they will send in a day or two (as they often do) such a number at once that she cannot get through them. . . . She has also perceived once or twice that they have sent to her drafts to approve when the originals have already been sent away, which of course renders her doing so useless. Perhaps Lord Palmerston could look into this and rectify these mistakes, which may arise from the quantity of business which has to be transacted". Palmerston's technique when confronted by such a reproach was to apologise profusely, blame his clerks, and carry on as before.

As time passed it became increasingly obvious that Palmerston was incorrigible. When the Queen discovered in 1850 that a draft despatch which Albert had laboriously amended had nevertheless been sent off completely "*unaltered*", she wrote to tell Palmerston plainly "that this must not happen again", and that it was not the first instance of such proceedings. "Lord Palmerston has a perfect right to state to the Queen his reasons for disagreeing with her views, and will always have found her ready to listen to his reasons; but she cannot allow a servant of the Crown and her Minister to act contrary to her orders, and this without her knowledge." For all his bland excuses and his habit of blaming subordinates, Foreign Office archives prove conclusively that he often gave instructions to send despatches abroad knowing perfectly well they had not been shown to the Queen: hence putting her in the position of seeming to sanction policies of which she, in fact, knew nothing.

The Queen made it her practice to consult the Foreign Secretary before corresponding with other Sovereigns, in case she might seem to be acting unconstitutionally. The one exception she made was when writing to close relations. Only too often she felt intensely mortified to be bound by Palmerston's advice. In 1847, for example, the Queen of Portugal, Maria da Gloria, sent her a plaintive appeal for help against the revolutionary Junta which threatened to depose her. When Queen Victoria showed the letter to Palmerston he required her to reply in most unfeeling terms, blaming Diez – a sort of Portuguese Stockmar – for provoking the insurrection. Her own sympathies were entirely with the Portuguese royal family, and nothing would have given her greater pleasure than to send a British squadron up the Tagus to annihilate the rebels: a policy which would normally have commended itself to Palmerston. Later the same year, the King of Prussia instructed his ambassador to St James's, Baron Bunsen, to hand H.M. a letter for her eyes only. When Palmerston heard what had happened, he required the Queen to reply in terms which were a travesty of her sentiments towards Germany. Naturally enough, the episode left her feeling humiliated, for few things exasperated her more than being treated as a cipher, nor could she happily accept the constitutional constraints which compelled her to profess opinions she did not hold. But one consolation was that nobody could prevent Prince Albert from writing on her behalf to whomever he pleased, be it the Pope or Garibaldi. Since the Constitution declined to recognise the existence of a Prince Consort, it could hardly be evoked to censor his correspondence.

For the Queen, the revolutions of 1848 were a dreadful nightmare, threatening the destruction of the monarchies of Europe in an orgy of bloodshed and violence. But Palmerston saw them in a much more favourable light, believing that they heralded enlightenment and liberty. "A disciple of Canning, with an Englishman's contempt and dislike of foreign potentates deep in his heart, the spectacle of the popular uprisings, and of the oppressors bundled ignominiously out of the palaces they had disgraced, gave him unbounded pleasure." While the Queen suspected him of giving covert support to rebels, he saw her as taking the part of tyrants. In 1859 he wrote her a letter in which he defined the issue between them. "The real question," he said, with reference to creating a North Italian Kingdom at the expense of the Habsburg Empire, "is whether a nation belongs to its ruler, or whether the ruler belongs to the nation. The first position is maintained by the despotic sovereigns of Europe, and was the doctrine of the House of Stuart and their adherents. The latter position is the foundation on which the thrones of Great Britain, of France and of Belgium rest." Presumably his purpose in dragging in Charles I and James II was to remind the Queen that their die-hard doctrines had cost both of them their crowns.

So wide was the gulf between the Queen and her Foreign Secretary that she told the Prime Minister in August 1848 that she was "highly indignant at Lord Palmerston's behaviour", and that she would "have no peace of mind" as long as he remained "at the head of the Foreign Office". It was one of the first of numerous appeals to Lord

John to dismiss his troublesome colleague. In September, while he was staying at Balmoral, she broached the subject again, and carefully noted the conversation in her journal. "I said to Lord John Russell, that I must mention to him a subject, which was a serious one, one which I had delayed mentioning for some time, but which I felt I must speak quite openly to him upon now, namely about Lord Palmerston; that I felt really I could hardly go on with him, and that it made me seriously anxious and uneasy for the welfare of the country and for the peace of Europe in general, and that I felt *very* uneasy from one day to another as to what might happen." Lord John acknowledged "the truth of all that I had said", but pleaded that "Palmerston was a very able man" and "entirely master of his office". The Queen replied that he "was distrusted everywhere abroad, which Lord John regretted", and went on to say that she had proof "that he was not always straightforward in his conduct and kept back things which he did not like should be known". Russell was in an intolerable dilemma for he had suffered enough himself from his insubordinate colleague to recognise the force of the Queen's objections, but at the same time he was only too well aware that the Government would disintegrate without him. The Queen consented to let the matter rest, but warned Lord John that some day she might have to tell him that she "could not put up with Lord Palmerston any longer, which might be very disagreeable and awkward".

In 1849 Palmerston diverted a shipment of arms, intended for the Royal Arsenal, to help Garibaldi free Sicily from King Ferdinand of Naples. He did so without consulting his Sovereign, or even informing his colleagues, who first discovered the news from an article in *The Times*. The Queen bitterly complained of having to work with a man in "whom she could not place the slightest confidence, who never dealt fairly towards her, and might at any moment endanger the most vital interests of the country".

The following summer, Prince Albert produced a new line of argument to stir the Prime Minister into action, by resurrecting an ancient scandal. Palmerston, whose promiscuity earned him the nickname "Cupid", was notoriously immoral, and while staying at Windsor as Her Majesty's guest, took a fancy to one of her Ladies-in-Waiting, a Mrs Brand, subsequently Lady Dacre. Never one to cherish an unrequited passion, he decided to visit her in the silent hours of the night. On entering her room, he locked one door and blockaded the other, but somehow his terrified victim avoided his embraces and managed to summon help. Lord Melbourne was "shocked beyond measure" by his brother-in-law's "atrocious attempt" on Mrs Brand's virtue, and protested that nothing would have induced *him* to force his attentions on a woman "against her will". In the end, the matter was hushed up to save the Queen from the scandal. But in 1850 the Prince decided to revive it in the hope of convincing Lord John that he was sheltering a rapist in his Cabinet. On July 11th, he took the Prime Minister aside and told him that reluctant as he was to discuss a matter which he had "studiously kept secret hitherto", it had become his duty to do so, if only to enable Russell to understand "the full extent of the Queen's objections to Lord P, which were connected with her knowledge of Lord P's worthless private character". He then rehearsed the whole sorry story of Palmerston's nocturnal rovings, and ended by asking him: "How could the Queen consent to take a man as her chief adviser and confidential counsellor in all matters of State, religion, society, Court, etc., etc., who as her Secretary of State and while a guest under her roof at Windsor Castle had committed a brutal attack upon one of her Ladies? Had at night by stealth introduced himself into her apartment, barricaded afterwards the door and would have con- summated his fiendish scheme by violence had not the miraculous efforts of his victim saved her?" Lord John agreed that Palmerston had behaved extremely badly, but argued that many years had elapsed since this episode took place, that Palmerston was now a happily married man devoted to his wife, and that the public might think it unjust, and possibly even ridiculous, to dismiss him for such an ancient misdemeanour. Indeed, it could prove a challenging task to form an administration if impeccable conduct was seen as pre- requisite. Gladstone, towards the end of his life, recalling the ten Prime Ministers he had known, admitted that "all but one of them had been adulterous".

On August 12th, the Queen brought matters to a head by sending Russell a memorandum, to be forwarded to Palmerston, which plainly spelled out his duties to the Crown. Part of it followed an earlier paper written by Stockmar; and Albert, as always, helped her to compose it. "The Queen," it began, "thinks it right, in order *to prevent any mistake* for the *future*, shortly to explain *what it is she expects from her Foreign Secretary*. She requires: (1) That he will distinctly state what he proposes in a given case, in order that the Queen may know as distinctly to *what* she has given her Royal sanction; (2) Having *once given* her sanction to a measure, that it be not arbitrarily altered or modified by the Minister; such an act she must consider as failing in sincerity towards the Crown, and justly to be visited by the exercise of her Constitutional right of dismissing that Minister. She expects to be kept informed of what passes between him and the Foreign Ministers before important decisions are taken, and to receive the Foreign Despatches in good time . . . before they must be sent off."

Russell at first believed that Palmerston would resign on receiving the Queen's memorandum. But, in fact, he accepted the royal terms without so much as a murmur. Indeed, he assured Lord John that he had taken a copy of the Queen's memorandum and would "not fail to attend to the directions which it contains". On August 4th he asked to see Prince Albert, who described him as "very much agitated". It was the first time the Prince had ever seen him without "a bland smile on his face" and a jaunty spring to his step. During the interview, he denied that "he had wanted in respect to the Queen, whom he had every reason to respect as his sovereign and as a woman whose virtue he admired and to whom he was bound by every tie of duty and gratitude". The Prince listened gravely to the old statesman's excuses, and thought him so low as almost to pity him, but he could not forbear to "remind him of the innumerable complaints and remonstrances which the Queen had to make these last years", and to point out that it was intolerable that she was so often kept in the dark. But contrite as Palmerston seemed, and for all his crocodile tears, nothing he subsequently did showed the slightest sign of amendment.

The battles between Palmerston and the Court reached their climax in 1850 and 1851, over four vexed issues: Don Pacifico, General Haynau, Kossuth, and Napoleon III, each crisis exacerbating the next. Don Pacifico was a Portuguese Jew, but being born in Gibraltar was technically British. In 1847, soon after he arrived in Athens as Portugal's Consul General, his house was burned to the ground by an anti-semitic mob. Understandably enough, he sought reparation in the courts, but improved the occasion by presenting a demand for over £80,000 damages. It should be remembered that Osborne had only cost the Queen some £26,000. The Greek Government rejected his lawsuit, and he thereupon turned to Britain for redress. After nearly two years of abortive negotiations, Palmerston lost patience and ordered the Mediterranean Fleet to seize sufficient ships in the Piraeus to meet Don Pacifico's claim. There can seldom have been a more blatant resort to gunboat diplomacy. The sum demanded was plainly preposterous and the method of collecting it outrageous. France immediately withdrew her ambassador, and Russia threatened to do the same. For some weeks Britain hovered on the brink of war, and the Queen blamed Palmerston for threatening the peace of Europe. On June 24th, Palmerston defended his conduct in one of the most compelling speeches heard in the Commons, which ended with a triumphant peroration in which he reminded the House that "as the Roman in days of old, held himself free from indignity when he could say 'civis Romanus sum', so also a British subject, in whatever land he may be, shall feel confident that the watchful eye and the strong arm of England will protect him against injustice and wrong". He sat down to "loud and prolonged cheers", having extricated himself from almost certain defeat with a blend of invective, reason and eloquence. Even the Queen was generous enough to admit that he made "a most brilliant speech". By the same token, she recognised that she would put her Crown at risk if she demanded his dismissal.

The next dispute arose only two months later over the visit of General Haynau to Barclay and Perkins' Brewery, which was on the south bank of the Thames, almost opposite St Paul's, and had once belonged to Dr Johnson's friends, the Thrales. The General had acquired an infamous reputation for his atrocities in Hungary and Italy, and was nicknamed the "Hyaena". During his visit to the Brewery on September 5th, he was met with shouts of "Down with the Austrian Butcher", beaten with brooms, and covered in horse dung. Eventually he managed to take sanctuary in the "George", a nearby public house, where he nursed his bruises and waited to be rescued. Palmerston, whose sympathies were entirely with the draymen, apologised in so perfunctory a manner as to compound the outrage, particularly as he maintained that the General was largely to blame for "having evinced a want of propriety in coming to England at the present moment". The Queen considered that Palmerston's apology was totally inadequate, and refused to believe that the General's assailants had been prompted by "feelings of just and honourable indignation". When she discovered that the objectionable draft had already been sent off, she insisted on recalling it. Palmerston, at first, threatened to resign rather than alter his despatch, but

Lord John, for once, proved adamant, and called his colleague's bluff.

In 1851, when Kossuth, the great Hungarian Patriot, was paying a visit to England, Palmerston received an address from a deputation of Radicals, which described the Emperors of Austria and Russia as "odious and detestable assassins". Far from reproaching them for such scurrilous language, he assured them that he was "extremely flattered and highly gratified" by their generous references to himself. The Queen complained bitterly of the Foreign Secretary's behaviour, and insisted that his silence would inevitably be seen as endorsing attacks on her fellow Sovereigns. But Russell refused to make an issue of his remarks.

By December 1851 Palmerston was like a cat who had already lost eight lives and could not afford to take risks. Nevertheless, he became involved in a crisis over France. In 1832 Napoleon's only son, the "King of Rome", died, leaving his cousin, Louis Napoleon Bonaparte, to claim the imperial title. Louis Napoleon's mother was Hortense Beauharnais, the Empress Josephine's daughter by her first marriage; and his father was Napoleon's younger brother Louis, the erstwhile King of Holland. Soon after Louis Philippe was deposed in 1848, Louis Napoleon was elected President of the Second French Republic. Three years later, on December 2nd, the anniversary of his uncle's victory at Austerlitz, Napoleon scrapped the Constitution by which he had been elected, dissolved the Assembly, and restored universal suffrage. Most Englishmen were horrified by this coup, partly because they feared a revival of French militarism, partly because a considerable number of eminent politicians had been imprisoned without trial, and partly because hundreds of Parisians were butchered in the Boulevard de Montmartre. The very next day, the French ambassador in London, Count Walewski, a natural son of the first Napoleon, gave Palmerston an account of the coup d'état in Paris. Immediately after this interview, he reported to Turgot, Napoleon's Foreign Minister, that Palmerston had expressed his "entire approbation of the act of the President, and his conviction that he could not have acted otherwise". In so saying, he blatantly ignored the Government's policy of remaining "entirely passive".

The British Ambassador in Paris, Lord Normanby, who was Colonel Phipps's eldest brother, was astonished to hear from Turgot that Palmerston had warmly endorsed Napoleon's coup: particularly as he had recently been sent the strictest instructions from the Foreign

Office to remain punctiliously impartial. News of the celebrated interview soon reached the Queen from a letter which Phipps received from his sister-in-law. Her first reaction was disbelief. Even Palmerston, she said, could hardly have been so reckless as to oppose the policy of the Government, and she suggested that the French had probably invented the story. But Lord John Russell confirmed that the rumour was true, and demanded to know from Palmerston why he had failed to consult his colleagues. Lord John, whose patience by now had been "drained to the last drop", had chosen his ground with skill, calculating that the Cabinet would be unlikely to endorse Palmerston's flagrant rejection of its advice, and that his radical supporters had been driven to despair by his staggering volte-face. How, they asked, could their idol, renowned for his zeal for liberty and democracy, suddenly see fit to congratulate a bloodstained tyrant on destroying a Constitution? It need hardly be said that when Russell decided to take issue with his Foreign Secretary, he did so, in part, in response to the Queen's prompting.

Palmerston's attempt to justify his conduct failed to carry conviction, and on December 19th Russell informed him that he had come to the "painful conclusion . . . that the conduct of Foreign Affairs can no longer be left in your hands with advantage to the country". Greville nearly dropped off his chair with astonishment at the news that Palmerston was "actually, really, and irretrievably out". Even the Queen was "quite taken by surprise when we learnt of the *dénouement*". That Christmas was the happiest of her life, and it would be idle to pretend that its celebration was confined to the birth of Christ. "Our relief was great," she wrote in her journal on December 20th, "and we felt quite excited by the news, for our anxiety and worry during the last five years and a half, which was indescribable, was mainly, if not entirely, caused by him! It is a great and unexpected mercy, for I really was on the point of declaring on my part that I could no longer retain Lord Palmerston, which would have been a most disagreeable task, and not unattended with a small amount of danger, in as much as it would have put me too prominently forward." When Palmerston's successor, Lord Granville, was sworn in to replace him, the Queen could hardly describe "the relief of having such a good, amiable honest man, in the place of one whom I grieve to think, I must with truth, consider an unprincipled man". Prince Albert, of course, was every bit as delighted, and told his brother that the year closed with the "happy circumstance, that the man who embittered our whole life" has "cut his throat himself. Give a rogue a rope and he will hang himself, is an old English saying."

The public tended to blame Prince Albert for the Foreign Secretary's dismissal, a view which was shared by Lady Palmerston, who denounced "the old Foreign Conspiracy over again", and suspected that the Orleanist exiles had poisoned the Queen's mind. Russell's behaviour she thought was "really too bad", and she felt sure that Normanby had been "intriguing with Albert and the Queen through Phipps". Lord Shaftesbury was equally convinced that his father-in-law's dismissal was "the result of the long cherished schemes of the Queen and Prince to get rid of Palmerston", and he predicted that "If this inter-meddling of the Royal Pair be not checked, if Albert is to preside at the Foreign Office, it will go hard with the Crown. Albert is utterly unEnglish and the Queen follows him".

In February 1852 the House of Commons debated the circumstances of Palmerston's dismissal, and during the course of his speech Russell read out the Queen's Memorandum of August 12th 1850, which helped to expose the late Foreign Secretary's overbearing conduct. In a sense, as Clarendon argued, Palmerston's foreign policy failed, at least in the short term. After all, for five years he had supported revolutions and encouraged liberty, but by the time he fell from power reactionary governments ruled throughout most of Europe. But one success he did achieve before February was out: he drove Russell from office by defeating his Bill to establish a local, rather than national, Militia. "I have had my tit-for-tat with Lord John," he exclaimed elatedly, "and I turned him out on Friday last."

The next ten months saw a period of Tory Government under the leadership of Derby and Disraeli, and the Queen began to have doubts about a victory which rewarded Peel's opponents. In a sense, of course, nothing could detract from the greatest political triumph of her reign: the overthrow of Palmerston. Most Victorians seemed to suppose that the role of the Crown was largely ceremonial, and it is curious, to say the least, that they continued to cherish this belief "after the Court had openly exercised a power, which in theory it did not possess, to dismiss the most popular politician in the country". Whatever doubts may remain over the heroic struggle between Palmerston and the Court, one thing at least is clear: nobody could afford to treat the Queen as a woman of no importance.

5

"A Foretaste of Heaven"
1851–1861

QUEEN Victoria's powers might be circumscribed, but there were no limits to her influence. In welcoming anaesthesia she set an example which helped put an end to appalling suffering. It might be supposed that so self-evident a blessing was scarcely in need of royal patronage, but, in fact, it encountered such vigorous opposition as to threaten its use in labour. Astonishing as it may seem, Sir Humphry Davy in 1800 published a monograph on Nitrous Oxide ("Laughing Gas") in which he pointed out that it could well be used to eliminate pain in surgery, but nobody thought it worth while to pursue the suggestion further. The subsequent history of the development of anaesthesia reveals only too plainly that the principal obstacle to its introduction was not ignorance of anaesthetic agents – by 1848 the properties of nitrous oxide, ether and chloroform had all been demonstrated – but reluctance to employ them. Important as it was to find effective drugs, it was equally essential to encourage people to use them.

The Queen's fourth son and eighth child was born on April 7th 1853, and named Leopold after his great uncle, the King of the Belgians. Sir James Clark, knowing how acutely his patient dreaded childbearing, invited Dr John Snow, whom he had first met when they were medical students at Edinburgh, to administer chloroform, an anaesthetic discovered in 1847 by their mutual friend, Dr Simpson, now Professor of Obstetrics at their old University. The fact that all three hailed from Scotland must have helped to persuade Her Majesty to put her life in their hands. After all, the use of anaesthesia was still experimental and the Queen was almost as much a pioneer

257

as Simpson himself. Happily she was delighted with the relief it gave her, and referred to her experience of "that blessed chloroform" as "soothing, quieting and delightful beyond measure". It would greatly have helped its proponents if that illustrious testimonial could have been printed on every bottle. Shortly after Prince Leopold's birth, Sir James wrote to inform Dr Simpson that "The Queen had chloroform exhibited to her during her last confinement. . . . It was not at any time given so strongly as to render the Queen insensible. . . . Her Majesty was greatly pleased with the effect, and she certainly never has had a better recovery".

The popular press was dismayed to learn that the Queen had been given chloroform. Who, they demanded, was responsible for using the Queen as a guinea pig? Even the Editor of *The Lancet* waxed eloquent on the dangers of anaesthesia. But the greatest storm of protest was raised by members of the clergy, secure in the knowledge that they would never have to endure the agonies of childbirth. The battle was joined by quoting scripture, a game at which two could play. Their favourite text was verse sixteen of the third chapter of Genesis, in which the Lord God told Eve "in sorrow thou shalt bring forth children". No one, so they claimed, was entitled to defy this injunction. It happened, however, that Simpson was as nimble a biblical scholar as he was dexterous with his forceps, and he referred his critics back to chapter two, verse twenty-one, which relates how "the Lord God caused a deep sleep to fall on Adam" before removing his rib. The Queen refused to concern herself with such absurdities, and in 1857, when her ninth child was due, sent for Dr Snow. Medical questions were not to be resolved by searching scripture. But even if they were, nothing would induce her to believe that a loving and merciful God demanded unnecessary suffering. Besides, she had always thought it unjust that men should enjoy the pleasures of procreation while women endured its pains. Ingenious as Simpson's arguments were, the Queen effectively won his battle for him, for how could her subjects go wrong by following her example? The fact that she asked for chloroform when her last two children were born provided a far more compelling reason in its favour than could ever be found in the use, or abuse, of Old Testament texts.

One afternoon in 1895 the Queen invited her granddaughter, Princess Marie, later Queen of Roumania, to accompany her on her drive through the grounds of Osborne. During the course of their conversation, the Queen suddenly asked her whether she had been

given chloroform when her children were born. Princess Marie confessed that she had, and waited for a reprimand. But instead of a
lecture, the Queen gave an "almost apologetic shrug of her shoulders", and said, "Quite right my dear, I was only given chloroform
with my ninth and last baby. (Presumably a lapse in Marie's memory
rather than the Queen's.) It had, alas! not been discovered before,
and I assure you, my child, I deeply deplore the fact that I had to
bring eight children into the world without its precious aid."

Nobody could accuse the Queen of worshipping her children, and
it was typical of her to describe her infant son, Leopold, as "common
looking" and "ugly". But it soon transpired that he was handicapped
by a far more serious defect: Haemophilia. Practically nothing was
known in the nineteenth century of this rare disease, apart from the
fact that the sufferer's blood refused to clot. Even today the mystery
of its origins remain hidden in the structure of the chromosomes,
although it has now become evident that the deficiency is almost
always inherited through the female line by male descendants, and
that Queen Victoria was an unwitting carrier of the disease. By the
end of the century her children, grandchildren and great grandchildren had innocently contaminated almost all the royal families of
Europe. It is impossible to say whether the defective gene which
wreaked such havoc was a product of spontaneous generation, or a
dormant legacy from the past. The Queen herself firmly maintained
it was "not in the family", and described the malady as "most extraordinary". But once it became recognised that the Prince suffered
from the disease, she naturally lived in "constant fear" that he might
fall and injure himself, and became so desperately overprotective
as to provoke the child to defy her: a sadly familiar syndrome in
haemophilic families.

The Queen's fifth daughter was born at Buckingham Palace on
April 14th 1857 at two in the morning. Princess Beatrice, otherwise
known as "Baby" or "Benjamina", was a strikingly beautiful child,
whom her mother described as "the flower of the flock". The royal
family fell into two age groups: the five eldest born between 1840
and 1846; and the four youngest, the so-called "Osborne set", born
between 1848 and 1857. The Queen and Prince, like George III and
Queen Charlotte, generally got on best with their younger children.
Regardless of the fact that she was thirty-eight when her ninth baby
was born, the Queen "longed for another child". But it seems that
Sir James Clark warned her against a further pregnancy, which led

her to ask him with a sinking heart: "Can I have no more fun in bed?"

Both royal parents made the common mistake of trying to force their children to conform to their own ideals. The example, of course, which the Queen had in mind for her sons was happily in their midst, and she never relinquished the hope that they would follow after their father. Princess Louise, when she was over eighty, expressed her satisfaction that the "habit of moulding all children to the same pattern" had fallen out of fashion. "It was deplorable," she said. "I know because I suffered from it. Nowadays individuality and one's own capabilities are recognised." History repeated itself in the next generation when the Princess Royal struggled in vain to prevent her eldest son (The Kaiser, William II) from developing into a coarse, reactionary Junker. In the end, she acknowledged defeat with all the philosophy at her command, and told her mother that she was trying to "guard against the fault of being annoyed with one's children for not being what one wished and hoped . . .".

In 1850 Lady Lyttelton resigned her post as governess, principally because of a tragedy in her family. Her daughter, Lavinia, had married Gladstone's brother-in-law, Henry Glynne, the rector of Hawarden. The couple were happy enough, but after producing four girls in a row longed for a son. Just as it seemed possible that their wish might be fulfilled, Lavinia died in labour, and Lady Lyttelton decided that she must leave the Court and look after her motherless grandchildren. When her trunks were packed and the time to depart had come, there was hardly a dry eye to be seen "she was so beloved". Fond as the Queen was of "dear Lady Lyttelton", and much as she hated to lose a familiar face, she had always been troubled by her "peculiar" High Church notions, and more recently had begun to suspect that she was a feeble disciplinarian with eccentric views on punishment.

Lady Lyttelton's place was taken by Miss Sarah Hildyard, or "Tilla" as the children preferred to call her. She first joined the royal nursery in 1844, on Stockmar's recommendation. She began life as the daughter of a devout and learned clergyman, and ended her days in the sisterhood of St Catherine. Not only did she possess a fine, unselfish character, but was remarkably well-read, combining an interest in botany and science with a love of history and literature. Prince Albert described her as a "lucky find" – as indeed she was – and the Queen was soon referring to her as "Dear Miss Hildyard", or as "Good Tilla". The job of royal governess was particularly demanding as the children were stubborn and tempestuous. Vicky, with whom "Tilla" was remarkably successful, needed especially skilful handling, as she was astonishingly precocious. In 1865, when Alice heard that Miss Hildyard's health had obliged her to retire, she told the Queen, "I shall never forget what I owe her, and I ever loved her most dearly".

The royal children were encouraged to be tolerant of all religions, and to adopt a broad view of Anglican doctrine. According to David Strauss, possibly the most controversial theologian of the nineteenth century, Prince Albert brought up his eldest daughters to follow critical principles regardless of where they led. Certainly Vicky and Alice were widely renowned for holding unorthodox views. There were few more contentious Anglicans than J. W. Colenso, the Bishop of Natal, who published five formidable volumes on the Pentateuch to prove that the Old Testament was historically unreliable. The consequence was that the Bishop of Cape Town, supported at home by his English colleagues, pronounced Colenso a heretic for questioning the infallibility of the Bible. In 1863, Vicky, who had followed the controversy with mounting indignation, told her mother that it reminded her "of the Middle Ages", and that there was "no nonsense too great for clergymen of all sorts – especially bishops – to talk on this subject; they invite scepticism instead of annihilating it. . . ." The Queen confessed that she had not been following the dispute, but had seen and heard enough "to feel just as you and dear Papa would". The fact that the Princess Royal supported Colenso, and that Princess Alice befriended David Strauss, was regarded as proof of the laxity of their parents.

In 1850 Disraeli picked up an intriguing bit of gossip, which he relayed with considerable relish to Lady Londonderry. He had heard the story from "the highest quarter and in the utmost confidence". It concerned the Prince of Wales's tutor, Henry Birch, "hitherto a prime favourite, and looked upon as a paragon. It seems that Albert, who has imbibed the ultra Lutheran (alias, infidel) doctrines, and holds that all Churches (reformed) are alike, etc., etc., etc., and that ecclesiastical formularies of all kinds ought to be discouraged, signified to Birch, the other day, that *he did not approve of the Prince of Wales being taught the Church catechism*, his R.H. not approving of creeds and all that. Conceive the horror and astonishment of Birch, a very orthodox, if not very high, Churchman at this virtual

abnegation of priestly authority! He at once informed H.R.H. that
he must then resign his post". There followed a week of scenes,
"some very violent", until eventually Birch consented to remain.
The "utmost efforts" were made to suppress the whole "esclandre"
in order to salvage what little remained of Prince Albert's reputation
with the clergy.

Both royal parents agreed that too much religious instruction
could prove its own undoing. When Prince Arthur told the Queen
in 1862 that besides attending Church on Sunday he was also given
an hour of religious instruction, she immediately wrote to his Governor, Major Elphinstone, protesting that Prince Albert had
"objected to this about 2 years ago, and the Queen thinks as the
service is long, a lesson *besides* (which none of the others used to
have) would be better *avoided*". Prince Albert played a prominent
part in founding Wellington College, the Nation's memorial to the
great Duke. From the moment it opened, he kept a vigilant eye on
its Lord's Day observance, and required Sir Charles Phipps to write
to its first "Master", Edward White Benson, requesting him to consider "the mode of spending the Sundays at the College . . . and
to think well whether there may not be excessive employment in
Religious Exercises in the present system". Phipps's eldest son,
"Charlie", was one of the first pupils to be enrolled, and supplied
his father with detailed ammunition, from which it appeared that
the Sunday programme included three Chapel services, Dormitory
Prayers, and two sessions of learning passages from the Bible. "His
Royal Highness" wrote Phipps, with Charlie's warmest endorse-
ment, "had the strongest feelings upon the inexpediency of thus
making the services of the Church and the study of the Bible irksome
to boys." Benson, a future Archbishop, endeavoured to justify his
policy, but without success.

The Queen encouraged her family to take a practical view of
religion, and taught them that "good works" were central to Christianity. In 1871 she explained her views to Vicky in the hope it might
help her to bring up her own children. It was of the first importance,
she said, that princes and princesses should not grow up believing
"that they were of a different flesh and blood to the poor – the
peasants and working classes and servants – and that going amongst
them – as we always did and do – was of such immense benefit to
the character of those who have to reign hereafter. To hear of their
wants and troubles, to minister to them, to look after them and be

kind to them (as you and your brothers and sisters were accustomed to be by good old Tilla) does immense good to the character of children and grown-up people. It is there that you learn lessons of kindness to one another, of patience and endurance and resignation which cannot be found elsewhere".

The Royal Family lived on closer and more affectionate terms with their parents than was usual at the time. While many of their contemporaries were cowed and crushed, on the principle that the young should be "seen and not heard", they were left to develop without undue constraint. The nursery over which Lady Lyttelton presided was more like the floor of the Stock Exchange than a Trappist Monastery. Both the Queen and Prince were determined that their family should have a happier childhood than either of them had known, and the wistful nostalgia with which Vicky and Alice recalled their early lives was a measure of their success. In 1869, after staying with Vicky at Potsdam, Alice told her mother how they had hardly stopped talking about "former happy days", and how she felt sure that "dear Papa and you, if you could ever hear how often, how tenderly, Vicky and I talked of our most beloved parents, and how grateful we are for what they did for us, would in some measure feel repaid for all the trouble we gave, and all the anxiety we caused. I ever look back to my childhood as the happiest time of my life". On another occasion, Alice told the Queen that she had been moved to tears looking back on those "happy, happy days", which she had tried to copy, as far as was practical, in her own children's lives.

Prince Albert has often been misrepresented as a "stern unbending Victorian Paterfamilias", a despot out of the same mould as Elizabeth Barrett's father. But, in fact, he achieved an unusual rapport with his offspring, six of whom were born before he was thirty. Once, Princess Feodore watched him playing with his children and was amused to see him behaving as if he was one of them. On the whole, he exerted a greater influence on his daughters than his sons. Just before Vicky finally left home, she told the Queen that she feared it would kill her "to take leave of dear Papa". As for Alice, she saw him not only as a parent but a "friend and even playfellow". Throughout her life she tried to model herself on her father, and the last words she uttered on her deathbed were "dear Papa".

Towards the end of her reign, it became hard to glimpse the Queen through the mists of mythology swirling around her. Obsequious authors, quick to point out an improving moral, fondly portrayed her as a matchless mother. But Prince Albert judged otherwise, and complained that she treated her children too "aggressively". She was, of course, an exceedingly formidable person, brusque, hot-tempered and censorious, quick to chide and slow to praise. When even Bismarck, the Iron Chancellor, trembled in her presence, it was hardly surprising that her family regarded her with awe. But there was another side to the coin, for she was "devotedly attached" to children, and few things amused her as much as their droll remarks. Like many parents, she was more tolerant of her grandchildren than her own sons and daughters, and so far from objecting to their boisterous ways, once told a relieved parent, "I love to hear the little feet and merry voices above". In the first months of her widowhood, the Queen begged Vicky to allow her daughter, Charlotte, then aged two, to stay with her at Windsor. "I need not tell you that it would be a little light in my darkness, for there is something refreshing, in the midst of misery and anguish like mine, even in an innocent little child."

Critical as the Queen was disposed to be of her family, she was also extremely proud of them, and constantly thanked God when she said her prayers that she was "happy and blessed" in her "home life". Like many shy people, she often preferred to express her feelings on paper. "Far or near," she wrote on Vicky's twentieth birthday, "My love and affection and my solicitude will ever be the same, my beloved Child. God bless you. Ever your devoted Mama." For all her sharp reproofs and caustic criticism, she doted on her children, and bristled in their defence if others dared to attack them. Nor did she ever cease to be concerned over the smallest details of their lives. When the Prince of Wales was over thirty and the father of five children, he set off on a state visit to India. The Queen was so anxious for his welfare that she plagued him with instructions, and worked herself into a frenzy over the question of his diet. Much as she loved her Indian Empire, she remained suspicious of "Bombay Duck". Most people might have supposed that the Prince was perfectly capable of picking his way through a menu without parental guidance. Naturally he ignored his mother's missives, but, nevertheless, was not best pleased when a runner arrived at a jungle camp with a telegram from Balmoral recommending him to stick to bottled water, or to be in bed by ten. Happily such messages were sent in code, but no doubt relieved the tedium of those privileged to decipher them. Yet for all its absurdity there was something rather touching about the Queen's concern.

Almost all the royal children were gifted but the Princess Royal was the most talented of the lot. Prince Albert described her as possessing "a man's head and a child's heart", while Stockmar regarded her as being clever "to the point of genius". She was never exactly beautiful, but few could resist her charm, or her sparkling green eyes and radiant smile. In 1856, Mr Buchanan, the American Minister in London, sat next to her during dinner at Buckingham Palace, and afterwards told Cobden, "he was in raptures about her". Apart from the fact that he found her "the most charming girl he had ever met", she had an "excellent head" and "a heart as big as a mountain". As a child she spent most of her pocket money on books which she devoured rapaciously, and such was the variety of her intellectual interests that in later life she became an impressive authority on architecture, sculpture, painting, economics, history, philosophy and politics. Nor was she backward in cultivating more practical concerns, such as gardening, hospitals, and women's education. But for all her learning, she was no mere blue-stocking, combining her father's brains with her mother's generous heart. Most of Vicky's faults were extensions of her virtues. She was invariably clever but not unfailingly wise, and her judgement was often impulsive. Notoriously tactless, and inclined to lay down the law, she made unnecessary enemies. Nor, as she readily admitted, was her temper a "first rate article". The impression she often gave was of a schooner in full sail with insufficient ballast. She lacked the massive weight of her mother's common sense to ensure that she kept on course.

Soon after Vicky had married and left home, the Queen reminded her what a troublesome girl she had been. She accused her, amongst other things, of being far too argumentative. "A more insubordinate and unequal-tempered child and girl I think I never saw! I must say so, honestly, now, dear. The tone you used to me, you know, shocked all who heard you and . . . the trouble you gave us all was indeed very great." The Queen concluded her critical retrospect by enquiring whether Vicky had conquered her former failings, such as "standing on one leg – the violent laughing – the cramming in eating, the waddling in walking". It did not take long for Vicky to learn that home truths are aptly so described, and that there was no shortage of them at Windsor. "If old Mama has a merit," the Queen remarked, "it is that of truth and the absence of all flattery."

The Royal parents were determined to play a part in their children's education and not leave everything to tutors and governesses. The Queen for a time gave Vicky instruction in history and religion, and in 1855 the Prince lent a hand in her confirmation classes. So wholeheartedly did she subscribe to his advanced religious views that she was later described as "quite Renan" in her thinking. Like her father, she believed that the Church had failed to adjust to the nineteenth century. Science and learning, she proclaimed, were "slowly preparing the ground" for a "New Reformation", and she welcomed attempts, such as that of Strauss, to separate the "purely historical and credible" elements in the Gospel "from all earlier and later embellishments". In 1884, she wrote a remarkable essay on religion in which she argued that "the eternal truths on which Christianity rests are true for ever and for all; the forms they take are endless; their modes of expression vary". Inevitably, the Gospel narratives were written in terms of the cultural outlook of the apostolic age. In so saying, she anticipated an important school of twentieth century theology.

When Vicky was fifteen, Prince Albert began to play a more prominent part in her formal education. For an hour every evening, starting at six, he instructed her in history and politics. No master could have wished for a more willing pupil or more ardent disciple. "To you dear Papa," she told him in 1858, "I owe most in this world. I shall never forget the advice it has been my privilege to hear from you at different times, I treasure your words up in my heart, they will have with God's help an influence on the whole of my life." Some days later, she told her mother that her first reaction to a problem was to ask herself "What would Papa say, What would he think? Dear Papa always has been my oracle." Delighted as the Queen was to hear Albert's praises sung, deep down in the unconscious recesses of her mind she could not but resent the affection he lavished on Vicky, or the fact that he looked to her for intellectual companionship.

If ever there was an inveterate match-maker it was Queen Victoria, who started considering a husband for Vicky before she had even been christened. But she drew the line at insisting upon a match unless those concerned had genuinely fallen in love. As she saw it, it was the duty of parents to ensure the right introductions, but it remained for their children to make the final decision. Her own marriage to Albert was the supreme example of a carefully contrived match which had blossomed into a deep and enduring devotion.

Prince Albert and Stockmar had long dreamed of seeing the independent German states united under the leadership of Prussia. If such a kingdom were ever, in fact, created, it would obviously prove an attractive ally. In 1840, the year Vicky was born, Frederick William IV became King of Prussia. Because his marriage was childless, his brother, Prince William, was next in line to the throne. Prince William was a traditional Prussian reactionary, but his wife, Princess Augusta, came from Saxe Weimar, the most progressive Court in Germany. As a girl she had known Goethe and breathed the spirit of the Enlightenment. Her liberal notions were regarded as highly suspect in Berlin, not least by her husband's family. In 1844 the Queen invited the Crown Prince and his son to visit Windsor, nominally to attend Prince Arthur's christening, but, in fact, to see whether young Prince Frederick William was suitable for Vicky. The Crown Princess strongly favoured the match, but lived in terror that her sister-in-law, Charlotte, who was married to the Tsar, might palm "Fritz" off on some Romanov Grand Duchess.

When the Queen met Prince William for the first time, she took him for a bluff, simple soldier, who appeared to listen spellbound to Albert's plans for the unification of Germany. In fact, he rejected most of Albert's ideas but thought it best not to argue. Barking out orders on a parade ground was more his line than dabbling in dialectic. Prince Albert mistook his silence for consent, and fondly imagined that the Crown Prince was as liberal as his wife. In 1845 the Queen met Augusta for the first time on her way to Coburg and the two became close friends. The Princess was almost the only person not related to the Queen with whom she could talk on equal terms. Early in 1848, the Year of Revolutions, Prince William was forced to seek asylum in England. During the three months he was a guest at Windsor, Albert lectured him on the British Constitution. Soon after it was thought safe for him to go home, he hanged the rebel officers who fell into his clutches. But Albert refused to think ill of William, and clung to his early belief that beneath his harsh exterior there beat a liberal heart.

In 1851 the Queen invited the Crown Prince and his family to the opening of the Great Exhibition. "Fritz" greatly impressed Prince Albert by echoing his mother's views, and the Queen by admiring

her dogs. He intended, he said, to resist "the old traditionary doctrine" of the Junkers. Although he was twenty and Vicky was only
ten, he fell for her flashing eyes, her vivacious smile, and astonishing
conversation. "You cannot form an idea," he said thirty years later,
"what a sweet little thing" the Princess Royal was, "such a childlike
simplicity, combined with a woman's intellect. She seemed almost
too perfect." So deep was the impression she made on him that he
was prepared to wait several years in the hope they might marry.
Naturally, no formal commitment was made, but an understanding
was reached which both families recognised.

Fritz returned home in love with the Queen, with Vicky, and
with England. Foremost amongst the impressions he took back were
memories of listening to Prince Albert's plans for Germany. According to Vicky, he thought her father "the best and wisest man alive",
but what astonished him most was to see so happy a family. The
Queen and Prince were such a devoted couple that it might be supposed they had only just married. Compared with Berlin, the life of
the Court seemed delightfully free and informal. Nor had he ever
before met children on such affectionate terms with their parents. It
was all so unlike the life he knew in Prussia, embittered by constant
feuds and animosity. Four years were to pass before he returned to
England, but he never forgot its beautiful May mornings, or the
wonderfully clever child who might one day become his wife. Meanwhile, he studied the British Constitution, corresponded with Prince
Albert about politics, and exchanged solicitous notes with the Princess Royal.

In September 1855 the Queen invited Fritz to stay at Balmoral,
only five days after the celebrations which greeted the fall of Sebastopol. Vicky by then was almost fifteen and was so fascinating that he
could not sleep for thinking about her. His mind was evidently not
on his stalking as he missed almost every stag he saw. Then, one
evening, Vicky squeezed his hand to show her affection for him. On
September 20th, Fritz plucked up courage to tell the Queen and the
Prince that he wished to belong to their family, that in so saying "he
had the entire concurrence and approval not only of his parents but
of the King", and that Vicky was so adorable that he could not
remain silent. The Queen, who had constantly prayed to hear such
a declaration, burst into tears, and between sobs protested how
happy she was. It was agreed that Fritz must wait until Vicky was
seventeen before formally proposing, but he was permitted to give

her a bracelet as evidence of his devotion. On the afternoon of September 29th an expedition set off from Balmoral to ride to the summit of Craig-na-Ban. Vicky and Fritz began to lag behind, while the Queen and Prince Albert rode on ahead, apparently unaware that the rearguard was straggling. Fritz began to tell Vicky about his native land and his hope that she might one day visit it. Suddenly he noticed a sprig of white heather, stopped his pony, dismounted, picked it, and pressed it into her hand. Towards the end of the ride he repeated "his observation about Prussia; she answered she would be happy to stay there for a year; he added he hoped always, always – on which she became very red – he continued, he hoped he had said nothing which annoyed her – to which she replied 'Oh! no,' – he added might he tell her parents, which she then expressed a wish to do *herself*". When they eventually caught up with the main party, he gave the Queen a meaningful look which told her the deed was done.

That evening, looking "*very* much agitated", Vicky confessed all, assuring her parents that she was "very fond of the Prince" and indeed had always loved him. "We kissed and pressed the poor dear child in our arms," wrote the Queen with breathless ecstasy. Then Fritz appeared, and Vicky hugged him again and again, and her mother would not for "the world have missed so touching and beautiful a sight". That night she could hardly find words to express her gratitude to God for enabling her "to see the happiness of two such dear, pure, young Beings".

Hardly had Fritz returned to Prussia, leaving his heart in the Highlands, than the secret somehow leaked out, and Delane, the editor of *The Times*, published a scathing leader which described Fritz's family as a "paltry dynasty" and Prussia as a "wretched German State". Prince Albert attributed this "infamous" article to the fact that *The Times* was "deeply offended that its permission was not first asked". Most Prussians disliked the match every bit as much as Delane, although some regarded it as a revival of the "Belle Alliance" which had saved Europe from Napoleon. It was furthermore widely believed that the match would offend the Tsar, seeing that England and Russia were still at war. Government circles in Berlin had traditionally tended to look eastwards, and Fritz's family had strong ties with Russia, not least his aunt, the Tsarina. Long before Vicky ever set foot in Germany, most of the Prussian Establishment looked on her as an enemy.

In the first letter the Queen ever sent Fritz, she told him that he would "be almost closer to us parents than our own son", and she signed herself "Ever your most devoted and loving Aunt and friend Victoria". In May 1857 she invited him to Osborne, and he thought Vicky even more beautiful than when they parted in Scotland. Some years later, Fritz complained that the Queen had been far too strict a chaperone. On the rare occasions he was left alone with her daughter, she sat in the next room with the door between them open. Unfortunately, she possessed, in her own phrase, "a particular aversion to being mixed up with *Braustand*" (Betrothal) and invariably felt embarrassed by courting couples. But all the same, she later confessed that perhaps "I was severer than I ought to have been".

The Queen was by nature exceptionally possessive, and admitted to Vicky that she "had to learn that one must put one's maternal feelings aside altogether if one is not to be very jealous". It was bad enough when her sons left home, but it was "nothing to the parting with a daughter; she is gone, as your own child, for ever; she belongs to another. . . ." It was an "awful moment to have to give one's innocent child up to a man", knowing "all that she must go through". The Queen recalled Vicky's last night at home before she and Fritz set sail for Germany. "When we took you to your room, and you cried so much, I said to Papa as we came back 'after all, it is like taking a poor lamb to be sacrificed'. You now know what I meant, dear. . . . It really makes me shudder when I look round at all your sweet, happy, unconscious sisters – and think I must give them up too – one by one!!'"

Soon after Vicky became engaged, her father began to prepare her for the role she should play in Prussia. Much of his advice was more suitable for a future Queen Regnant than a Queen Consort. The German States, he told her, must unite under Prussia and act in alliance with England. The second half of the nineteenth century, he prophesied, would be an era of enlightened liberalism, ever-growing prosperity, and European peace, already foreshadowed by the Great Exhibition and the union of two great Protestant nations in the persons of Vicky and Fritz. It was a noble ambition, but owed more to wishful thinking than reality. So successful was Prince Albert in indoctrinating Vicky that she came to regard it as her sacred mission to propagate his plans in the stony soil of Potsdam.

The authorities in Prussia suggested that the wedding should take place in Berlin, but the Queen dismissed the idea as out of the

question. She always disliked being compared with Queen Elizabeth, but her note to the Foreign Secretary had a distinctly Tudor
ring. "The assumption," she said, "of its being *too much* for a Prince
Royal of Prussia to *come* over to marry *the Princess Royal of Great
Britain* IN England is too *absurd*, to say the least. . . . Whatever may
be the usual practice of Prussian Princes, it is not *every* day that one
marries the eldest daughter of the Queen of England. The question
therefore must be considered as settled and closed. . . ."

The marriage took place on January 25th 1858 in the Chapel Royal
at St James's Palace, where the Queen had married Albert. "I felt,"
she wrote in her journal, "as if I were being married over again
myself, only much more nervous." Before she left Buckingham Palace the Princess Royal was daguerreotyped with her parents, but her
mother trembled so much that her picture came out blurred. Vicky's
brothers were dressed in kilts, and Fritz wore the uniform of a Prussian general. The bride's dress was of white moiré silk trimmed with
Honiton lace, and her veil was crowned with a ring of white roses.
On returning to Buckingham Palace, Vicky and Fritz appeared on
the balcony to acknowledge the cheers of the crowd. That night
London was illuminated, and "the loyalty shown by the country"
was "most truly gratifying". Meanwhile, the bride and bridegroom
set off for their honeymoon at Windsor. After dinner, they sat alone
in the Red Drawing Room for the first time in their lives. "I remember how we sat there," Vicky told Bishop Boyd Carpenter some
thirty years later, "almost too shy to talk to one another." But Fritz
saved the situation by taking her in his arms and pressing her to his
heart: a gesture far more eloquent than words.

Early in February, Vicky set sail for Prussia, her face swollen
with crying. The Queen managed to hold back her tears to the last
moment, but then her "breaking heart gave way" and she clasped
Vicky in her arms at a loss for words. As she watched the carriage
driving through the gates of Buckingham Palace it began to snow.
The Queen had seldom felt more miserable, particularly as "everything recalled the time now past – all programmes, dinner lists, etc.
lying about still, as if all were yet going on – and all over! Such
desolation!" Even the sight of Beatrice made her feel sad, "as dear
Vicky loved her so much, and only yesterday played with her".
A week later, the Queen told King Leopold that Vicky had been
brokenhearted at leaving home, "particularly at parting from her
dearest beloved Papa, whom she idolises. *How* we miss her, I can't

say, and . . . I am in a constant fidget and impatience to know everything about *everything*. It is a *great, great* trial for a mother who has watched over her child with such anxiety day after day. . . . The blank she has left behind is *very great* indeed".

When Vicky arrived at Berlin she was met with a rising tide of chauvinism, and few of Fritz's compatriots approved of his choice of a wife. The fact that she came from a notoriously liberal country only compounded his offence. Bismarck described her scathingly as "die Engländerin". Vicky was too candid, some said too tactless, to disarm her critics, and made no secret of her unshakeable belief that England was "far in advance of all other countries." It was hardly surprising that her manifest preference for English doctors, English dentists, English nannies, English meal times and English bathrooms, antagonised most Germans. What her enemies never recognised was just how Prussian she could be. So much so, that in 1864, during the Schleswig-Holstein War, the Queen accused her of selling her soul to Bismarck. Two years later, Vicky told her mother that she was "every bit as proud of being a Prussian" as of being English, "and that is saying a very great deal as you know what a 'John Bull' I am". When Frederick William IV died in 1861, he was succeeded by Prince William, and Fritz became Crown Prince. Vicky at once used her newly enhanced position to fight for women's rights, not least for her own to play a prominent part in politics.

During the first years of Vicky's marriage the Queen wrote to her several times a week. Their "dear Correspondence" ranged from the immortality of the soul to the way Bertie parted his hair. Both wrote so freely and naturally that Vicky described her letters as "thinking aloud". Unhappily, her parents' political advice was often specious, but being a dutiful daughter she followed it religiously, lured like a ship to its doom by a wrecker's lantern. Both the Queen and Prince refused to recognise that she would never be accepted by the Prussians unless she left the Englishwoman at home. All her mother told her was that she must never forget what she owed her country and family: both of which, the Germans complained, she remembered only too well. When Vicky tried to point out her dilemma, the Queen denied that her "two-fold affections need clash". The fact, however, remained that the divided loyalties inherent in her position could not be resolved by ignoring them, and her parents' refusal to recognise the difficulty itself became part of the problem.

Soon after Fritz became engaged, the Queen told Princess Augusta that her relationship with her daughter was "more like that of two sisters". Nevertheless, her letters to Vicky were crammed with maternal advice: recommending fresh air and exercise, scolding her for her wanton use of capital letters, and urging her to see her English dentist as soon as the chance arose. She was also concerned that there were so few "necessary conveniences" in Prussian palaces. "I am sure you would be benefiting all Germany if they could be introduced." In so saying, she was preaching to the converted, as the Crown Princess had already begun a crusade to introduce British plumbing.

The Queen, who spent most of her life in a valiant effort to curb her turbulent nature, welcomed an opportunity to blow off steam. In one of her letters to Vicky, she told her what a relief it was to pour out her "feelings quite openly to one who will feel for and understand me! And this I have found in you my dearest child! It has done my heart more good than words can express." According to Greville, when Lord Clarendon was in Berlin in 1858, Stockmar informed him that H.M. was behaving "abominably" to her daughter; and trying to "exercise the same authority and control over her that She did before her marriage". The Baron persuaded Prince Albert to speak to the Queen, as she later confessed to Vicky. "Papa says that I wrote far too often," and "has snubbed me several times very sharply on the subject." Her New Year's resolution for 1859 was to "try and bear patiently the utter change of position between parents and a married daughter". It would be idle to deny that the Queen was over demanding and over solicitous, but one has only to read her correspondence with Vicky to see how devoted she was to her.

In May 1858 Fritz wrote to his father-in-law to tell him that Vicky expected a child. The Queen described it as "horrid news" which "upset us dreadfully". It drove her "almost frantic" to think that she could not attend her daughter's confinement, "Where every mother is – and I ought to be and can't". But she did what she could to supervise arrangements in a flurry of "fidgety letters". In one, she encouraged Vicky not to "dread the dénouement; there is no need of it", and not to "talk to ladies about it, as they will only alarm you". Quite early on in her pregnancy, the Princess warned her German physician, Dr Wegner, that something was going wrong, but he brushed her misgivings aside as foolish fancy. Meanwhile, the Queen helped her to plan a nursery, to be run by an English nanny, Mrs Hobbs, with the help of English nurse maids.

Alarmed by her daughter's forebodings, the Queen sent out a medical team to assist at the birth, consisting of Sir James Clark, Dr Martin, another Scotsman, who had attended the Queen when Beatrice was born, and her trusted midwife, Mrs Innocent. Sir James insisted that there was no cause for alarm, but Mrs Innocent knew better and foresaw they were "in for trouble". When Vicky's labour began, Dr Wegner sent for Martin, but for some mysterious reason his note was posted instead of being sent by hand. The Princess endured the most "terrible" agonies which even two thirds of a bottle of chloroform only partly relieved. When Martin eventually arrived, almost a day late, he was told by one of the German doctors: "It is no use, the Princess and her child are dying." Martin immediately took charge and somehow contrived to save both lives. As Greville put it, "the child got twisted in the womb and came out with his bottom foremost". Such was the ignominious fashion in which the future Kaiser appeared on the world stage. Had Martin known what destiny had in store, he might have been tempted to follow Clough's advice:

> "Thou shalt not kill; but needst not strive
> Officiously to keep alive."

Vicky's distrust of German obstetricians became something of an obsession. They had, after all, left her for dead and said as much in her hearing. In 1860, when Charlotte was born, she was attended throughout by an English doctor.

Soon after the news reached Windsor that Vicky had had a son, Prince Arthur ran up and down shouting excitedly, "I am an uncle! I am an uncle!" The Queen was equally delighted at becoming a grandmother at the age of thirty-nine, and telegraphed to the Minister in Berlin "Is it a fine boy?" In fact, it turned out that the child was badly crippled. Because of the difficulty of bringing him into the world, his left shoulder socket had been torn away, leaving his arm useless. The life-long struggle he waged against his congenital weakness led him to over compensate: hence his aggressive posturing.

The infant Prince was christened on March 5th 1859. The Queen, detained in England by her parliamentary duties, sent Lord Raglan and Captain de Ros to represent her. So envious did she feel of her emissaries that she told Vicky "I wish I could go as their servant".

In 1860 she saw William for the first time when his parents brought him to a family gathering at Coburg. "It was a great happiness," she wrote afterwards, "to see you both so happy – and to see that dear, darling, little love . . . the parting from whom gave me quite a pang. . . . I am sure I shall be quite as foolish about him as all grand-mammas are supposed to be." A month later, she wrote to say that she felt as if "Darling William quite belonged to us – as much as our own children. He is such a little love, and such a darling, so pretty and intelligent." In later years, when his charm began to wear thin, the Queen remained strangely tolerant of his frailties.

Unlike Vicky, who was born with a love of learning, the Prince of Wales detested most of his lessons. Both the Queen and Prince proved over-anxious parents, for they were only too well aware of their grave responsibility for training a future King. The distracted couple "spent days and nights of worry and anxiety", discussing "the minutest details of the physical, intellectual and moral training of their eldest son. . . . Not a week, not a day, not an hour of the time of this precious youth could safely or properly be wasted". Only long after her son had grown up did the Queen belatedly recognise that "too great care, too much constant watching leads to those very dangers hereafter, which one wishes to avoid".

Stockmar never tired of proclaiming that the future of monarchy in Britain depended on moral foundations. The Crown had only survived the depravity of the Queen's uncles because of the strength of the Constitution. It was therefore imperative that the Prince of Wales should live a blameless life, surrounded by "those who are good and pure". The Baron preached to the converted, as the Queen was terrified of the tainted blood which surged through her son's veins. Prince Albert once told a Canon of Windsor that his principal object was to make the Prince of Wales "as unlike as possible to any of his great-Uncles", which considering the lurid history of the Dukes of Saxe-Coburg was decidedly ungracious.

Both the Queen and Prince were haunted by the fear of "young and carefully brought up boys mixing with older boys and indeed with any boys in general, for the mischief done by bad boys and the things they may hear and learn from them cannot be overrated". For this reason she consigned her sons to a form of moral purdah, presumably having forgotten how much she had suffered herself from the "Kensington System". In 1849 Bertie was handed over to the Reverend Henry Birch, who came to the conclusion that his pupil's "peculiarities" were to be attributed to two factors: his "want of contact with boys of his own age", and his "finding himself the centre round which everything seems to move". When several years later Lord Granville warned the Prince that his son should be permitted to mix with "boys of his own age away from home", he was grudgingly permitted the company of a few hand-picked Etonians on his carefully chaperoned travels.

Prince Albert's procrustean methods took little account of Bertie's disposition, as if it were usual for leopards to change their spots. The Queen wholeheartedly shared his aspirations, and fervently prayed that "Albert junior" would justify his nickname. In 1845 Lady Lyttelton reported that her pupil was "uncommonly averse to learning", and that there was no possibility of his becoming a student prince. In this respect, as in most others, he was the reverse image, not the duplicate, of his father. Prince Albert regarded tobacco with disgust. Bertie smoked twelve cigars a day. Prince Albert took wine as if it were castor oil. Bertie regarded it as nectar. Prince Albert appeared to be scared of women, but Bertie was never happier than in their company. Prince Albert read avidly, his student lamp remained a prized possession. Bertie preferred to gossip or visit the theatre. Prince Albert based his judgements on books and theories, while Bertie formed his opinions on experience. It was little wonder that they found one another hard to understand.

The moment that Bertie betrayed his repugnance for learning, his parents redoubled their efforts by lengthening his timetable and hiring more tutors. In 1852 Birch was replaced by Frederick Gibbs on the advice of Sir James Stephen. Earlier in his career, Sir James had helped draft the Bill which abolished slavery in the British Empire, a practice he now unwittingly revived within the Queen's four walls, seeing that his protégé proved as great a tyrant as any West Indian planter. In response to royal commands, Gibbs increased Bertie's lessons to seven hours a day, six days a week, not to mention such "leisure" activities as riding, gymnastics and drill. When Bertie showed signs of dropping from fatigue his parents were baffled, until it dawned on them that the boy was naturally lazy and required to be driven harder. Dr Becker, the Librarian at Windsor, vainly tried to warn them that their son was being overtaxed by demands which would have daunted the infant John Stuart Mill.

Part of Bertie's problem was that he was bound to appear backward in comparison with Vicky, whose precocity was not far short

of genius. "Other children are not always good," he once complained. "Why should I always be good?" Prince Albert was
permanently dissatisfied with the boy and the Queen echoed his
strictures. In 1858 she told Vicky "I am in utter despair! The system-
atic idleness, laziness – disregard of everything is enough to break
one's heart, and fills me with indignation. . . . To you I own I am
wretched about it. But don't mention this to a human being!" On
another occasion, she spoke of "the sorrow and bitter disappointment and the awful anxiety for the future this causes us". Even his
appearance aroused her displeasure. "Handsome I cannot think him,
with that painfully small and narrow head, those immense features
and total want of chin." The Queen subjected Bertie to such a barrage
of complaints that he came to believe he could never do anything
right.

In 1860, the young Prince made a triumphant tour of the United
States and Canada. Nobody, it seemed, could resist his youth, charm
and vitality. Only his father refused to give him credit and spoke
disparagingly of "our hero". But, for once, the Queen was proud
of her son, who had made himself "immensely popular", and "really
deserved the highest praise . . . all the more as he was never spared
any reproof". In fact, he had shown that he possessed precisely the
qualities which royal duties demand.

Greville maintained that the relations between the Queen and the
Prince of Wales provided yet one more example of "the hereditary
and unfailing antipathy of our Sovereigns to their Heirs Apparent".
It has also been argued that the Queen's indignation at having a
second child so soon, and the fact that she suffered severely in giving
him birth, might account for her feelings towards him. The Prince
was pre-eminently his mother's child, and she recognised in him the
very qualities she least liked in herself. "He is my caricature," she
once remarked, "that is the misfortune." If she sometimes felt ill
at ease with him, it was because he was the living ghost of her
"unregenerate Hanoverian self". However hard she struggled to
make him like his Papa, the spectre of the Prince Regent mocked her
efforts. Every time she looked at him, with his blue Hanoverian eyes
and his receding Hanoverian chin, she was reminded of her iniquitous uncle George, her outlandish uncle William, or her detestable
Uncle Ernest. Most tormenting of all was the thought that should
she die, her beloved husband would be thrust aside to make way for
her son.

Neither of the Prince's parents ever seemed to realise that they should have allowed him increasing freedom, even to make mistakes. They preferred, however, to keep him interned in a high security gaol than to leave him to sow wild oats. In 1858 he was given an establishment of his own at White Lodge in Richmond Park. Gibbs was replaced by Colonel Robert Bruce, a son of the seventh Lord Elgin who "rescued" the Parthenon Marbles. The Colonel was more accustomed to commanding a battalion of Grenadier Guards than handling a highly-strung schoolboy. Bruce was required to send frequent reports to the Queen, and the more critical they were the more convinced she became that he understood her son. Three distinguished young men were appointed to act as his companions: Lord Valletort, Lord Mount Edgcumbe's eldest boy, who was "thoroughly good, moral and accomplished"; Major Teesdale, who had won a V.C. in the Crimea; and Major Lindsay of the Scots Fusilier Guards, another V.C. who distinguished himself in the Battle of Inkerman. Prince Albert presented these three gentlemen with a lengthy memorandum setting out their various duties, which might well have been composed "for the use and guidance of a seminary for young ladies". It began with one of those resplendent truisms of which its author was master. The Prince of Wales, it proclaimed, had arrived at the transitional state between boy and man "which was the most critical and difficult period of a lifetime". In other words, he was an adolescent of sixteen. Rather than leave his friendships to chance, he was provided with a rota of carefully chosen Equerries to supply the want of companions. It was their duty to set the Prince an example of gentlemanly behaviour. Nothing "approaching to a *practical joke*" should ever be permitted, and the conversation at White Lodge must always be such as to encourage H.R.H. to cultivate his mind. "Mere games of cards and billiards, and idle gossiping talk, will never teach this." It is interesting to note that this list of forbidden occupations reads like a summary of the daily life of Sandringham. After more than a year at Richmond, Bertie was sent to Oxford, to stuff him with further learning. His parents refused to allow him to live in College, and made him reside in a separate establishment under the eye of his Governor. Nevertheless, he occasionally contrived to spend a riotous evening with such choice spirits as Harry Hastings, "the Wicked Marquis", or Lord Chaplin, the "Magnifico". So assiduously had he been sheltered from such companions that he found them irresistible. In 1861, he was transferred to Cambridge, of which his father was Chancellor. Even Bruce warned the Queen that the Prince had reached an age when it was hardly appropriate to treat him like a schoolboy. But he pleaded in vain, and it was decided to take the lease of Madingley Hall, some four miles from the University, where the royal student could be guarded from temptation.

During the Long Vacation of 1861, the Prince of Wales was attached to the Grenadier Guards in the Curragh Camp, near Dublin. Prince Albert, demanding as ever, required him to master "the duties of every grade from ensign upwards", and to be competent "to command a battalion" and "manoeuvre a Brigade in the Field" in less than three months. Naturally, it would never do for him to live in the mess, "having regard to his position both as a Prince of the Blood and Heir to the Throne". Hard as he tried, the Prince proved unable to learn in a matter of weeks what normally took some twenty years to perfect. When the Queen visited the Curragh at the end of August she had been led to expect that she would see her son marching at the head of a battalion. In fact, his commanding officer, Colonel Percy, only entrusted him with the duties of a subaltern, on the ground that his orders were indistinct and his grasp of drill imperfect. Prince Albert was greatly distressed, and remarked to the Viceroy that he doubted whether the boy took soldiering seriously.

The night before the Camp broke up, the Prince of Wales was the guest of honour at a ball in the Mansion House in Dublin. When he eventually returned to the Curragh for the night, he discovered that a vivacious young actress, named Nellie Clifden, had been smuggled into his quarters. She was a popular favourite with the army, and knew her way round the camp in the dark. Several of H.R.H.'s fellow officers had become so intrigued by his sheltered existence that they came to regard it as something of a challenge. Most of them thought nothing of keeping a mistress or two, so it was not particularly surprising that after a rowdy evening in the mess they persuaded Nellie Clifden to try her charms on the Prince. The chance was too good to be missed, but there is nothing to suggest that he took the liaison seriously. It began as a practical joke and as such he accepted it. But when rumours of what had happened reached Windsor, the Queen was not amused.

Alice was a great deal less troublesome as a child than either Vicky or Bertie, although just as liable to sudden squalls of passion. She was very small, instinctively graceful, and possessed more charm than was good for her. Her voice was as clear and melodious as her mother's, and she was the chatterbox of the family, with a mischievous sense of humour. But the most outstanding feature of her character was a dedication to others more common among saints than ordinary mortals. She was only fifteen when the Princess Royal left home, but did everything in her power to console her parents for the loss of their eldest daughter. The Queen found her "amiable", "gentle", "obliging", and "humble", and the Prince soon struck up the same rapport with her as he had with Vicky. So much so, that during his last illness he told her things he preferred to keep from the Queen. She, for her part, worshipped her father and looked to him as her "guiding star".

Alice proved such a treasure that the Queen was in no hurry to find her a husband. "I shall not let her marry," she told King Leopold in 1859, "as long as I can reasonably delay her doing so." But suitors were less patient, and the first to be thrust in her direction was Prince William of the Netherlands, alternatively known as "The Orange boy", or "Citron". For a time Prince Albert favoured the match, until Vicky warned him that the young man had inherited his father's taste for wine, women and song. Moreover, he was plain if not positively ugly. "Beauty I don't want," said the Queen, as if she were contemplating marrying "Citron" herself, "though I should be glad of it when it was there. But a nice, manly, sensible, healthy, gentlemanlike appearance is essential." In January, 1860, Prince William was sent to Windsor "on approval", where he was observed as closely as if he had been on day release from Broadmoor. Fortunately for all concerned, his manner was so offhand that Alice was glad to see the last of him. His subsequent escapades became the talk of Paris, and he died at an early age of dissipation, "with no real enemy in the world except himself".

Alice's next suitor was Prince Louis of Hesse-Darmstadt. His mother, Princess Elizabeth of Hohenzollern, had been born on the morning of the Battle of Waterloo, and consequently had both Blucher and Wellington as her godparents. His father, Prince Charles, was the brother and heir of the reigning Grand Duke, Louis III. In spite of the relative insignificance of the royal house of Hesse, Louis claimed descent from Charlemagne, and his aunt Maria was married to Tsar Alexander II. In June 1860 Prince Louis was invited to Windsor for Ascot, preliminary enquiries having established his moral credentials. The visit proved an outstanding success. Louis found Alice enchanting and she was delighted with him. Five months later he received a second invitation to give him a chance to propose. Several days passed without anything being said. Then Prince Albert broke the ice by telling Louis that he would be given "an early opportunity of expressing his hopes to Alice". During dinner that evening, the Queen noticed that her prospective son-in-law looked "dreadfully nervous and agitated". Afterwards, in the Red Drawing Room, she saw "Alice and Louis talking before the fireplace more earnestly than usual, and when I passed to go to the other room, both came up to me, and Alice in much agitation said he had proposed to her, and he begged for my blessing. I could only squeeze his hand and say 'certainly'." Lost for words, Louis kissed the Queen's glove and she embraced him fervently. Everyone was deeply moved and handkerchiefs were much in demand.

Nobody relished romance more fervently than the Queen, who was thrilled to see "the young lovers so happy". "We have perpetual sunshine in the house," she wrote to her uncle Leopold. As for Louis, he was unassuming, amiable, honest, warm-hearted and high principled. "He is so lovable, so very *young*, and like one of our children – not the *least in the way* – but a dear, pleasant, bright companion, full of fun and spirits." One great advantage she foresaw from the match was that "we shall be able to have them a good deal with us, Louis not having any duties to detain him much at home at present". Lord Clarendon was distinctly less rapturous, and described the Prince of Hesse as "a dull boy" coming from "a dull family in a dull country". But Alice, he reckoned, was "a girl in a thousand".

Soon after the engagement was announced, the Duchess of Cambridge "with wonderful good taste told Alice 'It is a very insignificant match, you will agree'." "As if that signified," wrote the Queen to Vicky. "Great matches do not make for happiness", and often cause nothing but "trouble and annoyance". Of course, "to be happily married" was "the greatest of blessings; but the contrary is dreadful – and better a thousand times never marry than marry for marrying's sake". Delighted, as she was, to see the two dear young people looking like "happy children" together, she was in no hurry to part with her daughter, and decreed that the wedding should not take place until 1862. Alice was too dutiful to challenge her parents' ruling, but at times she felt "like a bird in a cage beating its wings against the bars".

Until he grew up, Prince Alfred was almost as much a favourite as Prince Arthur. When he was twelve he was given an establishment of his own at Royal Lodge, Windsor, principally to shelter him from his elder brother's influence. His Governor was a promising young Officer of Engineers, John Cowell, who was later to serve the Queen for twenty-eight years as Master of the Household. From the earliest age, Prince Alfred was determined to go to sea, and much of his life was spent as a naval officer. Like his sisters, he had a natural gift for drawing and watercolours, and was passionately fond of music. At Royal Lodge he secretly learned to play the violin, an art which his critics alleged he never mastered, and surprised the Queen on her birthday by playing "a little composition of his own – very pretty and of which he is not a little proud". Soon after, he became the first member of the royal family to take up stamp collecting and photography, both then in their infancy. Most of his spare time was devoted to carpentry and mechanics. His greatest achievement was to make a musical box which performed a bizarre version of "Rule Britannia".

In 1858, Prince Alfred was sent to sea, much to the Queen's distress. "Papa is most cruel upon the subject," she complained to Vicky. His first ship, H.M.S. *Euryalus*, put in to Malta where she was welcomed with a royal salute. So outraged were Affie's shipmates to see a mere midshipman treated with such honours that they picked him up and bumped him on the deck every time a cannon fired. It seems that the treatment did him a world of good as the Queen found him "much improved" when he came home on leave. She was "truly happy", she said, to have the "darling boy" back, particularly as in so many ways he was like his "dearest Papa". He was not, of course as "beautiful" as his father, but he had "such a darling, handsome, round face" that it was always a pleasure to see him. "Bless him," she wrote, "he is such a dear, dear boy, and I must say we have not had a single fault to find with him since he has been here." She found it impossible not to contrast her sailor son with a certain "nameless youth": the one possessed of "such steam power" that he could hardly sit still, and the other so lethargic.

Princess Helena, the Queen's fifth child, was placid, plump and dowdy. Her mother described her as having "great difficulties with her figure", and little sense of dress. Like all the Queen's daughters she was an accomplished pianist, a talented artist, and a tireless supporter of charity. Not only was she a loyal and steadfast friend, but practical and business-like. If her manner was sometimes brusque and authoritarian, she knew how to get things done, and she became well known for the forthright way in which she expressed her opinions.

Princess Louise, the oldest member of the "Osborne Set", was the most beautiful of the sisters. When she was sixteen, the Queen described her as "so handsome", and "so graceful, and her manners so perfect in society, so quiet and ladylike". Carlyle once met her at one of of Dean Stanley's parties, and thought her "a very pretty young lady and clever too". Like most other members of her family, apart from Lenchen, Arthur and Beatrice, she had inherited her mother's volatile temperament, and her moods were as fickle as the English weather. There were times when the Queen found her almost too much of a handful. She was the first to admit that Louise was "decidedly clever" with "a wonderful talent for art", but she could also be "very odd, dreadfully contradictory, and very indiscreet". Her unconventional views and infectious sense of fun made her an exhilarating if capricious companion. Towards the end of her life, when she took up residence in Kensington, her high, penetrating, whooping laugh could often be heard ringing round the Palace.

Prince Arthur, the Queen's third son, was destined from infancy for the Army. The choice was entirely his own and from his earliest years he spent hours in the toy fort which his father and elder brothers had built in the grounds of the "Swiss Cottage". In a memo the Queen gave Albert in 1858, she described Arthur as "*dearer* than any of the others put together". The following year, Captain Howard Elphinstone, V.C., was appointed Arthur's Governor. Like Cowell, who recommended him, he was an engineer, besides being an excellent linguist and artist. In no time he became a great favourite with the royal family, and "few if *any* gentlemen" were ever on such "confidential terms" with the Queen. Prince Arthur saw little of his elder brothers, nor was he allowed to play with Prince Leopold because of the risk of injury. Elphinstone, like Gibbs and Birch before him, proposed that the boy might visit Eton to mix with his contemporaries, but the Queen preferred to restrict his companions to children of courtiers, such as General Grey's son, Albert, and little Lord Ely. On the first anniversary of Elphinstone's appointment the Queen wrote to thank him for all he had done, and went on to "*own* that she had adored our little Arthur from the day of his birth. He has never given us a day's sorrow or trouble." Elphinstone's task was not made easier by Her Majesty's detailed interest in her son's welfare. Sometimes he received several notes a day dealing with such topics as the need to exchange winter for summer underwear, whether to spell Mama with one m or two, and the precise moment to start lessons in Latin. But she was always careful to emphasise that "in *all* these things the Prince's (Albert) wishes *must* go before hers". Fuss as she might, she had the good sense to insist that Elphinstone was in ultimate charge of her son. If she wanted him to accompany her on an outing, she first asked leave from his Governor. "May Prince Arthur go with us to Portsmouth this morning," ran one typical memo, "to see the 32nd Regt (just returned from Lucknow) or does Major Elphinstone prefer that he should not? We shall be back by 12. Prince Leopold is going." It showed commendable humility that she preferred to plead than dictate.

It soon became clear to the Queen that her youngest son was "the *cleverest* and most studious". "His mind and head," she claimed, "are far the most like of any of the boys to his dear Father". Even before Leopold left the nursery, she described him as "very clever", but "very absurd". By the age of eight he had acquired a remarkable knowledge of early Italian painting, a passionate fondness for music, and a precocious command of languages. It was providential that his interests were so scholarly and artistic as illness prevented him leading an active life. The Queen fussed over him with ill-concealed anxiety which only provoked him to fret. Almost everything about him seemed to cause her distress. He was "dreadfully awkward", held himself badly, and had such a serious speech impediment that his French sounded "more like Chinese". Not even his mother succeeded in daunting his spirit. "I heard your musical box playing most clearly this afternoon," she once complained. "Impossible," he answered back, "for my musical box never plays." "But I know it was yours," she persisted, "as there was a drum in it I recognised." "That shows it wasn't my musical box," came the coup de grâce, "there is no drum in it."

Princess Beatrice, the baby of the family, was brought up in a more relaxed way than her brothers and sisters. The truth was that neither of her parents could resist her engaging ways. Even when she was cheeky they laughed too much to scold her. Once she came down to breakfast with a rueful face and told them: "Baby has been so naughty, poor Baby so naughty!" On another occasion, when the Queen insisted that some particular delicacy was "not good for

Baby", she cheerfully helped herself remarking as she did so, "But she likes it my dear". "I had such a funny thought today," she remarked to one of her mother's ladies, "but it turned out to be an *un*proper thought so I would not let it think".

The most constant theme of the Queen's prayers was thanksgiving to God for the "inestimable blessing" of her "perfectly united marriage", which had granted her the greatest happiness "which mortals are allowed to enjoy". On December 31st, 1855, when she took leave of the old year in her journal, she spoke gratefully of Albert's "unchanging love and wonderful tenderness". Six years later, she told King Leopold that she and Albert had "celebrated, with feelings of *deep gratitude* and love, the *twenty-first* anniversary of our blessed marriage, a day which has brought us, and I may say the *world* at *large*, such incalculable blessings! *Very* few can say with me that their husband at the end of twenty-one years is *not* only full of the friendship, kindness, and affection which a truly happy marriage brings with it, but the same tender love of the *very first days of our marriage!*"

Most of the Queen's letters to Vicky abound in wearisome praise of the Prince, but on rare occasions she sounded a dissonant note. In May 1861 she wanted to remain at Osborne as Prince Leopold was ill, but "Papa insists on our going to Town for no earthly reason but that tiresome Horticultural Garden – which I curse for more reasons than one. . . . I am very much annoyed and distressed at being forced to leave him (Prince Leopold) by the very person who ought to wish me to stay. But men have not the sympathy and anxiety of women." She also complained that she had "been shamefully deceived about Affie", who was supposed to have spent some time at home before being sent to sea, instead of which "he is to go away for many months and I shall not see him God knows when!" In October 1861, shortly before the Prince's fatal illness, the Queen replied to a letter from Vicky in which she had used the phrase "no one is perfect but Papa". "He has his faults too," she told her. "He is very often very trying – in his hastiness and over-love of business – and I think you would find it very trying if Fritz was as hasty and harsh (momentarily and unintentionally as it is) as he is!"

Supremely happy as the Queen was with Albert, violent squalls had become a great deal less common. There were three main reasons for her new mood of serenity. First she had learned to rely on the Prince's judgement and to accept his lead. Secondly, she had made considerable progress in achieving self-control and restraining her passionate outbursts. Thirdly, she had only three pregnancies to contend with after the birth of Louise in 1848, instead of six in less than eight years. The worst flare-up of all took place in October 1856 when she was three months with child, and all her old grievances erupted with pent-up force. In particular, she protested that Albert's obsession with business left her solitary and deprived. Being possessive by nature, she yearned to monopolise her husband.

Unlike the Prince, who seldom reached a decision without laborious premeditation, the Queen was exceedingly impetuous. Adolphus FitzClarence believed that impatience was one of her principal faults: "in sea phrase she always wants to *go ahead*". Early in 1860 the Queen alleged that Vicky was dragging her feet over Alice's marriage to Louis of Hesse, and accused her of trying to find a Prussian husband for her sister. When Prince Albert tried to make peace, the Queen flew into a passion and said that he ought to "trust" her. Later the same day, the Prince sent her a cogently argued note in which he examined their quarrel under a microscope in the vain hope of resolving it. The dispute, he claimed, was largely attributable to her "fidgety nature" and her "feverish eagerness" to enter into details rather than leaving well alone. Seeing that his dearest wish was to save her from herself, he felt "desperately" hurt to meet with such distrust.

If being "fidgety" was one of the Queen's most prominent shortcomings, her capacity for self-criticism was one of her foremost virtues. "I die in peace with all," she wrote in her will in 1897, "fully aware of my many faults." Her journal was crowded with entries expressing her resolve to mend her ways, and prayers that God might enable her "to become worthier, less full of weakness and failings". On January 1st, 1859, looking back on the old year, she asked: "Have I improved as much as I ought? I fear not. . . . Self is still far too prominent! I must crush it!" Often she noted, "Am trying energetically to overcome my faults", but was too honest to pretend that she met with much success. "I feel how sadly deficient I am," she confessed penitently in 1881, "and how over sensitive and irritable, and how uncontrollable my temper is, when annoyed and hurt." Towards the end of her reign she insisted that she felt unworthy of the devotion shown her by her subjects. "If they only knew me as I am," she remarked, "they would have less reason to be so attached to me."

The Queen always maintained that she had inherited her passionate nature from her maternal grandmother, Augusta, Duchess of Saxe-Coburg, but her Hanoverian relations were equally renowned for violent tempers. Throughout her journal she expressed herself "sadly dissatisfied" with "the little self-control I have", and she agreed with Albert that her "great task in life" was to restrain her feelings. Sometimes she suspected the problem was "irremediable". On January 10th 1859, the eighteenth anniversary of her wedding, she confessed that she had too often caused "annoyance to that most perfect of human beings my adored Husband" by being over sensitive, foolish and irritable. "Again and again," she wrote, "I have conquered this susceptibility – have formed the best of resolutions and *again* it returns." Soon after she became a widow, she told Gladstone that it grieved her to think that she had worried and fretted the Prince by being touchy and quick tempered.

It has often been suggested that Prince Albert's life was made wretched by the loneliness of exile and the hostility of Society. It is true, of course, that the Queen worshipped him, but idolatry was no substitute for understanding. His supposed despondency was traced to various causes: his sense of the futility of trying to arouse the English from their complaisant torpor, his deteriorating health, and Coburg melancholia. It was also suggested, and not without reason, that he suffered from being on show: the price which he had to pay for being Prince Consort. On the rare occasions when he dined alone with his family, he was the life and soul of the party. "How delightful these dinners *intimes* are without any *gêne*," wrote the Queen in her journal, "and Albert always so merry." It was even alleged that he sought solace from the wretchedness of his existence by chaining himself to his desk, in spite of the fact that he never tired of proclaiming that "genuine happiness is only to be found in work". Lady Lyttelton, one of the Prince's devoted admirers, felt sure when she heard him communing with the organ – the only instrument he once told her for "expressing one's feelings" – that she detected a note of sadness creeping in. The Queen, on the other hand, spoke of his "constant cheerfulness", and warmly endorsed a comment of John Brown's: "It's very pleasant to walk with a person who is always content." The best evidence of all, however, of the Prince's state of mind is to be found in a letter he wrote to the Duchess of Kent on the day his marriage "legally came of age", in which he thanked God "that He had vouchsafed so much happiness to us".

The longer the Queen was married the more she preferred the pleasures of family life to those of the fashionable world. Throughout the eighteen sixties her letters to Vicky sustained a vigorous diatribe against Society, and she even wrote to the editor of *The Times*, urging him to print "articles pointing out the *immense* danger and evil of the wretched frivolity and levity of the views and lives of the higher classes". A year later, G.H. Wilkinson, a fashionable Evangelical clergyman, preached a sermon at Windsor on the follies of Society. "What has all this to do with me?" the Queen asked reasonably enough. When a friend of John Brown remarked that he must have met "a lot o' grand folks in London", he scorned the suggestion. "Me and the Queen," he said airily, "pays nae attention to them."

It is a singular irony of nineteenth-century history that the Coburgs, who numbered amongst them some of the most dissolute princes in Europe, made Monarchy respectable. It was certainly a novel experience for Englishmen to be ruled by a sovereign who set them a good example. Naturally, the middle class and the Evangelical world welcomed the new morality. But many of the gentry, brought up in the days of George IV, denounced the Court as bourgeois and sanctimonious. They were deeply attached, for example, to the time-honoured custom of lingering over the port, and resented attempts to curtail any opportunity for drinking, gossip and bawdy. More objectionable still was the vigilant way in which Court appointments were vetted. In 1852, after Lord Derby had sent the Queen a provisional list of Household changes, the Prince reproached him for proposing to surround Her Majesty with the "Dandies and Roués of London and the Turf": a harsh if essentially accurate description of Derby's nominees. One by one he went through the list rejecting various names. When he came to that of Lord Wilton he remarked caustically that "a man bearing the nickname of the 'Wicked Earl' could hardly be put at the head of one of the Departments of the Queen's Household". It would seem to have been easier to become a novice in a nunnery than Master of the Horse. Lord Derby, who had previously sounded his friends before venturing to propose them, had the unenviable task of informing them that they lacked the necessary moral recommendations. The Prince was in favour of further reforms of the Court, which he hoped to make more intellectual. But the Queen was opposed to any such change, on the ground that learned people "alarmed her".

From the first, the English Establishment had never cared for Prince Albert, nor did they change their opinion on closer acquaintance. In 1850, after he had been married for ten years, the Cabinet debated the possibility of increasing his allowance, but Lord John Russell vetoed the proposal on the ground that "No government could last 4 and 20 hours that meditated such a thing". The fact was, in the phrase of Lord Henry Lennox, "the Swells as a class did not much like the Prince", largely because he insisted on trying to improve them. The Duke of Beaufort, who boasted descent from Edward III, insisted that it was beneath the dignity of the Somersets that a son of his should become a lord-in-waiting to a mere Prince of Saxe-Coburg; and when H.R.H. ruined his gloves while laying a foundation stone at Eton, the young gentlemen were so ill-bred as to show their satisfaction.

Prince Albert believed that the English were far too unphilosophical and he never succeeded in grasping their earthy pragmatism. They, for their part, saw him with his head in a cloud of German metaphysics, obscuring the simplest truths with effortless sophistry. His instinctive approach to problems was ponderous, and he never managed to learn the importance of being nonchalant. Just how little the Prince understood the British mentality was shown by the regulations he drew up for the Gold Medal for Good Conduct which the Queen presented to Wellington College. This prize was offered annually to a boy selected by the Master. A week was to elapse before the name was submitted to Her Majesty, during which time the Prefects were exhorted to denounce the chosen candidate if they had reason to doubt his integrity. The idea that Wellingtonians would cheerfully incriminate one another, in blatant defiance of the schoolboy's code of honour, could only have been entertained by one who knew nothing of their loyalties. Nor did the Prince succeed in understanding the English view of sport. The first time he watched a cricket match on the playing fields of Eton, he could hardly take his eyes off one of the players languishing in the out-field. For almost three hours this gilded youth sucked a blade of grass and occasionally stopped a ball which chanced to come his way. The Prince was astonished that such aimless pursuits were positively encouraged, and formed a most jaundiced view of England's national game. His attitude to shooting was if anything more offensive. He would appear dressed in a black velvet jacket with scarlet leather boots, and when shooting with his secretary, would "blaze away, miss, and then call out, 'Anson, di gonn' and seize Anson's gun before he had time to fire a shot".

It was bad enough, said the Prince's critics, that he was so totally un-English, but worse still that he was ostentatiously German, and made no secret of the fact that he regarded his fellow countrymen "as the embodiment of all that was lofty and wise". Both he and the Queen gave unnecessary offence by speaking together in German, thereby leaving the rest of the company out of the conversation. "In the way he talked, in the way he wore his clothes, in the way he rode a horse and shook hands, there was something unmistakably, and, so it seemed, determinedly, even arrogantly foreign." Lord Aberdeen, one of his most ardent supporters, regarded his "only fault" as "excessive Germanism". Nobody could blame the Prince for British xenophobia, which had a long and discreditable history, but it was folly to ignore it. In 1845 the Queen told Anson that "the continual and unbounded dislike (in England) of foreigners and *everything foreign*", was "*very* painful to her", particularly as her "hus-band, mother and all her dearest relations and friends *are* foreigners".

There was something in Prince Albert's manner which struck most Englishmen as decidedly ungracious. They thought him stiff, reserved and formal, and anxious to keep his distance. He might be the best of companions in the privacy of his family, but his public persona was chilling. It never occurred to him to "affect the interest in everyone's remotest concerns which the Queen really felt and expressed". During the Crimean War the Prince received General Williams after his heroic defence of Kars, and the quick, stiff, distant bow he gave him "struck like ice upon the beholders". So ill at ease did he feel when ladies were presented to him, that they felt insulted by his indifference to their charms. Lady Clarendon, having sat next to him at dinner, deplored his lack of "lady talk". But what gave graver offence than his lapses into silence was the fact that he was willing to sit through three acts of an opera while the Duchess of Sutherland stood behind his chair. Lord John Russell believed that the Prince's "rudeness to women" was inspired by his fear of provok-ing the Queen's jealousy. In fact, much of the trouble arose from his agonising shyness which he tried to conceal behind rigid etiquette. Brought up in the usages of a German Court, he had little idea how repugnant these were to the majority of Englishmen.

In some quarters even Prince Albert's virtues were regarded as telling against him. The childhood trauma of his parents' squalid divorce left him abnormally "disgusted" by the faintest hint of licentiousness. Indeed, such was his aversion to sexual impropriety that when his own brother was struck down by venereal disease, he wrote him a letter insisting that he had no alternative but to leave him "to perish in immorality". To some extent his attitude arose from political calculation, in that he believed that the very survival of Monarchy depended upon the purity of the Court, but most people found his self-righteousness oppressive, and would have preferred him to have shown a redeeming chink in his armour.

Between 1846 and 1868 no political party possessed a clear majority in the House of Commons, and hence for twenty-three years there was a succession of coalition Governments. There were three main parties in the aftermath of the repeal of the Corn Laws: the "Peelites", supported by Gladstone and Aberdeen; the "Protectionists" looking to Derby and Disraeli; and the "Whigs" led by Palmerston and Russell. Since no party could claim a clear mandate from the country, the Sovereign's role in appointing a Prime Minister was crucially important. By a fortunate coincidence, Prince Albert achieved his greatest political power at the precise moment that the Queen's influence also reached its zenith. When Derby resigned in December 1852, the Queen sent for her old friend, Lord Aberdeen, in the hopes that he would preside over a "Ministry of all the Talents". It had long been her dream to see the country governed by a national coalition. But the Peelites could not bring themselves to co-operate with Disraeli, whose vendetta against Sir Robert remained a festering wound. Since it proved impossible to re-unite the Tories, Aberdeen invited the Whigs to join his Government, with Palmerston at the Home Office, and Gladstone at the Exchequer. During the negotiations, he was astonished when Palmerston claimed an acquaintanceship dating back to their school days, and the Queen and Prince "could not help laughing heartily at the *Harrow Boys* and their friendship".

Prince Arthur was once reported as enquiring, "If Mamma is Queen why is Papa not King?" It was a question which had troubled his mother ever since 1840. Gradually she came to the conclusion that a titular King was a "novelty" in England, and that she would have to be satisfied with the title of "Prince Consort". In 1857, the Cabinet, having first favoured the proposal, suddenly changed its mind, and the Queen was obliged to fall back on Letters Patent. On

June 25th it was announced in the Gazette that it had pleased her to confer "upon His Royal Highness Prince Albert the title and dignity of Prince Consort", with "precedence next to Her Majesty", except where "otherwise provided by Act of Parliament". The following month, when the Prince went to Brussels for the wedding of his cousin, Charlotte, to the Archduke Maximilian, he was accorded precedence before the various Habsburg Princes who had come to support the bridegroom. The slight the King of Prussia had shown him in 1845 had been avenged.

The Prince was less concerned than the Queen over what he should be called. What mattered to him was that he effectively enjoyed substantial power and influence. So great were his services to the State that when he died Disraeli claimed "we have buried our Sovereign. This German Prince has governed England for twenty-one years with a wisdom and energy such as none of our kings have ever shown". In 1857 Granville told Greville that the Prince was better informed regarding the details and management of government departments than the ministers in charge of them, and that he "kept the Government out of innumerable scrapes", especially in foreign affairs. A few days later, Greville met Lord Clarendon, who confirmed what Granville had told him, and particularly praised the way in which Albert encouraged the Queen to hold each minister "to the discharge of his duty and his responsibility to her", by insisting upon being "furnished with accurate and detailed information about all important matters". Careful records were kept of all such reports to which she would often refer. For example, "she would desire to know what the state of the Navy was, and what ships were in readiness for active service" and would ask for returns "from all the arsenals and dockyards". Clarendon, moreover, agreed with Granville that the Prince had "rendered the most important services to the Government", and "had written some of the ablest papers he had ever read". The Queen praised her husband even more extravagantly and told King Leopold on the eighteenth anniversary of her marriage that her "beloved and perfect Albert" had not only brought "universal blessings" to Europe, but had "raised monarchy to the *highest* pinnacle of *respect*".

Prince Albert struggled with varying degrees of success to convince the Queen of three essential principles. First, that if Monarchy was to flourish it must be seen as a moral force, personifying justice, virtue and honour. Second, that the Crown must never descend into the arena of party strife. Third, that she must approach her duties in a calm and rational spirit. These precious lessons constituted the Prince's political legacy both to the Queen and his descendants, as she was the first to acknowledge.

In the summer of 1853 war clouds began to gather in the East. Tsar Nicholas I, an instinctive imperialist, lost few opportunities to exploit the decline of the Turkish Empire, "the Sick Man of Europe". His ultimate ambition was to dominate the Bosphorus and to achieve unhindered access to the Mediterranean. Successive British governments had pledged support to Turkey in a bid to discourage the threat of Russian expansion. In June, the Tsar overran the Sultan's Danubian Provinces, ostensibly to protect their Christian inhabitants, in reality to extend his territory westwards. Aberdeen was anxious to keep the peace, but Palmerston thought him weak and dilatory. He argued that it had long been the practice of the Tsars "to push forward their encroachments as fast and as far as the want of firmness of other Governments would allow it to go, but always to stop and retire when they met decided resistance". On October 23rd the Turks declared War on Russia, encouraged to do so by the British Ambassador at Constantinople, Lord Stratford de Redcliffe, who for several years had suspected the Tsar's intrigues. The Queen at first was as eager as Aberdeen to try to preserve peace, and pressed for Lord Stratford's recall. "The hundred and twenty fanatical Turks constituting the Divan at Constantinople," she complained, "are left sole judges of the line of policy to be pursued." In November, she wrote a conciliatory letter to the Tsar recalling his visit to Windsor in 1844, and expressing her belief that there were no differences between them which could not be settled amicably. But by February 1854, she came to recognise that the Russians were determined to capture Constantinople, and that Britain had no alternative but to fight. When Aberdeen spoke of his "terrible repugnance" for war "in all its forms", she told him sternly: "This will never do".

In the excitement of the moment, the gutter press turned on Prince Albert with unparalleled ferocity. Such wild rumours flew around, that people waited outside Traitor's Gate to see the Prince imprisoned in the Tower. One kind-hearted bystander was overheard saying, "Poor young man; we hope he may not be executed". The Conservative press joined in the hue and cry, and denounced the Prince's political interference. The *Morning Herald*, Lord Derby's mouthpiece, which had clearly been well briefed, deplored H.R.H.'s "leading

part" in the Queen's audiences with ministers. "It is too much," it
proclaimed, "that one man, and he not an Englishman by birth,
should be at once Foreign Secretary, Commander-in-Chief, and
Prime Minister under all administrations". Much play was made of
the fact that H.R.H. was an "irresponsible" adviser, although as
a Privy Councillor of some fourteen years' standing he had every
constitutional right to proffer advice to the Crown. Besides, as the
Queen pointed out to Lord Clarendon, she had heard a good deal
about the so-called "anomaly" of the Prince's political standing, but
was it not more anomalous to deprive her of "the advice and support
of her husband"?

The Court believed that the orchestrated attacks on the Prince
were instigated by Palmerston, who was notorious for cultivating
the press. War fever was also largely to blame. As Albert remarked
to Stockmar, "We might fancy we were living in a madhouse". Not
long before, the Queen had told King Leopold that the country had
learned to appreciate her husband and acknowledge what they owed
him. But now her words were flung back in her face and she was
left with "*very bitter* feelings". On January 31st 1854 the attacks on
Prince Albert were formally rejected in Parliament by spokesmen of
all parties. The Lord Chief Justice, Lord Campbell, pointed out in
the House of Lords, that in so far as the Prince had proffered his
advice it must have been "most salutary", seeing that Her Majesty
was "the most Constitutional Sovereign that ever reigned in this
country". Like most violent storms it soon blew over, but the Queen
found it hard to forgive politicians for stirring up ignorant passions
and taking so long to come to Albert's defence.

The moment fighting began, the Queen "*never* regretted more"
that she was "a *poor woman* and not a man" and she craved to share
the dangers of her troops with a deep, atavistic yearning. Throughout the campaign, she suffered "agonies of suspense and uncertainty
from hour to hour", but her heart always swelled with pride when
she read accounts "of such *gallantry*, such *devotion*, such courage
under privations" as was shown by her dauntless troops. She saw it
as her duty to do everything in her power to sustain her people's
courage. Lord Panmure, the Minister for War, remarked to Lord
Raglan, the Commander-in-Chief in the field, "You never saw anybody so entirely taken up with military affairs as she is". She got up
at six thirty in the morning to see the Guards embark for the East,
she reviewed the Navy before it set sail from Spithead, and she

offered the Royal Yacht to the Admiralty as a transport ship. Most of her evenings were spent writing consoling letters to Officers' widows, or knitting scarves and mittens. On Christmas Day she sent her cousin, the Duke of Cambridge, a comforter she had made him. "The whole female part of this Castle," she told him in an accompanying letter, "beginning with the girls and myself . . . are all busily knitting for the Army." So detailed was her knowledge of the Crimea that she astounded General Canrobert, one of Napoleon III's most experienced commanders. She was as familiar, he said, with "the position of the trenches, the camps and batteries" as he was himself. Despite things going wrong, and few wars were more incompetently conducted, she radiated confidence. When the Duke of Argyll was at Windsor in November 1854 he was much struck by her "high bearing under the anxieties of the time" and her refusal to be depressed. Such indeed was her spirit that James Buchanan, the American Minister, described her as "a fiery little devil".

Queen Victoria was proud to describe her soldiers as "her own", and even as her "children", just as they liked to think of themselves as "Soldiers of the Queen". To preserve the "personal connection between the Sovereign and the Army" she personally signed the Commission of every single Officer. In November 1855, Sir Colin Campbell considered resigning his command, in spite of the pleas of Lord Panmure. But when the Queen expressed her hope to this "chivalrous old Highlander" that he would return to the Crimea, he at once agreed to do so. Prince Albert, behind the scenes, fought a valiant campaign of his own against bureaucratic obstruction. Evidence of his stupendous industry may still be seen in the fifty bound volumes of his letters and memoranda on the Eastern Question preserved in the Royal Archives. He was one of the unsung heroes of the War who succeeded in chivvying the most somnolent of Departments into something approaching life, even if he never quite rivalled his wife's "Military Mania".

The Queen did everything in her power to reduce the avoidable suffering brought about by the incompetence of the War Office and the Army Medical Department, and she envied Florence Nightingale for "being able to do so much good and look after the noble heroes whose behaviour is so admirable". She particularly asked that the wounded should be told that "*No-one* takes a warmer interest or feels *more* than the Queen. Day and night she thinks of her beloved troops". Once the wounded began to return to England, she spent much of her time visiting them, although some of the sights she saw were exceptionally gruesome. Soldiers insisted on showing her cherished pieces of shrapnel removed from their eyes or bowels. Few things escaped her notice. After going round Chatham Hospital, she informed Lord Panmure that the wards were "more like prisons than hospitals", and that there was "hardly space to walk between the beds". The place was far too sombre, and everything should be done to keep patients cheerful. She hoped, she said, "to visit all the Hospitals at Portsmouth, and to see in what state they are". The Queen spent considerable sums on presenting wooden limbs to those who could not afford them, and used her influence to find the disabled jobs. In the past, the Sovereign's connection with the Army had been confined to officers and gentlemen, but Queen Victoria went out of her way to stress her concern for the rank and file.

In her anxiety for the welfare of her soldiers, the Queen never forgot that horses could also suffer, and wrote to the War Office demanding to know what steps had been taken to provide them with blankets to protect them against the Crimean Winter. Her compassion even extended to her enemies. When Nicholas I died in March 1855, she told Princess Augusta that "Although the poor Emperor has died as our enemy, I have not forgotten former and more happy times", and she asked her to "express to the poor Empress (Augusta's sister-in-law) as well as to the family, my heartfelt condolence".

Soon after the War was over, Sir James Clark invited Florence Nightingale to visit him at Birkhall, and the Queen was "enchanted" to meet her. One evening at Balmoral while they were looking at a photograph album of the wounded, they came across the portrait of a man without arms to whom the Queen had given a pension. His case was particularly sad as his friends insisted upon plying him with brandy. Prince Albert, she said, disowned him as incorrigible, but she believed he had taken the Pledge and refused to "give him up". So intrigued was she by Miss Nightingale's conversation, which ranged from theology to the merits of fresh air, that she drove over to Birkhall in a pony cart, unattended and unannounced, and insisted on taking her for a walk to continue their discussions. She even arranged for her to meet Lord Panmure to browbeat him into reforming Military hospitals. Miss Nightingale made a profound impression on the royal family, especially Princess Alice, who later became almost as legendary a nurse as "The Lady of the Lamp".

British troops in the Crimea, unlike the French, were only equipped for a summer campaign, presumably on the assumption that the war would be over by Christmas. Having won the Battle of Alma in September, Lord Raglan proposed an immediate attack on Sebastopol, but failed to persuade St Arnaud, his opposite number, to take the risk. The ensuing delay led to disastrous consequences: it gave the Russians time to fortify the town, and it necessitated a drawn out winter siege. Raglan warned the Government that his army was ill-prepared for fighting in winter, only to be told that the climate of the Crimea was "one of the mildest and finest in Europe". The British Army was therefore obliged to contend with devastating conditions, and, apart from the arctic cold, suffered from typhoid, dysentery and cholera. Newspaper reports and photographs showed the appalling conditions prevailing in the Crimea, and produced an explosion of anger against those responsible for them. John Roebuck, an independent Member of Parliament, proposed the establishment of a Select Committee to enquire into the condition of the Army outside Sebastopol. His motion was carried and Aberdeen resigned. The country cried out for Palmerston as the "pilot to weather the storm", but the Queen was desperately anxious to avoid him, and sent in turn for Derby, Lansdowne, and Russell. Finally, on February 5th 1855, she reluctantly sent for "Pilgerstein".

The Queen was a great fighter but knew how to yield with grace when the battle was lost, and got on amazingly well with her new Prime Minister. In no time she recognised his genius as a war leader, while he learned to recognise her energy and zeal. More remarkable still, he totally revised his attitude to Albert, whom he even described as a "far greater and more extraordinary man" than Napoleon III. "I had no idea," he told a close friend, "of his possessing such eminent qualities. . . . How fortunate it has been for the country that the Queen married such a Prince." After the war was over, the royal couple came to the startling conclusion "that of all the Prime Ministers we have had, Lord Palmerston is the one who gives the least trouble, and is most amenable to reason and most ready to adopt suggestions". Admittedly, he had been an impossible Foreign Secretary, but now that he "is responsible for the *whole*, everything is quite different". To commemorate the signing of the Peace, and as a tribute to his role in maintaining "the honour and interests of the country", the Queen went so far as to give him the Garter.

On December 2nd, 1852, the forty-eighth anniversary of the Coronation of Napoleon, the Second Empire was proclaimed, and the President of the French Republic was transformed into Napoleon III. Britain was the first nation to recognise the new Emperor, and the Queen in writing to congratulate him began her letter "My good Brother", and signed herself "Your Imperial Majesty's good Sister, Victoria. R." The Tsar, however, could not bring himself to address the royal upstart as "mon frère", and described him instead as "notre très cher ami". It proved only the first of a number of rebuffs which finally ended in war. For many centuries Englishmen had been taught to regard the French as their natural enemies. So much so that when George III chanced to meet an Etonian he would urge him to hate the French. But Louis Philippe began a diplomatic revolution which survived his downfall, and the worse Napoleon's relations became with Russia, the more anxious he was for England's support. Eventually, the exigencies of war led to a formal alliance, and in April 1855 the Emperor was invited to pay a state visit to Windsor, ostensibly to concert a joint strategy in the Crimea, in fact to dissuade him from taking command in the East. Lord Clarendon, Palmerston's Foreign Secretary and an old friend of Napoleon, failed to talk him out of it, and it was left to the Queen to see what she could do.

A month after proclaiming himself Emperor, Napoleon married Eugénie, the daughter of Count Montijo, a Spanish nobleman. Some people suggested that Lord Palmerston, or possibly Lord Clarendon, was her real father, but her mother dismissed such rumours by pointing out "les dates ne correspondent pas". On the evening of Monday April 16th the Queen waited expectantly under the porch of the Grand Entrance at Windsor for the Imperial couple to appear. At last a crescendo of cheering and a flourish of trumpets announced their arrival. After warmly embracing the Emperor and Empress on both cheeks, she presented her eldest children to them, and then led them up the Grand Staircase, lined by motionless Yeomen of the Guard. "I cannot say," she wrote in her journal, "what indescribable emotions filled me, how much it felt like a wonderful dream." The next few days passed in a whirl of pomp and pageantry as one entertainment succeeded another. On the second evening of the visit there was a state ball in the Waterloo Chamber, tactfully rechristened the "Picture Gallery". The Queen described the occasion with breathless excitement, amazed to think "that I, the granddaughter of George III, should dance with the Emperor Napoleon, nephew to our great enemy, now my nearest and most intimate ally". On the eighteenth, she invested her guest with the Garter which she left to Albert to buckle round his leg. The next day, they attended a gala performance of the opera, driving through "a sea of human beings, cheering and pressing near the carriage", and shouting "Vive le Hemperor" in Cockney French. On April 20th, there was the inescapable tour of the Crystal Palace, now re-sited at Sydenham, and the Queen kept a vigilant eye open for assassins as she pressed through the crowd on the Emperor's arm, hoping to protect him by keeping close to him. When she finally said farewell to her guests she could hardly choke back her tears, but at least she could console herself as she watched them disappear down the Mall that everything had gone off "beautifully, not a hitch nor *contretemps*, fine weather, everything smiling". After the ceaseless festivities of the past five days, her ordinary life seemed hopelessly humdrum.

The Emperor, a great believer in personal diplomacy, set out to court the Queen with all the expertise of a hardened old roué. Clarendon watched admiringly as he flirted with her in so chaste a fashion as "to flatter her vanity without alarming her virtue". She was delighted to be told that her irreproachable example had raised the moral tone of Courts throughout Europe, and to be assured – as if she doubted it – that her husband was a Prince amongst princes. But most of all she enjoyed being treated, as no other man could presume to do, as a young and attractive woman. Sometimes he sailed fairly close to the wind but never once capsized. Talking things over with Clarendon, she told him that it "was very extraordinary and unaccountable", but the Emperor seemed to know everything about her, including "what she wore" on great occasions. It never occurred to her that so accomplished a philanderer was used to doing his homework. Napoleon returned home in triumph, having made his greatest conquest, but the Queen too had won a decisive victory. Shortly before he left she got him to promise to give up his plan to take command in the Crimea on the ground that his life was far too precious to risk. The Emperor was so astonished by her innocence that he failed to notice her guile.

Before Napoleon's visit, the Queen regarded him as a "disreputable adventurer", who had driven the Orleanists from the throne. But the moment she got to know him she changed her mind. "There is something fascinating, melancholy, and engaging," she wrote, "which draws you to him." Throughout her life she tended to fall for exotic characters, like Lord Melbourne, Disraeli, and the "Munshi". As a girl, she had been deliciously agitated by the notorious Duke of Brunswick, and now, as a married woman, she was even more intrigued by her outlandish guest, with whom she felt she was playing with fire. Seldom before had she met anyone to whom she could speak so freely, or in whom she felt "more inclined to confide". "He is a most extraordinary, mysterious man," she decided, "whom one feels excessively interested in watching and knowing. . . . He always does the right thing, and behaves as if he had been all his life an Emperor!" As for the Empress, she thought her a "charming, lovable creature", who combined kindness and intelligence with grace and beauty. Albert had a "very great respect for her", and the children adored her. Looking back on the visit, she told Stockmar she could "*think* and talk of nothing else", and she described Napoleon as a "wonderful man", for whom she felt "a *real* affection".

In August 1855 the Queen paid a return visit to Paris, and was much intrigued to learn that she was the first reigning British Sovereign to enter the city since Henry VI was crowned there in 1430. She arrived at the Gare de Strasbourg on the evening of August 18th. "I felt quite bewildered but enchanted" she noted in her journal. "It was like a fairy tale, and everything so beautiful!" Sixty thousand soldiers lined the streets, including a regiment of Zouaves, "splendid troops in splendid dress, the friends of my dear Guards". As the cavalcade of carriages clattered down the Champs Elysées, it was too dark to see very much, but the noise was stupefying. Cannons roared, bands played "God Save the Queen" a dozen times, trumpets sounded, and the crowds cheered and shouted "Vive la Reine d'Angleterre! Vive l'Empereur! Vive le Prince Albert!"

The royal party stayed at the palace of St Cloud and the Queen was delighted with her apartments, which had been specially redecorated in white and gold to remind her of Buckingham Palace. Napoleon even gave orders that the legs of a table which had belonged to Marie-Antoinette should be cut short to suit his diminutive guest. The walls were hung with sumptuous Gobelin tapestries, and from the garden below there rose the murmur of fountains and scent of orange blossom. Standing on her sitting-room balcony, the Queen could make out the distant outline of the Arc de Triomphe looming over the city. She was so comfortable, she assured her host, that apart from the absence of her dog she felt completely at home. The

Emperor hardly seemed to have heard what she said, but instantly sent a courier to collect the missing animal. Next day, on returning from a drive, the Queen was astonished to hear excited yapping coming from her quarters. The Emperor spared no effort to make the visit magical. As his talent for entertainment verged on genius, it would hardly have been possible to surpass the magnificence of the occasion. The Queen wrote excitedly to King Leopold to say that no city was "more *beautiful* and gay than Paris" and that she was "*delighted, enchanted, amused* and *interested*" by everything she saw.

The Emperor not only invited the Queen and Prince but their two eldest children. Napoleon was fond of the young and treated them with unusual consideration. Bertie instantly warmed to the French, who seemed more concerned to relish life to the full than to meet its sombre duties. Vicky was so besotted by the Empress's charm and beauty as to become something of an embarrassment. When the time came to return, she and Bertie begged to remain behind. Eugénie protested that much as she would love to have them, she feared that their parents would prove reluctant to spare them. "Not do without us!" exclaimed the Prince of Wales. "Don't fancy that, for there are six more of us at home, and they don't want us."

On Monday, August 20th, Napoleon took his guests for a drive round Paris. As they passed the Palais de Justice, he pointed to a forbidding looking building where he had once been kept a prisoner. "Strange incredible contrast" thought the Queen, "to be driving with us as Emperor through the streets of the town in triumph." Next day they had luncheon at the Petit-Trianon, and the Queen told her host and hostess that she had once danced with old Lord Huntley who as a young man had been a partner of Marie-Antoinette at a Ball in the Tuileries. On Wednesday, she went on an incognito drive through Paris in a "common fiacre". The Queen, whose disguise consisted of a bonnet and a black veil, was greatly intrigued to see "people sitting and drinking before the houses, all so foreign and southern-looking to my eyes, and *so* gay". When somebody shouted, "Celle-la ressemble bien à la Reine d'Angleterre", she remarked crossly "They do not seem to know who I am". Often the purpose of assuming incognito was less to conceal her identity than to protect her from undue ceremony.

Nobody who saw the Queen in Paris could fail to be struck by her boundless energy and capacity for enjoyment. Lord Clarendon, having spent most of the day escorting her round the Tuileries and the Louvre, complained that "no royal person ever known in history comes up to her in indefatigability". One particularly portly member of Napoleon's suite gasped in despair, "Je donnerais tout – tout – la Venus de Milo incluse, pour un verre de limonade". It must be admitted that the Queen's clothes looked dowdy. Parisians were amazed by her enormous hand-bag decorated with a portrait of a poodle, her plain straw travelling bonnet, and her gown embroidered in geraniums reminiscent of a seed catalogue. But her total lack of dress sense did nothing to diminish her instinctive dignity. She might look as if she had borrowed the housekeeper's clothes, but nobody could mistake her regal assurance. She was a professional to the finger tips, compared with whom the Empress looked gauche for all her dazzling beauty.

The most dramatic moment of the Queen's visit took place at the Hotel des Invalides where she went to see the tomb of the great Napoleon, whose remains had been brought back from St Helena some fifteen years before. The coffin temporarily resided in the side chapel of St Jerome, while the crypt intended to receive it was being built. As they stood gazing at it, a violent thunderstorm raged. So moved was the Queen by the occasion, in which "old enmities and rivalries" were wiped out, that she told the Prince of Wales to kneel beside the coffin. At that sight, battle-scarred veterans, who had fought unflinchingly at Wagram and Waterloo, fumbled for their handkerchiefs.

The "delightful and never-to-be-forgotten" visit to Paris ended with a spectacular ball at Versailles, the first to be held there since the French Revolution. The Queen was greeted by the "dear Empress", whose white crinoline sparkled with diamonds. When the Emperor first caught sight of her, he was heard to exclaim, "comme tu es belle!" The royal party then passed through the Galerie des Glaces, which was "one blaze of light from innumerable lustres", to watch an extravagant display of fireworks, the like of which had seldom been seen before. The dancing then began, the Queen leading off with the Emperor, "who valses very quietly". During the evening she exchanged a few words with Bismarck, then the relatively unknown Prussian Minister at Frankfurt, with whom she conversed in German on the relative merits of Paris and St Petersburg. Supper was held in the theatre where four hundred guests sat down at forty tables. That evening the Queen set her seal on the social pre-eminence of the Second Empire by describing the ball as "one of the finest and most magnificent sights we had ever witnessed". It was nearly two in the morning before she left, Albert manfully fighting back sleep, and Vicky and Bertie "in ecstasies".

On returning to England, the Queen told Lady Churchill "that she had met many agreeable men in her life", but not one to compare with the Emperor. Towards the end of her visit she spent fourteen consecutive hours in his company but never once did the "interest and charm of his discourse" flag. The Queen played her part to perfection in strengthening the alliance: the serious purpose behind the show and glitter. Everybody, said Clarendon, praised "her grace and dignity, and some go so far as to think her pretty". Part of the secret of her success was her infectious enthusiasm. The fact that she was "*delighted, enchanted, amused* and *interested*" was written all over her face.

On September 8th, 1855, Sebastopol finally fell, and discussions began to end the war. Throughout the negotiations the Queen repeatedly urged the Foreign Secretary not to be too conciliatory. The peace treaty finally signed in Paris in March 1856 closed the Black Sea to warships, and guaranteed the integrity of Turkey. The Queen owned that the "peace rather sticks in my throat" as it hardly appeared to justify so much suffering and loss. In 1905, Lord Esher, who was editing Queen Victoria's letters, went through her papers on the Crimean War, and was "amazed" to discover just how influential she and the Prince had been. "*They* were the real ministers of the Crown", he concluded, who even obliged Palmerston from time to time "to take a back seat".

After the War, the Queen paid several visits to Aldershot to welcome regiments home from the East. At one such review, held on July 7th, the Commander-in-Chief, Lord Hardinge, had a serious stroke while talking to Her Majesty. At the time, she thought he had somehow slipped, as his mind remained perfectly clear, and he apologised "for making such a disturbance". Two days later he sent in his resignation as the whole of his right side was found to be paralysed. The Queen urged Palmerston to appoint the Duke of Cambridge to succeed him. On July 13th she sent for her cousin to tell him of his appointment. "We tried to give him good advice," she wrote in her journal, "and begged him always to consult us before anything definite was done." For the next thirty-nine years the partnership struck up that afternoon was to drive successive governments to despair as precious plans for military reform were blocked by royal obstruction.

The warm and close relationship between the Queen and the Emperor barely survived the war. Their first divergence arose over the generosity of the peace terms. The Prince Imperial was born a fortnight before the Treaty was signed, and the Queen suspected that his parents were more anxious to secure his inheritance than to bargain with the Russians. In January 1858 Anglo-French relations deteriorated dramatically after an attempt on the Emperor's life. Providentially he and Eugénie escaped with a few scratches when bombs were thrown at their carriage as they drove to the opera. "Don't bother about us," said the Empress, a moment after the explosions, "such things are our profession. Look after the wounded." The scene of carnage was sickening. Eugénie's dress was splattered with blood, injured horses thrashed about in agony, over a hundred people were injured, and ten were killed outright. It soon became clear that the assassins, chief of whom was Orsini, were a bunch of disgruntled Italians, who resented what they saw as Napoleon's failure to drive the Austrians from their fatherland. It also transpired that the plot had been hatched in London and the bombs came from Birmingham. The French press seemed more indignant with Britain for harbouring the conspirators than with the regicides themselves. When Palmerston tried to placate Napoleon by introducing a bill to make conspiracy to murder a felony, it was thrown out on its second reading. Parliament, it seemed, preferred to shelter assassins than protect a friendly Sovereign. The Queen's sympathies were with her Prime Minister, and she tried in vain to persuade him not to resign. For the next eighteen months Lord Derby contrived to carry on the Government in face of the Whig majority in the Commons, with Disraeli at the Exchequer and Lord Malmesbury at the Foreign Office.

In August 1858 the Queen and Prince visited Cherbourg and were dismayed to see that huge sums of money and enormous numbers of workmen had been poured into the town to extend its breakwater and fortify the harbour. The Queen was even more worried by the vast number of warships Napoleon was building, and naturally asked herself "Who were they intended to attack?" The Emperor seemed almost embarrassed by this display of naval might, and was "boutonné and silent". The moment the Queen returned home she tried to arouse Lord Derby to the danger, but he clearly preferred to bury his head in the sand. Albert was so exasperated that he told the Duchess of Kent, "The war preparations in the French Marine are immense! Ours despicable! Our Ministers use fine phrases, but they do nothing. My blood boils within me."

Orsini did Napoleon an injustice in assuming he would not help Italy. When in 1859 the Emperor Francis Joseph suspected a plot to drive him out of Lombardy and Venetia, he decided to launch a pre-emptive attack on Piedmont. Napoleon at once took the field and defeated the Austrians at Magenta and Solferino. Both the Queen and Prince Albert aligned themselves with Francis Joseph, the "legitimate" ruler of Northern Italy, and saw Napoleon as threatening the peace of Europe by his military adventure. But public opinion in England took an opposite view, denouncing the Habsburgs as tyrants, and applauding the way the Italian people fought to defend their soil. In the middle of this crisis, Lord Derby was forced to resign, and the Queen had no alternative but to summon Palmerston, knowing full well that he and Russell were eager to liberate Italy. On one occasion the Queen was so incensed by what she saw as incitement to revolution that she demanded that the Cabinet should be recalled so that they could consider her misgivings. This was the Monarch's "right to warn" with a vengeance. But whatever the views of her Government might be, the War of 1859 put an end to the Queen's cordiality with Napoleon. She refused to be duped by his claim that "the Empire stood for Peace", and described him in a letter to King Leopold as "the universal disturber of the world". By a curious irony, her relations with the Emperor followed much the same sequence as those with Louis Philippe: suspicion, affection, and alienation. But when they ended their lives as exiles, she welcomed them both with open arms and all old scores were forgiven.

Hardly had peace been signed with the Russians than a serious mutiny broke out in the Bengal Army. It had long been prophesied that the British would be driven out of India in 1857, the centenary of Clive's victory at Plassey. On Sunday, May 10th in that fateful year, three Sepoy regiments at Meerut seized a supply of arms, marched South on Delhi, and massacred every European in sight. In all India there were some forty thousand British troops, and it was not uncommon for them to be outnumbered twenty or thirty to one. Most of the fighting was concentrated on the military depots of Cawnpore, Lucknow and Delhi, where loyal forces were besieged by hordes of mutineers. The Queen told Lady Canning, one of her former Ladies-in-Waiting, and now wife to the Governor-General, that her thoughts were "almost *solely* occupied with India". Characteristically, the Cabinet refused to recognise the gravity of the crisis or the need for urgent action. "We are constantly digging our spurs in their sides" wrote Albert in despair.

Sir Hugh Wheeler held out in Cawnpore for several weeks against vastly superior forces, but when he ran out of water and ammunition accepted a safe conduct from Nana Sahib, a disgruntled native prince who had sided with the rebels. A bedraggled remnant of survivors, many of whom were women and children, tottered into the burning Indian sun to be herded into barges. No sooner had they embarked than their boats were set on fire, and troopers rode into the Ganges to sabre those who tried to swim to safety. All the men were killed, but over a hundred women and children survived and were thrown into gaol. When Sir Henry Havelock appeared with a relieving army, Nana Sahib decided to flee, but gave orders before doing so that his prisoners should be hacked to pieces and their remains thrown down a well. Naturally when news of his treachery reached England it seemed almost too awful to grasp. The Queen was haunted "*day* and night" by the horror of the massacre, and asked Lady Canning to let those "who have *lost* dear ones in so dreadful a manner *know* of my sympathy. A woman and above all a wife and mother can only *too well* enter into the agonies" of the bereaved.

One of the most deplorable features of the fighting was that bestial cruelty provoked the British to similar atrocities. Few prisoners were ever taken, and rebels were tortured, shot out of cannons, and hanged without trial. W.H. Russell, *The Times* correspondent, was disgusted by such savagery. In an effort to check reprisals, Lord Canning circulated a celebrated minute which earned him the contemptuous nickname "Clemency". Battling against the current of public opinion, he denounced the "rabid and indiscriminate vindictiveness", which was being shown "among many who ought to set a better example". British officers, claiming to be Christians, referred to "fine bags" of Indians, and one regiment hanged two hundred rebels in a morning while drinks were served and a band played. Newspapers in England bayed for blood and demanded Canning's recall.

The Queen regarded the public outcry as "too horrible and really quite shameful!" The trouble arose, she said, from people "judging of things from a distance, and not understanding them, and not waiting for explanations". Lord Canning told her that the bitterness of those "whose hearts have been torn by the foul barbarities inflicted upon those dear to them" was perhaps excusable, "but the cry is raised loudest by those who have been sitting quietly in their homes from the beginning". There could be little prospect of restoring tranquillity and good order in India in a spirit of revenge. The Queen entirely shared his "feelings of sorrow and indignation at the unchristian spirit shown by the public *without* discrimination". She thought, however, that the mood was unlikely to last, and was only a first reaction to "unspeakable atrocities against innocent women and children". No punishment, of course, could be too severe "for the perpetrators of those awful horrors", but "to the nation at large – to the peaceable inhabitants, to the many kind and friendly natives who have assisted us . . . these should be shown the greatest kindness. They should know that there is no hatred to a brown skin – none; but the greatest wish on their Queen's part to see them happy, contented and flourishing". She wholeheartedly agreed with her Governor-General that good government could not be based on reprisals and racial hatred, and she shared the sentiments of a working-class Member of Parliament: "We can never keep our 'old upon Hindia by the force of harms" alone. She was all in favour of "stern and inflexible justice", but not of being party to punishing the innocent in response to popular clamour. It was an immense comfort to Canning, who was sniped at from all quarters, to be told by the Queen that he had her steadfast support.

In 1858 the government of India was transferred from the East India Company to the Crown. Henceforth the Governor-General became Viceroy, and the easygoing rule of "John Company" was replaced by a rigid bureaucracy. The Queen, from the first, was passionately attached to India, the brightest jewel in her crown. When she was shown a draft proclamation setting out the principles upon which India was to be governed, she asked Lord Derby to re-write it, "bearing in mind that it is a female Sovereign who speaks to more than a hundred millions of Eastern people on assuming the direct government over them. . . . Such a document should breathe feelings of generosity, benevolence, and religious toleration". She particularly objected to a passage in the draft which referred to her power to modify the religions and customs of India, and suggested that it would be better to insist that "the deep attachment which Her

Majesty feels to her own religion, and the comfort and happiness which she derives from its consolations, will preclude her from any attempt to interfere with the native religions". In so saying, she showed herself wiser than her ministers who seemed slow to recognise that "fear of their religion being tampered with" was at the root of the Sepoy rebellion. When Canning congratulated her on the felicity of her Proclamation, she told him that it was a "source of great satisfaction and pride to feel herself in direct communication" with the sub-continent of India, and that she hoped that its publication would help "draw a veil over the sad and bloody past". The Queen's advocacy of religious toleration was particularly valuable and important given that the majority of her British subjects were not Anglicans, and the majority of her Imperial subjects were not Christian.

Sometimes in the heat of religious controversy, the Queen betrayed her principles by acting in a spirit of bigotry ordinarily alien to her nature. The very fervour of her Protestant faith encouraged her to defend it with greater ferocity than charity. Recognising that her ancestors had been placed on the throne in 1688 "solely to maintain . . . the *true* and *real principles* and *spirit* of the *Protestant* religion", she consequently felt *"more strongly* than words *can* express" the obligation imposed on her to maintain the reformed faith. Indeed, she went further and was *"most anxious* for a *very sweeping* Reformation of the English Church", in the belief that the work done in the sixteenth century "was *never* fully completed", and that there was still an urgent need to apply "the pruning knife more severely". But she drew the line at wanton provocation, and opposed a plan for a Lutheran festival in Britain, agreeing with Gladstone that "live controversies are bad enough without rekindling dead ones".

In 1833 a powerful religious revival began in Oxford, inspired by the threat of disestablishment and the spread of free-thinking. It derived many of its principles from seventeenth-century High Church traditions, and particularly stressed that the Church of England remained part of the "Holy Catholic Church". Unfortunately the distinction between Anglo-Catholic and Roman Catholic was so little understood that that even the "Supreme Governor of the Church" identified the former with the latter. The movement's most prominent leaders were Keble, Newman and Pusey, who published their views in a series of "Tracts for the Times". The emphasis "Tractarians" placed on the crucial importance of the Church and its clergy set new standards of parochial care and worship, but their insistence on the continuity of Pre-Reformation practices encouraged accusations of "Popery", a charge seemingly borne out in 1845 by Newman's defection to Rome. The Queen's sentiments were precisely those of Dr Arnold, the Head Master of Rugby, who in 1841 told Stanley "My feelings towards a Roman Catholic are quite different to my feelings towards a Newmanite (an early name for Tractarians), because I think the one is a fair enemy, the other a treacherous one. The one is a Frenchman in his own uniform; the other is the Frenchman disguised in a Red Coat", holding his post in the British Army "for the purpose of betraying it. I should honour the first and hang the second."

In 1874 the Queen told Archbishop Tait that she regarded Tractarians with the "greatest abhorrence" as they had poisoned the minds of the young, and were "*R Catholics* at *heart*, and *very insincere* as to their professions of attachment to the Church". Furthermore, she suspected that their emphasis on the divine origins of the Church obliquely threatened the Royal Supremacy. Like "every true Protestant" she regarded High Church rituals as a "mere aping of Catholic form", and was repelled by "the errors of a superstitious religion – full of strange observances repugnant to all the simplicity of our Saviour's teaching. . . . Thank God the Scotch Church is a stronghold of Protestantism, most precious in these realms."

In the first Tract of all, Newman urged his fellow clergymen to "exalt their office", and in so doing provoked a storm of protest which helped to enhance the Queen's aversion to priestcraft. Her vehement anti-clericalism seems to have originated in her poor opinion of Davys, the first clergyman she ever knew well. Later, Lord Melbourne and Prince Albert added fuel to the flames. "Those clergymen," Lord M warned her, "are always poking themselves into everything." In 1897 she held a reception for a hundred bishops who had gathered at Lambeth for a Pan-Anglican Conference. After the ceremony, she went out for her usual afternoon drive with her Lady-in-Waiting, the Dowager Lady Lytton. For some moments she brooded in silence and then suddenly remarked "A very ugly party", adding by way of explanation, "I don't like Bishops". Lady Lytton was so astonished that she nearly fell out of the carriage. "But your Majesty likes *some* bishops", she blurted out loyally. "Yes," said the Queen, "I like the man but *not* the bishop."

On three separate occasions in the first year of her reign, the Queen

promised to uphold the Protestant religion: at her first meeting of
the Privy Council, at the Opening of Parliament, and in Westminster
Abbey. In her Speech from the Throne she described the "Sacrifice
of the Mass" as "superstitious and idolatrous" with an emphasis
which confirmed the sincerity of her conviction, and during her
Coronation she swore on the Bible to "Maintain and preserve the
settlement of the true Protestant Religion". In 1894 she had occasion
to remind Lord Rosebery of the oath she had taken fifty-seven years
earlier to uphold the reformed faith, adding with unmistakable men-
ace that she proposed to "do all that lies in her power to be true to
this promise". It was only too apparent that she could be every bit
as obdurate as her grandfather, George III, who refused to give his
assent to Catholic Emancipation on precisely the same grounds. Lord
Rosebery was wise enough to recognise that when the Queen's inclination coincided with her duty she was virtually irresistible.

The Church of England was originally designed to comprehend
the widest possible spectrum of opinion in an effort to make it
national. Consequently, its Prayer Book was inspired by a judicious
compromise between the opposing views of traditionalists and
reformers. When Newman claimed that it was possible to interpret
the Thirty-Nine Articles in a "Catholic" sense, history was on his
side. The Queen, however, was so blinkered by her Protestantism
that she held the Tractarians solely responsible for the contention
they aroused, and cut herself off from some of "the noblest minds"
of the age. She at least respected men like Manning and Newman
who sacrificed their careers by their open apostasy, but she had no
time for covert Anglicans who clung to the privileges of the Church
while "betraying" it from within. In her eyes the saintly and
scholarly Pusey was an enemy and a traitor. Such, however, was the
religious confusion of the times, that even the Queen herself was
accused of High Church leanings. A newspaper once reported that
she had been seen to bow before the Altar. In fact, she was entirely
innocent of idolatry and had merely given her customary nod of
recognition to a group of friends and relations.

Soon after the "Great Famine", hordes of Irish immigrants poured
into Liverpool, Glasgow and the North of England, and it became
clear that the Roman Catholic Church would have to be recon-
structed to accommodate their needs. Consequently, in September
1850 Pope Pius IX issued a Papal Bull appointing Cardinal Wiseman
"Archbishop of Westminster", and dividing his province into twelve

new dioceses. These measures might hardly have been noticed had Wiseman not published a provocative Pastoral letter rejoicing that Catholic England had been "restored to its orbit in the ecclesiastical firmament". When the Queen opened Parliament there were cries of "No Popery", and Lord John Russell denounced what he chose to call "Papal aggression". Exploiting an outburst of public hysteria to revive his Government's fortunes, he alerted his fellow Protestants to "the danger within the gates from the unworthy sons of the Church of England herself". The Queen's initial reaction was one of outrage at "the extraordinary proceeding of the Pope", which she saw as "a *direct* infringement" of her prerogative. But she soon came to deplore the "feverish state of wild excitement" which had seized her subjects, and to "regret the unchristian and intolerant spirit" abroad in the land. "I cannot bear," she said, "to hear the violent abuse of the Catholic religion, which is so painful and cruel towards the many good and innocent Roman Catholics." In fact, as Greville astutely observed, "she is much more against Puseyites than Catholics". When the Duchess of Norfolk, one of the foremost Catholics in England, wrote her a letter deploring the proselytising efforts of some of the Roman Catholic clergy, the Queen replied that the "real danger . . . lies in our own divisions and in the extraordinary conduct of the Puseyites".

At first sight the Broad Church seemed to offer the best hope of healing Anglican wounds since it aimed to embrace the widest range of opinions. In fact, the closest it ever got to unity was to drive Tractarians and Evangelicals into an uneasy alliance against its liberal principles. In 1860, Pusey and Shaftesbury, hitherto bitter antagonists, jointly denounced the Broad Church Manifesto *Essays and Reviews* as heretical and profane. The Queen openly admitted to Gladstone that she was a "*broad* churchwoman", and claimed that her beliefs were "the only true, enlightened, Christian and intellectual view of religion which exists". She was partly drawn to the Broad Church because it opposed extremism, and partly because it "found something to admire in every creed and person". Moreover, its leaders, such as Coleridge and Arnold, shared her concern to make the Church national. So eager was she to make Broad Churchmen Bishops that Dean Wellesley felt bound to remind her that they represented the views of a small minority. Towards the end of her reign, Lord Salisbury expressed the fear that his Government would be accused of "rationalising" the Church if he appointed yet another theological liberal. "A very extraordinary idea I must say" was her unsympathetic response.

The Queen felt convinced that there was an "immense danger" that the Church would "*inevitably* fall, if MEN of intellect and enlightened views" were excluded merely because their opinions seemed too advanced. Besides, she could never "conscientiously agree" to the appointment of Ritualists and Evangelicals who threatened to "drive people to Atheism or Catholicism". "The Church," she warned Disraeli in 1875, was "in *great danger* from its divisions within, and from the outward danger of Romanism and Popery, as well as from Atheism and Materialism, and the only way to counteract this is by promoting pious, intelligent, well-informed, moderate, but large-minded and liberal-minded men in the Church". Prince Albert was even more vehement than the Queen in his hatred of dogma and bigotry. In his letter congratulating Samuel Wilberforce upon becoming Bishop of Oxford, he told him he should never "forget the insufficiency of human knowledge and wisdom". Those in high places, he added, with unabashed presumption, should be "meek, and liberal, and tolerant to other confessions" since nobody is entitled to say "I alone am right". The Queen was equally disposed to regard dogmatic differences as "very unnecessary", although it is difficult to see how the Church could resist attack without defining its doctrines. Her closest advisers amongst the clergy were all Broad Churchmen: Wellesley, Stanley, Tait, Macleod, Boyd Carpenter, and Davidson. So too were the authors and preachers she most admired, such as F.W. Robertson, Temple, Farrar, Westcott, Stopford Brooke and Kingsley.

The nineteenth century was notoriously litigious. Tractarians were dragged through the courts for illicit rituals, and Broad Churchmen were prosecuted for questioning the historicity of the Pentateuch, or suggesting that God might temper justice with mercy on the Day of Judgement. There was hardly a heresy trial in the course of her reign in which the Queen did not sympathise with the defendant, and on several occasions she let it be known that she did so. She spoke of the death of Dean Milman as "a great loss", although he had once caused uproar by calling Abraham a "Sheik". When Tennyson's son, Hallam, sent her a bunch of snowdrops, she told him that she was glad that he had such a "good and great" godfather as F.D. Maurice. That was certainly posterity's verdict, but not one shared by his academic colleagues who dismissed him from his professorship for depriving Christians of the "consolation" of everlasting Hell-fire.

In 1847 a hue and cry was raised against the appointment of Hampden to the vacant See of Hereford. It was said that he was guilty of disseminating heresy in his Bampton lectures, in which he argued that the primitive Gospel message had gradually been developed during the second and third centuries into a sophisticated system of Theology. This self-evident truism was regarded at the time as dangerously unorthodox, and consequently thirteen bishops, including Samuel Wilberforce, took the unprecedented step of reproaching Lord John Russell for so mischievous an appointment. Prince Albert, who blamed the Tractarians for stirring up the dispute, took up the cudgels on Hampden's behalf. It would not be long, he told Stockmar caustically, before the new Bishop's enemies would be clamouring to burn him at the stake. Wilberforce, hitherto a special favourite at Court, fell into deep disgrace. Had his path to preferment not been blocked by the Queen's and Prince's displeasure, he might well have succeeded Howley as Archbishop.

The publication of *Essays and Reviews* led to a storm of abuse against its authors. Two of its seven contributors were prosecuted in Ecclesiastical courts, and the rest were harassed and vilified. Not only did the Queen resent their persecution, but she subscribed to their belief that it was futile to try to dispose of religious doubts with anathemas or claims to infallibility. "Unbelief," she told Archbishop Tait, "can only be met by a full admission of the rights of reason and science", which was precisely what Jowett had argued in his contribution "On the Interpretation of Scripture". She also warmly endorsed the verdict of the Lord Chancellor, Lord Westbury, who declared that he could find nothing in the Formularies of the Church "to require us to condemn as penal the expression of hope by a clergyman, that even the ultimate pardon of the wicked, who are condemned in the day of judgement, may be consistent with the Will of Almighty God". It was really "monstrous", she wrote to Vicky, "to see how Christians can wish for others to be eternally damned". When she heard that eleven thousand clergymen had signed a Petition condemning the views of the Essayists, she described their behaviour as "disgraceful", "unchristian", and "humiliating".

The Anglican liturgy imposed a duty on Queen Victoria "to preserve her people in wealth, peace and godliness", and she took this commitment seriously. But she did not take quite so lofty a view of the Royal Supremacy as was implied in the Prayer Books used in St

George's Chapel, in which the pronouns employed for the Holy Trinity were spelt with small letters, but those which referred to the Queen were given capitals. Before she even came to the throne, King Leopold told her "that in England the Sovereign is the Head of the Church", and she was therefore astonished to read a report in 1874 of a speech by Gathorne Hardy in which he was quoted as saying that she was "*not* the *Head of the Church*". Hardy, in fact, was right. It is true that Henry VIII managed to browbeat the clergy into giving him that title, but in the Act of Supremacy of 1559 Queen Elizabeth was described as "the only Supreme Governor of this realm . . . as well in all spiritual or ecclesiastical, things or causes as temporal". Both Disraeli and the Lord Chancellor did their best to explain the true situation, but she remained unconvinced, and in 1893 entreated Gladstone "to pause before taking so *disastrous* a step as to attempt to *disestablish* part of the English Church of which she is Head". To her dying day she preferred the title adopted by Henry VIII to that assumed by his daughter.

When Henry VIII became "Head of the Church" he assumed the right to nominate new bishops. But over the years, as the power of Parliament developed, the exercise of prerogatives became increasingly dependent on ministerial advice. In fact, George III, as late as 1805, appointed an Archbishop (Manners Sutton) on his sole initiative, but when George IV tried to follow this precedent, Lord Liverpool threatened to resign, and established the principle that the Prime Minister was ultimately responsible for Crown patronage. Nevertheless, Queen Victoria succeeded in retaining a considerable influence over vacant sees and benefices, and frequently suggested particular candidates by name, or described the sort of person she hoped would be recommended. One residual prerogative she used unsparingly: her absolute right of veto. If she could not always succeed in pressing her nominees, nor could her Prime Ministers.

In 1854 the Queen made Gerald Wellesley Dean of Windsor, a post he retained for twenty-eight years. Wellesley, who looked remarkably like his uncle the great Duke of Wellington, gradually became one of her most intimate friends, "bound up with all the joys and sorrows of her family". Such was his growing influence that he acquired "an almost commanding authority in all Church affairs in which the Crown was involved". Gladstone, his exact contemporary at Eton, planned to make him Archbishop. Some people found him too formidable, but beneath his gruff exterior was a wealth of warmth and sympathy. The Queen could hardly have chosen a more gentlemanly, judicious and conciliatory adviser. Best of all, he combined piety with massive common sense. In 1856 he sent Prince Albert a memorandum on Crown Patronage in which he argued that the traditional practice of selecting bishops who supported the government of the day had produced some "very inferior specimens". It would be far better, he said, that they should be drawn from every shade of Anglican opinion than from one favoured faction. The Queen, who had been taught by the Prince that the Crown was above party, agreed that it was wrong to choose bishops because they were Whigs or Tories, but she refused to extend this principle to "*Puseyites* or Romanisers". The issue hardly arose before Gladstone came to power, as no previous Prime Minister, other than Aberdeen, had shown the slightest desire to recommend High Churchmen. It is a singular fact that the saintly Keble never received so much as a hint of official approval: not that he ever wanted it.

The Queen was almost as suspicious of Evangelicals as of Anglo-Catholics, and blamed their extremism for tearing the Church apart. She therefore repeatedly pressed the claims of "moderates" who tempered zeal with discretion. Such people, she could not resist pointing out, were likely to be Broad Churchmen. She particularly disliked the "sensational style of excitement" favoured by Moody and Sankey, the American revivalists, and deplored the brash vulgarity with which they handled sacred themes. Nothing, moreover, would induce her to observe Evangelical taboos against novel reading, card-playing, dancing, theatres, and the desecration of the Sabbath. In 1874 she went so far as to tell Disraeli that "the extreme Evangelical School do the Established Church as much harm as the High Church". In so far as a great part of what came to be seen as "Victorian" derived from the Evangelicals, the Queen's rejection of the majority of their tenets shows how far she transcended the shibboleths of her age.

Lord John Russell's ecclesiastical appointments were provocative and eccentric. Like many of his illustrious family he was obsessed by the Protestant ascendancy, but otherwise seemed to regard Anglicanism with an indifference bordering on scepticism. It is difficult to explain his choice of Hampden for Hereford except on the assumption that it was largely inspired by mischief. His most important appointment, that of Sumner to succeed Archbishop Howley, verged on the disastrous. In the first place his nominee was incapable of guiding the clergy through one of the most troublesome periods in their history, and in the second place, by discounting the claims of Wilberforce, he deprived the Church of the person best qualified to lead it. But the worse his mistakes, the more he could count on the Queen and Prince Albert's support, for no other Prime Minister campaigned so vigorously to undermine the Tractarians. Neither he nor they appreciated the pyrrhic nature of his victories which merely drove Anglican waverers to Rome.

When Palmerston died in 1865 he had appointed more than half the Bench of Bishops. During his ten years as Prime Minister he turned to Shaftesbury for guidance in exercising patronage. Naturally, Shaftesbury favoured his fellow Evangelicals, who soon achieved a predominance in the Church which neither their numbers nor ability could justify. The Queen was rightly critical of many of his appointments. She believed that Low Churchmen were sadly deficient in learning at a time when religion was under sustained attack. In 1860 she persuaded Palmerston to appoint the Master of St Catherine's College, Cambridge, to the diocese of Worcester; but before he finally yielded he could not resist telling her how "much mischief had been done by theological bishops". She was, however, unquestionably right to stress the importance of scholarship. After all, *The Origin of Species* had only just been published, and was ticking away like a time-bomb in a crypt.

6

Paradise Lost
1861–1901

I N 1859 Sir James Clark warned Prince Albert that he believed that the Duchess of Kent was suffering from a malignant tumour which would eventually prove fatal. The Prince decided to keep the news to himself. On March 9th, 1861, a few days after the sudden death of Sir George Couper, who had served her loyally for twenty-one years, the doctors decided to operate on a growth on her arm. At first she seemed to be making an excellent recovery for an old lady of seventy-four, but on March 15th she took so serious a turn for the worse that Sir James Clark urged the Queen to hurry to Windsor before it was too late. On reaching Frogmore she immediately went to her mother's darkened room. "I knelt before her," she wrote in her journal, "kissed her dear hand and placed it next my cheek; but, though she opened her eyes, she did not, I think, know me." That night she slept fitfully on a sofa, and at least three times "stole down with her little lamp, in her white dressing gown, and knelt kissing the hand and whispering 'Mama' so lovingly and earnestly as if the sound must rouse her". During her vigils, memories of her childhood at Kensington flooded back as she heard "the striking, at every quarter, of the old repeater, a large watch in a tortoiseshell case, which had belonged to my poor father".

At half past nine in the morning of March 16th, the Duchess ceased to breathe. The Queen, who had never before seen a person die, watched life ebbing away with mingled feelings of dread and fascination. "Her whole being, so instinct with vitality, recoiled in agony from the grim spectacle of that awful power", yet she could not but linger lovingly over the painful details of the last sad moments. When she went into her mother's sitting room "to weep and pray", her heart was wrung by the sight of the Duchess's "work basket with her work, and the little canary bird, which she was so fond of – singing". The Prince Consort was momentarily too upset to console the Queen and asked Princess Alice to "comfort Mama": a sacred injunction she never forgot, and which later that year she came to see as "a 'vorbedeutung' [portent] of what was to come".

So vehement was the Queen's despair that rumours began to spread that she had been driven mad by grief. Her one consolation was to sit in her mother's room, which was carefully kept as the Duchess left it. Some people even suspected she derived a perverse satisfaction from wallowing in her misery. On March 27th, she wrote to her "precious friend", Augusta, now Queen of Prussia, saying that her nerves were "terribly upset" and that she must have peace and quiet. "To lose a beloved mother is always terrible, but when you consider that this mother has lived for no one and nothing but me, that for 41 years I have never been separated from her for more than three months, that she was the gentlest, most tender and loving creature that one can ever imagine", then you can appreciate "how immeasurable is my loss and grief". "My dear husband," she added in a postscript, "has been a veritable angel of goodness to me in this terrible time." Never, said Lady Augusta Bruce, the Duchess's devoted companion and Lady-in-Waiting, had she seen "such tenderness, such gentleness, such tact as His – Oh! he is one in millions – well might She love Him as She did".

It took the Queen nearly six months to recover her shattered spirits, and there were times when "the grief and yearning" were almost too dreadful to bear. She lost her appetite, she felt "stupefied" and "stunned", she suffered from constant headaches, and could hardly endure "the least noise or talking". Even the sound of the wheels of her carriage on the gravel grated on her nerves. The Queen's despair was tainted by a strong vein of self-pity, and she fostered sorrow with a fond embrace. "You are right, dear child," she admitted to Vicky, "I do not wish to feel better. . . . The more others recover their spirits – the more trying it becomes to me." It was useless, she said, to exhort her to shake off depression. "I could not and would not." Lord Clarendon, who possessed a remarkably shrewd understanding of her self-indulgent nature, believed that she was so "determined to cherish her grief" that she almost resented attempts to console her. "I hope this state of things won't last," he told the

Duchess of Manchester, "or she may fall into the morbid melancholy to which her mind has often tended and which is a constant cause of anxiety to Prince Albert."

It would be idle to pretend that the Queen's orgy of grief was other than excessive, especially in view of the fact that her mother was nearly seventy-five when she died. But it must also be remembered that the Duchess's death was the first great sorrow she had encountered, and that she lived at a time when extravagant mourning was seen as proof of devotion. Moreover, her turbulent emotions were intensified by guilt over their earlier years of estrangement, particularly when she went through the Duchess's papers and found that her love for her was "beyond everything! Not a scrap of my writing – or of my hair has ever been thrown away – and such touching notes in a book about my babyhood". She was greatly helped in settling her mother's affairs by Lady Augusta Bruce, who became her resident "Woman of the Bedchamber" and "a kind of female secretary".

Prince Albert constantly tried to persuade the Queen "to take things as God sent them", but so accustomed had she become to having her own way that she found it exceedingly hard to submit to His will. In August, the Duchess's coffin was moved from St George's to her Mausoleum at Frogmore, which she had formerly used as a Summer House. When the Queen placed a wreath on her mother's granite sarcophagus, she "felt that it was only the earthly robe of her we loved so much was there – the pure, tender, loving spirit is above, and free from all suffering and woe".

Prince Albert went out of his way during their autumn migration to Scotland to revive the Queen's zest for living. The year before, they had made what she called their first "Great Expedition", and he decided to see whether another Highland journey could help to dispel her depression. In September 1860, they had travelled with Lady Churchill and General Grey, describing themselves as "Lord and Lady Churchill and party". Grant, the head keeper at Balmoral, and John Brown, who had entered royal service in 1851 and had subsequently been chosen to lead the Queen's pony, nearly destroyed their incognito by addressing them as "Your Majesty" and "Your Royal Highness". The expedition was decidedly arduous. The first day they covered some forty miles, travelling half the distance by pony, often being obliged to dismount to ford streams, cross boggy moors, or climb mountainous paths. Not until after dark did they reach the inn at Grantown where they planned to stay the night. While Brown and Grant made merry in the commercial room, the royal couple dined on vegetable broth, a fowl in white sauce, a leg of roast lamb, and a cranberry tart. When they retired to bed they had hardly room to move, as a huge four-poster took up most of the space. The Queen was particularly pleased with her Highland servants who proved so willing and cheerful. Brown, in particular, she thought "perfect – discreet, careful, intelligent, attentive . . .".

The Queen took an almost childish delight in travelling incognito: a recondite pleasure confined to the illustrious. The fun, however, was "not complete unless after a while there came disclosure; lacking that, it was like a play in which the highborn heroine takes a situation as a housemaid, and remains permanently unidentified". She was therefore gratified to learn that Albert had been recognised just before they left Grantown, and that its inhabitants "were ready to drop with astonishment and fright". She never failed to derive innocent satisfaction from failures to identify her. One evening at Windsor towards the end of her reign, she opened a window to breathe the night air, and was mistaken by a sentry for a servant. When he proposed that they should meet as soon as he came off duty, she hastily withdrew, but relished the incident so much that she often retold the story.

The second "Great Expedition" of 1861 consisted of the same party as before but with the addition of Princess Alice and her fiancé. This time they stayed at the "Ramsay Arms" at Fettercairn, some forty miles south-east of Balmoral. Prince Louis and General Grey were boarded out for the night in the nearby Temperance Hotel as there was not enough room for them all to stay under one roof. After dinner, the Royal Family took a stroll through the village by the light of the moon. Suddenly, they heard the sound of a drum and fifes and thought that they must have been recognised. On returning to their inn, they saw six Highlanders marching up and down outside, but it transpired that they often played there in the evening. Next morning, one of the guests at the Ramsay Arms insisted on breakfasting in the dining room assigned to the royal family, and was only persuaded to eat elsewhere when Brown told him that the room was occupied by "a wedding party from Aberdeen".

The next "great" expedition took place in October, and covered over one hundred and twenty miles in two days. On the first afternoon they stopped at an inn to water the horses, and were met by "a small, curious, chattering crowd of people" who seemed to suspect who they were. Brown, resourceful as ever, directed them to the wrong carriage, which the Queen thought "most amusing". They travelled for much of the day through torrential rain and wind, but the Queen contrived to keep dry "with the help of waterproofs and a plaid". It was not until quarter to nine that they reached Dalwhinnie, only to find that the inn was "not nearly so nice and cheerful" as the Ramsay Arms. Nor was the supper they were given particularly sustaining, consisting as it did of "two miserable starved chickens, without any potatoes", washed down with tea. But the discomforts of travel were all part of the fun, and the Queen described it as "the pleasantest and most enjoyable expedition I *ever* made", adding that nothing had cheered her so much since her "great sorrow". Her last expedition with the Prince took place a few days later on October 16th, 1861 It was a glorious sunny day but with ice and snow on the ground. They lunched in so precipitous a place that she could hardly bear to see anyone move backwards. Before they packed the luncheon baskets, the Prince "wrote on a bit of paper that we had lunched here, put it into the Selters – water bottle, and stuck it into the ground". On the way down, it was very slippery and the Queen had two falls, but, nothing daunted, claimed to be "much pleased and interested with this delightful expedition". Her beloved Highlands had soothed her bruised spirits and restored her eager appetite for enjoyment.

Prince Albert's passion for work was obsessive, if not neurotic. He began his day long before breakfast, in order to write letters, read despatches, and prepare drafts. So busy did he become that he would run down the corridors of Buckingham Palace and Windsor to save precious moments. Everybody seemed to want to consult him morning, noon and night. "Ask the Prince" was the solution to almost every problem. Occasionally he found time to relax over meals, but generally ate them in such a hurry that the Queen would warn him, "Not so fast, there is plenty of time". Like Peel, he never learned to delegate, and therefore spent far too long over trivial matters which could have been left to Phipps or General Grey. The consequence was that the Queen began to complain that she never saw him, and in 1862 she told Gladstone that towards the end of the Prince's life the demands on his time had so increased "that much of what they had formerly been used to do together . . . had been of necessity given up". Even Princess Beatrice was heard to echo her father's favourite excuse: "I have no time, I must write letters".

During the last ten years of Albert's life he was troubled by insomnia, which Sir James Clark attributed to "the mind". His appearance betrayed his sharp decline in health, and he looked middle-aged by the time that he was thirty. The Queen still regarded him as the incomparably handsome youth with whom she had fallen in love, but less partial observers remarked on his sallow complexion, his stooping gait, his portly figure, and his receding hair: intimations of mortality which he himself put down to worry and overwork. In 1859 the Queen told the Crown Princess, "My greatest of all anxieties is that dearest Papa works too hard", and "wears himself quite out by all he does".

During the Queen's visit to Coburg in 1860, the Prince had a merciful escape when the horses pulling his carriage suddenly bolted. Seeing that they were approaching a closed railway level-crossing, he decided to jump for safety, and only suffered from bruises and cuts to his face, hands and knees. Ernest, however, believed that his nervous system had been badly shaken, and that the accident was more serious than appeared. Just before the royal party was due to return to England, the Prince asked Ernest to join him on a walk. After a time, he stopped at one of his favourite views and felt for his handkerchief. "I thought," wrote Ernest, "his wound had begun to bleed afresh. I went up to him and saw that tears were trickling down his cheeks. He had become so absorbed in the thought that he would never see all this again, that his emotion got the better of him. When I tried to soothe him, he persisted in declaring that he was well aware that he had been here for the last time in his life." Some years earlier he had expressed a similar premonition to the Queen when he pointed to some saplings he had planted at Osborne and told her that he would never see them grow up. "Why not?" she asked. "You would be only sixty, and that is not so very old." "No," he said firmly. "I shall never see them grow up."

Soon after returning to England, the Prince had a bout of violent vomiting, shivering, and fever, which he put down to "English cholera". Hardly had he recovered from these distressing symptoms than he was attacked by agonising toothache, inflammation of the cheek, and swollen glands. The Queen was greatly distressed to see him so "despondent", and told Vicky she would willingly "have borne it all for him. . . . Sanders (the royal dentist) says it is the severest, most obstinate attack he has ever seen". Temporarily, his autumn migration to Balmoral cheered him up, but soon after returning to Windsor he was plunged into the deepest gloom by bad news from Portugal: King Pedro, and his brother, Prince Ferdinand, had both died of typhoid. "My Albert was very fond of him," wrote the Queen of "dear poor Pedro", and "loved him like a son." She, too had regarded her Portuguese "cousins" with special affection, and noted reproachfully, "We did not need this fresh loss in this sad year".

On November 22nd 1861 Prince Albert visited Sandhurst to see the Staff College building which had just been finished. It poured with rain all morning and he returned to Windsor soaked to the skin. On Sunday, November 24th, he accompanied the Queen to Frogmore to visit the Duchess's Mausoleum. That evening, he noted in his diary that he felt "thoroughly unwell", that he was "full of rheumatic pains", and that he had scarcely closed "his eyes at night for the last fortnight". But ill as he was, he set off next day to see Bertie and Colonel Bruce at Cambridge. So exhausted was he by this journey that on returning to Windsor on Tuesday he had to rest on a sofa.

A couple of weeks before this sudden descent on Cambridge, the Prince Consort had heard the "horrifying" news of his son's escapade at the Curragh, which the Queen insisted broke his heart. For a time he refused to credit the story, but searching enquiries confirmed that it was true. Had Bertie butchered his brothers and sisters and thrown their remains in the lake at Buckingham Palace, his father could hardly have been more indignant. On the first anniversary of his discovering the awful truth, the Queen recalled his "face of woe and sorrow". "Papa," she told Vicky, "was too perfect for this world", and his "pure, noble, heavenly spirit" was dreadfully grieved by its wickedness. Many Victorian fathers expected their sons to get into some sort of scrape, but Prince Albert saw the Prince of Wales's "Fall" as a devastating calamity. He had left nothing undone to shelter the boy from temptation, only to meet his match in a common harlot. If royalty was to survive in an age of revolutions it must be beyond reproach:

> "Wearing the white flower of a blameless life,
>   Before a thousand peering littlenesses,
>   In that fierce light that beats upon a throne . . ."

After twenty years' hard labour, he and the Queen had established a Court of impeccable propriety, only to see their life's work squandered by their son.

Before visiting Cambridge, the Prince Consort wrote Bertie a frenzied letter, accusing him of making himself the laughing stock of the town, and leaving himself at the mercy of Miss Clifden, who had it in her power to drag him through the courts, expose the "disgusting details" of their liaison, and break his parents' hearts. Unlike Charles II, Prince Albert would willingly have let "poor Nellie starve". This hysterical letter would have constituted an act of "gross deliberate cruelty" had his "own suffering not been apparent in every line". When father and son went for a walk together through the country lanes near Madingley, it became so clear that Bertie was deeply grieved by all the pain he had caused, that he was fortunately forgiven. Three days after his visit to Cambridge, the Prince told Vicky that he was at "a very low ebb", owing to "much worry and great sorrow". Like so much else, the Queen owed her conviction that Bertie was largely responsible for his father's illness to the Prince Consort himself.

News reached Windsor on November 28th of a grave incident off the American Coast, in which a British steamer, the *Trent*, had been stopped by an United States warship. Only after four Confederate envoys bound for Europe had been arrested, was she allowed to proceed for Southampton. When details of this episode reached England, eight thousand troops were sent to Canada to prepare for a possible war. On the evening of November 30th, the Queen received a copy of the letter which Lord John Russell planned to send to Washington. The Prince at once recognised that its tone was such as to deprive the American Government of a face-saving line of retreat. Consequently he got up at seven next morning to write to Russell proposing that the United States should be given an opportunity to withdraw gracefully, and that the Foreign Secretary should express the hope "that the American captain did not act under instructions, or, if he did, that he misapprehended them". Russell accepted the amendment, and the American Government, seizing the proffered excuse, blamed the incident on the excessive zeal of the officer concerned. It is hardly too much to claim that Prince Albert may have prevented an Anglo-American War. When he handed his draft to the Queen he told her that he had scarcely been able to hold his pen while he wrote it.

Somehow Prince Albert dragged himself to church on Sunday, December 1st, but next day felt too ill to get up, and lay shivering on a sofa. He insisted, however, on seeing Lord Methuen, who had just returned from Lisbon, in order to hear a detailed account of the deaths of his Portuguese cousins. It was a good thing, he said, that "his own illness was not fever as that, he felt sure, would be fatal to him". Lord Palmerston was so disturbed by H.R.H.'s symptoms that he urged the Queen to seek a second opinion. She thanked him frigidly for his "kind interest" – by which she meant unwarrantable interference – and assured him that the Prince was only suffering from a "feverish cold". The Queen's mood oscillated like a seismograph in an earthquake. The very evening she snubbed the Prime Minister for intervening, she confessed in her journal that she was "in an agony of despair" about her "dearest Albert", who seemed to have lost his interest in life. For the next three days the Prince refused all food, apart from a few sips of broth, and either wandered restlessly from room to room, or lay listlessly on his bed. The Queen was especially distressed by his "strange, wild look" and fits of irritability.

When the Prince awoke on December 7th after a restless, feverish sleep, it was clear he had taken a turn for the worse, particularly as a telltale rash had developed. "I went to my room," wrote the Queen, "and cried dreadfully and felt oh! as if my heart must break. Oh! such agony as exceeded all my grief this year." Sir James Clark, whose own wife was desperately ill at the time, temporarily left his patient to Dr Jenner, Professor of Clinical Medicine at University College. Nobody could have been better qualified to handle the Prince's case as he was celebrated throughout Europe for his research into typhoid and typhus. Nevertheless, he was not in charge of the patient, and was therefore obliged to defer to his senior colleague. In Sir James's absence, it fell to Jenner to explain to the Queen "in the kindest, clearest manner" that the Prince's rash confirmed earlier suspicions that his trouble was "gastric fever": a euphemism for typhoid. The Queen took the news surprisingly well. At first her "heart was ready to burst", but she soon cheered up when she remembered how many people had fever and survived.

Sir James Clark knew his patient well enough to recognise his obsessive fear of typhoid, and decreed that the word must never be used in H.R.H.'s hearing. There could be no point in impairing his chance of recovery by gratuitously demoralising him. Furthermore, he decided that everything must be done to disguise the gravity of the Prince's illness in view of the Queen's uncontrollable grief at the time of her mother's death. It was better, he thought, to permit her to cherish false hopes, than to leave her husband to read his fate in her eyes. Unfortunately this well intended conspiracy left her hopelessly unprepared for the final crisis. When Sir Charles Phipps wrote to the Duke of Cambridge to tell him that Prince Albert was suffering from "gastric fever", he ventured to suggest "Your Royal Highness knows the Queen well enough to be aware that Her Majesty cannot bear to be alarmed, and therefore if Your Royal Highness writes to Her Majesty it should be in a cheering tone". The doctors never ceased to hold out illusory hopes. One of them even told her on the day the Prince died: "I never despair with fever, my own son was left for dead and recovered". Phipps, on his own initiative, wrote almost daily to Palmerston, and endorsed Sir James's policy of doing everything possible to keep up Her Majesty's spirits. "The Prince himself, when ill," he warned, "is extremely depressed and low", and it required "no little management" to prevent the Queen "from breaking down altogether". In fact, elaborate precautions to keep H.R.H. in the dark were totally unnecessary. When Alice told him that she had written to let Vicky know he was seriously ill, he gently reproached her. "You did wrong: you should have told her I am dying."

On Sunday, December 9th, the Prince asked to be moved to the Blue Room: where George IV and William IV had died. But he was still allowed to wander about in his dressing gown, and his valet was left to nurse him. At times, his mind wandered, and he called for Colonel Bruce, but in lucid moments he asked Princess Alice to read to him. When the Queen saw him that evening, he was quite himself, called her "Liebes Frauchen", (dear little wife) and stroked her cheek affectionately. Next morning, she felt justified in writing to King Leopold to tell him that each passing day brought her "beloved invalid nearer the end of this tiresome illness". But on Friday, December 13th, the Prince's fever increased, as did his difficulty in breathing, and Jenner felt bound to warn H.M. how dangerous these symptoms were. She was so distraught by the news that she prayed and cried as if she was going mad, and Alice decided the time had come to send for the Prince of Wales.

During the night the Prince appeared to improve, and the Queen was told "there was ground to hope that the crisis was over". But even Sir James admitted to feeling "very, very anxious", despite a "decided rally". When she first saw Albert next morning she never forgot how "beautiful" he looked, "with his face lit up by the rising sun", and "his eyes unusually bright, gazing as it were at unseen objects". Soon after twelve, she went out for a breath of air with Alice, and strolled up and down the Castle terrace, while a distant band played martial music, and the sun shone as if all was right with the world. For the rest of the day she resumed her vigil by Albert's bedside, or sat in the next door room. Sometimes his mind began to wander and he mumbled a few words in French, but she never gave way in his presence and managed to seem cheerful. Towards evening, the doctors became more despondent, and were particularly disturbed by the rapidity of his breathing caused by the onset of pneumonia. At about six o'clock, the Queen left the darkened sick room and succumbed to "a terrible burst of misery", but soon managed to pull herself together and return with a confident smile. Bending over the Prince she whispered "Es ist kleines Frauchen!" (It is your own little wife!) and he leant forward and kissed her.

As the Prince's end approached, the Queen knelt by his side, holding his cold, left hand, while Bertie, Alice and Lenchen clustered round the bed. At about ten forty-five, he took two or three long gentle breaths and then "*all, all* was over". "Oh, yes, this is death," said the Queen as she watched the passing of that blameless soul. "I know it. I have seen it before." She then kissed the Prince's "dear heavenly forehead and called out in a bitter and agonising cry 'Oh! My dear Darling!'" For a moment or so, she addressed him "by every endearing name" and then sank to her knees "in mute distracted despair, unable to utter a word or shed a tear!" Eventually she allowed herself to be supported to the adjoining room where the Prince of Wales threw himself into her arms promising to help her in every possible way. "I am sure my dear boy, you will", she murmured, kissing him again and again. Supported by Alice, she consoled the doctors for what Lady Augusta called their "unsuccess", and then the Household filed past her, desperately searching for words of consolation. "You will not desert me?" she begged them, clutching each by the hand. "You will all help me?" Soon afterwards, she sent for the Duchess of Atholl and took her into the Blue Room. For a moment they stood silently gazing at the Prince, and then suddenly the Queen threw herself onto the bed, "with both her arms extended on the corpse", moaning "Oh! Duchess! he is dead! He is dead!" The poor Duchess watched helplessly, not knowing what to say, as the Queen was convulsed by grief.

The cause of Prince Albert's death was officially given as "typhoid", doubtless attributable to "the noxious effluvia" which escaped from the drains at Windsor. As one courtier put it, "There are more stinks in royal residences than anywhere else". Nevertheless, there are grounds for supposing that the Prince may have died from some other cause. In the first place, Sir James was notorious for errors in diagnosis. Indeed, most of the royal physicians, according to Lord Clarendon, were unfit "to attend a sick cat". Secondly, the doctors were plainly puzzled by some of their patient's symptoms. Thirdly, it is rare to find solitary victims of typhoid. It is possible therefore that the Prince's fatal illness was the terminal episode of a chronic disease, such as cancer of the bowels. In 1862 the Queen astonished Lord Derby by telling him that she had always feared that the Prince would not recover. "Some people," she said, "rally much better than others: it is all pluck." Derby suspected that she had picked up this expression from her children without fully understanding it. Presumably what she meant to say was that Albert preferred to submit to whatever God decreed than to put up a useless fight.

The night the Prince died, Phipps wrote to the Duke of Cambridge to break the "dreadful" news. The Queen, he said in the course of his letter, had shown "quite wonderful" self-control and good sense, although overwhelmed with grief. Next day, he informed Lord Palmerston that "the Queen's calmness and submissive resignation to the will of God in view of this stunning affliction is wonderful". Only a few months earlier, the Prince had lectured her "severely about giving way so completely on the death of her mother, and told her to remember that the blow was dealt by the hand of the All Wise". Those words kept coming back to her as she struggled to face the future without him. "Now you see I am calm," she would say, "I am profiting by his advice, I am doing what he wished."

On Sunday, December 15th, the Queen twice visited the Blue Room, and thought that the Prince looked as "beautiful as marble" as he lay in a sea of flowers. Much as she longed to see him once more, she decided not to do so, for fear that this last sad image would drive out happier memories. Four days later she left for Osborne, but not before choosing a site for a mausoleum in which she would one day be reunited with Albert. Meanwhile, Princess Alice telegraphed to Vicky: "Do come. Mama wants you so much." But the Crown Princess was expecting a child and her doctors refused to allow her to travel, so Alice was left to struggle alone to try to comfort her mother. Once, indeed, she did momentarily smile when Beatrice expressed her regret at being too young to have been at her wedding, but jokes lost half their savour when they could not be shared with the Prince. One of the few things which sustained her were mementoes of her husband. Wherever she went she carried his watch, keys and red handkerchief with her. No early Christian derived greater consolation from the jawbone of a saint than did the Queen from these sacred relics.

In order to appreciate why the Queen was so devastated by the Prince Consort's death, it is essential to understand that her loss was unique. On the day Prince Albert died, Lord Clarendon told the Duchess of Manchester that he could hardly bring himself to contemplate the consequences of the tragedy. "You know, just as I do," he wrote, "what the real relations were between him and her, and how different they necessarily were from those of any other man and wife; for no other woman has the same public responsibility or the same motive for being absolutely guided by . . . her husband." Very few people at the time had any idea how much the Prince assisted the Queen in her duties. Lord Stanley once overheard him at a dinner party prompting her in German "to enquire about this, that, or the other": advice she "never failed to follow". "What will happen?" Phipps asked Palmerston in despair. "Where can she look for that support and assistance upon which she has leaned in the greatest and least questions of her life?"

It was precisely because the Queen proved so successful in merging her personality in that of the Prince, that she suffered such violent symptoms of withdrawal, and was left with an aching sense of "belonging to no one any more". "Truly," she wrote, "he was my entire self, my very life and soul, yes even my conscience if I can describe it thus. . . . I only lived through him, my heavenly Angel! Surely there can never again be such a union, such trust and understanding between two people." As she saw it, a new reign began the moment the Prince died, and she was "changed from a powerful sovereign . . . into a weak and desolate woman". Her first instinct was to cling to his memory for posthumous support, to implement his policies and be guided by his advice. "I try," she said, "to feel and think I am living on with him, and that his pure and perfect spirit is leading me and inspiring me."

When Albert died, the Queen suffered "agonies of longing for her husband". "I am, alas! not old," she exclaimed, "and my feelings are strong and warm; my love is ardent." On December 18th, 1861, she informed Vicky that "sweet little Beatrice comes to lie in my bed every morning which is a comfort. I long so to cling and clasp a loving being." The trouble was that she possessed a particularly passionate nature – some said she had inherited the sexual libido of her Hanoverian ancestors – and was consequently tormented by unfulfilled desires. When Vicky eventually joined her at Osborne in February, 1862, she told Fritz, who had stayed behind in Berlin, that "Poor Mama has to go to bed, has to get up alone – for ever. She was as much in love with Papa as though she had married him yesterday". When she retired for the night, she cried herself to sleep, clutching "his dear red dressing-gown". The most obvious solution to her "wild longings" would have been to marry again, but this she refused to consider for one moment. She strongly objected to widows remarrying, although she herself was the child of just such an union.

A dominant theme of the Queen's letters for most of the eighteen sixties, was her sense of utter forlornness. "The two creatures who loved me most," she told Queen Augusta, "and to whom I was dearest on earth are gone: my dear mother and my Adored Angelic Husband, and I miss them so terribly. There is no one left to hold me in their arms and press me to their heart." In 1862 she spoke to Mrs Gladstone of her "awful loneliness", and told her that she found herself "constantly expecting to find the Prince – whether out walking or coming into the room and hearing his footsteps". Even as late as 1872 she still saw fit to describe herself as a "deserted child", almost as if she held Albert to blame for abandoning her so suddenly. Nor was she greatly comforted to be told that she could not possibly feel lonely when surrounded by her Court. Few things accentuate solitude more effectively than a crowd.

The very evening the Prince died, the Queen insisted that she would never allow her misfortune to interfere with her work. "They need not be afraid," she said, "I will do my duty." She began by being as good as her word and signed several urgent documents on December 17th. But soon after moving to Osborne, she seemed to forget her earlier resolution, and refused to see her ministers.

Presumably the sight of Lord Palmerston was more than her shattered nerves could stand. When it became imperative to hold a Privy Council, she grudgingly agreed to grace the proceedings through a half open door, and ministers were obliged to shout at the top of their voices while she sat unseen in the next room.

Throughout the Queen's first winter as a widow, she looked "thin and worn", complained of headaches and feeling cold, and was so weak that she hardly seemed able "to move one leg before the other". When Princess Mary of Cambridge saw her in March, she found her as "rigid as stone and the picture of desolate misery". One look sufficed to show how shattered she had been by the calamity which had befallen her. Her life, she insisted, was over. "Pleasure, joy – all is for ever gone." Nobody knew better than Alice what pain her mother endured. "How you suffered was dreadful to witness," she told her several years later, "it tore my heart to pieces."

In May, 1862, the Queen returned to Balmoral, "where everything, even down to the smallest detail, is somehow associated with him and his memory". "Oh! darling child," she wrote to Vicky, "the agonising sobs as I crawled up with Alice and Affie! The stags' heads – the rooms – blessed, darling Papa's room – then his coats – his caps – kilts – all, all convulsed my poor shattered frame!" Her plight reminded her of one of her favourite stanzas from "In Memoriam".

> "But I remained, whose hopes were dim,
> Whose life, whose thoughts were little worth,
> To wander on a darkened earth,
> Where all things round me breathed of him."

When the Duke of Argyll arrived at the Castle as Minister-in-Attendance, he was warned by the Factor, Dr Robertson, that the Queen had "had a day of the deepest waters to go through". Nevertheless, he was taken aback to find that she was momentarily struck dumb and could only shake her head in mute bewilderment. But gradually the Highlands began to work their magic, and the Queen felt consoled by the Prince's haunting presence, until, in the end, she came to regard Balmoral as a sanctuary and a shrine in which to assuage her grief and cherish her memories. In 1863 she told Queen Augusta, "the wild, grim, solitary mountains, where no human soul is, comfort me! The mountains, the woods, the rocks seem to talk of him, for he wandered and climbed so often among them".

The Queen's incessant concern for her suffering became a form of selfishness. So totally did she indulge in "the luxury of woe" that all she wanted to do was "to sit and weep and live only with Him in spirit and take no interest in the things of this earth". Florence Nightingale once remarked that H.M. reminded her "of the women in the Greek Chorus, with her hands clasped above her head, wailing out her inexpressible despair". The Queen herself admitted that she clung to grief, but claimed it was therapeutic. "For me," she wrote in 1862, "my very misery is now a necessity and I could not exist without it. Like Tennyson says:

> 'O sorrow, wilt thou live with me
> No casual mistress, but a wife,
> My bosom-friend and half of life,
> As I confess it needs must be . . .'

This is what I feel; yes, I long for my suffering almost – as it is blinded with him!"

Most people saw the Queen's profound mourning as a tribute to her devotion, but some believed that she overindulged in death and all its horrors. Marie Mallet, who accompanied her to Grasse in 1891, was astonished by the intensity of her concern over the obsequies of a housemaid, and her apparent obsession with funerals, "coffins and winding sheets". When Norman Macleod died she immediately wrote to his brother asking for all the details "of the last moments and illness of her dear friend". It is difficult to resist the suspicion that such blatant curiosity was not altogether wholesome, although it may partly be traced to the evangelical cult of "holy dying". The Queen's granddaughter, "Missy" (the Queen of Roumania), recalling her childhood, remembered "mysterious photographs of dead people . . . which, although they made us feel creepy, we always furtively looked at again and again". It was generally accepted by those who knew the Queen best that there were few things she liked better than organising funerals: a passion which her subjects also shared. Whenever she stayed at Windsor, she always carried the keys to Frogmore round her neck, and never returned from the mausoleum without seeming to be consoled.

There were widespread fears that the shock of the Prince's death might drive the Queen out of her mind, particularly as she had "trembled in the balance" after losing her mother in March. Nobody, least of all the Queen herself, could forget that her grandfather, George III, had apparently died insane, and there were grounds for fearing the malady might be hereditary. In June, 1862, she told Lord Clarendon that "her mind was strained to the utmost". She begged him to warn Lord Derby, the Leader of the Opposition, that a change of Ministry "would be more than her reason could stand", and that "three times at Balmoral she had thought she was going mad". Clarendon noticed that "while talking of the state of her mind, her eye and manner became excited", and that she was evidently in "a highly nervous state". More than once she murmured "My reason, my reason" and tapped her forehead to show where the problem lay.

By the spring of 1862, rumours were circulating that the Queen had gone out of her mind and refused to believe that her husband was dead: largely inspired, no doubt, by her fervent attempts to keep his memory alive. When Clarendon saw her at Windsor that March he could not help noticing that she repeatedly referred to "the Prince's opinions and acts as if he was in the next room", and he found it "difficult not to think that he was so for everything was set out on his table, the blotting book open with a pen upon it, his watch going, fresh flowers in a glass, etc., etc.; just as I have seen them all a 100 times". Reports that the Queen had lost her senses even reached St Petersburg, and when Prince Alexander of Hesse visited her in 1863 he promised to tell his sister, the Tsarina, whether she was "all there or not". In fact, he confounded the gossips by reporting that he had seldom met anyone more sane.

The deep feelings of insecurity which the Queen developed during her childhood led her to seek assurance in later life by clinging to the familiar. In 1895 Marie Mallet noted that "there seems a curious charm to our beloved Sovereign in doing the same thing on the same day year after year". Like the hands of a clock which have stopped at the precise moment of an earthquake, the life of the Court remained permanently stuck at December 1861. Ever after, the Queen observed the canonical year established by the Prince, and fiercely resisted the slightest attempt to modify her ritual. She always resented changes thrust upon her, whether by fractious ministers or divine decree; and especially deplored the deaths of those who had known her in happier days. Few people observed anniversaries more scrupulously, largely because they provided her with landmarks to guide her through the year. However threatening the future might appear, the past, at least, was unchangeable: hence the tenacity with which she clung to it. Indeed, at the time of her mother's death, the Prince reproached her for living too much in the past: a tendency which hardened into obsession in the early months of her widowhood. She was not, however, alone in her zeal. Gladstone's daughter, Mary, observed what her family called "dayums" with similar insistence. But not everyone proved so scrupulous. "Naughty Affie", when a midshipman of fourteen, forgot the eighteenth anniversary of his parents' wedding, until he received an indignant telegram asking him "if he remembered what day it was".

Naturally, of all days in the year December 14th was the one she recalled most vividly. So much so that in 1895, her grandson, Prince George (George V), was extremely concerned when the birth of his second son took place on that anniversary. The situation was saved by his father's suggestion that the best way to break the news would be to invite the Queen to become the boy's godmother, and to propose calling him "Albert". Much to Prince George's relief, she told him how "pleased and gratified" she was by his letter. Indeed, "this dear little boy (George VI), born the day when his beloved great-grandfather entered on a new greater life", would be especially dear to her.

During the early years of her widowhood the Queen longed to die and for a time persuaded herself that she would only survive the Prince by a few months at most. In 1862 she began putting her papers in order because she was "naturally much occupied with leaving this world". A year later, she was still convinced that her days were numbered and warned King Leopold that her life would "end *more* rapidly than any of you think; for *myself* this would be the *greatest, greatest* blessing . . .". In 1888, she confessed to Vicky that she had been tempted to put an end to her life in the early days of her widowhood, "but a *Voice* told me for *His* sake – no, 'Still Endure'." Eventually, she recovered her zest for living, and when she was eighty-one prayed for a few more years to "do what I can for my country and those I love".

The first time it was brought home to the Queen how much there was still to be done was in 1863, when she and Alice were driving home from Loch Muich. Some miles from Balmoral, their carriage began to lurch from side to side, as a "confused" coachman – a royal euphemism for drunk – lost sight of the snow-covered road. "We called out: 'What's the matter?' There was an awful pause, during which Alice said: 'We are upsetting.' In another moment – during which I had time to reflect whether we should be killed or not, and thought there were still things I had not settled and wanted to do – the carriage turned over on its side, and we were all precipitated to the ground!" Fortunately, she escaped with cuts and bruises, and was granted a further thirty-eight years to complete her unfinished business.

Towards the end of the Queen's reign hardly anyone could remember seeing her except in widow's weeds, and she imprinted herself on the public mind as a melancholy old lady, gazing morosely into the middle distance. In fact, the severity of her expression owed as much to the stress of being photographed – long exposures obliged the sitter to assume a frozen stare – as to her state of mind. Even by the late eighteen-sixties her clothes were already old-fashioned, and her ample skirts, with plenty of pockets for keys and handkerchiefs, were practical rather than elegant. Lady Wolseley described her as wearing "a black silk dress made *anyhow* and *nohow*", with a lace shawl draped over her shoulders. Some of her clothes were even bought from Caley's, the local Windsor draper, which was hardly the sort of couturier her Ladies-in-Waiting patronised.

Emily Tennyson, the Poet Laureate's wife, spoke of the Queen in 1863 as looking "small and childlike, full of intelligence and ineffably sweet". But Gladstone was less effusive, and told his wife that Her Majesty weighed eleven stone, eight ounces, "which was rather much for her height". Dejected as she appeared in repose, her whole "countenance lit up with unexpected radiance" the instant she laughed or smiled. Lord Ribblesdale attributed her "half cross, half tired expression", which Von Angeli caught so well when he painted her in 1875, to the fact that her mind was "overtaxed". The Queen herself thought the portrait "absurdly like . . . as if I looked at myself in the glass". She particularly admired the artist's "honesty, total want of flattery, and appreciation of character": three of her own pre-eminent virtues.

It has now become clear in the light of modern knowledge that Queen Victoria suffered a nervous breakdown in the early years of her widowhood. Naturally, given the ignorance of the time, nobody understood her disorder, but, in fact, she exhibited symptoms of "neurasthenia": fatigue, listlessness, irritability, anxiety, nausea, and headaches. The complaint is especially common in middle life and may often be traced to emotional trauma. The patient shows no obvious signs of disease, apart from a quickened pulse-rate or palpitations, but finds sustained exertion almost impossible. In so far as the neurosis is susceptible to remedy, the most promising treatment is rest and a change of scene. The Queen's breakdown lasted for most of the eighteen-sixties, the worst decade of her life.

In the summer of 1863 the Queen told King Leopold that she was suffering from "*violent* nervous headaches" and "*complete* prostration", which she attributed to "overwork, over-anxiety and the weight of responsibility and *constant* SORROW and *craving* and yearning for the ONE absorbing object of my love . . .". In other letters she spoke of herself as "failing in power, in memory, a *wreck*", and even as gradually "wasting away". Her pulse-rate was so high that she was terribly exhausted, and she was plagued by "bilious derangement". Even the noise of London traffic proved too much for her, as did "the slightest agitation or worry". This litany of ailments reads like a classic case-history of neurasthenia. It should also be remembered that the Queen's psychological breakdown coincided with what the Victorians called "le temps de la vie", in itself traumatic enough.

The fact that no one would take her illness seriously, increased the Queen's distress: a trouble inherent in psychogenic disorders. In 1863 she was furious with General Grey for giving King Leopold too favourable a report of her health, and she hastened to tell her uncle that she had "hardly been a day free from headache and nervous pains". Just because she was often "excited, flushed and feverish", it was absurd to conclude she was well. The following year she told Vicky that her "weakness, nervousness and trembling" had "greatly increased", adding reproachfully, "all this I know you can hardly understand, my good, dear child, for you think I have greater strength and courage than I have . . .". Five years later, she was still reprimanding the Crown Princess for wilfully refusing to acknowledge "how impossible it is for me to bear noise and excitement without feeling really ill, but so it is – and it gets worse every year".

It was widely suspected that the Queen's infirmities were conveniently selective. Clarendon once described her as "roaring well" and apparently capable of doing "everything she likes and nothing she doesn't". On what principle, it was asked, was it possible for her to remain at a Gillie's Ball long after midnight, while declining to spend even half an hour at a Drawing-room? Her well-known stamina helped to encourage scepticism. In reality, her physical condition was more or less irrelevant, seeing that her problem was mainly in her mind. Gladstone was one of the few people who recognised that "the woes of fancy are as real in their consequences as the most fearful dispensations of Providence", but somehow he never convinced the Queen that he understood how she suffered.

General Grey, a rugged old soldier, dismissed the Queen as a "Royal Malingerer", with whom he believed it was necessary to take a "peremptory" tone: the traditional, bracing, common-sense remedy of laymen confronting neurosis. Moreover, he saw the problem as mainly one of will. "The unchecked habit" of years of "self-indulgence", he once told Gladstone, made it impossible for her to give up a single whim without "nervous agitation". Grey maintained that she was totally unscrupulous in resorting to moral blackmail. "All she says," he confessed in 1869, "of 'the weight of work', 'weakened health' – shattered nerves, etc. – has simply no effect whatever on me. Neither health nor strength are wanting, were inclination what it should be." Gladstone suspected that Grey was over severe, but agreed that the Queen's exploitation of her health was a subtle form of selfishness.

Her Majesty's doctors tended to play safe by taking the view that their patient was always right. They soon discovered that it was wiser to accept her version of her ailments than to risk her wrath by challenging it. Nor were they disposed to repudiate her self-prescribed remedies: long periods of recuperation in the Highlands, and a virtual ban on public engagements. "Her Majesty's Physicians," Phipps warned the Prime Minister in December 1863, "are very decidedly of opinion that with a due regard to the preservation of Her Majesty's health", it would be highly undesirable for her to "appear in state upon public occasions". It was widely believed that Sir William Jenner, who succeeded Sir James Clark as the Queen's "Personal Physician" in 1862, encouraged her to malinger. From the first, she warmed to his jovial common sense and sympathetic nature, and when he died in 1898 she described him as "a most devoted and faithful servant, a most able doctor, and a truly kind friend to whom I could always speak frankly and confidentially". What especially commended him to her was that he endorsed her belief that worry and overwork were overtaxing her brain, and that what she needed was peace and rest. In 1866, at the Queen's prompting, he assured Lord John Russell that "the shattered state of her nerves" demanded an "entire change of air at least twice a year". Sir William was evidently an advocate of the maxim "a little of what you fancy does you good".

From time to time, Jenner sent letters to *The Lancet* in a bid to disarm the Queen's critics. Some of these communications were virtually written at her dictation. Nor were his duties confined to practising medicine. In 1869 he was employed as a "go-between" with Gladstone over Irish disestablishment, and in 1885 he was required to persuade Lord Salisbury to ally with the Liberal Unionists in an effort to thwart Home Rule. Throughout his career at Court, whether acting as a doctor or a political intermediary, he never forgot that his duty was to the Queen. On one occasion he justified the wording of a bulletin by suggesting that it was better to announce that "the Queen can't do so and so because of her health – which is to a certain extent true – than to say she won't".

Gladstone, in common with most of his colleagues, believed that Jenner was "an admirable doctor" but had allowed himself to become "a mere court tool". So single-minded was he in looking after the Queen, that he refused to make any allowance for the exigencies of politics. Grey, Ponsonby, and even her own children, shared Gladstone's conviction that Jenner was too malleable, and encouraged her "fancies about her health". The fact remains that Sir William's instincts were sound, and that any attempt to put her under pressure only made her more stubborn. Nobody ever succeeded in persuading him to compromise his judgement, or to risk the Queen's health for political purposes. The more successful he proved in preserving her peace of mind, the more he was bound to antagonise those threatening to disturb it.

It is impossible to decide how far the Queen was the victim of neurosis, and how far she exploited diplomatic illnesses. But whatever her motives might be, their outcome was clear enough: contentious disputes with ministers regarding her public duties. In 1867, to take one typical example, Lord Derby begged her to postpone her departure for Osborne for three days in order to receive the Sultan of Turkey during his visit to England. If Britain was to retain her influence at Constantinople it was imperative to fête him. The Queen, however, took a great deal of convincing of the need to change her plans. Lord Derby humbly apologised for proffering what he recognised was "unpalatable" advice, but felt bound to point out that Napoleon III had given the Sultan a spectacular reception, and that "a most unfortunate impression would be produced not only on the Sultan, but on the public mind of this country, if a very marked contrast could be drawn between the cordiality of his reception in Paris and an absence of any similar indication here". He therefore entreated Her Majesty to consider postponing her journey and receive the Sultan "if only for ten minutes". There was, he added, a distinct possibility that the Turks might be driven into the arms of France if they felt they had been cold-shouldered.

The Queen grudgingly consented to invite the Sultan to luncheon at Buckingham Palace, but not before pointing out that she was "almost driven to desperation by the want of consideration shown by the *public* for her health and strength". She warned Lord Derby that she foresaw "a *complete breakdown* of her nervous system . . . working and drudging as she does from *morning* till *night*, and weighed down by the responsibility and care of her most unenviable position and with the anxieties consequent upon being the widowed mother of so large a family". "Often," she said, "she wished that the time might come when she could go to that world 'Where the wicked cease from troubling and the weary are at rest'." It must plainly be understood that her shattered nerves "*prevented*" her from appearing in public, and she refused to "be dictated to, or teased by public clamour into doing what she physically CANNOT, and she expects Ministers to protect her from such attempts". In the course of these exchanges, she sent Dr Jenner to warn Derby that "any great departure from her usual way of life, or more than ordinary agitation, might produce insanity". Just as old men rattle their wills to bring their children to heel, so Queen Victoria browbeat her ministers with threats of a nervous breakdown.

Unlike most newspapers and politicians, Jenner had reason to know how hard the Queen worked. The public, however, appeared to believe she had virtually nothing to do, judging her duties in the light of her rare appearances. This ludicrous impression appeared to be confirmed by the publication in 1868 of *Leaves from the Journal of Our Life in the Highlands*. Given that these recollections concentrated on her rare moments of leisure, it was hardly reasonable to conclude that her life was one long holiday. When Martin published the second volume of his biography of the Prince Consort, he expressed a hope that it would show Her Majesty's subjects just how much work she was left to undertake when deprived of the Prince "who took from

the cares of royalty more than half their burden". Most of her waking
hours were spent at her desk, except for meals and exercise. "From
the hour she gets out of bed till she gets into it again there is work,
work, work – letter-boxes, questions etc. which are dreadfully
exhausting." Her whole life, she once told Vicky, was made up of
work and organised round it, and others must learn to accommodate
themselves to the rigours of her routine.

Only the Sovereign enjoys the unique privilege of serving a life
sentence of hard labour. Even the most enduring politicians spend
part of their time out of office. The last but one of Queen Victoria's
Prime Ministers was not even born when she came to the throne.
Yet few people seemed to think it unreasonable that she should work
for three hundred and sixty-five days a year. Nor could she ever
hope to escape for more than a few hours. It was not unknown for
despatch boxes to follow her half way up Loch-na-Gar. Never before
had an English Sovereign proved so assiduous a correspondent, or
so dedicated a bureaucrat. In 1878, at the height of the Eastern Crisis,
she wrote to Disraeli at least once a day and telegraphed every hour.
Four years later, at the time of Tel-el-Kebir, she sent the Secretary-
of-State for War seventeen letters in less than twenty-four hours.
During the course of her reign, she wrote, on average, two and a
half thousand words a day, adding up to a grand total of some sixty
million. If she had been a novelist, her complete works would have
run into seven hundred volumes, published at the rate of one a
month. In the archives at Broadlands there are twelve hundred of
her letters to Palmerston, and he was only one of twenty or more
ministers with whom she conducted a sizeable correspondence. She
also wrote countless letters to her children and grandchildren, an
increasingly arduous task as her family multiplied. Never a week
passed, from the time the Princess Royal married, until the dawn of
the twentieth century, without her hearing at least once from Windsor, Balmoral or Osborne.

The Queen spent a great deal of time reading as well as writing,
a task made more arduous by her resolve to follow Prince Albert's
plan "to *sign nothing* until he had read and made notes upon what he
had signed". In January 1901, when it became clear that she was
dying, Arthur Balfour hurried to Osborne and "was astounded at
the accumulation of official boxes that had taken place during the
last week, when Her Majesty was too unwell to deal with them".
Ten years earlier, Lady Waterford crossed the Solent in one of the

royal yachts and found herself wedged between two bags "as big as large armchairs". When she asked what they contained, she was told that they were the first of two deliveries of Her Majesty's daily mail. By dint of unrivalled diligence, the Queen transformed the Crown into a major Department of State, with no other help than that of her husband, and, later, her private secretaries.

There were two principal reasons why the Queen's work had increased, was increasing, and ought to have been diminished. Suddenly, overnight, she found herself forced to resume all the work which the Prince had been doing for her. Seeing that it was supposed to have killed him, the load was clearly crushing. It might, of course, have been mitigated by judicious delegation, but this she refused to contemplate. In some respects she was her own worst enemy, as much of the work she insisted on doing could have been done by others. It was not strictly necessary, for example, to check the proofs of the Court Circular, but she maintained that unless she did so, "the stupidest mistakes occur". The problem was further compounded by the growing trend to collectivism in the second part of her reign, which led to an increase in legislation and government departments. Precisely the same tendencies were at work within the British Empire. In 1858, to take one instance, the Crown assumed the responsibilities of the East India Company, which immediately increased the number of duties the Queen was required to perform: studying Indian despatches, approving draft instructions, confirming civil appointments, sanctioning proposed legislation, and corresponding with the newly created Secretary of State for India. The fact that Sir Henry Ponsonby and General Grey both died of strokes was gruesome evidence of the growth of royal business.

It was not in the Queen's nature to suffer in silence. The first time she saw Lady Lyttelton after Prince Albert's death, she told her between sobs, "I must work *so* hard – all day long – and no one to help or advise me. No one *above me*". In many of her letters, she spoke of being "fagged to death with work", "driven half mad with worry" and "overwhelmed with business". Indeed, she could seldom speak of herself without the note of self-pity creeping in. "I am well nigh worn out with all I have to do," she warned Vicky. "Anxiety, trouble and grief are all I have now – with nothing to cheer or brighten my sad life of constant incessant labour." Dr Jenner, at least, recognised how she suffered. In 1871, when he feared she was so ill that she might die within twenty-four hours, he threatened to publish a bulletin denouncing the Government for working her to death.

In August 1871, the Queen wrote to the Lord Chancellor, Lord Hatherley, protesting against the audacity of the Government in requesting her to delay her departure for Balmoral until Parliament was prorogued. At the best of times she resented attempts to alter her plans, but something in the tone of Gladstone's approach goaded her to frenzy, conceivably because "she knew, *au fond*, that she was defending the indefensible". "The Queen," her letter began, "has seen from long experience that the more she yields to pressure and clamour" the more she is "teased and tormented" with further demands. She had reluctantly decided to delay her departure by three days in response to the Prime Minister's appeal, but only on condition that there must be no further "interference with the Queen's personal acts and movements". The Government should plainly state that she could not "undertake any night work in hot rooms . . . nor any residence in London beyond 2 or 3 days at a time, as the air, noise and excitement make her quite ill", and caused her "violent headaches and great prostration". It was "abominable" that people refused to understand that there were limits to her powers. "What killed her beloved husband?" she demanded, in a powerful peroration. "Overwork and worry. What killed Lord Clarendon? The same. What has broken down Mr Bright and Mr Childers and made them retire, but the same; and the Queen, a woman, no longer young is supposed to be proof against all, and to be driven and abused till her nerves and health will give way with worry and agitation."

That autumn, Disraeli assured a rustic audience at Hughenden that only the Queen's ill-health prevented her from resuming those public duties which it had once been "her pride and pleasure to fulfil". But nothing had stopped her for one moment from carrying out "those much higher duties" which she was called upon to perform, and to which she brought a precision and punctuality unequalled by previous Monarchs. Ponsonby, who of all men was in the best position to judge, was "amazed at her industry". The editors of the nine volumes of the Queen's official Correspondence, were all agreed that nothing came out more strongly in the documents than "the laborious patience" with which she "kept herself informed of the minutest details of political and social movements both in her own and other countries". Si Monumentum requiris, circumspice.

Two forces combined to make the Queen invisible: her distaste for public appearances, and her yearning to hide from the world. It was "quite impossible", she told Prince Albert on their honeymoon, for her to leave London while Parliament was in session, but during the eighteen-sixties she visited it so rarely that Bagehot saw fit to describe her as a "retired widow". It is true that it was the custom of the mid-nineteenth century to make the most of mourning and withdraw for a time from society. But this could hardly be seen as entitling a Queen Regnant to succumb to that "fatal passion for retirement" which sorrow seems to beget. Even in happier days she was desperately shy and dreaded appearing in public. So much so, that in 1840 Lord Melbourne warned her that it was of the greatest importance that she should get over her "dislike of going amongst everybody: mustn't let it be known; it would be very injurious". But the moment her husband died, what began as a minor phobia became a major obsession. She dreaded, for example, breaking down as she drove through the streets with that vacant seat beside her. Soon, the very idea of performing a duty with which the Prince had formerly been associated plunged her into hysteria, and she implored Martin to use his influence with the press to make it clear that it was not merely sorrow but ill-health which forced her to live in seclusion.

One of the reasons the Queen gave for shrinking from the world was that she was more and more shocked by "the wickedness of mankind". She often spoke of her increasing desire "to lead a private life tending the poor and sick": a legacy of her cult of Florence Nightingale. Even during the time she shrank from the public, she privately visited workhouses, prisons and hospitals. The life which best suited her "broken and bleeding heart" was that of Balmoral. By the same token, she grew to detest London, particularly its noise, frivolity and ceremonial demands. Seldom at a loss to rationalise her phobias, she attributed her aversion to its "dreadful atmosphere". In 1862, she secretly visited Buckingham Palace for the first time since the Prince Consort's death, and saw enough to convince her that she could never "live there again except for two or three days at a time". From that moment on, she became as rare a visitor to London as snow in August.

For over two years the Queen's subjects respected her right to hide herself from view. But by 1864 they began to show less forbearance, and in March of that year posters were fixed to the railings of Buckingham Palace offering: "These commanding premises to be let or sold, in consequence of the late occupants declining business". In 1866, Kate Amberley, Lord John Russell's daughter-in-law, noted in her journal: "Everyone is abusing the Queen very much for not being in London or Windsor. . . . No respect or loyalty seems left in the way people allow themselves to talk of the Queen saying things like 'What do we pay her for if she will not work?' and 'She had better abdicate if she is incompetent to do her duty'." The press was almost unanimous in denouncing her seclusion. On April 1st, 1864, *The Times* printed a leading article remonstrating with H.M. Not long afterwards, the Editor received an unsigned communiqué, in the Queen's own hand, delivered by General Grey. The idea, it said, that the time had come for Her Majesty to reappear in public "cannot be too explicitly contradicted. The Queen heartily appreciates the desire of her subjects to see her, and whatever she *can* do to gratify them in this loyal and affectionate wish, she *will* do. . . . But there are other and higher duties than those of mere representation which are now thrown upon the Queen, alone and unassisted – duties which she cannot neglect without injury to the public service, which weigh increasingly upon her, overwhelming her with work and anxiety".

The Times returned to the attack on the third anniversary of the Prince Consort's death. "The living", it said, "have their claims as well as the dead; and what claims can be more important than those of a great nation, and the Society of one of the first European Capitals?" For three years, "every honour that affection and gratitude could pay to the memory of the Prince Consort had been offered", and it was now time for the Queen "to think of her subjects' claims and the duties of her high station, and not postpone them longer to the indulgence of an unavailing grief". Moreover, "for the sake of the Crown as well as of the public", it had to be recognised that it was "impossible for a recluse to occupy the British throne without a gradual weakening of that authority which the Sovereign has been accustomed to exert". The Queen was deeply distressed by such plain speaking, but, nevertheless, refused to be dictated to by a newspaper. There were after all, in her own phrase, "other and higher duties than those of mere representation".

It was widely felt in Court and Government circles that the Queen was failing in her duty to welcome foreign guests. She had lodged the King and Queen of Denmark in an hotel, had obliged the King of Sweden to stay at the Swedish Legation, and Prince Humbert of

Italy had been sent to the White Hart at Windsor as there was no room in the Castle! Naturally the Foreign Office felt badly let down when she refused to receive royal visitors. The fortunes of Claridges were built on her reluctance to entertain.

Formidable as were the Queen's critics, she was never without champions. In 1866, the great John Bright, one of the foremost Radicals of his time, sprang to her support. "I am not accustomed," he said, "to stand up in defence of those who are the possessors of crowns. But I think there has been, by many persons, a great injustice done to the Queen in reference to her desolate widowed position, and I venture to say this, that a woman, be she the Queen of a great realm, or be she the wife of one of your labouring men, who can keep active in her heart a great sorrow for the lost object of her life and affection, is not at all likely to be wanting in great and generous sympathy with you." His remarks were received with prolonged applause. Shortly before he died in 1889, the Queen told him how much she appreciated the way in which he had taken her part "when ignorant and unfeeling people attacked her for not going out into the world".

Ministers, courtiers, and even the Queen's children, waged a remorseless campaign to coax her out of retirement, but nothing they said was of any avail. She was far too obdurate, and her phobia too deep-rooted, to respond to appeals to reason. No one seemed able to convince her that people were anxious "to see a Crown and a Sceptre" and wanted "gilding for their money". In 1864 King Leopold warned her: "The English are very personal; to continue to love people they must see them". But she persisted in arguing that "mere representation" was only of minor importance. When Clarendon ventured to remonstrate with her he could feel the temperature drop as he spoke. Even poor Alice was scolded for forming a family "cabal" in an effort to alter her mother's "sad way of life".

It was true, as King Leopold said, that the English have always been anxious to see their sovereigns. They loved to watch Charles II stroll in St James's Park; and Edward VII owed much of his popularity to his cheerful rapport with the masses. Yet Queen Victoria not only refused to perform her public engagements, but would not permit the Prince of Wales to do so on her behalf. It appeared she was happier to neglect them than to relinquish them. There was, of course, some danger of over-exposure, and Bagehot warned of the risk of letting in "daylight on magic", but he did not intend to suggest that the Sovereign should be invisible.

The Queen was determined that her children should never forget their father. She even reproached Vicky for writing too rapturously about a holiday she spent in Italy some eleven months after his death. "Dear Child," she remarked disapprovingly, "I think no misfortune would crush you or break those elastic spirits." The worst blight fell on the younger children, brought up in a hushed and sombre Court, where everyone spoke in whispers. Somewhat to Lady Lyttelton's surprise, the Queen told her that she found the company of her youngest children soothing and liked their "gaiety": diminished as it was by her own pervasive grief. In the course of the conversation she also confessed to feeling "*less glad* than I ought when I see people happy – so *odd* and wrong! I *can't bear* to look at a man and his wife walking together". In 1865, when Princess Louise was seventeen, the Queen refused to give her a coming-out ball on the ground that the family was still in mourning. She was not, of course, setting a new fashion, but she certainly helped to sanctify current practice.

In 1865 the Queen's younger children revived the practice of staging a family play, and she sat through the performance as if her teeth were being drilled. But later she explained to Elphinstone "that if she appeared *listless* and did *not* applaud, it was only because the recollections of the *happy past* when the beloved Prince arranged everything . . . weighed her down and it was ALL she could do to sit thro' it!" In fact, she followed the play with her customary perspicacity. "Prince Arthur," she said, "was *excellent* and would have delighted his darling Papa". Prince Leopold spoke too softly and was "inclined to turn his *back* to the audience", while poor Albert Grey, the General's son, was a "stick". But apart from such lapses, "the whole was very successful" and a credit to those who took part.

In the short term, the Prince of Wales suffered most from the death of his father as the Queen blamed him for it. In January 1862, she told Vicky to put Stockmar "in possession of the sad truth" that it was the Curragh episode which had "made beloved Papa so ill – for there must be no illusion about that – it was so; he was struck down. . . . Oh! that cross!" When she told Lord Hertford, a month later, that it was "that dreadful business at the Curragh" which had killed her husband, he was so shocked that he contradicted her flatly. Clark was partly responsible for poisoning her mind, as it was he who had blamed the Prince's illness on "excessive mental excitement on one very recent occasion". Jenner, who knew a great deal more about typhoid, believed that the plumbing at Windsor was the culprit. One thing which seemed to confirm the Queen's theory was that when the Prince Consort's mind began to wander he kept calling for General Bruce. It never occurred to her that he was just as anxious over the prospect of war with America as he was about Bertie's "Fall", or that she herself had imposed a shattering strain on him after her mother died.

Given the nature of her delusion, it was not surprising that the Queen claimed that she could "never see Bertie without a shudder". When Lord Clarendon saw her in February 1862, he was greatly disturbed by her "positive monomania". It quite irritated her, she told him, to see her son in the room. Vicky implored her mother to be "kind, forgiving and loving". He knows, she said, that he is neither like you nor Papa, "and he feels it", but "he cannot help it poor boy. To give him up at 20 would not be right". Greatly to her relief, the Queen thanked her "a thousand times" for her "dear letter", acknowledged that what she had said was "quite true and right", and told her never to hesitate to "speak openly" for fear of her displeasure.

As the Queen came to terms with her bereavement, and the process was slow and bitter, she forgot the unjustified things she had said when out of her mind with despair. At the end of January, 1862, she told Palmerston that "Bertie was a good and dutiful son", and in June she began to refer to him as her "dear, darling boy". But it is doubtful whether she fully grasped how generous he had been in never so much as murmuring under the lash. Indeed, through her darkest hour, his only desire was to comfort and console her.

The day after the Prince Consort died, the Queen dedicated the rest of her life to carrying on his work. Soon afterwards, she told King Leopold that she had firmly and irrevocably resolved to make the Prince's plans and wishes about "*every* thing" her law, and that "*no human power*" would make her swerve "from *what* he decided and wished". Few things consoled her more, she told Mrs Gladstone, than "to carry out and finish" Prince Albert's schemes for his family and the country. It was a considerable comfort for her to recall his words and wishes, and to feel that his "pure and perfect spirit" watched over her. In death as in life, she turned to her "blessed Oracle" for guidance. When Vicky tried to persuade her mother that life remained worth living, she argued that no one was better placed to carry on the Prince Consort's work, which, "Heaven forbid . . . should be in vain". From the first she recognised that the Queen's resolve to promote the Prince's ideals would help her to keep her hold on life.

To her dying day the Queen never ceased to pay lip-service to her husband's wishes, provided they coincided with her own. But increasingly, without realising what she was doing, she tended to abandon them. Albert had always insisted that she should develop outside interests. In fact, she withdrew into monastic seclusion. Albert told her to look to the future, but after his death she lived in the past. Albert considered Disraeli something of an impostor, but she implicitly trusted him. Albert never tired of insisting that the Crown must remain impartial, but the Queen allowed her hatred of Gladstone's policy to make her a partisan. Soon Albert's so-called "wishes" became barely distinguishable from those of his widow. In the end it became little more than a pious pretence that the Prince still ruled from the grave. Palmerston warned Russell in 1862 that her determination to conform to what she persuaded herself were the Prince's wishes, promised "no end of difficulties" for those who had to advise her.

Not only did the Queen find solace in carrying on Albert's work, but also in doing whatever she could to honour his memory. Soon after he died, she took the Duchess of Sutherland to take a last look at him. As they stood by the bedside together, she asked despairingly: "Will they do him justice now?" Nothing she could do was left undone to put the record straight, and she made it her mission to tell the world that it had lost "one of the best, purest, most Godlike men" who had ever lived. Seeing that all he had said, thought, or written were "gospel now", she was anxious to publish his Letters and Speeches. Moreover, by so doing, people would see how wonderfully happy her marriage had been and how wretched she now was.

In so far as it was feasible, the Queen preserved the world around her precisely as Albert had known it. Even the glass from which he took his last dose of medicine remained where he put it down, and twice every day a macabre ritual was performed in which his clothes were laid out on a chair and soap and towels were replaced. Bishop Davidson recalled having an audience with the Queen in the last year of her reign, with a hot-water jug "actually steaming" on the washstand. The Prince's coat still hung in the hall at Osborne, and his desk remained untouched. Had he risen from the dead and returned to his island home, he would not have felt unexpected. Some people thought the Queen's behaviour morbid, but others applauded her delicacy of feeling.

Wherever the Queen was, whether at the Hotel Excelsior Regina at Cimiez, or in her sitting-room at Windsor, she surrounded herself with portraits of her family, and, above all, of "the late illustrious Prince". Her granddaughter, "Missy", described the Queen's apartments as full of photographs, statues and prints. "There was Grandpapa in full General's uniform, Grandpapa in his robes of the Order of the Garter, Grandpapa in kilt, in plain clothes, Grandpapa on horseback, at his writing-table, Grandpapa with his dogs, with his children, in the garden, on the mountains. Grandpapa with his loving wife gazing enraptured into his face." In case such reminders proved insufficient, statues appeared in all the royal residences, a cairn was built at the top of Craig Lourigan, and even the spot where he shot his last stag was hallowed with an inscription. The Queen knew perfectly well how much Albert disliked such memorials. "If I should die before you," he once begged her, "do not raise even a single marble image in my name."

On December 18th, 1861, the Queen "chose a spot in Frogmore Gardens for a Mausoleum for us". Lord Clarendon was astonished to learn that she had decided to abandon St George's Chapel, the burial place of the Kings of England, to "set up insignificant tombs in that morass at Frogmore which is constantly flooded." The building was constructed of granite and Portland stone, and cost £200,000, enough to rebuild the slums of Windsor. Its airy dome and light interior owed much to the Mausoleum at Castle Howard, one of Hawksmoor's finest works. When the Queen saw it in 1850, she described it in her journal as "just the sort of thing I wish one day to build for ourselves". It was no part of her philosophy that the Prince should be hidden away in some dank and cheerless crypt. On December 17th 1862, Samuel Wilberforce, Bishop of Oxford, consecrated the building, and next day the Prince's coffin was transferred from St George's to Frogmore. "The sight of our Queen and the file of fatherless children", struck Wilberforce as "one of the most touching sights" he had ever seen in his life. Some time later, Baron Marochetti completed a recumbent marble effigy of Prince Albert which was placed over his remains. The Baron's companion figure of the Queen was put into store for so long that when it was finally wanted only one person knew where it was.

The most imposing of all the Prince's memorials was that put up by public subscription near the original site of the Crystal Palace. Donations proved so meagre that the cost of the Albert Hall was finally undertaken by a joint stock company. Even Sir Gilbert Scott's monument could not have been built without a Government subsidy of £50,000. When it was finally unveiled by the Queen in 1876, the Prince was revealed seated under a gorgeous canopy, with a catalogue of the Great Exhibition open on his knees. Just in case some "traveller from an antique land" failed to recognise this most eminent of Victorians, the single word "Albert" was carved on the base of the statue.

Sculptures might serve to remind people of the Prince's appearance, but only the printed word could preserve his thought: hence Theodore Martin's biography, which took fourteen years to complete and ran into five volumes. The first book to appear was a collection of the Prince Consort's speeches, published in 1862. Nominally edited by Arthur Helps, it was largely the Queen's work, as she "sometimes saw the proof-sheets six times over, and would battle stoutly about a single sentence". Vicky thought Helps a grovelling toady, but the Queen was fond of him and valued his advice. The second book, *The Early Years of the Prince Consort*, which covered the period 1819 to 1840, was written by General Grey and published in 1867. Once more, the Queen played a prominent part in the book's production, and devoted bitter-sweet hours to selecting material for it. The original plan was for Grey to complete the work in a second volume, but, in fact, the task devolved on Martin, as the General had neither the time nor strength to complete it. Two years later, the Queen brought out *Leaves from Our Life in the Highlands* which she dedicated "To the dear memory of him who made the life of the writer bright and happy". She spoke of her book as "a simple record" of family life, but to many it seemed a work of hagiography.

None of the Prince's biographers dared to portray the Prince as anything less than perfect. Helps complained to Delane of the difficulties he encountered trying "to restrain the outbursts of affection of a most loving woman", and he was not altogether surprised that the public regarded his book as sugary. The English have always preferred their heroes to err as a token of their humanity. The saintly Henry VI was driven from the throne, while his reprobate father,

Prince Hal, was loved and admired. Nor could it be said that such popular Kings as Edward VII or Charles II were noted for their rectitude. Victorian readers were not to be satisfied with an "impeccable waxwork", they demanded a man of flesh and blood. The Queen, blinded by love, turned the Prince into a stereotype for Sunday-school sermons, forgetting the restless, tormented creature to whom she had actually been married.

Shortly before his death, the Prince affirmed his belief that the soul was immortal. "We don't know," he admitted, "in what state we shall meet again; but that we shall recognise each other and be together in eternity I am perfectly certain". The Queen shared his faith in a world to come, and spoke of her "*firm* conviction" of a "Blessed Eternal Reunion with her Angel". So definite was her assurance of an afterlife, that she was alleged to have objected to "the idea of allowing King David to be presented to her on account of his 'inexcusable conduct to Uriah'". The Duke of Argyll once warned Tennyson that the Queen greatly disliked the word "late" being applied to the Prince because of "Her belief in the *Life presence* of the dead". The "world to come" was for her so imminent a reality that she felt that she had only been "*outwardly* separated" from Albert. When Lord Clarendon saw her at Osborne a few months after her loss, she told him she felt sure that the Prince was constantly watching her, and that she had never ceased "to be in communion with his spirit . . .".

The Queen's views on Purgatory and "Prayers for the Dead" were virtually those of the Pope. Article twenty-two of the Thirty Nine Articles might denounce the "Romish doctrine of Purgatory" for being "repugnant to the Word of God", but she often spoke of an "Intermediate Life", and warmly endorsed Charles Kingsley's suggestion that "God takes those who have finished their career on earth to another and greater sphere of usefulness".

In 1882, when Canon Boyd Carpenter was bidden to dine and sleep at Windsor before preaching the Sunday sermon, the Queen cross-examined him on the life of the world to come, the crux of her religion. She was concerned, for example, to know how far it would be possible to renew companionship after a long interval of separation. "How shall we see them and known them? Clothed or unclothed? Men, women and children or how?" She had several conversations on the same subject with Tennyson, and told him how much she had been comforted by *In Memoriam*, parts of which she knew by heart. They both agreed in thinking that a God of Love could not be so cruel as to have inspired people with an utterly vain longing to be reunited with their loved ones, and she was much struck by his dictum: "You cannot love a Father who strangled you".

The Queen once admitted to Randall Davidson that she had "sudden qualms" that immortality was an illusion, but that fortunately such feelings never lasted. When the Duchess of Sutherland presented her with a Bible on behalf of the Widows of England, the Queen spoke of her "constant sense" of her husband's "unseen presence", and the "blessed thought of eternal reunion hereafter". She was also encouraged, she said, by the "spiritual joys which now fall to his share".

Some of the Queen's most unorthodox opinions were those she found most comforting. But she was also greatly consoled by her traditional belief in the existence of "an all powerful and loving Father who watches over us and overrules all for the best". Never once did she cease to feel His "love and power and strength". She learned by experience that the only way to survive the "trials, sorrows and difficulties of this life", was to trust in God's "merciful goodness". "Put your trust in God!" she told Vicky in 1866, when Fritz was fighting the Austrians. "Pray and trust in him, pour out your troubles to him as I do mine and you will find yourself strengthened and supported."

Prince Albert was largely responsible for persuading the Queen to "submit to God's will" and to put her trust "in the wisdom of his decrees". "All is in God's hands," she reminded Vicky, "as dearest Papa used always to say." As a girl, she could hardly refrain from reproaching the Almighty for his seemingly wayward behaviour. When the Duc de Chartres was killed in a carriage accident in 1842, her sorrow was mingled with indignation. But during the next twenty years she learned to accept that "God moves in a mysterious way". The letter she wrote Vicky two days after the Prince Consort's death, began: "My darling Angel's child – our First-born. God's will be done." In moments of stress she would often recite to herself a verse from Alice's favourite hymn:

> "If thou should'st call me to resign
> What most I prize, it ne'er was mine;
> I only yield thee what is thine;
> 'Thy will be done!' "

7

The Invisible Queen
1861–1874

A LTHOUGH the Queen refused to believe that time could assuage her grief, Clarendon thought it was starting to take effect after only three months. Princess Beatrice was the first person to encourage her mother to laugh again. "Baby was most amusing," the Queen told Vicky in August 1862, "and her sayings are charming. One is about Lot's wife; – 'Is it the salt I eat with my chicken?'" The following summer, the great geologist, Charles Lyell, was scavenging near the beach at Osborne when he saw the Queen and Alice rowing out to sea, pursued by Affie and Louise, and was amazed to hear them laughing and shouting at each other as if they were on a bank holiday outing. For a few glorious moments he watched his widowed Sovereign behaving like an over-excited schoolgirl.

The Queen's recovery was impaired by strong feelings of guilt. Dean Wellesley assured her that it was perfectly natural that initial despair should gradually subside into a "settled mournful resignation", and Alice pointed out that there "would be no justice or mercy were the first stage of sorrow to be the perpetual one . . .". The Queen, nevertheless, continued to reproach herself for disloyalty to the Prince. In 1866 she told Vicky that she was becoming a good deal more cheerful, but was ashamed that it should be so. In the eighteen-seventies, after Bismarck had overrun Europe, she even claimed to "feel thankful" that she "should have to bear alone much that would have hurt and distressed him so deeply".

Throughout the eighteen-sixties, the Queen was increasingly critical of what she chose to call "High-borns". Like George III and Queen Charlotte, she preferred the comforts of home to the

353

splendours of Chatsworth or Woburn. The more, therefore, the fashionable world denounced her for failing in her duty to "Society", the more she accused it of being frivolous and pleasure-seeking. It was monstrous, she said, to criticise her for failing to hold Drawing-Rooms, seeing that she was in deep mourning and in very poor health. But it was widely believed that her unwillingness to resume her public duties owed rather too much to her well-known distaste for performing them. It was rather as if a bishop declined to baptise, confirm or ordain.

By far the most serious of the Queen's grievances against "Society" was that it had cold-shouldered her husband, to which she now added the opposite charge that it led her sons astray. "Bertie," she wrote despairingly in 1867, "ought to set a good example by not countenancing any of these horrid people." Two years later she told him to his face that there was "a *very* strong feeling against the luxuriousness, extravagance and frivolity of Society", which was contrasted most unfavourably with her own simple life. It made her "blood boil", she said, when "the poorer and working classes" were "abused for the tenth part less evil than their betters commit without the slightest blame". It was, however, some consolation to know that the tone of Society was "*not near so bad* as it was 70 *or* 80 *years* ago" when, as Lord Melbourne used to tell her, "there was hardly *one lady* of high rank whose character was not well known to be most reprehensible!! And as for the gentlemen, beginning with her *own uncles*, it was as bad as possible".

Given the Queen's position and the age in which she lived, her views on class and race were decidedly unorthodox. Not only did she distance herself from the aristocracy, but formed close friendships with her humblest subjects. Mary Ponsonby noticed that both the Queen and the Prince seemed far more at ease with their servants than their guests. "I would as soon clasp the poorest widow in the land to my heart," she wrote in 1865, "as I would a Queen or any other in high position." In the last resort, we are all alike before God, and "while difference of position and of rank" are "necessary and must be supported", one can never be "sufficiently loving, kind and considerate to those beneath one". It was her belief that many of the humblest inhabitants of the Highlands were distinguished by being noble, high-bred, simple and unspoilt. Sorrow she saw as levelling all distinctions. In 1897, when she looked back over the year, she noted in her journal that she had lost several good friends, "including dearest Mary (Princess Mary of Cambridge, Duchess of Teck) and my good, faithful maid, Annie Macdonald".

Generally speaking the Queen was a thoughtful employer, who hoped that "the proper and kind feeling" she showed her servants would set a much needed example "among the higher classes". But sometimes she failed to practise what she preached and proved a demanding mistress. When things went wrong she was always very forgiving, believing that humble defaulters deserved to be judged leniently. For one reputed to be so censorious, she showed an amazing tolerance of drunkenness. The Ghillies' Ball at Balmoral was notoriously bacchanalian. The Queen's dinner began about two hours after the festivities began and many of those who waited on her were clearly the worse for drink. Loud crashes could be heard off stage as plates and dishes were dropped, and footmen would often pour wine all over the table in their effort to fill a glass. The Queen, however, would keep the conversation going as if nothing whatever was wrong, rather as a military chaplain might say prayers while shells exploded round him. Her published Leaves from her Highland Journal were full of descriptions of high spirited revels, and there were several circumspect references to people being "bashful", "confused", or "excited". When the Temperance Society requested her to expurgate references to drink, she refused to do so. Early on in her reign, a footman, with a long record of drunkenness, nearly set Windsor Castle on fire by dropping a lighted candle. Naturally, the delinquent expected to be dismissed, but when the Queen was sent a report of the incident, she merely wrote in the margin: "poor man". Indeed, such was her "persistent championship of the underdog" that, when such cases were brought to her attention, she would often connive at obstructing the course of justice by trying to keep matters secret from the Master of the Household.

The Queen always took a most detailed interest in her servants and their families, and tried to bring up her children to treat them with proper respect. She once told Vicky that to be brought "close to those beneath us . . . does one real good, by softening one's nature". She particularly commended the Prince of Wales for being kind to "high and low". He always had "a pleasant word and a smile" for every one, and was unfailingly gracious and charming to "servants, railway guards, and small functionaries". But Affie was sullen, brusque and offhand, and his quarterdeck manner was widely resented, not least by his mother, who was always reminding him that it cost nothing "to be *friendly* and *kind*", and gave "so much pleasure". Even Prince Arthur had to be warned "that stiffness is *not* requisite in *her* House", especially "towards the *faithful devoted* confidential servants who have known him since childhood".

In 1866, Lieutenant Stirling, a young cavalry officer, who had been seconded as Governor to Prince Leopold, had a terrible row with John Brown's youngest brother, Archie. The Queen instantly jumped to the conclusion that Stirling was trying to introduce military discipline in her Household, and maintained that it never did "to speak harshly and dictatorially to Highlanders" because of "their independence and self respect". Elphinstone took Stirling's part, much to the Queen's annoyance. It was not fair, she told him, to "support the stronger against the weaker" and to be sharp and unkind to "*inferiors*". Eventually, Stirling was sent back to his regiment, and the pride of the Browns was avenged. In fact, the Queen's behaviour was misguided. The support she gave to an insubordinate youth in defying his superior seriously undermined the morale of her Household. Moreover, in seeking to redress a minor injustice she perpetrated a major one.

John Brown, the most famous of all the Queen's servants, belonged to a supposedly Jacobite family. He was the second of nine brothers and his father was the schoolmaster at Crathie. John started his working life as one of Sir Robert Gordon's stable boys, and entered royal service in 1851 when he was twenty-five. He soon came to Prince Albert's notice and was made the Queen's "particular ghillie". As such, he immediately proved himself "*invaluable*" as a general factotum, "combining the offices of groom, footman, page and *maid*". In October, 1864, Jenner and Phipps hatched a plot to bring Brown to Osborne to encourage the Queen to start riding again. They knew that a strange groom would never do, but hoped that she might respond to this trusted Highlander. The plan was such a success that she appointed him to attend her "ALWAYS and everywhere out of doors, whether riding or driving or on foot; and it is a *real* comfort, for he is *so* devoted to me – so simple, so intelligent, so unlike an *ordinary* servant, and so cheerful and attentive". To mark his special status she decreed that he was to be known as "The Queen's Highland Servant".

Brown was a handsome, rugged Scot, with blue eyes, curly hair, and an aggressive chin concealed by a short beard. His shrewd judgement and curt wit made him a stimulating companion. One of the

Queen's Maids of Honour confessed that she found him "fascinating and good-looking". But most people thought his manner alarmingly forthright and deplored the way he spoke to his royal mistress. On one occasion, after struggling to pin a plaid round her shoulders, he was heard to say: "Hoots, wumman, canna ye hold yer head still!" If he disapproved of her dress he was liable to ask, "What's this ye've got on today?" Lesser mortals were treated with even more asperity. Ponsonby tells the story of a visit he had from the Mayor of Portsmouth with a request that the Queen should inspect a body of Volunteers. For some time, the two men sat chatting together awaiting her reply, when suddenly Brown poked his head round the door and announced without any softening civilities, "The Queen says saretenly not". Nor did he show any greater finesse when deciding which of her Household should have the honour of dining with her. Sometimes, he would come into a room, give a cursory glance at those assembled, and then bark: "All what's here dines with the Queen". She, however, relished his blunt ways, and allowed him the privileges which earlier Sovereigns granted their Court Jesters. The fact that he was a "child of the mountains" was part of his charm.

Even Brown's enemies were forced to admit that he was a wonderful servant to the Queen. Such was his dedication to her welfare, that for eighteen years he never took a single day's holiday. "His attention, care and faithfulness" she said in a footnote to her Highland journals, could not have been exceeded. So accustomed did he become to the pattern of her life that he generally knew what she wanted without her having to ask. Nor did she have to worry about his discretion, as she could trust him with "all the secrets in the Universe".

Despite jokes about Scottish meanness, Brown was exceedingly generous. He was the first to make a handsome contribution to a wedding present for a Lady-in-Waiting, or a monument to his friend Lord Beaconsfield, or to a footman in distress. But most generous of all was the way that he dedicated his life to the service of his Sovereign. That sacrifice did not go unappreciated, as she made clear in the message she wrote on the wreath which followed him to the grave: "A tribute of loving, grateful and everlasting friendship and affection from his truest, best and most faithful friend. Victoria. R.I." On several occasions he actually saved her life: sitting on a horse's head to prevent it upsetting her carriage, or seizing a pistol from the hand of an assassin. While she worked in a tent in the garden, Brown would patrol outside to see she was not disturbed. When she went out driving or walking, he would scatter those who dared to come too close. Understandably, she felt safe in his presence, and "terribly nervous" without him.

Brown knew better than anyone else how to console the Queen. His "strong, kind simple words" did her "an immensity of good", and it soothed and cheered her "to have one faithful friend near me – whose whole object I am – and who can feel so deeply for me and understand my suffering". Both he and Disraeli, at much the same time, began to restore her interest in life and confidence in herself. Different as was their approach, both treated her as a woman to be cherished. When Brown came down South, he brought a bracing tang of the Highlands with him, and a welcome reminder of "former happy days". Never before had she had anyone about her to whom the demands of Court etiquette remained so unfathomed a mystery. Like most formidable people she resented the terror she seemed to inspire, and respected those who refused to be cowed. Ponsonby always maintained that Brown was "the only person who could fight and make the Queen do what she did not wish". In her eyes, he embodied precisely those peasant virtues she found so refreshing. In many respects, "like called unto like", as both were "singularly straight-forward", both spoke the truth fearlessly, both were richly endowed with common sense, and both were fiercely loyal.

Those who reproved the Queen for favouring a "coarse" Highlander totally failed to recognise how lonely she was on what Tennyson called "that terrible height". Because she remained intensely shy, she was always happiest talking to old friends, or simple, humble people. If Brown felt at ease with her, so did she with him. From 1865 her letters to Vicky were spiced with his observations. For example, she told her that a proposal to arrange a meeting between two ladies involved in a bitter quarrel would end in "what Brown calls 'Hell and hot water'". On another occasion, when she sought to disparage the Belgian clergy, she described them as "'Nasty beggars' as Brown would say".

Deep down in the Queen's nature was the need to have people on whom she could lean. "God knows," she told Vicky, "how I want so much to be taken care of." In so far as Brown was able to satisfy this yearning, he became her "truest friend". Soon after his death, she copied an extract from her journal to send to his brother, Hugh. It described how Brown had told her "'I wish to take care of my

dear, good mistress till I die. You'll never have an honester servant.'
I took and held his dear kind hand and I said I hoped he might long
be spared to comfort me." Later, "I told him no one loved him more
than I did or had a better friend than me." Naturally, having won
such a place in her affection, he was granted exceptional privileges.
Although she detested the smell of tobacco, he was allowed to smoke
his "cavendish clay" in her presence: a concession she did not extend
to her sons-in-law. In 1872 she decreed that he was to be designated
"Esquire" and that his salary was to be raised to £400 per year, which
was a good deal more than Oscar Browning received as a Fellow of
King's. Towards the end of his life, she gave him two "princely
residences", the walls of which were covered with signed engravings
of the royal family.

It was only to be expected that Brown should become overbearing,
as most royal favourites before him. He was naturally domineering,
and the corruption of power enhanced his native arrogance. That
Highland independence, which his mistress so admired, struck others
as being the next best thing to insolence. When rows blew up, for
which he was often to blame, the Queen flew to his rescue, having
little idea how rude he could be to members of her Household. On
one occasion he cut Gladstone short in the full flood of his eloquence,
by telling him to his face "Ye've said enuf!" In 1874, the Tsarina
told her brother that Brown treated the Queen "like a small child
and seemed to regard her with a sort of condescension". Lord Derby
went further, and claimed she was "afraid of him", particularly when
he had had too much to drink. Even Brown's most charitable friends
were forced to acknowledge his fondness for the bottle, and it was
not unknown for him to approach the royal presence smelling like
a distillery. Once, at Balmoral, the Queen got into her carriage to
go for her afternoon drive, but no one could find Brown. Ponsonby,
suspecting what was wrong, went upstairs and sure enough found
him on his bed in no fit state to go out. "Having turned the key in
the lock he went down to the entrance and, without a word to the
Queen, himself mounted the box and they drove off. The Queen
knew what it was and knew that he knew. But on this as on other
occasions she turned a blind eye."

Naturally the Queen's family resented their mother's infatuation
for Brown, who in many respects was more privileged than they
were. Nor was it easy for them to tolerate his offensive manner
towards them. The Queen, of course, was ultimately to blame, not

only because his insolence was made possible by her protection, but because she appeared to trust him more than she did her own children. Sometimes she even suffered herself from Brown's surly behaviour. The older she grew the more she enjoyed spending part of the winter abroad, but he never held "with racketting about", and made his objection felt. At Baveno, in 1879, he refused to let her get out of her carriage in order to see a view, and showed his contempt for foreign parts by driving along a spectacular road "with his eyes fixed on the horses' tails." The Queen believed that the trouble was that the natives laughed at his kilt.

Brown had almost no friends at Court, and most of the Household detested him. Dr Robertson, the Factor at Balmoral, resigned because of his insolence, which persuaded the Queen for once to insist that he should apologise. The fact that four of his brothers were all found royal employment was bound to arouse jealousy. Even Princess Alice complained that "He alone talks to her on all things, while we, her children, are restricted to speak on only those matters which do not excite her, or of which she chooses to talk". Vicky believed that the Queen's tendency to fall under the spell of favoured individuals was largely to blame for the kitchen feuds in which she became embroiled.

The Queen gave Brown a free hand in disposing of fishing and shooting. It was not unknown for the Queen's sons to go out for a day's sport only to find that he had been there before them. In 1867 Brown was involved in a major political storm. The Queen had agreed to attend a military review in Hyde Park, but Lord Derby, the Prime Minister, was secretly warned that a demonstration was planned "to hoot J.B." which might get out of hand. It seemed that growing opposition to the Queen's long seclusion was finding increasing expression in protests against her favourite. Derby suggested that Brown should develop a diplomatic illness, but the Queen was deeply affronted by his attempt to prevent "her faithful servant going with her to the *Review* in Hyde Park". She was tired, she said, of "being teased and plagued with the interference of others", and she refused to "be dictated to, or *made* to *alter* what she had found to answer to her comfort". She was, in fact, "much shocked that Lord Derby COULD have listened to *what* must have been *merely* the result of *ill-natured* gossip in the higher classes, caused by dissatisfaction at *not forcing* the Queen *out* . . .". The matter was eventually resolved by the Review being cancelled owing to the "execution" of the Emperor Maximilian of Mexico, but not before the Queen had persuaded herself that the Prime Minister had been implicated in a malicious conspiracy against her Highland Servant.

The fact that the Queen was generally invisible provided the perfect climate for rumours to flourish. It soon began to be whispered that she had clandestinely married Brown, or, if not, that the two were lovers. Derby believed that Landseer was "active in making mischief", and that Lord Clarendon was also to blame for such gossip. Some people claimed that Brown had psychic powers and enabled the Queen to keep in contact with Albert. It was even suggested that rumours were spread by the Royal Household itself in the hope of getting rid of him. In July 1866, *Punch* printed an ironical "Court Circular" supposedly issued from Balmoral. "Mr John Brown walked on the slopes. He subsequently partook of a haggis. In the evening Mr John Brown was pleased to listen to a bagpipe. Mr John Brown retired early." In 1867, *The Tomahawk*, a new radical journal, published a series of articles and cartoons attacking the Queen's seclusion. That same year, a Swiss newspaper, the *Gazette de Lausanne*, hinted that she was in "an interesting condition", although it hastened to add that she had secretly been married for some time past. Such stories were not confined to the gutter press. Dr Jowett told Florence Nightingale that he was sorry to hear "that there is a foolish scandal going about respecting Majesty and a favourite ghillie and attendant of Prince Albert called John Brown, and the common people call her Mrs Brown – the great and good Augusta (Lady A. Stanley) in vain trying to hint that 'Majesty must be more careful'".

It is hardly surprising that Brown's position gave rise to salacious gossip, or that people began to say "there is no smoke without fire": as if no one had ever perjured themselves or broken the Ninth Commandment. But those who knew the Queen best remained confident of her innocence, in every sense of that word. In the first place, she was too straightforward to live a lie, and in the second place it never occurred to her for one moment that she needed to hide her feelings. On the contrary, she went out of her way to blazon them abroad. Her published *Leaves* dealt prominently with Brown. The first volume was dedicated to the Prince Consort, and the second to the memory of her "devoted personal attendant and faithful friend". Had there been anything remotely disreputable in the relationship, she would hardly have been at such pains to proclaim it to the world.

In 1866, Landseer painted a picture of her at Osborne, with Brown holding her horse's head, which was not only exhibited at the Royal Academy but published as an engraving. When she sent Elphinstone a copy, she described it as a "*very* good likeness" of "rather a portly elderly lady", and her "faithful attendant and friend". Nor did she conceal her feelings from her family. "I have lost my *dearest best* friend," she told her grandson, Prince George, in 1883, "who no one in *this* world can ever replace."

None of the stories about the Queen and John Brown were based on anything stronger than circumstantial evidence, and most of them flew in the face of probability. She was, for example, firmly convinced that widows should never remarry. Perhaps the most telling proof that she was blameless was her journal entry on May 24th 1871. "My poor old birthday, my 51st! Alone, alone as it will ever be!" Ponsonby, who of all men was in the best position to judge, told his brother that Brown was "certainly a favourite, but he is only a servant and nothing more – and what I suppose began as a joke has been perverted into a libel". "One had only to know the Queen," said Randall Davidson, who as Dean of Windsor was virtually her Father Confessor, "to realise how innocent it was."

During the eighteen-sixties the Queen sometimes spent five months of the year in Scotland, much to her ministers' disgust. Disraeli remarked that "carrying on the Government of the Country six hundred miles from the Metropolis doubles the labour", and Gladstone complained in 1869 that the Queen could have played a far more effective role "were she not six hundred miles off". It was virtually the only political problem on which the two men agreed. Nor did ministers relish the prospect of having to stay at Balmoral, where the discipline was stricter than in a reformatory, and the rigours of life were notorious. Both Disraeli and Salisbury detested the place, and when Campbell-Bannerman stayed there he found the Household bored to death, and the climate like that of Siberia. "It is the funniest life conceivable," he told his wife, "like that of a convent. We meet at meals . . . and when we have finished each is off to his own cell." Gladstone, however, enjoyed his rare visits, and walked and rode up to forty miles a day long after he was seventy. One reason why there were so many rows when the Court went north was that they helped to relieve the monotony. Sometimes the Queen would remain virtually unseen for days at a time, but her presence would still be felt. If anyone forgot for a moment that her eye was upon them, a sharp note of reprimand soon followed.

In 1868 the Queen built herself the remotest of all her retreats where the Allt runs into Loch Muich. The Prince had intended to build "in this favourite wild spot", hitherto only inhabited by the most venomous midges in the kingdom. It was, she wrote in her journal, "the first *widow's house* not built by him or hallowed by his memory". The "Glassalt Shiel" was little more than a hunting lodge, with a few simply furnished rooms, but the Queen thought it delightfully "warm and cosy". The first night she slept under the roof of her "own dear, pretty little shiel", she held a house-warming party in the dining-room. Her guests included Louise, Arthur, Lady Churchill, Brown, a dozen or so servants, and the policeman sent to patrol the grounds at night. "Animated reels were danced in which all (but myself) joined." The revelry was enlivened by a generous supply of hot toddy, and boisterous sounds of singing and cheering echoed across the loch. When the Queen retired, she noted that "all were very happy". Fortunately, the noise did not prevent her sleeping, "as the little passage near my bedroom shuts everything off". The Glassalt Shiel at once became the most favoured of all her retreats, with its "snug little sitting-room" and its glorious isolation. It was, she told Vicky, "the only place in the world where I can have complete rest". Ponsonby noticed that she always returned "the better and the livelier" from her Highland Petit Trianon. In 1876, Disraeli told Lady Chesterfield that he had received a letter from the Glassalt in which the Queen told him that "She never was so well: not only takes long walks, but climbs mountains. She is delighted with her romantic resting-place, where she hears nothing but the roaring of stags and the murmur of waterfalls and watches the snowy mountains in their sunset splendour".

Whenever the Queen was in residence at Balmoral, she regularly attended the Kirk at Crathie. Nowhere did she feel more spiritually at home. In 1867 she told Vicky, "I am very nearly a Dissenter – or rather more a Presbyterian": an astonishing confession for the "Head" of the Anglican Church. She was particularly impressed by the Communion Service at Crathie, held twice a year, which she attended for the first time in November 1871, and found "most touching and beautiful". What she admired most about it was its "grand simplicity" and the "perfect devotion of the whole assemblage". For a time she heeded warnings from Archbishop Tait that she would offend Anglicans if she received the sacrament at a Presbyterian Service, but in the autumn of 1873 she unobtrusively slipped out of her pew and took the sacred elements from the hands of Dr Robertson, an elder of the Kirk. When she was given the Cup, she was so overcome that her hand shook and she almost spilt the wine.

In 1868, the Queen lifted a corner of the veil in which her private life was shrouded, by issuing *Leaves from the Journal of Our Life in the Highlands*. The book had been privately printed the year before, and many who read it begged her to let it be published. Dean Wellesley, "among other wise and kind people", convinced her that it would do "much good" on account of "the kindly feelings it expressed to those below us". She therefore agreed to prepare a carefully edited version, with the assistance of Arthur Helps. His role might have daunted a lesser man. Nevertheless, he fearlessly chided her over bad grammar, waged war on colloquial phrases – in fact part of the charm of her style – and criticised her use of the word "so". When he temporarily took to his bed, she sent him a note to say that she was "so grieved (Perhaps Mr Helps will scold her for that 'so'!) to hear of Mr Helps feeling ill". In her private correspondence she sometimes employed the most improbable slang. "Now goodbye and God bless you", she ended a letter to Vicky, "and as Papa says, 'Keep up your pecker'".

The Queen's Highland Journal was a delightfully happy book: innocent, sincere, and written with great gusto. Her high spirits, her love of nature, the pleasure she took in little things, shine vividly through its pages. Disraeli described it as possessing "a freshness and fragrance like the heather amidst which it was written". It was more than an artless self-portrait, it was an idyllic tribute to the joys of family life. Simplicity was the keynote of her journal, which dealt with such homely matters as picnics, children and animals. Here was no gothic horror, but a placid, sunny world, in which almost the only disaster was when Vicky sat on a wasps' nest. The Queen believed that the "absence of all appearance of writing for effect" was what gave her *Leaves* such "undeserved success". She underrated her talent for terse but lively pen portraits. After meeting the great explorer, Henry Stanley, she described him as "a determined, ugly little man – with a strong American twang". Everything she wrote was "direct, simple, brief, vigorous and lucid". The style was the woman.

The fashionable world tended to ridicule the book, claiming that it was commonplace and bourgeois. On the whole, such critics were less than just, although right to suggest that it bordered on the banal. In one passage, for example, the Queen quoted Albert remarking on the weather, "We cannot alter it but must leave it as it is". Lord Shaftesbury denounced the work for exposing "the innermost recesses of her heart and home", which was just what her children thought. Vicky barely concealed her distaste for the publication, and the Prince of Wales went so far as to call it "twaddle". Several members of the Household had serious misgivings about "the domestic notes and histories" scattered throughout its pages, and feared that the fact that it hardly mentioned the Queen's incessant work might give a misleading impression. But whatever her critics might say, the book was a triumph. Within three months, one hundred thousand copies had been bought, and circulating libraries were said to be ordering it by the ton. It was even more successful in the United States, where it persuaded republican readers to look at royalty in "a new and more human light". When the Prince of Wales returned from India in 1876, he presented his mother with a translation of her book into Hindustani. It seems as if the public's appetite for the most trivial details of her life was as voracious in Pondicherry as Seattle.

"From all and every side," the Queen wrote elatedly in January 1868, "the feeling is the same, the letters flow in, I am known and understood." But she did not allow success to go to her head and inscribed a presentation copy to Dickens: "From the humblest of writers to one of the greatest". "It is very gratifying," she told Vicky, "to see how people appreciate what is simple and right and how especially my truest friends – the people – feel it. They have (as a body) the truest feelings for family life." If the public could no longer see her driving down the Mall, they at least had been granted a glimpse of her life in the Highlands.

During the first few years of her widowhood the Queen paid three visits to Coburg. On the first of these pilgrimages in 1862 she stayed with King Leopold at Laeken on her way to Germany. She was joined in Coburg by Vicky and Fritz who struggled to cheer her up. Just before she returned the following year, Stockmar died, which added to her gloom. She did, however, arrange to see the Emperor Francis Joseph. It was the first time they had met, and during the three hours they spent together they touched on the crisis in Schleswig-Holstein. Her third visit took place in 1865, when Duke Ernest invited her to unveil a statue of his brother in the market place of his native town. It was a rare family gathering, as all her children were present at the ceremony.

In 1868 the Queen decided to spend a month's holiday in Switzerland. Before, she had always travelled abroad as a guest of a foreign Sovereign, but this time she wanted to go on her own and remain strictly incognito. The previous summer, Elphinstone had been despatched to find a suitable house for her to rent, in "a quiet spot in true *mountain* scenery and fine *bracing* air". After an arduous search, he finally recommended the Pension Wallace, near Lucerne, which commanded a magnificent view over the lakes to the snow-covered Alps beyond. Some people suggested that the Villa's principal attraction was that it possessed a Scottish name. The Prime Minister, Disraeli, and his Lord Chancellor, Lord Cairns, raised no objection to the Queen leaving the country while Parliament was in session: a proposal which Gladstone would undoubtedly have resisted. In spite of the fact that she was travelling as the "Countess of Kent", Napoleon III put his Imperial Train at her disposal for her journey across France. It was a most welcome gesture as her baggage included her pony, "Sultan", her bed, her three younger children, John Brown, a considerable retinue of servants, Lady Churchill, Dr Jenner, Fraulein Bauer, and Colonel Ponsonby, who had been temporarily seconded from the army to act as an Equerry. Soon after their arrival, Princess Louise wrote to tell Elphinstone "how Mama likes this place. The view from the house is beyond all expectations". She signed her letter "Lady Louise Kent". During her visit, the Queen attended a Roman Catholic service for the first time in her life. She was deeply impressed by all that she saw and heard, but was able to reassure her anxious Household that she remained a staunch Protestant.

At dinner one evening during her Swiss holiday, the Queen asked Jenner how he had spent his day, and he told her that he and Fräulein Bauer, Beatrice's German governess, had joined a guided tour up the Rigi. The Fräulein was a formidable woman whose appearance was such as to ensure she would die a spinster. Ponsonby, without intending to be facetious, asked Jenner what their fellow tourists had supposed their relationship was. On learning that they had been mistaken for man and wife, and had hence been required to make the descent crushed together in a chair, everyone tried to look solemn. But soon Princess Louise began to choke and Jenner became convulsed. Eventually, the Queen herself gave way, and laughed till the tears rolled down her cheeks, later explaining that Ponsonby's face had proved her final undoing. When Lady Churchill tried to come to the rescue by asking, "Did you find it comfortable?" she only succeeded in forcing the good doctor to stuff a napkin over his mouth in a hopeless attempt to control his merriment. Never since 1861 had the Queen been so cheerful and talkative, nor her dinners so boisterous. She even made the ascent of Mount Pilate, which guards the entrance to the St Gotthard gorge, and whose precipitous aspect deterred all but the most adventurous travellers. Her Swiss holiday did her so much good, for all Brown's grumbles, that it gave her the taste for further visits abroad.

In 1872 the Queen spent a fortnight in Baden-Baden to see as much as she could of Princess Feodore, who had not much longer to live. Once more she described herself as the Countess of Kent, and stayed in a small Villa outside the town. Before setting foot on German soil, she asked Vicky to warn her father-in-law that the visit was unofficial, and that her sole purpose in coming was to see her "poor sick sister". Most of the time she spent sitting with Feodore, but she managed to take a look at the Casinos which had won the town its raffish reputation, and attracted some of "the worst characters of both sexes in Europe". Unhappily, amongst other pilgrims to this gambling Mecca were her two eldest sons.

In 1896 the Queen told Marie Mallet that she had "always *disliked* politics", which she did not consider "a woman's province", but the Prince Consort had "forced her to take an interest in them even to her disgust, and that since he died she had tried to keep up the interest for his sake". The Queen lacked the Prince's coherent approach to problems, and her enthusiasms were fitful and capricious. But from time to time, when some particular abuse caught her imagination, she demanded government action. Prominent amongst the matters which attracted her attention were unemployment, bad housing, vivisection, taxation, and safety on the railways. Otherwise she concentrated her energies on those areas where the Crown retained most influence: honours, appointments, the Empire, and Foreign Policy. One of her most outstanding gifts was her knowledge of what her subjects were thinking. Lord Salisbury went so far as to claim that once he had ascertained what the Queen thought, he "knew pretty certainly what view her subjects would take, and especially the middle class of her subjects".

In October, 1865, the Prime Minister, Lord Palmerston, died, having won a substantial electoral victory only a few months before.

"In many ways," the Queen told King Leopold, "he is a great loss", and one more link with the "happy Past" had been severed. But she could not forget "the terrible trouble" he had caused as Foreign Secretary, "Nor his conduct on certain occasions to my Angel". She was, however, magnanimous enough to propose a State Funeral, and to pay his widow a visit of condolence. Palmerston's successor was his old colleague, Lord John, who in 1861 had taken his seat in the Lords. His Ministry barely lasted eight months as he resigned in a fit of petulance when his Bill to reform the electoral system was sabotaged by a "Cave" of his own supporters, led by Robert Lowe. The Queen begged him to stay in office on the ground that Prussia having just declared war on Austria, it was hardly "consistent with the duty the Ministers owed herself and the country that they should abandon their posts . . .". But Russell refused to change his mind and she was forced to ask Derby to form an administration. His minority Government clung to power for almost two and a half years, largely because of the dexterity of Benjamin Disraeli, his Chancellor of the Exchequer.

The Queen never tired of insisting that politics was a man's world – as indeed it was in the nineteenth century – and that women were quite unfit for its rough and tumble. When ministers made too many demands upon her, she was quick to remind them "the Queen is a woman". But gradually after 1861 she became increasingly self-reliant and self-confident. Yet for all her success, she retained her disgust for the Feminist Movement. She dismissed a campaign to give votes to women as "mad and utterly demoralising", and described a suggestion that girls should study medicine as "an awful idea". When Gladstone sent her a pamphlet opposing Women's Rights, she told him that it would "be *sure* to meet with her *sympathy* as *she has* the strongest aversion for the so–*called* and most erroneous 'Rights of Women'". It grieved her deeply that her two eldest daughters became prominent supporters of a cause she deplored so deeply.

Not until June 1864 could the Queen bring herself to appear in the streets of London, and drive in an open carriage from Buckingham Palace to Paddington. Admittedly, she found doing so "*very painful*" but she was gratified by the warmth of her reception. Later the same year she visited Wellington College, which Albert had done so much to establish. Its first "Master", Edward Benson, proudly led her up one of the stone staircases to see a boys' dormitory, having earlier given instructions that it should be absolutely spotless. Owing, however, to some unexplained confusion, his orders were overlooked, and the Queen arrived to find the corridor littered with dirty linen and brimming slop pails. "You see us," said Benson, clutching at straws, "in our regular working-day appearance". Fortunately, she was greatly impressed by all she saw, and thought the Master "such a pleasing, nice, clever man": a vote of confidence which put his feet on the first rung of the archiepiscopal ladder. Just before she finally left, she told him that she hoped that some of the younger generation of her family would one day be sent to the College.

In 1866, the Queen began to make more frequent public appearances. She held two Garden Parties at Buckingham Palace, paid a visit to the Zoo, inspected troops at Aldershot, drove in state to the Royal Academy, inspected the South Kensington Museum, and opened a Water Works at Aberdeen, where for the first time since 1861 she consented to make a speech. During the course of the year, she also attended two family weddings: that of her daughter, Princess Helena, and her first cousin, Princess Mary of Cambridge. Eventually offspring of both these marriages were sent to Wellington.

The most important of the Queen's public appearances in 1866 was at the State Opening of Parliament. Hitherto, Sovereigns had always attended in person, but the Queen refused to do so after the death of her husband. In 1837, when William IV showed signs of absenting himself on the ground that his sister was ill, Lord Melbourne accused him of flouting the Constitution. Two years later, the Queen teased Lord M by pretending that she too would refuse to open Parliament if it met earlier than planned. "Oh, you must!" he said, believing she was serious. "Not to do so would not be right." The month before she married, she told Albert that she always found opening Parliament "a nervous proceeding", and that she was just as frightened each time she did it "as if I had never done it before". Once, when Lady Lyttelton stood behind her at the Prorogation of Parliament, she noticed how violently she was trembling.

Naturally the Queen's aversion to opening Parliament increased enormously after the Prince Consort's death, and in 1864 she told Russell that it "would be *totally out of the question* for her to do so". At the best of times she "was *always* terribly nervous on *all* public occasions, but *especially* at the opening of Parliament, which was what she *dreaded for days* before, and hardly ever went through without suffering from headaches before or after the ceremony".

Previously, however, "she had the *support* of her dear husband, whose presence alone seemed a tower of strength, and by whose dear side she *felt safe* and *supported* under *every* trial. *Now* this is *gone*, and no child can feel more shrinking and nervous than the poor Queen does when she has to *do* anything . . .". This register of woes was like a torrential river fed by the turbulent streams of the Queen's obsessions: her "demophobia", her morbid self-pity, her feelings of helplessness and loneliness, and the weight of work which threatened to overwhelm her. Even as late as 1880 she still thought it necessary to remind Lord Beaconsfield that there was "nothing she dreads and dislikes more" than opening Parliament.

In 1866 the Queen was persuaded to change her mind and agree to open Parliament. One reason for her belated acquiescence was the need to obtain a dowry for Princess Helena and an annuity for Prince Alfred. Such was the growing demand for her to resume her public duties, that the Commons might well have rejected her request had she declined to appear in person. Later, she was accused of only opening Parliament when she needed to make provision for her children, and Labouchère went so far as to describe her as "a voracious old woman who had been rattling the money box ever since she came to the throne". Long after she had decided in principle to brace herself for the ordeal, she still raised endless difficulties. A fortnight before the ceremony took place she sent Lord Russell an hysterical letter about "what SHE *can* only compare to an execution", complaining bitterly of the want of feeling shown by those who insisted on witnessing "the spectacle of a poor, broken-hearted widow, nervous and shrinking, dragged in *deep mourning* ALONE in STATE as a *show* . . .".

On the dreaded day, February 6th, 1866, the Queen felt so nervous that she hardly touched her luncheon. Shortly after two, she set off down the Mall with Louise and Helena sitting opposite her. In spite of a bitter wind, she insisted on opening both windows of the carriage so that her subjects might see her. The ceremony was deprived of much of its ancient splendour. Because of her deep mourning, the Queen decreed that there was to be no gilded State Coach, as few fanfares as possible, and instead of reading the "gracious" speech herself she left the Lord Chancellor to do so. When she entered the House she feared she was going to faint. "All was silent and all eyes fixed upon me." She felt, and she looked, a tragic, lonely figure. Her dress was black, relieved only by the Koh-i-noor set in a brooch and the blue riband of the Garter, her veil was black, her gloves were black, and she wore a black widow's cap on which was perched a small diamond and sapphire coronet. The crimson robes she had always worn before were draped over the throne, beside which was an empty chair bearing the arms of Saxony. Throughout the proceedings the Queen sat motionless, staring fixedly in front of her. Outwardly she appeared almost offensively indifferent, but inwardly she was a seething cauldron of emotions. She dared not relax for a moment for fear of breaking down. Lord Derby christened the Queen's impassive look her "Quandary Face", but interpreted it as a sign of irritation. Such was her relief when the ceremony was over that she was seen talking compulsively to her "dear affectionate girls" as they drove back to the Palace. For several days after, she remained "terribly shaken, exhausted, and unwell from the violent *nervous shock*". Princess Alice, who knew how panic-stricken the Queen became when obliged to appear in public, warmly congratulated her on conquering her phobia. "It was noble of you," she wrote effusively, "and the great effort will bring compensation. Think of the pride and pleasure it would have given darling Papa – the brave example to others not to shirk their duty." It was a shrewd thrust to suggest in passing how deeply the Queen was committed to opening Parliament.

In November 1866 the Queen visited Wolverhampton to unveil a statue of the Prince Consort, the first put up by an English municipality. It was with a "sinking heart and trembling knees" that she stepped onto the platform from the royal train, "amidst great cheering, bands playing, troops presenting arms etc.". She was accompanied once again by Louise and Helena as she drove through the streets of the town. The entire three-mile route was decorated with flowers, flags, and "endless kind inscriptions", and the pavements were crowded with people waving and shouting and singing "God save the Queen". "It seemed so strange," she remarked, "being amongst so many, yet feeling so *alone*, without my beloved husband! Everything like former great functions, and yet so unlike! I felt much moved, and nearly broke down at the sight of a banner on which was inscribed: 'Honour to the memory of Albert the Good'." The ceremony began with prayers and an address, both of which she complained were much too long. Before finally unveiling the statue, she made "several very deep curtsies" to the crowd gathered round it, and then took the Mayor completely by surprise by borrowing a sword from one of her entourage and knighting him. Such was his bewilderment that the poor man appeared to believe that she intended to behead him. As the monument was unveiled, the band played "the dear old Coburg March". Somehow she "remained firm throughout". The procession returned to the station by an entirely different route, this time through the "most wretched looking slums". Most of the inhabitants were "in tatters", but could hardly have been more "loyal and demonstrative". Much as the Queen dreaded appearing in public, when she finally screwed her courage to the sticking-place she thoroughly enjoyed herself.

During the eighteen-sixties, a number of secret societies sprang up on both sides of the Atlantic, dedicated to fighting for Irish independence. Foremost among such organisations were the Fenians, a group of republican revolutionaries who drew their principal support from Irish immigrants in the United States. In 1866, some twelve hundred Fenians invaded Canada in the vain hope that the American Government might assist them. In the following year, they transferred their campaign to Britain, and three of their number were hanged in Manchester for murdering a police sergeant. Instantly these "Manchester Martyrs" became national heroes in Ireland. Later, in 1867, the Fenians achieved their most spectacular triumph when they blew up part of the wall of Clerkenwell Gaol in the hope of releasing two colleagues. The explosion killed twelve people and injured over a hundred. Their indiscriminate violence proved totally counter-productive, and only succeeded in winning support for measures against terrorism. Some time before this attack, the Irish authorities warned the English police of what was in prospect. So precise was their information that they managed to supply a detailed account of the plan which was actually followed. But the Commissioner of Police, Sir Richard Mayne, ignored their report; and as Derby complained to Gathorne Hardy, his Home Secretary, no notice was taken "of persons placing a barrel against the very wall, and at the precise hour indicated, and in broad daylight applying a fuse of sufficient length to allow the operators to escape beyond the reach of the explosion". The immediate result of this astonishing incompetence was to encourage the authorities to take further warnings a good deal too seriously.

In October, 1867, the Chief Constable of Manchester told the Home Secretary that he had heard from a reliable informant that a plan was afoot to kidnap the Queen on her afternoon drive at Balmoral. This time the Government took no chances, and despatched a detachment of the 93rd Highlanders to Ballater. Meanwhile, plain clothes detectives watched incoming trains at Perth and Aberdeen for suspicious strangers. The Queen thought the whole thing "too foolish", and maintained that if the Fenians were "so silly" as to seize her, they would find her a "very inconvenient charge". The threat had been greatly "exaggerated", and needless precautions taken. "Amongst her beloved Highlanders she feels safer than anywhere else."

A few days before Christmas, when the Court was at Osborne, the Governor-General of Canada, Lord Monck, telegraphed to warn Lord Derby that two ships had set sail from New York with some eighty Fenians on board who had sworn to murder the Queen. Derby was so alarmed that he begged her to recognise that only the utmost vigilance could frustrate the threatened atrocity. He would hardly have ventured, he said, to have written so openly "if he were not aware that your Majesty is inaccessible, perhaps even, if he may be permitted to say so, too much so, to personal apprehension . . .". But the Queen was not to be moved, and refused to be escorted by anyone other than Brown. In fact, unknown to her, she was generally shadowed by men armed with revolvers. It was even suggested that she ought to return to Windsor, as Osborne was too exposed to attack from the sea. The moment the season of good-will was over, she began to complain that she was "little better than a state prisoner". Only two suspects were ever apprehended: the Queen's dresser and Prince Arthur.

General Grey became so agitated, that he begged the Queen "on his knees" to return to the mainland. Her reply was brief and emphatic. She was sorry, she said, "to see him *so very much* alarmed", but she believed it would be "most injudicious" to show any sign of panic or fear. She had no intention whatever of changing her plans and "must ask *not* to have this again mentioned". She took much the same line with the Home Secretary, pointing out that she valued her liberty "as much, and far more, for standing on such a pinnacle of lonely grandeur, as any of her subjects". Later, when it became clear that the threat had been fanciful, she declared that Lord Monck should be "utterly ashamed of himself for ever having credited such an *absurd* and *mad* story". She had lived, she told Gathorne Hardy, through "troubled times" for much of the thirty-one years of her reign: "'48 especially, when the troops were under arms every night" and she could hear mobs shouting in the streets. "She had been shot at 3 times, once knocked on the head, threatening letters have over and over again been received, and yet *we never* changed our mode of living or going on!" Recently, she said, "extraordinary measures" had been taken, "in consequence of this disgraceful hoax", during which almost everybody "lost their heads . . . excepting herself, her children, the ladies, and *one* or 2 other *men!*" In future, she positively refused to be tormented by unnecessary measures to safeguard her security.

The Queen's contemptuous disregard for danger and her common sense in assessing it were justified by events, but it was not altogether fair to blame her ministers for tending to over-react. In 1868, an Irishman, James O'Farrell, shot Affie in the back, which showed that the threat which his mother disdained was very far from imaginary. The Queen might be willing to take risks, but responsible ministers needed to be more cautious. The audacity of the attack at Clerkenwell proved how desperate Fenians were, and how rash it could be to ignore preliminary warnings. Slow as the Queen was to recognise danger, she was quick to suspect that a plot was afoot to force her out of retirement, by trying to represent her favourite retreats as vulnerable to attack. That, she came to believe, was what really explained the recent concern for her safety.

The defeat of Russell's Reform Bill only compounded the public demand for change. Once the principle of extending the franchise had been accepted, it was hard to stop short of conceding votes to all. Disraeli, having long believed that household suffrage was the logical basis of Parliamentary Democracy, was anxious to "dish the Whigs" by passing a Tory Reform Bill. Seldom did he display more dazzling virtuosity than in achieving this ambition. Not only did his opponents include the group of Liberals led by Robert Lowe, but such prominent Tory Ministers as Lord Cranborne (later Lord Salisbury), Lord Carnarvon, and General Peel. The Queen was so furious with these renegades that she refused to shake hands with them when they returned their seals of office. The Reform Act of 1867 gave votes to almost a million householders and virtually doubled the electorate. Derby described it as "a leap in the dark", Carlyle denounced it as "shooting Niagara", and Lowe prophesied that Disraeli would live to repent it.

The Queen, from the first, was in favour of reform, particularly as she detected "a growing feeling for it in the country amongst all the respectable classes". She had long maintained that working people were "becoming so well informed . . . that they cannot and ought not to be kept back". Moreover, Disraeli taught her to recognise that the broader the basis of the Constitution, the securer the Crown would be. What possible harm could it do to give votes to people like John Brown? Even Bradlaugh, the Republican MP for Northampton, was prepared to admit that the Queen showed more sympathy for the masses than any of her predecessors.

In February 1868, Lord Derby, who was increasingly crippled by gout, decided to resign, and the Queen invited Disraeli to succeed him. In accepting the "high honour" which she had "been graciously pleased to confer on him", Disraeli told her that he had nothing to offer her other than "devotion", but that it would "be his delight and duty to render the transaction of affairs as easy to your Majesty as possible". He further expressed the hope that she would deign to give him the benefit of her guidance, seeing that her life had "been passed in constant communion with great men, and the knowledge and management of transactions". The Queen told Vicky that she thought Disraeli would prove a good and loyal Minister as he had always behaved "extremely well" to her. "I enclose you a copy of his first letter to me which may interest you. He is full of poetry, romance and chivalry. When he knelt down to kiss my hand which he took in both of his, he said 'in loving loyalty and faith'."

Early on in the reign, both the Queen and Prince Albert regarded Disraeli with marked aversion because of the way he attacked their hero, Peel. In 1846 the Queen spoke of him as "that detestable Mr Disraeli", and denounced his opposition to repealing the Corn Laws as "unprincipled" and "reckless". Prince Albert went further and claimed that he "had not one single element of the gentleman in his composition". As late as 1870 the Queen told Theodore Martin that Disraeli's conduct to Peel "was and is a great blot", and "the more extraordinary as he seems a very kind hearted and courteous man". But he was, of course, very young at the time, and no doubt "urged on by others".

During the course of her reign the Queen changed her mind about three of her Prime Ministers. In 1839 she was wildly indignant with Peel and could hardly find anything too harsh to say about him. But by 1850 she saw him as one of her closest friends and grieved to learn of his death. In 1845 Disraeli struck her as little more than a ruthless adventurer, but in time he became the most favoured of all her Ministers. On the other hand, Gladstone began by being highly esteemed, but by 1876 was seen as a "mischievous firebrand".

When the Tories returned to power in 1852, the Queen warned Lord Derby that she "had not a very good opinion of Mr Disraeli". Later that year she invited him to dine at Windsor, and noted that he was "most singular" and his language "very flowery". By 1858, she was beginning to recognise his merits, but what finally won her over was the eloquent tribute he paid to the Prince Consort's memory. "One thing," she told Queen Augusta, "which has for some time *predisposed* me in his favour is his great admiration of my beloved Albert." For all his florid style, his sentiments were sincere, as his private letters show. During a debate in the House of Commons in 1863, he pleaded for a monument to the Prince which would demonstrate the nation's regard for "a sublime life and transcendent career". The Queen was so delighted that she wrote to tell him how much she was gratified by his tribute "to her adored, beloved and great husband. The perusal of it made her shed many tears, but it was very soothing to her broken heart". The letter was accompanied by a presentation copy of the Prince Consort's Speeches, which gave Disraeli a further opportunity "to touch on a sacred theme". The Prince, he wrote, was "the only person whom Mr Disraeli has ever known, who realised the Ideal. . . . There was in him an union of the manly grace and sublime simplicity of chivalry with the intellectual splendour of the Attic Academe". Lady Augusta told Helps that this was "the most striking and beautiful letter that Her Majesty had received".

In April 1868 Gladstone sponsored a resolution in the House of Commons to disestablish the Irish Protestant Church. The Tories, the Party of "Church and Queen", naturally opposed it, but on May 1st were defeated by sixty-five votes. Next day, Disraeli went down to Windsor to offer his resignation, but the Queen favoured a Dissolution in the hope that the Tories might win a working majority. The problem, however, was that the new electoral lists, required by the recent Reform Act, had still to be completed. In the end, she refused to accept the Prime Minister's resignation, on the understanding that he would appeal to the country at the earliest practical moment.

So far from sharing Lady Palmerston's "disgust" at "having a Jew for our Prime Minister", the Queen was enchanted by Disraeli. Unlike other Ministers, he seldom lectured or badgered her. "I never contradict," he once explained, "I never deny; but I sometimes forget." After his visit to Balmoral in September 1868, the Queen told Vicky that she had found him "most agreeable. . . . No Minister since Sir R Peel (excepting poor dear Lord Aberdeen) has ever shown that care for my personal affairs, or that respect and deference for me which he has". Lady Augusta confided in Lord Clarendon that part of the secret of Dizzy's success was that he wrote to the Queen daily "in his best novel style", telling her "every scrap of political news dressed up to serve his own purpose, and every scrap of social gossip cooked to amuse her. She declares that she has never had *such* letters in her life, which is possibly true, and that she never before knew *everything*!" Few people rivalled Disraeli in the art of delicious compliments. On receiving a box of primroses from Windsor, he claimed that "their lustre was enhanced by the condescending hand which had showered upon him all the treasures of Spring". His courtly flirtation captivated the Queen, and it was a great blow to her when he was crushingly defeated in December. At his suggestion, she agreed to reward his services by creating Mrs Disraeli Viscountess Beaconsfield.

Four years after being elevated to the peerage, Lady Beaconsfield died, and the Queen immediately wrote to Disraeli to say that she felt sure that he would "*not* consider the expression of her heartfelt sympathy an intrusion in this his first hour of desolation and overwhelming grief". She had always known and admired "the unbounded devotion and affection which united him to the dear partner of his life. . . . The only consolation to be found is in *her* present peace and freedom from suffering, in the recollection of their life of happiness and in the blessed certainty of eternal reunion". "Everyone grieves for poor Mr Disraeli's loss," she told Vicky, "for their marriage was so touching an example of mutual devotion and affection." From the moment they married in 1839, Mary Anne worshipped Dizzy with selfless devotion. On the day he carried his Reform Bill through the Commons, he was invited to celebrate at the Carlton Club, but he preferred to return to Mary Anne who was waiting with a bottle of champagne and a pie from Fortnum and Mason's. "Why my dear," he said as they toasted his triumph, "you are more like a mistress than a wife."

Disraeli was always something of an outsider and felt ill at ease in male society. He could not swap memories of Eton under Keate, or boast of his wild oats as an undergraduate. Sometimes he felt like an interloper at a Grand Lodge of Free Masons, debarred by ignorance of its rituals. "I owe everything," he once remarked, "to women; and if in the sunset of my life I have still a young heart, it is due to that influence." Above all, he "felt fortunate in having a female Sovereign", who was deeply moved when he told her that since his wife's death he returned to a "homeless home every night". She knew from her own suffering how desolate he must be, and the fact that they both had lost beloved partners enhanced their mutual sympathy.

Often the Queen and Disraeli failed to see eye to eye on ecclesiastical patronage, but he proved so willing to meet her wishes it seldom seemed to matter. Only when she asked him to make Charles Kingsley a Canon was he forced to point out the harm it would do his Government. Disraeli's principal problem with the Queen was that he distrusted Broad Churchmen. Indeed, in 1864 he publicly denounced them for threatening the traditional faith of Anglicanism at a meeting in the Sheldonian. His view was summed up in his warning to Stanley: "No dogma no Dean". Nor was he slow to recognise that progressive theologians generally voted Liberal. His own bias, he once told the Queen, was "towards the High Church", which appealed to his love of romance and history, but because he believed that the country was against them he declined to risk his Government's popularity by showing them any favour.

Disraeli was disposed to look on patronage "as the great State-engine of the Conservatives", while the Queen agreed with Dean Wellesley that political appointments produced "inferior specimens", and served to divide the Church. The immediate need, as Disraeli saw it, was to rally Protestant votes against Disestablishment, and he soon found himself torn between the advice of his High Church friends, such as Wilberforce, Gathorne Hardy and Lord Beauchamp; Evangelicals, like Lord Cairns; and, above all, the Queen, who was so much better informed than he was. During his visit to Balmoral, he sent his Private Secretary a despairing note: "Send me Crockford's Directory; I must be armed."

During the nine months of Disraeli's first Ministry an astonishing number of Church vacancies arose, including Canterbury, London and three other Sees, not to mention four Deaneries. When Archbishop Longley died on the very eve of the General Election, the Queen was quick to tell Dizzy that "there is *no* one so fit" to succeed him as the Bishop of London, A.C. Tait. The Bishop was descended from a family of Aberdeen yeomen, and early established his academic distinction. In 1834 he was awarded a Fellowship at Balliol, where he soon became known as a friend of leading Broad Churchmen. In 1842 he succeeded Arnold as Head Master of Rugby, and eight years later was made Dean of Carlisle. In 1856 he was appointed Bishop of London, where he won the Queen's admiration by the energy he displayed during a cholera epidemic which ravaged the East End. Disraeli, however, had a candidate of his own, Dr Ellicott, Bishop of Gloucester, whom Wellesley dismissed as an "amiable insignificant man talking constantly and irrelevantly".

Disraeli had several objections to Tait. First, he had learned to distrust schoolmaster prelates, who were "rarely men of the world", while "too often harsh, pedantic, self-conceited and dictatorial". Second, he deplored his "strange fund of enthusiasm", and his evangelical instinct to preach in the streets. Third, he objected to his "neological tendencies", which he caustically remarked were "his great recommendation in the eyes of H.M." Finally, he suspected him of supporting the Liberal Party, and believed that his appointment would please nobody apart from "a few clerical free-thinkers". But despite such powerful misgivings, he yielded to royal pressure when the Queen made it clear that she could not consent to Ellicott. In 1889 she told Davidson, then Dean of Windsor, "how entirely it was she herself who had got Archbishop Tait appointed to the Primacy, how earnestly Dizzy had pressed Ellicott, and how Dizzy often thanked her in later years for having taken the line she did!"

When Gladstone became Prime Minister for the first time in 1868 there was little to suggest that he would soon fall out with the Queen. Earlier that year she described him in her journal as "very agreeable" and "such a *good* man". Certainly he was was far the best informed of all her Prime Ministers on matters of church patronage. He was immensely painstaking over the most insignificant appointments, and "a vacant see excited him far more than a political crisis". Unfortunately, this obsession involved him in serious collisions with the Queen, which he was too obstinate to resolve by deferring to her judgement. Often, however, Dean Wellesley was able to keep the peace as his friendship with Gladstone dated back to Eton. As a young man, Gladstone had hesitated between entering the Church or Parliament, but finally took his seat in 1833. He did so in the belief that the political world was a battleground of moral forces, and that he could best serve God by ensuring that the State remained theocratic. He had been brought up an Evangelical, but gradually found himself drawn to the High Church. During his time as an Oxford undergraduate, some of his Christ Church friends became so alarmed by his fervent religiosity that they attempted to recall him to his senses by smashing up his rooms. He left Oxford with a Double First just as the Tractarian movement was beginning. Two legacies of his earlier faith persisted throughout his life: the evangelical intensity with which he embraced Christianity, and the sense of sin by which Calvinists are tormented. His High Church views were especially remarkable in the leader of a Party which depended on Non-Conformist support: an anomaly he resolved, at least to his own satisfaction, by maintaining the right to freedom of belief.

Naturally, given her views, the Queen deplored Gladstone's sympathy for Tractarians, even if she did not go so far as Brown in regarding him as a "Roman". She was far too straightforward to understand his casuistry, and was not alone in believing that he possessed "the mind of a Jesuit". The historian Lecky, for instance, found the subtlety of his intellect so bewildering that he reached the conclusion that he was "An honest man with a dishonest mind". Gladstone's first appointment to the vacant Canonry of Worcester, which the Queen had wanted for Kingsley, was seen as a straw in the wind. His choice fell on J.B. Mozley, Newman's brother-in-law, a close friend of Pusey, and a leading light of the Oxford Movement. Among other High Churchmen he recommended for promotion were Moberly, Head Master of Winchester; Liddon, Pusey's disciple and biographer; R.W. Church, the historian of the Oxford Movement; and the saintly Edward King. By 1874, the Queen had become so alarmed by the drift to Popery that she sent the Prime Minister a letter warning him of the danger. She had decided she said to write so "*openly*", as "Mr Gladstone is *supposed* to have *rather* a bias towards High Church views himself".

Gladstone replied at length to the Queen's letter. He began by humbly thanking her "for the very mild and circumspect terms of the allusion to himself". He went on to proclaim that he had always endeavoured "to make merit the passport to the royal favour". For example, he had recommended Charles Kingsley for a Canonry at Westminster, in spite of his notorious enmity to the Tractarians. There was, he suggested, an even graver threat to the Church than that posed by Dr Pusey, which came from those clergymen who denied "the Authority of the Holy Scriptures and of the Church whose Ministers they are". So palpable a hit at the Queen's Broad Church friends could hardly miss its mark.

One of the main issues at the election of 1868 was Gladstone's plan to "pacify" Ireland by disestablishing the Protestant Church, which he saw as a symbol of oppression. The Queen was strongly opposed to the plan, fearing that it might "ultimately prove fatal to the continued existence of the Established Church even in England itself". Moreover, having sworn at her Coronation to defend the Protestant Faith, she had no desire to assent to undermining it. From the first she made it clear how much she disliked the proposal, but she never denied that Gladstone's electoral triumph entitled him to pursue it. In January 1869 the Prime Minister sent her a draft copy of the Bill, with a covering letter supposedly elucidating it. It was the first of a number of similar "explanations" which left her totally mystified. Earlier in the reign, Melbourne had warned Peel to present his policies shortly and clearly: advice which Gladstone seemed disinclined to follow. No sooner did it become clear that the Tory Peers intended to use their majority to destroy the Bill, than the Queen begged Derby to think again. She was subsequently much praised for exerting her influence to support a measure she obviously detested. In truth, she was neither inspired by respect for the Constitution nor the principles of Democracy, but was deeply concerned to prevent the House of Lords from rushing to destruction. Nobody knew better that an hereditary second chamber was a vital bulwark of monarchy.

Gladstone's great reforming ministry was far too radical to please the Queen, or many of her subjects, as they showed by their votes in 1874. In a sense, as Dilke once remarked, "the Liberals are continually doing, and exist for the purpose of doing, the things she does not like". During the brief period when the Queen and Gladstone both supported Peel, the fact that they were travelling in opposite directions was temporarily concealed. But one thing they shared as they drifted further apart: an ever-increasing conviction that their policies were right.

Lord Morley believed that Army reforms were what turned the Queen against Gladstone. Some sort of military overhaul was long overdue, but the Prime Minister's earlier record convinced H.M. that his main concern was "Peace and Retrenchment". Cardwell, his Secretary of State for War, had won his laurels at the Treasury under

Peel, and was known to be looking for ways to cut costs. The Queen, however, never forgot the lesson taught by the Crimean War: that unless the Army was kept up to strength in peace-time it would never be ready when needed. Nobody could persuade her that it was feasible to reconcile the interests of economy with national security. In October 1871, she told Cardwell that his plans for short service and his recall of colonial garrisons caused her "deep regret", and threatened to destroy "a system which had worked so well for so long". She did not need the Duke of Cambridge to persuade her of "the *idiocy* of the English Constitution taking an ignorant *civilian*, a stupid lawyer full of theories, to organise an Army!!!" In particular, she regarded Cardwell's plan to subordinate the Commander-in-Chief to the War Office as an attack on her royal prerogative. Military men were even more dismayed by a Bill to abolish the purchase of commissions, a system which being "utterly illogical, iniquitous and indefensible, commended itself heartily to the British public". The measure was so badly mauled in the Second Chamber that a serious crisis threatened. Eventually it was suggested that since the practice had originated in a Royal Warrant, it could equally be ended by one. The Queen was by no means averse to accepting Gladstone's "advice" to revive an ancient prerogative, but hesitated to do so to outwit the House of Lords.

By 1868 the older generation of the Queen's advisers had more or less disappeared. Palmerston and King Leopold had died in 1865, Russell retired in 1866, and Derby two years later. Disraeli and Gladstone were the first Prime Ministers of the reign to have entered Parliament after the 1832 Reform Bill. Increasingly, the Queen was acquiring greater political experience than those supposed to advise her. Writing to Vicky in 1869 she referred to herself as "the *doyenne* of the Sovereigns", and proudly pointed out that after reigning for thirty-two years she had far more experience than most public men of the day. In 1870, General Grey died after a series of strokes, and his successor, Henry Ponsonby, was six years younger than she was.

In 1870 Colonel Ponsonby was already well known to the Queen, partly because he was a nephew of Lord Melbourne's wife, Caroline; and partly because he married Mary Bulteel, one of Her Majesty's Maids of Honour. Mary became a close friend of the Queen although she was totally unlike her. Amongst other things, she corresponded with George Eliot, supported working-class rights, and was a tireless advocate of higher education for women. She was rightly thought to be "clever", a quality not much esteemed in Court circles. Ponsonby came from a distinguished Whig family, and started his royal career as one of Prince Albert's equerries. Like his wife, he was, in the Queen's phrase, "a very decided Liberal". His successor, Arthur Bigge (Lord Stamfordham), described him as "one of, if not the, greatest gentlemen I have ever known", who treated Princes and paupers with equal charm and courtesy. Such was his sense of the ridiculous that he could often be tracked down by shouts of laughter. Once, in 1865, the Queen sent a chilly note to the Equerries' Room, where he was being entertained, to say that "it would be as well if Mr Ponsonby was cautioned not to be so funny".

Some people reproached Ponsonby for lacking Grey's courage in standing up to the Queen. Indeed, she herself once complained that he lacked "backbone" in that he always appeared to agree with her. Perhaps this was only another way of saying he was exceptionally diplomatic, and saw it was wiser to coax her than to browbeat her. On the rare occasions he persisted in offering disagreeable advice, he found it proved counter-productive. "No one," he once remarked, "can stand admitting they are wrong, women especially; and the Queen can't abide it." The keynote of Ponsonby's method of handling the Queen was "never to risk completely losing his influence". It was calculation not cowardice which led him to acquiesce. His "gingerly" approach was admirably illustrated when she asked him in 1880 whom she should send to represent her at the funeral of the Tsarina. He suggested Prince Alfred, the late Tsarina's son-in-law. The Queen said "No, of course he couldn't", and Ponsonby agreed. But later he remarked "It was a pity he couldn't". Whereupon she telegraphed to ask him if he could, he replied "Yes", and went.

Gladstone showed little of Ponsonby's skill in managing the Queen, who was not alone in finding him forbidding. Emily Eden complained he "does not converse – he harangues – and the more he says the more I don't understand. . . . If he were soaked in boiling water and rinsed until he was twisted into a rope, I do not suppose a drop of fun would ooze out". The tragic irony was that he held the Crown in the deepest veneration: a vestigial relic of his Tory past. Indeed, he was so concerned for its welfare that he almost drove the Queen to despair in his efforts to uphold it. Mrs Gladstone begged him to "*pet* the Queen", as did his friend, Dean Wellesley. "Everything," wrote the Dean in November 1865, "depends upon your manner of approaching the Queen. . . . You cannot show too

much regard, gentleness, I might say even tenderness towards her."
But this admirable advice proved unavailing. To him, Queen Victoria was an institution, not a woman of flesh and blood. He talked
at her too much to listen to what she said. Even the Ponsonbys, who
greatly admired him, deplored his "terrible earnestness". He hardly
knew what it was to relax, and when playing a friendly game of
backgammon would rattle the dice so vigorously that one might
have supposed his immortal soul was at stake.

The gravity of Gladstone's approach derived from religious con-
victions, which Rosebery believed were the "motive power of his
life". Beneath the aquiline exterior of the great Liberal Statesman
lurked a clergyman manqué. Hence the cosmic significance with
which he invested so many of his opinions, hence his *ex cathedra*
pronouncements, and hence the Queen's belief that he was a "fanatic
in religion". In 1894 she protested to Archbishop Benson that the
only suggestions to which Gladstone paid any attention were those
he had made himself. Twenty years earlier, she told Vicky that she
found him "arrogant, tyrannical and obstinate": precisely the adjectives he was known to use about her. No wonder that Ponsonby
described their encounters as those of two "ironclads". Lady Augusta
believed that part of Gladstone's problem was his lack of humour.
When Prince Albert facetiously suggested that the Royal Ordnance
planned to commandeer Burlington House, Gladstone solemnly
listed three conclusive reasons why the site would be unsuitable. In
reality, he was not without a capricious sense of fun, and sometimes
was even known to choke with laughter. But he rarely indulged this
lighter side of his nature except with his wife and children. Certainly
he never said anything to the Queen which she thought remotely
amusing. Instead, he bored her by his relentless pertinacity. Nobody,
she once told Ponsonby, could be sure at any moment "what he may
persuade himself to think right", and he had grown so "dictatorial"
that he would "listen to *no* reasoning or argument" and appeared to
expect her "to do what *he* liked".

The Queen was supposed to have complained that when Gladstone
addressed her he seemed to forget she was not a public meeting.
Obsessed as he was by great causes, he took it for granted that others
were equally engrossed, and once having launched himself on a
favourite theme mowed down his audience like a juggernaut. The
image which best conveys his mode of "conversation" is that of a
flood sweeping all before it, and "gathering fresh force from every

obstacle it encounters". The Queen, of course, with her instinctive preference for simple speech and straightforward argument, felt nothing but disdain for his copious vocabulary and Byzantine reasoning. Those "occasional flashes of silence", which characterised Macaulay, would have been rather more to her liking. The truth was that Gladstone took the whole world for his audience, and would address a fourteen-year-old Etonian with the same profundity of argument as he would Professor Huxley. Ponsonby once noted that Gladstone always drove people into a groove of his own choice, while Disraeli pursued whatever theme they preferred. The story goes that a young lady had the honour of sitting next to these two great statesmen on consecutive evenings. After meeting Gladstone she concluded that he was the cleverest man in England, but after talking to Dizzy she came away convinced that she was the cleverest woman in England.

Both Gladstone and the Queen were inclined to express themselves rather too vehemently on paper, and generally got on better when they met. Gladstone's Private Secretary, Edward Hamilton, maintained that the Queen was "always nicer and more considerate in conversation than in writing", and that her natural courtesy and graciousness "came out much more when face to face with Her Ministers than when She has the pen in her hand". The sad thing was that Gladstone was deeply distressed by the Queen's increasing displeasure. It grieved him, he wrote, looking back on his career, "to be troublesome to anyone, especially among women to a Queen".

Soon after the establishment of the Third French Republic on September 4th 1870, a meeting was held in Trafalgar Square to demand that the Queen be deposed. France had sneezed and England once more caught cold. Naturally, English Republicanism drew part of its strength from the Queen's persistent seclusion, although, curiously enough, she appeared more often in 1871 than over the past ten years. Labouchère, an Old Etonian Radical, maintained that the Queen had forfeited all respect by her constant demands for money for her children. During a debate in 1871 about a proposed annuity for Prince Arthur, the question was raised why this "princely pauper" needed such ample provision. Macaulay's nephew and biographer, G.O. Trevelyan, published a pamphlet under the nom de plume "Solomon Temple", entitled "What does she do with it?" In it he claimed that the Queen was salting away some £200,000 a year – the first time the Hanoverians had ever been censured for thrift – and that there was "not a lady in Christendom better able to provide for every one of her family". Others pointed out that the President of the United States, the greatest Republic on earth, seemed capable of jogging along on an income of £10,000.

Republican agitation reached its climax in November 1871, when Sir Charles Dilke, the Radical MP for Chelsea, indicted the Queen for dereliction of duty in a forthright speech at Newcastle. He made much of the vast sums spent on the royal family, and claimed they were not worth the money. Was the country really intent, he asked, on financing a Lord High Falconer, or a Lithographer-in-Ordinary? Much of what he said was wildly inaccurate, but no less effective for that. *The Times* condemned his remarks as bordering on criminal recklessness, but described them as being received with "great enthusiasm". Joseph Chamberlain, then making his name in municipal politics in Birmingham, prophesied that "The Republic must come, and that at the rate at which we are moving it will come in our generation". In fact, Dilke was a somewhat half-hearted Republican, prepared to denounce Monarchy as a "cumbersome fiction", but unwilling to take to the barricades. The Queen was deeply distressed by the Newcastle speech, particularly as Dilke's father had been associated with the Prince Consort at the time of the Great Exhibition. Indeed, she first met young Charles at the Crystal Palace when he was only eight years old. Twenty years later, recalling that brief encounter, she remembered stroking his hair, and supposed that she must have done so "the wrong way".

Soon after the Newcastle speech, the Queen urged Gladstone to refute its grosser errors, but although he had long been concerned by the growth of republican views, he felt bound to agree with the tenor of some of their arguments. In December 1870, for example, he told Lord Granville: "To speak in rude and general terms, the Queen is invisible, and the Prince of Wales is not respected". Mary Ponsonby was by no means alone in believing that had Gladstone decided to "show his teeth about Royalty" he could have destroyed the Monarchy. Fortunately, he was too loyal and chivalrous to do so, and incurred the ill-will of many of his supporters for defending the Queen so staunchly. It must be confessed that she never fully recognised the extent of the debt she owed him. In her view, he ought to have silenced Dilke and Chamberlain, instead of maintaining their right to freedom of speech.

Gladstone believed that the Crown was seriously threatened, but the Queen maintained her subjects were sound at heart. For almost a year, English republicanism produced billowing clouds of smoke like a bonfire of damp leaves, and then was extinguished by one sharp shower of rain. In August 1871, the Queen became seriously ill, and four months later the Prince of Wales nearly died. Between them, these two events evoked such loyalty that Dilke was howled down in the Commons. Shortly afterwards, a French secret agent, sent over to England to stir up revolution, returned with the news that republicanism was dead.

The Queen's illness began at Osborne with an infection of the throat. On August 18th she travelled to Balmoral, and three days later said she had never felt so ill since 1835. Jenner at one moment warned Ponsonby that he feared she might die within twenty-four hours. She seems to have suffered simultaneously from an inflamed throat, an abscess on the arm, and spasms of gout and rheumatism. She lost two stone in three months and was so badly crippled that she had "to be fed like a baby". On September 3rd, Professor Lister was summoned to lance the abscess, making use of his carbolic spray to destroy all possible germs. Alice, who happened to be visiting Balmoral at the time, tried to keep up her mother's spirits by playing the piano for her. Beatrice, meanwhile, made herself useful by writing letters at the Queen's dictation and keeping up her journal. By November 5th she felt well enough to attend a Service at Crathie, but complained of being stiff and "aching". Even those who had earlier shown themselves sceptical acknowledged how ill she had been.

Late in November 1871 the Prince of Wales caught typhoid and the Queen hurried to Sandringham to be with him. The moment she arrived she took charge, and guarded his door like a sentry. Inevitably, she was reminded of "dearest Albert's illness", but was greatly consoled by "the quite marvellous and most touching" feeling "shown by the whole nation", which proved "how sound and truly loyal the people really are". The crisis came on December 13th, and it seemed so probable that the Prince would follow his father to the grave on the tenth anniversary of his death, that bell ringers stood by at St Paul's in case they were required. Meanwhile, the Queen sat by Bertie's bed, holding "his poor hand" and looking forward "with anxious forebodings" to the dreaded Fourteenth. In the intervals of fearful fits of coughing, when it seemed he must choke at any moment, he mumbled deliriously. Then, suddenly, he looked wildly at the Queen and asked her who she was, but before she could answer whispered: "It's Mama. It's so kind of you to come." December 14th dawned "with the cheering news" that Bertie had slept quietly and was breathing far more easily. It seemed hardly possible for the Queen to believe on that "dreadful anniversary" that her son was actually recovering. "How deeply grateful we are for God's mercy" she wrote in her journal that evening. When the Duke of Cambridge heard that the Prince was better, he told his mother gleefully: "The Republicans say their chances are up. Heaven has sent this dispensation to save us."

On February 27th, 1872, a Thanksgiving Service was held at St Paul's Cathedral, which the Queen attended, but not before making it clear to Gladstone that "public religious displays" were not to her taste. When the great day arrived she was profoundly moved by "the wonderful enthusiasm and astounding loyalty shown" as she drove with her son to the City. The Prince looked worn and haggard, and the Queen elated and happy. On returning to Buckingham Palace she appeared several times on the balcony and waved at the crowds in the Mall. Meanwhile, Bertie lay on a sofa at Marlborough House, exhausted by his ordeal. Two days later, the Queen sent Gladstone a letter for publication in which she said that she had been deeply touched and gratified by "the immense enthusiasm and affection exhibited towards her dear son and herself from the highest down to the lowest". Several times during the "Day of triumph" she felt a lump in her throat, not least when she glanced behind her and saw Brown in his "handsome full dress". The Poet Laureate contributed to the occasion by adding an epilogue to his "Idylls of the King" in which he spoke of a "Crowned Republic": thus neatly turning the flank of Citizens Dilke, Bradlaugh and Chamberlain.

Two days after the Service at St Paul's, a sixth attempt was made on the Queen's life. While she was out driving in Hyde Park, a seventeen-year-old youth, Arthur O'Connor, a great nephew of the Chartist leader, Feargus O'Connor, slipped into the grounds of Buckingham Palace and waited for her return. Eventually, the Queen's open carriage drew up at the Garden Gate, and O'Connor rushed forward waving a pistol a foot from her head. But Brown was too quick for him, and "with wonderful presence of mind" jumped down from the rumble and seized him by the neck. It later transpired that the pistol was unloaded, and that O'Connor's plan was to force the Queen to sign a document ordering the release of

Fenian prisoners. This madcap scheme led many to conclude that the youth was out of his mind, but the Queen refused to believe it and objected strenuously when a quirkish Judge only gave him a twelve-month sentence.

By the spring of 1872 English Republicanism had been swamped by a tidal-wave of loyalty – in which O'Connor played his part. When Dilke attempted to speak at a meeting in Bolton, his remarks were drowned by raucous renderings of "Rule Britannia", and "God Save the Queen". On March 19th, 1872 he delivered a speech in the House of Commons in favour of a Select Committee to look at the Civil List. Gladstone opposed the suggestion with a battery of artillery, while the Tory Benches cheered him to the echo and his own supporters listened in glum silence. Of the two hundred and eighty Members present, only two supported Sir Charles's motion when it was put to a division. Relieved as the Queen was by his humiliating defeat, she seems to have taken Gladstone's support for granted. Several years later, Dilke publicly recanted "the opinions of political infancy", made when he was only twenty-three and still "rather scatter brained". Chamberlain's conversion to royalty was even more dramatic as in 1897 he was the principal architect of the greatest imperial demonstration ever seen: Queen Victoria's Diamond Jubilee.

Gladstone believed that it was his duty as Prime Minister to urge the Queen to remain near London while Parliament was in session. In 1872 he told his sister, Helen, that it was only what he called "The Royalty Question" which deterred him from giving up politics. "I must say," wrote Lady Augusta, "I honour him for pressing her duty on her." In 1869, for example, he urged her to open Blackfriars Bridge, only to be told that it would be quite impossible as "the fatigue and excitement would be *far too* great . . .". Gladstone, who seldom took no for an answer, wrote back to say that such appearances were an "indispensable means of maintaining the full influence of the Monarchy", and that it was "not given to any to occupy the Throne of the British Empire without special and heavy sacrifices". Few letters could have been better calculated to infuriate the Queen. She thought it presumptuous to lecture her on her duty, and knew in her heart of hearts that Gladstone was right. In the end she agreed to open the bridge in December, and the ceremony went off splendidly. "I never saw more enthusiastic, loyal, or friendly crowds," she wrote in her journal. "Felt so pleased and relieved that all had gone off so well."

The only time that the Queen opened Parliament for Gladstone was in 1871. He could hardly, however, have failed to notice that on the rare occasions when her shattered nerves permitted her to undertake the ceremony, her appearance was accompanied by requests for dowries or annuities for her children. She only opened Parliament four times in the ensuing thirty years: three times for Disraeli and once for Salisbury.

In 1873 the Queen was persuaded to entertain the Shah, who was making a tour of Europe. She was particularly concerned by the cost of his fortnight's stay, and insisted that the Treasury must help to meet the expense. The Government attached particular importance to the visit in view of the threat of Russian imperialism in Turkey and Afghanistan. The Queen, who had heard alarming rumours of the Shah's "uncivilised notions and habits", was delighted to find her oriental "Brother" so suave and courteous. During his visit he met the Queen on three occasions at Windsor. The first took place on June 20th, the thirty-sixth anniversary of her accession. Before luncheon, they sat side by side on two chairs in the middle of the White Drawing Room while the Grand Vizier acted as an interpreter. "Very absurd it must have looked," she noted in her journal, "and I felt very shy." During the meal, the Shah ate nothing but fruit, washed down with iced water, and was particularly intrigued when pipers marched round the table playing Highland airs. On his third visit the Queen gave him a personal tour of the Castle, and Prince Leopold took him to see the Mausoleum at Frogmore. Delighted as she was by his lively intelligence, exotic jewels and unassuming dignity, what pleased her most was to discover that he had specially arranged to have her *Leaves* translated into Persian.

Just before the Queen became seriously ill in the summer of 1871, Gladstone became obsessed with the idea that she ought to postpone her intended visit to Scotland until Parliament was prorogued. It was precisely the sort of suggestion she most detested: partly because she resented attempts to control her private life, and partly because the dates of her annual migrations were far too sacred to change. Lord Kimberley noted in his diary on August 5th that the Prime Minister had "worked himself up into a tremendous pitch of excitement" over the Queen's departure for Scotland. "The only wise thing to do in such circumstances is to remember that she must have whims like other women, to shrug one's shoulders and bear these little annoyances. Unfortunately, this is just the last thing Gladstone can do." Eventually, the Queen became so distressed by his importunate demands that she complained to the Lord Chancellor of his "abominable" interference, pointing out furthermore that *"No earthly political object"* was to be gained by delaying her departure "except gratifying a *foolish* and unreasonable fancy": a phrase which admirably summed up Gladstone's view of her own intractable conduct. Two months later, when he met his ailing Sovereign at Balmoral, he immediately found himself "on a new and different footing with her", and was made to feel "the repellent power which she so well knows how to use".

Soon after becoming Prime Minister, Gladstone proposed that the Queen should be found an Irish residence as a means of cementing the Union. To that end, he persuaded a Dublin banker, John La Touche, to offer her an estate, but she firmly declined this "noble" gesture on the ground that she found the climate too debilitating. In fact, she secretly bore a grudge against the Irish because of their hostility to Prince Albert. Nor did she find it easy to understand why the Prime Minister should press her so vehemently on the subject, when he himself had never set foot in the country.

In December 1870 Gladstone produced a further plan to encourage Irish loyalty: to appoint the Prince of Wales as Viceroy. Lord Bessborough, the Lord Lieutenant of Ireland, described the scheme as "the wildest and most visionary I ever heard of". The Prime Minister revived it in a letter he sent the Queen in 1872, in which he outlined his "Plan of Life" for her son. It was vital, he thought, to find H.R.H. employment, or the Devil would occupy his idle hours. Knowing perfectly well he was picking his way through a minefield, he once again stressed the importance of "the visible functions of Monarchy". He went on to suggest that the Prince should spend November to March in Dublin performing Viceregal duties, the next three months in London representing Her Majesty at Court, and the rest of the year between army manoeuvres and visits to Sandringham and Balmoral. It was hardly a very enticing programme to set before a sybarite. Gladstone's letter gave deep offence, because, as the Queen told him, the Prince's future was a question which "more properly concerns herself to settle with the members of her family as the occasion may arise". Lord Granville begged him to let the matter drop, but he refused to do so, maintaining that the Queen had suffered too much in the past from "want of plain speaking". Accordingly, on July 17th, he sent her another immensely long letter, to which she replied by saying that Ireland was in no state for experiments and that she "therefore trusted that his plan may now be considered as *definitely* abandoned". He still refused to give up, and sought her permission to discuss his ideas with the Prince and his advisers. Only when the Queen wrote back to say that it was "useless to prolong the discussion", was he prepared to admit that she had put "an extinguisher" on his proposals. Before finally dropping the matter, he made a private note expressing the hope that when these negotiations eventually became known they would take their "proper place in any account of our relations with Ireland".

In March 1873 Gladstone resigned when his Irish University Bill was rejected by the Commons. Disraeli, however, declined to form a minority Government and forced the discredited Liberals back into office. When Parliament was dissolved in January 1874, the Conservatives won a great electoral victory and returned to power with a decisive majority for the first time since 1846. It was perhaps inevitable that the greatest reforming Ministry of the nineteenth century should have alienated so many powerful interests. The Licensing Act of 1872, to take only one example, turned virtually every public house into a recruiting ground for the Tories. "We have been borne down in a torrent of Gin and Beer" was Gladstone's sardonic verdict. On February 17th, he set out for Windsor with a copy of Thomas à Kempis to read in the train. He told the Queen that he planned to abandon politics and devote himself to writing, having decided that the best possible use he could make of his talents was to take up his pen in defence of "belief in God and the Gospel of Christ". On returning to London, he told his colleagues how kind and gracious the Queen had been when he proffered his resignation. Presumably it never occurred to him what had made her so affable.

During the first decade of her widowhood the Queen was more occupied by family affairs than political problems. Even after her children grew up she dominated their lives as Head of the Royal Family. Ponsonby once described them as being "in terror" of her. But they were not her children for nothing and could sometimes prove as stubborn and candid as she was. Naturally, they often felt irritated by her "interference", but they knew it was largely inspired by maternal concern. "I think you can hardly know," Vicky told her in 1874, "how tender is my love and devotion to you. I have not the gift of showing it, and a sort of funny shyness, I think also respect and reverence makes me as stiff as a stick. . . . At any rate one thing never changes – that is the love and devotion, the grateful and dutiful affection of your most loving and obedient daughter Victoria." It would be hard to conceive of a more articulate tribute from one supposedly tongue-tied.

Vicky's family grew at a rate which distressed the Queen. "It is very sad," she warned, to be pregnant too often, as "the poor children suffer for it, not to speak of the ruin it is to the looks of a young woman". But in spite of all such warnings, six more grandchildren appeared at regular two-year intervals: Prince Henry in 1862, Sigismund in 1864, Victoria in 1866 (known as "Moretta" to distinguish her from her mother and grandmother), Waldemar in 1868, Sophie in 1870, and Margaret, the last of the family, in 1872. Unhappily, "little Sigi", the joy of his parents' life, died of meningitis when he was only two. "Your suffering child", Vicky wrote to the Queen, "turns to you in her grief sure to find sympathy from so tender a heart, so versed in sorrow".

The Prussian Court was run with military discipline and Vicky was forced to appear at endless balls until she collapsed with fatigue. What was supposedly a pleasure reminded her of the treadmill. Moreover, it galled her to see her "existence wasted in joyless frivolity". Nobody in royal circles, other than Fritz and his mother, showed any interest in art, literature, or philosophy. Prussian princes talked only of soldiering, while their wives were obsessed by the latest Paris fashions or the gossip of Berlin. It was as if George Eliot was stranded on a desert island with a gang of cattle-drovers. Just like her father, Vicky turned to artists, musicians and scholars: deplorable company for a Princess. The Queen thoroughly sympathised with her daughter's disdain for the "busy idleness" of fashionable Society. In 1864, Fritz bought a country retreat at Bornstadt, where they managed to live a relatively simple life away from prying eyes. Here Vicky was able to re-create the joys of her own childhood and share them with her family.

One thing which Vicky never lacked was good advice from home. No detail was too trivial to escape the Queen's notice, and she was particularly anxious that her grandchildren should be brought up on the nursery system established by "dear Papa". It was she who chose Mrs Hobbs as William's nanny, a treasure if ever there was one. The nursery became the centre of family life, a cheerful English oasis. The Queen was especially distressed by the treatment prescribed for

William's withered arm. Nor did she approve of him starting Latin
so early. "Our boys only began at 10 – and Willy is not 9." Stranger
still, she begged Vicky to ensure that her sons were "not overworked, I have such a horror of that". "Don't press poor dear Henry
too much," she wrote in 1870. "Believe me, dear child, more harm
than good is done by forcing delicate and backward children." Belatedly experience had taught her "that youth is so wayward and foolish
that all one's wishes to make them do what is for the good and what
is the best is useless! Often when children have been less watched
and taken care of – the better they turn out!!" The Queen greatly
enjoyed the company of her grandchildren, provided they did not
get too excited or noisy. "Dear little things," she once said, "I like to
see them at home with me." In November 1863, Vicky left William,
Charlotte and Henry at Windsor while she was staying at Sandringham. "I love William so dearly," the Queen wrote reassuringly,
"that I would do anything for the darling child. Both he and Charlotte are very affectionate to me but I don't spoil them and insist on
obedience."

In September 1862 the Liberal majority in the Prussian House of
Representatives voted to shorten military service, which led William
I to send for Bismarck, a man whom the late King had described as
"only to be employed when the bayonet reigns supreme". Bismarck
promised to ride roughshod over the Constitution rather than yield
to the Liberals. "The great questions of the day," he proclaimed, are
not decided "with speeches or parliamentary resolutions . . . but
with blood and iron". The dream which Vicky and Fritz had shared
with the Prince Consort was shattered in a sentence. In December
1870 Fritz noted in his journal that instead of uniting Germany by
democratic consent, the "insolent brutal 'Junker'" resorted to force
and fraud. From the first, Vicky warned her mother that "the great
Otto" was an "unprincipled adventurer" who was determined to
make himself "the sole and omnipotent ruler" of Prussia and govern
the country on "mediaeval lines". Soon, she and Fritz were confronted by an agonising choice between disobeying the King or
betraying their liberal principles.

On June 1st 1863, William I was persuaded to sign an emergency
decree authorising the Government to silence the press. Fritz
immediately reminded his father that he was breaking his oath to
preserve the Constitution, and told Bismarck that those who led His
Majesty "into such courses" were "the most dangerous advisers for

Crown and Country". Four days later he made a speech at Danzig defending the rights of the press. The King was so furious that he sent Fritz a peremptory letter ordering him to retract. Much as Vicky relished "a pitched battle", the Crown Prince was disarmed by his loyalty to his Sovereign. "Think if it was *your* father," he told her, "would you like to disobey him and make him unhappy?" On June 7th he sent his "beloved Papa" a contrite letter, but nevertheless made it clear that he could not take back his Danzig speech. "God knows," he concluded, "what a struggle it cost me" to be forced to oppose a royal decree. For Vicky the issue was unmistakably clear, and she never ceased to urge him "to place his opinions and his political conscience above his filial feelings". "I shall stand by him as is my duty," she told her mother, "and advise him to do his in the face of all the Kings and Emperors of the whole world." "My little wife," Fritz wrote on the eve of his Danzig speech, "is my most devoted adviser, my whole support, my indefatigable comforter, and no words can adequately express this."

Bismarck never forgave the Danzig speech, and resolved to show that not even an heir to the throne could defy him with impunity. *The Times* made matters worse by congratulating Fritz on his wife's progressive opinions. Such remarks were the kiss of death, and over the next twenty-five years the "Iron Chancellor" did everything in his power to discredit the royal pair in the eyes of the King and the nation. The day after the Prussian press was muzzled, the Queen urged Vicky to "prevent Fritz getting at all identified with such terrible misconduct". On no account, she argued, must he compromise his own or his children's position, or "shrink from separating himself from all his father's unhappy acts". If needs be, he must even leave Prussia. "This house," she said, writing from Windsor, "your old home – sad and shaken as it is – is open to you. . . . I speak in beloved Papa's Name, I hear his voice, and his blessed words: 'You should come here'." In so saying, she plainly deluded herself, for the last thing Prince Albert would ever have recommended was to leave the field to Bismarck. When King Leopold learned that his niece was preaching sedition, he hastened to point out what a "dangerous precedent" it was "to *disobey* the Sovereign. . . . You cannot in your position promote the disobedience of children, to which after all they are sufficiently inclined". The Queen could hardly have acted more inconsistently. On the one hand she never tired of reminding her children of the duty they owed their

Sovereign. On the other, she exhorted her son-in-law to defy his father's authority.

The most urgent family problem of all was to find Bertie a wife. Fortunately, as the Queen told Bruce, she had had "many conversations with her beloved angel" about her son's future. Before he died, he had arranged for the Prince to visit the Near East after coming down from Cambridge. To this end, he consulted Arthur Stanley, then Professor of Ecclesiastical History at Oxford, who had written a learned work about Sinai and Palestine. Stanley was one of the most eminent Broad Churchmen of the day, who owed his liberal principles to his father, the late Bishop of Norwich, and to Dr Arnold of Rugby. His biography of his Head Master, published in 1844, contributed almost as much to the fame of its author as to the subject of the book. Early in 1862 the Queen begged Stanley to take charge of the expedition, with the help of General Bruce, and made it difficult for him to refuse by telling him that the Prince Consort had said that there was no one else he could trust to undertake it. The royal party set out on February 6th 1862, sailed up the Nile to the First Cataract, spent Good Friday at Nazareth, and returned home by way of Constantinople, Athens and Paris. During the journey, the Prince turned out to be a charming companion, although a good deal more interested in shooting crocodiles than visiting "tumble-down" ruins. Somewhere in the Holy Land, General Bruce caught fever, and had to be left behind. His illness eventually proved fatal, and he was replaced as the Prince's "Comptroller" by General Sir William Knollys, who "possessed beloved Papa's esteem and confidence".

During the Prince's absence the Queen began to miss him, and forgot the foolish things she had said when almost demented by grief. Towards the end of May, she sent him such a loving letter that it made him beam with pleasure, and she welcomed him home like the Prodigal Son. In July she invited Stanley to Osborne to thank him for all he had done to reform her wayward boy. During his visit she was greatly impressed by his broad-mindedness and sympathy, and, above all, by the fact that he was "the most unclerical clergyman" she had ever met. Later that year, she invited him as a special mark of her favour to take a service in the Blue Room on the first anniversary of the Prince Consort's death, and when the Deanery of Westminster fell vacant in 1863 she virtually forced Lord Palmerston to offer him the post. Thereafter, the new Dean, according to Lord

Shaftesbury, entered upon his infidel career, "corrupting society by the balmy poison of his doctrine".

As early as March 1858, when Bertie was only sixteen, the Queen asked Vicky "to look out for Princesses" for him. Vicky was almost as fond of match-making as her mother, and eagerly thumbed through the Almanach de Gotha in search of a suitable bride, but she soon found that the wealth of the Queen's demands rendered her task impossible. Where could she hope to unearth a Princess who was not only beautiful, resolute, virtuous and dutiful, but also German and Protestant? For several months she considered the merits of countless young ladies, but all were found to be wanting. So, at length, in December 1860, she suggested Prince Christian's daughter, Alexandra, who possessed almost all the qualities required, apart from being Danish. At first, the Queen was scathing and dismissive, and declared that "the beauty of Denmark is much against our wishes". Both she and the Prince regarded Princess Christian, who was a niece of the Duchess of Cambridge and came from Hesse-Cassel, with unmerited suspicion. The family, she said, "would never do", and was "the *very* worst society for Bertie possible". But she began to have second thoughts once she heard that Tsar Alexander II was showing an interest in Alix and her younger sister, Dagmar. When Prince Albert first saw a photograph of the Danish "beauty" he said that "on that evidence he would marry her at once", and the Queen was inclined to agree with Vicky that "it would be dreadful if this pearl went to the horrid Russians".

In June 1861 Vicky and Fritz visited the Grand Duchess of Mecklenburg-Strelitz to meet Princess Alexandra. The Grand Duchess was the Queen's first cousin, Princess Augusta of Cambridge. Vicky was instantly bewitched and wrote to tell her mother that Alix was "as simple and natural and unaffected as possible" and could not have been more lovely and charming. "Oh if she was only not a Dane and not related to the Hesses I should say yes – she is the one a thousand times over". What with such glowing reports from Strelitz, and the threat of the "horrid Russians", the time had obviously come for Bertie and Alix to meet. On September 24th a carefully contrived encounter was arranged, and Vicky reported back that her brother had never seen any "young lady who pleased him so much".

The moment Prince Albert died, the Queen became more insistent than ever that Bertie should marry Alix. It was, she proclaimed in

January 1862, "a sacred duty, he, our darling Angel, left us to perform". But before proceeding further, she resolved "to see the girl" for herself, not, as might be supposed, to discover what sort of a wife she promised to make, but to judge, as she candidly put it, if "she will suit me". They met that September at Laeken. Alix looked ravishing in a simple black dress with her hair falling over her shoulders. "How he would have doted on her and loved her!" was the Queen's verdict. A few days later, Bertie arrived in Belgium, and after four days in Alix's company decided to propose. I assured her, he told his mother in a "touching" letter, that "you would love her as your own daughter", and I said "how *very* sorry I was that she could never know dear Papa. She said she regretted it deeply and hoped he would have approved of my choice. I told her that it had always been his greatest wish. . . ." According to Lady Augusta, the Prince was "desperately in love, and his mother *much* pleased with him". As for Alix, she told the Crown Princess that if Bertie had been "a cowboy" she would have "loved him just the same".

In November, the Queen invited Alix to Osborne, while Bertie was cruising with Vicky and Fritz round Italy. It was a terrifying ordeal for a seventeen-year-old girl to have to face alone. But soon her sunny nature thawed the Queen's chilled heart. "We cannot thank you enough," she told Vicky, for finding us this "jewel". She is "one of those sweet creatures who seem to come from the skies to help and bless poor mortals and brighten for a time their path! She lives in complete intimacy with us and she is so dear, so gentle, good, simple, unspoilt – so thoroughly honest and straight forward – so affectionate". But fond as she was of Alix, the match was not without drawbacks. "Oh! if Bertie's wife was only a good German and not a Dane!" she exclaimed in 1864 when her family was torn apart by Prussia's invasion of Denmark. Yet for all that, she noted in her journal on the tenth anniversary of Bertie's wedding that she was "ever thankful" for the day as it had given her "such a dear sweet daughter as darling Alix".

The Queen planned the wedding mainly to suit herself. She insisted, for example, that it should be held in St George's Chapel, Windsor, which severely restricted the number of guests and the public's chance of seeing it. Nothing could persuade her to invite Frederick VII of Denmark, a notorious profligate, or most of Princess Christian's other relations. Naturally, the Danish Royal Family felt aggrieved, which merely increased the Queen's antipathy to them.

In her looking-glass world, it was they not she who were selfish and intractable. She also contrived to affront the clergy by holding the service in Lent. When the Archbishop of Canterbury complained, she told him "in my young days there was no Lent". Presumably she took the view that Easter was a Tractarian invention. On the eve of the wedding, the Queen took the bridal pair to visit the Mausoleum, which had only just been finished. "I opened the shrine and took them in. I said '*He* gives you his blessing!' and joined Alix's and Bertie's hands, taking them both in my arms. It was a very touching moment and we all felt it". In her eyes, that ceremony was every bit as sacred as the service held next day.

The Wedding Day, March 10th, 1863, was somewhat overshadowed by the Queen's resolute gloom. Before the guests arrived, she told the Crown Princess to use her influence to check "noise and joyousness". On the day itself, she looked down on the congregation from Catherine of Aragon's closet, rather as she might watch an opera from her box at Covent Garden. There were two especially agonising moments. Early in the proceedings, a flourish of trumpets brought back her "whole life of twenty years at *his* dear side", and almost overwhelmed her. More moving still was the performance of Albert's chorale sung by Jenny Lind. As her magnificent voice soared above the choir, the Queen raised her eyes to heaven and "seemed to be with Him alone before the throne of God". When the ceremony was over, and the Bride and Groom had departed for Osborne, the Queen drove to "the beloved resting place" at Frogmore to "soothe and calm" her nerves. A few days later, Vicky reported that Bertie was "blissful", "beaming" and "radiant". "Love," she declared, "has certainly shed its sunshine on these two dear young hearts."

Alix's first child, Prince Albert Victor, known to his family as "Eddy", was born in January 1864 two months before expected. In June the following year, her second son, George, was also born prematurely. Three daughters followed in rapid succession: Louise in 1867, Victoria in 1868, and Maud in 1869. The Queen regarded these children as "frail" and "puny", and itched to interfere. "Alix and I," she complained, "never will or can be intimate; she shows me no confidence whatever especially about the children." But the moment they met, such grievances disappeared. Barely a month after she protested that she could never be "intimate" with her daughter-in-law, she went for a "walk and drive with dear Alix and nothing could be nicer or dearer than she is". The Queen's moods were as fickle as the English climate. At one moment she spoke of her grandchildren as "fine sweet, dear, merry simple things", and at the next she claimed they were terribly spoilt and as "wild as hawks". Rumours reached Windsor that their family life was one long boisterous romp, and that Alix was known to toboggan downstairs on a tray. Lady Geraldine Somerset, the Duchess of Cambridge's Lady-in-Waiting, spoke of the boys as badly in need of discipline, and the girls as "rampaging hoydens". The Queen was occasionally even more censorious, and once went so far as to claim that they were so "ill-bred" and "ill trained" that she could "not fancy them". In fact, she loved them dearly, and was especially fond of Eddy.

Long after the Prince of Wales married, the Queen continued to regulate his life as if he were still a schoolboy. It was only when he became King that he knew what it was to be his own master. Lord Stanley noted in 1863 that all London was gossiping about the "extraordinary way" in which the Queen insisted on directing "the Prince and Princess of Wales in every detail of their lives. They may not dine out except at houses named by her: nor ask anyone to dine with them, except with previous approval. . . . In addition, a daily and minute report of what passes at Marlborough House" had to be sent to Windsor. But what proved more serious was the Queen's insistence on meddling in the nursery. Her earliest exercise of her dubious prerogative was over her grandsons' names. "I felt rather annoyed," the Prince told her firmly, "when Beatrice (aged six) told Lady Macclesfield that you had settled what our little boy was to be called before I had spoken to you about it." Next there was an acrimonious exchange about taking Eddy to see his Danish grandparents. During the course of a heated correspondence, the Prince exposed his mother's double standards by pointing out that when Vicky or Alice came over to England she asked them to stay for two or three months at a time, but when Alix went home she was only allowed to remain there for a fortnight.

The Prince and Princess of Wales presided over the London Season of 1863 with such verve and panache, that people recalled the days of the Prince Regent. The Queen, however, frowned on the "Marlborough House Set" with its "fast" ways and late hours. Nor was she amused by the practical jokes which were part of the terrors of Sandringham. Rumours reached her of guests being offered mince-pies filled with mustard, or finding live lobsters in their beds. But what she deplored most was her son's choice of friends. When Tsar Nicholas II visited Sandringham he described the house-party as consisting mostly of "horse dealers". Worst of all was his growing promiscuity. Alix might comfort herself by saying "he always loved me the best", but the Queen took a less indulgent view of his "pleasant little wickednesses".

Racing was always a bone of contention between the Prince and his mother, but nothing she said could persuade him to turn his back on the Turf. "I fear dear Mama," he told her in 1870, "that no year goes round without your giving me a jobation on the subject of racing." Yet whatever Lord Shaftesbury might say, one hardly risked one's immortal soul by occasional visits to Ascot. "I am always most anxious to meet your wishes in every respect, and always regret if we are not quite *d'accord*, but as I am past twenty-eight, and have some considerable knowledge of the world and society, you will I am sure, at least I trust, allow me to use my own discretion in matters of this kind."

In November 1863, King Frederick VII of Denmark died. His successor, Alix's father, Christian IX, was immediately faced by rival claimants to the Duchies of Schleswig and Holstein, which ever since 1533 had been governed as Danish dependencies. Seizing the pretext of this disputed succession, Prussia and Austria intervened and occupied both territories, heedless of Palmerston's warning that it "would not be Denmark alone with which they would have to contend". The British public blamed Bismarck for what they saw as a blatant act of aggression, and displayed a chivalrous sympathy for Alix and her family. But Palmerston's bluff had been called, and his colleagues refused to embark on a war they could not possibly win. The Queen, having carefully studied Prince Albert's papers on this vexed and ancient problem, convinced herself that he would have supported Prussia, and told the Crown Princess that she was "grieved and distressed" by the prevailing belief in England, which she knew to be false, "that Prussia wants to have the Duchies for *herself*". The moment fighting began, she assured her daughter, with breathtaking inconsistency, that she was totally impartial, and that her "heart and sympathies" were all "German". For the first time since 1861 she began to discover how self-sufficient she was.

During the Winter Campaign of 1864, in which Fritz played a prominent part, Vicky identified herself so whole-heartedly with the war that her mother accused her of selling her soul to Bismarck. But

when the fighting was over, she started to speak of "bullying" and
"injustice". In February, the Queen told Vicky that Alix was "in a
terrible state of distress" and that Bertie was quite "frantic". Indeed,
he espoused the Danish cause so fervently that the Prussian Ambassador in London complained of his partisanship. Wherever he went,
he made his view known that the "horrible war" was a blot on
Prussia's honour, and that Denmark had been betrayed by the British
Government. "It is terrible," the Queen wrote, "to have the poor
boy on the wrong side." Alix never forgave the "bestial Germans"
for their wanton attack on her country. Many years later, when her
second son was made honorary Colonel of a Prussian regiment, she
complained that her "Georgie boy had become a real live, filthy,
blue-coated Pickelhaube German soldier!!!" "It is your misfortune,"
she added magnanimously, "not your fault."

The war realised the Queen's worst fears that foreign marriages
would lead to rifts in her family: an endemic complaint of royalty.
"Oh! would to God," she exclaimed, "I had not to be plagued with
politics." It so happened that when Frederick VII died there was a
large family party at Windsor, which included Princess Feodore,
whose daughter, Adelaide, was married to Prince Frederick of
Augustenburg, one of the claimants to Schleswig-Holstein. Naturally, Alix insisted that "the Duchies belong to Papa", which led the
Queen to complain that she came "from the enemy's camp", and
"was not worth the price we have paid for her". Equally naturally,
Princess Feodore pressed the claims of her son-in-law, and Fritz
those of Prussia. The Queen became "almost frantic" without Albert
beside her "to *put* the *others* down", and only restored a semblance
of peace by forbidding her guests to discuss the matter at all.

The Prince of Wales's open support for Denmark convinced the
Queen that he lacked discretion and judgement. How could she trust
him with confidential documents when he was known to betray
state secrets over the dinner table? She seemed unwilling to make
allowance for the fact that he was only twenty-two at the time, and
that it was natural that he should show some sympathy for the
Danes. Nor did it ever occur to her that she had herself openly sided
with Prussia. It was, of course, true, as she told Lord Clarendon,
that it was "fearfully dangerous for the heir to the throne to take up
one side violently", but she should not have held this error against
him for close on forty years. Only during the last decade of her
reign, when the Prince had become a grandfather, did she finally

permit him to see Cabinet papers and Foreign Office despatches. For most of his life, the royal understudy was kept hanging about in the wings, not even allowed to prepare for the role in which destiny had cast him.

In 1872, when Gladstone proposed his "Plan of Life" for the Prince, the Queen told him that she doubted her son's "fitness for high functions of state". Many years earlier she spoke of the prospect of his becoming King as "too awful" to contemplate. Gladstone, of course, was right to protest against wasting the Prince's talents. It was absurd to pretend that opening bazaars sufficed to keep him occupied. But the Queen refused to recognise the problem, apart from lecturing him on the aimless life to which she had consigned him. In 1868, for example, she told him that his plan to visit Punchestown Races would merely confirm the "too prevalent" belief that he only lived for "amusement". In one breath she complained she was grossly overworked, and in the next refused to allow her son to share her most trivial duties. In 1847, when Bertie was only six, Prince Albert suggested that it was never too early to accustom him to "work with us and for us". The Queen agreed wholeheartedly. "How true this is!" she noted in her journal. "So wise and right; and the more confidence we show him the better it will be for himself, for us, for the country." She was not, however, unique as a parent in knowing the right procedure without being willing to follow it.

In February 1870 the Queen was distressed to learn that her son had been summoned as a witness in what became known as the "Warwickshire Scandal". It was the first time since the reign of Henry IV that a Prince of Wales had appeared in a court of law. Four years before, Sir Charles Mordaunt had married Harriet Moncreiffe, then a girl of eighteen. In 1869 she gave birth to a premature son who threatened to go blind. The shock drove her out of her mind and she told Sir Charles that Lord Cole was the child's father. She also confessed to having affairs with a number of well-known men, including the Prince of Wales. When Mordaunt broke into her desk, he found a number of letters in H.R.H.'s hand. Somehow this correspondence found its way into the newspapers, but proved about as salacious as an Evangelical tract. No sooner had Sir Charles filed a petition for divorce than Harriet's parents entered a plea that she was out of her mind when she made her so-called "confession".

The moment the Queen received Bertie's letter about his subpoena, she sent him a telegram in which she expressed her sympathy and support. "I cannot sufficiently thank you," he wrote back, "for the dear and kind words you have written me." The trial unfortunately took place at precisely the moment that Queen Victoria's popularity reached its lowest ebb. Naturally, the Radical press made a meal of the Prince's shady associates: the "frivolous, selfish and pleasure-seeking" set whom the Queen deplored every bit as much as they did. The whole affair, she told Vicky, was "painfully lowering", not "because he is not innocent, for I never doubted that, but because his name ought never to have been dragged into the dirt, or mixed up with such people". To judge from republican newspapers one might have supposed that the Prince himself was on trial. In fact, the court decided that Lady Mordaunt was suffering from puerperal mania, and that the Pope could well be found guilty if her testimony was allowed.

However much the Queen might scold the Prince, she was ready to admit that he was "so full of good and amiable qualities" that it helped her "forget and overlook" much that she could have wished otherwise. "No Heir apparent," she once proclaimed, "was so nice and unpretending." In 1873, after Vicky had sent her a letter singing her brother's praises, the Queen wrote back to say what pleasure it gave her to hear her "speak so loving of dear Bertie. He is such a kind, good brother, a very loving son and a very true friend".

For several months after the Prince Consort's death, Alice slept in the Queen's room, issued orders to the Household, and acted as an intermediary with ministers. In a matter of days she changed from a carefree girl of eighteen into a woman of the world. Lady Lyttelton described her as "an angel in the house", and *The Times* declared that it was largely due to her that Her Majesty had "been able to bear the irreparable loss that so suddenly befell her". The Queen herself was the first to agree that "no one can sufficiently estimate" just what a "support" and "comfort" her "dear excellent child" had been. As the day of Alice's "wretched marriage" approached, her mother began to wish it was "years off". The ceremony, which eventually took place in the dining-room at Osborne on July 1st 1862, "was more like a funeral than a wedding". Winterhalter's portrait of the royal family, dominated by Prince Albert, looked down on the scene from above the improvised altar. The Queen was concealed from the congregation by her four sons who clustered protectively round her. Vicky had been forbidden to attend, as her third child was expected shortly. At the close of the ceremony, the family withdrew and the Queen gave way to grief. Clasping her younger sons in her arms she sobbed as if she would never see them again. It was more like a scene at a pithead disaster than a royal wedding. After Alice returned to Darmstadt, she sent her mother a ceaseless stream of letters, overflowing with love and solicitude, but tactfully avoiding the subject of her own happy marriage.

No sooner had Alice settled in Hesse than her mother complained that she ought to stay more in England. "The good children," she said, "have no duties at present to perform at home (Hesse). No house to live in, and ought to be as much with me as possible. A married daughter I MUST have living with me, and must *not* be left constantly to look about for help, and to have to make shift for the day, which is too dreadful." Liberal as she might be in interpreting awkward passages of Scripture, she took the biblical view of duty to parents absolutely literally. Nothing that Alice could say persuaded the Queen that she had obligations to Darmstadt. Whenever she visited England there were complaints of her long absences, and whenever she went back she was told that the Hesses "monopolised" her.

Not only did the Queen cling desperately to her daughters, but she seemed to believe that her ladies-in-waiting should always remain old maids. When Dean Stanley had the temerity to propose to Lady Augusta Bruce, the Queen wanted to know why he "could not see as much of her as he wished" without actually marrying. "Dear Lady Augusta," she told King Leopold, "at forty-one, without a previous long attachment, has most unnecessarily decided to marry!! It has been my *greatest sorrow* and trial *since* my misfortune! I thought she *never* would leave *me*!" How, she asked herself, could anyone be so selfish as to prefer their own happiness to the welfare of their Sovereign?

Alice's first child, dutifully christened "Victoria Alberta", was born at Windsor on Easter Sunday, 1863. The Queen, who insisted when possible on attending the births of her grandchildren, sat up all night with her daughter. Later, she described her self-imposed vigil "as the most dreadful thing to witness possible. Quite awful! I had far rather have gone through it myself!" The following year, a second girl was born, called Elizabeth, or "Ella" for short. Naturally, Alice hoped for a son to maintain the Grand Ducal line, but in 1866 a third daughter appeared named "Irène", after the Goddess of Peace. At last, in 1868, Alice produced a boy, christened "Ernest", a favourite name in his father's family. Two years later a brother followed called "Frederick William" after his uncle, the Crown Prince. "Frittie", as he soon became known, suffered from haemophilia, and was so wild and boisterous that it was almost impossible to prevent him from being injured. One morning in May 1873 he fell out of an open window, while playing a game of hide and seek with Ernie. He was picked up unconscious from the stone terrace some twenty feet below, and died in his mother's arms. No bones were broken and his injuries proved fatal only because of haemorrhage of the brain. Two more daughters were born in 1872 and 1874. The eldest, Alexandra, laughed so much that her mother called her "Sunny", a name which her husband, Tsar Nicholas II, was later to make his own. The younger, who was born on her grandmother's birthday, May 24th, was christened Marie Victoria Feodora Leopoldine, and was known as "May".

In the late eighteen-sixties Alice's relations with her mother began to come under strain. In a sense it was her turn to be in disgrace, and the principal charge against her was her supposed love of meddling, particularly when she had the temerity to oppose her mother's plans for Princess Helena's marriage. But worse was to come. If there was one thing the Queen bitterly resented it was any attempt to dictate to her, yet Alice was rash enough to try to persuade her to alter her way of life. She might just as well have attempted to persuade a Moslem Fundamentalist to toast her in champagne. In 1867, Vicky was told that her erring sister, who had recently stayed at Osborne, "grumbled about everything – the rooms, the hours, wanting me to do this and that". If she wished to visit, "she should accommodate herself to my habits" and recognise that as "my life is made up of work, I must live as I find I best can to get through the work. . . . I therefore require to shape my own life and ways". The Queen furthermore blamed Alice for forming a family cabal to force her out of seclusion, and even accused her of falling for "fine Society", in spite of her work for the poor, the sick and the suffering. They also fell out over money, as Alice could never restrain her generosity. Some people thought she was too demanding in asking her mother for help, although no one was better equipped to resist such requests. In hard times, as the Hesses soon discovered, she was as generous with advice as she was niggardly with money.

Both Alice and Vicky were deeply disturbed by Bismarck's growing hostility to Austria. In 1866 he hardly concealed the fact that he was looking for a pretext to attack his former ally in the hope of uniting the German princes under the King of Prussia. The Queen, in a desperate attempt to avert the threat of war, begged William, "for the memory of him who was your friend, (my beloved husband)", not to destroy the precarious peace of Europe. Her letter proved unavailing, and for the second time in two years there was civil war in the family. Vicky described her "cruel contradiction of feelings" in a bewildered letter home. "You will not think it unnatural," she told her mother, "that my feelings are on the side of my country and husband", but that did not mean that she relished treating fellow Germans as enemies. "How cruel it is," she wrote a few days later, "to have one's heart and one's head thus set at right angles."

Hesse and Hanover threw in their lot with Austria, and Louis went off to war on the fourth anniversary of his wedding. It need hardly be said that the Duchy was no match for Prussia. When somebody asked the Grand Duke how many guns should be moved to the front, he replied majestically, "Send both". Alice remained in Darmstadt, but Victoria and Ella were packed off to Windsor to stay with their grandmother. Fritz played a prominent part in Austria's defeat and was given the order "Pour la Merite" on the battlefield of Sadowa. In July, a Prussian army advanced on Hesse, and Alice could hear the sound of distant gunfire as she visited military hospitals. On July 22nd Darmstadt was occupied, and not long after the Grand Duke was forced to surrender. Prussia's peace terms were devastatingly harsh, and Hesse was impoverished by the cost of the war. Hanover fared even worse, and George V, the Queen's first cousin, was left a penniless exile. Vicky was so bewildered by events that she hardly made any sense. At one moment, she was deeply moved by the "distressing position" in which "darling Alice" found herself, and in the next exulted over the fruits of Bismarck's iniquity.

In 1870, when France declared war on Prussia, Vicky and Alice at least could be thankful to be on the same side. The Queen, of course, shared their concern over Fritz and Louis, and felt sure that "Papa would have gone to fight if he could". She saw the struggle in black and white as a conflict between "civilisation, liberty, order and unity", as symbolised by Germany; and "despotism, corruption, immorality and aggression", as represented by France. Although Government policy remained one of strict neutrality, she looked back to Waterloo when British and Prussian troops had fought side by side against the Emperor's uncle. "How my heart bleeds for you all," she assured the Crown Princess. In October 1870 a republican meeting condemned her Court as a "pack of Germans", and she was deeply distressed by the suspicions aroused "on account of her relationships and feelings". Surprised as she was by Prussia's early victories, she believed that they showed the righteous judgement of God. When Norman Macleod preached a sermon at Crathie in which he described France as "reaping the reward of her wickedness and vanity and sensuality", she was seen to nod approvingly. She had long been convinced that the Second Empire had done "frightful harm to English Society and was very bad for Bertie and Affie". "Surely," she said, on being told of the fall of Paris, "that Sodom and Gomorrah as Papa called it deserves to be crushed."

Soon after the outbreak of war, Count Bernstorff, the Prussian Ambassador in London, sent a despatch to Berlin claiming that the Prince of Wales had publicly expressed the hope that the French would prove victorious. The Queen assured Vicky that the story was "quite untrue" and that Bernstorff was "a shocking mischief maker" who ought to be recalled. But the damage was done, and Bismarck exploited such lies to discredit the "English Princess". "Mothers' and wives' hearts," wrote the Queen in despair, were "not made for such fearful trials".

On September 2nd 1870, Napoleon was captured at Sedan, one of the most decisive battles of the nineteenth century. Two days later, the demise of the Second Empire gave birth to the Third Republic. On September 9th the Queen received two telegrams: one to say that Lehzen had died, and the other to tell her the Empress had landed at Hastings. Immediately the Prince of Wales heard the news of her escape, he wrote her a letter recalling happy memories of all her kindness to him since his first visit to France in 1855, and offering her the use of Chiswick House, "notre maison de campagne près de Londres". Lord Granville, the Foreign Secretary, fearing such chivalry would offend the newly established Republic, was greatly relieved to learn that the Empress had decided to live at Camden Place, Chislehurst. When the Queen was told of the Prince's intervention, she thought it presumptuous and inopportune. Not that she did not sympathise with the "poor dear Empress", whom she visited at Chislehurst and invited back to Windsor.

Before the Prussians began the Siege of Paris, the Queen implored William I not to bombard the city: an appeal which Bismarck dismissed as "petticoat" interference. Not long after, the forces of "civilisation" began to rain down shells on "Sodom and Gomorrah". When peace was at last concluded, the terms proved so severe that a whole generation of Frenchmen summed up their hopes in the single word "revanche". No settlement could be permanent, said the Queen, which sowed such seeds of hatred and resentment.

In January 1871 Bismarck persuaded King Ludwig of Bavaria to invite William I to accept the Imperial Crown of Germany on behalf of his fellow princes. When the Empire was proclaimed on January 18th, in the Salle des Glaces at Versailles, the new Kaiser looked sullen and dejected. Indeed, so deeply did he resent the honour thrust upon him, preferring his time-honoured title of King of Prussia, that he refused to speak to Bismarck during the ceremony. Fritz wore the Garter for the occasion "as an omen of an ultimate union of the Empire with England". In March, Napoleon III was released and joined his wife in exile. A week after his arrival at Chislehurst, he was invited to Windsor, and the Queen at once succumbed to the old magic. Soon after, she returned his visit, and was met at the door of Camden Place by the young Prince Imperial. She was particularly struck by the Emperor's stoicism. Never once did he rail against misfortune or blame those who had helped to bring it about. When the Empress begged him to defend himself against slanders, he replied that it was the "highest prerogative of a Sovereign" to shoulder "the responsibilities incurred by those who had served him" or "betrayed him".

Only a few hours after Napoleon died in 1873, a letter arrived by hand from Windsor so full of affectionate sympathy that the Empress claimed that if anything could have mitigated her sorrow it was the Queen's kindness. The Prince of Wales insisted on attending the funeral, in defiance of fears of imperialist demonstrations. "One cannot be wrong," he said, with habitual generosity, "in showing respect to fallen greatness". For once, the Queen supported him, although Gladstone complained of his want of judgement "inherited or acquired". A month later, she placed a wreath on Napoleon's tomb and went on to visit the Empress at Camden Place. There the two widows sat in a darkened room discussing the details of the Emperor's agonising illness and "terribly sudden" death. "Nobody would ever believe," the Empress once said, what "delicate attentions" the Queen lavished upon them from the moment they landed in England. Regardless of the fact that her Government had recognised the legality of the Republic, she continued to treat them as Sovereigns. On one occasion in 1892, while the Empress was staying at Birkhall, she was invited for dinner at Balmoral. When the time came for her to leave, the Queen accompanied her to the door, and a tussle took place over who should go through it first. In the end, they both curtsied low to each other, and passed through together, the Queen, if anything, lagging slightly behind.

For most of the eighteen-sixties, Affie, like Alice, was frequently in disgrace. In 1862, while serving with the Mediterranean Fleet, he got into trouble with a young lady in Malta, news of which reached the Queen and caused her "bitter anguish". His conduct, she said, "dealt a heavy blow to her weak and shattered frame", and showed that he "was both heartless and dishonourable". "How could Affie be such a goose?" Vicky asked, in the hope of defusing the crisis. Nothing, however, could alter the fact that he was the least agreeable of all the Queen's children. She did not herself suffer from his abominable temper, but she knew that he loved to make mischief in the family, and that he was inconsiderate to servants. When it came to women, his morals were little better than those of his uncle Ernest. The Queen's feelings for her sailor son changed with the ebb and flow of her volatile nature. At one moment, she described him as "a great, great grief" and a "source of bitter anger". At the next, she thought him greatly improved and quite like his old self. But the fact had to be faced that he spent too much time with Bertie's "fast" friends. "We do all we can," she told Vicky, to "keep him from Marlborough House as he is far too much 'épris' with Alix to be allowed to be much there without possibly ruining the happiness of all three". Ponsonby, always a shrewd judge of character, said there was something about the Duke's eyes which inspired distrust. Nor did he relish being kept up half the night listening to Affie talking about himself.

In 1866, Affie was given the order of the Garter and the title "Duke of Edinburgh". Later that year he met his future wife, the Grand Duchess Marie, whose father was Alexander II of Russia, and whose mother was Louis of Hesse's aunt. They met at a royal house party in Denmark, as Marie's brother, "Sacha", who later succeeded his father as Alexander III, was married to Alix's sister, Dagmar. By 1869 Affie had set his heart on Marie, not least of her attractions being her stupendous wealth. Given his passion for money, amounting to disease, he found the thought of her dowry irresistible. Neither the

Tsar nor the Queen showed much enthusiasm for the match. Alexander had no wish to lose his much loved daughter, and Queen Victoria regarded the Romanovs as "false", "unfriendly", and "*half Oriental*". She was also painfully aware of the fact that no member of her family had married a non-Protestant since 1688. "We must be very firm" she said, "or else we may pack up – and call back the descendants of the Stuarts". The young couple, however, were determined to marry, and became engaged in July 1873. "The murder is out!" wrote the Queen to Vicky in her letter announcing the news. It was not, she said, "what I wished or like – religion – politics – views of Court – and nation, are all contrary to ours, but I shall receive Marie with all love and affection". She naturally longed to inspect her new daughter-in-law, and was furious with the Tsar for refusing to bring her to England. In an effort to be conciliatory, the Tsarina, Marie, suggested a meeting at Cologne, a proposal which Alice was rash enough to second. "You have entirely taken the Russian side," wrote the Queen indignantly, "and I do *not* think, dear child, that *you* should tell *me* who have been nearly 20 *years longer* on the throne than the Emperor of Russia and am the Doyenne of Sovereigns, and who am a *Reigning* sovereign which the Empress is *not, what* I *ought to do.* I think *I* know *that.*" It was quite out of the question to suppose that she could be ready to travel at twenty-four hours' notice at the behest of the "*mighty Russians*".

Affie's wedding took place at St Petersburg on January 23rd, 1874. He wore the uniform of a Russian naval captain (a wedding present from the Tsar) and was supported by Bertie and Fritz. After an interminable Orthodox service, Dean Stanley conducted the Anglican rites in a room lit by ten thousand candles. When the Queen finally met her new daughter-in-law, she described her as a "treasure". Many of Marie's qualities were those she most admired, and she was delighted to find her "pleasingly natural and unaffected", "easy to live with", and "even-tempered" and kind. Furthermore, she was intelligent, "fond of serious books", and anxious to work for charity. "Pretty really I cannot think her." Her chin was too short, her neck too long, and her stance ungainly. Having been brought up with six obstreperous brothers, it was not surprising that she was something of a tomboy. The Queen always respected people who refused to be overawed by her, and Marie's courage was legendary. "You only have to give her a good fight," she told the Tsarina,

"to make her draw in her horns." In spite of her massive trousseau
– sufficient to stock an emporium – the Duchess dressed dowdily.
But on state occasions, her dazzling diamonds and sapphires, many
of which had belonged to Catherine the Great, made even the Queen
envious.

The Queen's fifth child, Princess Helena, took Alice's place the
moment she left for Darmstadt, and soon became an invaluable companion. "I *don't* intend *she* should marry," her mother wrote in 1863,
"till nineteen or twenty." Eventually she would look out for "a
young sensible prince" who would make Windsor "his *principal*
home. Lenchen is so useful and her whole character so well adapted
to live in the house that I could *not* give her up without *sinking* under
the *weight* of my desolation." The search for a suitable husband was
fraught with difficulties. She was the least prepossessing of all the
sisters, and not every suitor would willingly live with his mother-in-
law. The Queen, with her customary candour, acknowledged that
"poor dear Lenchen, though most useful and active and clever and
amiable . . . had great difficulties with her figure". The problem was
finally solved by finding a consort as unbecoming as she was: Prince
Christian of Schleswig-Holstein-Sonderburg-Augustenburg. Christian was fifteen years older than Lenchen, and "the best and dullest
of men". At first sight it was difficult to find much to commend
him, as he was bald and penniless. Moreover he smoked cigars from
morning until night, which in most circumstances would have
proved fatal to his chances. But the Queen was prepared to overlook
his shortcomings because of the "noble and right view" he took of
her "very forlorn position". Hence the warm welcome she offered
the homeless exile who agreed to live at her Court. Even before he
married she began to take him in hand. "I shall see to Christian's
cough and teeth", she said soon after their first meeting.

Prince Albert taught the Queen to believe that the family needed
"strong, dark blood". When her cousin, Princess Mary of Cambridge, married the Duke of Teck in 1866, she welcomed the match
on precisely that ground. Equally, she regretted the fact that Christian's mother had "fair hair and blue eyes" which made "the blood
so lymphatic". Some of the family, however, saw that as the least
of their objections to the "miserable starveling German Princeling"
the Queen had chosen for Lenchen. In 1864, Prince Christian had
joined the Prussians against the Danes on behalf of his elder brother,
Frederick, Duke of Augustenburg, a claimant to Schleswig-Holstein.

What made matters worse was that Alix's brother, the Crown Prince Frederick, had been seen as a possible suitor for Helena's hand, until the Queen made it clear that the match was out of the question. At first, Bertie was so opposed to the marriage that he threatened to boycott the wedding, but after a long discussion with his mother was finally won round. Alix, however, refused to relent, and Alice was also critical of the match, mainly because she feared that her sister's future was being sacrificed to suit her mother's convenience. Not only did she warn Lenchen that it might be a great mistake to continue to live at home, but she also advised Christian not to be "put upon". The Queen was so furious that she accused Alice of being "heartless", and "disrespectful", and of wanting "her own way". It was perfectly "monstrous", she said, when "your parent and your Sovereign settles a thing for her (Helena's) good" to raise selfish and jealous objections. Fortunately, Alice fell into line when her sister expressed the fear that Christian might slip through her fingers.

The marriage took place at St George's Chapel, Windsor, on July 5th 1866. To many people's surprise, the bride was given away by her mother. "I was the only one to do it," she explained for Fritz's benefit. "I never would let one of my sons take their father's place while I live." The Christians had four children: Christian Victor, born in 1867, another son, Albert, born two years later, then Helena Victoria, born in 1870, and finally Marie Louise, born in 1872. The family was mainly brought up at Windsor, first at Frogmore House and later at Cumberland Lodge, very much under their grandmother's eye. Besides looking after her children and waiting on her mother, Lenchen devoted herself to numerous charities. She was far too businesslike to put up with dithering. When discussions became too discursive, she would bring matters to a head with the formula: "So we all agree don't we?"

Princess Louise, who was thirteen when the Prince Consort died, grew up under the shadow of her mother's grief. The Queen took it for granted that her children would be as inconsolable as she was, and told General Bruce in 1862 to warn the Prince of Wales not to indulge in "worldly, frivolous, gossiping kind of conversation", but to accept "in a proper spirit the cureless melancholy of his poor home". Four years after Prince Albert's death, she refused to open the Ballroom at Buckingham Palace to give Louise a coming of age party. In 1864 the Princess nearly died of tubercular meningitis, a

disease which can cause infertility. When Lenchen married it soon
became clear that Louise could never replace her. As her mother said,
she was "dreadfully contradictory" and regrettably "indiscreet". By
the time she was eighteen, she was full of fun and vivacity, but was
often betrayed by her sharp, uncharitable tongue. "Mama," she once
said disconcertingly loud, "was not too unwell to open Parliament,
only unwilling." Even her critics had to admit her remarkable skill as
a sculptress. In 1869 her marble bust of her mother was prominently
displayed at the Royal Academy and justly admired by almost all
who saw it.

The Queen was resolved that Louise should marry an Englishman,
and began to browse through Burke's Peerage in search of a suitable
husband. She demanded three prerequisites of a suitor: impeccable
integrity, a considerable fortune, and noble lineage. By the summer
of 1870 she had narrowed the field to five contestants. One after the
other they were paraded at Balmoral like prize bulls in a cattle ring.
The victor was John Douglas Sutherland Campbell, the eldest son
of the eighth Duke of Argyll, who until he succeeded his father was
known as the Marquis of Lorne. In 1868 he was presented with
a safe Liberal seat in the House of Commons. What particularly
commended him to the Queen was the fact that he was a grandson
of her "dearest, kindest, truest friend", the Duchess of Sutherland,
her former Mistress of the Robes, who had attended her on her
Wedding Day and had been at Windsor the evening Prince Albert
died. The Queen, at first, did not take very kindly to Lorne. "Il ne
faut pas disputer des goûts", she told Vicky in June 1870, "but I do
not fancy him. He has such a forward manner and such a disagreeable
way of speaking, but I know he is very clever and good." The nasal
twang, which she found so distasteful, was the consequence of an
injury he received on the playing fields of Eton. By October, she
changed her mind, and thought him "very good looking", as well
as "clever" and "amiable". On October 3rd Lorne proposed as he
and the Princess climbed the path from the Glassalt Shiel to Loch
Dhu. The last time that a child of a reigning sovereign had become
engaged to a subject was in 1515, when Henry VIII's younger sister,
Mary, married Charles Brandon. Louise had dithered for some time
between her dazzling suitors, but when Lorne actually asked her to
be his wife her doubts seemed to melt away.

The idea that Louise should marry a mere nobleman did not appeal
to her family. Even the Queen, whose idea it was, found intimacy

with a subject rather trying, and thought that the Duke was disposed to be too familiar when discussing his future daughter-in-law. Vicky, who wanted her sister to marry a Prussian Prince, sent her mother "a *very* unamiable letter" on learning of the engagement. But as Lorne's ancestors had been kings when no one had ever heard of the Hohenzollerns, he remained unmoved by such protests. The Queen, rather undiplomatically, told the Crown Princess, "the English do not like the Prussians", although they were willing to make an exception of Fritz. Besides "the prospect of comfort, peace and unity" was infinitely preferable to "dreadfully painful divided interests". Everywhere, she claimed, the match had been hailed as "the most popular act" of her reign. Not only would it invigorate the Monarchy by connecting it with one of "the great families of the land", but infusions of new blood were an "absolute necessity" if the dynasty was to flourish.

Louise's marriage took place at St George's, Windsor on March 21st 1871. Lorne processed down the aisle to the strains of "The Campbells are Coming", and the Queen gave her daughter away with a heavy heart. The Lornes spent most of their early married life between Number One Grosvenor Crescent, Argyll Lodge (Camden Hill), and Inveraray. In 1873 they were given apartments at Kensington Palace, which the Princess retained for the next sixty-six years.

Just when Prince Arthur needed his father most, the Prince Consort died. His Governor, Major Elphinstone, was an admirable person, but had little experience of looking after the young. The Prince was a late developer, and much of his childhood was rather sad and solitary. The Queen was most anxious that her "darling boy" should be brought up to take pride in his German ancestry, particularly as he might succeed to Coburg. At the time of his Confirmation, she trembled "to think to what his pure heart" might be exposed, but thanked God that he had so far remained unblemished. Until he was eighteen, he could hardly do wrong in her eyes, and of all her sons he was far the most amenable.

In 1866 Prince Arthur passed into Woolwich, but lived separately from the other Cadets in the Ranger's House at Greenwich. Her experience of Bertie and Affie had taught the Queen how easy it was for young men to be corrupted. The last thing she wanted was the trauma of a second Nellie Clifden. In 1869 the Prince was commissioned into the Rifle Brigade and sailed for Canada to join the Regiment. After a year's "active" service at Montreal, he returned to England where military life was more leisurely. In 1874 he was created Duke of Connaught, less to reward him for his services than to enhance his marital prospects.

Naturally, when Prince Arthur came of age in 1871, he thought that the Queen would relax her maternal vigilance. But Elphinstone failed to discern any falling off of her "crisp and incessant" notes, reminding him, for example, that the Prince's rooms should be kept at sixty degrees, or deploring his habit of keeping his hands in his pockets, which his father had always "hated". Hunting was discouraged because it was dangerous, smoking because it was obnoxious, and yachting because "the *very worst people*" seemed to take part in regattas. So exhaustive was the Queen's list of prohibited entertainments, that little remained apart from tennis and croquet. Obsessed by the groundless fear that Arthur had sold his soul to the "fashionable world", she repeatedly exhorted him to "BREAK with the higher classes", and repudiate racing and gambling, "the *ruin* to hundreds of families and the heart-breaking of Parents". The Prince was wonderfully patient, but sometimes let out a momentary murmur of protest. On one such occasion, she objected indignantly that it was very wrong for "*a boy* of twenty-one" to "put his *feelings* against the experience of his mother, 24 years on the Throne". In 1879, when he was a Lieutenant-Colonel, she sent Elphinstone a note in which she said that her son looked out of sorts and ought to be "*dosed*" at once. Apparently the Prince could not even be trusted to reach for the syrup of figs.

Prince Leopold was the most unruly of all the Queen's children and the most liable to defy her. When he was five years old, she told Vicky that he was "amusing" but not "engaging". Inevitably, their relationship was overshadowed by her "constant fear" of his suffering a haemorrhage. Her incessant anxiety made her helplessly over protective. It was a natural mistake for a mother to make and totally counter-productive. In 1872 she complained to Vicky that Leo was wilfully negligent of his health. The Crown Princess, who thought it was time to set her brother free, replied with exquisite tact. It was the way of the world, she said, for the young to chafe at restraint and the old at opposition, and she quoted a German proverb: "If the string of the bow is drawn too tight it will snap". There was a considerable risk, she argued, that if Leo was kept "pining for liberty" he might over-react once he got it. The Queen remained unconvinced, and urged the Crown Princess to use her influence to remind her youngest brother and sister of the duty they owed to their "sorely tried mother".

Between 1866 and 1870, Leopold's tutor and Governor was the Reverend Robinson Duckworth, a delightful and brilliant young man. He was a Fellow of Trinity, Oxford, and a friend of Charles Dodgson (Lewis Carroll), who portrayed him in *Alice in Wonderland* as the "Duck". All went splendidly until Princess Louise developed a school-girl crush on him. In 1872 Prince Leopold insisted on going up to Oxford, in spite of the Queen's opposition. During his time at Christ Church he became acquainted with Ruskin, Dr Jowett, Gounod and Sullivan; and even found time to fall in love with the Dean's daughter, Alice Liddell. His undergraduate days were the happiest of his life, partly because of his scholarly disposition, and partly because he was able to live a fairly normal existence.

During Prince Albert's lifetime there could hardly have been a more boisterous child than Beatrice, but after he died she was forced to adjust to a world of mourning and grief. Many years later, the Queen told Tennyson that she could not allow her daughter's life to be darkened by her own "trials and sorrows", seemingly unaware that this was precisely what she had done. Absorbed as she was by her own wretchedness, she turned Beatrice into a solemn-faced young lady, who tiptoed down the corridors of Windsor like an undertaker's mute. Once an enchanting extrovert, she became awkward, shy and withdrawn.

By the time that Beatrice was sixteen, she was already established as "a dear, unselfish companion" to her mother. "I may truly and honestly say," the Queen informed Vicky, "I never saw so amiable, gentle, and thoroughly contented a child as she is." She had been taught from the earliest age to believe that her principal role in life was to help to support her widowed Mama. In 1863, when she was barely six years old, she used to watch Frith at work on his huge canvas of the Prince of Wales's Wedding. One day he asked her if she would have liked to have been one of her brother's bridesmaids. "No," she replied emphatically, "I don't like weddings. I don't like weddings at *all*! I shall never be married. I shall stay with mother!" Over the next thirty-eight years she never said anything to suggest that she questioned that commitment. The Queen, of course, was by no means alone in believing that a daughter's first duty was to her parents. Cheltenham, Bath and Torquay were peopled by selfless spinsters who had surrendered their chance of happiness for the sake of some ailing relation. The tragedy was that such heroic sacrifices were simply taken for granted.

The Queen was so anxious for Beatrice to stay at home that she determined to "keep her as young and childlike as possible". Long after she was eighteen, she referred to her as "baby". "She is the last I have, and I could not live without her." Because in her heart of hearts the Queen must have known that it could not be right to retard her daughter's growth, she rationalised her decision. "All of your sisters," she said in a letter to Vicky, "have come out too early and have been made grown-up too soon. I mean to hold her (Beatrice) back much more – for her own good as well as for my comfort." In 1874, the Crown Princess provoked an explosion of anger by casually remarking that she hoped that "Baby" might one day prove as good a wife and mother as she already had a daughter. The Queen was never more impossible than when defending the indefensible, and so heated was the subsequent exchange that she later burned her letters. To suggest that Beatrice might one day wish to marry was like playing Russian roulette with a bullet in every barrel.

8

The Queen Empress
1874–1887

B Y the mid eighteen-seventies, the Queen's capacity for enjoying the simple pleasures of life was once more reasserting itself, and she seemed to become more adventurous with every year that passed. One of the earliest signs of her recovery was her renewed zest for travelling. Whenever she stayed abroad for any length of time, she insisted on taking her bed, desk, a gallery of family portraits, one of her own carriages, and several horses and ponies. She was also accompanied by well over sixty people, amongst whom were six or so dressers, M. Ferry, her French chef, a small battalion of scullions, grooms, footmen, doctors, secretaries, ladies-in-waiting, and, of course, John Brown. The royal train, which included her own sleeping-car and drawing-room, was restricted to a maximum speed of thirty-five miles an hour – twenty-five at night – as it trundled across Europe. When its occupants were disgorged onto the platform of Nice or Cannes station, bystanders were supposed to believe that the majestic elderly lady in black was the Countess of Balmoral: an incognito which began to wear rather thin when the royal standard fluttered above her hotel.

In the spring of 1879 the Queen visited Italy for the first time, and stayed for a month in the Villa Clara on the eastern shore of Lago Maggiore. During her outward journey she spent a night at the Embassy in Paris where she met M. Grévy, the French President, who particularly pleased her by bowing to Brown. When she went out for drives with an escort of Carabinieri, she was surprised to find that "the children on the roads knew me quite well", and called out "La Regina d'Inghilterra". She was forced, however, to cancel a visit to Venice because Brown was afflicted by erysipelas. During her stay she managed to see Milan, but insisted on doing so privately. Nevertheless, when a crowd in the Cathedral began to push and jostle, she complained there were too few police. Otherwise she was delighted by the beauty of the country and the welcome she received. Three years later, in 1882, she paid her first visit to the French Riviera in search of spring sunshine. She stayed at the Chalet des Rosiers, to the east of Menton, which she described as "a nice little quiet chalet surrounded by a wood of olives", with "a beautiful view of the sea and coast". Not only did she capture the scene in water-colours, but her letters were full of descriptions of its beauty.

Throughout her life, Princess Beatrice was plagued by rheumatism, and had difficulty in writing and playing the piano. In 1883 her doctors advised her to take the waters at Aix les Bains, and she was so delighted by the resort that in 1885 the Queen decided to accompany her. They stayed at the Maison Mottet, later renamed the "Villa Victoria". "The scenery here is quite splendid," the Queen told one of her grand-daughters, "like Switzerland and the Lago Maggiore and some of our large Scotch lochs." She relished the "snowy range of the Alps", which she thought "so wild and grand", and which gave her particular "pleasure" as she always delighted "in mountains and hills". By the time of her second visit in 1887 she had already made her mark on the town, and relics of her patronage remain to this day in such place names as "Avenue Victoria", "Villa Beatrice" or "Hotel Windsor". Shortly before she arrived, there was a series of earthquakes in the neighbourhood, and she was naturally apprehensive. Soon after retiring to bed on the very first night of her stay, she heard ominous rumblings below, and rang her bell to discover what was amiss. It transpired that the disturbance came from a nearby room, and was nothing more threatening than her private secretary's snoring.

During the Queen's stay, she was shown over the monastery of La Grande Chartreuse, about which she had heard from the Empress Eugénie. The monastery was perched some three thousand feet up a mountain, and involved a risky journey over narrow, precipitous roads, made more dangerous by melting snow. Few travellers undertook the arduous climb, and it was a measure of her fortitude that she insisted on making the ascent. As always, she was hugely intrigued by all she saw, and little escaped her notice. At luncheon, she was offered a glass of wine, but asked for a taste of the monks' famous liqueur which she later described as "excellent". She was particularly intrigued by a young Englishman who had joined the Order soon after becoming eighteen. When they met, he knelt and kissed her hand, and told her that he was proud to be her subject. The Queen, who even in old age had an eye for a handsome youth, noted that he was "very good-looking and tall, with rather a delicate complexion and a beautiful, saintly, almost rapt expression". Some people in England protested at a Protestant Sovereign fraternising with Catholics.

On March 2nd, 1882, a seventh attempt was made on the Queen's life, a year after the assassination of President Garfield of America and Alexander II of Russia. As she drew out of Windsor station late that afternoon a shot was fired at her carriage. At the time she saw nothing, and supposed that the pistol's report was an engine letting off steam. The first she knew that anything was amiss was when she noticed a man being "violently hustled, and people running in all directions". Then Brown opened the coach door and told her "That man fired at Your Majesty". Princess Beatrice, who accompanied her mother, saw everything, but "showed great courage and calmness and never moved or said a word". Two Eton boys, who had been standing in the crowd, rushed forward and belaboured the would-be assassin with their umbrellas, until Superintendent Hayes of the Windsor Police seized him by the collar and managed to disarm him. For once Brown was almost last on the scene, for by the time he had clambered down from the rumble the incident was over. That evening, when the Queen recorded the episode in her journal, she described him as "greatly perturbed". This was the most dangerous of all attempts to kill her, as the revolver used was loaded with live ammunition. Next day Brown showed her the weapon, which she noted "could be fired off in rapid succession" and possessed "six chambers".

So eager was the crowd to tear the culprit to pieces, that Inspector Hayes summoned a cab and bundled him off to the Police Station. As they drove up Windsor hill, he learned that the suspect was Roderick Maclean, who came from Scotland and professed to be a poet. On March 6th, the Queen "received an address from the Eton boys in the Quadrangle", and promised the two who had come to her rescue "a commission in my guards". Such was the outburst of loyalty which greeted her escape that she claimed it was "worth being shot at – to see how much one is loved". From the first she remained convinced that Maclean although "thoroughly bad and eccentric" was "*not* insane". In April, Maclean was charged with High Treason and tried at Reading Assizes. During the proceedings the police disclosed that they had found a poem dedicated to Her Majesty amongst the prisoner's effects, to which was pinned a letter from Lady Biddulph, written from Buckingham Palace, explaining that the Queen "never accepts manuscript poetry". It further transpired that Maclean had spent fifteen years in the Bath and Somerset Lunatic Asylum following a serious injury to his brain. Montagu Williams, his defending counsel, declared that "few who looked upon him had any doubt that insanity had marked him for its own", a verdict later endorsed by eight medical experts. The consequence was that Maclean was found "not guilty of attempting to murder the Queen on grounds of insanity": a form of words which made her so indignant that she protested "if this is the law, the law must be altered". How could it be argued that Maclean was "not guilty" when it had been conclusively proved that he had fired at her? In 1883 an Act was passed substituting a new formula: "Guilty but insane". Not until eighty-one years later was the original wording restored.

On Easter Monday, March 25th, 1883, Brown woke up with a high fever and swellings all over his head. It soon became clear that he was suffering from erysipelas, which had first attacked him in 1865 and more recently in Italy. Unfortunately, his resistance was undermined by drink, and on Tuesday symptoms appeared of delirium tremens: a complication mercifully kept from the Queen. Indeed, at ten o'clock that evening Jenner told her that she need not be too much alarmed as Brown's "pulse was better". His illness could hardly have come at a more inconvenient time, as only the week before she had slipped at Windsor and badly injured her leg. For several months she could only walk with difficulty, and was never again free from pains in her knee. Much as she longed to "see after" Brown, she was "tied" to her chair and forced to depend on the doctors' reports. Early on Wednesday morning, Prince Leopold came into her dressing room and "broke the dreadful news" that Brown had died in his sleep.

The Queen was "utterly crushed" by John Brown's death. "I feel so stunned and bewildered," she told Vicky. "He protected me so – that I felt safe! And now all, all is gone in this world, and all seems unhinged again in thousands of ways." There was something at once touching and ludicrous in her desperate outbursts of grief. "Weep with me," she wrote to Jessie Brown, who had married John's brother, Hugh, "for we have all lost the best, the truest heart that ever beat." Tennyson managed to sound the right chord and touched her by his sympathy. "I *do* need it," she told him, writing in the first person, "for few have had more trials and *none* have been or still are in such an exceptionally solitary and difficult position. . . . Friends have fallen on all sides, and, one by one, I have lost those I cared for and leant on most. And now again lately, I have lost one who humble though he was – was the truest and most devoted of all! He had *no* thought but for me, my welfare, my comfort, my safety, my happiness. Courageous, unselfish, *totally* disinterested, discreet to the highest degree, speaking the truth fearlessly . . . and *ever* at hand – he was *part* of *my life* and quite invaluable." The void he left was "terrible, the loss irreparable".

Of all the Queen's letters of condolence, the most inept was that of her Prime Minister, who spoke of Brown as an "attached" and "intelligent domestic": a description which fell far short of Her Majesty's estimate. In her own words, written on his tombstone, he was a "devoted and faithful personal attendant and beloved friend". Gladstone finished his letter by hoping that she would find "a good and efficient successor" – as if John Browns were as common as rabbits in Windsor Park. Had Disraeli still been alive he would have described her loss as a national disaster.

A funeral service was held for Brown in his room in the Clarence Tower. The Queen hobbled painfully up the staircase leaning heavily on Beatrice. When the rites were over, the coffin was closed, and taken by rail to Deeside. Two wreaths accompanied it on its final journey: one from his "best and most faithful friend, Victoria, R.I.", and the other from the Empress Eugénie. Seldom, if ever, before had so humble a subject been treated so majestically. When the Queen arrived at Balmoral that May, the first thing she did was drive to Crathie to see Brown's grave in the churchyard. The headstone had not been finished, but a heap of withered wreaths marked where he lay. The most impressive of his memorials was a life-size statue by Boehm, which was placed where he had often stood guard while she worked in the grounds of Balmoral. On the plinth was a tribute written for her by Tennyson.

"Friend more than servant, loyal, truthful, brave!
Self less than duty, even to the grave!"

At Frogmore she arranged for a bronze tablet "In loving and grateful remembrance" of her "faithful and devoted personal attendant and friend". It was the only memorial in that sacred shrine not dedicated to her family.

In 1884, the year after Brown's death, Queen Victoria published a second volume of extracts from her diary: *More Leaves from the Journal of a Life in the Highlands*. It covered the twenty years of her widowhood from 1862 to 1882, and showed, as she wrote in the preface, "how her sad and suffering heart was soothed and cheered by the excursions and incidents it recounts". *More Leaves* was dedicated to her "Loyal Highlanders and especially to the memory of my devoted personal attendant and faithful friend JOHN BROWN". Naturally, he figured prominently in its pages, and it ended with this striking tribute. "His loss to me (ill and helpless as I was at the time from an accident) is irreparable, for he deservedly possessed my entire confidence; and to say that he is daily, nay, hourly missed by me, whose lifelong gratitude he won by his constant care, attention, and devotion, is but a feeble expression of the truth."

The Queen's second book was received so rapturously that she was "startled" by its success. Possibly she under-estimated the influence of sycophancy in forming literary judgements. Her own family remained critical and grudging. On February 20th 1884 she told Vicky of the touching sympathy and affection with which her journal had been received, and added ruefully "though I know it don't interest you much". The truth was that the Crown Princess deplored the fulsome prominence given to Brown. Hence she took refuge in silence. The most she was ever prepared to say was that the book described the charm of Balmoral "so well". In the end, the Queen felt obliged to point out how deeply it pained her to know that her children refused to share in the general satisfaction.

The Prince of Wales was even more critical than his sister of his mother's publication. But then, he said, there was "no one to prevent her committing such acts of insanity". Before it came out, he begged her to confine its circulation to her family and friends. "You will, dearest Mama, I am afraid not agree in this, but I hold very strong views on the subject." The Queen, as expected, remained totally unconvinced, and the Prince returned to the fray with a new and ill-judged grievance. People, he claimed, had been greatly surprised to find no mention made of his name. She immediately wrote back asking him whether he had ever actually read her book, or whether he had left it to "so called friends" to do so on his behalf. If he had read it, he could hardly have failed to notice that he was mentioned on pages 1, 5, 8, 331 and 378. She would happily have referred to him more often, had he proved less reluctant to visit her. There can be little doubt that she won the encounter "game, set and match".

In the summer of 1883, the Queen asked Theodore Martin to write a memoir of Brown. He was horrified by the commission which he lamely declined on the grounds of his wife's ill health. Eventually, she decided to write the life herself and wrestled for months with its problems. In February, she sent Ponsonby a draft of her "little Memoir". When he failed to make any response, she asked him point blank what he thought of it. If Ponsonby had a fault it was moral cowardice. He did his best to persuade her not to publish, but the full force of his objection was lost in a mist of diplomacy. The "Life", he told her was "invested with a degree of interest which must be felt by all who knew Brown", but he could not help wondering "whether this record of Your Majesty's innermost and most sacred feelings should be made public to the world. There are passages which would be misunderstood by strangers, and there are expressions which will attract remarks of an unfavourable nature towards those who are praised. . . . Sir Henry cannot help fearing that the feeling created by such a publication would become most distressing and painful to the Queen." That was as far as he dared to go, and he prayed he would never be asked to provide her with chapter and verse.

Ponsonby's son, Arthur, claimed that his father killed the project, but this was not, in fact, so. The decisive role was that of the Dean of Windsor. Davidson was almost thirty years younger than the Queen, but soon became one of her most influential advisers. On March 6th, 1884, in the course of thanking her for his copy of *More Leaves*, he told her that there were those "especially among the humbler classes" who had shown themselves unworthy of her "confidences", and that there was a very real risk, to quote Her Majesty's own words, that "the sacredness of deep grief may be desecrated by vulgar hands". Before she committed herself to any further publication, he begged her to recall the unbecoming spirit displayed by some of the popular press. But the Queen insisted on going ahead. Nothing daunted, he wrote again to persuade her to desist. This time, she let it be known that she expected him to withdraw his opposition, but he still refused to be cowed. Naturally, he assured her, he was deeply distressed to have grieved her in any way. Nevertheless, he could not withhold advice he felt it his duty to proffer. He concluded his letter by offering to resign if she thought that he had been guilty of abusing his position. For a fortnight he neither saw nor heard from her. Then, quite suddenly, he was summoned, and all was smiles and sunshine. He had clearly been forgiven. In the long run, as Davidson later said, "her sound common sense judgement always prevailed, and she was much too good *au fond* to let things continue to rankle harmfully. My belief is that she liked and trusted best those who occasionally incurred her wrath provided that she had reason to think their motives good." Discretion triumphed, Brown's memoir was set aside, and the world is a sadder place for its loss.

Several of the Queen's New Year's greeting cards to Brown are preserved in the Royal Archives. If her Memoir was written in much the same spirit, it is easy to understand why Randall Davidson risked his career to suppress it. Not that he doubted her virtue for one moment, but he saw how the world would react to her artless sentiments. On New Year's Day, 1877, she sent Brown a card which portrayed a pert little parlour-maid, below which the following verse was printed:

> "I send my serving Maiden
>   With New Year Letter laden,
>   Its words will prove
>   My faith and love
> To you my heart's best treasure.
> Then smile on her and smile on me
>   And let your answer loving be,
>   And give me pleasure."

Underneath, in her own hand, she added:

> "To my best friend J.B.
> From his best friend. V.R.I."

Those who did not know how astonishingly innocent she could be, in every possible sense of the word, can hardly be blamed if they misconstrued such effusions.

When Disraeli became Prime Minister in 1874 the Queen wrote in her journal: "It shows that the country is not *Radical*. . . . What a good sign this large Conservative majority is of the state of the country." That summer, when Dizzy visited her at Osborne, he told Lady Bradford, "I really thought she was going to embrace me. She was wreathed with smiles as she talked", and "glided about the room like a bird". Knowing that he suffered from gout, she insisted that he sat down, but he carefully replaced his chair at the end of the audience so that no one should know how privileged he had been.

In the cold light of print, Disraeli's approach to the Queen can only be seen as bizarre, but his blandishments proved magical. Such was the power of his spell that he turned a plaintive recluse into one of the best-loved sovereigns of history. When in 1874 she asked him to form a Government, he assured her without a blush: "I plight my troth to the kindest of Mistresses". Nothing which Gladstone had ever said prepared her for such language, but she warmed at once to the chivalrous terms in which he expressed his devotion. Some people thought his audacious flirtation bordered on the ludicrous, but then he had always looked on life through a haze of poetic romance. It was his misfortune, he once remarked, that his heart refused to grow old. Where others could only see an elderly, portly matron, he beheld a dazzling "Faery Queen". For all his flowery phrases, he meant what he said. "I love the Queen," he confessed in 1879, "perhaps the only person in this world left to me that I do love." When he was finally forced to resign, he told her that his relations with Her Majesty had been "his chief, he might almost say his only, happiness and interest in this world".

Disraeli was just as concerned by the "Royalty Question" as Gladstone, but tackled it in a totally different way. Instead of attempting to browbeat the Queen, he set out to restore her confidence. "Everyone likes flattery," he remarked to Matthew Arnold, "and when you come to royalty you should lay it on with a trowel." The Queen, of course, was far too shrewd to fall for sugary phrases, of which she already had her fill. But Dizzy's "delicious absurdities" amused her, and she knew that much that he said was sincere. When he first declined her offer of the Garter on the ground that no honour or reward could "equal the possession of Your Majesty's kind thoughts", his action spoke louder than words.

Throughout his political life, Disraeli had seen the role of the Crown as crucial, and found the Queen only too willing to agree.

Whereas Gladstone had made her feel like a worthless schoolgirl, Disraeli conveyed the impression that he and she were running the country together. In 1878, he told her that her "imperial courage had sustained him through immense difficulties" and that "all really depends upon Your Majesty". The year before, they had behaved like co-conspirators when they sent Colonel Wellesley on a secret mission to Russia. This startling initiative showed, in Disraeli's phrase, "how great is the power of the Sovereign over this country". For the first time in her life she was made to feel that politics could be thrilling, and to relish her role in the drama. Sometimes Disraeli would even send her a note while changing trains at a station. "Your Majesty must pardon these rough lines," he wrote on one such occasion. "They are, as it were, from Your Majesty's 'own Correspondent'" and written "in the saddle".

The secret of Dizzy's success with the Queen, according to Lady Derby, was that he always appeared "to consult Her and take Her pleasure" before decisions were reached. Nor was he slow to acknowledge how greatly he valued her judgement. "It may be unconstitutional for a Minister," he wrote, "to seek advice from his Sovereign instead of proffering it," but he hoped she would forgive him for respectfully requesting her to give him the benefit of her "almost unrivalled experience". In all their dealings, he exploited her tendency to see political problems in personal terms. When he gave her the news of the Government's coup in gaining control of the Suez Canal, he did so in these words: "It is just settled: you have it, Madam".

It was widely suspected that Dizzy had "rubbed the lamp too hard", and could not return the genie to the bottle. During the tunnel years of the eighteen-sixties, the Queen looked back with regret to happier days, but now she began to look forward again and to pray for strength for the future. "What nerve! What muscle! What energy!" Disraeli exclaimed in 1879, amazed by her tireless strength. By the time she was sixty, she no longer complained of overwork, but showed a remarkable zest for life. On the eve of Beatrice's twenty-first birthday, she held an impromptu party at Osborne. "I danced a Quadrille and a valse," she noted with satisfaction, "which I had not done for eighteen years, and I found I could do it as well as ever." Two years later, she attended a military review at Edinburgh in a violent storm of rain. "There was nothing for it," she said gamely, "but to start out with waterproofs and umbrellas" and drive in an open landau. For two hours she sat in a pool of water while her loyal troops marched by. On returning to Holyrood she seemed chiefly concerned that Arthur's uniform had been ruined "by the green of the ribbon of the Thistle coming off on his tunic!" In 1884, when she was almost seventy, she visited Liverpool under worse conditions still, and insisted once more on driving through the city in an open carriage. Even Gladstone felt bound to acknowledge her resolution, but could not resist reminding her how long it had been since her last visit to Merseyside. Most amazing of all was her childlike interest in everything which went on. One of her Ladies-in-Waiting, desperately clutching at a conversational straw, once blurted out: "Yesterday, Ma'am, I heard a barrel organ playing in the Park." "A barrel organ?" muttered the Queen. "But I was not told, I am never told anything." A stunned silence followed during which the two old ladies contemplated the enormity of a Government which had proved too indolent to notify Her Majesty of this hastily improvised concert.

In many respects Disraeli appealed to the Queen for precisely the same reasons that had attracted her to Napoleon. Both were of foreign appearance, both were raffish and romantic, both yearned for female companionship, and both saw her first and foremost as a woman with whom they conducted a chaste flirtation. She excused his flamboyant ways as "Oriental", and welcomed his audacity in breaking through the ice in which convention trapped her. He was, moreover, one of nature's listeners, and she knew she could always depend on his sympathy. "So long as he was there," she told the Empress Augusta, "one felt as with the old Duke of Wellington, a sense of security."

The Queen showed Disraeli many signs of affection. When in 1876 she gave him her portrait, he described the scene in a letter to Lady Bradford. "After admiring it, what could I do but say, 'I think I may claim, Madam, the privilege of gratitude', and dropped on my knee; and she gave me her hand to kiss which I did three times very rapidly, and she actually gave me a squeeze." Two years later, she was writing to him in the first person, and signing herself "yours very affectionately".

Disraeli's political partnership with the Queen was based on shared ideals. Naturally, she welcomed his respect for the Crown, the Church, and the House of Lords. But most of all she responded to his vigorous foreign policy and his faith in the British Empire.

Because they so often thought as one, she trusted him unreservedly, and consulted him on her family's private affairs. Such was the extent of their personal correspondence that Ponsonby complained that he was kept totally in the dark about much that was going on. One touching token of their special relationship was the deal boxes she sent him full of his favourite primroses. Sometimes, of course, they failed to agree, but nobody "managed the lady" better than he did. Soon after becoming Prime Minister in 1874 he persuaded her to postpone her departure for Scotland, in order to meet the Tsar. Both the Prince of Wales and the Foreign Secretary had pleaded with her in vain, and she only agreed to stay "for Mr Disraeli's sake". "My head is still on my shoulders" he told Lady Bradford, describing his perilous triumph. Towards the end of her life, the Queen told Lord Rosebery how irresistible Dizzy could be, and how he would put his head on one side and say "'Dear Madam' so persuasively".

Disraeli was far more successful than Gladstone in getting the Queen to appear in public. Between 1874 and 1880 she actually opened Parliament three times. In fact, he left the decision entirely to her as he knew that "a long and impending engagement harasses and disquiets. The gracious act, if it occur, should be quite spontaneous". In 1876 she agreed on a State Opening in order to smooth the path of a bill to make her Empress of India. In 1877 she did so again, this time to show "her special support" for the Government's foreign policy. Finally, in 1880 she drove down to Westminster in a new State coach just a few weeks before the Conservatives went to the country. "She will make the sacrifice", she told Disraeli, "to do what she can to support the present Government and to gratify her people".

The Tories traditionally believed in paternal government and were far less hesitant than the Liberals in resorting to legislation to try to improve society. Disraeli had always belonged to the radical wing of his party, and began his career by calling on the Country to recognise that Britain was fast becoming "Two Nations". When he became Prime Minister, he was so occupied by the demands of foreign policy, that he was forced to delegate social reforms. Between 1874 and 1876, his Home Secretary, Richard Cross, carried six major bills which did much to improve the lives of the British people. This "Policy of Sewage", as its detractors chose to call it, encouraged the working class to support the Conservative Party. Cross became a personal friend of the Queen, and not only helped to arouse her social conscience, but to dispel her suspicion of publicly sponsored philanthropy.

On two notable occasions, Disraeli committed himself to legislation mainly to please the Queen: the Public Worship Regulation Act of 1874, and the Vivisection Act of 1876. One consequence of the Oxford Movement was a revival of interest in liturgy, especially amongst Tractarian clergy working in the slums. Most of them – despite rumours to the contrary – were not "Romanizers", although they naturally tended to copy the church which retained the traditional liturgy. The Queen regarded their emphasis on ritual as "*new and very* dangerous", and described it as "most extraordinary" to hold a weekday service. On November 5th, 1873, presumably choosing the date advisedly, she sent Ponsonby a sharp note of protest about the number of Anglican clergymen who insisted on imitating "ALL the Romish forms", and were "ashamed to be called Protestants". A week later she told Dean Stanley that she thought "the Archbishop should have the *power* given him by *Parliament* to *stop all* these Ritualistic practices, dressings, bowings etc., and everything of that kind, and, *above all, all* attempts at *confession*". Disraeli, however, was not so sure of the wisdom of legislation. Indeed, he had partly absorbed the High Church principles of his "Young England" friends, and warmly endorsed their views on the "beauty of holiness". Furthermore, he knew that to wage war on Ritualists was to run the risk of antagonising his High Church supporters, the very people who founded the Tory Party. Nevertheless, he finally decided to meet Her Majesty's wishes.

Several attempts had been made in the eighteen- sixties to legislate against Ritualism, but none had had Government backing. Consequently, in January 1874, Archbishop Tait decided to draft a bill designed to win widespread support. In March, the Queen wrote to Disraeli to say that "No measure so important affecting the Established Church should be treated as an open question", and she further expressed "her *earnest* wish" that he should "*go as far as he can without embarrassment* to the Government in *satisfying* the Protestant feeling of the country". When the Cabinet proved hesitant, she instructed him to tell them that she was "deeply grieved" by their "want of Protestant feeling", and to remind them that her family had been placed on the throne "to defend and maintain" the Reformed Religion. Later, Disraeli assured her, with a minimum of embellishment, that "the Act would never have passed, nay, would never have been introduced, had it not been for Your Majesty". At no other time in her life did she prove so willing to render to Luther the things that were Christ's. Looking back on her reign in 1899, she agreed with Bishop Creighton that it was "dreadful" to see how much persecution there was at the end of the nineteenth century, forgetting, no doubt, the part she had played in waging war on Tractarians. It is fair, however, to say that this momentary aberration was not at all characteristic: except in so far as being typically inconsistent.

Between 1877 and 1884, a number of turbulent priests were thrown into prison for exposing themselves to the charge of "contempt of court". Even their staunchest enemies were appalled to see them treated as criminals. Nor was it easy to understand why prominent Broad Churchmen were permitted to challenge the resurrection of Christ, while Tractarian Clergy risked being sentenced to gaol for elevating the host. In 1880 Disraeli felt tempted to blame this ill-starred Act for his party's defeat at the polls.

The second occasion on which Disraeli committed his Government to a bill entirely to please the Queen was in 1876 when Parliament passed an act to regulate vivisection. Such was her devotion to animals that she sometimes appeared to prefer their welfare to that of her Court and family. In 1878 Brown brought her two "bonnie" puppies, which had been sent by the Crown Princess. "You know how I adore doggies," she said in the course of her letter of thanks, "and these two are darlings." When her collie, "Noble", died at the age of sixteen, she "cried a great deal", and had to be given a sedative. She was, however, firmly convinced that they would meet again in Heaven, and quoted Charles Kingsley as her authority for believing that dogs have souls. "I feel so much for animals," she once told Vicky, "poor, confiding, faithful kind things, and do all I can to prevent cruelty to them which is one of the worst signs of wickedness in human nature!" In 1875 she sent Disraeli an account from the *Daily Telegraph* of the slaughter of young seals which he found so "harrowing" that he brought in a bill to protect them. Soon afterwards, she began to subject him to "an hurricane of words" on the subject of vivisection. The practice, she said, should be stopped, "if the nation is not to be disgraced by cruelty under the shameful plea of humanity". Ten years later, she wrote an impassioned memorandum, in which she pleaded that "her poor dear friends the dogs" should never be destroyed unnecessarily, or kept in muzzles unless they were known to be vicious. In the same memorandum she suggested that abattoirs should be subject to strict regulation. "Nothing brutalises human beings more than cruelty to poor dumb animals, whose plaintive looks for help ought to melt the hardest heart." To mark her Golden Jubilee, she was asked to remit a number of prison sentences. This she was happy to do with one exception: that of a man convicted of cruelty to animals.

No Prime Minister was more anxious than Dizzy to meet the Queen's wishes, but they nonetheless frequently disagreed over problems of Church patronage. In November 1875, Wellesley did what he could to extricate him from a "very painful correspondence" over the vacant Deanery of Chichester, by telling H.M. that her views were neither those "of Mr Disraeli's supporters, nor, as yet, of the majority of the Church of England". Her incessant advocacy of Broad Church prelates led the Prime Minister to warn her "that the utmost discretion" was necessary in offering them preferment, seeing that "the great mass of the Conservative party" viewed them "with more suspicion and aversion than they do the Ritualists". She remained unconvinced, and pointedly remarked that the interests of the Church were further reaching and longer lasting than even the "best of Governments". In his efforts to find a suitable Dean for Chichester, Disraeli asked Lord Salisbury whether he could suggest a High Churchman who "was not a damned fool". The name finally proposed only partially overcame "this formidable restriction". It was that of John Burgon, an old-fashioned Anglican, who hated the Pope even more than he loved controversy. Had it not been for the Prime Minister's constant anxiety to meet Her Majesty's wishes, their differences over patronage might have poisoned their relationship.

In 1875 Disraeli delighted the Queen by his daring coup to control the Suez Canal. Soon after it was opened by the Empress Eugénie in 1869, it became clear that three quarters of the ships passing through it were registered in Britain. In 1875, the Khedive of Egypt was forced to sell half his shares in the Canal in order to meet his debts. He had all but completed a deal with France when Disraeli intervened. There was no time to debate the matter in Parliament, so he borrowed £4,000,000 from Baron Rothschild and purchased the shares for Britain. "The Faery", he told Lady Bradford, "is in ecstasies about 'this great and important event'." The Crown Princess was equally delighted and regarded the news with "a thrill of pleasure and pride". Even her eldest son described it as very "jolly!!!" The British public and press were inclined to agree with Prince William, as were many leading Liberals. Gladstone, however, condemned the venture as mischievous and reckless, and reproached the Government for incurring an open-ended commitment. The Queen in a letter to Theodore Martin contrasted the Prime Minister's style with that of his great rival. The coup, she claimed, was "entirely the doing of Mr Disraeli, who had *very large ideas* and *very lofty views* of the position this country should hold. His mind is so much greater, larger, and his apprehension of things great and small so much quicker than that of Mr Gladstone".

Ever since 1858, when the Crown took over the government of India, the Queen had pressed her right to the title of "Empress". In 1871, the newly proclaimed Emperor of Germany infuriated her by hinting that Fritz should be given precedence over the Prince of Wales. Three years later, the Tsar put forward a similar sort of claim when his daughter married Affie. The Queen dismissed such proposals as preposterous, but felt handicapped in her battles over protocol by not being an Empress: a title her eldest daughter would one day inherit. Disraeli believed that "you can only act upon the opinion of Eastern nations through their imagination", but was far from convinced in 1876 that the moment was ripe for change. Nevertheless, anxious as ever to meet Her Majesty's wishes, he embarked on a bill to alter her royal title. The measure was passed on May 1st, after a bitter battle. The Queen was greatly "shocked and surprised" by the violence of the debates, but recalled Prince Albert's advice: "*Never* yield to clamour and misrepresentation – if a thing is right". Understandably enough, she saw attacks on the Bill as a personal affront, and thought it "perfectly disgraceful" that over a hundred and thirty members voted against the measure. The whole sorry episode showed only too clearly "the wickedness of party". Believing, as she did, that the Opposition was anxious "to injure Mr Disraeli", she sent him a touching letter in which she said she was mostly to blame for all his troubles and worries. She was especially incensed by the vituperative way in which Gladstone attacked the proposal. The imperial title was proclaimed at Delhi by the Viceroy, Lord Lytton, on January 1st 1877. That evening, the Queen gave a banquet at Windsor to celebrate the occasion, and astonished her guests by being covered in Indian jewels. Prince Arthur proposed a toast to the "Queen Empress", to which she responded with a smile as dazzling as the diamonds she was wearing.

The strains of Government, and especially late night sessions in the House of Commons, began to tell on Disraeli's health. The Queen became so worried that she told him in June 1876 that "she would be very happy to call him up to the other House, where the fatigue would be *far less*". "*No* one", of course, could "replace him in the House of Commons", but the most important thing of all was that he should continue as Prime Minister. For a time it seemed that he might decide to retire, but eventually he was prevailed upon to accept a peerage and take his seat in the Lords as the Earl of Beaconsfield. Sir William Harcourt paid him a handsome tribute on behalf of the Opposition when he wrote to say "You have made the House of Lords much too rich and you have left the House of Commons far too poor. Henceforth the game will be like a chess-board when the queen is gone – a petty struggle of pawns".

One reason which made the Queen so anxious to retain Disraeli's services was the growing eastern crisis. In the summer of 1875 Bosnia and Herzegovina rebelled against the Sultan of Turkey, who had totally failed to implement promised reforms. Their example was followed in 1876 by Serbia and Bulgaria. The Sultan, "Abdul the Damned", suppressed these revolts with unsurpassed ferocity. Twelve thousand Christians in Bulgaria alone were cruelly massacred by a regiment of Bashi-Bazouks. On June 23rd 1876, the *Daily News* published reports of atrocities. Unfortunately, Disraeli, misled by false assurances, dismissed them as "Coffeehouse babble". Gladstone, who in 1875 had resigned from leading his party, was so incensed by the Prime Minister's apparent indifference that he set aside his theological studies to devote his time to the fate of the Sultan's subjects. In less than three days, he completed one of the most incendiary pamphlets ever written: "The Bulgarian Horrors and the Question of the East". Britain, he argued was morally bound to throw in her lot with "Holy" Russia, and drive the Infidel Turks "bag and baggage" from the provinces they "had desolated and profaned". Disraeli dismissed the pamphlet as "vindictive and ill written", and "of all the Bulgarian horrors, perhaps the greatest".

Gladstone possessed a dangerous gift for isolating "one issue from the web of all those that were interwoven with it". In 1876 he concentrated so exclusively upon what he perceived as a moral crisis, that he failed to see that Russia's intervention was largely inspired by self-interest. His horror of Turkish atrocities blinded him to the savagery of the Bulgarians. The consequence was that he appeared to be willing to surrender the hard-won gains of the Crimean War, and to expose the British Empire to precisely those threats which the victors had fought to avert.

When the Queen first learned of the shocking barbarity of the Turks, she wrote to the Foreign Secretary, Lord Derby, requesting him to protest. Nevertheless, she had no desire to see the Mediterranean becoming a Russian lake, and endorsed Lord Beaconsfield's policy of maintaining Turkey's integrity. She never forgot the lessons taught at the time of the Crimean War: that Aberdeen's attempts at appeasement encouraged the Tsar to fight, and that Russia's control of the Dardanelles threatened the sea-route to India. Rather than fall into the trap of mawkish sentimentality, she persuaded herself that the Russians were largely to blame for "the blood of the murdered Bulgarians". She hardly needed Disraeli's persuasion to see the issue in personal terms. The question was who was to be master: the Queen Empress, or the Tsar of all the Russias?

The Queen's deep aversion to the Russians derived from Crimean memories. "They will always hate us," she told the Prince of Wales in 1878, "and we can never trust them." Reprehensible as her prejudice may have been, there was no escaping the fact that Russia was backward, despotic and treacherous. It was clear to her from the first that the Tsar's policy was "to obtain possession of a portion of Turkey, if not of Constantinople", under the "pretext of wishing to protect the Christians" in the rebel principalities. He must therefore be told "that we will *not allow* him to go to Constantinople and that that would be a *casus belli*". The problem of taking a firm line was "the stupid shortsightedness and really mad folly of the philanthropists". Gladstone's behaviour illustrated what Lord Melbourne had often told her: "that nobody ever did anything very foolish except from some strong principle". The Queen told Vicky in 1878 that she could never forgive the Liberals for the "irreparable" harm they had done by making "a *party question*" out of a national crisis. Their "*disgraceful proceedings*" threatened "to hand over the interests and honour of their country" to the Tsar. "Oh if only the Queen were a man, she would like to go and give those Russians such a beating!"

By 1878, the Queen's distrust of Gladstone had become almost pathological. The only excuse, she thought, for his "shameful" conduct was that he had "taken leave of his reason". Shortly before the

Tories went to the country, she let it be known that she never could "take Mr Gladstone as my Minister again, for I never COULD have the slightest *particle* of confidence" in him "after his violent, mischievous and dangerous" betrayal of "the honour and interest of this country" and "our Empire in India and the Colonies". The Duke of Sutherland went further and accused the Liberal leader of being a "Russian agent".

Lord Beaconsfield was not only prevented from taking decisive action in the East by the strength of Liberal opinion, but by renegades in his Cabinet. In particular, his Foreign Secretary declined to say "boo" to the Russian goose. Even the Opposition was divided as both Hartington and Granville questioned Gladstone's strategy. The issue, in fact, proved so divisive that it cut across party lines. As usual, the royal family championed opposite factions. Just as the Queen had "always feared and dreaded", Affie was quick to take his father-in-law's part and obliged her to "warn him strongly" not to meddle in politics. On the other hand, the Prince of Wales was an ardent Turkophile, who blamed the Liberals for emboldening the Russians to pursue their expansionist policy. The fact that his views coincided with those of his mother led her to show more confidence in his judgement.

In April 1877, no doubt reassured by Gladstone's compelling rhetoric, the Tsar declared war on the Sultan. The Turks put up an astounding fight against the Cossack hordes. For five months the Fortress of Plevna resisted all attacks, but when it eventually fell on December 10th, there was little to stop the victors marching on Constantinople. Throughout the summer and autumn, public opinion in Britain began to come round to the Queen's way of thinking. Four days after the fall of Plevna, the Cabinet met to discuss plans to recall Parliament, and increase the size of the army. When Lord Beaconsfield put these proposals to his colleagues they were greeted in dead silence. On Saturday, December 15th, the Queen and Beatrice set out for Hughenden, the Prime Minister's country estate. Before luncheon, they talked about world affairs and dissensions in the Cabinet, and afterwards she planted a tree and was shown the garden. No one was left in any doubt that the principal purpose of her visit was to "support Lord Beaconsfield's policy" and to help win over the waverers in the Government. It is true that agreement was only reached after Beaconsfield spoke of resigning, but his victory owed much to the Faery's unfailing assistance.

In March 1878 the Russians imposed peace terms on the Turks at the Treaty of San Stephano. The Queen was especially dismayed to learn that the Sultan had been deprived of several Aegean ports, thus providing the Black Sea Fleet with Mediterranean bases. There could be only one policy, she said, and that was to force the Tsar to disgorge his ill-gotten gains: preferably by diplomacy, but, if necessary, by war. Lord Beaconsfield was equally eager to see the Treaty revised, and looked once more to his Sovereign for support. Nothing proved too much for her. She drove over to Aldershot to review her troops, inspected a naval task-force at Spithead preparing for "special service", and telegraphed almost every hour to Downing Street. Throughout the mounting crisis, Dizzy kept her informed of the views of his fellow ministers. He once asserted that there were seven parties in his Cabinet: ranging from those, like Lord Derby, who insisted on "peace at any price", to others who held Her Majesty's views and those of her Prime Minister. On several occasions she sent him notes to be read out to his colleagues, in which she exhorted them to show a "bold and united front to the enemy in the country as well as outside it".

Lord Derby was the most recalcitrant of all Beaconsfield's colleagues. When the Russians began their attack on Plevna he told the Queen that the majority of Englishmen wanted "nothing so much as the maintenance of peace". She replied by saying that she found it difficult to imagine "from what sources Lord Derby gathers his opinion that the British people are in favour of Russian supremacy". It is interesting to note that this sharp remonstrance was drafted by Lord Beaconsfield, who was happy to use the Queen's pen to reproach his Foreign Secretary. The most remarkable instance of their partnership was Colonel Wellesley's mission in 1877. The Colonel, who was the Military Attaché to the Embassy at St Petersburg, was briefed by the Queen and Prime Minister to tell the Tsar that it was his distinct impression that if Russia seized Constantinople Britain would go to war. This virtual ultimatum was delivered without reference to the Foreign Office, and behind the back of the responsible Minister. Lord Carnarvon, the Colonial Secretary, tried the Queen's patience almost as much as did Derby. In January 1878, she scolded him for making a "lamentable" speech, and for advocating policies "which *she must consider* as *most* detrimental to the position of her great Empire". Later that month, she told the Crown Princess that she had "pitched into him with a vehemence and indignation – which was at any rate inspired by the British Lion. . . . Oh! that Englishmen were now what they were!! But we shall yet assert our rights – our position – and 'Britons never will be slaves' will yet be our motto". In her journal, she described the wretched "Twitters" as shrinking from her presence like "a naughty schoolboy".

In March 1878 Derby and Carnarvon belatedly resigned: a decision the Queen described as an "unmixed blessing". Three months later a Congress was held at Berlin to consider the terms of the recently signed Treaty. It was attended by the Prime Minister and his new Foreign Secretary, Lord Salisbury, with Bismarck playing the role of an "honest broker". Eventually the Russians were forced to revise those portions of the Peace of San Stephano which had most alarmed the great powers, and Britain was given Cyprus as a naval base to protect her interests in the eastern Mediterranean. On July 16th, Beaconsfield returned home bringing "Peace with honour". As he drove to the door of Ten Downing Street, Ponsonby emerged from the crowd clutching a bunch of flowers. "From the Queen," he yelled at the top of his voice in an effort to make himself heard above the cheering. The tonic effect of the crisis on her morale could hardly have been more potent. Instead of her ministers having to pester her to take an interest in politics, it was she who badgered them to uphold her Imperial Crown. Indeed, Dizzy had almost been overwhelmed by the frenzy of her concern.

No sooner had Beaconsfield brought back peace from Berlin, than he was confronted by war and dishonour in South Africa. Sir Bartle Frere, the Governor of Cape Colony, had long been anxious to destroy the power of the Zulu King, Cetewayo. His opportunity came when the Zulus raided Natal and gave him a pretext for occupying their country. On January 22nd, 1879, an expedition, led by Lord Chelmsford, was taken completely unawares and massacred at Isandhlwana. Beaconsfield had little choice but to send out reinforcements. Naturally enough he was greatly dejected by the distressing news from South Africa, but the Queen, with her customary courage, told him "not to be downhearted for a moment, but show a bold front to the world". Eventually, Cetewayo was crushed at the Battle of Ulundi and deported to the Cape of Good Hope, but the Government's setbacks handed its critics valuable ammunition. When the Queen congratulated Beaconsfield on restoring "the honour of Great Britain", she added a plea that the deposed King of the Zulus should be treated generously.

Soon after passing out of the Royal Military Academy at Wool-wich, the young Prince Imperial persuaded the War Office to allow him to go to South Africa. Although he was only supposed to be a "spectator", he contrived to get killed in June 1879 while out with a scouting party led by Lieutenant Carey of the 98th Regiment. The Prince at the time was resting under a tree, and the moment the Zulus appeared his horse decided to bolt: as did Carey and his com-panions. The young Napoleon received seventeen wounds from ass-egais before he finally died, fighting like a lion. When John Brown broke the news to the Queen at Balmoral, she decided to travel south to comfort "the poor dear Empress". It was "quite heart-breaking to see her", she wrote a few days later, "and one can say *nothing* to *comfort* her! I never felt anything more, and am quite miserable and overwhelmed by it! Poor dear! She asked me, did I think it *possible* it might not be true, and that it might be someone else?" That question was answered with horrifying finality when she unpacked her son's boxes from South Africa and found "the poor little Prince's shirt, all covered in blood".

The least that the Queen could do was arrange a magnificent funeral. When the Government began to make difficulties, she sum-moned Lord Beaconsfield to Windsor and remonstrated with him until she got her way. On July 12th, she watched the Imperial cortège set off from Camden Place, having placed a wreath on the coffin inscribed in her own hand: "To him who lived the purest of lives, and died the death of a soldier, fighting for our country in Zululand". Three of her sons were amongst the pall-bearers: the Prince of Wales, the Duke of Edinburgh, and the Duke of Connaught.

Some months later, the Queen was deeply distressed by what was revealed at Carey's Court Martial. The Empress behaved nobly and wanted the matter dropped, although she had seen letters written by Carey in which he admitted leaving the Prince to his fate. Her one consolation, she said, was that her dear boy had died like a soldier. "Enough of recriminations. Let the memory of his death unite in a common sorrow all those who loved him. . . . I, who desire nothing more on earth, ask it as a last prayer." Her chief anxiety seems to have been to avoid repaying her generous welcome in England by casting slurs on its army. That autumn, the Queen offered the Empress the use of Abergeldie, a couple of miles from Balmoral. Hardly a day passed without her visiting her old friend and taking her out for a drive. On one such expedition, they strolled together through the desolate landscape of Glen Gelder, talking of happier times. Only John Brown saw the poignant sight of the two Empresses, shrouded in black, disappearing down the glen, pursued by a cluster of dogs.

Towards the end of 1878 the Government found itself committed to war in Afghanistan as well as South Africa. In July of that year, the Amir, Sher Ali, accepted a Russian mission to Cabul, which provoked the Viceroy, Lord Lytton, to demand a similar privilege. The strategic position of Afghanistan on Russia's eastern border made it vital to stop it becoming a dependency of the Tsar. When Sher Ali rejected the British request, the Viceroy instructed Sir Neville Chamberlain to storm the Khyber Pass and occupy Kandahar. The Amir appealed, in vain, to the Russians for help, and died shortly afterwards. In May 1879, his son and successor, Yakub Khan, agreed to recognise Sir Louis Cavagnari as British Minister in Cabul. On September 2nd, Sir Louis sent Lytton a telegram to say that all was well. The very next day, rebel Afghan troops stormed the Residency and slaughtered all its occupants. The Amir protested that he was innocent of this treachery, although it was clear that he had done nothing to prevent it. Lord Beaconsfield was so dismayed by the disaster that he told the Queen he was unequal to writing about it. She, however, proved more robust, and telegraphed back: "We must act with great energy" and allow nothing to "deter us from strong and prompt measures. . . . Pray urge this on the Viceroy." During the punitive war which followed, General Roberts conducted a brilliant campaign in a hostile and mountainous country. In a matter of months the Afghans were crushed, Cabul was reoccupied, and the Amir replaced by his cousin, Abdur Rahman.

Preoccupied as the Queen was, she found time to write to Lady Cavagnari. "Though I am a total stranger to you and never had the pleasure of knowing personally your distinguished and noble husband, I cannot remain silent at this terrible moment, and must intrude on your overwhelming grief to express my deep sympathy. It is quite impossible for me to express what my feelings are or *how* my heart bleeds for you! To me, to my country, and to India, the loss of your most distinguished husband is immense. . . . That God may in His infinite mercy sustain and comfort you as He alone can the widowed and bleeding heart, is the sincere prayer of your truly and sympathisingly, Victoria. R and I."

Princess Helena once told Lord Esher that her mother possessed an almost "unbounded sympathy for others". Her dark night of the soul in 1861 gave her a special insight into grief. As she herself said, she had drunk "so deeply of the cup of sorrows" that she could not but feel "acutely for the suffering and misfortune of others". When Lord Rosebery's wife died, he told the Queen that it was partly because she spoke from the "sad summit of her experience" that she showed such understanding of his anguish.

In January 1879 Gladstone agreed to stand for Midlothian, a marginal seat in a part of the world from which Liberals drew strong support. That November he travelled north to meet his new constituents. Lord Rosebery, who was in charge of the visit, decided to copy electioneering techniques borrowed from America. Gladstone's fortnight campaign resembled a royal progress. Wherever he went, he was met by excited crowds, triumphal arches, addresses of welcome, and fireworks. People flocked to hear him from all over Scotland and even the outer Hebrides. Throughout his "Pilgrimage of Passion", he harangued his listeners with a moral fervour which appeared to owe more to the pulpit than the hustings. Opponents might scoff at his "wearisome rhetoric", but his audiences never tired of it. They loved to hear him denounce the evils of "Beaconsfieldism" like an Old Testament prophet. The Queen, however, deplored his "disgraceful spite and personal hatred of the Prime Minister", and complained of him rampaging about Scotland "like an American stumping orator, making most violent speeches". Hitherto politicians had seldom appealed to voters outside their own constituencies, but Gladstone saw the whole world as his parish.

Gladstone's first Midlothian speech was delivered at Edinburgh on November 25th. The Government, he proclaimed stood convicted of wanton profligacy, of pursuing "false phantoms of glory", of annexing Cyprus, fighting the Zulus, waging war on the Indian frontier, and attempting to subjugate Egypt. Next day, he told an audience at Dalkeith to "remember that the sanctity of life in the hill villages of Afghanistan among the winter snows, is as inviolable in the eyes of Almighty God as can be your own". He did not, however, see fit to mention the rights of those slaughtered in Cabul. On December 5th, he assured a vast crowd at Glasgow that ten thousand Zulus had been put to death "for no other offence than their attempt to defend against your artillery with their naked bodies, their hearths and homes, their wives and families". The Queen read his speeches with growing distaste and deplored the novel techniques he employed to appeal to a mass electorate.

In February 1880, the Tories won a by-election at Southwark, and the Queen telegraphed to Beaconsfield: "I am greatly rejoiced at the great victory at Southwark. It shows what the feeling of the country is." In fact, it did no such thing, but succeeded in luring the Government to destruction. On March 8th, the Cabinet decided to hold a general election, and Gladstone turned to the masses for support in a patent appeal to class warfare. Contrary to expectation, the Liberals achieved a landslide victory, mostly because the late eighteen-seventies were years of growing recession.

The Queen regarded the Tory defeat as a "great public misfortune", and told Lord Beaconsfield that she was deeply grieved by the prospect "of having to part with the kindest and most devoted as well as one of the wisest Ministers the Queen has ever had . . .". He at once replied that he was tormented by the thought of "separation from your Majesty", and that their partnership had "inspired and sustained him" at the loneliest time of his life. On receiving this letter, she wrote back insisting that it was not "a real parting", and that they could continue to keep in touch by correspondence. She went even further and told him always to write in the first person. "When we correspond – which I hope we shall on many a *private* subject and without anyone being astonished or offended, and even more without anyone knowing about it – I hope it will be in this more easy form. You can be of such use to me about my family and other things and about great public questions." In so saying, she evidently chose to forget how Albert had reproved her for writing to Lord Melbourne when Peel became Prime Minister.

In spite of the part which Gladstone had played in the Liberals' election victory, the Queen was resolved to do all in her power to prevent his becoming Prime Minister. "In common," she claimed, "with many sound Liberals or Whigs", she had been "*deeply* grieved over" and "*indignant* at the *blind* and *destructive* course pursued by the *Opposition*", which threatened to "ruin the country". When Ponsonby tried to persuade her to take a more charitable view, she objected to being told that Mr Gladstone was "'*loyal and devoted to the Queen!!!*' He is *neither*; for *no one* CAN be, who spares no means . . . to *vilify* – *attack* – accuse of *every* species of iniquity" the Prime Minister of the day. "Is this *patriotism* and devotion to the sovereign?" She would "sooner *abdicate*", she said, "than send for or have any *communication* with *that half-mad* firebrand", who wished to become a "Dictator". "Others but herself *may submit* to his democratic rule, but *not the* Queen". Fortunately, as Gladstone was no longer the Liberal leader, she was perfectly free to invite whomever she chose to attempt to form a Government. On Sunday, April 18th she summoned Beaconsfield to Windsor to discuss the impending crisis. She began by making it clear that she would not consider Gladstone. Dizzy proposed that she should send for Lord Hartington, who was at "heart a Conservative, a gentleman, and very straightforward in his conduct". After forty-eight hours of feverish consultations, it became clear that neither he, nor anyone else, could hope to form a Liberal administration without the "Grand Old Man". Consequently, the Queen was left no alternative but to send for him. It was at least some consolation that when he kissed hands, he looked "very ill, very old and haggard". Little did she suspect that this "exhausted volcano" would spew forth fire and brimstone for a further fourteen years.

Beaconsfield was invited to Windsor three times between May and December 1880. On his first visit the Queen told him how happy she was to see him again, and that she could almost believe that his fall from power was "only a horrid dream". In September, she informed him that she never wrote to Gladstone "except on formal *official* matters", and that she looked to him for "ultimate help". Towards the end of March 1881, Beaconsfield took to his bed after catching a chill. The Queen telegraphed almost every day and insisted he sought a second opinion. From the first he felt sure he was dying, whatever the doctors might say. On March 30th, she sent him a touching note in which she said, "I meant to pay you a little visit this week but I thought it better you should be quiet and not speak. And I beg you will be very good and obey the doctors and commit no imprudence. Ever yours very affectionately, V.R.I." On April 5th she assured him that he was constantly in her thoughts, and that she wished she could be "of the slightest use or comfort". It was the last letter she ever wrote him.

The day after Beaconsfield died, the Queen sent for his Secretary, Lord Rowton, to hear an account of Dizzy's last moments. "I passed hours," he wrote later to Lady Bradford, telling H.M. all that " she wished to know of her loved friend. And she did love him." The funeral took place at Hughenden on April 26th, the Queen being represented by Prince Leopold. The evening before, a wreath of primroses arrived from Osborne inscribed "his favourite flowers, a tribute of affection from Queen Victoria". Lord Rowton sent her a detailed account of the ceremony and informed her that there would "ever lie, close to that faithful heart the photograph of the Queen *he* loved; that which your Majesty gave him signed, two years ago". Shortly after the funeral, the Queen drove over to visit his tomb and to choose the site of a memorial tablet she planned to place in the church. Some days later, she told Lord Salisbury that she was "overwhelmed with this dreadful loss, irreparable to the country and Europe, to his many friends, and above all to herself! His devotion, unselfishness and kindness she can *never, never* forget; her gratitude is everlasting".

Disraeli was the last major influence on the Queen's life. He had found her withdrawn, insecure and neurotic, he left her defiant, vigorous and imperious. During six enhancing, glorious years of partnership, he set the stage for her final apotheosis. "The old Queen who drove through the clamorous streets of imperial London in 1897 was very much his masterpiece." Indeed, Gladstone complained that he had proved a good deal too successful in restoring her self-confidence.

The Queen felt threatened by Gladstone and put up a resolute fight to preserve her Throne and Empire. She was far too tenacious an imperialist to accept the Prime Minister's policy of withdrawal, and asked Ponsonby to make it clear to the incoming Government that "There must be no democratic leaning, no attempt to change the Foreign Policy, no change in India, and *no* cutting down of estimates. In short *no lowering* of the *high position* this country holds, and *ought always* to hold". It would hardly have been possible to have predicted more precisely the drift of Gladstone's policy. In 1883, after he reached an agreement with France over the future of Madagascar, she told him how much she deplored his "growing tendency to swallow insults and affronts and not taking them in that high tone" displayed by her previous Government. Throughout his administration he had no more vigilant critic than his Sovereign. "This Government," she told Vicky in 1884, "is the worst I have ever had to do with." Even the mellowing influence of age appeared to pass them by. The older they grew the more certain they both became that the other was in the wrong.

Between 1880 and 1885, Gladstone was almost worn out by the

weight of his royal correspondence. During these years he wrote over a thousand letters to the Queen, all in his own hand, and many demanding careful research and drafting. In 1883 he told Lord Rosebery that "the Queen alone is enough to kill any man", and would never be satisfied until she had "hounded him out of office". During their relatively rare meetings, she sheered away from points of difference. After one such audience, he listed the topics discussed, which ranged from the prevalence of fogs at Windsor, to the health of the Bishop of Rochester, and the fact that Mrs Gladstone's nephew was a master at Eton. The nearest they broached a controversial theme was to touch on the agricultural depression. Increasingly, Gladstone came to agree with Hamilton that the Queen's hostility to him was largely inspired by jealousy. She resented, for instance, "the big type in which the newspapers head 'Mr Gladstone's Movements' and the small type *below* of the Court Circular". It was certainly true she hated to be upstaged, nor was she best pleased to see his portrait hanging beside her own in a crofter's cottage. But this was only part of the story. She might have swallowed the pills he forced down her throat had he proffered them in jam.

Gladstone became convinced that the Queen's mind had been poisoned because of his work for prostitutes. When Lord Stanmore expressed his belief that she questioned his motives in "rescuing" fallen women, his response was truly heroic. "If the Queen thinks that of me," he said, "she is quite right to treat me as she does." He had begun his work for "the Church Penitentiary Association for the Reclamation of Fallen Women" in 1848, but it was not until twenty years later that his friends began to worry: especially when he was seen talking to street-walkers whom he met on his way home from the House of Commons. It was not unknown for him to offer such ladies shelter, but only, of course, with the blessing of his wife who helped him in his work. Edward Hamilton was greatly "exercised" by Gladstone's "unfortunate craze". His concern was shared by Lord Rosebery and Lord Granville, neither of whom doubted their leader's integrity, but both of whom thought him exceedingly rash to offer so tempting a hostage to fortune. In May 1882 the Prime Minister was seen conversing with a prostitute on the Duke of York steps. In a matter of hours, stories of this encounter were winging their way round London. "It may be true," Gladstone informed a well-wisher, that "the gentleman saw me in such a conversation, but the object was not what he assumed, or, as I am afraid, hoped." The Queen as always was well aware of such gossip, but nothing she said or wrote suggests that she believed it.

In July 1881, Gladstone told his son, Herbert, that the Queen, while always polite, held him "at arm's length". Nevertheless, when they did meet face to face, she was generally gracious and friendly. In 1882, she invited Mr and Mrs Gladstone to stay at Windsor to attend Prince Leopold's wedding: an "unparalleled civility" with which they were both delighted. Later the same year, he noted in his diary that he had had "a most difficult" audience with H.M., which passed off better than expected because of her "beautiful manners". In 1884 he was "particularly pleased" with a visit to Osborne, where he talked to the Queen for over an hour and found her "unusually gracious". Before he left, she gave him a signed copy of *More Leaves* with a rather chilly inscription. Nevertheless, her courtesy was a "slender bridge" to span the gulf which divided them.

Many of Gladstone's supporters complained that there were too many Whigs in the Cabinet in spite of the tide of radical votes which had swept the Liberals to power. The Queen, on the contrary, protested that the Government consisted of "very advanced Radicals", and that Dilke should retract his extremely "offensive speeches" before becoming a minister. In 1882 she begged the Prince of Wales to persuade his friend, Lord Hartington, to restrain "this dreadfully Radical Government which contains many thinly-veiled Republicans". It was clear, she said, that the Prime Minister was unwilling to curb his colleagues, and so far from stemming the "downward course of Radicalism" was anxious to encourage it.

In 1883 the Queen read a pamphlet by the Reverend Andrew Mearns with the arresting title: "The Bitter Outcry of Outcast London", which described how the poor lived in the world's richest capital. It painted a gruesome picture of squalor, of houses in which effluent trickled down the staircase, of dead bodies rotting in overcrowded basements, of stench, damp and filth. The Queen, who had long felt a special concern about housing, was deeply moved and shocked; while Vicky was so disturbed by Mearns's disclosures that she begged her mother to press for legislation. "How much good it would do," she wrote, "if the people knew you wished everything to be done to change and improve this state of things. . . . I can imagine how dear Papa would have taken it up. . . ." In fact, the Queen had already written to Gladstone to say how distressed she was to read "of the deplorable condition of the Houses of the Poor in our great towns", and suggesting that other matters should wait "till one involving the very existence of thousands – nay millions – had been fully considered by the Government". Later that year, she discussed the matter with Sir Charles Dilke, the Head of the Local Government Board, Sir William Harcourt, the Home Secretary, his predecessor, Richard Cross, and the Reverend Harry Jones, an East-End curate, who lived and worked in the slums. In 1884, a Royal Commission was set up, under Dilke's chairmanship, to consider working-class housing, and the Queen agreed to the Prince of Wales becoming one of its members. So seriously did he take this novel challenge, that he insisted upon visiting the worst areas of Holborn and St Pancras, disguised in a "slouch" hat and a ready-made ulster. Soon after, he made a speech in the House of Lords in which he described the conditions of "darkest London" as "perfectly disgraceful", and urged the Government to take "drastic and thorough" measures.

The Queen continued to show her concern for housing to the very end of her reign. In 1900, she read a report exposing the negligence of the Windsor Town Council. It was shameful, it said, that people were living in a state of degradation "within almost a stone's throw of your Majesty's home", particularly as "some of the worst of the hovels" were named "Victoria" Cottages. The Queen was so outraged that she instructed Sir Arthur Bigge (Ponsonby's successor) to write to the Mayor to tell him how pained she was by the wretched conditions in which her neighbours lived. When the Mayor blamed the Press for "garbled" reports, Bigge proved unrelenting. "Surely," he asked, "a rent of six shillings and sixpence for a cottage in which 'for two years the rain has fallen on to the bed; the floor falling in, etc., and no repairs carried out', vide page 12 of Report, is exorbitant and extortionate?. . . . It certainly must make the task of effecting reforms somewhat hopeless if the Corporation fail to obtain one conviction . . . against the owner of Victoria Cottages."

In February 1884 the Government introduced a Bill to enfranchise rural householders, thus increasing the total number of voters from three to five million. At the same time they promised further legislation in 1885 to adjust the constituency map to accommodate the change. Lord Salisbury, however, maintained that the measures had to be taken together: mostly because they were logically inseparable. The Queen, at first, was in favour of reform, and thought the House of Lords wrong to reject the Bill on the ground that it failed to provide for boundary changes. During the summer recess, Gladstone's radical colleagues fought a violent campaign to discredit the Second Chamber. Chamberlain summed up the issue as "the Peers versus the People", and denounced the "insolent pretensions of our hereditary caste"; while Morley coined the ominous slogan, "Mend them or end them". The Queen was disgusted by the extravagance of such language, and maintained that "to threaten the House of Lords" was "to threaten Monarchy". Once the hereditary principle was rejected, it was hard to see how the Crown itself could survive.

For three months the Queen worked tirelessly to bring about peace between the Lords and Commons, working on Gladstone's behalf to persuade the Tories not to reject his Bill, but whenever it seemed a settlement was in sight he made a provocative speech. "Mr Gladstone," she wrote, after he had visited her at Balmoral, "was plausible and amiable when here, but as soon as he got amongst his foolish adorers, all was forgotten." He even had the audacity to indulge in "his *stump* oratory under her very nose". In the first stages of her protracted negotiations, the Queen used Lord Rowton and the Duke of Richmond to mediate with Lord Salisbury, and relied on the Duke of Argyll to try to bring pressure on Gladstone. At the end of September, the Prime Minister made it clear that if the Bill was thrown out, he would ask for a mandate to curb the power of the Lords. In view of this threat, the Queen begged the Duke of Richmond to persuade Lord Salisbury not to force the issue. "The great object must be to maintain the important position of the House of Lords unimpaired", even if this meant paying the price of accepting the Bill as it stood. On October 31st, the Queen wrote directly to the Tory and Liberal leaders proposing that they should meet in an effort to solve the problem. Lord Salisbury, who had hitherto proved more intransigent than Gladstone, wrote back to say that it would give him "great pleasure to consult with anyone with whom Your Majesty wishes him to consult: and in obedience to your Majesty's commands he will do all that in him lies to bring this controversy speedily to a just and honourable issue". The two men met over tea and scones at Downing Street on November 22nd and each was surprised to find the other so reasonable. Five days later they managed to reach a deal.

The moment terms were agreed, Gladstone telegraphed to Windsor: "Points of substance all settled this afternoon. Humbly congratulate". Later, he wrote "to tender his grateful thanks to your

Majesty for the wise, gracious, and steady influence on your Majesty's part, which has so powerfully contributed to bring about this accommodation and to avert a serious crisis of affairs". When she first discussed the Downing Street conferences with Lord Salisbury she thought he "seemed rather depressed". "I think we could have made a good fight of it," he told her ruefully. "But at what a price!" she replied. Had it not been for her intervention, he might have been tempted to make a last-ditch stand, with fatal results for the House to which he belonged.

It was hardly to be expected that the Queen and Gladstone would concur over Church patronage, particularly as his closest advisers were friends of the Oxford Movement. Hamilton was the son of the first Tractarian bishop, and R.W. Church was one of its prominent leaders. Nevertheless, he went out of his way to appoint Broad Churchmen like Temple, and Low Churchmen like Bickersteth. The Queen, however, refused to acknowledge just how impartial he was, and could not forgive him for going to Pusey's funeral. During his second Ministry he decided to promote three eminent High Anglicans: Wilkinson as Bishop of Truro, Stubbs as Bishop of Chester, and King as Bishop of Lincoln. Even the Queen could hardly exclude them for ever, particularly as Lord Salisbury favoured their claims.

In little over a year, the Queen suffered three "dreadful" losses amongst her closest clerical advisers. In July 1881, she learned of the death of her "valued friend", Dean Stanley, and could not restrain her tears when she went into the dear sacred Blue Room" and recalled how he "had stood by me and comforted me on that first anniversary of December 14th". Her initial choice of a successor was Dean Liddell, who told her that he would do anything to honour Stanley's memory "except to attempt to wear his mantle". Her second choice was Bradley, an intimate friend of the late Dean and a fellow Broad Churchman. Hamilton noted that "Mr G does not at all like this dictation from the Crown, or rather these strong hints. He regards such action as tending to invert the Crown and the Minister".

In September 1882, the Queen suffered a deeper loss in the death of the Dean of Windsor, who was "bound up with the happy past and with all the joys and sorrows of her family". The third death was that of Archbishop Tait, who sent her a message before he died, "with earnest love and affectionate blessing". Eventually, both she and Gladstone agreed that the best man to succeed him was Edward Benson, whom she had known since 1858 when he became the first

"Master" of Wellington. He was, in fact, the third of four successive pedagogues to become Archbishop of Canterbury, starting with Longley, a former Head Master of Harrow, then Tait, and finally Temple, both Head Masters of Rugby.

After a brief interregnum, the Queen chose Randall Davidson, the late Archbishop's Chaplain and son-in-law, as Wellesley's successor. She first met the new Dean in December 1882 and was deeply impressed. Less than a fortnight later she began to consult him about Gladstone's church appointments. "I should be *most thankful*", she wrote from Osborne, "if you could help me with names . . . losing as I have done the two dear Deans, Stanley and Wellesley, I am left without anyone to turn to for advice and help". Before the year was out, Ponsonby provided Davidson with a code so that they could communicate by telegraph in cipher. In a remarkably short time he became as valued an adviser as his predecessor, Dean Wellesley.

The most intractable of all Gladstone's problems was that of governing Ireland, where simmering discontent was brought to the boil by the growing depression in farming. In 1880 alone, some ten thousand tenants were evicted for failure to pay their rents. All over the country landlords were murdered, houses burned down, and cattle slaughtered. Charles Parnell, the Irish leader, who succeeded Isaac Butt in 1879, had been brought up to hate the British ascendancy and to see Home Rule as the only hope for Ireland. His plan was ruthlessly simple: to reduce Parliament to impotence by never-ending obstruction, and by violence to render Ireland ungovernable.

The moment that Gladstone returned to power he withdrew the coercive measures he found in force, in the fond belief it would help to restore good will. Next, in the summer of 1881, he passed a great Land Act designed to get at the roots of Ireland's problems. This radical measure inevitably threatened the powerful landowning class, who never forgave him for undermining their interests. The Duke of Argyll and Lord Lansdowne resigned in protest, and the Queen became further convinced that the Grand Old Man had completely lost his wits. Before the year was out even Gladstone's patience wore thin, when nothing he did diminished violence or crime. In April 1882, Lord Frederick Cavendish, the new Irish Chief Secretary, was brutally hacked to death as he strolled through Phoenix Park. The Queen was in no doubt that the Prime Minister's policy was responsible for the tragedy. "Surely his eyes must be opened now," she commented in her journal. The lawlessness of Ireland convinced her that its people were impossible, and the only thing that they understood was force. The worst mistake of her whole career was her dogged neglect of the suffering of the Irish, and her failure to see that their grievances were justified. It was no sort of a policy to insist that the Union was sacred, while at the same time rejecting proposals to strengthen her links with Ireland. Had Balmoral been built on the shores of the Lake of Killarney, there might never have been a demand for Home Rule or an Irish Republican Army.

The crux of Gladstone's foreign policy, in so far as he had one, was to destroy what he called "Beaconsfieldism". It was hardly a programme to win the Queen's favour. Strangely enough, many of his radical supporters tended to share her views. Both Chamberlain and Dilke were as far to his right on foreign affairs as they were to his left on domestic reforms. As early as 1868 Sir Charles wrote a book called *Greater Britain* vindicating Imperialism, and when Chamberlain dined at Windsor in 1884 the Queen thought him "very sensible and reasonable about the question of Egypt". The Prime Minister always suspected grandiose plans, and preferred to react to events in a piecemeal fashion. It was, after all, a well-tried British tradition to decline to meddle in other people's affairs.

No sooner had Gladstone become Prime Minister than trouble broke out in Afghanistan, when the late Amir's brother, Ayub, attempted to overthrow Abdur Rahman. In July 1880 he besieged the British in Kandahar, only to be annihilated by Sir Frederick Roberts. "This double triumph," wrote Beaconsfield from Hughenden, "this march of Xenophon, this Victory of Alexander – must relieve your Majesty's mind." Gladstone was less elated by the news, and refused to believe that the town was worth keeping, regarding it, in the words of one of his generals, as "a hateful, useless, abominable hole". The Queen, however, was strongly opposed to withdrawal, which would only encourage the Tsar to get up to his old tricks. Besides, long experience had taught her that hasty retreats only led to costly returns.

On January 5th 1881 the Queen held a Council at Osborne to approve the draft of the Speech from the Throne. From it she learned that the Government proposed to abandon Kandahar. She was so furious that she postponed the meeting, and telegrams flew between Hawarden and Osborne. Harcourt told Ponsonby that unless she agreed to approve the Speech, Gladstone would have to resign. In the end, she gave her consent on two conditions: that the Cabinet was told how much she deplored the measure, and that the Government undertook to remain in Kandahar if the situation changed. When she finally held the Council Meeting, she did so in total silence, and "the Ministers nearly tumbled over each other going out". Never before, she claimed, had she been "treated with such want of respect and consideration". It was not merely that she objected to the Government's policy but that she thought they were trying to keep her in the dark in order to force her hand. Even Gladstone acknowledged that she could hardly be expected "to express satisfaction at the withdrawal from a place to which only a few months ago she had by Her late Ministers been made to attach so much importance".

The Government's proceedings in Afghanistan had at least followed a victory, but its policy in South Africa arose from a major defeat. In 1877, Sir Theophilus Shepstone annexed Transvaal to the Crown, but three years later the Boers decided to fight for their independence. In February 1881, they achieved a decisive victory at Majuba Hill, killing the British Commander, General Colley. Gladstone regarded demands for revenge as a legacy of Jingoism, and agreed to sign a truce. "Our 'Patriots'", the Queen complained, "intend to take the side of the Basutos and the Boers. That fearful sentimentality for our enemies is simply disgraceful." The thought of the Prime Minister grovelling at Kruger's feet was one she found deeply distressing. Moreover she strongly objected to seeking peace before giving the Army a chance to retrieve its honour. In August, the Transvaal was given its independence, subject to acknowledging the suzerainty of the Crown. On learning of the peace terms, the Queen insisted that the natives should be assured that if the Boers attempted to "crush and oppress them", we would "not abandon them to the tender mercies of a most merciless and cruel neighbour".

The most catastrophic of all Gladstone's mistakes was his policy towards Egypt. In 1879, while Lord Beaconsfield was Prime Minister, the Khedive, Ismail, decided to repudiate his international debts. This proved too much for Britain and France, who engineered his overthrow. Ismail was replaced by his son, Tewfik, who agreed to accept the help of Major Baring, later Lord Cromer, and M. de Blignières, in administering the country. Britain could not afford to lose control of the Suez Canal, or to see the collapse of the Government in Cairo. In September, 1881, the Khedive's War Minister, Arabi Pasha, rebelled against the "Dual Control" and made himself virtual master of Egypt. Gladstone half-heartedly drifted into a war to reassert Britain's authority, while the Queen bombarded her ministers with advice about hospitals, food and equipment. Almost a year to the day after Arabi's revolt, Sir Garnet Wolseley landed at Port Said, defeated the rebels at Tel-el-Kebir, and bivouacked in Cairo. When news of the battle reached Balmoral, the Queen had a bonfire lit on Craig Gowan to celebrate the victory. The Government meanwhile was so overwhelmed by its inadvertent triumph that it hardly knew what to do.

The Khedive's dominions included the Sudan, where the Mahdi raised his standard, and virtually drove the Egyptians out of the country. In 1883 Tewfik gave a British Officer, Hicks Pasha, command of an expedition to crush the rebels, but his army was cut to pieces. This dismal failure confronted Gladstone with a formidable dilemma: whether to abandon the Sudan, or undertake its reconquest. Eventually, he sent Gordon to report on the best way to withdraw.

Gordon, who had briefly been Governor of the Sudan before the Mahdi's revolt, could hardly have been worse qualified to carry out a retreat. His reputation rested on victories not surrenders, and there can seldom have been a more insubordinate officer. "I know if I was Chief," he once admitted, "I would never employ myself for I am incorrigible." It should not have been too difficult for the Government to have foreseen that this wayward eccentric would claim the "hero's privilege" of disobeying his orders. Moreover, the Cabinet was in two minds about how to treat the Sudan. Gladstone was disinclined to fight for the Khedive, while most of his colleagues believed that the Mahdi threatened the peace of the world. Given the absence of an agreed policy, it was far from clear what Gordon was meant to do.

Gordon arrived at Khartoum in February 1884, with wide discretionary powers from the Khedive to act as Governor-General. Hardly had he arrived than he tried to persuade the Government to reject their plan to withdraw. In April, he attempted to force the pace by proposing to annihilate the rebels, or leave ministers to suffer the "*indelible disgrace* of abandoning the garrisons". Nor did he hesitate to exploit the fact that his communications were constantly being cut, thus giving him every excuse to act on his own initiative. As early as March, the Queen telegraphed to warn Hartington at the War Office that "General Gordon is in danger", and a couple of months later Khartoum was besieged and escape had become impossible. Gladstone, however, refused to listen to mounting appeals to send out an expedition. Forster, a former colleague, remarked despairingly that the Prime Minister could "persuade most people of most things", and "himself of almost anything". The Queen echoed his verdict when she described Mr G as wrapping "himself up in his own *incomprehensible delusions*". Not until August was Wolseley finally authorised to march on Khartoum. It naturally took a couple of months to collect and transport the necessary troops and equipment. Eventually, in October, the expedition set off on its eight hundred and fifty mile journey up the Nile. The following January, an advanced column defeated the Dervishes at Abu Klea, a week's march from Khartoum.

The Queen, who knew how the Army had suffered, sent a telegram to congratulate all concerned, a copy of which appeared in the Court Circular. When Lord Hartington saw it, he wrote to tell Ponsonby that he thought it would be better for such messages to be forwarded through the Secretary of State. Sir Henry relayed the suggestion to Her Majesty, who not surprisingly thought the proposal "*impertinent*". It had always been her practice, she said, to telegraph to her Generals, and it always would be, "as they value *that*, and *don't* care so much for an official message". "The Queen," she insisted, has "the *right* to telegraph congratulations and enquiries to *any* one, and won't stand dictation. She *won't* be a machine." It was typical of Ponsonby that when she told him "to *make* Lord H understand his impropriety", his letter was so diplomatic that it seemed more like an apology.

The relief expedition reached Khartoum on January 28th, only to find that the garrison had succumbed a couple of days before, and that Gordon had suffered a hero's death at the hands of fanatical Arabs. "Dreadful news after breakfast," the Queen wrote in her journal. "Khartoum fallen. It is too fearful. The Government is alone to blame, by refusing to send the expedition until it was too late." As further details emerged, she became more than ever convinced that the Government had "Gordon's innocent, noble, heroic blood on their consciences", and she told Ponsonby that she held "*Mr. Gladstone responsible* by imprudence and neglect, for the lives of many thousands though unwittingly". Nothing, she said, would persuade her to offer him the Garter in view of all the "*incalculable harm*" he had done.

The Queen gave vent to her feelings in an unciphered telegram to

Gladstone. Soon after the Battle of Omdurman in 1898, she told
Lord Kitchener that she had sent the message en clair "so that everyone should know" what she thought of the Prime Minister. "These
news from Khartoum", she proclaimed, "are frightful, and to think
that all this might have been prevented and many precious lives
saved by earlier action is too frightful." In so saying, she had clearly
forgotten how "beloved Papa" had "never permitted" her to express
opinions in public which could later be quoted to undermine the
Government. Only the admirable discretion of the Post Office prevented a constitutional crisis. Gladstone at first took the view that
the Queen's telegram was a *public* vote of no confidence, and hence
a resigning matter, but when it became clear that no one was any
the wiser, he decided to stay in office. Nevertheless, for a time he
was so angry that he assured Morley that he would "never set foot
in Windsor again".

On February 17th, the Queen wrote to Gordon's sister to convey
her "inexpressible" grief at the death of her "dear, noble, heroic,
brother", who had "served his country and his Queen so truly", and
she told her how "keenly" she felt "the *stain* left upon England" by
the general's cruel fate. Miss Gordon was so moved that she presented H.M. with her brother's Bible, to which he had constantly
turned for guidance. The Queen, as so often, reflected the national
mood in blaming Gladstone: a view which the voters clearly
expressed by rejecting him at the polls. It would, perhaps, have been
fairer to admit that the problems of the Sudan were so intractable as
to be virtually insoluble.

For some months after the relief of Khartoum the Government
hardly knew what to do next. The Queen, suspecting that it might
well decide to withdraw, begged Wolseley to resist all talk of retreat.
"She fears," she wrote, "*some* of the Government are very unpatriotic, and do *not* feel what is a *necessity*." In spite of the fact that her
letter contained nothing which she had "not said to her Ministers
over and *over* again", she asked him to destroy it as it was "so very
confidential". Shortly before, she had written in "*strict confidence*" to
Lady Wolseley, to tell her that the Government was "*more incorrigible
than ever*", and to urge her to encourage her husband to
"THREATEN to resign if he does *not* receive strong support. *It must
never appear* or Lord Wolseley *ever let out* the hint I give *you*. But I
really think they *must be frightened*". The stress she placed on secrecy
shows that she knew very well how improper it was to incite Lord

Wolseley to sabotage the Government. In April, she sent Gladstone a message saying that it would "be fatal to our reputation and honour" to evacuate the Sudan, and that she could not give her consent "to such a humiliating step", which "would be seen as a *triumph* of savages over British arms". Later, she made a final appeal to Lord Hartington, in which she expressed her surprise that he was prepared "to carry out a total reversal of policy" against the "*earnest advice*" of the military authorities. "To see her brave soldiers as the Queen did yesterday gashed and mutilated for nothing is dreadful! And to see for a second time our troops recalled – *most probably* only to have to send them out again in a little while – is to make us the laughing stock of the world". Thirteen years later her prophecy was fulfilled when it became necessary to despatch yet another expedition to destroy the power of the Mahdi.

The Government was defeated in June 1885 when Parnell and his supporters decided to join the Tories in a snap vote on taxing beer and spirits. Seeing that the revised electoral rolls demanded by the 1884 Reform Act would not be completed until the autumn, it was impractical to hold an election until the end of the year. The ensuing crisis was intensified by the Queen's objection to leaving Scotland, and Gladstone's reluctance to travel north. "The Queen declines to come down from Balmoral", Hamilton noted on June 10th, and "many disagreeable things will I fear be said about Her, and not without reason. She is the Constitutional instrument whereby alone there can be a transfer of political power; and if the instrument is not ready at hand, it is not unnatural to ask what is the use of it?" The Prince of Wales telegraphed to inform her that her "presence near London" was "earnestly desired" and that her "position as Sovereign might be weakened" by her absence. "Forgive me for saying this but universal feeling is so strong I could not help telegraphing". In spite of his plea, the Queen showed no inclination to interrupt her holiday, and thought it "impertinent" of Gladstone to propose that she should do so. "He forgets," she said, "I am a lady. He seems to think I am just a machine to run up and down as he likes." "The Railway authorities," she told the Prime Minister, "unless *previously* warned," did "*not* consider it *safe* for her to start without some days' notice". Furthermore, as "a lady nearer seventy than sixty, whose health and strength have been most severely taxed during the forty-eight years of her arduous reign", she was no longer able "to rush about as a younger person and a man can do". Finally, it would be

"extremely inconvenient and unpleasant" for her to stay at Windsor
during Ascot Week "owing to the noise and crowds". Gladstone
regarded her various woes as nothing more than ingenious rationalis-
ations. Experience had taught him that she seldom appealed in vain
to such pliant authorities as the obliging Dr Jenner, or the Station
Master at Ballater, whose advice suspiciously echoed their Mistress's
voice. Nor did he find it easy to believe that the London and North
Eastern Railway was incapable of providing a special train at relatively short notice.

The political crisis was finally resolved when Lord Salisbury
agreed to form a caretaker Government. The Duke of Cambridge,
who saw the Queen at Osborne a fortnight later, described her as
"like a school girl set free from school" so delighted was she "to be
rid of Gladstone". "I have accepted the resignation," she told Vicky,
"of the man who has caused such fearful mischief, who dragged
England in the dirt, and has deprived us of any friend abroad." When
the Crown Princess expressed surprise that her mother objected so
strongly to the Liberals, she was firmly reminded that "Republicanism and Destructivism" were not "true Liberalism". The moment
Salisbury agreed to form a Government, the Queen offered Gladstone an earldom "as *a mark* of her *recognition* of his long and distinguished services". He was "greatly touched" by her letter, which
he described as "a pearl of great price", but nevertheless felt obliged
to decline her "gracious offer", as he felt that his destiny lay in the
House of Commons.

Lord Salisbury was the first Prime Minister to be younger than
the Queen: indeed he had been a page at her Coronation. Most
people had expected her to send for Sir Stafford Northcote, who for
the past five years had led the Opposition in the Commons, but she
preferred her former Foreign Secretary, who shared her views on
Britain's imperial destiny. The new Ministers were sworn in at
Windsor on June 24th, and the Queen noted in her journal that
"Bertie came to be with me during the Council, and lunched with
us . . . which was the greatest help to me". In an effort to retain
Parnell's support, Lord Carnarvon, the newly appointed Lord Lieutenant of Ireland, held a secret meeting with him in an empty house
in Mayfair, at which he expressed his willingness to suspend
coercion, and go further than ever before towards self-government.
In September, a month before the General Election was held,
Chamberlain stormed up and down the country like a "new Jack

Cade". His so-called "Unauthorised Programme" included pro-posals for free education, manhood suffrage and death duties: too heady a brew for some of his own supporters, let alone his critics. Nevertheless, it appealed to radical working men. Parnell, encour-aged by his discussions with Carnarvon, instructed his supporters to back Salisbury. Largely owing to Chamberlain's initiative, the Lib-erals won a majority of eighty-six: precisely the number of seats held by the Irish Nationalists. Hence the "eighty-six of '86" achieved their dream of holding the balance of power in a "hung" Parliament.

Some time during the summer of 1885 Gladstone reached the momentous decision that the only way to solve the problem of Ireland was to offer it Home Rule. He had long sympathised with nationalist movements in Italy and the Balkans, and gradually came to the conclusion that the policies he had advocated in Europe were right for Britain. He decided, at first, to keep his conversion to himself, in case it might seem to be an electoral stunt. Nor did he wish to split the Liberal Party by prematurely committing it to so polemical a programme. His hand, however, was forced by his son, Herbert, who chose to announce his father's conversion in the hope of persuading Parnell to abandon the Tories.

The moment that Herbert flew his "Hawarden Kite", Lord Salis-bury's days were numbered. The Queen, none the less, fought a frantic campaign in an effort to stem the tide. Her strategy was to exploit the discontent of Liberal Unionists by persuading them to recognise that supporting Gladstone would lead to "UTTER ruin". "Patriotism", she told Ponsonby, "*must now* be the *one aim* of *all* who love their country and are loyal to their Sovereign." She particularly looked to Goschen to save her from "a wild and fanatical old man of 76". "Let me urge and implore you", she pleaded, "by your devotion and love for our dear, great country, to do *all* you can to gather around you all the moderate liberals, who indeed ought to be called '*Constitutionalists*' to prevent Mr Gladstone recklessly upsetting the Government. . . . I do not speak of *myself*, but I may say I think a Queen, and one well on in years who has gone through terrible anxieties and sorrows, ought not to appeal in vain to British gentle-men, who have known and served her long." In a last attempt to whip up support for the Tories, she even agreed to open Parliament. Never before had she shown such scant regard for her duty to be impartial.

On January 26th 1886, Parnell joined the Liberals in a vote of censure, and Goschen and Hartington voted with the Government. When Lord Salisbury resigned, the Queen told him that she trusted that "a very short time" would elapse "before he returned to office", and went on to thank him for "the admirable manner in which he had conducted public affairs". Such was his "triumphant success" that in seven months he had "raised Great Britain to the position which she ought to hold in the world". Personally, it had been "a pleasure and a comfort" to her, "to transact business with him, and she felt the blessing of having a minister in whom she could thoroughly confide".

Once Gladstone acknowledged his conversion to Home Rule, neither Hartington nor Goschen was willing to serve under him. Chamberlain, at first, accepted a post in the Government, but resigned when he learned that it was proposed to delegate power to a Parliament sitting in Dublin. Early in April, the Prime Minister introduced his Bill in a speech of astonishing power, while Lord Randolph Churchill warned that "Ulster will fight and Ulster will be right". Hartington spoke so eloquently of the dismemberment of the Empire, that the Queen wrote to tell him how gratified she was to see "that patriotism and loyalty go, as they always should, before party". A fortnight later, she told Goschen that if the Liberal Unionists were still not prepared to make any pact with the Tories, "We must . . . organise the opposition separately, and then act together". Her remarkable choice of pronoun showed how closely she identified herself with the battle against Home Rule. On one occasion, after she complained of Gladstone's attacks on the House of Lords, he could not resist pointing out "Your Majesty's argument might doubtless have been used with great force from the Opposition Bench".

Throughout Gladstone's third Ministry the Queen remained in contact with Lord Salisbury, even sending him copies of the Prime Minister's letters to keep him in touch with events. In May, a rumour reached her that attempts were being made to try to win back Chamberlain, and she immediately telegraphed to Hatfield: "Pray advise me how to protest agst such a fearful danger and *possibility* and consult *together* HOW this contingency can be stopped". On June 8th, the Commons rejected the Irish Bill by 343 votes to 313: ninety-three Liberals voting against the Government. "There goes the man who killed Home Rule" said Parnell as he watched Chamberlain voting with the Tories. Gladstone refused to give up without a fight and decided to go to the Country. In spite of his indefatigable efforts, Home Rule won scant support. The Tories emerged with a majority of 115 over the Liberals. The seceding Unionists, or "Loyalists" as the Queen preferred to call them, won 78 seats. During the course of the campaign Gladstone tried to steal the Radicals' thunder by denouncing the privileged classes. When the Queen protested, he said that long experience had taught him that on almost all questions of "humanity and justice" the masses had proved right and their so-called "betters" wrong. That July, she told Princess Victoria, Alice's eldest child, that "the G.O.M. writes most dreadful letters setting class against class, and behaves abominably. I really think he is cracked". When he saw her at Osborne to hand in his resignation she could scarcely conceal her delight.

Lord Salisbury's second Ministry began with a crisis precipitated by Lord Randolph Churchill, a younger son of the Duke of Marlborough, and a friend of the Prince of Wales. His career may be best described in a metaphor from Tom Paine: He rose like a rocket and fell like the stick. In 1886, when he was only thirty-seven, he became Chancellor of the Exchequer and Leader of the House. Almost as soon as "Lord Random" joined the new Government, he quarrelled with most of his colleagues. "I could do very well with two departments," said Salisbury, "in fact I have four – the Prime Ministership, the Foreign Office, the Queen and Lord Randolph Churchill – and the burden of them increases in that order." In December, Lord Randolph put forward his budget proposals, conceived in the spirit of Tory Democracy. Trouble, however, arose because of his insistence on reducing the army estimates, which the Secretary of State for War, W.H. Smith, regarded as unacceptable. The Chancellor could easily have found the sum required from the estimated surplus, but chose instead to try to force the Prime Minister to overrule Smith. When the strategy failed he decided to resign, presumably imagining that he would be swept back on a wave of popular feeling. In the event, not a dog barked, and Lord Randolph was taught the chastening lesson that no man is indispensable. Not only had he forgotten Goschen, who replaced him at the Exchequer – the first Liberal Unionist to join a Conservative Government – but he could not defend his actions as budget proposals are secret. The Queen was happy to see him go, having long regarded him as one of the most dissolute members of the Marlborough House Set. As

Chancellor, he had been "a perpetual thorn in the side of his colleagues", and she was particularly incensed by the "want of respect"
he had shown her by dining with her at Windsor and talking about
the future, without so much as a hint of his intentions. Then, later
"that *very night at the Castle*, he wrote to Lord Salisbury resigning
his office!" She was right, of course, in thinking Lord Randolph
"impossible", but as Rosebery pointed out, besides being "pug-
nacious, outrageous, fitful" and "petulant", he was also "eminently
lovable and winning".

The Queen was not only Head of State but of a rapidly growing
family. Affie's daughter, Marie, described her as "the central power
directing things", whose "'yes' or 'no' counted tremendously". Her
gift for prising out family secrets was uncanny. "*Who* is it tells the
Queen these things?" asked Knollys, when she somehow got wind
of a most unsavoury morsel. Ponsonby thought that she was too
despotic, and might have had "ten times more influence" over her
children if she had treated them less peremptorily. On the other
hand, to quote her own phrase, "love of opposition" was "a family
defect", and she needed to be strong-willed to maintain her authority. Nor should it be forgotten that her maternal instincts were
exceptionally strong. When Beatrice aged twenty-four, and Arthur
aged twenty-seven, got soaked to the skin during a military review,
she "ran down" to make sure that they had changed into dry clothes
and were none the worse for their drenching. It is easy to be misled
into supposing that the Queen's relationships were more abrasive
than they were, largely because Prince Albert had taught her that the
best way to deal with domestic disputes was to write a letter. By the
same token, the procedure ensured that the most trifling disagree-
ments were meticulously recorded, while years of untroubled harmony could easily pass unremarked.

From the moment the German Empire was proclaimed, Bismarck
ensured that Vicky and Fritz were left outside in the cold. Sometimes
Vicky was almost driven to despair by the oppressive régime of
Berlin. She considered it an "insupportable tyranny" that Fritz at
forty should be "treated like a boy of six" and required to ask his
father's permission merely to leave Potsdam. The accident of the
Emperor's long life – he was ninety-one when he died – forced her
to watch Germany growing ever more reactionary. Looking back
on those years of barren apprenticeship, she told the Queen: "We
had a mission. We felt and we knew it – we were Papa's and your

children!" Their dream was to see Germany "strong and great, not only with the sword, but in all that was righteous in culture, in progress and liberty". For years, the Chancellor kept up his campaign to destroy what he could of the Crown Prince's reputation, by portraying him as the puppet of his wife: an unforgivable crime in Prussian eyes. Two things sustained them through adversity: the knowledge that their days of waiting were numbered, and their passionate love for each other.

In March, 1879, Vicky's third son, Waldemar, died from diphtheria. He was an enchanting boy of ten: boisterous, affectionate, and intelligent. Once, while staying with his grandmother at Buckingham Palace, he released a small crocodile under the table at which she was writing. She let out a shriek of terror, and a footman rushed to the rescue, only to find that the reptile was not well disposed to being captured. Eventually, Waldemar retrieved his improbable pet, but not before having extracted the last possible ounce of amusement from its exploits. The Queen was staying at the British Embassy in Paris when she received a telegram containing the "terrible words: 'Have just taken a last look at the beloved child. He expired at half past three this morning. Your brokenhearted daughter Victoria'." Two days later, she wrote to her "poor dear darling child", to say how her heart bled for her, and how anxious she was to do anything to help in "this terrible affliction". Vicky's Prussian relations might think her absurd for feeling such grief for a child of ten, but at least she knew she could look to her mother for understanding and sympathy.

The Queen was so interested in the welfare of her grandchildren, that Vicky once ventured to ask her to scold Henry for biting his nails to the quick. More importantly, she shared her daughter's concern that German governesses confused their charges by speaking "too much of Hell and of the Devil and the Trinity", rather than stressing "the simpler notions of Christianity", and telling them "the touching stories of the Bible". Vicky was particularly eager that her eldest son should learn to be tolerant of divergent creeds. In 1893, during one of his visits to Osborne, William intrigued Bishop Davidson by telling him that he had preached a sermon to a congregation of sailors avoiding "dogmatic trash". The language was plainly his, but the sentiments those of the Prince Consort.

William at fifteen was a turbulent adolescent, whose principal pleasure in life was to drive his parents to frenzy. Vicky described his behaviour as that of a child who "pulls off a fly's legs or wings and does not think the fly minds it". He belonged to the first generation to grow up under Bismarck, and hence rejected the liberal ideals which his parents held to be sacred. A trivial incident illustrates how cantankerous he could be. A year after Waldie's death, Vicky was greatly distressed when a "stupid Jäger" killed a cat to which she and Waldie had both become deeply attached. William, so far from expressing sympathy, went out of his way to praise the keeper's zeal. The Queen was horrified to learn of his heartlessness, and hastened to say how grieved she was to hear of the cat's death. It was perfectly proper, she wrote, to mourn "truly and deeply", and added on a more practical note, "We always put a collar with V.R. on our pet cats and that preserves them". As for William, she rightly foresaw trouble, partly because the "greatest object" of children was "to do precisely what their parents do not wish and have anxiously tried to prevent!"

Much of the antagonism between William and his mother arose from the fact that their characters were similar but their outlook very different. The Queen believed William's problems sprang from Prussian pride. Why does he always sign himself "William of Prussia?" she asked. "His father never does." The trouble was that his head had been filled with ridiculous notions about "the immense position of Kings and Princes", and he needed to be taught that he was of the same "flesh and blood" as the rest of mankind. What was required was a German John Brown to put him in his place. William's mistakes, in Churchill's words, were as much his fate as his fault. His grandfather insisted that he should be brought up on military principles and that his "young soul" should be "guarded against errors": by which was meant "his father's and mother's wishes and opinions". "Willie and Henry," the Crown Princess told the Queen, "are quite devoted to the Bismarck policy" which seems to them "sublime", and at times she felt "like a hen which had hatched ducklings". But even when she was at her wits' end, she was eager to make excuses for her son, and blamed his waywardness on "all the nonsense with which his head had been stuffed".

It is not uncommon for parents of troublesome children to pin their hopes on marriage. Vicky was therefore delighted when William became engaged to Princess Augusta of Schleswig-Sondeburg-Augustenburg, who answered to the diminutive "Dona". Dona's mother was Princess Feodore's daughter, Adelaide, and

Prince Christian was her uncle. The wedding took place in February 1881, and the bride soon proved a bitter disappointment in that she fawned on William instead of trying to improve him. When her eldest son was born he was given his father's name. "How absurd," the Queen wrote to Vicky, "of Willie and Dona to call the child William." Seeing, however, that they omitted to inform her of their decision, she decided to write to say "Of course you will call him Fritz after his two grandpapas".

Charlotte was almost as troublesome as her brother. The Queen insisted that Vicky was "forcing" her too fast and spoke disparagingly of over-education. The Princess relished gossip, and was quoted as saying that her parents would ruin Germany. She possessed the seductive charm of a cat, not to mention its sharp claws. Vicky regarded her as "very nineteenth century", and complained that she smelt "like a walking cigar box". In 1877 she fell in love with Prince Bernard, Duke of Saxe-Meiningen, a shy, retiring, studious friend of William. The wedding took place the following year, but Charlotte was slow to settle to family life. "Married children," the Queen warned Vicky, "are very often a great trial at first," but one soon gets used "to their follies as time goes on". In May, 1879, Charlotte gave birth to a daughter, Feodora. "Received the news," wrote the Queen, "that Charlotte had been delivered of a little girl, and I have become a great-grandmother! Quite an event." She was sixty at the time, and Vicky was thirty-eight. Lord Beaconsfield wrote from Downing Street to congratulate "the royal great grand mother" on becoming "the mother of many nations" while "still in the freshness and fullness of life".

Moretta was next to lose her heart at the age of seventeen, having fallen for the handsome young Prince of Bulgaria. "Victoria," the Queen wrote in 1883, is "violently *in love*", and insists that she "never cared for anyone else, or ever *will* marry anyone else". Prince Alexander, or "Sandro" as he was known to the family, originally came from Hesse. In 1851, his father, yet another Prince Alexander, was morganatically married to Julie, Countess Hauke, whom he met while visiting his sister Marie, the future Tsarina of Russia. They were given the title "Serene Highness", and the family name "Battenberg". In 1879, in pursuance of the terms of the Congress of Berlin, Sandro became ruler of Bulgaria. As he principally owed his position to the Tsar, it was naturally expected that he would look to him for guidance. The Tsarina wrote to her brother to assure him that Queen Victoria was well disposed to his son, and "John Brown had deigned to approve" of him.

In 1881 Alexander II was murdered, and the new Tsar, Alexander III, thought Sandro was too inclined to follow a line of his own. He therefore encouraged a group of dissident officers to force him out of the country. The Queen was sickened by such treachery. "I really could hardly have felt much more for my own son," she wrote from Balmoral in 1886. The whole wretched affair rekindled memories of Russia's past duplicity.

Unfortunately for Moretta, Bismarck was vehemently opposed to the Battenbergs, and warned the Emperor that an alliance with them would taint the Hohenzollerns. He even succeeded in representing the match as aimed at ensuring "a permanent estrangement between ourselves and Russia". "The old Queen," he told his crony, Busch, "is fond of match-making, like all old women". The Emperor appeared to agree and forbade the marriage: a decision endorsed by William, Henry and Charlotte, the more so because they knew that their mother favoured it. The Queen regarded their attitude as "shameful" and accused them of being resolved to break Moretta's heart.

Bismarck was right to describe the Queen as a match-maker, but she, nevertheless, was strongly opposed to marriages of convenience. It was enough for her that Moretta had fallen in love. From the first, she thought Sandro "very fascinating and (as in beloved Papa's case) so wonderfully handsome. He is a person in whose judgement I should have great confidence." Moretta was deeply grateful to her grandmother for all the support she gave her. "You are ever and constantly so loving and kind to me," she wrote appreciatively. "It is such a comfort to have at all events one Grandmama who loves me and to whom one can tell everything." The Queen was furious with Willie for discouraging the match, and let it be known that she would refuse to see him if he insisted on visiting England. At the height of the Bulgarian crisis in 1886, she wrote a note to Lord Cranbrook, then Minister in attendance at Balmoral, to say that she feared she must have tried his "patience very much", but she hoped he would understand that she had felt unusually concerned over the fate of "the chivalrous and distinguished young Prince".

In the autumn of 1886, the Crown Prince caught a severe chill while driving in an open carriage with the King and Queen of Italy. His hoarseness failed to clear up, and the following spring his physician, Dr Gerhardt, diagnosed cancer of the throat. He consulted Professor Bergmann, the President of the Association of German Surgeons, who proposed to remove a lump in Fritz's larynx from outside: a procedure known as "thyrotomy". Like all exploratory operations its seriousness largely depended on what it exposed. Bismarck insisted on seeking a further opinion, and the German doctors agreed to consult Dr Morell Mackenzie, a Harley Street specialist, and author of a text book on *Diseases of the Throat and Nose*. Mackenzie hurried to Berlin and saw the Crown Prince on May 20th. He was strongly opposed to drastic surgery before it was proved that the growth was carcinomatous, not only because of the risk to life, but because he believed that so major an operation might leave him in a "condition worse than death". The following day, Mackenzie succeeded in removing a small portion of the growth, which he sent to Professor Virchow for analysis. When it transpired that the tumour was not malignant, the doctors agreed to abandon all thought of surgery.

A fortnight or so later, the Crown Prince was well enough to attend the Queen's Jubilee. Indeed, Mackenzie welcomed the opportunity of treating him in London. The plan was extremely unpopular in Germany, but it sufficed for Vicky that Fritz was determined to go, and would be in the hands of "the only person" who seemed to think he could "cure him". On the great day, June 21st, 1887, Fritz set out from Buckingham Palace to the Abbey, mounted on a white charger, and wearing the uniform of the Pomeranian Cuirassiers, with a silver breastplate and an eagle-crested helmet. His star of the Order of the Garter glinted in the sunshine, and he held his Field Marshal's baton in his hand. The Queen that evening wrote in her journal that "he looked so well and handsome". Mackenzie, who watched his patient riding down the Mall, claimed that "Few could have thought on seeing him then, in the very prime of his magnificent manhood, that behind the hero of Königgrätz, Wörth and Sedan, there rode on that day of triumph a grimmer Conqueror, who before another year had passed, would have laid that stately form in the dust."

A few days after the Jubilee, Mackenzie managed to remove what remained of Fritz's growth by means of special forceps, and Virchow reported the fragment was benign. That August, Vicky and Fritz moved north to be near Balmoral, and stayed at the Fife Arms, Braemar. The Queen was delighted to hear her son-in-law speaking again in his normal voice instead of a hoarse whisper. On September 7th, she knighted Dr Mackenzie at the Crown Prince's request. In November, the royal couple settled at San Remo, having rented the Villa Zirio on the shores of the Mediterranean.

No sooner had they arrived, than a new tumour appeared in Fritz's throat. When he asked if it was malignant, Mackenzie felt bound to reply: "I am sorry to say, Sir, it looks very much like it." There was a moment's silence, and then Fritz grasped his hand and said with a gentle smile, "I have lately been fearing something of this sort, I thank you Sir Morell for being so frank with me." In fact, his suspicions dated back to May, but he kept his thoughts to himself for Vicky's sake. While she sought to protect him from the despair of confronting the truth, he strove to keep up the pretence that she had succeeded in deluding him. In November, Prince William arrived at San Remo and attempted to take charge on the "Emperor's orders". Vicky, who had been nursing the Crown Prince night and day for a month, barred Willie's way to his father's room, and refused to allow him to take Fritz back to Berlin. Later, the Queen received two very different accounts of this hapless visit. The first was from William himself, who merely spoke of his father accepting his fate like "a Hohenzollern and a soldier". The second came from Vicky. "You ask," she wrote, "how Willie was when he was here! He was as rude, as disagreeable and as impertinent to me as possible when he arrived, but I pitched into him, with, I am afraid, considerable violence, and he became quite nice and gentle and amiable." She ended by trying to excuse his behaviour. "He thought he was to save his papa from my mismanagement!! When he has not his head stuffed with rubbish at Berlin he is quite nice and 'traitable', and then we are very pleased to have him." A few days later she wrote to tell her mother that Willie's advisers had persuaded him that Fritz was too ill to reign, and that he should hand on the Crown when the Emperor died. "That is a monstrous idea," the Queen replied, which "must never be allowed – Fritz is quite capable of doing and directing anything and this must be stopped at once."

The Crown Prince, who by now had lost his voice, decided against a major operation, preferring to trust himself to God than Professor Bergmann. The German press, which was largely controlled by Bismarck, launched a series of shabby attacks on Vicky, inspired by a common hatred of "die Englanderin". Some papers even claimed that she would welcome Fritz's death as "the moment of deliverance". Others alleged that she had prevented the German doctors from operating, because she preferred to risk her husband's life than to forfeit her chance of becoming an Empress. The truth was far simpler. She did whatever she thought was best for him. Every attempt to find other explanations merely exposed the malice of her enemies. At one stage, the Queen wrote to Sir Edward Malet, the British Ambassador in Berlin, to say that she thought "it very wicked and unpatriotic to torment and irritate the Crown Prince and Princess by these shameful attacks". Malet took up the matter with the Government, but Bismarck was too anxious to discredit the English Princess to put the record straight.

Vicky learned to ignore the Prussian press but not her own family. "Henry," she told the Queen, "maintains that his Papa is lost through the English doctors and me. . . . It is hard enough to hear myself abused, and everything found wrong that is done for Fritz. . . . But it is harder still to see one's own children side violently with these people and refuse to hear or believe a word one says. Henry is quite dreadful in this respect!! He is so prejudiced, and fancies that he knows far better than his Mama and all the doctors here." "You have every reason to feel angry and annoyed," the Queen replied, but allowance had to be made "for the fearful anxiety of the nation about their beloved, noble and heroic Prince."

Even as late as 1887, when Bertie was forty-six, his mother remained convinced he was not to be trusted with secrets. "I often pray," she told Vicky a few years earlier, "he may never survive me, for I know not what would happen." "Dear uncle," she once warned a granddaughter, "cannot keep anything to himself but lets everything *out*." It was hardly surprising therefore that the Prince complained that he was "not of the slightest use to the Queen, that everything he says or suggests is pooh-poohed, and that his sisters and brothers are more listened to than he is". One thing which helped to convince her that Bertie was not to be trusted was his attitude to Gladstone, whom he entertained at Sandringham. Alix was so hospitable that she actually tucked Mrs Gladstone in bed on the last night of her visit. One of the Prince's greatest virtues was his gift for remaining on friendly terms with those of opposing political views, in which respect he was wiser than his mother.

In 1885, Gladstone asked the Queen's permission to follow the precedent of the previous Government which had forwarded Cabinet Papers to the Prince. The Queen refused to believe that Beaconsfield had made such communications, and declined to give her consent. "I was afraid," noted Hamilton, that "the Queen would raise difficulties. She is very jealous of anything tending to derogate sovereign powers." The Prince's obsessive desire for Government Boxes sprang from a deep malaise: his lack of rewarding work. Only in 1892 did the Queen finally agree that H.R.H. should be given access to all official papers, not realising that she was only regularising a practice of many years' standing.

Throughout most of the eighteen-sixties the Queen and her son were at odds over foreign policy. He basically supported Bismarck's victims, while she instinctively took the side of Prussia. In the next decade, however, their views converged. Both applauded Disraeli's coup over Suez, both shared a common suspicion of Russia, both were in favour of staying in Kandahar, and both were opposed to abandoning the Sudan. If the Queen was a somewhat belated convert to Palmerston, the Prince was a fervent disciple, and the more their opinions began to coincide, the more she was willing to trust him.

In 1875 Disraeli prevailed on the Queen to agree to the Prince of Wales paying a visit to India. She began by raising a fine crop of objections. India, she said, was far too hot to be healthy, and the Prince was no longer strong. Besides, who should be given precedence, her son or the Viceroy? Then what if she should die when her heir was thousands of miles away? When she grudgingly gave her consent, she refused to leave the arrangements to H.R.H. and supervised them herself. Yet for all her misgivings, the tour proved a huge success, "an unresting progress of durbars, receptions, dinners, visits, processions, ceremonies, speeches, addresses, entertainments, investitures and reviews". "The Royalty Problem" was triumphantly solved, at least for a few months, and the Prince was given a chance to do something of real consequence.

Parliament made a special grant to meet the cost of the Indian tour. The Prince, of course, already received a considerable income from the Civil List and the revenues of the Duchy of Cornwall. Nevertheless, he was by no means the richest of the Queen's subjects, although possibly one of the most extravagant. The Duke of Buccleuch, for example, had three times his income, and lived in a style which made Sandringham look frugal. It was certainly arguable, and H.R.H. did so argue, that when he performed the duties of the Sovereign, the Queen should foot the bill. In 1874 *The Times* published a leading article, no doubt inspired by Marlborough House, putting forward this very proposal. Ponsonby did not deny that the Prince deserved more money, but failed to see why the Queen should be asked to provide it. "I may as well tell you," he wrote to Knollys, that "We do not applaud *The Times* proposals here."

In her youth the Queen learned from personal hardship the penalties of improvidence. Believing, as she did, that her children were far too extravagant, she saw no reason to help them to be more so. It was not in her nature to lavish money on those disposed to squander it. On the other hand, she was only too willing to help in cases of genuine hardship. In 1887, for example, she told the Crown Princess that she would gladly give Moretta the bulk of her German investments. Some forty years earlier, the exiled Louis Philippe told one of his English friends, "I should not have had this house (Claremont) to cover my head, or the plate or anything which is on the table" were it not "for the generosity of the Queen of England".

The Queen was shocked by the Prince of Wales's associates. "Believe me dearest child," she once wrote, "the Duchess of Manchester *is not a fit companion for you.*" "If you ever become King," she later warned him, "you will find all these friends *most* inconvenient, and you will have to break with them *all.*" No doubt she would have reminded him of the repudiation of Falstaff had she felt sure he would grasp her meaning. The Prince, however, parried her protests with customary forbearance. In 1887, for instance, she complained that he lived "far too intimately with everyone irrespective of character and position", and failed to "keep up the right tone". "You are," he replied, "rather hard on me when you talk of the round of gaieties I indulge in at Cannes, London, Homburg and Cowes. . . . With regard to London, I think, dear Mama, you know well that the time we spend there is not *all* amusement, very much the reverse." The gulf between Marlborough House and Windsor was as deep as the Grand Canyon. The Queen's dinners were sedate to the point of being sombre. As Ponsonby once remarked, "We subdue our voices considerably while eating the royal beef". But when the Prince and Princess entertained the sounds of revelry echoed down the Mall.

In the winter of 1876, while the Prince of Wales was sailing home from India, rumours began to spread round London concerning his closest associates. It seemed that Lord Aylesford, familiarly known as "Sporting Joe", was resolved to divorce his wife for running off with Lord Blandford. Aylesford was married to General Williams's sister, Edith; and Blandford to the Duke of Abercorn's daughter, Albertha. While Aylesford accompanied the Prince to India, Blandford rented a property a mile or so from Edith, and could often be seen leaving her house in the early hours of the morning. In February, Lady Aylesford wrote to her husband to say she proposed to elope, which led him to take the next ship back to England, breathing fire and slaughter. The Prince was deeply distressed by this turn of events, and denounced Blandford as "the greatest blackguard alive". Naturally, the whole affair proved an even greater trial for Blandford's father, the Duke of Marlborough, whose dissolute sons had already brought shame on the family.

When Lady Aylesford recognised that she would be banished by Society the moment she was divorced, she decided to do whatever she could to keep matters out of court, and persuaded Lord Randolph Churchill, Blandford's younger brother, to act on her behalf. Randolph's plan was to force the Prince to avert an open scandal by threatening him with letters he had earlier written to Edith. So confident did he feel, that he openly boasted that "he held the Crown of England in his hand". His plan, however, miscarried, as the Prince defied him to "publish and be damned". Knollys sent Ponsonby copies of Randolph's letters, assuring him that H.R.H. had "never in his life written a line to Lady Aylesford which might not be read out at Charing Cross". The Prince, he added, "feels sure that H.M. with the affection she had never ceased to bestow on him will afford him her support". As always, when the going got rough, the Queen came to the rescue, and sent the Prince a reassuring telegram. "Her Majesty," Ponsonby hastened to tell Knollys, had "not the slightest doubt" that the letters were "not compromising, from the minute she read that the Prince of Wales said so". At the same time, she added with a rueful smile, "writing letters was a family failing". The Prince was especially touched by his mother's magnanimity, seeing how concerned she was for the family's reputation.

The matter was further complicated when Randolph and Lady Aylesford dragged Alix into the scandal, by calling on her at Marlborough House. Alix would never have dreamt of seeing Edith, had she not misheard her footman announce a visit from "Lady Ailesbury". The Queen was furious, and said that "Alix's dear name should never have been mixed up with such people". When the Prince heard what had happened, he was beside himself with rage, and actually went so far as to challenge Randolph.

Early in May, 1876, Lord Aylesford dropped his divorce to save any further scandal. Soon after, he sailed to America, where he drank himself to death. Eventually, Randolph's parents forced him to apologise for his conduct to the Prince. Some four years later, the two agreed to meet, after Randolph's American wife, Jennie, had exercised her charm. Thenceforward, nobody supported him more loyally than the Prince and Princess of Wales. Sandringham was one of the few houses which was still prepared to invite him when his mind began to wander. The day he died, the Prince wrote to Jennie to offer his consolation. In the course of his letter he spoke of "a cloud" which had once overshadowed their friendship, but which he was happy to say had "long been forgotten by both of us". It was a remarkable tribute to pay to a man who had done his best to blackmail him.

The Queen's affection for Alix grew over the years, and she knew very well that her lot was far from easy. What she particularly admired was her "simplicity and humble-mindedness", and the way she remained unspoiled by the "frivolous, flattering, pleasure-seeking world". Alone of the family, she rushed to Windsor on learning of John Brown's death. "Nothing," wrote the Queen, "could exceed her tender sympathy and complete understanding of all I feel and suffer." Nevertheless, on many occasions they failed to see eye to eye. The Queen believed that if Alix was given her way, the interests of Britain would always take second place to those of the Danish Royal Family, and she found it hard to forgive her inveterate dislike of Germans.

The Queen, as ever, itched to interfere in bringing up the Prince of Wales's children. It was imperative, she said, that "the *dear boys*" should be kept "*apart* from the society of fashionable and fast people". Nor could she help remarking that Eddy was frail and lethargic, while his sisters were plain and retiring. The trouble was that their mother over-cosseted them. Alix in many respects was a sort of Peter Pan, fighting a rearguard campaign against growing old, and retarding her children's development. When Prince George was a young naval officer in command of a gunboat, she ended a letter to him "with a great big kiss for your lovely little face". Some people even claimed that her main concern was to hide her own age. Like the clock at Grantchester, she stopped the hands of time in the afternoon of life. Unfortunately, she was so devoted to her family that she clung to them possessively. Nothing, she told Prince George before he married, could diminish the love that a mother feels for her child, and "nobody can, or shall ever, come between me and my darling Georgie boy". No doubt her letter was meant as a benediction, but it sounded more like a threat.

In 1877 the Prince of Wales sent his sons to HMS *Britannia*, agreeing, no doubt, with William IV that there is "no place for making an English gentleman like the Quarter-deck of a Man of War". He was particularly anxious for them to mix with other boys, a thing he had never himself been allowed to do. The Queen suggested, in vain, that the curriculum of a training ship was likely to prove too narrow, and wanted them sent to Wellington. Two years later, they joined HMS *Bacchante* and circumnavigated the world, watched over by their tutor, the Reverend John Dalton. Before they left, the Princess of Wales begged him to see that they were not allowed to get "grand". The Queen was equally anxious that nobody should treat them as "great princes". In fact, they were royally received wherever they went.

Prince George decided to make his career in the Navy, but his brother remained a problem. After three years at Cambridge, he joined the Tenth Hussars, but it soon became clear that he was even more hopeless as a soldier than he had been as a student. Sometimes he was so sunk in apathy that he would sit for hours staring into space. When the Duke of Cambridge inspected him at Aldershot, he discovered that he had never heard of the Battle of the Alma, and had no idea how to drill. Dalton maintained that Eddy's "dormant condition" arose from some physical abnormality, which Ponsonby thought might well be hereditary deafness. It is equally possible that he suffered from "petit mal". His problems were not made easier by the Prince of Wales, who did nothing at all to hide his disappointment. While Eddy was still at Cambridge, he told his friend, Lionel Cust, that he was "rather afraid of his father", whose expectations he clearly failed to meet. The Queen, however, was far more tolerant of her grandson's peculiarities, and Alix was deeply grateful for her forbearance. "I am so glad," she wrote in 1883, that "you seem to have understood his disposition", and that you recognise that "he is a very good boy at heart", though perhaps "a little slow and dawdly, which I always attribute to his having grown so fast".

In the early eighteen-seventies, the Queen became concerned that Alice was working herself to death on behalf of the people of Hesse. Her charities ranged from Hospitals, Orphanages and Lunatic

Asylums, to Women's Rights, education and the housing of the poor. Her first love, however, remained nursing. When the Franco-Prussian War broke out in 1870, she lent her house to the Red Cross. Not content with presiding over committees, she insisted on dressing wounds and emptying slops. Seldom before had a Princess been so steeped in filth, stench and horror. Eventually, incessant overwork began to tell on her health. In 1876, before visiting her mother at Balmoral, she felt bound to warn her that she was far from well, and felt "dull, tired and useless. . . . I live on my sofa and see no one, and yet go on losing strength". Nobody knew better than Alice how stoically the Queen bore other people's afflictions, and how sceptical she could be about inconvenient illnesses. In 1877, on the death of his uncle, Louis became Grand Duke, thus adding a further load to his wife's burden. It was typical of her that when her doctors ordered her to recruit her strength at Eastbourne, she spent much of her time visiting the poorest parts of the town and spending what little money she had in her endless fight against suffering. Indeed, it was only because the Queen was paying for her holiday that she had anything to give.

Soon after returning from Eastbourne, Alice's children went down with diphtheria. Expertly as Alice nursed them, nothing could save May. "Our sweet little one is taken," she telegraphed the Queen. "The pain is beyond words, but God's will be done." "I can't but say in all one's agony," she wrote a few days later, "there is a mercy and peace of God, which even now He has let me feel." The supposedly "infidel" Princess was sustained by a deep if unorthodox faith. The doctors decided that Ernest was far too ill to be told of his sister's death: a pretence which tortured his mother. When he asked her to give May a book he thought she might like to read, Alice smothered him in kisses, knowing full well the risk she ran from contagion. On December 8th, it became clear that she had succumbed to the infection, and the Queen at once sent Sir William Jenner to help the stricken household. Naturally, she dreaded the approach of December 14th, the seventeenth anniversary of Prince Albert's death. Just as she sat down to breakfast on the fatal morning, Brown brought her an incoherent telegram from the Grand Duke. "Poor Mama," it said, "poor me, my happiness gone, dear, dear Alice." Soon after, she was handed a further message from Jenner "with the dreadful tidings that darling Alice sank gradually and passed away at half past 7 this morning! It was too awful! I had so hoped against hope. Went to Bertie's sitting room. His despair was great. As I kissed him, he said, 'It is the good who are always taken'."

If Vicky was the cleverest of the family, Alice was the most saintly. She was like her father in being both practical and artistic, and her mother in being direct and unpretentious. Both instinct and necessity compelled her to live frugally, and she taught her daughters to cook and sew: unexpectedly useful accomplishments for life in Bolshevik gaols. Generally when she travelled she chose unfashionable resorts, dowdy hotels, and second-class railway carriages. She "walked with Kings" but kept "the common touch". At one moment, she lived in a world of diamond tiaras, powdered flunkeys, champagne and caviare: at the next, of slum tenements, seaside boarding houses, tripe and onions. She was always refreshingly sceptical about royalty, and surprisingly humble for a Grand Duchess. Shortly before she died she told Jenner, "I am so sorry for all the anxiety this causes dear Mama". In death, as in life, her first thought was for others.

The moment the Queen heard the news from Darmstadt, she took charge of her Hessian grandchildren. "You are doubly dear," she told one of them, "as the children of my *own* darling child I have lost and loved so much." Early in 1879, the whole family was invited to stay at Osborne, and when they returned home they were accompanied by a new governess, Miss Pryde, despatched at the Queen's expense, with strict instructions to write to Her Majesty virtually every day. Even the patterns of the Princess's dresses needed the royal assent. The Queen kept in constant touch with Victoria, the eldest of Alice's children. Most of her letters ended "Ever your devoted Grandmama. V.R.I.", but sometimes she absently signed herself "Your devoted Mama", thus revealing the role she saw herself assuming. In 1880 she paid a special visit to Darmstadt to attend Victoria and Ella's Confirmation, and to see Princess Alice's grave.

In June 1883, Prince Louis of Battenberg, Sandro's eldest brother, proposed to Princess Victoria. He, by then, was a naturalised British subject and an officer in the Navy. She shared her mother's radical views, and believed that the days of royalty were numbered. The fact that the Battenbergs were only "Serene Highnesses" recommended them in her eyes. Elsewhere, however, the match was viewed with disdain. Fortunately, the person who mattered most gave the marriage her blessing. "Darling Victoria," the Queen wrote from Balmoral, "You will I know be anxious to know what I think. I think you have done very well to choose only a husband who is *quite* of your way of thinking and who in many respects is as English as you are . . . and who dear Mama liked." The one possible drawback was that neither had any money. "I don't think *riches* make happiness, or that they are necessary, but I *do* think that a certain amount is a necessity so as to be independent." "Of course," she told Vicky a few days later, "people who care only for 'great matches' will not like it. But they do not make happiness." The Queen, having initially said it would be impossible to be present at the wedding, changed her mind, partly because she saw it "as a sacred duty" to "darling Mama's eldest child", and partly because "as some are *not* pleased at the marriage, *my* presence *would* be a support". Before the great day, Victoria was summoned to Osborne to make sure that she understood what was expected of a wife, and would always remember "*that* the *husband must* be the person to *look up to and obey* – and that a woman can only really be happy and in her right place when she *can* do so". The marriage took place at Darmstadt on April 30th, 1884, and seldom before had Hesse entertained such a gathering of royalty, prominent amongst whom were Uncle Bertie, Uncle Fritz, Aunt Alix, Aunt Vicky, and Aunt Beatrice. After the ceremony, the Queen appeared on a balcony of the New Palace to acknowledge the cheers of the crowd.

No sooner had the bride and bridegroom left for their honeymoon, than the Louis of Hesse himself was secretly married. For some time since Alice's death, he had sought consolation with Alexandrine de Kalomine, the divorced wife of a Russian diplomat. Five days before her wedding, Victoria was forced to make "the painful communication" to the Queen that her father intended to marry his mistress. Shocked as she was by the news, she at once announced "I shall never turn against or away from dear Papa – I know how attached he is to me and mine", and "how happy he made dear Mama, how much she loved him and how much he loves you all". Nevertheless, there was no disguising the fact that his "marrying such a person – a divorced Russian lady – would lower him so much" that she would be forced to see rather less of him. It would have made better sense had he chosen "to make a morganatic marriage with some nice, quiet, sensible and amiable person", but "to choose a lady of another religion who has just been divorced" would be "a *terrible mistake* and one which he would soon repent of, when too late. . . . I do *most earnestly* ask him to *pause* and put it off at least for a time". The Grand Duke's decision faced the Queen with an impossible dilemma.

If she stayed, it might seem that she sanctioned his marriage. If she left, the scandal would devastate the family. The moment she heard that the ceremony had actually taken place, she instructed the Prince of Wales to arrange an annulment. Before long the knot was untied, Madame de Kalomine was paid off, and the marriage successfully dissolved. Some people expressed surprise that the Grand Duke should have allowed himself to be dictated to, but as the Prince of Wales remarked, "We are a very strong family when we agree".

The Queen was determined that Victoria should have her first child at Windsor, in the very same room and the very same bed in which she herself had been born. Early in the morning of February 25th 1885, the Queen was warned that the Princess was in labour. For the next nine hours she sat holding her granddaughter's hand and whispering words of encouragement. Shortly before five a baby girl was born: Victoria Alice Elizabeth Julie Marie, who was always known by her second name.

During the course of the celebrations at Darmstadt in 1884, Ella announced her engagement to the Grand Duke Serge, the Tsar's (Alexander III) younger brother. Ella was as remarkable for her beauty as she was for works of charity; while Serge was morbidly pious, immensely rich, and savagely reactionary. His political views were learned in a hard school when he saw his father (Alexander II) blown to bits by a bomb. The Queen deplored the match. Ella, she argued, would "*never* stand the climate", which had killed her poor Aunt Marie, and there was furthermore a serious risk that her head would be turned by Serge's prodigious wealth. "I know," she wrote to Victoria from Balmoral, that "dearest Mama was *against* the idea (tho' *personally* she liked Serge), and I also feel that Ella will be *quite lost to me* for a Russian Grand Duke is a *person* belonging to Russia, and Russia is *our real enemy* and totally antagonistic to *England*. This is *very painful* for you know *how* dear you are to me – how like my own children – and that therefore it is a great wrench and trial to me." In spite of the Queen's forebodings, Ella and Serge proved perfectly happy, apart from the fact that their marriage was childless and both longed for children.

The Eastern Crisis of 1876 put a dangerous strain on the Queen's relations with the Duchess of Edinburgh. It is true that in 1877 she admitted that Affie was "fortunate" to have found himself such a wife, but she grew rather less complimentary with every Turkish reverse. "Poor Marie," she wrote a few months later, "is at Malta

. . . and reads the *Daily News*!!'': a paper which championed Bulgaria. From the first, the Duchess never much cared for England. "Marie thinks London hideous," the Tsarina told her brother, "the air there appalling, the English food abominable, the late hours very tiring, and the visits to Windsor and Osborne boring beyond belief". The anti-Russian hysteria of 1877 only increased her dislike for her husband's country. Nevertheless, her growing estrangement from Affie had little to do with politics. The trouble was that she found him bibulous and bad-tempered. It was only because he spent much of his time at sea that their marriage somehow survived.

The first of Marie's children, "young Affie", was born at Buckingham Palace in 1874. He was followed by a succession of girls: Marie ("Missy") in 1875, Victoria Melita ("Ducky") in 1876, Alexandra in 1878, and Beatrice ("Baby Bee") in 1884. In 1876 their father was given a Mediterranean command and the family moved to Malta. For the next fourteen years he spent most of his time overseas, which encouraged the Queen to complain that she hardly knew his children. In 1878, about the time of the Treaty of San Stefano, Affie was sent to join the fleet patrolling the Sea of Marmara. Prominent amongst the officers serving under him was a future First Sea Lord, Prince Louis of Battenberg. When they anchored off Constantinople, Louis arranged to meet his brother Sandro, who was then an aide-de-camp of the Russian Commander-in-Chief. Shortly afterwards, Affie invited Sandro to dine on board his ship, and gave him a tour of the *Temeraire*, the finest ironclad afloat. The Queen was so furious to hear how Sandro had been fêted that she went so far as to call him "a Russian spy". "It was *most injudicious* and *imprudent*", she told Affie angrily, "and you will hear of it from the Admiralty. . . . I own I should hardly believe you *capable* of such imprudence and want of (to say the least) *discretion*". When the Duke threatened to demand a Court of Enquiry to clear his name, Disraeli complained that these royal tantrums gave him more trouble than the Eastern Question itself. Meanwhile Sandro, the innocent cause of the storm, poured out his heart to the Tsarina. "The poor boy," she told his father, "is beside himself that the Queen, crazy old hag, made him the pretext for persecuting Alfred and more especially Louis." In the end, the Prince of Wales persuaded his mother that it was natural that Louis should wish to meet Sandro, that none of the Navy's secrets had been betrayed, and that Russia and England were not, after all, at war. The crisis blew over, but the stresses and strains which had caused it remained at work like a fault in the earth's crust.

Of all her married children the Queen saw most of Helena, who lived at Cumberland Lodge within walking distance of Windsor. Hard as she tried to please her Mama, she often fell out of favour. In 1873 the Queen complained to Vicky that Lenchen was so touchy that it was "difficult to live with her". Part of her problem was her foolish habit of taking laudanum for real or imagined ills. On several occasions the Queen and Prince Christian begged Dr Reid to persuade her to stop. In many respects her common sense approach was much like that of her mother's, and few things annoyed her more than sanctimonious cant. One Sunday, at the time of a damaging dock dispute, she discovered a special Prayer of Intercession lying in her pew, which spoke in rather fanciful terms of the "Brotherhood of Man". Having scrutinised it with evident disdain, she proclaimed in a stage whisper: "That prayer won't settle any strike".

Prince Christian's duties as Ranger of Windsor Park hardly sufficed to occupy his time. Most of his days were spent shooting, or riding, or pottering in his garden. His leisurely style of life appears to have taken its toll. In 1881, the Prince of Wales chanced to meet him in Berlin. "Who is the old German General?" he asked, pointing at his brother-in-law. "I am sure I have seen him before." Worthy as Christian was, the Queen found him a bore. One day, when she looked out of her sitting-room at Osborne, she saw him lolling dreamily under a tree, and immediately sent him a note to say that he ought to find something better to do with his time.

In September, 1875, the Queen spent a week with the Duke and Duchess of Argyll at Inveraray. Throughout her stay she treated her host as if he kept an hotel. Only on rare occasions did she eat with the family. Generally speaking she took her meals separately, with Beatrice and Louise, in the Duchess's drawing-room overlooking Loch Fyne. "Evidently," said Ponsonby, "she considered herself as paying a visit to Princess Louise", and hence regarded the rest of the household as "merely accidental". Even the Duke's footmen were expected to take instructions from John Brown. Louise spent much of the time complaining to her mother that "her rooms were not good enough", and that her husband's family treated her too familiarly.

In 1878 Lord Beaconsfield nominated Lorne as Governor-General of Canada: possibly the only thing he ever did which met with Gladstone's approval. The proposal, the Queen told Vicky, was "carrying out beloved Papa's views" as "he wanted our children to be useful in the Colonies". Louise presided over Ottawa society in rather bewildering style. At one moment she was rigorously royal, at the next defiantly maverick. Nobody ever felt sure which way she might choose to jump. She seldom attempted to hide the fact she was bored, and would talk for hours with those who took her fancy, while honest aldermen hovered in the wings. In 1880 she was involved in a serious accident when a sleigh in which she was travelling overturned. Her injuries were so grave that she almost lost an ear, and her neck was badly strained. The Queen believed that the trauma of this accident explained her growing estrangement from Lorne. Clearly the fact that the marriage proved childless lay at the heart of the matter. It was also rumoured that Lorne had a penchant for handsome young guardsmen. The story goes that she bricked up a window at Kensington Palace to stop him indulging his fancy. Be that as it may, she certainly looked elsewhere for affection.

The Queen was extremely anxious that Lorne and Louise should try to keep up appearances. Provided they nominally lived under the same roof, and were seen together in public, she accepted their right to spend much of their time apart. Throughout the stormiest periods of their marriage she contrived to remain sympathetic, without taking sides or apportioning blame, and for thirty years she showed her son-in-law "nothing but kindness and affection". Louise's long absences from Ottawa were put down to her shattered health and the rigours of Canada's climate.

In 1878, the year in which Princess Louise made her debut in Canada, her brother, Prince Arthur, proposed to her namesake, Princess Louise of Prussia. Louise was a daughter of Prince Frederick of Hohenzollern, a brutal cousin of Fritz's, who ill-treated his wife and children. Much as the Queen had longed for her son to marry, she questioned his choice of a partner. What on earth possessed him, she wondered, to have fallen in love with a girl from a broken home who was ten years younger than he was? "I could not help saying," she admitted in her journal, "that I dislike the Prussians, and told him he should see others first, but he said it would make no difference." The moment, however, the Queen met Arthur's fiancée, her earlier doubts were dispelled. "Had I seen 'Louischen' before Arthur spoke to me of his feelings," she wrote later, "I should not have grieved him by hesitating for a moment in giving my consent to their union. She is a dear, sweet girl of the most amiable and charming character and . . . I feel sure dear Arthur could not have chosen more wisely." The Prince was married on March 13th 1879 at St George's Chapel, H.M. having made it clear that it was out of the question that she should travel to Berlin. The Bride's father was in a foul temper and told the Queen how much he disliked England.

In 1882 the Duke of Connaught was given command of the First Guards' Brigade and sent out to Egypt. "When I read that my darling precious Arthur was ready to go," the Queen confessed in her journal, "I quite broke down. . . . Still I would not on any account have him shirk his duty." When she finally saw him off, she said that her heart was almost "torn in two – for no child (excepting her beloved Beatrice) was ever so loved by her as that precious Darling son is, her darling from his birth". It was "a new and terrible anxiety" for her to be the mother of a serving soldier, and one she felt "very deeply". On September 14th, Sir Garnet Wolseley, writing from the battlefield of Tel-el-Kebir, informed the Queen that he had heard "loud praises" from all sides of the Duke's "cool courage" under the hottest fire he had ever seen in his life. "He is a first-rate Brigadier General, and takes more care of his men and is more active in the discharge of his duties than any of the Generals now with me." The Queen replied that she was "*immensely* gratified and proud" of this tribute to her "dear soldier son", who "had never given her a day's sorrow or anxiety". When Arthur returned home he presented her with a magnificent Turkish carpet taken from Arabi's tent. On November 18th, the Queen reviewed her victorious troops, and her heart was in her mouth when her son "rode past at the head of the brave men he led into action – and looking so like darling, beloved Papa. It was almost overpowering".

Between 1883 and 1890 the Duke of Connaught spent most of his time in India: first in command of the troops in Bengal, and then as Lieutenant-Governor and Commander-in-Chief at Bombay. Throughout those seven years he did everything in his power to break down racial barriers. He even learned Hindustani on the ground that those who aspired to govern India should know how to speak its languages. He was very much his mother's son in deploring the brutality and contempt only too often shown to her native subjects. In 1874 she informed Lord Carnarvon of "her very strong feeling (and she has few stronger) that the natives and coloured races should be treated with every kindness and affection, as brothers, not – as, alas! Englishmen too often do – as totally different beings to ourselves, fit only to be crushed and shot down!" A year later, she showed Disraeli a letter in which the Prince of Wales spoke of the "disgusting" way in which the officers and civil servants he met in India spoke of its sundry races as "niggers". It was Britain's mission, she said, to protect native populations, not to treat them as savages.

The Duchess of Connaught had three children: Margaret born in 1882, Arthur in 1883, and Victoria ("Patsy") in 1886. When she joined her husband in India, she left them behind in their grandmother's care. The Queen found Margaret congenitally disobedient, but often forgave her because she was so "funny". Arthur took after his father and was much less of a handful. She loved having children around and was always refreshed by their visits. In 1886, Lord Kilmarnock wrote to Ponsonby to say that he had been "horrified" to discover that one of his sons had written to Her Majesty and had actually posted the letter. "I hope," he said, "his extreme youth may be accepted as an excuse for his indiscretion." "Pray tell Lord Kilmarnock," the Queen replied, that she was "delighted with the little letter . . . as nothing pleases her more than the artless kindness of innocent children. She has written him an answer and has posted it to him."

"No one knows," the Queen once wrote of Leopold, "the constant fear I am in about him." While he did what he could to assert his independence, she never ceased to complain of his "wilful neglect of advice", and "disregard of his doctors". The Prince was undoubtedly her most cultivated son, although Martin told Esher that he "had no real capacity" and that the "excellent addresses he delivered in the style of his father's were written by Dean Stanley". In 1876, Disraeli, recognising the fervour of Leopold's Tory principles, wrote him a letter proposing that he should help the Queen "in the most confidential portion of her labours". "You would become acquainted," he told him, "with all the most secret springs and motives of public action", and, in due course, would "find yourself in a position to influence events". Naturally, this enticing offer could only have been proposed with Her Majesty's approval. Not long afterwards, Prince Leopold pulled a key from his pocket and showed it to a friend, proudly proclaiming that it had once belonged to his father and opened the Queen's despatch boxes. "Dizzy gave it to me," he said, "but the Prince of Wales is not allowed to have one." It was an extraordinary state of affairs that the heir to the throne should be kept in the dark while his brother was trusted with state secrets.

Prince Leopold deliberately did everything in his power to persuade his mother that Gladstone was her enemy. Sir Almeric Fitzroy, one of Greville's successors as Clerk to the Privy Council, maintained that the Prince's "persistent interference" was a constant cause of "friction". The Queen, however, forgave his indiscretions, largely because he reinforced her prejudices.

Apart from the last two years of his life, Prince Leopold lived at Court in a smouldering state of rebellion, and from time to time made precipitous dashes for freedom. For instance, in 1878, he suddenly proclaimed his "intense aversion" to Balmoral, voicing what many had felt but few had dared to express. The Queen was so stunned that she accused him of subverting the "authority of the Sovereign and the Throne", and tried to enlist his brothers and sisters to help her to deal with the threat. "He must," she insisted, "be made to feel that such conduct cannot be tolerated." The squall eventually blew over and Leopold was forgiven, but not before he had spent a week in Paris instead of in the Highlands. In 1881 the Queen made him Duke of Albany, "a fine old Scottish title" which Mary Queen of Scots had conferred on Darnley, and had last belonged to his great-uncle, "the Grand old Duke of York". In spite of this new honour, his mother decreed that he was "always to be called Prince Leopold in my house". "I always say," she explained, that "no one can be a Prince but anyone can be a Duke."

The Queen was opposed on principle to the idea of Leopold marrying, not least because she wished to retain her unpaid political secretary. Besides, he was far too much of an invalid to survive the strains of matrimony. Nevertheless, as usual, he went his own way, and in November 1881 proposed to Princess Helen of Waldeck-Pyrmont. The Queen, in breaking the news to Vicky, explained that he had long been anxious "to find a nice wife", and that she had consequently suggested that he might take a look at Princess Waldeck's daughter. For once he took her advice, and soon afterwards wrote to say "how much struck he was by Hélène (or rather Helen as she is generally called)". After several further meetings, they took "a decided fancy to one another", and eventually decided to marry. It was typical of the Queen that she should proudly announce "It was entirely my own idea", and then go on to complain that she could not get over the "grief" and "shock".

Helen turned out to be all the Queen could have wished. "I am much pleased with his choice," she wrote, "for I have heard such very high and excellent character of her." Moreover, she was well educated, well read, and exceptionally intelligent. She liked to read Descartes on a train journey, and thought mathematics fun. Like Florence Nightingale, she was dedicated to good works, and like her husband to be, was one of the few people who dared to stand up to the Queen. In 1904, she told Arthur Benson, her son's House Master at Eton, how, shortly after her marriage, she found that her mother-in-law had chosen a maid for her without bothering to consult her. She was so angry that she "flounced into the Queen's room" and protested so vigorously that she got her own way. "I can do nothing with the Duchess," her mother-in-law complained, "but unfortunately in this case she is quite right. It is what I should have done myself."

Prince Leopold was married at St George's Chapel on April 27th 1882, and spent his honeymoon at Claremont. In February, the following year, the Duchess gave birth to a daughter, who was christened "Alice" after her late aunt. The Queen was delighted with her new grandchild, but could "scarcely believe" that "dear Leopold" had succeeded in being a father. Only two years later, on March 28th, 1884, her worst fears were realised when she learned that "darling Leopold had died at 3.30 quite suddenly in his sleep, from a breaking of a blood vessel in the head. Am utterly crushed. How dear he was to me, how I watched over him! Oh! What grief, and that poor loving young wife. . . . Too, too dreadful! But we must bow to God's will and believe that it is surely for the best. . . . He was such a dear charming companion, so entirely 'the child of the House'." The Queen described herself in her journal as "stunned, bewildered and wretched. I am a poor desolate old woman and my cup of sorrows overflows". It did not escape her notice that by an "extraordinary and awful" coincidence, the Prince had died on the first anniversary of his telling her that Brown had passed away in the night.

It was left to Princess Christian to break the news to Helen, who was expecting a second child. On March 29th, the Queen drove over to Claremont and was "much overcome" by the sight of her widowed daughter-in-law, looking "so sweet, young and touching". The occasion was made more poignant by Alice's merry chatter. Four months later, the Duchess gave birth to Leopold's posthumous son, Prince Charles Edward, Duke of Albany. The children were often invited to stay at Windsor. "Mind you curtsey at the door," Alice's Nanny would whisper, "and kiss Grandmama's hand and don't make a noise and mind you are good." They would then be left to play, while the Queen got on with her letters. Their favourite game was to build a wall round her feet with discarded despatch boxes. Sometimes a footman would announce an illustrious guest, and Alice and "Charlie" would be told to say "How do you do?" and then be packed off to the nursery to face a barrage of questions.

In 1873, when Beatrice was only sixteen, the Queen told Vicky that she was "the apple of her eye", and that she "could not live without her". She could hardly "thank God enough for the blessing of such a devoted daughter and child", who was like "a sister as well as a daughter". Leopold's death meant that Beatrice assumed his political role and became even more indispensable. Nobody else understood her mother as she did, or served her so devotedly.

Towards the end of her life, the Queen was inclined to agree "with the Mohammedans that duty towards one's parents goes before all others". The principle appealed to her more as a mother than a daughter. She had not shown much sign in 1840 of preferring the claims of the Duchess of Kent to those of the Prince Consort. When Ponsonby casually mentioned at dinner "that someone they all knew was engaged to be married" he was curtly informed that the subject "must never be mentioned in Princess Beatrice's presence". Nevertheless, while the Prince Imperial lived, the Empress Eugénie cherished the hope that he and Beatrice might marry. There was even some talk of her marrying her widowed brother-in-law, the Grand Duke of Hesse, if the law could be changed to allow it.

In 1884, when the Queen was at Darmstadt for Princess Victoria's wedding, she failed to notice that Beatrice had fallen in love with Prince Henry of Battenberg, a dashing young officer in the Prussian Household Cavalry, and the bridegroom's younger brother. The truth was that she was so preoccupied by Ella's engagement to Serge, and the Grand Duke's liaison with Madame de Kalomine, that her customary vigilance lapsed. Prince Henry, or "Liko" as he was known to his relations, was widely regarded as exceptionally good looking, and Beatrice could hardly be blamed for finding him attractive. Soon after returning to England she confessed that Liko had taken her fancy. The Queen was so displeased that she refused to talk to her for some months. Beatrice visibly pined and hardly ate a morsel, but none the less stood her ground. In the end, the Queen relented, but only after her future son-in-law promised to live at Court. "It would have been *quite out of the question*," she told the Duke of Grafton, for Beatrice to have left home. Indeed, "She would *never* have *wished* it herself, knowing well how impossible it was for her to leave her mother."

The Queen's attempts to thwart her daughter's marriage were heartless, selfish and cruel. In all probability it was the most discreditable thing she ever did in her life. Plainly she put her own convenience before her daughter's happiness. Nevertheless, it is only fair to point out that her principal aim was not to prevent the marriage, but to force Prince Henry to agree to live under her roof. Unforgivable as her conduct was, it is easy to understand. To insist on her duty to let the Princess leave her was like asking a cripple to throw away his crutches. A sad succession of deaths deprived her of those upon whom she chiefly depended, and led her to cling to her last unmarried child. When the Queen wrote to tell Vicky that her sister was engaged, she explained that it was only because she was very fond of Liko, who had agreed to give up his career and live at Court, that she had finally consented. A few days later, she told the Crown Princess that the fearful shock had made her "quite ill". For some time, she confessed, she had refused to hear of Beatrice marrying, "and had hoped against hope that it would not be! But alas she was so determined that her health would have suffered if I had not relented".

Considering the Queen's "horror and dislike" of the very idea of her "precious baby's marriage" (Beatrice was twenty-eight at the time), she was surprised to discover how quickly she came to accept it. It was "really Liko himself", she decided, who managed to convert her. "He is so modest, so full of consideration for me, and so is she." Nevertheless, it still pained her to hand over her daughter "to a stranger to do unto her as he likes", and she found herself counting "the months, weeks and days" that Beatrice remained her "own sweet, unspoilt, innocent lily and child". "The nearer the fatal day approached", the more depressed she became, and the more "invincible" her dislike of Beatrice's marriage, although "NOT to dear Liko. Sometimes I feel as if I *never* could take her myself to the marriage service – and that I wish to run away and hide myself".

The wedding took place on July 23rd, 1885, at St Mildred's, Whippingham, barely a mile from Osborne. It was the first time that a Sovereign's daughter had been married in an ordinary parish church.

Shortly before, the Queen gave Prince Henry the Order of the Garter and the title of "Royal Highness". The Hesse family arrived for the ceremony looking "green and yellow" after an extremely rough crossing. "I stood very close to my dear child," the Queen wrote in her journal, who looked "sweet, pure and calm". Never before had she "felt more deeply" when giving a daughter away. Nevertheless, she "bore up bravely" until she took leave of the bridal couple. Only when she heard their carriage rattling down the drive did she finally burst into tears. Just before Beatrice left, the Empress Eugénie gave her a last hug, explaining wistfully that she had always looked on her as a possible daughter-in-law. The "honey couple" were only allowed two days' leave of absence before being recalled to Osborne, where Beatrice was needed once more to run errands for her mother.

The Russians and Prussians agreed that Beatrice had married beneath her, and that England's apparent attachment to the Battenbergs might pave the way for Moretta's marriage to Sandro. The Empress Augusta wrote the Queen a "very unamiable letter" which more or less ended their thirty years' friendship, and even "dear Fritz" sent a disagreeable note in which he spoke "of Liko as not being of the blood" as if he was merely an animal. The Queen regarded such sentiments as "outrageous" and told the Crown Princess that she could not "swallow affronts". The Empress, she claimed, appeared bent on "persecuting and insulting" the Battenbergs, "now so nearly allied with me and you . . .". But the worst offenders of all were William and Dona. Willie, she said, deserved a "good skelping" for his "extraordinary insolence" towards his aunt Beatrice. As Lord Granville remarked, "If the Queen of England thinks a person good enough for her daughter what have other people got to say?" The marriage had proved "immensely popular" with her subjects, who rejoiced to know that "she, sweet child, remains with poor, old, shattered me". In defending the match, the Queen returned to a favourite theme: the need for new blood in the family. "If no fresh blood was infused occasionally the races would degenerate finally – physically and morally."

Prince Henry entirely won the Queen's heart and enlivened the gloom of her sombre Court. She found his youthful gaiety irresistible. In November 1886, Beatrice gave birth to a son, Alexander, who at once became known as "Drino". The Queen sat by her bedside for most of the night and was the first member of the family to hold her grandson. When she finally went to bed the sun was rising over the eastern ramparts at Windsor. In October, the following year, the Princess gave birth to a daughter: the first royal child to be born in Scotland since the time of Queen Elizabeth. This "Jubilee" baby was baptised at Crathie with water from the Jordan. Her mother intended to give her the old Gaelic name "Eua", but the presiding minister misread her handwriting and christened the child "Victoria, Eugénie, Ena". The Queen was as anxious as Beatrice that the Empress Eugénie should be the girl's godmother. When it was pointed out that the Presbyterian rubric made no provision for sponsors, she altered the service to suit her requirements.

In June 1887 the Queen celebrated the fiftieth anniversary of her accession. Only three previous sovereigns had reigned as long: Henry III, Edward III and George III. According to the Lord Chamberlain, she "was consulted *on every point*, as she knew more about etiquette than any one else". So many demands were made upon her that she told Ponsonby to make it clear that she would "not be teased and bullied about the Jubilee". The morning of June 21st, the great day of national thanksgiving, was so bright and beautiful that it reminded the Queen of the opening of the Great Exhibition in 1851. She had insisted that the Jubilee should be celebrated on June 21st to avoid the day on which William IV died. Her family did all in their power to persuade her to drive through the streets in state, but she would not hear of wearing a crown or dressing in royal robes. When Alix attempted to raise the matter, she "never was so snubbed". Only Prince Arthur had slightly better luck. "Now Mother," he said persuasively, "you must have something really smart." In the end, she appeared in "a dress and bonnet trimmed with *white* point d'Alençon", covered in diamonds and all her orders. One of the Jubilee photographs taken for the occasion was so unflattering that her daughters wanted it banned, but the Queen insisted she thought it was "*very like*". "I have *no* illusions," she said, "about my personal appearance." She often described herself as a "portly" old lady, and made no attempt to affect to be anything else. Holstein was too severe when he referred to her as "an undersized creature, almost as broad as she was long", but he did not entirely miss the mark when he said she looked like a cook.

The Queen left Buckingham Palace for the Abbey soon after half past eleven. She sat alone on the back seat of an open landau, with Vicky and Alix opposite. Her procession was headed by her three sons, five sons-in-law, and nine grandsons or grandsons-in-law. The Duke of Cambridge rode beside her carriage, recalling no doubt that he might have been sitting beside her had destiny not decreed otherwise. From time to time Vicky glanced over her shoulder to see if Fritz was all right, and more than once her mother took her hand and squeezed it reassuringly. Lady Geraldine Somerset told the Duchess of Cambridge, who was too infirm to watch her niece drive past, that "It was the "greatest and most *perfect* success ever known!" Seldom had there been a more thrilling spectacle than Her Majesty driving down Constitution Hill, escorted by four Kings and a caval-cade of Princes, and seldom had there been a more "touching and magnificent display of loyalty and attachment": commodities in short supply when it came to the Cambridge Household. The scene, said Lady Geraldine, beggared description. "The millions of people, thronging the streets like an anthill, and *every* window within sight and every roof of every house. . . . It was one continuous roar of cheering from the moment she came out of the door of her Palace till the instant she got back to it! Deafening." One observer, who watched the procession from a stand outside St Margaret's, noted that the loudest cheers were reserved for "the Queen of the Sandwich Islands and the driver of a water cart", but then English crowds are renowned for their wry sense of humour.

For several hours the congregation in the Abbey waited restively, while munching sandwiches or reading the morning newspapers, until a crescendo of cheers ended their tedious vigil. Slowly a great procession of kings, princes and clergy wended its way up the nave, but one small figure leaning on a stick was more conspicuous in her simple grandeur than all that glittering throng. Now at last it was plain to see how inspired she had been to refuse to wear a crown. Previous Empires had been symbolised by swords and sceptres, but she preferred a widow's bonnet bought from her local draper. Throughout the service, the Queen "sat *alone*", thinking how proud her beloved Prince would have been to have shared in the celebration. Before leaving the Abbey her family paid her homage. The Prince of Wales was first to make his bow and reverently kiss her hand. Fritz came next, and as he made to withdraw, she pulled him back and embraced him in her arms.

Not until four o'clock did the Queen sit down to luncheon, with the King of Denmark on her right, and the King of Saxony on her left. Afterwards, she snatched a few moments' rest on her sofa, half buried under a pyramid of telegrams. Dinner was held in the Supper Room, for which she wore "a dress with the rose, thistle and shamrock embroidered on it." Towards the end of the meal, her pipers marched round the table relieving her guests of the need to make conversation. Next, she held a reception in the Ball Room where foreign dignitaries mingled with Indian princes. Eventually, "half dead with fatigue", she "slipped away" to her room. As she drifted off to sleep feeling tired but "very happy", she could hear the strains of "Rule Britannia" coming from the Mall.

The following day, June 22nd, the Queen drove to Hyde Park where some thirty thousand urchins were drawn up for her inspection. She was particularly touched by "a beautiful bouquet" to which was attached the embroidered message: "God bless our Queen, not Queen alone, but Mother, Queen and friend". She was less impressed to hear the National Anthem sung "somewhat out of tune". That evening, she returned to Windsor making the last stage of the journey in an open landau. As she drove through Eton, its buildings glowed in the light of the setting sun, and the town "was one mass of flags and decorations". Later that night, the boys marched up to the Castle in a torchlight procession, and sang the "Eton Boating Song". Delighted by their performance, the Queen said in as loud a voice as she could, "I thank you very much". "These two days," she later acknowledged, "will ever remain indelibly impressed on my mind, with great gratitude to that all-merciful Providence, Who has protected me so long, and to my devoted and loyal people."

On June 29th, the Queen held a Jubilee Garden Party in the grounds of Buckingham Palace. Soon after four o'clock, she joined one of the most distinguished gatherings of her reign. "I walked right round the lawn with Bertie," she wrote, and "bowed right and left talking to as many as I could." It was an exceedingly hot afternoon and she was greatly relieved to take tea in the shade of a tent. She could not, however, escape being waylaid by her former Prime Minister. "Do you see Mr Gladstone?" she asked the Duke of Cambridge. He has been standing there "hat in hand" for the past half hour, "determined to force me to speak to him!" A ludicrous game of hide and seek ensued, which ended in her being forced to give him her hand.

Although the Queen was nearly seventy, she made more public appearances in the summer of 1887 than in any year since the death of the Prince Consort. During June and July alone, she entertained the visiting Princes from India with a dazzling reception at Windsor, attended a Garden Party at Hatfield given by Lord Salisbury, laid the foundation stone of the Imperial Institute, inspected the London Volunteers in the grounds of Buckingham Palace, took a march past at Aldershot, and inspected the Fleet at Spithead. On the day of the Naval Review, not a cloud could be seen in the sky as the *Victoria and Albert* steamed past lines of Ironclads. The Queen stood on the quarterdeck, waving her handkerchief to acknowledge the cheers of her sailors. When her yacht finally dropped anchor, the captains of the assembled ships were invited to come aboard, including some French officers on a courtesy visit. Standing beside the Queen was a lady in deep mourning who could hardly keep her eyes off them. Not until some time after did they learn that the mysterious stranger was their former Empress. To most people the sight of the Solent black with ships seemed visible proof of Britain's power and greatness, but expert observers knew that this mighty fleet was virtually obsolescent.

Even during the Jubilee celebrations a few discordant notes were sounded, apart from those of the children in Hyde Park. In June 1887, *Reynolds' Newspaper*, notorious for its republicanism, demanded to know "one good thing" that the Queen or her children, or "her inexhaustible brood of pauper relations 'made in Germany'", had "ever done for the people of this land?" It went on to denounce the obsequious worship of "a pampered old woman of sullen visage and sordid mind", whose only recommendation was her supposed descent from that "devotee of Sodom and Gomorrah, James I". It needed a somewhat fevered imagination to recognise the sedate old lady behind this lurid portrait. Lord Rosebery succeeded in catching the public mood a good deal more felicitously. Few people, he told the Queen, could have watched unmoved "the procession from the Palace to the Abbey with its proud cavalcade of Princes, its majestic representation of the Sovereignties of the world, and the enthusiastic multitudes that hailed its passage; but fewer still that touching and magnetic moment in the Abbey when your Majesty appeared alone and aloft – symbolising so truly your Majesty's real position – to bear silent testimony to the blessings and the sorrows which it has pleased God to bestow on your Majesty and your people during two generations. . . . All was worthy of your Majesty and of the Empire; all has tended to strengthen and to deepen the foundations of a

monarchy which overshadows the globe, and represents the union
and aspirations of three hundred millions of human beings. . . ."
The Queen thanked Rosebery warmly for his "beautiful letter", and
told him *"how deeply, immensely touched"* she had been by the "universal" enthusiasm with which her Jubilee had been celebrated. In
1887 the last sediments of earlier discontents were washed away in
a flood of love and loyalty.

9

Indian Summer
1887–1901

THE older the Queen grew, the more she enjoyed what remained of her lease on life. The brooding introvert of earlier days had become a merry widow. In 1890 she told her granddaughter, Princess Victoria of Hesse, that she had spent a "very *gay* autumn" at Balmoral, enlivened by an "excellent band" and "a *very* successful Tableaux". When Lord Esher dined with her a few days after her eightieth birthday, he found her "extraordinarily vivacious, full of smiles and chaff – a wonderful thing". Marie Mallet, who became a Maid of Honour in 1887, was amazed to see the Queen enjoying a fire-work display as if she had never seen anything like it before.

"Carriage exercise" was an essential part of the Queen's ordered life, and she always took an afternoon drive regardless of the weather. In March 1890, when the Court was still at Windsor, she went out with Marie Mallet in a biting north-east wind. Although it snowed without ceasing, the Queen refused to put up the hood of the carriage. "I cannot conceive," Marie wrote to her husband, "why the Queen never catches cold. She is tremendously strong and will outlive us all." In the autumn of 1891, the composer, Ethel Smyth, was invited to stay at Birkhall by the Empress Eugénie. On the third day of her visit, the Queen drove over to tea in a raging storm. She had hardly eaten a scone, when a ghillie banged on the door to say she must leave at once as the horses were growing restive. Miss Smyth, discreetly concealed behind a curtain, watched the royal departure, and was astonished to see Her Majesty, sitting bolt upright in the back of an open landau, disappear down the drive in a cloud of rain and spray. The first time Lord Redesdale was summoned to Balmoral it was bitterly cold and the ground was covered in snow. On being shown to his room he was handed a note from Ponsonby. "Please order tea," it read, "and make yourself comfortable. We are off to a picnic."

Even when the Queen was well past seventy, there was nothing she liked more than to push the furniture back for "a little impromptu dance". "We had a Quadrille," she noted with evident satisfaction in the autumn of 1890, "in which I danced with Eddy! It did quite well, then followed some waltzes and polkas." Nobody seeing her cavorting with her grandson would ever have guessed how lame she was, so "prettily" did she execute every figure with "light airy steps" in "the old courtly fashion". Neither age nor infirmity seemed to impair her vigour. "We had a most cheerful Ladies' Dinner last night," wrote Marie Mallet in 1898. "The Queen in excellent spirits, making jokes about her age and saying she *felt* quite young." The following year, she inspected three Squadrons of the Household Cavalry before they embarked for South Africa, having spent the previous seventeen hours travelling by train from Balmoral. *The Times*, in congratulating her on her stamina, referred in glowing terms to her "habitual subordination of ordinary personal comfort to ceremonial requirements". Clearly whoever paid her this tribute had failed to consult back numbers of his paper.

The Queen celebrated her eightieth birthday at Windsor, and was never in "better health or higher spirits". She began the day by expressing her "deep gratitude to God" for having preserved her "so long to my dear children, all my friends, and the whole nation", and she asked that He might "mercifully preserve" her to work for the good of the country. Having dressed, she went to the Audience Room to see her presents, which included "three very handsome candelabras" from her children, and "a very interesting miniature of Prince Charles Edward", given her by Lord Rosebery. After breakfast, she knighted the Mayor of Windsor, attended a march past of the Scots Guards, and planted a tree. There followed a huge family luncheon and in the afternoon she drove through the streets of the town and returned to the Castle by way of the Mausoleum. The celebrations ended after dinner with a magnificent performance of "Lohengrin" in the Waterloo Chamber. "I was simply enchanted," she wrote in her journal. "It is the most glorious composition, so poetic, so dramatic, and one might almost say, religious in feeling.

. . . The whole opera produced a great impression on me", and provided "a fine ending to this memorable day".

Towards the end of her life the Queen's vigour if anything seemed to increase. She is "full of business", wrote Ponsonby in 1893, "and sending ticklers all round, as much as to say 'I'm back, so look out!'" Two years later, Lord and Lady Ribblesdale were invited to stay at Windsor, and were amazed by the Queen's industry. I hear, Lady Ribblesdale told her son, she retires at eleven, "but does not go to bed till about two o'clock in the morning, particularly at present, when she is tremendously interested in the elections". When Lord Esher was summoned to Osborne in 1899 he found her working at her despatch boxes as vigilantly as ever. Who else, he wondered, worked so hard at eighty? On one occasion, Lord Clarendon, emboldened by senility, ventured to ask the Queen the secret of her stamina. "Beecham's Pills", she replied with mischievous solemnity.

The closing years of the Queen's reign were the happiest of her widowhood, as agonising recollections subsided into a painless glow of nostalgia. Furthermore, she drew increasing strength and courage from knowing how loved she was. But, above all, she owed her refreshment of spirit to Princess Beatrice's marriage. Prince Henry turned out to be an ideal son-in-law: dashing, handsome, fearless, vivacious, thoughtful and understanding. His presence, she said, was "like a bright sunbeam" in her home. She rejoiced once again to have a man at her side, whose sense of fun relieved the gloom of her Court. Like the late John Brown, or Princess Helen of Albany, Liko refused to be overawed by the Queen, and Beatrice was often kept "on thorns" by the way he spoke to her mother. He even contrived to persuade her to relax her ban on smoking and give him a comfortable room in which to indulge his vice. Her new-found happiness, and the mellowing influence of age, combined to make her more charitable and forgiving. One night over dinner, when the conversation became a shade too censorious, she remarked "We are all growing very ill-natured", and deftly changed the subject.

So rigorous was the Queen's mourning for Prince Albert that for twenty years she never watched a play. Eventually, in 1881 the Prince of Wales persuaded her to see a private performance of *The Colonel*, a comedy which satirised the aesthetes of the day much in the manner of *Patience*. Beerbohm Tree, then relatively little known, took the part of Lambert Streyke, modelled on Oscar Wilde. The play was performed in the Coach House at Abergeldie, and was intended, in the Queen's words, "to quiz and ridicule the foolish aesthetic people who dress in such absurd manner, with loose garments, large puffed sleeves, great hats, and carrying peacock's feathers, sunflowers and lilies". In 1887 she invited Mr and Mrs Kendal to present a double bill at Osborne, which proved such a huge success that it was followed by some twenty or more "command" performances. In 1893, for example, the Comedie Française performed "two charming pieces" in the Waterloo Chamber at Windsor. She thought the players "perfection" and insisted on thanking the cast in French for giving her so much pleasure. Later the same year she persuaded Squire and Marie Bancroft to come back from retirement. "How you made me laugh!" she told Marie, "and it is so nice to be merry." In 1895 she invited the St James's Theatre Company to present their popular comedy *Liberty Hall* at Balmoral. As usual, she sat in the front row dauntingly close to the actors, who were greatly encouraged to see her laughing so much that she kept dabbing her eyes with a handkerchief.

Some of Her Majesty's subjects regarded the stage as the work of the Devil, and were distressed by the interest she showed in actors and actresses. Even her daughter, Vicky, drew the line at her meeting Sarah Bernhardt, whose acquaintance, she claimed, "no *lady*" could make on account of her "reputation". The Queen, however, thought her manner "most pleasing and gentle". Sarah was later invited to sign the Queen's "Birthday Book", and took almost a whole page to write in enormous letters: "le plus beau jour de ma vie". The news that Queen Victoria had consented to receive her was greeted with some astonishment. It was rather as if the Vatican authorities had stamped their imprimatur on a collection of bawdy poems.

The Queen's "command" performances included several operas. In 1891 she saw *The Mikado* at Balmoral, but thought the plot rather fatuous, and the music inferior to that of *The Gondoliers*. She was far more impressed when the Covent Garden Opera Company sang "Carmen" at Windsor in 1892. "So unspoilt was dear Grandmama," wrote Missy of this occasion, "that her joy and interest was almost childlike. Of all the audience in the stately hall, no one was more pleasurably excited than the great little old lady." She had never seen the opera before, and followed its plot with growing consternation. It was not, after all, the sort of story which often reached her ears. Towards the end of the second act she gave voice to her agitation. "My dear child," she whispered to Missy, "I am afraid she is not really very nice!" In 1898 she saw Gounod's *Romeo and Juliet* and described the music as "heavenly". She enjoyed it so much, that she insisted on meeting the entire Company, and it was two o'clock by the time she got to bed. Amongst several other musical "treats", Melba sang for her, and young Henry Wood conducted the Good Friday music from *Parsifal*. "I knew Richard Wagner quite well," she told him afterwards, and went on to say that as she was now too old to travel to Bayreuth, she hoped he would come again and play some more *Parsifal*.

The Court spent part of its leisure time in the early eighteen-nineties rehearsing plays of its own. The Queen was fortunate to possess in Alick Yorke, who joined her Household in 1884, an outstandingly talented actor and producer. Some people thought him a trifle too flamboyant, as he wore an enormous carnation in his buttonhole, and covered himself with jewelled rings and scent, but the Queen was extremely fond of her Court Jester, who kept her in "fits of laughter" with "killingly funny" songs. On one occasion, however, he fell from grace when a neighbour led him astray. The Queen overheard him laughing at dinner and asked him to tell her the joke. The company fell silent, and Alick was forced to repeat a rather improper story. When he came to the end of it, the Queen looked at him as if she had found a caterpillar in her salad, and told him icily, "We are not amused". It was not that she minded herself, but she thought it her duty to shield her Maids of Honour. The Kaiser loved to tell a story which showed that his grandmother was not so strait-laced as people seemed to imagine. It arose from the sinking of HMS *Eurydice* with three hundred cadets on board: not in itself a promising subject for laughter. Somehow the ship was raised and towed for repair into Portsmouth. The Queen, stunned by the tragedy, summoned the Superintendent of the Dockyard, Admiral Foley, to report to her at Osborne. The Admiral, a weather-beaten old sea-dog, had grown deaf in Her Majesty's service. During luncheon, he told her rather more than she wanted to know about the recovery of the stricken ship, and eventually she decided to change the subject by asking after his sister. Nobody knows what he thought she said, but he clearly misheard her question. "Well Ma'am," he yelled in resonant tones, his mind still fixed on salvage, "I am going to have her turned over and take a good look at her bottom and have it well scraped." The effect of his answer was such that the footmen took refuge behind a screen to try to regain their composure, and H.M. "put down her knife and fork, hid her face in her handkerchief, and shook and heaved with laughter until the tears rolled down her face."

The Queen so loved watching rehearsals that she almost knew the plays by heart by the time they were performed. Had the prompter fallen ill, a replacement was always at hand. It was not unknown for her to rewrite plays to meet her own requirements, and she even took it upon herself to expurgate Tennyson's *Becket* to rid it of "coarse" language. In 1889, Bigge wrote to tell Ponsonby, who was away on leave, that Her Majesty had "extracted the maximum amount of fun and interest out of the fortnight's preparation" of *L'Homme Blasé*. During one rehearsal, she told Bigge that she could not permit him to address Princess Beatrice as "a degraded woman", whatever the script might require. Some of the younger members of the royal family were not best pleased to be dragged to Osborne merely in order to see some "tiresome theatricals". Eddy, for instance, thought it "quite extraordinary" that the Queen should take such a naïve delight in amateur productions. "There!" she would say triumphantly, as the drama reached its dénouement, "You didn't expect *that* did you?" In the heat of the moment she was rather inclined to provide a running commentary to ensure that nobody missed the finer points of the play. Once Princess Beatrice became so exasperated by her mother's incessant chatter, that she ordered her to stop talking. "I will be good!" said the Queen meekly, hiding her face in her hands. "I will be good!" Occasionally, she even took part in a musical evening herself. One night after dinner, she sang a duet from "Patience" with Alick Yorke. After a couple of verses, she suddenly broke off to tell him, "You know, Mr Yorke, I was taught singing by Mendelssohn". Sometimes she still played the piano, in spite of her rheumatism, but was tempted to give it up when one of her granddaughters rather ineptly asked: "How can *you* practise now, and what for?"

Few people faced old age and its infirmities as intrepidly as the Queen. Towards the end of her reign she was so crippled by rheumatism that she could only walk with the help of a stick, or leaning on somebody's arm. Eventually, she was forced to resort to being wheeled about in a chair. When Vicky saw her at Osborne in 1893 it broke her heart to find her "showing traces of age" and hardly able to walk at all. In common with most of the rest of the population she assumed that she was immortal. But "lame and infirm" as the

Queen might be, she made wonderfully light of it all, and "her mind and spirits" remained "as bright as ever". Unfortunately, she had to contend with an even graver problem. As early as 1872 she began to have trouble with small print, and was forced "to read with 'specs'". At the back of her mind there was always the fear that she might become blind like her grandfather, George III. By 1893 she could hardly read at all. Neither drops of Belladonna nor gigantic print dispelled the closing mist. In 1896 she apologised to Princess Victoria of Battenberg for taking so long to reply to her letter, explaining that she had been ordered to cut down her correspondence and spare her eyes. "Pray write with as black ink as you can," she begged Lord Salisbury, in the hope that she still might be able to read what he wrote. In the end, she was forced to depend on others for help. Apart from Princess Beatrice, she turned to Harriet Phipps, who began her career in 1862 as a Maid of Honour, and ended by being an "assistant private secretary". By 1895 there was a serious danger of her losing control of things which demanded the supervision of the Sovereign. Had she lived much longer, her blindness could well have precipitated a constitutional crisis.

In 1881, the Queen decided that the time had come to appoint a resident doctor, and her choice fell upon James Reid, a gifted young man of thirty-two. Naturally, his medical qualifications were impeccable, and he came with the further recommendation of being an "honest straight-forward Scotchman". From the first, he became a favourite with the Household, whom he handled with tact and humour. Both Bigge and Ponsonby found him excellent company, and the Queen was quick to recognise that he could always be trusted to say what he thought and not what she wished to hear. Soon she began to consult him on every subject, and no other courtier enjoyed such privileged access. When Sir William Jenner retired in 1889, Reid took his place as Her Majesty's chief physician. Six years later, she knighted him with a claymore in the drawing-room at Balmoral. As he rose from his knees when the ceremony was over, she told him she had never realised before that his "hair was so nearly gone!"

Shortly after her Diamond Jubilee in 1897, the Queen was mortified to learn that Sir James had "snapped up" one of her Maids of Honour under her "*very nose*". The young lady concerned was Susan Baring, one of Lord Revelstoke's daughters and a niece of Lady Ponsonby. The Queen believed that the husband did not exist who was able to keep a secret from his wife, and she set her face against marriages in her Household. "It is too tiresome," she said, in break-ing the news to Vicky, "and I can't conceal my annoyance." For several weeks she saw Sir James at least four or five times a day, but never once referred to his engagement. When she finally relented it was only to send him a rather ungracious note. "Before leaving Osborne," she wrote in the third person, "the Queen is anxious to express to Sir James Reid her sincere good wishes for his happiness in his intended marriage with Miss Susan Baring." She went on to say that she could not deny that "their position" was likely to cause "many difficulties". Reid hastened to assure her that "neither his marriage nor anything else" would "make the slightest difference" in the way he discharged his duties to Her Majesty. It was long believed that he finally placated her by promising never to marry again.

The image of Queen Victoria as a benign old lady, hunched in the back of a carriage, is so powerfully stamped on the public mind as to drive out other impressions. But many who knew her best maintained that her voice was what they remembered most about her. In 1895 she made a recording for the Emperor of Abyssinia, who expressed his surprise that Her Majesty spoke so firmly and distinctly although she was nearly eighty. Unfortunately, the British Minister at Addis Ababa was required to destroy the cylinder once he had played its message. Lady Paget, who encountered the Queen in Florence, never forgot the bell-like precision with which she ordered the coachman to drive to "the Ponte Vecchio". Most elusive of all was her wonderful smile, which no photographer ever seemed able to catch. Lady Ponsonby thought it provided the key to her character. There was hardly a nuance of feeling it could not express, from a gentle reproof to a shared sorrow. Her hair might grow white and her eyes dim, but her smile and her laugh remained young.

Soon after her Golden Jubilee in 1887, the Queen began to employ a number of Indians at Court, who combined an uncanny gift for hovering in the background, with always being close at hand when-ever needed. She was so delighted with them that she told Sir Henry Ponsonby that they proved Lord Dufferin's claim that Indians made wonderful servants. After a couple of months she singled two out for special duties: Abdul Karim, a slim, good-looking young man, and Mahomet Buksh, who was plump and cheerful. Abdul, she said, was "most handy in helping" and learned with "*extraordinary assiduity*", while Mahomet was wonderfully "quick and intelligent" and seemed to understand "everything". There can be little doubt that much of the spice of the late Victorian Court derived from the Indian contingent. Indeed it was hardly possible to escape the exotic fragrance of curry and onions wafting from their apartments.

Abdul Karim somehow persuaded the Queen that his father was a Surgeon-General in the army, and that he himself was a clerk, or "Munshi". In August 1888 she noted in her journal: "Am making arrangements to appoint Abdul a Munshi, as I think it was a mistake to bring him over as a servant to wait at table. . . . I particularly want to retain his services as he helps me in studying Hindustani, which interests me very much, and he is very intelligent and useful". When she first told Hélène Varesco (Missy's Lady-in-Waiting) that she was learning a new language, she begged her not to laugh, and advised her to follow her principle of always living "as if we were immortal". The Munshi's duties including looking after the Queen's despatch boxes, helping her deal with her Indian correspondence, and keeping her briefed on eastern religions and customs. She once told Lord Salisbury that she had more Mohammedan subjects than the Sultan, a statistic presumably gleaned from her new adviser. By 1892 his name began to appear in the Court Circular as "The Munshi Hafiz Abdul Karim, Her Majesty's Indian Secretary", and two years later he became a Companion of the Order of the Indian Empire. Like John Brown before him, he was given furnished cottages at Osborne, Balmoral and Windsor, and like John Brown grew far too big for his boots. In 1895, Lord Wolseley, who had just been appointed Commander-in-Chief in place of the Duke of Cambridge, was summoned to Balmoral, and was somewhat surprised to be met at Ballater Station by a common or garden "fly" instead of a royal carriage. Some days later, while walking with Colonel Bigge in the Castle grounds, he was forced to stand in a pile of snow to allow a landau to pass, in which he caught a fleeting glimpse of the Munshi. "One must have been in India," Wolseley later wrote to his wife, "to realise the position of a man who is thus provided with a carriage, while the Field-Marshal, at the Head of the Queen's Army, drives in a Fly."

It is something of a mystery that so shrewd a judge of character as the Queen could believe that Abdul Karim was a "refined and gentle young man". Not even his fellow countrymen had a good word to say for him. To some extent he aroused her maternal instincts, and she could not help feeling responsible for him. Soon after she first set eyes on him at Balmoral, she gave him a "warm tweed dress and trousers", made in "the Indian fashion", to prevent him from catching cold in that bracing climate. The favours and privileges thenceforth showered upon him helped to make him insufferable. Behind his bland and smiling features lurked a furtive scoundrel, for ever making mischief. The disdain with which he chose to treat his inferiors was barely more despicable than the umbrage he took when he thought himself ill-used. In 1894, when the Queen insisted on taking him to Florence, he refused to allow his fellow Indians to share his railway compartment, and immediately on arrival deprived her maids of their bathroom. On the other hand, he never ceased complaining about imaginary slights. Such was his effrontery that he saw fit to protest that the Viceroy of India had failed to acknowledge a Christmas card he had sent him. Glamorous as he might seem in the royal presence, he lived in appalling squalor, and the inside of "Karim" Cottage resembled the slums of Calcutta. Reid always maintained that when he was summoned to visit the Munshi's "wife", a different tongue was put out each time he called. So promiscuous were his tastes that only an endless stream of "aunts" and "nephews" could satisfy his appetite. In 1897, the Queen was greatly distressed to learn that he had contracted gonorrhoea, but as he could do no wrong decided to overlook it.

It is hardly surprising that members of the Household resented the Queen's attempts to thrust the Munshi upon them. Ponsonby, to whom everyone appealed, confessed to his wife "These injuns (sic) are too much for me". The Queen became so obsessed by Abdul's ruffled feelings that she refused to make any attempt to understand the hostility he provoked, except to put everything down to racial hatred. It was absolutely *"outrageous"*, she told Sir Henry, to try to pretend that the Munshi was some sort of outcast. His "father saw good and honourable service as a doctor and he feels cut to the heart at being thus spoken of". Anyway, what would it matter if it was true? "She had known 2 Archbishops who were the sons respectively of a Butcher and a Grocer", and "Sir D. Stewart and Lord Mountstephen both ran about barefoot as children." It so happened that Fritz Ponsonby, Sir Henry's second son, was just about to return from India to join the Royal Household, and she therefore asked him to visit the Munshi's father to investigate his credentials. When Fritz announced that he had found the old man working as an apothecary in a gaol, the Queen maintained that he must have made a mistake and talked to the wrong person. It was not a propitious start to his long career as a courtier.

Most of the royal family were as eager as the Household to thwart the Munshi's pretensions. The Prince of Wales made no secret of the fact that he did not trust him an inch. When the Munshi died in 1909, a remarkable document was found amongst his papers in Queen Victoria's handwriting. It was headed: "Extracts from the Prince of Wales's letters to the Queen in answer to hers". The first, dated September 29th 1899, read: "I shall always be ready to notice and speak to the Munshi when I meet him." The second, dated October 2nd, authorised the Queen to assure him "that I have no ill will against him and only trust that matters should go smoothly and quietly". The Duke of Connaught shared his brother's sentiments, but was too much in awe of his mother to protest. During the Braemar Games in 1890 the Duke sent for Ponsonby and complained that the Munshi was mingling with the gentry. Sir Henry replied that "Abdul stood where he was by the Queen's order", and that if it was wrong, as he "did not understand Indian Etiquette and H.R.H. did, would it not be better for him to mention it to the Queen". Discretion being the better part of valour, the Duke decided to let the matter rest.

In 1894 it became evident to the authorities that confidential information was leaking out in India. The two prime suspects were Abdul Karim, and his friend, Rafiuddin Ahmed, who was known to intrigue with subversive organisations. The Government took the threat so seriously that in 1895 Lord George Hamilton, the Secretary of State for India, persuaded the Queen that it would no longer be possible for him to send her secret despatches if she showed them to the Munshi. But nothing he said could convince her that she was harbouring a spy, and she never ceased to pester Lord Salisbury to find employment for Ahmed.

Sir James Reid was one of the few people who dared to tackle the Queen on sensitive issues, and in 1897, while she was wintering at Nice, was brave enough to tell her that there was "a very general belief" that she was "entirely under the influence of the Munshi". It was high time, he said, for her to consider her own reputation, and not just Abdul's feelings, and he went on to warn her that there were people in high places, who knew Her Majesty well, who thought she was "mad on this point". Furthermore, he felt bound to tell her that Sir Edward Bradford, the Commissioner of the Metropolitan

Police, possessed incontestable proof of the Munshi's subversive intrigues. At first, the Queen "caved in", and said that she knew "she had played the fool about the Munshi", but later took up the cudgels once more and worked herself into a frenzy. In the last resort, she tried to resolve her dilemma by closing her eyes to unpalatable truths.

Shortly after the Diamond Jubilee, when the Queen was at Balmoral, the *Daily Graphic* published a photograph of her which caused a storm of derision. It showed her working at a table, while the Munshi towered above her, surveying the scene with a supercilious smile, as if to proclaim "I am the King of the Castle". The caption beneath it read: "The Queen's life in the Highlands. Her Majesty receives a lesson in Hindustani from the Munshi Hafiz Abdul Karim, C.I.E." She was "terribly annoyed and upset" by the "whole stupid business", and not best pleased to learn that the Munshi was responsible for the photograph appearing. The episode proved the last straw for Reid, and his health succumbed to the strain. Blind as the Queen might be to the faults of others, she was quick to acknowledge her own, and immediately sent Sir James an endearing note. "I must write a line," she began, "to say how distressed I am at your getting unwell (as I well know) from the worry I caused you the last few months and especially the last week which might *all* have been prevented but for my senselessness and want of thought." She might so easily have sheltered behind the regal formula: "The Queen writes to say . . ." but she chose to admit her fault in the first person. It was one thing, of course, to see what was wrong, and another to mend her ways. In 1899 she was back to her old tricks and nearly provoked a Household revolt by expecting the Munshi to eat with them. Harriet Phipps was given the unenviable task of having to remonstrate with her. During the course of a heated exchange, the Queen became so incensed that she brushed everything off the top of her desk with an angry sweep of her hand.

Long experience taught the Queen that the quickest way to undermine her authority was to be seen to give in to clamour. The more she came under pressure, the more she felt bound to resist. She was also incredibly loyal to those who served her. The Munshi was only the last of a long line, from Lehzen to John Brown, for whom she was eager to take up arms against a sea of troubles. She saw him as the victim of oppression, not as the pampered upstart she had made him. In fact, the fervour with which she fought his cause served to increase the aversion in which he was held. In 1890, she even crossed swords with the Viceroy to ensure the Munshi a privileged seat at the Durbar; and in 1897, she made him a C.V.O. and gave him a prominent place in the Jubilee procession. Some people thought that she was frightened of him and that he bullied her into rewarding him. "I quite dread seeing him," she once admitted to Reid, "for I fear more trouble and mischief." Nevertheless, had she really felt intimidated, there was nothing to stop her packing him off to India. The truth seems to be, as Salisbury pointed out, that she rather relished their brawls, "being the only form of excitement she can have".

It is clear that the Queen saw the battles she fought for the Munshi as part of her lifelong campaign against racial prejudice. She believed that discrimination was not only "reprehensible", but "never intended by the law of nature". In 1898 she wrote to ask Lord Salisbury to warn Curzon, her last Viceroy of India, "not to be guided by the *snobbish* and vulgar overbearing and offensive behaviour of many of our civil and political agents". Curzon replied that Her Majesty's "wise injunctions" would "furnish his Rule of Conduct", and agreed that the English were insular and arrogant. Few people did more than Queen Victoria to champion the rights of "lesser breeds without the law". She supported "Clemency" Canning after the Mutiny, she insisted that harsh, crushing policies disgraced a Christian nation, and she never wearied of pleading the cause of outcasts and untouchables.

Princess Beatrice once told Lord Rosebery that her mother had always yearned to visit India, but feared that she could not face the climate. It was some consolation, however, to surround herself with souvenirs of her Empire, such as Abdul Karim, and the Durbar Room at Osborne. This wondrous edifice, built by Bhai Ram Singh in the Saracenic style, was filled with exotic trophies from the Orient. It would be difficult to conceive of a more incongruous appendage to Albert's Italian villa.

Before 1890, most of the Queen's visits abroad were to Germany, but once William became its Kaiser she found it more restful to look elsewhere for her holidays. Wherever she went, whether to a villa or hotel, she turned it into a replica of Windsor, keeping the same hours, and surrounding herself with familiar faces. She even insisted on taking her own bed and desk, and a van load of family portraits. Naturally, she needed a special train to transport the hundred or so people who accompanied her abroad. Sometimes its progress was so leisurely as to disrupt the entire railway network through which it passed.

In 1888, 1893, and 1894, the Queen visited Florence, a favourite haunt of the English. On the first two occasions she stayed at the Villa Palmieri, the setting of Boccaccio's "Decameron". The natives of the city, who had long grown accustomed to English eccentricity, were nevertheless dumbfounded by the royal retinue of Highlanders and Indians. Like all good tourists, the Queen inspected the Churches of San Marco and Santa Croce, and spent several hours being wheeled round the Uffizi. Her "holidays" were more of a change than a rest. In the first place, she was a tireless sightseer and occupied her leisure with gruelling expeditions, and in the second place she could never escape her relentless pile of despatch boxes. Most of her mornings, and often much of her evenings, were necessarily devoted to studying state papers, and keeping up with her mountainous correspondence. Not a day passed without a Queen's Messenger bringing her a fresh supply of homework. On her last visit to Italy, one such messenger arrived so late at night that there was no one to answer the bell. Rather than sleep in the garden, he tapped on a ground floor window in the hope of attracting attention: a plan which proved an overwhelming success. At first there was no response, but then suddenly he was seized by a swarm of half-dressed footmen who dragged him into the house. By a singular stroke of misfortune he had chosen to wake his Sovereign.

In 1889, the Queen decided to spend the spring in Biarritz, where the Comte de la Rochefoucauld lent her a stately villa. All went splendidly until it came to her notice that the Comtesse had been involved in a most unsavoury divorce, which meant that she could not possibly be "received". The Comte besieged Ponsonby with a battery of arguments, pointing out that his wife was not a British subject, and therefore her conduct need not concern H.M. He even suggested that traditional morality did not apply to a family such as his. But nothing he said was of any avail. Apart from this little awkwardness, the Queen enjoyed her visit. The country reminded her of the Isle of Wight – probably the only time the resemblance has ever been noticed – and she claimed that nothing could exceed the extraordinary kindness and civility of "the French high and low". Wherever she went, the Basques shouted "Viva la Reina", just like the denizens of East Cowes.

During her stay at Biarritz, the Queen crossed the frontier into Spain to meet the Queen Regent, Maria Christina, who three years before had borne a posthumous son to her husband, Alfonso XII. On crossing the border at Irun, the "Countess of Balmoral" dispensed with her incognito and admitted to being the Queen of England. No reigning British Sovereign had ever before set foot on Spanish soil. On arriving at the railway station at San Sebastian, H.M. embraced Maria Christina, kissing her on both cheeks. They then drove together through the streets of the town, drawn by a team of black horses which reminded the Queen of paintings by Velásquez. Their attempts to converse in German were drowned by cheering crowds, military bands, and exploding squibs. The two Queens lunched alone, and then returned to the principal Plaza of San Sebastian for a reception by the Municipality. Before they left, they were given a "quite undrinkable" cup of tea in deference to English usage.

Later the same year, the Queen returned to Wales for the first time since 1832. The Gladstones proposed that she should stop off at Hawarden on the way, but were told that her time was so fully engaged that "she was reluctantly compelled" to decline their "kind invitation". Martin, who played a leading part in organising the tour, arranged for her to stay at Paté Hall, an Italianate villa set down in Merioneth, the property of the railway magnate, Sir Henry Robertson. The maids at the Hall were so terrified by the Indian servants imported to help them out, that the butler locked them up in a bathroom in order to keep the peace. The highlight of the tour was the Queen's visit to Sir Theodore and Lady Martin at Brynstysilio, a few miles from Llangollen. The day chosen, August 26th, was especially auspicious as it was the seventieth anniversary of the Prince Consort's birth. Sir Theodore proudly showed H.M. the table to which he had chained himself for almost quarter of a century writing the Prince's life. Before leaving for Balmoral, the Queen instructed Ponsonby to inform the Prince of Wales "how much this naturally *sensitive* and warm-hearted people *feel* the neglect" he had so long shown them, and that it was "very wrong of him not to come here". Seeing that she had last visited Ireland in 1861, and had barely set foot in the West Country for the past fifty years, it was probably wise to leave Sir Henry to pass on her rebuke.

In the spring of 1890, the Queen and Princess Beatrice paid their final visit to Aix-les-Bains. In addition to all her usual impedimenta, she brought her donkey "Jacquot", a wonderfully docile beast, who seemed to show no objection to her grandchildren pulling his tail. She had acquired him three years before from a peasant farmer whom she chanced to meet on the shores of the Lac du Bourget. M. Xavier Paoli, the French detective who escorted her on such outings, watched the bargain being sealed. "The animal was still young, but so thin, so very thin, and so ill groomed that he was very little to look at. The Queen stopped her carriage and beckoned to the fellow: 'Would you care to sell me your donkey?' she asked." Not knowing to whom he spoke, he grunted: "All depends." "How much did you pay for him?" "A hundred francs and he was cheap at the price." "Very well, I'll give you two hundred. Will you take it?" The deal was agreed, and the half starved animal was "duly washed, combed and groomed", and above all fed. Soon he was harnessed to a little trap in which he transported his mistress down narrow paths where no ordinary carriage could go. Like Cinderella, he was whisked overnight from a tumble-down barn to the lushest of royal pastures. The Queen loved him dearly as she did almost all animals. Whenever her carriage approached a steep gradient, the ghillie, who sat on the box beside the coachman, was obliged to climb down and walk to reduce the load. The phrase "Home James, and don't spare the horses!" played no part in her vocabulary.

In 1891 the Queen stayed at the Grand Hotel at Grasse. "I need hardly tell you," Marie Mallet wrote home to her mother, describing the journey from Cherbourg, that "the Queen was less tired than any of us" and "looked as fresh as a daisy". That Good Friday, the Mistral raged so furiously that the hotel shook, but H.M. insisted on taking a two-hour drive, in spite of the wind and dust. She enjoyed herself "as if she were 17 instead of 72", and returned from the expedition as "white as a miller". The views were enchanting, and the wild flowers so lovely that Miss Mallet wanted to stop and pick them in armfuls. There was only one cloud in an otherwise sunny sky: that disreputable old reprobate Duke Ernest of Saxe-Coburg was staying in the neighbourhood. As the grounds of the Grand Hotel were open to visitors, the Queen thankfully availed herself of Alice de Rothschild's garden. In order to open up one of its finest views, Alice decided to build a new road for Jacquot and his mistress, which she hoped would be a surprise. H.M. was far too observant not to see signs of the work being undertaken, and Lady Battersea had to warn her that she was not supposed to know about it until she was asked to open it. "It is a secret, a secret", she said, "with a smile and a twinkle", as she promised to join the intrigue.

Between 1895 and 1899, the Queen spent five successive springs in the neighbourhood of Nice. The first two years she stayed at the Grand Hotel, Cimiez, and the next three at the Hotel Excelsior Regina, from which she looked over the red tile roofs of the town to the Bay of Angels beyond. Lord Salisbury, who owned a villa not far down the road, described the Riviera as suffering from two drawbacks: "Flies in summer, royalties in winter". In the early eighteen-nineties the Empress Eugénie bought a house on the west slope of Cap Martin with grounds sweeping down to the sea. Naturally the Queen was eager to see it and in 1897 drove over to luncheon. Afterwards, she hobbled round the garden and gazed through the pine trees to Monaco. She never missed the annual "Battle of Flowers", and bombarded passing floats so vigorously that footmen had to be sent to scavenge for ammunition to replenish the royal arsenal. On the final day of her last visit to Nice, she noted in her journal how grieved she was to leave "this Paradise of nature" to which she grew more attached every time she came.

The Conservatives held power for ten of the last thirteen years of the Queen's life, and as she and Lord Salisbury saw eye to eye she ended her reign on a tranquil note. Throughout his time as Prime Minister he did everything in his power to spare her unnecessary trouble, and to resist what he saw as unreasonable claims on her time. "I will not have the Queen worried", he would tell importunate Ministers. Not only was she "a woman and must not be over-pressed", but "she was also the Queen and must not be dictated to". The reforms of his second Ministry were hardly such as to agitate Her Majesty, who was chiefly concerned with the turn of events in Ireland, where "The Plan of Campaign", designed to ensure fair rents, ended in murder and "moonlighting".

Towards the end of 1891, Gladstone began to prepare for the coming election. In a rousing speech at Newcastle he committed his party to a wide range of reforms, in the hope of attracting as many voters as possible. He offered Ireland Home Rule, Scotland and Wales disestablishment, and Trade Unions "Employers' Liability". The election took place in July 1892, and Gladstone returned to power for the fourth time. The Court Circular announced that the Queen had accepted Lord Salisbury's resignation "with great regret", which was certainly true but should never have been acknowledged. Privately she attributed his defeat to "abominable misrepresentations", and thought it lamentable that "one of the best and most useful governments" she had ever known should be forced out of office "merely on account of the number of votes". So much for the democratic principles of the Newcastle Programme!

There was, of course, no escaping the people's verdict, and the Queen was obliged to send for Gladstone. When he arrived at Osborne to kiss hands, she thought him "greatly altered and changed, not only much aged, walking rather bent, with a stick, but altogether; his face shrunk, deadly pale, with a weird look in his eyes, a feeble expression about the mouth, and the voice altered". During dinner, the Prime Minister sat next to Ponsonby's daughter, and the moment the ladies retired the Queen wanted to know what he had been talking about so elatedly. "Home Rule, Ma'am!" "I know!" she said ruefully, "He always will!" When Gladstone finally got to bed, he noticed two old sparring partners amongst the engravings looking down from the wall: Archbishop Tait and Lord Beaconsfield.

The moment it became clear that the Liberals had won the election, the Queen told Ponsonby to let Gladstone know that she would "insist" upon Rosebery becoming Foreign Secretary. However unsound his politics might be, he was, at least, an Imperialist. There was no denying, however, that she had been "dreadfully disappointed and shocked" by one of his recent speeches at Edinburgh, in which he had launched a ferocious attack on Lord Salisbury, and committed himself to views which were "almost communistic". The trouble was, she said, that Lady Rosebery was no longer there "to keep him back". Sir Henry was not only instructed to tell the Prime Minister that Lord Rosebery was "necessary to quiet the alarm of the foreign powers who are beginning to intrigue right and left against us", but to warn him that he would find "the Queen very determined and firm on *all* that *concerns* the *honour, dignity and safety* of the *vast Empire* confided to her care and which she wishes to hand down unimpaired to her children and their children's children". Earlier, she suggested that "Sir H., who knows all these people well", could make it clear to them that she would "*resist any* attempts to abandon our obligations towards Egypt and any truckling to France or Russia". She might be compelled to accept a change of Government, but she did not intend to endorse a reversal of policy.

Gladstone, for once, agreed with the Queen and offered Lord Rosebery his former post, but the problem was to persuade him to accept it. His ambitions, he said, were buried with his wife. In fact, he also resented the way in which Gladstone confided in Morley. Fortune had smiled so favourably upon him that he was apt to behave like a spoilt child. As Cory remarked in one of his Eton reports, he wanted "the palm without the dust". No sooner did Rosebery learn of the Liberal victory than he set off on a cruise of the west coast of Scotland. It looked as if he might prove as temperamental as a prima donna refusing to go on stage. The Queen, recognising that she "could not personally *communicate* with Lord Rosebery", proposed that the Prince of Wales might act as an intermediary. It was the first time she had trusted him with such an important role. Naturally, he was only too eager to help, and wrote as an old friend to implore him to take office. I know, he said, how much the Queen "wishes for it", and he begged him for her sake to join the Government. Gladstone finally resolved the problem by telling Rosebery that he proposed to submit his name to the Queen that very day "in conformity with her wish". Like some hesitant swimmer dreading to take the plunge, he was pushed into the water to help him make up his mind.

Early in January 1893 the Government revealed its legislative plan for Home Rule. Initially Gladstone spoke of a bill "for the better Government of Ireland", but the Queen refused to allow such words to be used in the Speech from the Throne. No one could fail to admire the relentless zeal with which he confronted a stormy House of Commons. Young Winston Churchill watched him from the Strangers' Gallery, looking "like a great white eagle at once fierce and splendid". Eventually, the Bill was passed with a majority of thirty-four. A week later, it was rejected in the Lords by four hundred and nineteen votes to forty-one. Gladstone, still spoiling for a fight, wanted to make a final appeal to the Country, but his colleagues described the idea as "absolutely insane".

For some time Gladstone had been thinking of retiring because he was growing increasingly deaf and his sight was beginning to fail. His final decision to do so was precipitated in 1894 by a row over naval estimates. Lord Spencer, the First Lord of the Admiralty, responding to Germany's rapidly growing Fleet, insisted he needed more money for the Navy. Gladstone, however, refused to acknowledge the danger. The dead he said were with him, and the Admirals were "Mad! Mad! Mad!" From the first, Lord Rosebery, in common with most of the Cabinet, took the side of the Admiralty. When he told the Queen that the authority of the Foreign Office would be bound to suffer if the Navy was starved of funds, he was preaching to the converted.

Gladstone held his final Cabinet on March 1st 1894, and went to Windsor the following day to hand in his resignation. Not one syllable of thanks did he receive for his lifetime of public service. It is true that the Queen expressed her gratitude for his help in a trivial matter relating to Coburg, but the most she could otherwise bring herself to say was that she trusted he would enjoy some "peace and quiet" after "so many years of arduous labour". "This," he said bitterly, "is the only record that will remain of fifty-one years as a Privy Councillor." The Queen's heartlessness haunted his dreams, and he felt that he had been treated as if she were settling a long-standing bill.

The last time the Queen and Gladstone met was at Cimiez in March, 1897. He thought her "decidedly kind", and she even shook hands with him, a privilege "rare with men". They exchanged a few words about the Grand Hotel, but otherwise she spent most of the time talking to Mrs Gladstone. When he died the following year, the Queen sent her a telegram in the course of which she said: "I shall ever gratefully remember his devotion and zeal in all that concerned my personal welfare and that of my family". Even this grudging tribute had taxed her ingenuity. The funeral took place at Westminster Abbey on May 28th 1898. Strangely enough Lady Geraldine Somerset had foreseen that when "Heaven in its mercy delivered us from the curse of Gladstone's existence", the Prince of Wales would rush up from Sandringham "with ten special trains and twenty extra engines" to pay honour to his memory. In fact, he went further, as he, and his son, Prince George, insisted on acting as pallbearers. The Queen was so incensed that she telegraphed to enquire what advice he had sought and what precedent he had followed. The Prince's reply was unusually curt. He had sought no advice and knew of no precedent. There was but one Gladstone.

Sometimes during his lifetime Gladstone spoke in "unmeasured" terms of his treatment by the Queen. What made him particularly bitter was the way she ignored his loyalty to the Crown. In 1889, for example, he supported Lord Salisbury's plan to increase the Royal Family's grants, much to the fury of his radical supporters. Yet not one word of thanks did he get from Windsor. But in spite of his private anguish, he was anxious the public should never know of his squabbles with the Queen, as the last thing he wanted to do was to injure the Monarchy. It was his "strong desire", he instructed his executors, that they should "be most careful to keep in the background all information respecting the personal relations of the Queen and myself during these later years down to 1894, when they died a kind of natural death". It was only after the Queen's Letters were published, in which the vendetta was given a new lease of life, that his sons decided to put the record straight by releasing the relevant papers.

In 1896, the Queen told Lord James of Hereford, a Liberal renegade, that Gladstone "was very dangerous". Their differences, she said, were confined to matters of principle. Yet the fact remained that she thought Lord Rosebery "almost communistic" and, nevertheless, regarded him as a friend. "What I most dislike about President Kruger," she once told Cosmo Lang, "is the way he brings his politics into religion and his religion into his politics. I am bound to say that in Mr Gladstone also I disliked this mixture of politics and religion." On another occasion, she told Archbishop Benson that Gladstone refused to listen to what she said. "I have told him two or three facts of which he was quite ignorant" but to no effect. "He only says 'Is that so? Really?'" The Queen perhaps was unusually spoiled by the deference most people paid to her opinions, and hence found it hard to accept the off-hand way in which Gladstone brushed them aside. No woman – let alone a Sovereign – relishes being ignored. "I cannot think he was a 'great Englishman'", she told Vicky soon after his death. "He was a clever man, full of talent, but he never tried to keep up the honour and prestige of Great Britain. He gave away the Transvaal and he abandoned Gordon, he destroyed the Irish Church and tried to separate England from Ireland, and he set class against class. The harm he did cannot be easily undone."

It would hardly be fair to Gladstone's reputation to leave the last word to the Queen. No other statesman in the nineteenth century pursued ideals more fervently, or with such disregard for political calculation. His heroic cast of mind was matched by volcanic energy and awesome eloquence. In many respects there could hardly be a more exemplary liberal. No one could doubt his attachment to peace, his trust in the masses, or zeal in the cause of freedom. Yet in some ways he never entirely discarded his early conservative instincts. "I do not like changes for their own sake", he admitted in old age. "I have a great reverence for antiquity." Few things were more characteristic of him than the deference he felt for the institution of Monarchy, or the way in which, nevertheless, he handled his Sovereign.

One of the Queen's most momentous prerogatives was to choose a Prime Minister. Had Gladstone been consulted about his successor he would have suggested Lord Spencer. But, in fact, she invited Lord Rosebery to form a ministry. Rosebery pleaded with Ponsonby to persuade H.M. that he was "altogether unfitted for the post", and that "a liberal peer as Prime Minister is in a wholly false position". Next day, he told the Queen herself that he wished to avoid being committed to pledges he knew she would find distasteful. She at once wrote back to say that she was "sorry to hear that he apprehends any trouble which might alienate him from her", but she hardly thought "this possible or at any rate probable". She had no objection to Liberal measures which were not revolutionary, and she did not believe that Lord Rosebery would "destroy well-tried, valued and necessary institutions for the sole purpose of flattering useless Radicals . . .".

"I am very fond of Lord Rosebery," the Queen told Vicky, "he is so much attached to me personally." She looked on him as a wayward son in constant need of her guidance. Rosebery himself recalled her telling him "quite maternally" that he could always rely on her to offer him "good advice". Shortly after he became Prime Minister she warned him "*very* openly" that "he should take a more serious tone" in his speeches, and be rather less "jocular". Presumably she remembered Disraeli's dictum that "the British people being subject to fogs, require grave statesmen". She was not alone in thinking him too frivolous. Edward Hamilton noted in his diary: "His speeches have not been up to the mark. They have been a little too flippant, and made people think that, for a Prime Minister, he is not serious enough or sufficiently in earnest". Fritz Ponsonby thought that the secret of Rosebery's success with H.M. was that he "was always good company, and took the greatest pains to explain his policy". She even encouraged him to buy an estate near Balmoral, assuring him "we should so like to have you for a neighbour".

The first serious misunderstanding between the Queen and her new Prime Minister arose over the wording of the draft Speech from the Throne, which included proposals for disestablishing the Anglican Church in Scotland and Wales. "I was horrified," she wrote in her journal, "and sent for Sir H. Ponsonby, who was at once to write to Lord Rosebery and tell him that I could not sanction this being put into my Speech." Rosebery was dreadfully distressed, and explained that he had been under the impression "that all this was discussed and settled by the Queen and her late Prime Minister". After all, the policy had been plainly foreshadowed in the Newcastle Programme. In the end, a compromise was agreed and honour was satisfied, but the threat to the Church remained.

After only a few weeks in office, Rosebery warned the Queen that his problems might prove insuperable. The House of Lords was "almost unanimously opposed to his Ministry", and he "might as well be in the Tower of London" for all the good he could do there. Harcourt, who led the party in the Commons, was "bitterly hostile" to him, and "ostentatiously indifferent to the fate of the Government". He was pledged to policies the Queen was known to deplore, and all he could do was try to ensure that "the interests of Your Majesty's Empire are maintained abroad". Such was his feeling of despair that the moment the Ministry fell he was resolved "to extricate himself from politics for ever". The Queen replied that she fully realised "the extreme difficulty of his position", and that he had inherited a legacy of "dangerous and almost destructive measures" from his predecessor, but she nonetheless looked to him to "act as a check and a drag" upon hotheads amongst his colleagues.

Rosebery's toughest problem was to reform the House of Lords. The fact that only forty-one peers had voted for Home Rule was a measure of the problem. His first step was to try to persuade the Queen that some sort of change was essential. The 1884 Reform Bill, he argued in a trenchant memorandum, had inevitably accentuated the difference between the hereditary House of Lords and the representative House of Commons. Since 1886, when the majority of Liberal peers went over to the Tories, the Second Chamber had become a "permanent barrier" to progressive legislation. "When the Conservative Party is in power, there is practically no House of Lords. . . . But the moment a Liberal Government is formed, this harmless body assumes an active life, and its activity is entirely exercised in opposition to the Government." The Queen was prepared to agree that the House of Lords "might possibly be improved", but it was "*part* and *parcel* of the *much vaunted* and *admired British Consti-*

tution and CANNOT be *abolished"*. Moreover, she could not agree, to quote Lord Rosebery's phrase, that "the House of Lords does not represent anybody". On the contrary it represented "the opinion of those who have the greatest stake in the country: land, commerce, employers of labour, legal, church, and men of science". Above all, she begged him not "to excite the passions of the people . . . but rather to strive to restrain them".

The Government's policy was to promote bills which the Lords were bound to oppose, in order to win a mandate for reform. The Peers were obliging enough to rise to the bait, but the measures they chose to reject had little appeal for the public. Few Englishmen were wedded to Welsh Disestablishment, or wanted to see a local veto on drink. On October 10th, the Prime Minister warned the Queen that the Government intended to move a "Declaratory Resolution" in the House of Commons insisting that it was impossible for the elected representatives of the people to allow "their measures to be summarily mutilated and rejected by the House of Lords". This, he claimed, was the least that could be done when so many of his supporters were outright abolitionists. He deeply regretted being forced to reiterate opinions "with which he has too much reason to fear your Majesty does not agree", but nothing less would satisfy his party. The Queen at once telegraphed from Balmoral: "Your letter of yesterday caused me much concern. . . . Earnestly appeal to you to support me in preserving that which I am bound to uphold. Surely national interest should be considered before your party?"

On October 27th, Lord Rosebery addressed a public meeting at Bradford in which he denounced the House of Lords as "a permanent party organisation", and "a great national danger". He concluded his strictures with a challenging appeal: "We fling down the gauntlet. It is for you to back us up." After reading his speech, the Queen immediately wrote to protest that he had publicly announced the Government's intention to deal with "the greatest constitutional question which has arisen in England for two centuries", without obtaining her leave. "The fact of such an important declaration being made by the Prime Minister implies that it has the sanction of the Sovereign." The Queen next played her ace by suggesting that "the sense of the country should be taken" before people's passions were further excited.

Nothing the Queen could say convinced Lord Rosebery of the need to retain a permanent Tory veto on Liberal legislation. Nor could he accept her view that he should have obtained her consent before discussing his policy in public: a principle which would drag the Crown into every political dogfight. He told her that he would happily resign if he thought it would do any good, but since most of his Cabinet favoured a single legislature it would probably open the floodgates to revolution. The Queen agreed that the House of Lords would be safer with him than if left to his radical colleagues, but begged him "to bear in mind that fifty-seven years ago the Constitution was delivered to her keeping, and that, right or wrong, she had her views as to the fulfilment of that trust". When they met in December at Windsor, he assured her that the Resolution would prove "much ado about nothing", and that the Liberals stood little chance of surviving a general election. So hard was she to please that she later described his attempt to console her as unbecoming his office.

On October 25th, the Queen sent Lord Salisbury a letter marked "Very Private", in which she described the Government's Declaratory Resolution as "mischievous" and "disloyal". She then put three questions to him to help her to make up her mind on proroguing Parliament. First, would it be safe to allow the Liberal campaign more time to develop? Second, "Would it not be right to warn Lord Rosebery that she cannot let the Cabinet make such a proposal (the Declaratory Resolution) without ascertaining first whether the Country would be in favour of it?" Third, "Is the Unionist Party fit for dissolution *now*?" In effect, the Queen was consulting the Opposition about bringing down the Government. Lord Salisbury replied that no minister of the Crown was entitled to persist in proposals "unacceptable to Your Majesty". To do so would be to clothe them with a sanction "they did not really possess". The Queen, therefore, had every right to demand a dissolution. As for her last question, the Unionists were ready to fight an election and "likely to fare well". Later, however, he warned her that people might "be startled" if she directly intervened, and that he thought it probably best to let the matter drop.

The two major achievements of Rosebery's Government were the introduction of death duties and the appointment of Lord Wolseley as Commander-in-Chief. On May 4th 1895, the Duke of Cambridge wrote to the Queen to say that she was no doubt aware of "serious attacks being made in some of the newspapers on the authorities of the War Office and on myself in particular. . . . It is specially pointed out that my *age* (seventy-six) is much against me, and that if I don't retire voluntarily, I ought to be forced to do so by a vote of the House of Commons". Such sentiments were not confined to the Radical press, but shared by the Government and Campbell-Bannerman, the Secretary of State for War. Three days later the Queen had a long interview with her cousin, who expressed his "anxiety to do what is best for the Crown. . . . He was ready to resign but could not allow himself to be turned out, and his last words were 'I place myself in your hands'." Some days later he showed himself less conciliatory, having been buffeted round the compass by contradictory advice. When he next met the Queen he was firmly against resigning, although she did all in her power to persuade him to do so. She could not "have said more" she later told Colonel Bigge, "Without being rude". Finally, on May 19th, she was forced to write to him to say that she had "given much anxious thought" to his remaining Commander-in-Chief, and had "come to the conclusion, on the advice of her Ministers, that considerable changes in the distribution of duties among the officers constituting the Head Quarter Staff of my Army are desirable. The alterations cannot be effected without reconstituting the particular duties assigned to the Commander-in-Chief. . . . This necessary change will be as painful to me as it is to you, but I am sure it is best so." The Duke wrote back to say that he was surprised that it had been necessary to reach a decision so soon, "but of course I accept the inevitable, though I deeply regret it". He continued to raise so many difficulties that the Queen telegraphed to Bigge: "Think Duke wrong not to have retired some years ago, and that it is undignified to cling to office." Not until June 21st was Campbell-Bannerman able to tell the House of Commons that the Commander-in-Chief had sent in his resignation after thirty-nine years in office.

The Duke blamed the Queen for surrendering to her ministers and giving him "the sack". In truth, by turning a deaf ear to her endless hints and entreaties, he forced her to act brutally. At least, he could still depend upon Lady Geraldine Somerset, his mother's Lady-in-Waiting. "A little before seven," she wrote on June 24th, "came the Duke! He had tea. Much depressed and disgusted with the whole thing! . . . *All* had behaved so shamefully! Rosebery a regular cur! The worst of all the Queen! Who bowls him over altogether! Utterly selfish, without a particle of consideration for him! Who has so long and gallantly fought her battles for her." Lady Geraldine described

H.M. as sending the Duke away "like a footman in disgrace. . . . It does make my blood boil how abominably she behaves to him!" In fact, it is hard to see what more the Queen could have done to mitigate the blow. Not only did she appoint H.R.H. her "Personal Aide-de-Camp", but she formally thanked him for his great services. "Believe me that I feel deeply for you in this severance of a *tie* which existed so long between you and the Army. It is not, however, a *real* severance, for you are a Field Marshal and Colonel of many regiments".

On the very night that Campbell-Bannerman announced the Duke's resignation, the Government was defeated in a snap vote and decided to resign. Lord Rosebery told the Queen that it "was an immense relief to give up his office, and the unfortunate inheritance of Mr Gladstone". Next day, he wrote her a letter in which he declared that his only regret was the ending of their partnership. "May I then, once for all, and from the bottom of my heart, thank your Majesty for your abundant and gracious kindness to me? Whether in public or private life I shall always remember it with the deepest gratitude, and pray for the continuance of your Majesty's health and glorious reign." The Queen wrote back to say that his "very kind letter" had deeply touched her, and thanked him warmly for it. "I shall ever remember your personal kindness and sympathy on all occasions, and shall ever take the warmest interest in you and yours." Gladstone had only been given a "two-penny halfpenny" photograph, but Rosebery received a marble bust of the Queen "which I hope will recall me to your memory, and that you will not forget me". "There are two supreme pleasures in life," wrote the retiring Prime Minister. "One is ideal, the other real. The ideal is when a man receives the seals of Office from his Sovereign, the real pleasure comes when he hands them back."

Early in January 1895, after thirty-eight years in royal service, Sir Henry Ponsonby suffered a crippling stroke from which he eventually died. Reid, who spent half the night with him at Osborne Cottage, reported that "He was not absolutely unconscious; but his speech was affected, and his right arm and leg were paralysed". Davidson wrote to console the Queen, and said in the course of his letter that no Sovereign had "ever been more loyally, capably and diligently served than has your Majesty by Sir Henry Ponsonby". She, in her turn, offered Lady Ponsonby the use of Osborne Cottage as long as it was "*considered right* for dear Sir Henry to remain there.

I wish I could be of far more use, but you *know how* distressed I am at this sad and trying illness of your beloved Husband, and I would say much more when I see you, but I am afraid of upsetting you. But I *do* feel so deeply for you. May God help you and strengthen you to bless and relieve Sir Henry is the earnest prayer of your affectionate V.R.I." Ponsonby lingered on for almost a year, but it soon became clear he could never recover. When he died in November, the Queen told Mary how deeply she felt the loss of one "who was so universally beloved", and "always so kind and fair and just that I miss him terribly – his memory will ever be gratefully remembered by me and mine. It is a comfort to have one of his sons (Fritz) with me, to keep up a tie with you and your children."

Randall Davidson, who liked and admired Ponsonby, nonetheless thought he failed to stand up to the Queen. His dilemma, however, was virtually insoluble. When he opposed her too vigorously she simply refused to listen, and when he handled her too gingerly she ignored the force of his protests. She was particularly caustic about his friendship with Gladstone, but was quick to exploit it whenever it suited her book. "Sir Henry should speak very strongly to the Government," she once instructed him, "and *ought* to be *able* to do so the *more* for belonging to that side." She never fully grasped the value of his liberalism, but knew very well how fortunate she was to be served with such dedication. "The longer I live," wrote Bigge, "the more remarkable he seems to me to have been." He completely lacked "conceit, side, or pose". Nor did he ever complain of the crushing burden of work which eventually killed him.

Ponsonby was succeeded by his assistant, Arthur Bigge, who began life in a Northumberland parsonage, joined the Royal Artillery, and fought in the Zulu War. In 1879 the Empress Eugénie invited him to Scotland, as he was one of the Prince Imperial's closest friends. During his visit, he was presented to the Queen, who described him as "a charming person – of the very highest character, clever, amiable and agreeable as well as good looking." So taken was she with the young lieutenant that she made him Sir Henry's assistant. In 1880 he accompanied the Empress on her pilgrimage to Zululand to visit the spot where her son had met his end. Lord Stamfordham, as he became, died in harness in 1931, having served the Crown for over half a century. He could hardly have wished for a finer epitaph than that of George V: "He taught me how to be a King". Bigge was a born conservative with all the congenital caution of a courtier, which earned him the nickname "Better Not". His assistant, Fritz Ponsonby, was far more exuberant and provoked the Queen to tell him that he "should learn not to express views which no one wished to hear".

Between 1880 and 1901 the Queen's Prime Ministers had one thing in common: they were all old Etonians. When Salisbury returned to power in 1895 he was joined by a number of prominent Liberal Unionists. Chamberlain became Colonial Secretary, Lansdowne went to the War Office, Goschen took over the Admiralty, the Duke of Devonshire was appointed Lord President of the Council, and Sir Michael Hicks Beach returned to the Treasury. Salisbury himself undertook the double role of Prime Minister and Foreign Secretary, while Balfour once more led the party in the Commons. This exceptionally talented team was further strengthened by a great electoral victory during their first month in office, in which the Conservatives won a majority of one hundred and fifty-two over the Liberals and Irish Nationalists.

Lord Salisbury's belief that it was his "paramount duty" to maintain the Crown's prerogatives encouraged the Queen to trust him unreservedly. Moreover, they held the same views on virtually all policies, other than Church appointments. When Salisbury resigned in 1886 the Queen told him what a "comfort" it had been to have him as her Prime Minister, and now he was back in office most of her worries seemed over. Soon after her Diamond Jubilee he became her longest serving Prime Minister, and "every day", so she told him, "I feel the blessing of a strong Government in such safe hands as yours". Lady Milner, who was once invited to tea with the Queen and Lord Salisbury at Cimiez, said, "I never saw two people get on better. Their polished manners and deference to and esteem for each other were a delightful sight and one not readily forgotten". The Prime Minister was a fervent if unsentimental monarchist, who saw the Crown as a vital link holding the Empire together. His friendship with H.M. was one of "the warmest and closest" of his life. Discussing public affairs with her he said "was like talking to a man". Amused as he was by her foibles, he had enormous respect for her "unrivalled experience", "inflexible conscience", and "unflagging industry". At first the Queen suspected that Chamberlain might insist on the sort of Tory radicalism which Randolph Churchill had preached, but, in fact, he was too preoccupied with the Empire to devote much time to domestic reforms.

The one issue on which the Queen and Lord Salisbury fell out was ecclesiastical patronage, as became evident early on in his second Ministry. "It is a great pity," she told Randall Davidson in 1889, "that he should so lack liberality in his view of church appointments". When Salisbury referred to Boyd Carpenter as a "prominent Low Churchman", she got Ponsonby to tell him "Dr B. Carpenter is not Low, but is a Broad Churchman". Some years before she even corrected Gladstone on this point. Carpenter in his youth, she told him, had been an Evangelical, but for some time past had been "what would be termed broad, but which really is the only true enlightened, Christian and intellectual view of religion which exists".

In 1888, Salisbury proposed to offer the Bishopric of Oxford to Canon Liddon: the biographer of Pusey, and an erstwhile supporter of Gladstone's campaign denouncing Turkish atrocities. His well-known Tractarian sympathies and his bitter attacks on Disraeli were hardly qualifications to commend him to the Queen, who told Ponsonby in July that she was "greatly opposed to Canon Liddon being made a bishop, but Bishop of Oxford he must never be. He might ruin and taint all the young men as Pusey and others did before him . . .". The Dean of Windsor agreed that Liddon's sympathies were narrow, but maintained that it would hardly be possible to veto so eminent a champion "of what is undoubtedly a large party of the Church of England . . .". One way to resolve the dilemma would be for H.M. to insist that Lord Salisbury should enquire into Liddon's health. Ponsonby accordingly wrote to the Prime Minister to say that the Queen required him to assure her that the Canon was "in sufficiently vigorous health to enable him rightly to undertake the extremely heavy and harassing duties of the Bishopric of Oxford". Liddon, who suffered from a painful spinal disease, was the first to admit that the strain would prove too much for him. Salisbury's next choice was the historian Stubbs. The Queen, who approved of appointing learned men, especially strong Conservatives, made no further difficulties, but someone who spoke of Pusey as "the Master" was not her idea of a bishop.

It was generally accepted that the Queen's veto was decisive, but that she did not possess the power to insist on a nominee. Nevertheless, more often than not, she got her own way. In December 1889, Bishop Lightfoot of Durham died, and she pressed the claims of Westcott as his successor. Westcott began his career as a Fellow of Trinity, Cambridge, where he was Benson's and Lightfoot's tutor.

Then he spent eighteen years as a Master at Harrow before returning to Cambridge as Regius Professor of Divinity. Few English scholars rivalled his fame or influence on theology. Lord Salisbury, however, was strongly averse to appointing him, having got it into his head that he possessed "little personal influence". In fact, he could hardly have been more wrong as events were soon to show. Shortly before the New Year, Davidson dined with the Queen at Osborne. "She thinks Lord Salisbury not very wise in his nominations", he noted in his diary, "and means 'decidedly to take the matter largely into her own hands . . .'". The Dean, who had been a member of Westcott's House at Harrow, agreed that he was Lightfoot's obvious successor. But Salisbury remained adamant, and accused him of "socialist tendencies". On March 4th, 1890, the Queen summoned Salisbury to Buckingham Palace, intending "to prevail", and pressed her views so forcefully that he finally capitulated. Later that month, Davidson dined with H.M. and found her "greatly amused by Lord Salisbury's jubilation" at the public response to the choice. "He talks," she said, "as if he had done it, instead of having opposed it with all his might for weeks." In 1892, after Westcott's triumphant role in resolving the Durham Coal Strike, the Queen sent Davidson a letter from the Prime Minister in which "he took special credit to himself" for the wisdom of his appointment.

In the summer of 1890, the Queen suffered a rare defeat over the vacant See of Winchester, which she wanted given to Davidson. On August 20th, she wrote to Salisbury proposing that the Dean should go to Winchester, especially as Osborne came under its jurisdiction. He would, she admitted, be "a serious loss" to her, "but she would feel consoled if he were placed in a *post* of real usefulness". Lord Salisbury, however, maintained that if the Dean were suddenly advanced "to so high a dignity . . . it would generally be felt that excessive favour had been shown to him". Furthermore, he believed it was high time to appoint an Evangelical to avoid a possible rift in the Church. The Queen made two further appeals, and persuaded Benson to write on the Dean's behalf, but was forced in the end to accept that Thorold should go to Winchester, and Davidson to Rochester. It was not in her nature to hide her displeasure. "Did Lord Salisbury," she asked, "never receive the last letter she wrote to him on the subject?" The Archbishop had spoken to her "in the very strongest terms" on Davidson's behalf, and she "thinks he must also have written to Lord Salisbury. She is quite at a loss to know why he rejects such advice and the opinion of the First Dignitary of the Church. . . . It is painful to the Queen to say all this; but Lord Salisbury knows that she is always frank in all her dealings with him."

No sooner had Davidson accepted Salisbury's offer than he received a salutary lecture from Balmoral. "The Queen must honestly confess that she has never found people promoted to the Episcopate remain what they were before. She hopes and thinks that will not be the case with the Dean. . . . She cannot help mentioning this as it strikes her from experience." She expressed the further fear that his duties would threaten his health, and urged him to take all the exercise he could. "Her motherly heart," wrote Davidson, was "all taken up about fears that the strain of the work" would prove too much for his strength. When he finally took his departure, she noted in her journal: "I grudge him very much." The moment Lord Salisbury returned to power in 1895, Thorold died. This time the Queen got her way and Davidson went to Winchester.

During the Queen's autumn holiday at Balmoral in 1896, she received a telegram from Gladstone to say that Benson had suddenly died that morning while attending communion at Hawarden. "We are all most dreadfully shocked", she wrote later that day, "for he was such a dear, kind excellent man, and so charming." Recognising what a blow his death must have been to Mr and Mrs Gladstone, she telegraphed back: "Fear this sad event happening in your house must be a great shock to you. . . ." They were deeply touched by the Queen's "tender thought" for them. "What we feel so very especially is that Your Majesty, stunned with grief and the sense of personal loss, should have thought of *us*". On October 14th, Salisbury wrote to H.M. suggesting that Temple was Benson's obvious successor as "unquestionably the greatest man on the English Bench". If, as seemed probable, he thought himself too old, then his second choice would be Davidson. Temple, a disciple of Arnold, started his working career as a Fellow of Balliol, and then, like Tait, was appointed Head Master of Rugby. In 1860 he contributed a harmless piece to *Essays and Reviews* and discovered that those who supped with Jowett needed a long spoon. It took him twenty years to live down the accusation of heresy. In 1869, Gladstone appointed him Bishop of Exeter, and some sixteen years later Bishop of London. The Queen acknowledged that Temple was "very clever" and "very worthy", but she thought him too old for Canterbury:

presumably having omitted to calculate that he was three years younger than she was. Grudgingly she consented to his being offered the succession in the hope that he would decline it. "You will perhaps have guessed," she wrote to Davidson, "what I wished for the Primacy? It was *yourself*." When Temple died in 1902, Davidson succeeded him.

Since Rosebery inclined to the liberal school of Theology, the Queen, on the whole, approved of his Church appointments. Nevertheless, she agreed with Davidson that no recent Prime Minister had "made his political bias quite so prominent in his ecclesiastical nominations". When the Queen reproached him for being too partisan, he complained of victimisation. "The Queen wishes Lord R to know," wrote Bigge on her behalf, that she "never hesitated to criticise, and even when she thought it necessary to veto, submissions for Church preferment by Lord Salisbury, or any other Prime Minister."

In January 1895 Rosebery proposed to appoint Dr Percival to the vacant See of Hereford. Percival, the first Head Master of Clifton, subsequently became President of Trinity College, Oxford, and then Head Master of Rugby: a breeding-ground for Bishops. He was also the "*only* prominent clergyman in England" to favour Welsh Disestablishment. The Queen begged Davidson to suggest "*how* she could refuse Dr Percival, as she will on no account appoint a Disestablisher". Rosebery, while professing to understand her reservations, maintained that the Anglican Church in Wales was "very much what Gibraltar is to Spain, a foreign fortress placed on the territory of a jealous, proud and susceptible Nation . . .". In the end, Davidson felt bound to warn her that were she simply to say, "I will not have a man who is in favour of Welsh Disestablishment", she would, in effect, be demanding that "Bishops must be of one political party". She was therefore obliged to consent to Dr Percival, but not before making it clear that she thought it a great mistake to force a bishop on Hereford who was known to hold views unacceptable to the Diocese.

There were two respects in which the Queen's influence on patronage was unhelpful if not detrimental. First, she prevented some of the best men in the Church from holding high office merely because they showed Tractarian sympathies. Liddon, for instance, was the obvious choice for Oxford. Secondly, she was so terrified of clerical domination, that she tended to undervalue pastoral qualities: hence the perverse way in which she dismissed Champneys, one of the greatest slum pastors of her reign, as "an insignificant Low Churchman". But in other respects her influence proved salutary. Not only did she discourage patronage being used for political ends, but she constituted "a kind of jury of perfect integrity" whom ministers had to convince of the wisdom of their choice. Her mistakes were principally those of omission, and Victorian Bishops were justly renowned for holiness, learning and wisdom. It would be difficult to fault her judgement in pressing the claims of Westcott, Davidson, Lightfoot, and Tait.

As the Queen became older she grew more tolerant, even of Tractarians. In 1888 the Church Association decided to prosecute Bishop King of Lincoln for countenancing rituals which they claimed were against the law. They charged him, amongst other enormities, with adopting the "Eastward position" during communion, profanely lighting candles on the "altar", and making the sign of the cross during absolution. Throughout the proceedings, which took place in the Archbishop's Court, Benson depended on Davidson for advice. The Dean was strongly in favour of ceremonial latitude, but dared not speak out for fear of involving the Queen. During the Trial, Davidson found her "much exercised by the proceedings", and made it his business "to try to put the *good* side of High Churchmen before her". In February, 1889, he dined at Windsor where there was "much talk about the Lincoln Prosecution – the Queen objecting equally to the Bishop's doings and the prosecutors". In the end, the Archbishop decided in favour of King on the ground that the Church was sufficiently broad based to comprehend "catholic" traditions: just as Newman had argued in Tract Ninety.

For a short time during the eighteen-fifties, the Queen allowed fear of "papal aggression" to vitiate her judgement, but otherwise sought to defend religious minorities. When in 1887 she was handed a petition reproving her for thanking the Pope for his Jubilee message, she said that the signatories seemed to forget "how many thousand Catholic subjects" she had, "who cannot be ignored". Three years later, while staying at Aix-les-Bains, she received the Archbishop of Chambéry, whom she described in her journal as "a dignified, portly old man", wearing a "purple cloak and a red skull cap, a very fine cross hanging from a chain, and episcopal ring of a single amethyst surrounded with diamonds". In spite of her growing blindness, she retained her sharp eye. The Archbishop read her a "beautiful address" which greatly pleased and touched her. "I doubt," said Davidson, "whether any parallel could readily be found for an Address couched in these particular terms, emanating from a Roman Catholic dignitary, and addressed to a Protestant Sovereign." During her last visit to Ireland, she went out of her way to mix with her Catholic subjects. "I am their Queen," she said, "and I must look after them."

Britain's Foreign Policy during the last years of Queen Victoria's reign was dominated by growing fear of Germany. Early in 1888 news reached San Remo that William I was dying. On the morning of March 10th, as Fritz was strolling in the grounds of the Villa Zirio, he was handed a telegram from his son, addressed to "His Majesty, the Emperor". For some moments he was overcome by grief at his father's death, and the knowledge that all his hopes for the future were likely to come to nothing. When the new Kaiser met his Household in the Drawing-room there was little to show how short his reign was to be. Taking off his order of the Black Eagle, he made a reverent bow to Vicky and put it round her shoulders, having first thanked Mackenzie for having enabled him "to live long enough to recompense the valiant courage of my wife". For once she lost her composure and gave way to a flood of tears. "This time it was he who tried to encourage and soothe her, he who told her to hope, although he knew full well that there was no hope left either for him or her."

Fritz's first official act as Emperor was to send Queen Victoria a telegram. "At this moment of deep emotion," it read, "my feelings of devoted affection to you prompt me, on succeeding to the throne, to repeat to you my sincere and earnest desire for a close and lasting friendship between our two nations. Frederick." Clearly England had little to fear while Fritz was ruler of Germany. Before the day was out, Vicky scribbled a hurried note to her mother to say that the thought of "poor Fritz succeeding his father as a sick and stricken man is so hard!! How much good he might have done! Will time be given him? I pray that it may be and he may be spared to be a blessing to his people and to Europe". "My OWN dear *Empress Victoria*," the Queen wrote that very same evening, "May God bless you! You know how little I care for rank or titles – but I cannot *deny* that *after all* that has been done and said, I own I am *thankful* and *proud* that dear Fritz and you should have come to the Throne."

Knowing full well the risk he ran in returning to Berlin, Fritz nevertheless insisted on moving to Charlottenburg. The Imperial Train accordingly left San Remo on March 10th, in warm spring sunshine, only stopping at Leipzig for Bismarck to board it. The old man wanted to kneel to kiss his Master's hand, but Fritz refused to allow him to do so. Soon after eleven the following night, the royal party drove through the gates of Charlottenburg, which could hardly be seen for snow. Such exaggerated reports had preceded Fritz that there were murmurs of astonishment when he walked up the Palace stairs as if he was perfectly well. Like the loyal soldier he was, he intended to stay at his post while breath remained in his body, but he knew he had neither time nor strength to embark on liberal reforms. For thirty years he and Vicky had looked forward to his accession as "the sunrise of their day", but now all that seemed to remain was a "brief and tortured sunset". Bismarck's son, Herbert, spoke of the Emperor as an "encumbrance", and watched his demise with barely concealed satisfaction. Early in April, Professor Bergmann, who was clearly the worse for drink, replaced a cannula in Fritz's throat so clumsily that it produced a further abscess. Soon after William succeeded to the throne, he appointed Bergmann a Commander of the Hohenzollern Order. It is difficult to see what he had done to merit it, apart from shortening his patient's reign.

Vicky was well aware that Fritz was seen as a "passing shadow", and that most politicians preferred to pay court to her son. It was some consolation, however, to be left to decide for themselves what was best for Fritz's health. Moreover, as Queen Victoria pointed out, it was high time to remind William, "who was always speaking of the 'Emperor and Empress', who they are now!" Having made such play of his "Grandfather's orders", and professed such respect for the Head of the Family, he owed it to Fritz to show him similar deference. When he not only failed to do so, but could hardly contain his impatience to succeed, the Queen told Vicky "I have no words to express my indignation and astonishment. . . . This must not be allowed".

Fritz was naturally anxious to settle Moretta's future, particularly as the objections hitherto raised no longer seemed to apply. In 1886 Sandro had been kidnapped and then compelled to abdicate. Since then he had lived in Darmstadt, where, unknown to Vicky and Fritz, he had fallen in love with an operatic soprano. Queen Victoria, from whom no secrets were hidden, knew of the liaison through Sandro's brother, Prince Henry. While keeping the matter to herself, she ceased to encourage the marriage. When Bismarck discovered that the late Prince of Bulgaria had been invited to Berlin, he protested that such a visit would deeply offend the Tsar. Meanwhile, he let loose a virulent press campaign denouncing the match as a British intrigue intended to alienate Russia. "There was a terrible report and fuss in the papers," wrote the Queen on April 6th, "that Bismarck intended resigning, as Vicky and Fritz wanted to insist on young Vicky marrying Sandro".

Before the Queen returned home from her spring visit to Florence, she decided to visit the Emperor at Charlottenburg. Bismarck was convinced that she would bring the parson "in her travelling bag and the Bridegroom in her trunk". Lord Salisbury warned her that the Chancellor was "in one of his raging moods about the marriage", and that her visit would expose her "to great misconstruction and possibly to some disreputable demonstration". He also pointed out that there was considerable anxiety amongst highly placed officials "with respect to the meeting of Prince William with Your Majesty. It appears that his head is turned by his position", and that "if any thorny subject came up in conversation, the Prince might say something that could not reflect credit on him; and that, if he acted so as to draw any reproof from Your Majesty, he might take it ill, and a feeling would rankle in his mind which might hinder the good relations between the two nations". Unhappily, it was an inescapable fact that the Crown Prince's impulses, "however blameable or unreasonable", would henceforth be of "enormous political potency". The Queen reacted angrily to such pressure. Nothing, she said, would persuade her to postpone her purely private visit to her "dear suffering son-in-law".

In the spring of 1888, it was still assumed that the Queen supported the Battenberg match, so in March of that year she told Ponsonby to write to Sir Edward Malet, the British Ambassador in Berlin, making it clear that she was, in fact, opposed to it. Later the same month, she told Vicky that she understood her natural wish to settle Moretta's future, but begged her not to take any step without William's acquiescence. "You must reckon with him, as he is Crown Prince, and it would never do to contract a marriage which he did not agree to." She did not, however, see fit to mention that Sandro's affections had strayed.

Queen Victoria set out for Berlin on April 22nd, 1888, stopping at Innsbruck for a rapid luncheon with the Emperor Francis Joseph, who had travelled for seventeen hours for this brief encounter. Two days later her train drew into Charlottenburg station, where Vicky and all her children were waiting to greet her. On arriving at the Palace, she was shown her "charmingly arranged" rooms, which had once belonged to Frederick the Great but had never been lived in since. "After I had tidied myself up a bit," she wrote in her journal, "Vicky came and asked me to see dear Fritz. He was lying in bed, his dear face unaltered: and he raised up both his hands with pleasure at seeing me and gave me a nosegay. It was very touching and sad to see him thus in bed." Later that afternoon she drove down the Unter den Linden to visit the Dowager Empress, and was shaken to find her "quite crumpled up and deathly pale, really rather a ghastly sight". Only on rare occasions did Vicky contrive to see her mother alone. "Sat talking for some time in my room," wrote the Queen on the first day of her visit. "Vicky cried a good deal, poor dear. Besides her cruel anxiety about dear Fritz, she has so many worries and unpleasantnesses." Naturally, they discussed Moretta's future, and the Queen took the line that the engagement had dragged on so long that the time had come to "forget the whole business".

Shortly after twelve on April 25th, the Queen had "a most interesting conversation" with Prince Bismarck. Before being granted his audience, he was "nervous and ill at ease", and after it was over came out mopping his brow. Several times he asked Bigge "whereabouts in the room the Queen would be", and whether she "would be seated or standing". One reason for his evident agitation was that he thought he would have to thwart her plans for Moretta. The Queen asked him to sit down and was "agreeably surprised to find him so amiable and gentle". They spoke of the might of the German Army, their mutual desire for peace, and Fritz's tragic illness. "I appealed to Prince Bismarck," she noted, "to stand by poor Vicky, and he assured me he would." They both agreed that William was hopelessly inexperienced, having hardly travelled at all. They then turned to various "personal" matters, of which no record remains, but presumably she told him that she no longer wished for Moretta to marry Sandro. Bismarck was very much gratified when she asked to meet his wife, whom she later described as "an elderly, rather masculine, and not very *sympathique* lady". On leaving the royal presence he was heard to mutter: "That was a woman! One could do business with her!" But once she was back in England he spoke more condescendingly. "Grandmama," he said, "was a jolly little body", who "behaved quite sensibly at Charlottenburg".

Next day, after an early dinner, the Queen took leave of her son-in-law. She knew she would never see him again, but tried to avoid too final a note of farewell. She hoped, she said, as she gave him a parting kiss, to see him in England as soon as he was stronger. It was the nearest thing to a lie of which she was capable. Vicky accompanied her mother to the station and spent some moments with her in her carriage. "I kissed her again and again," wrote the Queen that night. "She struggled hard not to give way, but finally broke down, and it was terrible to see her standing there in tears, while the train slowly moved off, and to think of all she was suffering and might have to go through. My poor child, what would I not do to help her in her hard lot!" The visit was both a "great joy and a great comfort" to Vicky. "Your motherly kindness and affection," she wrote, "has done me good."

A month after the Queen's visit, Vicky's sailor son, Henry, was married to Princess Irene of Hesse, his first cousin. Fritz insisted on being present at the ceremony, which took place in the rococo chapel at Charlottenburg. He appeared in the full dress uniform of a Prussian General, wearing the blue ribbon of the Garter, and an order given him by his brother-in-law, the Grand Duke of Hesse. Pale and wasted as he was, he looked every inch a king. The sight of the dying man, struggling for breath while attempting to hide his infirmity, was pitiful to see. That evening he ran a high temperature. Old Field Marshal Moltke remarked after the service: "I have seen many brave men, but none as brave as the Emperor has shown himself today!"

Soon after the wedding, Vicky and Fritz decided to move to the Neue Palais. They made the journey by river, and as they steamed past the Isle of Peacocks they recalled how they had visited it by moonlight with Queen Victoria and Prince Albert. Towards the end of the voyage, Fritz decided to rename the Palace "Friedrichskron". So little did his successor respect his parents' wishes, that one of the first acts of his reign was to restore its former title. Early in June, Fritz began to have difficulty in swallowing and had to be fed through a tube. On the morning of June 14th his symptoms were so grave that a telegram was sent summoning the Crown Prince. When he and Dona arrived, they took "possession of the Palace", chose their apartments, and issued "orders left and right". That afternoon, Sir

Edward Malet called on Vicky. On returning to the Embassy, he telegraphed to Balmoral to say that the Emperor "desired to send his love to Her Majesty".

The morning of June 15th was fine and sunny. Fritz tried to write something but had not the strength to do so. "My one thought," wrote Vicky to her mother, "was to help him over the inevitable end, gently, softly, contentedly and quietly." She asked him if he was tired, and he whispered "Oh very, very". Just after eleven he took three deep breaths, and then "closed his eyes tight and convulsively as if something was hurting him". There was a moment of utter silence which marked the end of his ninety-nine day reign. Thus, in Mackenzie's words, "passed away the noblest specimen of humanity" it had ever been "my privilege to know". To Vicky it seemed as if a "noble ship" had sunk at sea "with all the Nation's hopes, its freedom, its progress and with its bright clear future!" Distracted as she was, she wrote at once to her mother: "On 14th December 1861, you found time and strength to write me a line in your overwhelming grief, and I, through agony, yet must send you a few words. . . . The wrench is too terrible – when two lives that are one are thus torn asunder. . . . I am his widow, no more his wife! How am I to bear it! You did, and I will too. Now all struggles are over! I must stumble on my way alone."

The moment the Queen learned of Fritz's death she dashed off a note to Vicky. "Darling, darling unhappy child," she wrote, "I clasp you in my arms and to a heart that bleeds, for this is a double and dreadful grief – a misfortune untold and to the world at large! You are far more sorely tried than me. I had not the agony of seeing another fill the place of my Angel husband. . . . May God help to support you as he did me and may your children be some help – some comfort – as so many of mine were." No sooner had she finished this letter than she telegraphed to William. "I am broken hearted. Help and do all you can for your poor dear mother and try to follow in your best, noblest, and kindest of father's footsteps. Grandmama. V.R.I." Seldom has good advice fallen on deafer ears.

Fritz's funeral took place on June 18th, the seventy-third anniversary of the Battle of Waterloo. It was one of the rare occasions when Alix agreed to set foot on German soil. The Prince of Wales told his mother that he had found his meeting with William and Dona "trying". He thought it best not to mention that the Court Chaplain, Adolf Stöcker, had laughed and joked throughout the service, and that Bismarck had claimed to have "too much work" to attend his master's obsequies.

From the summer of 1888 the future of Germany was in the hands of an impetuous young man who was "perilously intoxicated with the sense of his own power". The Prince of Wales might encourage Prince George to regard his uncle Fritz as "one of the finest and noblest characters ever known", but William was taught by his military friends to deplore his father's memory. In no other epoch of history would Fritz have been so denounced for his choice of an English Princess. It was his misfortune to come of age in an era of militant nationalism. He was born with qualities often lacking in rulers: unfailing honesty, instinctive compassion, and a horror of war. "If he had a fault he was too good for this world." Seldom was fate more cruel than in striking him down just when he came to the throne, almost as if to ensure that the peace of Europe would follow him to the grave.

In 1871, after three victorious wars, Bismarck assured the world that Germany was a "sated" power which intended to live in peace with its neighbours. For the next twenty years he proved as good as his word, but the moment that William II succeeded, the tiger began to snarl and show it was still hungry. It has often been said that the Kaiser's mind was warped because of his crippled arm. His magnificent uniforms, his theatrical display, his claim that he was the reincarnation of Frederick the Great, have been seen as attempts to compensate for his injury. Indeed, at times, his egotism was such as to border on insanity. He seriously regarded himself as the "All-Highest", and never forgave his English relations for failing to take him seriously. He loved to boast of "My" Navy, and "My" Army, and "My" Empire, and elicit applause by sabre-rattling speeches. Sarah Bernhardt described him as always being "on stage", and claimed that they got on so well because they were "both troupers". In 1914 he was relegated by his own High Command to being little more than a figure-head. "The supreme War Lord", for all his swagger, was a strangely vulnerable creature.

In the early years of his reign, the Kaiser constantly gave offence to most of his English relations, who deeply resented the way he treated his mother. So far from doing his best to try to console her, he added to her grief. "Just at this moment," she once complained to the Queen, "there is a big parade going on in front of my window." William "does do the oddest things, the element of show-off – noise and 'sensation', dramatic effects, etc. – is very preponderant and, in these serious times, seems to me very youthful. All the clanging bands – passing the windows of this empty house – the cannons firing salutes – so that I dread my windows being shivered – crowds hurrahing – all this is most painful to me! William is in his element and glory." Despite his ludicrous posturing, Vicky continued to love her wayward son. Indeed, he could hardly have hurt her so much had her feelings not been so strong. Nor was their relationship improved by her nagging sense of frustration. She had little to look forward to but a "diminished and crippled existence", and the role of a helpless spectator. She remembered Fritz once saying, "I must not die; what would become of Germany?" Unhappily, she lived long enough to see that question answered, although she was spared the final act of the tragedy.

Even a hundred years later, it is difficult to describe temperately the way the Kaiser behaved when his father died. Vicky succeeded better than most in remaining calm when his "first act as Ruler was to have our sanctuary, our quiet house of mourning, cordoned off by a regiment of Hussars". The "Neue Palais", as it now had to be called, was completely sealed off from the outside world, and Queen Victoria telegraphed to the British Embassy demanding to know what was happening. Fritz's writing-desk was twice ransacked in Vicky's presence in a search for secret documents. Later William himself arrived in full dress uniform to supervise the proceedings. While he strutted about complaining that his mother seemed bent on concealing state papers, she and her daughters sat numb and bewildered amidst the clamour and bustle. When the Queen heard of her grandson's grotesque behaviour, she said that she feared he was not quite right in the head.

Neither Vicky nor Fritz had wanted a post-mortem, but William insisted on holding one. "I was mad with sorrow, anger and agitation," his mother wrote to the Queen, "that they dared to touch his dear, sacred remains." Next followed a long and distressing dispute about Fritz's medical treatment. It began in July of 1888 with an official publication intended to show "that the sagacious, experienced and high-minded German Professors had always been right, and the ignorant, clumsy, and untrustworthy English doctors always wrong". It even accused Mackenzie of postponing an operation which it claimed would have saved the patient. The fact that this pamphlet was "authorised by William" was an outrage to Vicky's feelings. "He had no heart," she protested to her mother, "he cannot understand how insulting it is to have all the details which concern so harrowing and painful a thing as the illness of one's own dear husband, officially dragged before the Public in order to satisfy the spite and vanity" of Bergmann and Gerhardt. Three months later, Mackenzie replied by publishing *Frederick the Noble*. One hundred thousand copies of the book were sold in a matter of weeks, in spite of the fact that the German edition was banned. Even friendly reviewers described it as "injudicious", although few seemed aware of the vicious attacks to which its author responded. Mackenzie's real "offence" was that he helped Fritz to die with the least possible suffering. In 1889 Vicky told the Queen that William had publicly announced: "An English doctor killed my father, and an English doctor crippled my arm – and this we owe to my mother who would not have Germans about her".

During the controversy over *Frederick the Noble* the German press condemned Vicky almost as much as Mackenzie. She maintained that the purpose behind such attacks was to make the Kaiser believe that she and her friends were "a danger to the state". The Queen wanted Lord Salisbury to complain to Bismarck, but he preferred to ignore what newspapers chose to print. In the very first speech which William delivered to the Reichstag he promised to be guided by the example of his grandfather, but made no mention of Fritz. "The ruling party here", Vicky told her mother, are determined to "wipe out all trace" of the last reign. "Frederick III has been happily removed by Providence", and "the sooner he is forgotten the better". The Queen felt "too savage" to say all she felt on the subject, and merely remarked that her grandson's behaviour was "shameful and undignified".

Towards the end of 1888 the Queen decided that Vicky needed to get away from Germany, and invited her to spend the winter in England. Both the Prince of Wales and Lord Salisbury were agreed that the visit should be postponed for fear of offending William. The Queen, however, was adamant, and telegraphed to the Prime Minister to say that "it would be impossible, heartless, and cruel to stop my poor broken-hearted daughter from coming to her mother for peace, protection and comfort". She was astonished that everyone seemed frightened of the Emperor and the Bismarcks, "which is not the way to make them better. Tell the Prince of Wales this, and that his persecuted and calumniated sister has been for months looking forward to this time of quietness. Please let no one mention this again". The fact had to be accepted that her grandson was "a hothead" and that deferring to him only made matters worse. What was needed was someone to put him in his place, and she would "always be happy" to "set William right".

The Prince of Wales met his sister at Flushing and escorted her back to England. When the Royal Yacht tied up at Gravesend the Queen was waiting to greet her. Never before had she gone further than her own front door to meet the most illustrious of her guests. She was not, however, concerned to follow precedent, but to teach the Kaiser a lesson. On November 21st Vicky celebrated her forty-eighth birthday with most of her family at Windsor. Consoled by familiar surroundings and her mother's affection, she laughed for the first time since she lost her beloved Fritz. When she finally had to leave, the Queen accompanied her to Charing Cross Station. In spite of a biting February wind, they sat side by side in an open carriage and drove down the Mall through cheering crowds: a pleasant change from the surly welcome which greeted her in Berlin.

Few people were more willing than the Queen to criticise her children, or quicker to defend them if others usurped that privilege. It was therefore entirely consistent with her character that she took the part of her eldest son in his squabbles with the Kaiser. The Prince, who was almost the perfect uncle, told the Queen in 1878 that it would be "impossible to find two nicer boys than William and Henry". But soon he began to have second thoughts when he saw how his nephews behaved towards their parents. Such confidence as he still retained in William was finally shattered in 1885, when he learned through his sister-in-law, the Tsarina, that Willy was trying to poison her husband's mind against any attempt to improve his relations with Britain. In a number of secret letters, he tried to persuade the Tsar that the Prince of Wales, abetted by "my mother and the Queen of England", had repeatedly urged the German Emperor to launch a preventive strike against Russia. "But these English have accidentally forgotten that I exist. And I swear to you my dear cousin that anything I can do for You and Your country I will do." When William visited England two years later at the time of the Golden Jubilee, he complained that his uncle seemed anxious to avoid him.

In 1888, the Prince of Wales was disgusted by William's behaviour. Sometimes he found him more absurd than sinister, and spoke disdainfully of "my illustrious nephew". But he never forgave the heartless contempt with which he treated his mother. "His conduct towards you," he told her in November, "is simply revolting. But alas! he lacks the feelings and usages of a gentleman! Qualities which his ever to be regretted father and grandfather possessed to a high degree." It was some consolation, however, to know that "Master William" was "getting into a nice scrape with the press, and that the time may come quicker than he expects when he will be taught that neither Germany nor Prussia will stand an autocrat at the end of the 19th century". Alix was even more incensed than the Prince by the way in which William had "gone over to Bismarck and Co", and was trying to "crush" Vicky. Nevertheless, the Queen was resolved to try to make peace in the family, and the Prince reminded his sister that whatever the Kaiser might do, he remained "his father's eldest son, and your first born".

One of the most serious disputes between the Kaiser and his uncle took place within months of Fritz's death. In the autumn of 1888 the Emperor Francis Joseph invited the Prince of Wales to attend the Austrian army's annual manoeuvres. When H.R.H. heard that William would also be present, he wrote him a courteous letter, to which he received no reply, saying how pleased he was by the prospect of their meeting. Soon after his arrival in Vienna, he was astonished to be told that his presence in the city during the Kaiser's state visit was "unacceptable" to his nephew. Tactfully he decided that the wisest thing to do was to make himself scarce while the two Emperors met. Count Hatzfeldt, the German Ambassador in London, tried to explain to Lord Salisbury "the political reasons which made the presence of the Prince of Wales at Vienna 'inadvisable'". The gist of his argument was that it would irritate the Emperor of Russia, at a moment when matters were very delicate. He also passed on a complaint that the Prince had treated the Kaiser "as an uncle treats a nephew, instead of recognising that he was an Emperor". The Queen would have none of it, and told her Prime Minister that it was "simply absurd" to allege that the Tsar – "the Princess of Wales's own brother-in-law" – would have raised an objection to "uncle and nephew meeting". As for "the Prince's not treating his nephew as Emperor", it was "too *vulgar* and too absurd *to be believed. We have always been very intimate with our grandson and nephew, and to pretend that he is to be treated in private* as well as in public as 'His Imperial Majesty' is *perfect madness*. He has been treated just as we should have treated his beloved father and even grandfather, and as the Queen *herself* was always treated by her dear uncle King Leopold. *If* he has *such* notions, he had better *never* come *here*. The Queen will not swallow this affront!"

When Vicky first heard that William had snubbed his uncle, she told the Queen how "ashamed" and "indignant" she felt. "Any want of respect, or gratitude or courtesy to Bertie from a son of mine I resent most deeply, as he has been the very kindest of uncles to all my children. Here Bertie was blamed for having left Vienna in order not to see William, and to be purposely uncivil to him." Long before Dr Goebbels, the German press had learned to stand truth on its head. Lord Salisbury was anxious to patch up the quarrel, and begged the Prince to forgive his insolent nephew. In August 1889 Prince Christian was sent to Berlin to try to persuade the Kaiser to apologise. William, however, resorted to a lie and denied he had ever refused to meet the Prince. He was even brazen enough to insist that the whole affair was nothing more than a figment of "uncle Bertie's imagination". In the end the Queen was reluctantly forced to accept this worthless assurance to prevent a serious breakdown in Anglo-German relations.

The Queen, like her son, was deeply disturbed by the news coming out of Germany. "Had a touching letter from darling Vicky", she noted in her journal. "Her trials and troubles are dreadful." One of the things which "sickened" her most was "to see Willy, not two months after his beloved and noble father's death, going to banquets and reviews. It is very indecent and unfeeling". Vicky, too, was "inexpressibly" hurt to learn that William proposed to visit Russia in the very first month of his reign, "as if he could not wait to show himself, to go out, to be fêted, and to enjoy the outward honours of his position". "All I can say," wrote the Queen, who favoured at least a year of mourning, "is that he is very young and foolish" and "is not well surrounded". Vicky, of course, agreed, and further concurred in her mother's view that he ought to have visited England rather than Russia. "You are his Grandmother," she argued, and the longest reigning Sovereign. "My darling Fritz always used to say: 'First I will visit Mama and then all the others'."

Early in 1889 the question arose of the Kaiser visiting England, but the Queen at first was reluctant to invite him. "William must *not* come *this* year," she told the Prince of Wales. "*You* could not meet him, and I could *not*" after the way he behaved at Vienna. In the end, however, she was persuaded to relent, partly because Lord

Salisbury maintained that a visit was highly desirable, and partly because she had formally accepted her grandson's explanations. When the Kaiser received his belated invitation, he said he could hardly wait to revisit that "dear old home at Osborne". But what excited him even more was the Queen's decision to make him a British Admiral. "Fancy wearing the same uniform as St Vincent and Nelson," he wrote to Sir Edward Malet, "it is enough to make one quite giddy." On the afternoon of August 2nd, the Kaiser arrived off Spithead in the *Hohenzollern*, with an escort of twelve warships. Soon after landing, the Queen "received him at the door", and he kissed her "very affectionately on both cheeks". That evening, she noted, he was "very amiable", and looked most dashing in his admiral's uniform.

Most of the brunt of entertaining the Kaiser was borne by the Prince of Wales, who proposed his nephew for membership of the Royal Yacht Squadron. Even as early as 1889, the Kaiser began to dream of building a German Navy which might one day be able to challenge the British Fleet. When a great review was held for him in the Solent, he could not resist delivering a lecture on armaments and gunnery. *The Times* watched dubiously as the Imperial spy was shown official secrets. On August 8th the Queen took the salute at a march past, led by William himself. "The men," she noted, "march beautifully, though in that peculiar Prussian way, throwing up their legs." The visit was seen as a huge success, and William went out of his way to treat the Queen with deference. On returning home, he sent her a telegram from Wilhelmshaven which read: "The German Emperor to Queen Victoria. I reiterate from the depth of my heart the thanks for your unbounded love and kindness to me." "It gives me great pleasure," she telegraphed back, "to hear you liked your stay and were happy here. My prayers and good wishes for yourself and your Empire will always accompany you. V.R.I." William's bread-and-butter letter began rather ominously by declaring that he now felt able to take an interest in the British Navy "as if it were my own", and he spoke of the "keenest sympathy" with which he would henceforth watch "every phase of its further development. British Ironclads, coupled with mine and my army, are the strongest guarantees of peace." But if, unhappily, a war should ever break out, "then may the British fleet be seen forging ahead side by side with the German, and the 'Red Coat' marching to victory with the 'Pomeranian Grenadier'".

Two years later the Kaiser paid his first state visit to Britain. It began with his staying four days at Windsor, but most of his time was spent at Buckingham Palace, where the Prince of Wales was left to entertain him. When he was given the Freedom of the City at a ceremony in the Guildhall, he assured his audience that the principal aim of his policy was "the maintenance of peace". Moreover, he claimed, as far as it lay in his power, he intended to preserve "the historical friendship between our two nations". William returned in 1892, nominally to compete in the Cowes Regatta, but also to keep an eye on naval developments. This time he made the mistake of proposing himself, and was firmly told by the Queen that she had no room to house his enormous suite. However, she said, if he wished to stay on his yacht she would happily entertain him to luncheon or dinner. There were few things that she hated more than a threat to her routine, and she instructed Sir Edward Malet to let it be known "that these regular annual visits are not quite desirable". It would seem that Sir Edward failed in his delicate mission, as the Kaiser returned to Cowes every year until 1896. One thing which drew him back was his new-found passion for yachting. Throughout Regatta Week he could be seen taking the helm, hauling on sheets, and urging his crew to victory. In 1893 he had the supreme satisfaction of defeating *Britannia*, his uncle's pride and joy. There is nothing like sport for promoting ill-will, and when William began to behave like the "Boss of Cowes", the strain became intolerable, particularly as *Meteor I* and *Meteor II* outclassed their British rivals. On one occasion, members of the Royal Yacht Squadron were horrified to read a telegram from the German Emperor, pinned to their noticeboard, withdrawing his entry to a race on the ground that "your handicaps are appalling". The Prince of Wales was driven to despair and decided to give up racing. "The Regatta at Cowes," he explained, "was once a pleasant holiday for me, but, now that the Kaiser has taken command there, it is nothing but a nuisance." Part of his growing antipathy for his nephew was, no doubt, inspired by jealousy: conscious or unconscious. How could he not but resent the fact that the world hung breathlessly on William's lightest word, while nobody showed the least concern to find out what he thought?

Lord Salisbury encouraged the Kaiser's visits, partly because he believed that the Queen exerted a wholesome influence over him, and partly because he wanted to know what was going on in his mind. On the other hand, Eckardstein, the First Secretary of the

German Embassy in London, thought the Emperor's "perpetual visits" were "clumsy" and "injudicious". The Kaiser's visit to Cowes in 1894 was one of his most successful. The Queen described it as having "passed off very pleasantly", and was delighted to find her grandson so affectionate. On his return to Berlin, he told his "Beloved Grandmama" that his stay at Cowes "was enhanced by the dinners at dear old Osborne which I so adore, and which my *entourage* has come to love as much as I do; fascinated by the kind and benevolent accueil (welcome) of the much revered Queen. The 'Week' is my real holiday, and I must with all my heart thank you for the kind and warm reception which I met at your hands." He signed his ecstatic letter: "Ever your most devoted and dutiful Grandson, William".

Next year the Kaiser came back once more, but his visit proved such a disaster that he did not return until 1899. The day after the *Hohenzollern* dropped anchor in the Solent was the twenty-fifth anniversary of the Battle of Wörth (August 6th 1870), and William decided to celebrate the victory by making a speech on board the cruiser of that name which had escorted him to Cowes. In the course of his remarks he boasted that the defeat of France had proved that his army was invincible. There could hardly have been a worse occasion for such an aggressive harangue. Regatta Week was a time for bands to play excerpts from *HMS Pinafore*, for nibbling cucumber sandwiches on the lawn of the Royal Yacht Squadron, for flags gently fluttering in the breeze. Then suddenly, with all the delicacy of an inebriated drayman, the Kaiser destroyed this peaceful summer idyll with his reckless tirades, his menacing ironclads, and his brazen attempts to win every trophy in sight. The English press denounced the Emperor's speech in a manner to which he was not accustomed in Germany. Nothing, they said, could have been in worse taste than to make such offensive remarks while a guest in Great Britain. The Queen was just as angry as the newspapers, and deeply deplored her grandson's speech. The visit was further marred by the Kaiser referring to his uncle as "the old Peacock". When the *Hohenzollern* finally headed home there were sighs of relief at Osborne.

Anglo-German relations were not only affected by tensions within the family, but by conflicts of interest in various parts of the Empire. From the middle of the nineteenth century, the great imperial powers were lured into the heart of Africa in their search for raw materials and markets. Inevitably arguments arose over territorial claims and

rival spheres of interest. Although Britain's Empire had been growing steadily, "Imperialism" only caught the voter's fancy towards
the end of Queen Victoria's reign. Bernard Shaw spoke wryly of the
Englishman's "burning conviction that it is his moral and religious
duty to conquer those who possess the things he wants". Certainly,
at the time he wrote, Imperialism was a dangerously heady brew.

When Salisbury invited Chamberlain to join his Ministry in 1895,
he offered him virtually any post he wanted. Most people were
astonished when he chose the Colonial Office, which was generally
reckoned a dead-end job. But the fact was, that having "discovered"
the Empire, he intended to make it the Government's chief concern.
There were few politicians the Queen distrusted more. His overt
republicanism, and the "dangerous and offensive language" to which
he seemed addicted, had led her to see him as "Gladstone's evil
genius". But when he resigned in 1886, because he opposed Home
Rule, she changed her mind completely. Fritz Ponsonby believed
that she found him peculiarly intriguing because she regarded him
like "a wild man who had been tamed". When he stayed with her
at Windsor she thought him "very agreeable", and his American
wife "charming" and "very ladylike".

The earliest European settlements on the African continent were
mainly confined to the coast, but gradually missionaries and traders
began to penetrate inland. Such initiatives, however, owed nothing
to the Government. In so far as the map of Africa was painted red,
it was because of entrepreneurs like Sir George Goldie and the Royal
Niger Company, Sir William Mackinnon and the British East Africa
Company, and Cecil Rhodes and the British South Africa Company.
Bismarck, a hesitant convert to Colonisation, belatedly joined in
the "scramble for Africa" by establishing German Protectorates in
Tanganyika, the Cameroons, and South-West Africa. On the whole,
the Great Powers contrived to divide the spoils with surprisingly
little acrimony, but two areas threatened to spell trouble. The first
was Fashoda in the Upper Sudan, where Britain and France pursued
rival claims. The second was in the south, where Germany's plan
for a "Mittel Africa", stretching from the Atlantic to the shores of
the Indian Ocean, conflicted with Rhodes's idea of a Federal South
Africa under the British Crown.

In December 1895, Dr Jameson of the British South Africa
Company attempted to overthrow Kruger, then President of the
Transvaal. His raid proved a total disaster, and Chamberlain was

forced to apologise. The Kaiser, seizing a splendid chance to meddle, sent Kruger a telegram commending his "energetic action against armed bands which invaded your country as disturbers of the peace", and congratulating him on safeguarding "the independence of the country against attacks from the outside". When the message was despatched he remarked ruefully that it would put an end to his invitations to Cowes. He also intended to land a German force at Lourenço Marques and send it to Pretoria, but fortunately the Portuguese forbade it to disembark. Had it done so, according to Salisbury, "War would have been inevitable". As it was, the Kaiser's telegram provoked an explosion of anger. The Queen noted that the newspapers "were full of very strong articles against William, who sent a most unwarranted telegram to President Kruger, congratulating him, which is outrageous, and very unfriendly towards us". An article in the *Saturday Review* proclaimed "Germania delenda est", and the *Morning Post* prophesied that "the nation will never forget this telegram". The First Royal Dragoons, of which the Kaiser was honorary Colonel, were so incensed that they cut his portrait in pieces and threw them on the fire.

The Prince of Wales was every bit as indignant as the *Morning Post*, and appealed to the Queen to give William a "good snubbing". Knollys was instructed to write to Bigge to tell him that H.R.H. regarded "the German Emperor's message as a most gratuitous act of unfriendliness", which showed "the worst possible good taste and good feeling in congratulating the Boers on their victory over a body of men composed exclusively of the Queen's subjects". Moreover, what business did the Emperor have to send any message at all? "The South African Republic is not an independent state in the proper sense of the word, and it is under the Queen's suzerainty". The Queen neither sought nor needed advice about how to handle her grandson, and sent him a very discerning letter in which she told him that his telegram had caused her "much pain and astonishment", and that it had generally been seen as "very unfriendly" to England: "not that you intended it as such I am sure". Dr Jameson's raid had been "totally unwarranted, but considering the very peculiar position in which the Transvaal stands to Great Britain, I think it would have been far better to have said nothing". She hoped, she added, that he would take her "remarks in good part, and believe that they are entirely dictated by my desire for your good". Lord Salisbury described the letter as "entirely suited to the occasion", and gratefully acknowledged his debt to her for employing language no subject could use to a Sovereign. Home truths lose much of their pungency when delivered on bended knee.

The Kaiser's reply was a dextrous mixture of fantasy and falsehood. "Most beloved Grandmama," he wrote, "never was the telegram intended as a step against England or your Government." He had sent it with three ends in view: to preserve peace, to protect the lives and property of German nationals, and to show that he regarded rebels acting against the will of her "most gracious Majesty" as the "most execrable beings in the world". In short, his only ambition had been to stand up for "law, order, and obedience to a Sovereign whom I revere and adore". The Queen noted in her journal on January 10th that she had received a letter from William "in answer to mine, declaring he never intended to offend England, but the explanations are lame and illogical". The Queen sent the Prince of Wales the whole correspondence, with a covering note explaining why she had been conciliatory. It would not have done, she argued, "to have given William 'a good snub'. Those sharp, cutting answers and remarks only irritate and do harm, and in Sovereigns and Princes should be most carefully guarded against. William's faults come from impetuousness (as well as conceit); and calmness and firmness are the most powerful weapons in such cases." When the Kaiser asked her to close down *Punch* to stop its offensive attacks, she patiently explained that her prerogatives did not extend to silencing the press. For all that, she did, in fact, ask Sir Theodore Martin to let it be known in Fleet Street that she feared that the newspaper war was a serious threat to peace.

The Kaiser's abortive attempt to intervene in South Africa taught him a number of lessons, the most important of which was that Tirpitz was right to plan to expand the Navy. Imperialism would never prosper without a powerful fleet. Not only did his telegram to Kruger do permanent damage to Anglo-German relations, but it steeled the Boers to be even more intractable in dealing with English settlers. In so far as German support served to fortify their arrogance, it played a subsidiary part in provoking the Boer War.

"Today is the day on which I have reigned longer, by a day, than any English Sovereign," wrote the Queen on September 23rd 1896. There seemed no bound to her Empire nor end to her reign. Many of her subjects had virtually come to assume that she was part of the order of nature: sans peur et sans rapproche. Chamberlain was determined to make her Diamond Jubilee a celebration of Empire, and invited all the Prime Ministers of the self-governing dominions to share in the rejoicing. It was his ambition to produce a heroic pageant which would show that people of different races could join as a single family to pay homage to the Crown. Native levies from India and mounted riflemen from Australia would march through the capital with soldiers from Borneo, Cyprus, South Africa and Hong Kong. The Queen was a willing convert to Chamberlain's proposals, not only because she shared his imperial fervour, but because they gave her a perfect excuse for not inviting the Kaiser. She was adamant that no crowned heads should attend, most of all her grandson. "It would *not* do," she said with a finality which left no room for argument.

The sixtieth anniversary of the Queen's accession happened to fall on a Sunday, so it was decided to hold the public celebration on Tuesday, June 22nd. "How well I remember this day sixty years ago," she recorded on June 20th, "when I was called from my bed by dear Mama to receive the news of my accession." At eleven o'clock she and all her children attended "a short and touching service" at St George's Chapel, Windsor. It began with the hymn "Now thank we all our God", and later "Dear Albert's beautiful 'Te Deum' was sung". Services were held throughout the Kingdom at precisely the same time as that at Windsor, in oratories, churches, chapels and synagogues. Next day, she travelled by train to Paddington and drove with a Sovereign's Escort to Buckingham Palace. "The streets, the windows, the roofs of the houses, were one mass of beaming faces, and the cheers never ceased." So many telegrams kept pouring in that "it was quite impossible even to open them". That evening she dined in the Supper Room with her family. For once, she discarded black and wore a dress embroidered in gold and specially worked in India. During the meal she sat next to the Archduke Ferdinand of Austria, whose assassination at Sarajevo in 1914 plunged the world into war.

Next morning the Queen had breakfast with Vicky, Lenchen and Beatrice, by which time the head of the procession had already passed the Palace. At a quarter past eleven she set off in an open landau drawn by eight creams. Earlier, the sky had been overcast, but the moment she left Buckingham Palace the sun burst through the clouds and never ceased to shine. There could hardly have been a more impressive demonstration of "Queen's Weather". She was dressed in "black silk, trimmed with panels of grey satin veiled with black net and some black lace", and her bonnet "was trimmed with creamy white flowers and white aigrette". Round her neck she wore the "lovely diamond chain" given her by her younger children. Mrs Gladstone thought that the most "thrilling moment" of all was "the sound of the first gun, punctual to 11.15, signifying the Queen's start. The vast crowd seemed to vibrate with indescribable emotion, which found vent in cheers and then broke into 'God save the Queen'." It was said that the population of London had tripled for the day. Just before H.M. left the Palace, she "touched an electric button" which "started a message which was telegraphed throughout the whole Empire. It was the following: 'From my heart I thank my beloved people. May God bless them!'"

Princess Helena and the Princess of Wales accompanied the Queen in her landau because Vicky's "rank as Empress prevented her sitting with her back to the horses". "Dear Alix" looked "very pretty in lilac" and Lenchen achieved a certain portly grandeur. The Queen felt "a good deal agitated" in case anything went wrong, and had earlier written several letters to the Home Secretary about "overcrowding the roofs of the poorer classes of houses". She was haunted by the dreadful catastrophe near Moscow only the year before when hundreds of people were crushed while waiting to see the Tsar. Not much escaped her as she drove to St Paul's, although she told Randall Davidson that she had "been in a bad position" to see the procession. She was particularly intrigued by a little group of veterans who had fought with the Light Brigade at Balaclava. How dear Lord Beaconsfield would have relished the occasion, and how he would have laughed to see the immaculate Mr Chamberlain presiding over the revels! Lord Dundonald, who rode just behind H.M.'s carriage, kept shouting to his mare: "Steady, old lady! Whoa old girl!" It was some time before the Queen realised that he was not addressing her.

When plans for the Jubilee were first discussed, the Queen was greatly concerned by the length of the Thanksgiving Service, and even threatened to give it up if it could not be kept to twenty minutes. She was too lame to mount the Cathedral steps, but agreed to sit in her carriage while the service took place outside. "The scene in front of St Paul's was most impressive," Vicky told her daughter Sophie, "and when the bells pealed out from the dark old Cathedral, and the cheers rang out again, and the sun shone on all the glitter of the escort and carriages, it was as fine a sight as you could wish to see." The Queen's cousin, Augusta Cambridge, now Grand Duchess of Mecklenburg-Strelitz, was a good deal less impressed, and indignantly complained that nothing better could be found than "to thank God in the street". It would appear that she had forgotten where the Gospel was first preached. One of the earliest films ever made of a public occasion recorded part of the service. The Queen described it as "Very wonderful", but "a little hazy and too rapid". Her verdict was almost too charitable as the ceremony appeared to have been conducted in a snow storm, and the venerable participants moved hither and thither like leaves caught in a whirlwind. During his exile at Doorn, the Kaiser subjected his guests to this primitive documentary, and dwelt nostalgically on memories of his grandmother. The moment the royal carriages moved off from St Paul's, an eager chorister stuffed his pockets with some of the gravel on which the Queen's landau had rested. Archbishop Temple, a former Head Master of Rugby, accused the Bishop of London of "spoiling those boys".

On leaving St Paul's, the Queen crossed London Bridge and passed through some of the poorest districts of the East End of London. Everyone, as she expressed it, "seemed delighted to see their little old Queen". The procession crossed the river again over Westminster Bridge, and passed through the Horse Guards and down the Mall back to Buckingham Palace. The heat was so great during the last hour of the drive that she was obliged to shelter under a parasol, and poor Lord Howe fainted and fell off his horse with a terrifying clatter. So moved was the Queen by the warmth of her reception that tears ran down her cheeks. "How kind they are!" she kept saying again and again, as if she could hardly believe how much she was loved. No one, she later proclaimed, had ever "met with such an ovation as was given me, passing through those six miles of streets. The crowds were quite indescribable, and their enthusiasm truly marvellous and deeply touching. The cheering was quite deafening and every face seemed to be filled with real joy".

The ensuing fortnight was one of the busiest of the Queen's life. On June 23rd she received an Address from the Houses of Parliament and inspected a huge crowd of school children in Hyde Park. Five days later she held an enormous Jubilee Garden Party at Buckingham Palace, moving amongst her guests in a victoria drawn by two greys. She then took tea in an open tent and could be seen by her loyal subjects munching buttered toast. Irving, Ellen Terry, the Bancrofts,

Albani and Tosti all received invitations. On July 2nd, there was a military review in Windsor Great Park, and the Queen addressed her Sikh soldiers in halting Hindustani. Finally, on July 3rd, there was yet another Garden Party, especially for Members of Parliament. "Some of the Labour Members were presented", and were greatly gratified by the warmth of Her Majesty's welcome. Possibly the most bizarre of all the Jubilee celebrations took place in the French Republic, where the village children of Berneval were provided with a banquet of strawberries and cream, and a gigantic iced cake on which was written in letters of pink sugar: "Jubilee de la Reine Victoire". The benefactor to whom this feast was owed, was none other than Oscar Wilde, who only a couple of months before had languished in Reading Gaol.

When the last of the bunting had been packed away and the Jubilee was over, it was generally agreed that there had never ever been anything like it. Kipling was almost alone in sounding a note of warning.

> "Lo, all our pomp of yesterday,
>   Is one with Nineveh and Tyre!
> If drunk with sight of power, we loose
>   Wild tongues that have not thee in awe . . ."

Just how sound the poet's instincts were, was shown when the "glad, confident morning" of 1897 gave way to "Black Week".

After the fall of Khartoum and the subsequent British withdrawal, the country fell prey to anarchy. In 1896 Sir Herbert Kitchener was given command of an Anglo-Egyptian army with orders to crush the Dervishes. On September 2nd 1898 he virtually annihilated the followers of the Mahdi in a battle fought at Omdurman, where reckless courage proved no match for machine guns. Next day, the Union Jack fluttered over Khartoum, and a Memorial Service was held for Gordon on the steps where he was murdered.

No sooner had Kitchener established himself in Omdurman than he learned that a French expedition, led by Captain Marchand, had reached Fashoda, some five days' journey southwards. For many years, increasing rivalry in Africa between Great Britain and France had poisoned their relationship, and when Marchand battled his way to the banks of the Upper Nile a major crisis ensued. On September 7th, Kitchener told the Queen that he intended to set off down river with five gunboats and a hundred Cameron Highlanders in the hope of persuading the French to withdraw. As he approached Fashoda, he was met by a rowing boat, flying an enormous tricolour. Some minutes later, a black Sergeant scrambled aboard his steamer, and handed him a note from Captain Marchand informing him that Fashoda was a French Protectorate. Soon afterwards, the General met the Captain, and the two agreed to refer the dispute to the British and French Governments. Marchand's position could hardly have been more desperate. His eight Frenchmen and one hundred and twenty native troops were dangerously short of food and ammunition. Nevertheless, he steadfastly refused to haul down his flag without instructions from home.

The Queen followed the crisis with a mixture of emotions. On the one hand, she warmly supported her Government's claim to control the Upper Nile, if only by right of conquest. "We cannot give way," she telegraphed from Balmoral, when she thought she saw signs of weakening. But, on the other hand, she could well understand the reluctance of France to haul down its flag in response to Lord Salisbury's dictation, and she went so far as to warn him that she might refuse to consent to "a war for so miserable an object". Her most constructive suggestion was that everything possible should be done to help the French find a way "out of the foolish and horrible *impasse* they had got into". "We must try to save them from humiliation", she insisted, and help them to find an honourable escape. Eventually, M. Delcassé, the French Foreign Minister, who had long advocated better relations with England, announced his intention to evacuate Fashoda, on the ground that it served no useful military purpose now that the Dervishes had been crushed. In March, 1899 Britain and France signed a convention agreeing their territorial claims in Africa.

The problems in South Africa were not so easily resolved, and after fruitless discussions the Boers resorted to arms on October 12th, 1899. Before reinforcements arrived, the Afrikaners outnumbered the British by over three to one. They further possessed an intimate knowledge of the terrain and all the advantages of interior lines of communication. But instead of invading Cape Colony, they concentrated their resources on individual sieges, thus giving the British time to send more troops. In December, Sir Redvers Buller disembarked at Cape Town with a considerable army. Unfortunately, he was too rigid a traditionalist to adapt to the novel demands of war in South Africa. Before taking up his command he told the Queen that he did not think "there would be much hard fighting". Soon after landing, he divided his forces into three: part under General Gatacre to defend Cape Colony, part under Methuen to relieve Kimberley, and part, which he chose to command himself, to march on Ladysmith. None of these armies was adequate for the tasks demanded of them, and all were repulsed in the second week of December: the notorious "Black Week". When the Queen learned of this catalogue of disasters, she said that she hoped that the Government would now take her advice and "send out Lord Roberts and Lord Kitchener", as she had "urged them to do from the first". This, in fact, was precisely what they did, Roberts being given overall command, with Kitchener as his Chief of Staff. Nothing in Buller's career became him more than the magnanimity with which he accepted demotion.

The Queen followed the fighting in South Africa almost as closely as Lord Roberts, and felt sure in the end that all would "become right". According to Fritz Ponsonby, her mood was at first "bellicose", and she was all "in favour of teaching Kruger a sharp lesson", but later she tended to dwell on the "senseless waste of lives" which doing so entailed. She never took leave of departing troops without a lump in her throat, and she begged Lord Wolseley to do everything in his power for the horses sent out to the front. When the Chancellor of the Exchequer proposed a tax on beer to help to finance the war, she pointed out that the burden would fall on her poorest subjects. For the first time for forty years she remained at Windsor for Christmas. Never one to abandon those in adversity, she telegraphed New Year's greetings to Buller.

By January 1900 reinforcements were pouring into Cape Town. On the fifteenth Kimberley was retaken, and six weeks later Buller marched into Ladysmith. The Queen's "joy was unbounded", although it distressed her to learn that the garrison had been reduced to a diet of horse meat. At last, on May 19th, it became known that General Baden-Powell had been relieved at Mafeking and people went "mad with delight". The Queen at the time was visiting Wellington College, where her grandson, "Drino", had started his first term. As she drove down the "Long Walk", she passed under an arch on which was inscribed: "Welcome to the Queen of Mafeking". That evening, on returning to Windsor, she watched an excited crowd of Etonians singing and cheering with patriotic abandon. One especially observant youth noted her being handed a glass of whisky to sustain her through the evening. Five days later she celebrated her eighty-first birthday. "God," she wrote in her journal, had been very merciful to her, but her "trials and anxieties had been manifold." In July, Kruger fled to Europe, and some months later Britain annexed the Transvaal and Orange Free State. Believing the war was all but over, Lord Roberts returned home, and Lord Salisbury exploited the mood of jubilation to win the "Khaki Election". In fact, it took Kitchener another eighteen months to wear down Boer resistance.

Throughout the winter and spring of 1900 the Queen was indefatigable in reviewing troops, visiting the wounded, consoling widows, and encouraging the army in South Africa. No one could fault her devotion to duty, or fail to admire her battle against infirmity. If she dozed off for a few minutes after luncheon, she reproached herself for wasting valuable time. She never despaired of victory, but often broke down and cried over the long list of casualties. Most evenings, she knitted scarves and comforters for "her dear brave soldiers" almost "as if her bread depended on it". "I like to think," she would say, "I am doing something for them, although it is so little." The trouble was that "they *would* give them to the officers, not at all what I intended". In 1899 she sent her front-line troops a personal Christmas present of a hundred thousand tins of chocolate. The gift was so greatly prized that many preferred to preserve both the tin and its contents: some of which still survive after two world wars.

In February 1900 the Queen paid her last visit to the military hospital at Netley, and was distressed to find "so many with heart disease brought on by over marching and hard work". Marie Mallet was amazed by the way she stood up to this strenuous expedition, but the Queen explained that her "interest was so keen that she felt no fatigue whatever". On March 8th, she drove in state to Blackfriars to show how grateful she was to the City of London for the part it had played in the war. The crowds lining the route showed even greater enthusiasm than those at her Diamond Jubilee. Next day, she drove through West London, and was thrilled and touched by "the deep devotion and loyalty" of her people. Lord Rosebery wrote to tell her that he had seen her both times, "and my overpowering feeling was 'what a glorious privilege to be able to make millions so happy'". Those March days, he said, in which she appeared in the streets of her capital, were "the most remarkable" he had "ever passed in London".

By the summer of 1900 it was widely believed that the war was virtually over, but the Queen was one of the few who foresaw the risk of further fighting. On June 4th, she telegraphed to Lord Salisbury to warn him of the danger, in the light of her "former experiences". "The great fault," she said, "we always commit is withdrawing our troops too soon: then fresh troubles arise and more have to be sent. . . ."

In April 1900 one of Lord Roberts's confidential despatches to the War Office was published in the newspapers, in which he blamed Buller and others for what had gone wrong. Not long before, the Queen had urged Balfour to resist "unpatriotic and unjust criticism of our Generals". When she learned that Roberts's strictures had appeared in print, she told Lord Lansdowne that "the publication will only do harm, and lower the officers named in the estimation of their commands". Next day, she wrote to Lord Salisbury to express her "astonishment" and "concern" at the "publication *now* of the very secret and confidential despatch from Lord Roberts", which she saw as both "cruel and ungenerous" to Sir Redvers. "I must protest most strongly", she added, "against any such important steps having been taken without my knowledge and approval." Lord Salisbury wrote back to say that he quite agreed "in deprecating what had been done". All he could say was that Lansdowne had misunderstood the intentions of the Cabinet.

The Queen did not live to see the signing of peace, but she would certainly have endorsed the generous terms of the Treaty of Vereeniging. Britain's initial defeats destroyed the self-confidence of the eighteen-nineties. The rejoicing which marked the relief of Mafeking was a measure of the trauma of "Black Week". The triumphant age of Imperialism came to an end in the last years of the reign of the Queen Empress. Thereafter, repentant politicians, disarmed by feelings of guilt, seemed almost as anxious to haul down the flag as their forefathers had been to raise it.

In 1899 the Kaiser let it be known that he wanted to pay another visit to England. The Government eagerly welcomed the suggestion, hoping that it would demonstrate "that the alleged coalition in favour of the Boers had no real existence". The Kaiser, the Kaiserin, two of their sons, and Count Bülow, the Foreign Minister, landed at Portsmouth some six weeks after the outbreak of war in South Africa. Most Germans objected to the visit, which Dona tried to prevent on the ground that the British were "only out to make use

of us". It so happened that Lady Salisbury died on the day that
William arrived, so the Queen was left to handle her grandson without much help from the Government. On November 21st a banquet
was held in his honour. "When the guests had assembled," wrote
Bülow, describing the scene in St George's Hall, "the Queen
appeared, a little old woman, not of striking appearance, brought in
in a priceless litter by four Hindus. Alongside the litter walked the
Kaiser, showing every mark of deep respect for his grandmother.
. . . In these moments this woman ruler of a world empire reminded
me of some old soul in Hanover, Hamburg, or Holstein, as she
carefully prodded the potatoes on her plate to find the softest . . .".
He was not alone in discerning the bourgeois vein beneath the regal
crust.

In March 1900, the Government at Pretoria sought Germany's
help to bring the war to an end. The Kaiser immediately telegraphed to Windsor to ascertain Britain's reaction. The Queen
replied that she was "most grateful" for his "friendly interest"
and his refusal to act unless both sides consented. On the same
day, she sent a ciphered telegram to her ambassador in Berlin, Sir
Frank Lascelles. "Please convey to the Emperor," she said, "that
my whole nation is with me in a fixed determination to see this
war through without intervention. The time for, and the terms
of, peace must be left to our decision, and my country, which is
suffering from so heavy a sacrifice of precious lives, will resist all
interference." Knollys told Bigge that he thought this message
"worthy of Queen Elizabeth".

Several attempts were made during the last years of Queen Victoria's reign to establish an Anglo-German alliance. One of the first
was made by Bismarck in 1889, but met with little encouragement.
Later, Count Hatzfeldt, the German Ambassador in London, tried
to point out the risks of isolation, but Lord Salisbury remained convinced of the greater "danger of being dragged into wars which do
not concern us". The Queen was not so sure, and warned him that
the world was now "so different" that she could not "help feeling
our *isolation* is dangerous". By 1898 even Salisbury had come to
agree on the need for closer relations with Europe. During the
Kaiser's visit, Chamberlain told a meeting at Leicester that "no
farseeing Statesman could be content with Britain's permanent isolation on the continent. . . . The natural alliance is between ourselves
and the German Empire". Both religion, "interest and racial senti-

ment united the two peoples". That was precisely what the Prince Consort had argued half a century earlier.

It soon transpired that the principal problem of negotiating with Germany was the Kaiser's volatility. At one moment he spoke of his ardent love for England, at the next he conspired to stab her in the back. "I wish," wrote the Queen on his fortieth birthday, "he were more prudent and less impulsive." On one occasion, when he tried to exploit her Russophobia by telling her stories of lurid intrigues, she wrote to Nicholas II to warn him "that William takes every opportunity of impressing upon Sir F. Lascelles that Russia is doing all in her power to work against us. . . . I need not say that I do not believe a word of this. . . . But I am afraid that William may go and tell things against us to you, just as he does about you to us. If so, pray tell me openly and confidentially. It is so important that we should understand each other and that such mischievous and unstraightforward proceedings should be put a stop to". When the Kaiser urged the Tsar to invade India, it never struck him that such blatant treachery only increased the distrust in which he was held. When his plan misfired, he tried to persuade the Queen that she owed it to him that the Russian "plot" had been foiled.

Throughout the War, the French supported the Boers and attacked their British "oppressors". Not a day passed without some scurrilous abuse of the Queen in the Paris newspapers. She therefore abandoned her holiday on the Riviera and visited Ireland instead: partly to show her gratitude for the gallant way that the Irish had fought in South Africa. When the Kaiser heard the news, he wrote to tell her that "she had a wonderful gift of always doing the right thing at the right moment". Her critics, however, maintained that the gesture was somewhat belated as she had never set foot in the country since 1861. The Queen landed at Kingstown on April 4th, and drove in an open carriage to Dublin. The journey lasted two and a half hours and took her through some of the poorest parts of the city. Fritz Ponsonby, who had escorted her on numerous such occasions, claimed that he had never seen anything to approach the "frenzy" with which the Irish greeted her. For the next three weeks she stayed at Viceregal Lodge and carried out a strenuous round of engagements. When she took what was known as "carriage exercise", she often drove twenty miles on public roads, trusting her safety to a crown equerry and the loyalty of her subjects. Sometimes she fell asleep, and when

Ponsonby saw a crowd gathered ahead, he would dig his spurs in his horse in the hope that the clatter would rouse her.

On Primrose Day, April 19th, the Queen wrote to tell Lord Salisbury "how wonderfully kind, loyal and enthusiastic" the Irish people had shown themselves. "Such real affection," she said, amply repaid her "for the considerable but unavoidable fatigue" of appearing so often in public. She was not altogether to blame for being so slow to arrive at this conclusion. In 1897, at the time of her Diamond Jubilee, when congratulations poured in from Newfoundland to Pondicherry, not a squeak was heard from the City Fathers of Dublin. "Felt quite sorry that all was over", she wrote on returning to England. "I can never forget the really wild enthusiasm and affectionate loyalty displayed by all in Ireland, and shall ever retain a most grateful remembrance of this warm-hearted sympathetic people."

10

Grandmother of Europe
1887–1901

THE Queen's ascendancy over her family increased the older she grew. She was not accustomed, as Bismarck once remarked, to contradiction in settling its affairs. When her children spoke of her they did so with "bated breath". If at times she was meddlesome and dictatorial, she could also be wise and compassionate. "How can I live without her?" was Vicky's *cri de coeur* when she heard that her mother had died.

In 1898, after falling off her horse, Vicky was plagued by "lumbago". When she failed to improve, it became increasingly clear that she was suffering from cancer of the spine. For a time she kept her death sentence to herself, merely telling her daughter, Sophie, that she was "not quite well". In spite of increasing pain, she struggled to live a normal life, but in 1899 was obliged to tell her mother that her "stupid lumbago" prevented her from joining the family for her eightieth birthday. Gradually, as she grew worse, not even morphia could relieve her pain, and she went so far as to suggest that she would "feel intensely grateful" if somebody put her out of her misery. When she was finally forced to let William into her secret, he belatedly did what he could to make amends. Vicky survived her mother by six months, and when she died the disgraceful scenes at Friedrichskron in 1888 were re-enacted. Her house swarmed with soldiers and police searching for secret papers. In fact, they found nothing, as earlier that year, her godson, Frederick Ponsonby, had smuggled two trunks of her letters from under the Kaiser's nose: one labelled "Books" and the other "China with care".

Unlike William, Charlotte and Henry, Vicky's three youngest

daughters accepted their parents' ideals and did all they could to console their widowed mother. In 1890, a year after Sandro finally married his opera singer, Moretta became engaged to Prince Adolphus of Schaumburg-Lippe: not because she had fallen in love, but from fear of ending her days as an old maid. Earlier, the Queen had warned Vicky that it "would *never* do" to press Moretta "to marry for marrying's sake". In July, Adolphus was summoned to Windsor to see if he was suitable. The Queen was satisfied that he was "amiable" and "good looking", but recognised that her grand-daughter could not "feel the *same* as she did for Sandro. That was a *passion* and *1st* attachment. Still I think she will be happy and make a good wife. He is *very* fond of her." The marriage turned out to be childless, and Moretta never got over this bitter blow. If her life with Adolphus was not exactly wretched, it hardly put people in mind of Tristan and Isolde.

During the Jubilee celebrations in 1887, Sophie was introduced to Crown Prince Constantine, who was staying at Marlborough House. His father was Alix's brother, King George of the Hellenes; and his mother, Queen Olga, was one of the Tsar's half-sisters. While Fritz was being treated in Dr Mackenzie's clinic, Sophie and "Tino" were busy falling in love. The young man was only nineteen at the time, and few could resist his spell. Sophie was married in Athens in 1889 in the presence of half the crowned heads of Europe. In July 1890 she gave birth to a son, a future King of the Hellenes (George II). "Dear Grandmama," wrote Vicky, has "worked a little quilt in crochet" with "her own dear hands." The Queen longed for the latest news from Athens, and was heard to complain that "Sophie never writes to me". She was particularly anxious to find a British nanny to take charge of her new great-grandson. In so deciding, she was preaching to the converted. Sophie's children seldom spoke Greek at home, and the greatest event of their young lives was their annual visit to Eastbourne.

When Sophie was in Berlin for Moretta's wedding, she announced her conversion to the Greek Orthodox Church. Dona was horrified by the news and told her that William would never give his consent, and that she risked everlasting damnation. "Whether I go to Hell or not is my own affair," was Sophie's angry reply. As for William, he had "absolutely no religion. If he had, he would never have behaved as he did." The Kaiser immediately sent the Queen a lurid account of his sister's behaviour, hoping, no doubt, to forestall objections

17a Princesses Helena, Louise and Beatrice, at the Prince of Wales's Wedding. 1863

17b Major Elphinstone with Princes Arthur and Leopold. 1864

17c Prince Alfred and his bride. 1874

17d Fritz, Vicky and family. 1875

18a Arthur, Duke of Connaught, and his bride, Princess Louise Margaret of Prussia. 1878

18b The Queen with the Grand Duke of Hesse and his children. 1879
(Left to right) Princess Victoria, Prince Ernest Louis, Princess Irene, Princess Elizabeth and Princess Alix.

18c Prince William of Prussia and his fiancée. 1880

18d The Duke and Duchess of Albany with their daughter, Princess Alice, July 30th 1883

19a Unveiling of Prince Albert's Statue at Coburg. 1865

19b The Queen knights the Mayor of Wolverhampton. 1866

20a Lord Palmerston.
1844-5

20b W. E. Gladstone.
1859

20c Earl of Beaconsfield. 1881

20d The Marquis of Salisbury

21a Christmas at Windsor. 1850

21b Maclean attempts to shoot the
Queen. 1882

22a The Drawing room at Balmoral. 1875

22b Birthday party for Princess Helena. Balmoral. 1868

23a The Queen and John Brown.
[See 362]

23b The Queen presenting colours at Balmoral. 1898

Von Angeli's portrait of
Queen Victoria. 1875.
[See 335]

25a Aix-les-Bains. 10th April 1890
(Left to right) Princess Margaret of Connaught, Queen Victoria, Prince Henry of Battenberg, Princess Patricia of Connaught, Prince Arthur of Connaught, The Marquis of Lorne, Beatrice Princess Henry of Battenberg

25b The Queen at Grasse 1891

26 The Queen and the Dowager Empress Frederick. 1889

27a The Golden Jubilee. London, 1887

27b The Diamond Jubilee procession leaving Buckingham Palace. 1897

28a Princess Beatrice at the time of her
wedding. 23rd July 1885

28b The Queen at Windsor lunching with
Prince and Princess Henry of Battenberg and
their children. 1895
(*Left to right*) Prince Leopold, Prince Alexander and Princess
Victoria Eugenie.

29b The Queen Empress. 1876

29c The Queen and the Munshi. 1897.
[See page 505]

30a Princess Beatrice reading to the Queen.
1895

30b A rare photograph of the
Queen smiling. 1887(?)

31a The Queen's Funeral. Windsor,
2nd February 1901.

31b The Queen's coffin in the Albert Memorial Chapel, Windsor Castle,
1901

32a The Queen's Statue
outside Government
House Mauritius

32b Queen Victoria's Statue at Newcastle.

32c Unveiling of Queen Victoria's Statue outside Buckingham Palace. 1911

from Windsor. "Sophie," he wrote, "made an awful scene in which she behaved in a simply incredible manner," and had upset Dona so badly that she later gave birth to a premature son. If the baby dies, he said, "it is solely Sophie's fault and she has murdered it". The Queen was so disgusted by the hysterical tone of his letter that she decided the best thing to do was to leave it unanswered.

The Kaiser's next step was to disown his sister and banish her from Germany. "He seems," wrote Vicky, "to be copying Peter the Great, Frederick William I, Napoleon, or some such preposterous tyrant. To a free-born Briton, as I thank God I am, such ideas are simply abhorrent; and this my own son!" Sophie tried but failed to persuade him to change his mind. "Keeps to what he said in Berlin", she telegraphed to her mother. "Mad. Never mind." Vicky was torn between trying to console her daughter, and finding excuses for William. It was true, she said, that he had "no heart", but perhaps it was "not his fault, and therefore one ought not to be angry with him". Much of the trouble arose from his "silly vanity and pride of being 'Head of the Family'". Besides, in dealing with religion, it was far wiser to seek for "points of *union* and *similarity*" than those that "*separate* us from our Brothers in other Churches. 'In my Father's House are *many* Mansions' says the Bible. . . . Whether you lift up your soul to God in a Greek Church or a Latin or a Protestant one is the same to the one Spirit, whom all *try* to seek each in their different ways".

The Queen regarded the Kaiser's behaviour as that of a "tyrant and bully". "I need hardly tell you," she wrote to Queen Olga, that "as soon as I heard of the matter, I sent word to William that I could not blame Sophie, as I considered that where another person's conscience was concerned one must be tolerant." In her letters to Vicky she said that Dona was largely to blame as she loved to interfere. In the spring of 1891 Sophie was formally received into the Greek Orthodox Church, and later the same year defied the Kaiser by visiting her mother. Naturally, he was furious, but dared not protest for fear of displeasing the Queen. The dispute was finally put to rest in 1895 when the Crown Princess was invited to Kiel for the opening of the Canal: an event which threatened the peace of the world but ended the family quarrel.

In 1897 the family was once more divided when the Greeks provoked the Turks to attack them. The Kaiser supported the Sultan, as did Lord Salisbury; but Vicky, Bertie and Alix favoured King

George. Sophie kept begging her mother to appeal to the Queen for help, in spite of the fact that it was the policy of her Government to champion the Ottoman Empire. The very most she could do was "soften asperities and cool down angry spirits". Vicky, who described herself as living with "a padlock" on her mouth, told Sophie that William was "violently for 'order' and the 'right' as he considers it, which in his eyes is represented by the Sultan!" "My poor dear Mama," she added, "feels very sad and depressed that all this political trouble should take place in the year of her Jubilee." One thing the Queen could do was to try to prevent her grandson from making matters worse by denouncing the Greeks in public. On February 21st, she telegraphed to Lord Salisbury suggesting that he should instruct the Ambassador in Berlin "to tell the German Emperor from me, that I was astonished and shaken by his violent language against the country where his sister lives".

Vicky's youngest daughter, "Mossy", was a particular favourite of the Queen. At one time it was proposed that she should marry her cousin, Eddy, but, as Knollys pointed out to Ponsonby, it would not have been "agreeable to the Princess of Wales on account of her being a Prussian and a sister of the German Emperor". In 1892 Mossy fell in love with Prince Frederick Charles of Hesse-Cassel, better known as "Fischy" to his relations. Of all her sons-in-law, he was the one to whom Vicky warmed the most, as he shared her artistic and scholarly interests. At first, the Queen was disposed to reproach Mossy for abandoning her mother, but Vicky was less concerned by the prospect of living alone than seeing her daughter happy. In spite of the Queen's fears, Mossy remained her mother's constant companion, particularly during the closing years of her life.

Relations between the Queen and the Prince of Wales prospered during the last decade of her reign. Both were fervent Imperialists, both agreed in deploring the Kaiser's blunders, and both had become mellower as they grew older. In October 1887, the Queen described "a most pleasant visit", which Bertie had just paid her. "He had not stayed alone with me, excepting for a couple of days in May '68, at Balmoral, since he married! He is so kind and affectionate that it is a pleasure to be a little quietly together." Sometimes, they would be found sitting on a sofa "rocking with laughter". Four years later, after a similar visit, she noted in her journal that he had told her "how happy he had been here, that he had liked to come here alone and stay, it reminded him of old times. He was most dear and affectionate". Nevertheless, for all their new found harmony, the Prince could still be daunted by his mother. One one occasion, when he was late for dinner at Osborne, through no fault of his own, he hid behind a pillar and wiped the sweat from his forehead while summoning up the courage to apologise.

On March 10th, 1888 the Prince and Princess of Wales celebrated their Silver Wedding. The Queen attended a family dinner party at Marlborough House. It was the first time she had ever had a meal there. "Alix," she wrote in her journal, "was in white and silver with lovely jewels, looking more like a bride just married than the silver one of twenty-five years." While praying God to prosper their marriage further, she could not resist the temptation of reminding Him: "To me it was not permitted to celebrate this happy anniversary with my husband Albert".

The following spring, the Queen paid a four day visit to Sandringham. During her drive from Wolverton Station in an open landau, "Dear Alix insisted on sitting backwards with Louise, in order that I might be better seen". As she passed through the gates of the house she was reminded of "the terrible time" in 1871 when she feared that Bertie was dying. On her last evening, the Ballroom was converted into a theatre, holding some three hundred people, "including all the neighbours, tenants, and servants. We sat in the front row, I between Bertie and Alix. The stage was beautifully arranged and with great scenic effects." Over sixty actors took part, not to mention a small orchestra. The main piece was a performance of *The Bells*, a celebrated and "very thrilling" melodrama. Sir Henry Irving acted the main role "wonderfully", although in a rather "mannerist" fashion. "He is a murderer, and frequently imagines he hears the bells of the horses in the sledge, in which sat the Polish Jew, whom he murdered. The way in which Irving acted his own dream, and describes the way in which he carried out the murder, is wonderful and ghastly." There followed a scene from *The Merchant of Venice* between Irving and Ellen Terry. Soon after the performance, Shylock and Portia joined the Royal Family for supper. Later, the Queen spoke to them in the Drawing-room, and it was not until one o'clock that she "got upstairs", enchanted by being a guest "under dear Bertie and Alix's hospitable roof", and "greatly touched" by "their kindness and affection".

In 1891, for the second time in his life, the Prince of Wales was obliged to give evidence at a trial. The year before, he had accepted an invitation to stay with the Wilsons at Tranby Croft for the week of the St Leger. Amongst those invited to meet the Prince were three of his old friends: Lieutenant-Colonel Sir William Gordon-Cumming, Lord Coventry and General Owen Williams. On the third day of the visit, Wilson's son, who had recently come down from Cambridge, told Lord Coventry that Sir William had cheated at baccarat two nights running. Having discussed the matter with some of his family, they too had watched, and had seen Sir William adding to his stake after his hand had won. It was generally agreed that the Prince would have to be told and the episode hushed up. Unfortunately, H.R.H. allowed himself to be persuaded that the evidence was conclusive, without even hearing what Cumming might have to say. It would have been much better had he acted on the principle: "Honi soit qui mal y pense" (Shame be to him who thinks evil). Eventually, Lord Coventry and General Williams persuaded Sir William to sign a document agreeing never to gamble again in return for a promise of secrecy. They pointed out that if he refused to sign he would drag the name of the Prince of Wales through the mud. In the end, he agreed to do as they asked while still maintaining his innocence. His "friends", in acting as they did, seemed more concerned to protect the Prince's honour than to see that justice was done.

As was only to be expected, the scandal at Tranby Croft soon became common knowledge. Most people blamed the Prince of Wales for letting the secret out, and Sir William had little choice but to sue the Wilsons for slander. Sir Edward Clarke and Charles Gill, who appeared for him in court, were both convinced of his innocence. In the first place they pointed out that the Defendants had dined and wined so royally before sitting down to cards that they were in no fit state to give evidence about anything, let alone the finer points of baccarat. But worse still, they were so ignorant of its rules that they had never even heard of the "*Coup de trois*", the system according to which Sir William played. His basic plan was to increase his stake by multiples of three after a winning hand. Thus, if he bet five pounds and won, he would leave his original counter on the table, to which he would add his winnings and a further five pounds from his own supply of counters. Unfortunately, being total novices, his accusers jumped to the conclusion that he was increasing his stake with a view to defrauding the Bank. The presiding Judge, Lord Coleridge, was reputed to "favour the defendants", and his final address to the Jury was very one-sided. It was hardly surprising, therefore, that they found in favour of the Defendants, and Sir William left the court a ruined man.

On the day the Prince was summoned to the witness box, there was not an inch of standing room left. Inevitably, the fact of his having to appear was enough to blacken his name. Newspapers, particularly those of a religious turn, "trumpeted their horror, like great moral elephants piously running amok". As Macaulay once remarked, there is "no spectacle so ridiculous as the British public in one of its periodical fits of morality". The Prince was buried under an avalanche of petitions. The Free Church of Spalding told him that it deeply deplored the encouragement he had given to "so harmful and fascinating a vice", while the Primitive Methodists of North-ampton begged him to follow more closely in the steps of his royal parents. They were certainly right in supposing that Her Majesty was not in the habit of whiling away her evenings playing baccarat.

The Prince's critics condemned him for a variety of shortcomings. Some, for instance, maintained that he should never have demeaned himself by staying at Tranby Croft with upstarts like the Wilsons. Others argued that he had far too readily accepted Sir William's guilt on little more than hearsay. It was also suggested that he had deliberately broken article forty-one of the "Queen's Regulations", which clearly required him to refer the matter to the Commander-in-Chief of the Army. Nothing, however, annoyed him more than a letter his nephew sent him. "The young man," as Bismarck called him, had the effrontery to rebuke his uncle, as a Colonel of Prussian Hussars, for "embroiling himself in a gambling squabble, and playing with men young enough to be his sons". This sanctimonious epistle was all the more unpalatable because it contained a provoking germ of truth.

The Queen's views on baccarat were barely distinguishable from those of the Free Church of Spalding. When the Prince of Wales won the Derby in 1896, she told Lady Lytton that she disapproved of his gambling as "it encouraged it so much in others". Prince Albert, she said, had always insisted: "Il faut payer pour être Prince". Neverthe-less, not wishing to be unkind, she telegraphed to congratulate him. In 1891, she was so outspoken in condemning baccarat that the Prince implored Ponsonby to do what he could to see that she did "not allow the strong views which she entertains to get about". During the course of the trial, she told Vicky that it was "a fearful humiliation to see the future King of this country dragged (and for the second time) through the dirt". Later, she claimed that the Monarchy was in danger, and that the light thrown on the Prince's habits had shocked and alarmed the country. Moreover, "his signing that paper was wrong (and turns out to have been contrary to military regulations)". Yet distressed as she was by the whole unhappy affair, she never forgot that a mother's place was to stand by her son and support him in adversity. When Clarke suggested that Sir William had been sacrificed in an effort to save the Prince, the Queen described his remarks as most "unjust" and "unfair".

Tranby Croft was bad enough, but worse was to follow. In 1889 the Prince fell madly in love with Lady Brooke, a discarded mistress of his friend Lord Charles Beresford. It was his most passionate affair, and he even went so far as to call her "my own darling Daisy Wife". When Lady Brooke discovered that Lady Charles Beresford was expecting to have a child, she accused Lord Charles of "infidelity", and told him that he had treated her disgracefully by returning to his wife. The Prince was so besotted by Lady Brooke that he took her side, and pronounced a sentence of social death on her rival. In spite of the fact that Beresford was a notoriously wayward husband, his pride was injured, and he accused the Prince of behaving like a blackguard. Some people said that he actually struck H.R.H. to lend emphasis to his argument. In December 1891, the season of good will, an ultimatum arrived at Marlborough House: either the Prince must apologise and banish Lady Brooke, or the newspapers would be given the story. Four frantic days of negotiations followed, involving the Queen and the Prime Minister. When all seemed lost, a compromise was agreed, and the gutter press was deprived of a succulent morsel. The Princess of Wales was so distressed that she refused to return from Lividia for her husband's fiftieth birthday. Male infidelity was taken for granted in the Danish royal family, but the mixture of Tranby Croft and Lady Brooke proved more than she could bear. Throughout the crisis, the Queen remained calm, and while she made no attempt to defend the indefensible, stayed on affectionate terms with her prodigal son.

On the whole the Queen and the Prince agreed about whom his children should marry, but Alix was less compliant. In 1895, when the Princess was over fifty, the Queen complained: "She will not be *advised* as is common with *young* people". The problem was that H.M. was disposed to choose German brides for her grandsons.

Much as she liked to disclaim the role of a match-maker, she itched to find Eddy a wife: partly because she would probably be Queen Consort, and partly because she might help him to settle down. The Prince of Wales agreed that what the boy needed was "a good sensible wife": which was just what people had said about him. The Queen's first choice for her grandson was Alice's youngest daughter. As early as 1887 she secretly confessed that her "heart and mind" were "bent on securing dear Alicky for either Eddie or Georgie". Two years later her plan appeared to prosper when Eddy obligingly fell in love with his ravishing first cousin. But Alicky had the sense to turn him down and his fancy moved elsewhere. "I fear," wrote the Queen to the Empress Frederick, all hopes of her "marrying Eddy are at an end. . . . It is a real sorrow to us." Nevertheless, in rejecting his proposal, she had shown "gt strength of character, as all her family and all of us wish it, and she refused the greatest position there is".

Eddy's second choice of a bride was Princess Hélène, whose father, the Comte de Paris, was head of the House of Orleans. It would have needed more ingenuity than the Prince possessed to have made a worse match. "I have heard it rumoured," the Queen wrote from Windsor in May 1890, "that you have been thinking and talking of Princess Hélène d'Orléans. I can't believe this for you know that I told you (as I did your parents who agreed with me) that such a marriage is utterly *impossible*." Under the terms of the Act of Settlement of 1701 he would forfeit his right to the throne if he married a Catholic. "Besides which *you* could not marry the daughter of the Pretender to the French Throne." When Eddy insisted that he would rather abdicate than abandon the love of his life, Alix decided to further the ill-judged romance. So successful was she that on August 20th the pair became engaged, while staying at Mar Lodge some twelve miles from Balmoral.

The Princess of Wales, knowing the Queen's romantic disposition, suggested that Eddy and Hélène should seek her blessing. Ignoring her son's reluctance to confront his grandmother, she bundled him into a carriage and ordered the coachman to drive to Balmoral. Her stratagem proved successful as Eddy told Prince George. "I naturally expected Grandmama would be furious at the idea, and say it was quite impossible etc. But instead of that she was very nice about it and promised to help us as much as possible, which she is now doing. . . . I believed what pleased her most was my taking Hélène into her, and saying we had arranged it entirely between ourselves without consulting our parents first. This as you know was not quite true but she believed it all. . . ." Lord Salisbury was on holiday at the time, so his nephew, Arthur Balfour, was summoned north to advise on the Prince's engagement. "Will it be believed," he wrote to his uncle, "that neither the Queen, nor the young Prince, nor Princess Hélène see anything which is not romantic, interesting, touching and praiseworthy in the young lady giving up her religion *to which she still professes devoted attachment*, in order to marry the man upon whom she has set her heart! . . . The Queen is much touched by the personal appeal to *herself*. With admirable dexterity (this surely cannot be the young man's idea) they came hand in hand straight to her, and implored her to smooth out not merely the political difficulties, but the family difficulties also. In making her their confidante, they have made her their ally. She would have been in a much less melting mood if the approaches had been conducted in due form through the parents." Lord Salisbury sent the Queen a memorandum in which he made no attempt to disguise his objections to the match. In the first place, he argued, the Princess was only nineteen and the marriage would need her father's consent. As it was well known that he objected to her changing her religion, he was hardly likely to give it. In the second place, "this marriage is a State Act of the greatest gravity", which could "profoundly affect the feelings of the people towards the throne and of foreign countries toward England". Much to Salisbury's relief, the Comte refused to permit his daughter to change her faith. The Queen consequently agreed that the match was out of the question, which proved the end of the dubious "royal idyll".

Eventually, Eddy became engaged to Princess Mary of Teck, whose mother was Princess Mary Adelaide, the Duke of Cambridge's sister. When Princess "May" was summoned to Balmoral in October 1891, her excited parents guessed she was "on approval". And approved she was. "We have seen a great deal of May," the Queen told Vicky, "and I cannot say enough good about her. May is a particularly nice girl, so quiet and yet cheerful." Soon afterwards, the Queen expressed the hope that Eddy would marry her, as "she has no frivolous tastes, has been very carefully brought up and is very well informed". This was a particularly notable tribute since the Queen was disposed to regard the Cambridge family as mischievous and worldly. On December 3rd, Prince Eddy became engaged, and the Prince and Princess of Wales were absolutely delighted. The only person who seemed to have reservations was Princess Mary herself, who hardly knew her fiancé. Later, the Queen insisted bluntly: "May never was in love with poor Eddy." She had only accepted him from that sense of duty for which she became famous.

The wedding was fixed for February 27th 1892, and on January 4th Princess May and her parents joined a family party at Sandringham for Eddy's twenty-eighth birthday. An epidemic of influenza was raging at the time which claimed the Prince amongst other notable victims. The day before his birthday he felt so wretched that he was forced to take to his bed. On January 8th, Alix telegraphed to the Queen: "Poor Eddy got influenza, cannot dine, so tiresome". The following day he developed pneumonia. By the thirteenth he was delirious and fighting for his life. In moments of frenzy he spoke of his love for the Queen, who had always regarded him with the forbearance she reserved for drunken ghillies. Above all, his wandering mind meandered through his past. Again and again, the watchers by his bed heard him calling for Hélène. In the early hours of January 14th he lapsed into a sleep from which there was no awaking. "Darling Aunt Alix," May told the Queen, "never left Him for a moment, and when a few minutes before the end she turned to Dr Laking and said 'Can you do nothing more to save Him?' and he shook his head, the despairing look on her face was the most heart-rending thing I have ever seen." On the day Eddy died, Alix told Princess May "it makes one more link with heaven". Deeply as Eddy was mourned by his parents and family, his death was a merciful dispensation of Providence. Even his doting relations could find no more flattering adjectives to describe him than "poor", "dear" and "kind". Anyone further removed from Albert's ideal of what a ruler should be would be difficult to conceive. Apart from a certain charm, he lacked every quality demanded of a king.

Prince George's life was transformed by his brother's death and he had to abandon his naval career. In May 1892 he became Duke of York, but ignored his grandmother's wish that he should use his last name. "Like his father before him and his second son after him, he well knew the importance of not being Albert." In spite of this decision, the Queen was quick to recognise his worth. "I think dear George so nice, sensible, and truly right-minded," she told his aunt Vicky in 1892, "and so anxious to improve himself." Naturally, she was eager to find him a suitable bride, and encouraged him to propose to Princess Marie of Edinburgh. In February 1891, Prince George told the Queen that he understood why she wished him to marry "as soon as possible", but that, nevertheless, as "Missy" was only sixteen, he thought it best to wait. Alix, who regarded the Edinburgh girls as too German, told him the plan was "ridiculous". Much to her relief, the Princess became engaged to Crown Prince Ferdinand of Roumania.

The Queen's thoughts began to return to May, who was "very *un*frivolous" and would "set an example of a steady quiet life". There was, in fact, an important family precedent for such an union. In 1865, Alix's sister, Dagmar, became engaged to the Grand Duke Nicholas of Russia, who died before their wedding. Instead of returning to Denmark, she stayed on at St Petersburg, and eventually married his younger brother, "Sasha" (Alexander III). At the time of Eddy's funeral, the Queen remarked to one of her German cousins: "The present Empress of Russia married the next brother and it is a most happy marriage". The difficulty was that both Prince George and his parents felt hampered by the "reproachful shade" which hovered over Sandringham. Not until 1893 did Prince George at last propose. Queen Victoria was delighted and wrote to say how thankful she was "that this great and so long and ardently wished for event is settled". Alix was rather less rapturous, and in writing to her son expressed the hope that he would manage to make up to "May all she lost in darling Eddy": not an impossibly arduous task.

The wedding took place in overpowering heat on July 6th 1893 in the Chapel Royal at St James's Palace. The Kaiser was represented by his brother, Prince Henry, and the Tsar by his son, Nicholas, who looked so like the bridegroom that the two were often confused. The Prince and Princess of Wales gave a gigantic Garden Party the day before, at which one of their guests, imagining that he was addressing the Tsarevich, asked the Duke of York whether he had come to London on business or just to attend the wedding. The Queen was also involved in a misunderstanding. Mr Dawson Damer, who had evidently drunk at least one toast too many, offered her his hand in a most convivial fashion, remarking as he did so, "Gad! How glad I am to see you! How well you're looking! But, I say, do forgive me – your face is, of course, familiar to me; but I can't for the life of me recall your name!" The Queen replied with a gracious smile, "Oh, never mind my name, Mr Damer, I'm very glad to see you. Sit down and tell me all about yourself." Next day, she drove to the Chapel Royal in the new glass State Coach, accompanied by the Duchess of Teck, radiantly happy to see her daughter marry the heir apparent. According to protocol, the Queen should have been the last to arrive, but owing to some oversight was nearly the first. So far from being annoyed, she thought it "very amusing to see everyone come in", and rather enjoyed the consternation she caused. As Georgie and May took their place at the altar, she recalled that she "had stood, where May did, fifty-three years ago, and dear Vicky thirty-five years ago, and that the dear ones who stood where Georgie did, were gone from us! May these dear children's happiness last longer!" The better the Queen came to know the Duchess of York, the more she came to admire her. "Each time I see you," she told her in 1897, "I love and respect you more and am so truly thankful that Georgie has such a partner." When the Queen died, May wrote to her aunt, the Grand Duchess of Mecklenburg-Strelitz, to say how miserable she felt to have lost so "kind" a "friend and counsellor". Nevertheless, there had been times when she found H.M.'s "everlasting questions . . . rather an ordeal", and had felt a trifle oppressed by her unremitting advice.

In 1894 May gave birth to a son, and the Queen proudly told Vicky that never before had there been "3 direct Heirs as well as the Sovereign alive!" Almost as soon as the news reached Windsor, she ordered a special train to take her to Richmond to see her great-grandson: "a very fine strong boy". Prince George wished to call him "*Edward* after darling Eddy", but H.M. was quick to point out that the late Prince had been christened "Victor Albert". Eventually, he was baptised: Edward Albert Christian George Andrew Patrick David. It was by this last name that the future Edward VIII was best known to his family. The following year, on December 14th, the thirty-fourth anniversary of the Prince Consort's death, the Duchess of York gave birth to a second son (George VI). His father, with some trepidation, broke the news to the Queen, who decided the child was a "gift from God", and that the date of his birthday would probably prove "a blessing". This time there was no haggling over names and the boy was christened Albert Frederick Arthur George, after the Prince Consort, the Emperor Frederick, the Duke of Connaught, and his father.

The Prince of Wales's daughters were disappointingly plain. Only Maud, her father's favourite, had any pretension to beauty. In the family circle the girls were vivacious and uninhibited, but in company they were diffident and gauche. It was not their fault that they were overshadowed by their mother. Louise was the first of the family to marry. Her husband, Lord Fife, was a friend of her father, a Liberal politician, and gratifyingly rich. He could be excellent company when he chose, but was coarse and selfish by nature, and his language was that of Billingsgate. For some unfathomable reason the Queen loved him dearly, although he never did anything to deserve it. Indeed, he took liberties with her which horrified her Court. Once, at a servants' ball at Balmoral, he coolly suggested that they should dance a reel together. "Her Majesty, after a moment's hesitation, consented, retired, and reappeared in a few minutes wearing – poor old lady – a short skirt. They danced together, but 'Macduff' (doubtless invigorated by his well-loved alcohol) chose the kind of reel usually danced by sweethearts – hands locked across the bosom; and danced it in rather an improper way. Of course, the innocent old royal lady in the short skirt knew nothing of this, and equally, of course, nobody dared tell her." Fife and Louise were married in 1889 in the private Chapel of Buckingham Palace. The bridegroom, who had been created a Duke as a wedding present, might easily have been mistaken for Louise's father. After her marriage, the Duchess became something of a recluse, and devoted much of her life to trying to catch fish on her husband's estates in Scotland.

Louise's sister, Victoria, the most intelligent of the trio, never found a husband, and died an embittered spinster. When the Queen told the Prince of Wales that it was high time she married, he pleaded that he was powerless to interfere. "Alix," he said, found her daughters "such good companions that she would not encourage their marrying," and besides, "they themselves had no inclination for it." When it was rumoured that "Toria" fancied the widower, Lord Rosebery, her mother insisted that she could only marry a Prince, regardless of the fact that Fife was already her son-in-law. Towards the end of her life, the Princess told a friend that Lord Rosebery would have been "perfect for her, but they wouldn't let her marry him, and we *could* have been so happy". Instead, she became her mother's companion and unpaid Lady-in-Waiting. Toria's cousin, the Grand Duchess Olga of Russia, thought she was treated like a drudge. Whenever Alix needed her she would ring a bell, and her daughter "would run like lightning" to see what she wanted.

Maud, the youngest of the family, was a cheerful tomboy, who peppered her conversation with schoolboy slang. What she really enjoyed was a simple outdoor life devoted to dogs and horses. The Queen, at first, intended that she should marry her cousin, Ernie, Alice's son, but then decided "it would not be advisable" on account of his family's history of haemophilia. Maud nearly decided the matter for herself by falling in love with Prince Francis of Teck, May's dissolute younger brother, who was always being rescued from scrapes. When he was only sixteen his parents were obliged to remove him from Wellington College for coming to blows with his House Master. The Prince neither returned his cousin's affection nor answered her letters, and was packed off to India in 1895 in the hope he might mend his ways. Later that year, the Princess became engaged to Prince Charles of Denmark (elected King Haakon VII of Norway in 1905), a handsome if impecunious naval officer, whose father, Crown Prince Frederick, was Alix's brother. Charles proposed during a family reunion at Fredenborg, and they were married the following summer. The Queen thought the Prince charming and much to be preferred to the ne'er-do-well Francis of Teck.

In March 1892 the Queen heard that the Grand Duke Louis had suffered a serious stroke. When he died on the thirteenth, a month after Eddy, she could hardly accept "the dreadful truth! He was so dear and joyous – so loving and so young for his age. . . ." It added to her distress to think of his orphaned children, especially Ernest and Alicky, neither of whom were married. Later that spring, after her holiday at Hyères, she arranged to return via Darmstadt to see her grandchildren, and to brief the new Grand Duke on his duties. As the train drew into the station she remembered how "darling Louis" used "to jump into the railway carriage and welcome us with such joy". Now she was met by "Dear Ernie, in plain clothes, and the three poor dear girls, Victoria, Irène and Alicky, in deepest mourning with long veils. . . . No Guard of Honour, all silent and sad."

Of all her Hessian grandchildren, the Queen saw most of Victoria, whose husband, Prince Louis of Battenberg, was an officer in the Royal Navy. In the summer of 1889, the Princess gave birth to a second daughter, Louise, who later became the wife of King Gustav VI of Sweden. The infant arrived prematurely, and the nurse, whom the Queen had sent out to Hesse, was only just in time. The Princess's third child, Prince George, was born soon after the Grand Duke's death. Sometimes, when Prince Louis was overseas, the Queen, who was "thankful to be of use", would look after his children. "I must tell you," she wrote from Osborne in 1893, "*how* I enjoyed those 10 quiet days with your beloved ones! I don't know when I felt happier during the last few years." Victoria's second son, Louis, was born at Frogmore in June 1900: the last great-grandchild born in H.M.'s lifetime. He was christened in the Duchess of Kent's drawing-room on a blazingly hot day. The baby proved almost too lively. The moment "he was handed over to Grandmama, he waved one of his little arms about so violently that he knocked her spectacles off, and his hand became entangled in her cap-veil". When the Queen agreed to become the boy's godmother, she insisted that his first name should be Albert, but for everyday use his parents called him "Dickie": the name by which Lord Mountbatten was always known. Princess Victoria died in 1950 but not before she had seen her grandson, Prince Philip (her daughter Alice's only son), married to Princess Elizabeth.

Once Ella married Serge, she lived most of her life in Russia. They were perfectly happy together, apart from the fact that she longed for a child and proved unable to have one. The Grand Duke was richer than his mother-in-law, which led her to fear that Ella might well be spoilt by the "glitter of jewelry and grandeur". Her fears were utterly groundless as Ella was almost a saint. In 1905, when her husband was blown to bits by a bomb, she gave her wealth to the Church and devoted her life to the poor. Thirteen years later she was thrown alive down the shaft of a disused mine. In the eyes of the Bolsheviks it was a capital crime to be royal.

Irène was happy enough with Henry whom she helped to make more tractable. Vicky became very fond of her, and often sought refuge from the pressures of Berlin by staying with her at Kiel. But like most of the Hesse family, her marriage was dogged by tragedy. Two of her sons suffered from haemophilia; and during the First World War, her husband fought for his brother, while her sisters were all in the "enemy" camp. Marriages sown in goodwill were harvested in rancour. As Queen Victoria pointed out, "divided interests" were so "dreadfully painful" that she could not "wish to continue them".

When Ernest succeeded his father as ruler of Hesse he was still a young man. Being an only son, he had been spoiled by his parents and pampered by his sisters. More of an aesthete than a soldier, he preferred rehearsals at the court theatre to drilling on the parade ground. During his student days at Leipzig he devoured the works of Ruskin and William Morris, and spent much of his time studying poetry, painting and music. Politically his views were so progressive that his critics portrayed him as the "Red Grand-Duke". One thing about him which greatly distressed the Queen was his failure to answer her letters. "I do wish," she told his eldest sister, "you *could* get Ernie to be less neglectful in answering letters. . . . I have to send message on message by telegram . . . so I entreat you do what you can to make him more punctual and more attentive."

It was generally agreed that Ernest lacked ballast and urgently needed a wife. As early as May 1892, the Queen consulted Jenner about the desirability of his "marrying one of his Edinburgh cousins". Sir William told her that there was "no objection as they are so strong and healthy", and that "intermarriage" would probably lead to "greater strength and health". The girl she particularly had in mind was Victoria Melita, known for short as "Ducky". When the Queen invited the cousins to Balmoral, she was happy to see how well they got on together. Both showed "high spirits", and were "very funny together". But Ernest, as usual, proved so dilatory that the Queen was obliged to write to him "*twice* about the necessity of his showing some attention and interest". "Georgie" she warned, "lost Missy (Ducky's sister) by waiting and waiting". Not until January 1894 was Affie able to telegraph: "Your and my great wish has been fulfilled this evening. Ducky has accepted Ernie of Hesse's proposal".

The wedding took place at Coburg on April 19th 1894, and attracted one of the largest gatherings of royalty ever seen in Europe. Queen Victoria was present to bless the match she had done so much to foster. It was her first visit to Albert's birthplace for eighteen years. She had never forgiven the late Duke for banishing Brown to a distant part of the Castle, but now that her son ruled Coburg, she could hardly wait to return. Four generations of her family attended the wedding, and every night there were two sittings for dinner to feed the "royal mob". Prominent amongst the glittering array of guests were the Emperor William, the Dowager Empress Frederick, the Prince of Wales and the Tsarevich. Naturally Ella was there with her husband, the bride's maternal uncle. During the service, Vicky kept glancing at her mother, who "looked so nice in her white cap and veil and diamonds", and who watched her two grandchildren making their vows with tears rolling down her cheeks.

The Grand Duke and Duchess had only one child, who was born at Darmstadt in 1895. The Queen insisted on sending out Dr Champneys to supervise the delivery. She perfectly understood that Ducky's mother wanted a Russian nurse, and that Ernie wished to avoid offending "German prejudice", but she could never forget "that *similar* ideas were the *cause* of *William's* arm and a *lifelong* injury and blemish . . .". The baby, christened Elizabeth, turned out to be enchanting. One afternoon in 1899, she was taken out for a drive and happened to meet the Queen. They stopped to talk, and having thanked her great-grandmother for lending her a pony carriage, she offered her a peppermint.

It is difficult to understand how the Queen could have thought that Ducky would make a suitable wife for Ernie. She had inherited her mother's temperament. At one moment, she would be carefree and exuberant, at the next morose and sullen. When her temper was aroused she became a "little spitfire". Life with the Grand Duchess was as trying to the nerves as living near a volcano. She loved to gallop through the woods near Darmstadt on a fiery black stallion, and spoke with withering scorn of her husband's phobia about horses. While he was deeply concerned over his duties as a ruler, she forgot official engagements, and chafed at his dull Court. It is hardly surprising,therefore, that their marriage ran into trouble, especially when both of them sought consolation outside it. In 1896, during the Tsar's Coronation in Moscow, Ducky fell head over heels in love with her cousin, the Grand Duke Cyril. Meanwhile Ernest showed an unhealthy interest in good-looking footmen. "No boy," according to his wife, "was safe with him."

It was not long before the Queen became aware that trouble was brewing. Distressing stories reached her of violent quarrels. In an effort to find out exactly what was happening, she sent for Sir George Buchanan, the Chargé d'Affaires at Darmstadt, and rigorously cross-examined him. Eventually, he was forced to tell her that both the Grand Duke and Duchess had separately confided in him, and that he could not betray their trust by repeating what they had told him. The Queen remained silent for a moment, and then told him with tears in her eyes: "I quite understand. I arranged that marriage. I will never try and marry anyone again." When Ernie and Ducky implored her to let them divorce, she made it clear that to do so was out of the question. What particularly troubled her was the future of Princess Elizabeth. The Grand Duchess was therefore obliged "to bear the irksome bondage of her marriage" for several years to come, and remonstrated in vain against the Queen's "unalterable horror of divorce".

Concerned as the Queen was for all Alice's children, she felt especially responsible for her youngest daughter. Such was her solicitude, that her granddaughter later acknowledged, "a dearer, kinder being never was". "Have you not always," she asked in 1894, "been as a mother to me since beloved Mama died?" Nobody understood better than the Queen what Alicky suffered from shyness. Diffident and withdrawn, she longed to take refuge from her brother's boisterous Court and steal away to her room to read or pray. However much the Queen might protest that she was not a match-maker, she was strongly in favour of Alicky marrying Eddy. Had her dream been realised, she would virtually have ensured that the throne would eventually pass to a haemophiliac. Even when it became clear that Alicky was indifferent to the Prince, the Queen continued to plead his cause, suggesting that "she should be made to reflect sincerely on the folly of throwing away the chance of a very good husband, kind, affectionate and steady", and of "a very good position which is second to *none* in *the world*". Nobody, other than his doting grandmother, had ever described the Duke of Clarence as "steady". Above all, she insisted, there could be no question of "those dreadful Russians".

The Queen's dislike of the Romanovs dated back to the Crimean War, and had recently been revived by the way they had treated Sandro. In December 1890 rumours reached her that the Tsarevich, the future Nicholas II, had fallen in love with Alicky, and that Ella was doing her best to encourage his suit. Princess Victoria, who did not much relish the role of her sisters' keeper, received a broadside from Osborne, assuring her "that in spite of *all* your (Papa's Ernie's and your) *objections*, and still more *contrary* to the *positive* wish of *his Parents* who do *not wish* him to *marry* A, as they feel, as everyone must do, for the *youngest* sister to *marry* the *son of the Emperor* would never answer, and lead to no happiness – well in spite of all this behind *all* your backs, Ella and Serge do *all* they *can* to bring it *about*, encouraging and even urging the Boy to do it!" The Queen had learned this from the Princess of Wales, who had heard it from her sister, the Tsarina. "Papa," she continued, "*must* put his foot down", and "*this* must *not* be *allowed to go on*". Her letter provides an interesting glimpse into her sources of information. How could the Foreign

Office hope to rival an intelligence service which counted the Empress of Russia amongst its agents?

The morning after Ernie's wedding, Ella informed the Queen that her sister and Nicky had just become engaged. "I was quite thunderstruck," wrote H.M., "as though I knew Nicky much wished it, I thought Alicky was not sure of her mind. Saw them both. Alicky had tears in her eyes, but looked very bright, and I kissed them both. Nicky said 'She is much too good for me'." In spite of the obvious drawbacks to the match, such as "the question of religion", they had become so deeply attached to one another that it was "perhaps better so". That summer, the Tsarevich and his fiancée stayed at Windsor. During their visit, they accompanied H.M. to White Lodge for the christening of May's eldest son, the future Edward VIII. The Queen was completely won over by Nicky's charm. "He has lived this month with us like one of ourselves," she told Vicky, "and I never met a more amiable, simple young man, affectionate, sensible and liberal-minded." She even agreed with Lord Rosebery that the marriage offered a prospect of better relations with Russia. To that end she instructed Princess Alix to become a true Russian, while never forgetting, of course, that she was the Queen of England's granddaughter.

As the wedding drew nearer, the Queen became more apprehensive, "on account of the country, the policy and differences with us and the awful insecurity to which that sweet child will be exposed". In October, it became clear that Nicky's father was dying and the Queen's blood ran cold to think of one "*so* young" being placed "on that very unsafe Throne, her dear life and above all her Husband's constantly threatened. . . . It is a great additional anxiety to my declining years". Alexander III died on November 1st 1894, and his son became the Tsar of all the Russias. Next morning, Princess Alix was received into the Orthodox faith, and it was decided to hold her wedding immediately after the funeral. The Queen was deeply disappointed that she would never again see her "*sweet* innocent *gentle* Alicky" as when they next met she would be a "*mighty* Empress!!" The marriage took place on November 26th, and the Queen sent her granddaughter a piece of myrtle from the tree at Osborne which had been grown from a sprig from the Empress Frederick's wedding bouquet. That evening, she gave a dinner at Windsor, and having proposed "the health of their Majesties the Emperor and Empress of Russia, my dear grandchildren", stood to attention "whilst the Russian anthem was played". Throughout the Tsar and Tsarina's tragic lives, their love endured without faltering, from the moment they took their marriage vows in the Winter Palace, until death did them part in the cellar at Ekaterinburg.

"Grandmama tells me," wrote Vicky to Sophie in 1895, "that Nicky and Alicky write to her often, and seem very happy." In 1896 there was a great family reunion at Balmoral. During what Bigge described as the "Russian occupation" the Castle was so full that the footmen's quarters resembled the hold of a slave ship. When the Tsar left, he handed the Master of the Household a thousand pounds to be given to the servants. On Sunday, September 27th, the royal guests were packed off to church at Crathie, regardless of the weather or their differing religions. "The most awful stormy morning," wrote Lady Lytton, "but all was arranged for going to Kirk so we all went, for Her Majesty never gives in. It was very interesting seeing the two pews full of the Royalties and the Emperor and Empress standing by the Queen even in the Scotch Kirk, where all is simple and reverent." On the last day of the visit, the Queen and her guests were "photographed by the new cinematograph process, which makes moving pictures by winding off a reel of film. We were all walking up and down and the children jumping about." The Queen was delighted by the Emperor's visit, but Nicky complained to his mother that the Castle was colder than Siberia, that his uncles insisted on taking him "out shooting all day long", and that he seemed incapable of hitting anything.

Desperately as the Tsar longed for a son, he seemed destined to have nothing but daughters, three of whom were born in the Queen's lifetime: Olga in 1895, Tatiana in 1897, and Marie in 1899. It was not until 1904, three years after the birth of Anastasia, that Alexis was born. But fate, so far from smiling upon them, could hardly have been more cruel, as it soon transpired that the child had haemophilia. Alicky brought up her children at Tsarköe Selo in the rigorous English fashion. For all the barbaric splendour of their surroundings, they lived a life of Spartan simplicity: washing in cold water and sleeping on camp beds. The irony was that during the First World War, the Russians insisted on calling the Empress "Nemka", the "German Woman", although she never forgave Prussia for fighting Hesse in 1866, and her sympathies were wholly with the allies. "Why do people think I am siding with Germany and our enemies?" she asked Kerensky in 1917. "I am English by education and English is my language."

During the last years of her life the Queen saw little of Affie or his children. Between 1886 and 1889 he was Commander-in-Chief of the Mediterranean Fleet, and then spent the next four years stationed at Devonport. In 1893 he left England for good, having succeeded as Duke of Coburg. There was not much love lost between the Queen and her brother-in-law, but she, nevertheless, was a "good deal upset" by his death. "I thought of the happy past," she wrote, "when he was so much with us, of his frequent visits formerly, of dear Coburg, and that my child, our son, was now reigning Duke, a foreign Sovereign!!" The new ruler, while a good deal less disreputable than his predecessor, was an alcoholic. When his niece, Princess Alice of Albany, was invited to tea, she was startled to find him drinking champagne. In 1897 Sir James Reid, having received "a dreadful account" of the Duke's habits, "had a talk with the Queen on the subject".

By 1900, Affie's health was deteriorating fast, and when it became clear that he was suffering from cancer of the tongue he had to be fed through a tube, a fact which he somehow concealed from his family. On July 24th the Queen received a telegram to say that the Duke was "seriously unwell". Two days later, she was sent a further alarming account which made her "terribly anxious". On July 30th, Affie died in his sleep at the Rosenau. "It is awful to reflect," wrote Marie Mallet, "that his own acts have largely contributed to his premature death. Alas, intemperance was his ruin as it is of so many." The shock was all the more stunning for the Queen as she had never been told the whole truth. "Felt terribly shaken and broken," she noted in her journal, "and could not realise the dreadful fact." She found it almost impossible to believe that she had lost her "poor darling Affie", her "third grown up child, besides three very dear sons-in-law. It is hard at eighty-one!" Nevertheless, she managed to smile through her tears on being shown a telegram which read: "Sincere condolences. Poem follows."

The Queen held the Edinburgh children in high regard. When they stayed with her at Windsor in 1890, she described the girls as "handsome", "strong" and "healthy". Young Alfred, too, she said, was "a dear good boy". It was not long before she was forced to eat her words. By the time he was twenty-five, the Prince had contracted syphilis and suffered from "nervous depression". In 1899, shortly before his parents began to celebrate their Silver Wedding – admittedly a hollow anniversary – he shot himself after a violent row with his mother. His injuries, although serious, were not immediately fatal, and the Duchess decided to bundle him out of the country before her guests arrived. When the doctors told her the journey might prove fatal, she brushed their objections aside. Accustomed to believe that she always knew best, she despatched him to the Tyrol. Some days later, the Duke received a telegram to say that the Prince had died. So shattered was he by his son's death, which he mostly blamed on his wife, that he more or less lived on his own from that time onwards.

Affie's eldest daughter, Marie, was a born romantic. When the sun shone, she was ecstatic, but when it became overcast she sank into Russian gloom. The Queen, she wrote in her memoirs, was the arbiter of her fate. "Even Mama, who, according to us, was omnipotent, had to listen to her." Approaching her was an awe-inspiring experience, like entering the inner sanctuary of a shrine. "Silent, soft-carpeted corridors" led to her apartments, and those who trod them spoke in hushed whispers. But when the door of her room was eventually opened, "there sat Grandmama not idol-like at all, not a bit frightening, smiling a kind smile, almost as shy as us children . . .".

The Duchess of Edinburgh did everything she could to forestall the Queen in finding Missy a husband. As she explained to her son-in-law, Prince Ernest, she "could not really like" her English relations, whom she regarded as "nasty and spiteful", and she begged him not to keep dragging Ducky to England "in perpetual adoration of Granny". In the autumn of 1891, when Missy was only sixteen, the Duchess more or less forced her into the arms of Prince Ferdinand of Roumania. "Nando", as he was called, belonged to the Catholic branch of the House of Hohenzollern, and was heir-presumptive to his uncle, King Carol I. He had protruding ears, melancholy eyes, and a shy, nervous laugh. Normally, he was tongue-tied, unless discussing his favourite subject, botany. For many years he lived at Court with his aunt, Queen Elizabeth, who published exotic poems under the pen-name "Carmen Sylva". When Missy accepted him, she did so to please her mother. The Duchess saw to it that the Duke's permission was only sought when it was virtually too late for him to prevent the match. "Papa," Princess Marie admitted, "said very little, though his face was rather glum." Lady Geraldine Somerset represented the views of the English royal family when she expressed herself "disgusted" by the engagement. "It does seem too cruel," she wrote, "to cart that nice pretty girl off to semi-barbaric Roumania." Queen Victoria was equally indignant that her grand daughter's future had been settled behind her back. "We have been much startled to hear of Missy's *Engagement to Ferdinand* of *Roumania*," she told Princess Victoria of Battenberg. "He is nice I believe and the Parents are charming – but the Country is very insecure and the immorality of the Society at Bucharest *quite awful.*"

Soon after Missy became engaged she and Nando were summoned to Windsor. It was a trying experience for both of them. For all "Mama's smiles and reassurances", she could not help feeling "a little bit of a traitor". She need not, however, have worried. The Queen could hardly have been more kind. Later in life, Missy recalled waiting with Nando in the corridor at Windsor. First, they heard the tap, tap, tap, of Grandmama's stick and "the rustle of her stiff, silk gown". Then, there she was, "wee and smiling and rather shy", addressing the Crown Prince in German. "I see her looking up at him and asking him about his parents, and telling him that she had a picture of his mother in her own private room. 'Sie war so wunderschön.'" During their visit, the Queen noticed Nando dipping a bread roll in his coffee, to the dismay of his fellow guests. "You must have breakfast with me," she said coming to his rescue, "and *then* we will break our rolls into our coffee together *in the good old German fashion.*" It would be difficult to conceive of a more tactful way of pointing out a faux pas.

Before Missy returned to Coburg, the Queen told her that the Munshi was anxious to meet Prince Ferdinand. They therefore presented themselves at the appointed hour in "Her Majesty's inner sanctuary. She was sitting at her writing-table; as usual the air was sweet with the scent of orange flowers peculiar to her rooms". Winterhalter's portrait of Nando's mother stood on an easel beside her. Graciously the Queen pointed to the canvas with a captivating smile and said: "Wunderschön". The Prince gazed at it in silence, feverishly trying to think of something to say. Momentarily the tension was relieved by the arrival of the Munshi, dressed in gold for the occasion. "Putting his hand to his heart, lips and forehead, he saluted us Eastern-wise and then froze into immobility." There was an awkward silence, which Missy finally broke by crossing the room, shaking hands with the Munshi and introducing Nando.

At first, Marie was miserable in Roumania. "The heavy German atmosphere of the royal palace, the dark, stiff furniture, the thick curtains, the closed windows, stifled and oppressed her." Nor did she take readily to the despotism of King Carol, the dominant force in her life. But eventually she learned how to get her own way, and to turn a deaf ear to poor Nando's pathetic appeals not to provoke his uncle. By the time she became Queen in 1914 she had totally fallen under the spell of the Balkans. In 1893 she learned that she was pregnant, and a series of furious battles broke out between the King and her mother, both of whom had their own ideas on childbirth, and both of whom were accustomed to have their way. For some months Nando was caught in a hail of crossfire which left him dazed and shell-shocked. Finally, the Queen resolved their disputes by sending Dr Playfair to supervise the delivery. "We want to be on the safe side," she said, so the future King Carol II was ushered into the world with the help of an English specialist.

Princess Helena's life was based on that of the Court, and followed its annual migrations. Her eldest son, Prince Christian Victor, joined The King's Royal Rifle Corps and saw active service in India, the Sudan, and South Africa. In October 1900, "having passed through endless hardships and danger", he died of enteric fever. The Queen at the time was staying at Balmoral, where she was joined by the Prince's sister, "Thora" (Helena Victoria). "I could not believe it," she wrote, "it seemed too dreadful and heart-breaking, this dear, excellent, gallant boy, beloved by all, such a good, as well as a brave and capable officer, gone!" It made her feel miserable to think of "poor dear Lenchen, who so worshipped this son, and poor Thora, so dear, so courageous, trying to comfort me by saying so sweetly she knew 'he was happy'." Seldom had her ladies seen her "so dreadfully shaken and upset". Marie Mallet told her husband that "when she breaks down and draws me close to her and lets me stroke her dear hand, I quite forget she is far above me and only realise she is a sorrowing woman" in desperate need of compassion. In public, she made an heroic attempt not to appear downhearted, but her face in repose betrayed the extent of her suffering. The day after she heard the news from Pretoria, she went out for a drive with Lady Lytton. Little was said as they sat in the back of the carriage, but the tears rolled down her cheeks as she gently squeezed Lady Lytton's hand to show how she valued her sympathy.

In 1889, Princess Helena's second daughter, Marie Louise, met Prince Aribert of Anhalt, a handsome young cavalry officer in the German Army, to whom she became engaged in the following year at a family party at Potsdam. In view of what transpired, it seems probable that the Prince only married her because she was a grand-daughter of Queen Victoria and the Kaiser's first cousin. The wedding took place in St George's Chapel, Windsor in July 1891. When the "honey couple" drove off, they were greeted "with shouts and shrieks of joy and hurrahs" from hundreds of Etonians, more because they had been given a whole holiday than to register approval of a measly German prince. The marriage proved a disaster. So great was the strain on the Princess, that in 1900 her doctors advised her to take a long holiday. Soon after arriving in Ottawa, where she stayed with the Governor-General, Lord Minto, she received two telegrams. The first was from her father-in-law, the Duke of Anhalt, ordering her to return at once. The second came from the Queen and was addressed to Lord Minto. "Tell my grand-daughter," it read, "to come home to me. V.R." It was only on returning to Cumberland Lodge that the mystery was resolved when Prince Christian showed her a letter from her husband announcing his intention to have the marriage annulled. Naturally, Prince Christian demanded to know the charges against his daughter, but the reply which came back was so patently absurd that he rejected it contemptuously. Only two accusations were true: her passionate love of England, and her failure to bear him a son. The one thing he did not dare to allege, "because he could not, was the charge of infidelity". Princess Marie Louise never married again: partly because her experience of matrimony did little to commend it, but mostly because she thought marriage vows were binding. Rumour has it that the official account was a fiction, devised to conceal a more lurid truth. It was rumoured that Prince Aribert had been found sleeping with a man and that the Queen agreed to hush the matter up.

Princess Louise was by far the most waspish of all the Queen's children. Like her mother, she was a warm-blooded Hanoverian, and loyal to people in trouble, but she was totally ruthless and suffered from paranoia. Provided her interest was aroused – and she held decided views on a variety of topics – she was an animated conversationalist. Ponsonby claimed that he did not know what he would have done to relieve the gloom of dreary evenings at Court had it not been for her vivacity. Nevertheless, he was disturbed by the "bitter things" she said, in spite of her "sweet smile and soft language". The bonbons she dispensed were sugar coated but their centres reeked of cyanide. While the Queen admired her daughter's artistic talent, she disliked her Bohemian friends and eccentric habits. It might just be acceptable to ride a bicycle but not to smoke cigars. Like Vicky and Alice, Louise was deeply concerned with Women's Rights, particularly her own, and even wrote articles under the pen name "Mira Fontenoy".

Louise got on particularly well with the Prince and Princess of Wales, and felt more at home when her brother became King than she had in their mother's reign. Her relations with Beatrice were often strained, mainly because she was fond of making mischief. "Princess Louise has just arrived," wrote Marie Mallet from Osborne in 1891. "She is fascinating but oh, so ill-natured. I positively dread talking to her, not a soul escapes." Some months later, Marie decided that she had never "come across a more dangerous woman", who would "stick at nothing to gain her own end". Not content with stirring up trouble in the family, she enjoyed provoking political storms. In 1894, Campbell-Bannerman had several conversations with her while he was minister in attendance at Balmoral. He came away convinced that "she favours Home Rule all round", and deplored attempts by the House of Lords to reject it. He even persuaded himself that she was a "divine influence" on the Queen, and helped predispose her towards his Liberal colleagues. The truth was very different. The Princess thrived on excitement and rarely missed a chance to stir up controversy. Put her in a field with a bull and nothing thrilled her more than waving a red flag at it.

Princess Louise, like her husband, was so attracted to men that "she ran after anything in trousers". She was known to be very fond of Sir Edgar Boehm, who gave her lessons in sculpture. The fact that she visited him alone was enough to cause tongues to wag. Indeed, she had the misfortune to be with him when he died. "Good Sir E. Böhm (sic)," wrote the Queen, with her customary concern for the minutiae of death, "died quite suddenly in a moment and poor Aunt Louise was *with him at the time*, when he was showing her some of his newest Busts – when he gave a shriek and fell forward and never spoke again – and she only heard a gurgling in his throat. She undid his collar, moved his arms, felt his pulse – but all in vain. She ran for help to his neighbour and pupil Mr Gilbert, and he sent for a Doctor and asked her to leave. It has been as you may *easily* imagine, a most terrible shock to her, and she was dreadfully upset, for besides the horror of such a thing, he was a very kind friend of hers and she was his pupil."

In so far as Lord Lorne lived a separate life from Louise, he cultivated the company of his uncle, Lord Ronald Gower, who decided to pay an extended visit to Europe on learning that Oscar Wilde had been sent to prison. Until his sudden departure, Lorne was a frequent guest at his house parties, which involved what were known as "masculine entertainments". Neither Lorne nor Louise was the easiest of companions. She suffered from rheumatism and insomnia, which left her depressed and petulant, and he was equally moody and hot-tempered. One evening, when he was dining at Inveraray, he became so angry that he threw his plate half way across the room. Nevertheless, in spite of their problems, their marriage began to pick up in the eighteen-nineties: partly because they had learned to agree to differ. Gradually their lives reconverged, and the common interests which originally brought them together assisted in re-uniting them. When Lorne died in 1914 he was seldom out of her thoughts. He "would have been so interested" she would say when one of his favourite topics was being discussed. She was even once seen gazing at his portrait with tears streaming down her cheeks.

Between 1886 and 1890, when Prince Arthur was Commander-in-Chief at Bombay, the Queen only saw him once, in 1887. Indeed, even then it required a special Act of Parliament to allow him to attend her Golden Jubilee. It was fortunate that he returned, because nobody else was able to persuade her not to wear black when she drove in state to the Abbey. "Now Mother," he said, as if addressing a squad of dishevelled recruits, "you must have something really smart!" At least the Queen saw rather more of his children, who were sent back to England when Poona became too hot. Prince Arthur was sent to Eton, then joined the Seventh Hussars, and briefly saw service in South Africa. Unlike "Young Alfred", the Queen had every right to be proud of him.

In 1890, the Duke returned from India to take up the Southern Command. Nobody could pretend that his new duties were as exotic as those in Bombay, and he soon became restless. Throughout his career he could always rely on the Queen to fight his corner. The problem was that politicians had suffered so much at the hands of the Duke of Cambridge that they refused to consider another royal prince who might prove equally immovable. The Queen, however, refused to "submit to the *shameful principle* that Princes are to suffer for *their birth* in a monarchical country. Have a Republic at once if that is the principle." The Duke, after all, had served with "honour and distinction" in Canada, Gibraltar, Egypt, and India. It was "abominable" that he should be regarded as disqualified merely because he happened to be her son. In 1893, partly because of his mother's relentless pressure, the Duke was given the Aldershot Command. Two years later she took up the cudgels again when the Duke of Cambridge retired. Nevertheless, in spite of her vigorous advocacy, the Government preferred the claims of Lord Wolseley. Once they reached this decision, the Queen sent Bigge to Aldershot to tell the Duke "how grieved she was that it was considered inexpedient now to appoint him as Commander-in-Chief", but that she "hoped to live to see him in that position, and would do all possible to insure this being carried out". Four years later, Lord Salisbury personally assured her that "Arthur would have the next appointment after Lord Wolseley".

Nobody was more anxious than Prince Arthur to volunteer for South Africa, and he begged his mother to bring pressure on the Prime Minister to permit him to play an active part in the fighting. Painful as it would be for her to see her son go, she recognised "what a laudable wish it was". The Government, however, refused to encumber Lord Roberts with further responsibilities, no doubt recalling the fate of the Prince Imperial. "Feel most deeply for you," the Queen assured the Duke, "and share your feelings. I pressed your wishes strongly against my own." Eventually, it was decided that the Prince should be given command of the British Army in Ireland. In 1900 Lord Roberts was appointed to succeed Lord Wolseley as General Commander-in-Chief, in spite of Lord Salisbury's promise. "I was much surprised," the Queen telegraphed, on hearing of the proposal. "I had always hoped the Duke would, after Lord Wolseley, be appointed to the position for which his zealous and conscientious service and great experience at home and abroad have fully qualified him."

No other members of the royal family were more in need of support than Leopold's widow and children. On the other hand, no one was more courageous or self-sufficient than the Duchess. "I do love and respect her, poor darling," the Queen told Vicky. She is "always thinking of others and not herself", and accepts her fate with "unwavering resignation". Until her children grew up, she devoted her life to their welfare, and taught them to share her own strong Lutheran faith.

When "Young Affie" died in 1899 a problem arose over who should succeed his father as ruler of Coburg. The Duke of Connaught was next in line but refused to give up his army career, and his son was equally disinclined to live in permanent exile. The Connaughts, therefore, renounced their family rights, and the Queen decided that the young Duke of Albany should succeed his uncle Alfred. "I have always tried to bring up Charlie as a good Englishman," his mother complained, "and now I have to turn him into a good German." When Charlie's Etonian friends heard of his elevation they greeted him with the goose-step. The Kaiser arranged for his young cousin to be sent to Leichterfelde, a German Sandhurst, and the Duchess and Alice moved to a nearby villa. In 1900, Charlie was proclaimed ruler of Coburg with the title "Carl Eduard". Eighteen years later, he was forced to abdicate, and was stripped of his British titles by George V. Subsequently he became a Nazi, and was briefly interned in 1945. In some ways the Duke was the most unfortunate of all Queen Victoria's grandsons. Having lost his father before he was born, he was forced to become a German prince, and then was condemned for serving the Reich "not wisely but too well".

During the last years of the Queen's reign, Princess Beatrice spent much of her day reading aloud to her mother, or writing on her behalf with fingers crippled by rheumatism. The Empress Eugénie once told a friend that "Poor Princess Beatrice" was "nearly driven wild" by overwhelming demands. Not until after eleven o'clock at night could she and her husband "enjoy each other's society". When Beatrice occasionally claimed that she needed a holiday, she was told she was thoroughly selfish. In 1889, for example, she announced her intention of accompanying Prince Henry on a shooting trip to Albania, only to be informed that it was a "foolish expedition" which would greatly annoy and inconvenience her mother. Everything about Beatrice, from her drab appearance to her shy and distant manner, showed how the Queen's constraining influence had turned her into a sombre drudge, very unlike the pert, vivacious child who had once delighted Prince Albert.

Prince Henry's life at Court, surrounded by women, was rather too placid to occupy his talents. In 1894 he made a dash for freedom by joining his brother Louis on a yachting trip off Corsica. When rumours reached Beatrice that he was "keeping low company" in Ajaccio, a man-of-war was despatched to bring him home. "Have you ordered *Surprise*?" she kept asking Ponsonby. "Has *Surprise* left harbour? Has it been made clear to Captain Tillard that under no circumstances must he return without the Prince?" The Queen did everything in her power to keep Liko happy: except to give him his freedom. She made him a Knight of the Garter, a Privy Councillor, and Governor of the Isle of Wight, but it was not in his nature to relish undeserved honours. Inevitably, he chafed at his life of leisure. He was happy enough for a time to ride and play tennis with Beatrice, to shoot with his brothers-in-law, or to sail his yacht in the Solent, but his aspirations were hardly satisfied by such trivial pursuits. On one occasion he told the Empress Eugénie how tired he was of his futile existence, "continually opening this, that and the other institution", or "presenting prizes day after day". On the whole, however, he kept such thoughts to himself, and was greatly loved at Court, where he endeared himself "to the Ladies of the Household by his gaiety and charming manners", and to the gentlemen by persuading Her Majesty to allow them more comfortable quarters for smoking. He was an ideal son-in-law: thoughtful, enterprising, and a veritable master of revels.

In October 1895, the British Government demanded that the King of Ashanti should put an end to the Slave Trade. When this ultimatum expired unanswered, an expedition was sent to enforce compliance. Prince Henry, who longed for a chance to do something more useful than being Honorary Colonel of the Isle of Wight Rifles, immediately volunteered to go to West Africa. The Queen told him that "it would never do", but he refused to take "no" for an answer. He came, he said, from a family of soldiers, but unlike his three brothers had never seen active service. The Queen fell back on an intermediary and encouraged Sir James Reid to persuade the Prince that the climate of the Gold Coast might undermine his health. But Liko stuck to his guns, nobly supported by Beatrice. In the end H.M. succumbed to three unanswerable arguments. First, that fever was the common lot of armies. Second, that she had already authorised Prince Christian, Helena's son, to join the expedition. Third, that he longed for the chance to show how devoted he was to the country which had adopted him. Newspapers had mocked him for whiling away his time bicycling and playing billiards, and now was his chance to prove he was made of sterner stuff.

On January 10th 1896, Beatrice received a telegram to say that Prince Henry was suffering from malaria and had been sent back to the coast. Reassuring messages followed to the effect that H.R.H.

had "slept well", had "taken nourishment", and that his symptoms showed "great improvement". On January 16th Beatrice received a telegram from the Prince, who had arrived at Cape Coast Castle, to say that he had been very ill, but, thanks to the care of his doctor and manservant, had recovered enough to begin the journey home. Four days later he suffered a sudden relapse and died off Sierra Leone. The blow was all the more devastating as the crisis was thought to be over. "There is such grief in the house," the Queen wrote in her journal. "Dear Liko was so much beloved. Went over to Beatrice's room and sat a little while with her, she is so gentle, so piteous in her misery. What have we not all lost in beloved, noble Liko, who has died in the wish to serve his country!"

On the morning of February 4th, the Prince's body, preserved in a makeshift tank of rum, arrived at Portsmouth on board HMS *Blenheim*, where it was reverently transferred to a more conventional coffin. That same afternoon, the Queen, with Beatrice's children, went down to Trinity Pier to greet the *Alberta*, which was carrying Prince Henry's remains on their last journey to the island of which he was Governor. "The minute guns began their sad solemn salute, the bells in the ships tolling, and the *Alberta* with the Royal Standard fluttering at half-mast [surely a solecism?], slowly passed through the Flying Squadron, gliding noiselessly up to the pier." The Queen "was rolled across the gangway, and then walked to where, on deck, between the funnels and the saloon, covered with the Union Jack and flowers, the beloved remains were resting". After adding her own wreath, H.M. could hardly "realise it was *he*, dear bright Liko, who was always going down to Cowes", and was "so devoted to sailing and boating, and anything to do with the sea". On the very evening that Liko died, the King of Ashanti surrendered without fighting.

The depth of the Queen's despair was a measure of the extent to which Prince Henry had made her old age happy. "My grief is great," she wrote on the day that she learned of his death, "and I am quite unnerved by the shock of this dreadful news." Few people understood her feelings better than her cousin, the Duchess of Teck, who told Princess May that "Dear Liko was the one being who brought a little of the outward world and of *life* and animation into her otherwise so monotonous, deadly dreary existence!" The Queen felt put to shame by Beatrice's unmurmuring resignation, and longed "to do everything in the world to save her every additional trouble" and to "lessen her bitter anguish". One afternoon at Osborne, while taking a drive in the grounds, her Lady-in-Waiting attempted to cheer her up by remarking how wonderful it would be to meet our dear ones in Heaven. "Yes," said the Queen to whom the thought had already occurred. Failing to recognise that the signals had turned to red, her companion went on to speak of meeting "in Abraham's bosom". "I will *not* meet Abraham," Her Majesty replied, oblivious to the fact that in the World to Come she might not be left to decide on questions of protocol. One of the Queen's memorials to her son-in-law was the Royal Victorian Order, a mark of "personal service to the Sovereign and her Successors". Nobody deserved the honour more than the Prince whom it commemorated. When Princess Louise heard the news of Prince Henry's death, she told Lady Minto that "He was almost the greatest friend I had. I too miss him more than I can say". Soon after the funeral, the Duchess of Teck found Princess Beatrice in tears. It appeared that her sister had just announced "that *she* (Louise) was Liko's *confidant*" and that Beatrice meant "nothing to him".

Beatrice's four children were an endless source of happiness for the Queen, and helped her retain her youthful outlook on life. "Once more small feet scampered down the corridors, and small children trotted into her bedroom to say 'Good morning Gangan'." One of her grandchildren recalled going out for drives with her, and giggling and joking so much that they ached with laughter. But for all her sense of fun, few liberties were permitted. Princess Ena, for example, was magisterially rebuked after the Duke of York's wedding. She had been warned beforehand to keep absolutely silent as nobody was supposed to speak in church, but when the Archbishop began to read the service, she exclaimed indignantly, "But mummy *that* man is talking". On returning to Buckingham Palace, the Queen reproached her for being "very pert". Sometimes, when she and her brothers were staying at Balmoral, their grandmother would give them Bible talks which were a great ordeal as she generally lost her temper when they were stupid. The Battenberg children, being resident members of the family, "were always given dull nursery meals – beef, mutton and milk-puddings – but visiting children were allowed éclairs and ices". Once Princess Ena, by way of a protest, said as her grace: "Thank God for my dull dinner." The Queen was furious and punished her severely.

Alexander (Drino), who claimed to be the Queen's favourite

grandson, was badly spoiled by his grandmother. The party she gave for his eleventh birthday included a troop of performing dogs. Two years later, he was sent to Wellington, where he discovered that his contemporaries were "a lot of bloodthirsty hooligans". Unaccustomed to handling money, he soon got into difficulty, and wrote a despairing appeal to the Queen begging her for assistance. Her response consisted of a stern warning to keep within his allowance. Some days later she was amused to receive a letter informing her that the problem had been resolved by his selling her letter for the sum of thirty shillings. His younger brothers, Prince Leopold and Prince Maurice, were a cause of constant concern as they suffered from haemophilia. Both, however, contrived to survive their grandmother: Leopold dying in 1922, and Maurice in 1914 on the retreat from Mons.

Ena, the only girl of the family, was a mischievous child. In 1894 she had a serious accident while riding her pony at Osborne. She sank into a coma, and Reid was obliged to warn the Queen how dangerous this might prove. "I love these darling children so," she noted apprehensively, "almost as much as their parents." Some five years after her grandmother's death, Ena married the King of Spain, Alfonso XIII. It later transpired that she, like her mother, had sons with haemophilia.

"I am not very happy about the beloved Queen," wrote Marie Mallet from Osborne in February 1900. "She has changed since I was here last (July 1899) and looks so much older and feebler my heart rather sinks." By the summer, H.M. was reluctantly forced to concede that her strength was failing. "I now rest daily," she admitted in her journal, "which is thought good for me but loses time." Lord James of Hereford, Chancellor of the Duchy of Lancaster, noticed a serious decline in her health between May and October. In May, she "was quite as of old – very cheerful and enjoying any anecdote or smart conversation according to her nature". By October, she "had lost much flesh, and had shrunk so as to appear about one-half the person she had been. Her spirits too had apparently left her." The Queen herself was aware that all was not well, and apologised to Vicky for being "a poor old thing not almost myself".

The most obvious sign that the Queen was growing old was her tendency to doze. "My evening task is no light one," wrote Marie Mallet in February 1900. "The Queen sleeps soundly and yet adjures me to keep her awake, even shake her if necessary, this I cannot bring myself to do, so I read and rustle the paper and wriggle on my chair and drop my fan and do all in my power to rouse my Sovereign, but she would be much better off in bed and so should I." On November 11th, the Queen noted in her journal: "Had a shocking night, and no draught could make me sleep, as pain kept me awake. Felt very tired and unwell when I got up. . . . Could do nothing for the whole morning. Rested and slept a little." Nevertheless, she continued to work to the very last week of her life. Nobody who saw her heroic battle with infirmity could fail to admire her indomitable spirit.

Some of the Queen's symptoms had a considerable history. She had long suffered from rheumatism, made worse by her love of fresh air and indifference to rain. Her failing sight was also an old problem, but getting rapidly worse. By the end of her life she was so blind that she even had to be helped to sign documents. She also began to have trouble with her digestion. At first she was slow to accept a sensible diet, preferring roast beef to chicken. When Reid "at last persuaded her to try Bengers", instead of "substituting it for other foods she added it to her already copious meals". But in the autumn of 1900 she lost her appetite and the sight of food disgusted her. Unfortunately, the servants at Balmoral served her "abominably". The chefs took no trouble to "prepare tempting little dishes" which might have encouraged her to eat, and the "footmen smelt of whisky". She once complained that she was "the only person in England who could not get good tea". When the Court returned to Windsor the arrangements were not much better. One evening she ordered vermicelli for her dinner, but it "was entirely forgotten, so she had nothing". By the end of the year she had the greatest difficulty in eating anything, and found it "most trying" sitting through meals, toying with milk and blancmange. Marie Mallet maintained that the cooks should have been "drawn and quartered and the Clerks of the Kitchen strung from the Curfew Tower; their indifference makes me boil with rage".

The Queen's health was visibly affected by worry over the Boer War. She suffered "intensely" as the casualty lists mounted, and began to look haggard, anxious and "careworn". She herself thought her visit to Ireland was largely to blame for her troubles. "It was very hard and trying work," she told Lord James. "I had a great deal to get through, and I was so anxious that everything should pass off well. I am afraid it was too much for me." Nevertheless, she refused to give in, and struggled to do what she could for her country. Before leaving Windsor in December 1900, she visited the Irish Industries Exhibition in the town hall, where she was "rolled round" the stalls to inspect their wares and to talk to the ladies attending them. It was the last of a lifetime of public appearances.

The Christmas festivities at Osborne proved a joyless ritual. The Queen's insomnia had become so bad that she had to be dosed with chloral, and hence spent much of the morning sleeping off its effects. On Christmas Eve she was taken to see her tree in the Durbar Room, and complained that the candles were very dim. Next day, she was shattered to learn that Lady Churchill had died after forty-six years in her service. First, Beatrice warned her that "dear Jane Churchill had had one of her bad heart attacks". Then Reid informed her that her condition was so grave that he had telegraphed for her son. Later, he finally broke it to her that "all was over". That evening, the Queen dictated her journal to Beatrice. "They had not dared to tell me," she said, "for fear of giving me a shock, so had prepared me gradually for the terrible news. . . . The loss to me is not to be told." The month ended with a series of fearful storms which prevented the Queen going out for her afternoon drives.

The opening entry in the Queen's journal for 1901 reads: "Another year begun and I am feeling so weak and unwell that I enter upon it sadly". On January 2nd she conferred the Garter on Lord Roberts, who noticed with some dismay how frail and infirm she was, and on Saturday, January 12th, she had a twenty-minute discussion with Joseph Chamberlain. "I was the last Minister to see her before her death," he wrote a fortnight later, and "was much relieved to find her looking much better than I expected with bright eyes and clear complexion. Her voice was distinct as usual and she showed not the slightest sign of failing intelligence." Little did he realise the massive effort of will required to collect her thoughts. On Sunday, she dictated the final entry in the journal she had begun at Kensington in 1832. The day began with Lenchen reading despatch boxes. In the afternoon, she went for a short drive, and at five-thirty attended a service in the Drawing room, conducted by the Vicar of Whippingham, "who performed it so well" that it was "a great comfort" to her. "Rested again afterwards, then did some signing, and dictated to Lenchen." On Monday, she saw Lord Roberts and discussed the war in South Africa for an hour. Somehow, like the great professional she was, she rose to the occasion, although Reid could see that she hardly knew where she was.

On Tuesday, January 15th, the Queen went out for a drive with the widowed Duchess of Coburg. It was the last time that she left the house alive. Next morning, she kept mumbling that she must get up and then drifting back to sleep. When Reid was told that she was too drowsy to notice him, he decided to take a look at her without waiting to be summoned. He had never seen her in bed before, and "was rather struck by how small she appeared". It was not until after six that she finally got dressed, and appeared downstairs looking dazed and bewildered. Under these circumstances, Sir James decided that the time had come to warn the Princesses that their mother was showing signs of "cerebral degeneration", and to write to the Prince of Wales to the same effect.

When Reid first saw the Queen on Thursday, he feared she had suffered a mild stroke, as her left cheek was "drooping" and her speech showed signs of impairment. Suspecting that her days were numbered, he sent for Sir Richard Powell, an eminent London consultant and former assistant of Jenner. The Queen raised no objection. Indeed, she had previously said that "he must have help" or the strain might prove too much for him. Powell first saw her at 8 p.m. that evening, and agreed with Sir James that her mind appeared to be failing. During a lucid moment she wanted to know whether people had commented on the fact that she had missed her afternoon drive. Princess Helena assured her that the weather had been so bad that no one had been surprised, but her mother was not convinced and shrewdly observed that everyone knew "she always went out in the rain".

Reid, having promised the Kaiser that if the Queen became seriously ill he would let him know at once, telegraphed on January 18th: "Disquieting symptoms have developed which cause considerable anxiety. This is private." As the Duke of Connaught happened to be in Berlin, the Kaiser suggested that he should accompany him back to England. The Duke dropped a hint that the Emperor might not be welcome, but William insisted that as the Queen's eldest grandson his place was at her side. "The Old Trouper", as Sarah Bernhardt called him, instinctively hogged the limelight. It was he who drove the Imperial Train to Flushing, and he who took the helm of the ship in which they crossed the Channel. Throughout the journey, he was so full of fun that nobody could have guessed the nature of his mission. His suite attributed his high spirits to the absence of the Empress, but his own explanation was that Uncle Arthur needed cheering up. Some forty years before, the Queen told Vicky that to die "peacefully surrounded by all one's children" would be "a great blessing". But later she changed her mind, and described it as "very dreadful" to have one's relations swarming around like a cloud of starving vultures. "That I shall insist is never the case if I am dying. It is awful."

At first the Prince of Wales was reluctant to issue a public statement for fear of creating alarm, but on Saturday, January 19th, he authorised Reid to issue his first bulletin. "The Queen," it said, "has not lately been in her usual health, and is unable for the present to take her customary drives. The Queen during the past year has had a great strain upon her powers, which has rather told upon Her Majesty's nervous system. It has, therefore, been thought advisable by Her Majesty's physicians that the Queen should be kept perfectly quiet in the house, and should abstain for the present from transacting business." While Sir James was naturally anxious to reassure the public, he was equally eager to warn the Prince of Wales that the Queen might die within days. The Prince therefore decided to stay at Osborne, but no sooner had he arrived than his sisters persuaded him to go back to London to try to head off the Kaiser. It was agreed that it would be best for him not to see the Queen, or to let her know he had come, so that he could truthfully argue "that not even *he* had been allowed to see her". When Reid visited his patient at 6 p.m. that evening, she seemed quite her old self, apart from the fact that her speech remained slurred. "Am I better?" she asked, "I have been very ill." "Yes," said Sir James cheerfully. "Your Majesty has been very ill, but you are now better." Once more she expressed her concern for his own health and told him he must have help.

In 1875 the Queen wrote a memo explaining what she wished to be done if she ever became too ill to issue instructions. In particular, her doctors must understand that "The Queen wishes never to be deceived as to her real state". Sir James was naturally anxious to comply, but not at the price of discouraging her from putting up a fight. Indeed, when he saw her on Saturday evening, she told him that she wanted "to live a little longer" as she still had "things to settle". Meanwhile, in response to a warning telegram from Bigge,

Davidson embarked on the late boat from Southampton, intending to stay with Canon Smith at Whippingham. It was a stormy night and exceptionally rough, but more disagreeable still was a crowd of drunken football supporters returning from the mainland: strange companions, the Bishop thought "in an hour of such anxiety".

Throughout Saturday night the Queen was confused, and next day remained semi-conscious. Sir James became so alarmed that he telegraphed for Sir Thomas Barlow, Holme Professor of Clinical Medicine at University College, and also advised the Prince of Wales to return as soon as possible. Shortly before midnight a carriage was sent to Whippingham to summon Davidson. On Monday, the Queen rallied and even asked for Turi, one of her favourite dogs. When he was eventually put on her bed, she "patted him and seemed pleased to have him beside her". Just before noon, the Prince of Wales arrived with the German Emperor. The Queen at the time was asleep so both tiptoed into her room and gazed at her from the doorway. That evening, however, the Prince had a talk with his mother, who was obviously pleased to see him. Shortly afterwards, Reid returned to her bedside and was surprised when she grasped his hand and kept on kissing it, until it dawned on him that she thought he was her son.

For most of Monday night, Barlow, Reid and Powell remained by the Queen's side. Next morning, January 22nd, the family were summoned as Powell believed she might die at any moment. After Davidson said a few prayers, the Queen asked Beatrice to send for Canon Smith in case "he might be hurt". When Reid asked her to take a little food, she smiled at him and said, "Anything you like!" Later, he asked the Prince of Wales for permission to take the Kaiser to see her. "Certainly," he replied, "and tell him I wish it." For a few moments the Queen's bedroom was cleared, and Sir James told her: "Your Majesty, your grandson the Emperor is here; he has come to see you as you are so ill." Early that afternoon she had another relapse, and the Bishop and Canon Smith resumed their vigil. Most of the family kept coming and going, but the Kaiser never left her, kneeling for hours by her bed and helping Reid to support her. At four p.m. a bulletin was issued warning the world "The Queen is sinking". Shortly before she died, she held out her hand to the Prince of Wales and murmured "Bertie". Meanwhile Davidson read her one of her favourite hymns, "Lead Kindly Light". At first she did not appear to be listening, but when he came to the lines:

"And with the morn those Angel faces smile,
Which I have loved long since and lost awhile"

it was clear she had grasped their meaning. In the silence that followed, her children and grandchildren called out their names as if to arouse her from the eternal sleep into which she was peacefully drifting.

While the Queen's life slowly drew to its close, Balfour sat waiting in the Equerries' room, contemplating the mountain of despatch boxes which had piled up over the past few days: impressive testimony to a lifetime of hard labour. Just before the end, the Queen suddenly raised herself and gazed towards the window. There was a look of joy and recognition in her eyes. "Oh, Albert . . ." she cried, and sank back on her pillow. "I shall never forget," wrote Princess Helena, "the look of radiance on her face. . . . One *felt* and knew she saw beyond the Border Land – and had *seen* and *met* all *her loved ones*. In death she was so beautiful, such peace and joy on her dear face – a radiance from Heaven."

When all was over, the family shook hands with Reid, and the new King told him he would never forget his services to his mother. "Her Majesty," read the final Bulletin, "breathed her last at 6.30 p.m. surrounded by Her Children and Grandchildren." For once, the Kaiser had behaved impeccably, with a "gentleness and selflessness" foreign to his nature. Edward VII was so disarmed that he told his sister, Vicky, he would always remember William's "simple" and "touching" devotion to the Queen. When George V in 1911 invited the Emperor to attend the unveiling of Queen Victoria's Monument in the Mall, he replied that he was "over-joyed at the prospect". "Never in my life," he insisted, "shall I forget the solemn hours in Osborne at her death bed when she breathed her last in my arms! These sacred hours riveted my heart firmly to your house and family, of which I am proud to feel myself a member. And the fact that for the last hours I held the sacred burden of her – the creator of the greatness of Britain – in my arms, in my mind created an invisible special link between her country and its people and me. . . ." Three years later these grandiloquent phrases were blown to bits on the battlefield of the Marne.

The moment the journalists huddled outside the house were handed the final Bulletin, they leapt onto their bicycles and raced towards Cowes, shouting as they hurtled down the road: "Queen dead! Queen dead!" Such unbecoming hubbub was entirely alien to Her Majesty's "whispery" Court, or the calm and peace with which she was still surrounded. When Reid helped her maids to lay out her body, he discovered that "she had a ventral hernia and a prolapse of the uterus". Evidently, during his twenty years with the Queen, he had never before had the chance to examine her properly. After dinner, the Prince of Wales, as he still wished to be called, asked Davidson to hold a brief service. Accordingly, the family gathered in the Queen's bedroom to say a few prayers, while she lay where she had died, "with quantities of white lace and a few simple flowers". In her hand was "the little crucifix which had always hung over her bed". Not many years before, recalcitrant High Churchmen had been prosecuted for venerating the Cross.

Newspapers throughout the world spoke of a feeling of universal grief. Robert Bridges caught the prevailing mood when he said that "It seemed as though the keystone had fallen out of the arch of Heaven". Most of the Queen's subjects felt her loss personally, and some went so far as to speak of a cosmic catastrophe. When a Zulu Warrior Chief was told the news, he announced, "Then tonight I shall see another star in the sky". At Oxford, the streets were filled "with dim figures wandering aimlessly here and there without a word spoken". Only the tolling of the great Bell of Christ Church broke the silence.

When Vicky was told that her mother had died it is said she exclaimed, "I wish I were dead too". On January 23rd, she wrote in her diary "Oh, how can my pen write it, my sweet darling beloved Mama; the best of mothers and greatest of Queens, our centre and help and support – all seems a blank, a terrible awful dream. Realise it one cannot." The page of her journal on which these words were written is smudged and stained with tears. The same day she also wrote to Sophie. "Is she *really* gone?" she asked in numbed bewilderment. "Gone from us to whom she was such a comfort and support. . . . What a Queen she was and what a woman!" Her feelings were shared by the Empress of all the Russias. "I cannot really believe she has gone," she wrote. "England without the Queen seems impossible." Even Henry James, the American novelist, confessed that he "felt her death much more than I should have expected; she was a sustaining symbol".

The Queen, who "loved funerals", gave considerable thought to her own, and left detailed instructions about what she wanted done.

As befitted a soldier's daughter, she wished for a military funeral, but, above all, a white one. When she took Tennyson to see the Mausoleum in 1873, he told her he thought that funerals should always be white: a seed which appears to have fallen on fruitful soil. For forty years the Widow of Windsor had rarely been seen in anything other than black, but now that she hoped to be reunited with Albert the time for mourning was over. Soon after breakfast on January 25th, Reid took charge of preparing the Queen's coffin, in obedience to her commands. Amongst the relics she wanted buried with her was the Prince Consort's dressing gown embroidered by Princess Alice, a plaster cast of his hand, and a number of family photographs. When all was ready, the Queen's body was lifted into the coffin, with the help of the King, the Kaiser and the Duke of Connaught. The family then withdrew, and Sir James, having helped to drape her in her wedding veil, placed John Brown's photograph in her hand, "according to her private instructions". Before the mourners returned to take their last look, Reid tactfully hid his handiwork under a pile of flowers. The King, with his customary magnanimity, sent for the Munshi to give him a chance to bid farewell to his mistress. The coffin was then closed, and a party of blue jackets carried it down to the Dining-Room. When the King returned to London, he left his nephew and Princess Beatrice in charge. Later, the Kaiser was heard to boast that his most treasured possession was the Union Jack which had covered the Queen's remains while she lay in state at Osborne.

On Friday, February 1st, the Queen's coffin was placed on the quarterdeck of the *Alberta*. When she set sail shortly after three, she was followed by the King, on board the *Victoria and Albert*, and the Kaiser in his Imperial Yacht. The *Alberta*, "small, dark and dignified", looked "strangely like the Queen herself" as she glided through two long lines of warships stretching from Cowes to Portsmouth. To the east, lay the mighty battleship *Hatsuse*, a tribute from the Mikado. Throughout the voyage, guns thundered their salutes, and the strains of Chopin's Funeral March drifted across the water. By the time the *Alberta* came to rest under the shadow of Nelson's *Victory*, the sun began to set, and the Victorian era expired in one last glorious blaze. It was just such a scene as Turner loved to depict.

Next morning, the coffin was taken by train to Victoria, and those who travelled with it saw people kneeling reverently by the track. Colonel John St Aubyn (the author's great-uncle) commanded the troops in Buckingham Palace Road. At about eleven fifteen, after several hours of waiting, he caught sight of the gun carriage drawn by eight cream horses. "Some people," he wrote later, "thought the white horses inappropriate, but, as they never conveyed anyone but the Queen during her life, I do not think so myself. The coffin covered with a white pall, and with the Imperial Crown, Orbs, Sceptre and Collar of the Garter on it, passed within a couple of yards of me. Although my head was bowed, I could see the King, the Emperor, and the Duke of Connaught as they moved by very slowly." The procession wended its way to Paddington through densely massed crowds. Spectators were struck by the silence of the ceremony. Few sounds were heard apart from a distant booming of guns, the jingle of swords and curb chains, and the noise of horses' hoofs clattering along the road.

When the coffin was taken by train to Windsor and placed on a waiting gun carriage, the horses kicked and plunged so violently that they managed to break their harness. Meanwhile the front of the procession had marched up Windsor High Street and had to be stopped by an NCO sent by Fritz Ponsonby. Back in the station forecourt, Admiral Sir Michael Culme-Seymour shouted reassuringly: "My boys will soon put things right." Ponsonby, having obtained the King's permission for the Blue Jackets to drag the gun carriage up the hill, instructed the Artillery officers to get their horses clear. Bigge was furious, and told him that he was "ruining the ceremony". Somehow the sailors managed to rig up a harness with the help of a length of communication cord, and to manhandle the gun carriage to the steps of St George's. The Duke of Cambridge shuffled behind on foot, leaning heavily on his son Adolphus's arm. One of the few members of the family to miss the funeral was the Duke of York, who was recovering from measles.

The congregation gathered in St George's shivered as they waited for the procession to arrive. Whoever stoked the boilers evidently shared the late Queen's views about heat. At last, the West Doors were flung open and the service began. That night and the next, the Queen's coffin remained in the Albert Memorial Chapel, beside the recumbent effigies of the Prince Consort, Prince Leopold and Prince Eddy. Day and night, four officers stood motionless on guard: a duty shared alternately by the Grenadiers and the Life Guards. As each hour struck, the relief officers marched in slow time up the aisle of the Chapel, and the senior member of the old guard handed over his duties with the words: "I commit to you the charge of the body of her late Majesty Queen Victoria, Queen of Great Britain and Ireland, Empress of India, together with the Regalia of the British Empire." On Sunday afternoon, two Eton boys, Shane Leslie and his cousin, Hugh Frewen, persuaded a verger to let them see the coffin. Hugh wrote a poem describing the scene for the "Eton College Chronicle", and the King "was kind enough to express the wish that Frewen might one day become the Poet Laureate".

The following afternoon, the Queen set off on her final journey. It was almost impossible to believe that the coffin, which looked like that of a child, contained the remains of the world's greatest Empress. Many of those who walked behind the gun carriage had often accompanied her on that very journey. For the past forty years, whenever she was at Windsor, she seldom allowed a day to pass without a visit to Frogmore. Above the door of the royal shrine were the words: "His mourning widow, Victoria the Queen, directed that all that is mortal of Prince Albert be placed in this sepulchre. A.D. 1862. Farewell, beloved! Here, at last, will I rest with thee; with thee in Christ I will rise again." Now that promised day had dawned.

A simple Prayer Book service was held inside the Mausoleum, and when it was over the royal mourners filed by the open grave. The King went first, and knelt beside his parents' remains. Of all those present, the young Duke of Coburg seemed the most affected. By the time the family returned to the Castle, the ground was dusted with snow, just as it had been when Charles I was buried. Heaven itself had conspired to ensure that the Queen should be given her white funeral.

There is hardly a page of the political history of Queen Victoria's reign which does not bear her impress. She was responsible for inspiring at least four Acts of Parliament: the Public Worship Regulation Act (1874), the Vivisection Act (1876), the Royal Titles Act (1876) and the Law allowing the verdict "Guilty but insane" (1883). Her influence over appointments was second to none. Several of her Prime Ministers, and at least one Archbishop, owed their positions to her favour; while other politicians, such as Labouchere and Dilke, languished in the wilderness because she disapproved of them. When Gladstone was forming his third administration in 1886, the Queen snubbed Vicky for appearing to believe that he ignored her recommendations. "You speak," she complained, "as if I was 'pour rien' – or a mere puppet", whereas, in fact, she had "insisted" on Lord Rosebery for the Foreign Office, and had "refused to accept Mr Childers at the War Office or Admiralty and Lord Ripon for the India Office".

Strangely enough, the Queen herself was to blame for the loss of important prerogatives, in spite of the fact that her policy was to preserve them. It was her decision alone, in defiance of her ministers, to make the Opening of Parliament the exception and not the rule. Instead of identifying the Monarchy with the Houses of Parliament, she managed to suggest that the two were somehow distinct. Moreover, unlike any of her predecessors, she repeatedly travelled abroad without so much as a minister in attendance. It was hardly surprising therefore that some should conclude that the country could do without her. Nor did the fact that she spent so much of the year six hundred miles from London suggest that she played a vital role in the day-to-day business of Government. The impression, of course, was entirely false. The busiest telegraph office in the Kingdom was probably that at Balmoral. But, nevertheless, the Crown's reputation suffered from the delusion that it had virtually ceased to function.

The British Constitution demands that the Sovereign should always remain impartial. Allowing the wish to father the thought, it was widely believed that the Queen never strayed from the paths of political rectitude. Throughout her lifetime this fiction survived "the direst proof of the contrary", although it was known to be false by most of her closest Ministers. What finally destroyed it was the publication of her Letters. She herself was prepared to admit to being partisan. "Do you know, my Dear," she told one of her granddaughters, "I sometimes feel that when I die I shall be just a little nervous about meeting Grandpapa for I have taken to doing a good many things that he would not quite approve of."

From time to time, the suggestion was heard that the Queen should step down in favour of her son, a proposal which Princess Louise and Gladstone both appear to have favoured. The Queen, however, was far too wise to follow their advice. Had she done so, her reign would have ended with a whimper instead of a blaze of triumph. So far from being too old to perform her duties, she possessed an increasing asset: her lifetime of experience. It was all very well to pity her eldest son for having to wait so long to succeed, but that hardly sufficed to justify a change in the Constitution. Besides it is nonsense to suppose that the life of a Prince of Wales only begins when he comes to the throne. The very fact that his role is ill-defined allows him the freedom to fashion it as he chooses.

The fact that the Queen lived to be over eighty transformed her into a national institution, who appeared to be part of the permanent order of nature. She outlived every one of the Privy Councillors who welcomed her on her accession. During her reign she had eleven Lord Chancellors, ten Prime Ministers and six Archbishops of Canterbury. When Campbell-Bannerman sought to win her approval for his plans for Army reform, he made the mistake of telling her they were new. "No, Mr Bannerman," she said, "Lord Palmerston proposed exactly the same thing to me in '52 and Lord Palmerston was wrong." She enjoyed almost all the advantages which civil servants possess in handling ministers: experience of the past and continuity of office. But no official, however permanent, could rival the Queen's unbroken years of service. Often those whose duty it was to advise her were obliged to confess they had more to learn than impart. Knowledge, as ever, meant power.

If the Queen was sometimes slow to respond to sweeping political change, that was not to say that she somehow remained the only fixed star in the firmament. On the contrary, it is possible to identify six different Victorias, related and yet distinct, and evolving according to inner laws of development. The first of these multiple personalities was Victoria I (1819–1837), the frustrated prisoner of Kensington Palace, battling against hostility and intrigue. Next, came Victoria II (1837–1839), the Young Queen revelling in her new-found freedom and the charms of her Prime Minister. There followed Victoria III (1840–1842), Albert's devoted bride, absorbed by her love for her husband but reluctant to share her duties. After two years, there emerged Victoria IV (1842–1861), who struggled in vain to make Albert King, and who could not select a bonnet without his help. Peel, who had proved anathema to Victoria II, had now become her hero. In 1861, Victoria V (1861–1874) appeared – or rather disappeared – the shattered, despairing widow, hiding away in the Highlands wrestling with grief. But, eventually, revived by Dizzy's magic, she made a triumphant return as Victoria VI (1874–1901), this time in the role of an Empress. Had Palmerston survived into the reign of Victoria R.I. he would not have been unwelcome.

On the whole the Queen's subjects were far more concerned with her social and moral influence than her constitutional rule. No previous age had so fervently believed in the sanctity of the family, or looked so confidently to their Sovereign to personify its virtues. The Queen was survived by six children, thirty-two grandchildren and thirty-seven great-grandchildren. It is little wonder therefore that her subjects saw her as "the mother" of her people, and rejoiced in her "happy and blessed family life". It would be wrong to suggest that the Queen began the Victorian cult of the Family, but no one did more to popularise it.

In 1858, Lord Shaftesbury assured the Queen that working people "valued and loved a moral Court and a happy domestic home". Later, Disraeli said much the same when he claimed that the hearth was "sacred". Naturally therefore the Nation looked to a family to represent it, although there were some who complained of the cost of so doing. Labouchère suggested that the National Anthem should end with the following verse.

> "Grandchildren not a few,
> With great-grandchildren too,
> She blest has been.
> We've been their sureties,
> Paid them gratuities,
> Pensions, annuities,
> God save the Queen!"

In 1896 Davidson told the Queen that she wielded "a personal and domestic influence over the thrones of Europe without precedent in the History of Christendom". Three factors help to explain her remarkable dominance: she was the acknowledged head of the European royal family, she was the longest reigning Sovereign of them all, and she presided over the world's greatest Empire. One clear sign of Britain's new ascendancy was the fact that English increasingly replaced French as the language of diplomacy. Nowhere was the Queen's influence more apparent than in Europe's royal nurseries. From Athens to St Petersburg, British nannies wielded an authority which Genghis Khan would have envied. Even the Empress Eugénie was persuaded to engage a Miss Shaw to bring up the Prince Imperial. Reading the Queen's correspondence, it would be easy to suppose that she earned her living managing an employment agency for nurserymaids and nannies.

When hostilities broke out in 1914 almost all the rulers involved

were related to Queen Victoria. Yet in spite of that fact they failed
to prevent war, thus putting an end to the Prince Consort's dream of
peace being preserved by a closely related royal family. Something,
however, survived of his and the Queen's ideals. Their daunting
example of industry, their informal home life, and their stern commitment to duty, became the model for most of their successors.

In the nineteenth century, perhaps more than ever before, people
looked to the Court as a yardstick of social behaviour. The story
goes that an elderly lady was taken to see Sarah Bernhardt act Cleo-
patra. When the curtain came down on her frenzied histrionics, she
saw fit to remark: "How different, how very different from the
home life of our own dear Queen!" Certainly the Queen saw it as
her duty to set a moral example, and she always remembered Albert
showing her a passage he had marked in Saint-Simon which argued
that the best way to promote religious principles was to live a blameless life.

One entirely new factor which helped her to spread her influence
throughout her three kingdoms was the coming of the railway.
George III never went further north than Worcester, but his granddaughter travelled from London to Aberdeen in the course of a single
night. In 1877, the United States Minister in London, Edward
Pierrepont, told Ponsonby that his fellow countrymen felt a "deep
and sincere admiration for the Queen", whom they regarded as "*a
true and most exemplary woman*". The Royal example, however, was
not invariably elevating. One old lady remembered how "as children
we were allowed to gnaw our chicken bones because, according to
our nurse, Queen Victoria did so, and 'What's good enough for the
Queen is good enough for you my dears!'"

It has often been argued that one of the Queen's chief strengths
was the fact that she shared the views of the "Man on the Clapham
Omnibus". Yet in many important respects she was less typical of
her age than the fact that she lent it her name might first suggest.
Indeed, several of her views were so blatantly unorthodox as to
make her one of its critics. On the other hand, nothing was more
characteristic of the Victorians than to insist that the world was out
of joint. Carlyle's incessant grumbling was just as typical of the
Zeitgeist as the trumpetings of Macaulay.

A spate of improving books about the Queen appeared at the time
of her Golden and Diamond Jubilees. In 1887, to take one instance
of the genre, an anonymous work was published entitled *Queen*

Victoria: Her Character brought out by Incidents in Her Life. The book shared much in common with the devotional writings of Thomas à Kempis, being primarily concerned to exhibit her Majesty's character "in the hope that many who admire her may be induced to imitate her". The Jubilee biographies lingered a little too fondly on the Queen's legendary virtues. There was even a "Jubilee Song" which, for all its problems with scansion and rhyme, struck an uplifting note:

> "Let ev'ry English Maiden make this her frequent prayer;
> That she the same high purpose may with her Sovereign share."

Ten years later, the Sunday School Union, published a volume in its *Splendid Lives Series* called *The Story of Victoria, R.I. Wife, Mother, Queen*. Its author, W.J. Wintle, had already achieved success with his life of *Albert the Good*. In a sense he disposed of his theme on his title page by quoting the late Lord Tennyson.

> "Her Court was pure; her life serene;
> God gave her peace; her land reposed;
> A thousand claims of reverence closed
> In her as Mother, Wife and Queen."

Just how far Wintle allowed piety to run riot may be seen from his reference to the "stainless life" of her father, the Duke of Kent. Greville, who knew the Duke personally, was a good deal nearer the mark in describing him as the "greatest rascal that ever went unhung".

Inevitably the Queen's life lent force to those campaigning for Female Emancipation, in spite of her marked dislike for the movement. H.G. Wells remembered his mother telling him "that among school-mistresses and such like women", there was a stir of emancipation associated with the claims of the Princess Victoria to succeed King William IV. In 1895, Mrs Henry Fawcett, the militant suffragette leader, published a life of Her Majesty. It was the first in a new series on *Eminent Women*, "strongly bound in cloth" and costing a shilling a volume. Presumably the Queen would have raised no objection to finding herself in the company of Elizabeth Fry or Susanna Wesley, but would she have welcomed that of George Sand and Mary Shelley? Mrs Fawcett lavishly praised her for remaining aloof from party political squabbles, and went on to insist that there was "probably not a mother in England who had given more loving thought and care" to her children. Seldom has the line between biography and fiction been drawn so imprecisely. There is no particular evidence to suggest that the Queen's example transformed the moral tone of the country. If she could not succeed in persuading the Prince of Wales to copy her way of life, it is difficult to believe that the citizens of Windsor restrained their "amorous inclinations" merely because she was known to frown on adultery, or that the inhabitants of Glasgow "corked up their whisky bottles" for fear of risking her censure. As has often been pointed out, the problem is not to know what is right but to do it.

It was but one step from portraying the Queen as a model of virtuous living, to conceiving her as being little less than a goddess. Although she dismissed such talk as "twaddle", it did at least show how profoundly feelings had changed since Dilke and his friends had talked of a Second Republic. The story is told of an old African Chief who greeted a new Governor with two questions: "How am Queen Victoria, how am 'postle Paul?" If she was not actually divine, she kept impeccable company. Her greatness, however, did not depend on her being a latter-day Saint, and she greatly disliked attempts to portray her as such. "If they only knew what I really am like," she remarked on being shown an over-effusive pen portrait. On almost the only occasion that Gladstone resorted to flattery, she told him curtly: "She does not like to be praised for what she does not deserve". When she unveiled her statue in Kensington Gardens at the time of her Diamond Jubilee, she received a rapturous welcome. On her way back to Windsor, Princess Marie Louise asked her whether she did not feel proud to be so loved. "No dear Child," she replied, only "very humble". On an earlier occasion, she drove to Kensal Green to put a wreath on "dear Janie Ely's" tomb. "We could not understand," she wrote, why there was such a crowd, "and thought something must be going on, but it turned out it was only to see me." She was not always, of course, so self-effacing. Her practice of writing in the third person encouraged her to think of herself as a disembodied being, as an institution not as an individual. In 1885, when she appealed to Goschen to help her destroy Home Rule, she insisted "I do not speak for myself" but as "Queen of England".

No previous British Sovereign was anything like so well known as Queen Victoria. The invention of photography, the coming of the railway, and the rapid growth of literacy, combined to spread her fame. State education also played a part in adding to her prestige. Not a schoolday began without saying a prayer for the Queen and the Royal Family. Towards the end of her reign the popular press was hungry for crumbs of gossip from the Court. It was only by keeping it firmly at arm's length that she succeeded in resisting its encroaching triviality. Much as her love of seclusion was denounced, it helped to protect the mystical aspect of Monarchy. "Secrecy," wrote Bagehot, is "essential to its utility. . . . Above all things, our royalty is to be reverenced, and if you begin to poke about it you cannot reverence it. . . . Its mystery is its life."

Early obituaries of the Queen struck far too fulsome a note. Not until April 1901 did the *Quarterly Review* venture to print some mildly critical comments. The author, who preferred to remain anonymous, was Edmund Gosse, briefed by Lady Ponsonby. The time had come, he announced, "to abandon the note of purely indiscriminate praise" which had hitherto prevailed, and to put this "revered personage into the crucible of criticism". His insistence that none is without fault, not even the late Queen, created a major sensation. Arthur Benson, who knew what he was talking about, described Gosse's article as "a noble and transparent piece of character-drawing". Even its most daring revelation, that "The Queen was less ready to yield to ministerial dictation than was commonly supposed", was hardly news to Lord Rosebery or Lord Salisbury. Otherwise, the worst it saw fit to confess was that sometimes she seemed to prefer her own interests to those of her family and friends.

In the aftermath of the First World War, the *Quarterly's* tentative steps became a headlong stampede. The world had changed, and people refused to accept the restraints of the nineteenth century. They tried to drown their memories of the horrors they had survived in a reckless search for pleasure. To their eyes Queen Victoria was a symbol of repression: hence their accusations of hypocrisy and cant. In fact, the charge was absurd, but they managed to make it stick. It is always easier to demolish a caricature than prevail against the truth.

In retrospect, the nineteenth century seems relatively peaceful and stable, but distance lends enchantment. At the time, the future looked stormy and unsettled, but everyone knew they could always depend on the Queen as a guiding light amidst the "encircling gloom". Whatever else might change, she was there to guarantee continuity. In 1899, when her grandson, the Kaiser, was showing his retinue round Windsor, he pointed at the Round Tower and informed them: "From this Tower the World is ruled". In fact, it only contained the Royal Archives, but he was right to stress how wide her bounds were set. Much the same thought occurred to Hélène Varesco, Missy's Lady-in-Waiting. In 1897, Hélène was given a room in the Castle overlooking the Queen's. Long after everyone else had gone to bed, she noticed the lights opposite still blazing, and confessed to feeling awestruck at the thought of "the frail little old lady" working into the early hours of the morning, and holding "the threads of her Empire" in her hands.

Those who knew the Queen best found her irresistible. Marie Mallet described her as "wonderfully dear and kind", and Lady Augusta Bruce thought her "so innocent and lovable" that she spoke of her as "the blessed One". Such devotion was not confined to those who knew her personally. Like Elizabeth before her she had every right to boast: "This I count the glory of my crown: that I have reigned with your loves." When she came to the throne in 1837 she was an unknown schoolgirl of eighteen. When she died in 1901 the whole world mourned her passing.

Queen Victoria's Prime Ministers
1837–1901

Viscount Melbourne 1837–1841
Sir Robert Peel 1841–1846
Lord John Russell 1846–1852
Earl of Derby 1852
Earl of Aberdeen 1852–1855
Viscount Palmerston 1855–1858
Earl of Derby 1858–1859
Viscount Palmerston 1859–1865
Earl Russell 1865–1866
Earl of Derby 1866–1868
Disraeli 1868
Gladstone 1868–1874
Disraeli 1874–1880
Gladstone 1880–1885
Marquis of Salisbury 1885–1886
Gladstone 1886
Marquis of Salisbury 1886–1892
Gladstone 1892–1894
Earl of Rosebery 1894–1895
Marquis of Salisbury 1895–1901

Chronology

Note on Sources

John van der Kiste has produced a useful "select bibliography" of *Queen Victoria's Family*, Clover Publications 1982, which lists "the main volumes of biography, published correspondence, and journals of Queen Victoria, the Prince Consort, and their immediate family". Most books discussed in the following note are mentioned in "Books Cited". Those which are not are provided below with details of publication.

Lady Longford's *Victoria R. I.*, written in 1964, is the envy and despair of those who venture to follow her. In 1972 Mrs Woodham-Smith brought out the first volume of *Queen Victoria Her Life and Times 1819 – 1861*, but unhappily died before completing its sequel. Her book throws fresh light on Queen Victoria's childhood, and her bitter feelings for Conroy. Three earlier biographies remain especially well worth reading. In 1902, Sidney Lee published *Queen Victoria*, based on his article for the *Dictionary of National Biography*. Its lucid account of her reign and career owed much to the help of those who had known her personally. During and after the First World War, a new school of biographers emerged, whose principal purpose seems to have been to speak ill of the dead. Not for them such inconceivable heroes as Martin's Prince Consort, but men and women of flesh and blood, teeming with human frailty. In 1918, Lytton Strachey, a pioneer of the movement, went on the rampage, toppling four *Eminent Victorians* from their pedestals. While many rejoiced to see his victims humbled, others deplored his reckless virtuosity. Soon after it became known that he was writing about the Queen, his mother begged him to remember that she had won "a reputation in our history which it would be highly unpopular, and I think not quite fair, to attempt to bring down". His most serious problem was shortage of primary evidence. Strachey's portrait of *Queen Victoria* published in 1921 has not altogether survived the test of time, but remains a literary triumph: perspicacious, stylish and sparkling. It was, moreover, a remarkable tribute to the Queen that Strachey, like Baalam before him, "went out to curse and stayed to bless". He "analysed, he dissected, he derided, but at the end he could not help admiring". In 1935, E.F. Benson, Archbishop Benson's second son, published *Queen Victoria*, in which he was able to draw on family recollections and his own exceptional insight into character.

"The truest service to the Queen", according to Lord Esher, was "to let her speak for herself." Authorised selections from *Letters of Queen Victoria* have been published in nine volumes. The first three came out in 1907, covering the years 1837–1861. Three further volumes appeared between 1926 and 1928 dealing with the period from 1862 to 1885. The last three volumes came out between 1930 and 1932 bringing the record down to 1901. The First series (Volumes I to III) was edited by Lord Esher and Arthur Benson, and the remaining two series were edited by George Buckle, a former editor of *The Times* and biographer of Disraeli. His handling of the Queen's correspondence with Gladstone was plainly inspired by his high regard for Lord Beaconsfield. Viscount Gladstone in his book *After Thirty Years* denounced Buckle's "positive cataract of aspersion and disparagement", and felt justified in ignoring his father's plea that nothing he wrote which might harm the Queen should ever appear in print.

Just before the Second World War, Hector Bolitho edited *Further Letters of Queen Victoria* consisting of letters from the Queen to the Prussian royal family. In 1964 Roger Fulford produced the first of five volumes of correspondence between the Queen and her eldest daughter, Vicky. (See below 629). Richard Hough's *Advice to a Grand-daughter*, consisting of letters from Queen Victoria to Princess Victoria of Hesse, is particularly interesting for the light which it throws on H.M.'s views of the duty of a wife. The Queen's correspondence with Lord Tennyson, edited by Hope Dyson and Charles Tennyson, has been published with the title *Dear and Honoured Lady*. The letters discuss the problems of immortality, and show how much *In Memoriam* meant to the Queen. Brian Connell's *Regina v Palmerston*, and Philip Guedalla's two volumes, *The Queen and Mr Gladstone*, are important sources of letters to and from the Queen on vexed political issues. Guedalla's introductory remarks are especially penetrating in their analysis of the Queen's evolving persona.

The Queen kept a diary from the time she was fourteen until eight days before her death (see 29) In 1912 Lord Esher published *The Girlhood of Queen Victoria* in two volumes, which mainly consist of extracts from her journal from 1832 to 1840. The early extracts are disappointingly reserved, presumably because the Duchess of Kent and Lehzen insisted on reading them. But the moment the Princess became Queen, and her journal was written for her eyes alone, it could hardly have been more candid. The portrait she painted of Lord Melbourne was enchanting, as was the innocent way she charted her growing affection for Albert. Her journal accounts of Napoleon III's visit to Windsor in 1855, and her return visit to Paris later that year, are printed in *Leaves from a Journal*, introduced by Raymond Mortimer. The Queen herself published two volumes of extracts from her journal during her lifetime: *Journal of Our Life in the Highlands* in 1868 (see 364) and *More Leaves from the Journal of a Life in the Highlands* in 1884 (see 424).

During the first four years of Queen Victoria's reign, Sallie Stevenson, whose husband was the American Minister to the Court of St James's, spent a good deal of time at Windsor and Buckingham Palace. Her letters to her family in Virginia, edited by Edward Boykin in *Victoria, Albert and Mrs. Stevenson*, provide a discerning portrait of the young Queen, and lively accounts of her Coronation and Marriage.

The Greville Memoirs 1814–1860, edited by Lytton Strachey and Roger Fulford, are a mine of information and gossip. Charles Greville was Clerk to the Council from 1821 to 1859, and a leading figure in London Society. He was exceedingly well connected, being descended from the Dukes of Portland and Devonshire, and seems to have known almost everyone of note. His journals are amongst the most fascinating in English literature, partly because of his inside information, partly because of his appetite for gossip, and partly because of his shrewd assessment of character. When extracts from his diaries were published in 1874, Disraeli described the book as "a social outrage".

The *Correspondence of Sarah Spencer Lady Lyttelton*, edited by Mrs Hugh Wyndham, gives a less abrasive account of the royal family. Lady Lyttelton was governess to the Queen's eldest children between 1842–1850 (see 174) and her letters describe the Queen's home life, her views on education, and her devotion to her husband. Lady Lyttelton became very fond of her pupils and their mother, and greatly admired Prince Albert. Miss Charlotte Stuart, who in 1835 married "Clemency" Canning, was one of the Queen's Ladies-in-Waiting between 1842 and 1856. Her letters and diaries are full of descriptions of everyday royal life. The Queen was particularly fond of her, and after she left for India in 1856, kept up a close correspondence. *Charlotte Canning* by Virginia Surtees, and Charles Allen's *A Glimpse of the Burning Plain*, print letters from the Queen and extracts from Charlotte's journals and correspondence.

Lady Augusta Bruce (Lady A. Stanley) was one of the most beloved of all the Queen's ladies. Her letters to her younger sister "Fanny" (Lady Francis Baillie) contain vivid portraits of the Queen, Prince Albert, and the royal children. They are particularly valuable for being affectionate but not adulatory. Lady Augusta's letters have been edited by Hector Bolitho, with the help of her nephew, Albert Baillie (Dean of Windsor 1917–1944). They were published in two volumes: *Letters of Lady Augusta Stanley*, (1849–1863) and *Later Letters of Lady Augusta Stanley* (1864–1876).

Lord Clarendon, who was Foreign Secretary three times between 1853 and 1870, wrote a series of wonderfully indiscreet letters to the Duchess of Manchester, which he posted under the impression that they were burnt after being read. He referred to the Queen as "Eliza", and denounced her seclusion after Prince Albert's death. "Eliza," he wrote in 1869, "is roaring well, and can do everything she likes and nothing she doesn't." Nevertheless, he understood better than most the devastating nature of her loss. A.L. Kennedy's *My Dear Duchess* offers a selection of Clarendon's letters to the Duchess written between 1858 and 1869.

Few people knew the Queen better than Sir Henry Ponsonby, her private secretary from 1870–1895. Sir Henry's son Arthur (Lord Ponsonby of Shulbrede) wrote a biography of his father, *Henry Ponsonby. His Life from his Letters*. The book makes extensive use of letters to the Queen, on behalf of the Queen, and from the Queen. Ponsonby's son, Fritz, (Lord Sysonby) supplemented his father's and brother's portrait of H.M. in *Recollections of Three Reigns*, and *Sidelights on Queen Victoria*. The Ponsonby family were famous for their wit and liberal principles, and the Court was less astonished than dismayed when Arthur Ponsonby became Leader of the Labour Opposition in the Lords. The whole family took a refreshingly detached view of royalty, and their correspondence with one another about the foibles of the Queen was highly entertaining, but none the less affectionate. Sir Henry would have been greatly disturbed to see his lightest remarks mulled over by historians with ponderous solemnity. They were not intended as definitive judgements but as passing jests.

In 1881 Dr James Reid became Queen Victoria's resident medical attendant, a post he retained for the rest of her reign. Soon after his appointment, the Queen began to depend upon him for a great deal more than medical advice. In 1985 Michaela Reid published a biography of her husband's grandfather, *Ask Sir James*, based on scrapbooks, diaries and some two hundred notes from H.M. Her book offers important new evidence about the Queen's health during the last twenty years of her life, and provides a fascinating picture of her Household, of the way she employed Sir James as a political intermediary, and of her obsessive regard for the Munshi.

In 1883 the Queen appointed Randall Davidson, then a young man of thirty-five, to be Dean of Windsor, and soon began to turn to him for spiritual advice, and help with family problems. (See 451). Dr Bell's two volume biography *Randall Davidson* contains many important letters from the Queen, and not only shows how Crown patronage was exercised, but the extent to which she regarded the Dean as a "father confessor". The book provides the most authoritative account of the Queen's projected life of John Brown, and Davidson's role in persuading her not to publish it.

Courtiers were not supposed to keep diaries, but several ignored this requirement. General Grey's daughter, Louisa, Countess of Antrim, kept a detailed journal, extracts from which have been published by Elizabeth Longford in *Louisa Lady in Waiting*. Her portrait of life in the royal Household, supplements that of Edith, Countess of Lytton. Like Lady Antrim, Lady Lytton kept a journal, extracts from which may be found in *Lady Lytton's Court Diary*, edited by her granddaughter Mary Lutyens. In 1887, Marie Mallet (née Adeane) was appointed a Maid of Honour, and struck up an intimate friendship with the Queen. Her letters to her mother and husband have been published by her son, Victor Mallet, in *Life with Queen Victoria*. Between them these three books give first-hand accounts of what life was like at Windsor, Balmoral and Osborne in the last decade of the reign.

In April 1901 *The Quarterly Review* printed an unsigned obituary of the Queen, in fact written by Edmund Gosse, briefed by Lady Ponsonby. It struck a new note of cautious candour (see 607). Early the following year, Sir Theodore Martin privately circulated a memoir of the Queen designed to redress the balance. It was eventually published in 1908 with the title *Queen Victoria as I knew Her*, and portrays a simple, kindly and humble human being.

Countless biographies of the ten Prime Ministers of Queen Victoria's reign deal with their relations with the Crown. Of these, David Cecil's *Lord M* provides an engaging account of Melbourne's education of his Sovereign, and the affectionate friendship which soon sprang up between them. Robert Blake's *Disraeli* performs a similar service for a Conservative Prime Minister. The six volumes of Monypenny and Buckle's *The Life of Benjamin Disraeli, Earl of Beaconsfield*, quotes extensively from the Queen's correspondence between 1868 and 1881. Gladstone's endless wrangles with the Queen are discussed at length in Lord Morley's *Life of Mr. Gladstone* (3 volumes), Philip Magnus's *Gladstone*, and *The Diary of Sir Edward Walter Hamilton 1880 – 1885* (Gladstone's private secretary) edited by Dudley Bahlman. David Brooks, in *The Destruction of Lord Rosebery*, prints further extracts from Sir Edward's journal, covering the years 1894–1895. Lady Gwendolen Cecil's four-volume biography of her father, *Life of Robert Marquis of Salisbury*, contains ample evidence of the Queen's confidence in the last of her Prime Ministers. Unfortunately, Lady Gwendolen never finished her book which ends with the fall of the Conservative Government in 1892.

There are surprisingly few lives of Queen Victoria's parents. David Duff's *Edward of Kent* (Stanley Paul. 1938) offers a charitable account of her father's life and career; while Dulcie Ashdowne's portrait *Queen Victoria's Mother* is almost too congenial, particularly as it appears to ignore the devastating evidence to be found in Mrs Woodham-Smith's *Queen Victoria 1819 – 1861* about the Duchess's complicity in Conroy's machinations. Philip Ziegler's *King William IV* (Collins. 1971) gives a fascinating account of Princess Victoria's relations with her uncle, and his quarrels with her mother. Roger Fulford's *Royal Dukes* provides masterly vignettes of George III's sons (the Queen's father and uncles). The Queen's brother-in-law published his *Memoirs of Ernest II* in four dreary volumes, and Joanna Richardson in *My Dearest Uncle* presents an intriguing account of Leopold I of the Belgians, the éminence grise of his age. *The Life and Letters of Princess Feodore* (Robert Hale. 1967) by Harold Albert offers a pleasing portrait of the Queen's half-sister. There are three biographies of her first cousin, George, Duke of Cambridge, who was Commander-in-Chief of her army for thirty-nine years, the most recent being the present author's *The Royal George*. The Duke's sister, Queen Mary's mother, was the subject of Sir Clement Kinloch Cooke's two-volume *A Memoir of H.R.H. Princess Mary Adelaide, Duchess of Teck*. This cumbersome portrait does scant justice to a scatty but lovable character.

In 1862 Arthur Helps published an edited version of *The Principal Speeches and Addresses of H.R.H. the Prince Consort*. Selections from the Prince's letters, edited by Kurt Jagow, were published in 1938 with the title *Letters of the Prince Consort 1831 – 1861*. Hector Bolitho's *The Prince Consort and his Brother* prints some two hundred further letters. Soon after her husband's death, the Queen commissioned General Grey to write an official life of the Prince. The General died before getting further than 1841, and his book appeared in 1867 as *The Early Years of H.R.H. the Prince Consort*. It was left to Theodore Martin to complete the undertaking (see 350). Martin's *The Life of H.R.H. the Prince Consort* ran into five volumes. The book prints large numbers of the Prince's letters, and extracts from the innumerable memoranda he so delighted in writing, and is rather more valuable for the raw material it contains than for its portrait of the Prince, who is represented as virtually exempt from human imperfection. His task was not made easier by the meticulous interest shown in his work by Albert's adoring widow. Among the best modern biographies of the Prince are Roger Fulford's *The Prince Consort*, Frank Eyck's *The Prince Consort: a political biography*, Daphne Bennett's *King without a Crown*, and Robert Rhodes James's *Albert, Prince Consort*. Two recent books concentrate on the Prince's domestic life: Tyler Whittle's *Victoria and Albert at Home*, and Joanna Richardson's *Victoria and Albert: a study of a marriage*.

There are three outstanding biographies of Queen Victoria's eldest daughter, Vicky: Egon Corti's *The English Empress*, Daphne Bennett's *Vicky*, and Andrew Sinclair's *The Other Victoria*. In 1928 Frederick Ponsonby, the Empress's godson, published *Letters of the Empress Frederick*. Shortly before she died, she asked Ponsonby to smuggle her letters out of Germany (see 557). When Ponsonby printed them, the former Kaiser, and several members of the British royal family were shocked by their publication, but Vicky's surviving daughters, Sophie and Margaret, were delighted to see that justice at last had been done to the memory of their mother. Roger Fulford devoted much of the last years of his life to editing five volumes of the Queen's correspondence with her eldest daughter, starting with *Dearest Child* and ending with *Beloved Mama*. (See Books Cited for the complete list.) Fulford's editing is exemplary and the letters provide the most intimate revelations of the Queen's thought and feelings that have ever appeared in print. Fulford died before covering the years 1886 to 1901, but Agatha Ramm completed his task in *Beloved and Darling Child*. From the moment that Vicky's daughter Sophie married Crown Prince Constantine and went to live in Greece, the Dowager Empress wrote her some two thousand letters (1889–1901). These have been edited by Arthur Lee in *The Empress Frederick writes to Sophie*.

King George V invited Sir Sidney Lee, a distinguished biographer and a former editor of the Dictionary of National Biography, to write his father's official life. Sir Sidney's book came out in two massive volumes with the title *King Edward VII*. The first appeared in 1929 and covered the years 1841–1901 from birth to accession. The second was published two years later and dealt with the King's reign, 1901–1910. The chief value of Lee's study lies in its detailed documentation. The standard modern biography is Philip Magnus's *King Edward the Seventh*. Two more recent books have helped to supplement Magnus: Gordon Brook-Shepherd's *Uncle of Europe* (Collins. 1975) and Giles St Aubyn's *Edward VII, Prince and King*, which draws on the hitherto unpublished papers of Francis Knollys, the King's private secretary from 1870 to 1910. The best life of King Edward's much tried and much loved consort is Georgina Battiscombe's *Queen Alexandra*.

Soon after the death of her daughter Princess Alice, Queen Victoria asked a Darmstadt clergyman, Dr Carl Sell, to write a brief biographical sketch of the Grand Duchess. Dr Sell's book was published in 1884, with a preface by Princess Helena. The book was called *Princess Alice Grand Duchess of Hesse*, but the title page made no mention of its author. Gerald Noel's *Princess Alice*, subtitled "Queen Victoria's forgotten daughter", is an admirable recent study. David Duff's *Hessian Tapestry* begins with a portrait of the Princess, and goes on to trace her children's tragic history. Duff's survey of the family demonstrates the political ramifications of the descendants of Queen Victoria. John van der Kiste and Bee Jordaan, co-authors of *Dearest Affie*, do justice to the Prince's merits without concealing his failings. Jehanne Wake's biography *Princess Louise* provides a lively and kindly portrait of a gifted but waspish woman. It also shows how generous her mother was when her marriage ran into trouble. Sir George Aston's *H.R.H. The Duke of Connaught* is a rather wooden account of the Duke's career, and in spite of describing itself as an "intimate study" does not even mention Leonie Lady Leslie, whom the Duchess accepted as part of a *ménage à trois*. Sir Howard Elphinstone V.C. the Duke's Governor and later Treasurer and Comptroller, was a great favourite of Queen Victoria, who wrote of him that "few if *any* gentlemen ever were on such confidential terms with me as dear excellent Sir Howard". Elphinstone's daughter, Mary McClintock, in *The Queen thanks Sir Howard* provides interesting glimpses of the royal family between 1858 and 1867, and prints many revealing letters from H.M. on the upbringing of her children. There are two lives of Princess Beatrice: M.E. Sara's *The Life and Times of H.R.H. Princess Beatrice* (Stanley Paul. 1945) and David Duff's *The Shy Princess*. Both struggle gallantly with a somewhat unpromising subject. Marlene Eilers' *Queen Victoria's Descendants* surveys more than six hundred and seventy of the Queen's offspring, and is an invaluable genealogical guide to her family. Dulcie Ashdown's *Queen Victoria's Family* (Hale, 1975) and *Victoria and the Coburgs* (Hale, 1981) are both studies of the way in which the "Royal tribe" – the Queen's phrase – wielded "power and influence from one end of Europe to the other." Theo Aronson discusses the same theme in his *Grandmama of Europe*, but concentrates especially on those descendants of the Queen who *first* occupied one or other of ten European thrones. Meriel Buchanan, the author of *Queen Victoria's relations*, grew up in various embassies before the First World War. Her father, Sir George Buchanan, succeeded the present author's grandfather, Sir Arthur Nicolson, as ambassador at St Petersburg. In writing her book Miss Buchanan was able to draw on recollections of many of those she describes.

The Kaiser, William II, is probably the subject of more books than all Queen Victoria's grandchildren put together. E.F. Benson's *The Kaiser and his English relations* gives an entertaining account of William's dealings with his grandmother and his uncle the Prince of Wales. A more recent work, based on a mass of material published since Benson's book appeared in 1936, is Michael Balfour's *The Kaiser and his times*. (Penguin, 1975) The Kaiser's autobiography *My Early Life* offers a slightly unreal account of his youth. In 1889, his sister, Princess Victoria (Moretta) was invited to stay with their grandmother. During this visit, she wrote a number of letters to her mother describing the Queen's life and that of her Court. These have been edited by James Pope-Hennessy in *Queen Victoria at Windsor and Balmoral*. Egon Corti's *Alexander von Battenberg* (Cassell. 1955) tells Sandro's story, which reads like that of a prince of Ruritania, and describes his thwarted engagement.

Michael Harrison's *Clarence* is the only modern biography of the Duke of Clarence and Avondale. The book perhaps dwells a little too fondly on the lurid side of the Duke's career, and appears to take seriously the ludicrous suggestion that he was actually Jack the Ripper. Those who believe that can believe anything. George V has been singularly fortunate in his biographers. Both Harold Nicolson's and Kenneth Rose's *King George V* are models of their genre, as is James Pope-Hennessy's *Queen Mary*. These three books show that meticulous scholarship does not have to be couched in turgid jargon.

The Queen's granddaughter, Victoria of Hesse, was especially close to H.M. after Princess Alice's death. She, and her husband, Prince Louis of Battenberg, are the subjects of Richard Hough's biography *Louis and Victoria*. Her cousin, Princess Marie of Edinburgh (Missy), who later became Queen of Roumania, wrote *The Story of my Life* in three volumes. In the first, she describes her childhood memories of her grandmother, and gives interesting portraits of her parents. Helena's daughter, Princess Marie Louise, also wrote an autobiography: *My Memories of six reigns*. It is especially valuable for its descriptions of her mother, about whom little else has been written, and for the account it gives of the Queen's help and sympathy when her odious husband deserted her. Leopold's daughter, Princess Alice (Countess of Athlone) decided to write her reminiscences when she was over eighty, partly, as their title suggests, *For My Grandchildren*. Her recollections include awesome memories of Queen Victoria, an affectionate portrait of her mother, and a firsthand account of the way in which her brother "Charlie" became heir to the Dukedom of Coburg (see 586).

There are a number of interesting books concerned with the Queen's home life and the way she spent her leisure. Vera Watson's *A Queen at Home* gives "an intimate account of the social and domestic life of Queen Victoria's Court", largely derived from the Lord Chamberlain's records. John Matson's *Dear Osborne* (Hamish Hamilton. 1975) and Ivor Brown's *Balmoral* give detailed histories of these residences, and the holiday life of the royal family. There were few things the Queen enjoyed as much as going to a play, and nothing shows more clearly how devoted she was to Prince Albert than the fact that she never entered a theatre after 1861. Nevertheless, towards the end of her life, she revived the practice of amateur theatricals, and invited professional companies to perform for her at Court. George Rowell in *Queen Victoria goes to the Theatre*, has drawn on material in the Royal Archives to discuss almost every performance she ever saw, and to show what a shrewd and decided critic she was. Marina Warner's *Queen Victoria's Sketchbook* charmingly illustrates the Queen's artistic gifts. Her paintings and drawings provide visible proof of the range of her enthusiasms, her power of observation, and her innocent zest for life: le style est l'homme même.

Not much has been written about the Queen's religion, in spite of its importance. In 1902 Walter Walsh published *The Religious Life and Influence of Queen Victoria*. He was severely hampered by ignorance as virtually nothing had then appeared in print. Walsh was an Evangelical Anglican who hoped to establish that there had never been "a more truly God-fearing Sovereign" since "the birth of Christianity": a view which the Queen would have swept aside as "twaddle". Walter Arnstein's article "Queen Victoria and Religion", in Gail Malmgreen's *Religion in the Lives of English Women* (Croom Helm. 1986) is briefer and more informative.

The success of the Monarchy depends in part on its invisible advisers. Paul Emden's *Behind the Throne* investigates the work of the Queen's private secretaries, and shows how her secretariat, like the royal families of Europe, was intricately inter-related. More recently, Louis Auchinloss in *Persons of Consequence: Queen Victoria and her Circle* (Weidenfeld and Nicolson. 1979) has also studied the role of those who help to sustain the Monarchy. Frank Hardie's *The Political Influence of Queen Victoria 1861 – 1901*, which came out in 1935, has inevitably been overtaken by modern research, but still remains a masterly survey. Theo Aronson's *Queen Victoria and the Bonapartes* gives an entertaining account of a bizarre but enduring friendship. Finally, Baron Hermann Eckardstein (Chargé d'Affaires at the German Embassy in the last years of the Queen's reign) shows in his recollections of *Ten Years at the Court of St James'* just how volatile his imperial master could be.

Books cited

I am extremely grateful to the authors and publishers of the books listed
below whose works I have quoted, and I am particularly indebted to
those marked with an asterisk for permission to make use of copyright
material.

Abbott, E. Campbell, L. The Life and Letters of Benjamin Jowett. Murray.
   2 vols. 1897.
Aga Khan. Memoirs. Cassell. 1954.
Alice, Countess of Athlone. For My Grandchildren. Evans. 1966.
Allen, C. A Glimpse of the Burning Plain. Joseph. 1986.
Allinson, R. (ed) The War Diary of the Emperor Frederick III. Stanley
   Paul. 1927.
Amery, J. The Life of Joseph Chamberlain. Macmillan. 2 vols. 1951.
Ames, W. Prince Albert and Victorian Taste. Chapman and Hall. 1967.
Anon. The Empress Frederick. J. Nisbet and Co. 1913.
Antrim, L. Recollections of Louise, Countess of Antrim. The King's Stone
   Press. 1937.
Argyll, Duke of. Autobiography. Murray. 2 vols. 1906.
Aronson, T. Grandmama of Europe. Cassell. 1973.
Aronson, T. Queen Victoria and the Bonapartes. Cassell. 1972.
Aronson, T. Victoria and Disraeli. Cassell. 1977.
Arthur, G. Not Worth Reading. Longmans. 1938.
Arthur, G. Queen Alexandra. Chapman and Hall. 1934.
Arthur, G. The Letters of Lord and Lady Wolseley. Heinemann. 1923.
Ashdowne, D. Queen Victoria's Mother. Robert Hale. 1974.
Ashwell, A. Life of Samuel Wilberforce. Murray. 1880.
Asquith, H. Memories and Recollections. Cassell. 2 vols. 1928.
Askwith, B. The Lytteltons. Chatto and Windus. 1975.

Askwith, Lord. Lord James of Hereford. Benn. 1930.

Aston, G. H.R.H. The Duke of Connaught. Harrap. 1929.

Bagehot, W. The English Constitution. Oxford University Press. 1929.

*Bahlman, D. The Diary of Sir Edward Walter Hamilton. Oxford University Press. 2 vols. 1972.

Bancroft, S. The Bancrofts. Murray. 1909.

Barkeley, R. The Empress Frederick. Macmillan. 1956.

Battiscombe, G. Queen Alexandra. Constable. 1969.

Battiscombe, G. Shaftesbury. Constable. 1974.

Beatrice, Princess. In Napoleonic Days. Murray. 1941.

Bell, G. Randall Davidson. Oxford University Press. 2 vols. 1935.

Bell, H. Lord Palmerston. Longmans. 2 vols. 1936.

Bennett, D. King Without a Crown. Heinemann. 1977.

Bennett, D. Queen Victoria's Children. Gollancz. 1980.

Bennett, D. Vicky. Collins. 1971.

Benson, A. Edward White Benson. Macmillan. 1901.

Benson, A. The Letters of Queen Victoria. First Series. Murray. 3 vols. 1907.

Benson, E. As We Were. Longmans. 1930.

Benson, E. Daughters of Queen Victoria. Cassell. 1939.

Benson, E. King Edward VII. Longmans. 1933.

Benson, E. Queen Victoria. Longmans. 1935.

Benson, E. The Kaiser and his English Relations. Longmans. 1936.

Beresford, C. The Memoirs of Admiral Lord Charles Beresford. Methuen. 2 vols. 1914.

Bing, E. The Letters of Tsar Nicholas and Empress Marie. Nicholson and Watson. 1937.

Blake, R. Disraeli. Eyre and Spottiswoode. 1966.

Bloomfield, G. Reminiscences of Court and Diplomatic Life. Kegan Paul. 2 vols. 1883.

Blunt, W. My Diaries. Secker. 1919.

Bolitho, H. Albert the Good. Cobden-Sanderson. 1932.

Bolitho, H. A Victorian Dean. Chatto and Windus. 1930.

Bolitho, H. Further Letters of Queen Victoria. Butterworth. 1938.

Bolitho, H. Letters of Lady Augusta Stanley. Howe. 1927.

Bolitho, H. Later Letters of Lady Augusta Stanley. Cape. 1929.

Bolitho, H. The Prince Consort and his Brother. Cobden- Sanderson. 1933.

Bolitho, H. The Reign of Queen Victoria. Collins. 1949.

Bolitho, H. Victoria and Albert. Cobden-Sanderson. 1938.

Bolitho, H. Victoria the Widow and her Son. Cobden-Sanderson. 1934.

Boyd Carpenter, W. Some Pages of My Life. Williams and Norgate. 1911.

*Boykin, E. Victoria, Albert and Mrs Stevenson. Muller. 1957.

Briggs, A. The Age of Improvement. Longmans. 1959.

Brodrick, G. (ed) Ecclesiastical Cases Relating to Doctrine and Discipline. Murray. 1865.

Brooks, D. The Destruction of Lord Rosebery. Historical Press. 1986.

Brown, I. Balmoral. Collins. 1955.

Buchanan, M. Queen Victoria's Relations. Cassell. 1954.

Buckle, G. (ed) The Letters of Queen Victoria. Murray. 6 vols. 1926–1932.

Bülow, Prince. Memoirs. 1897–1903. Putnam. 1931.

Bunsen, F. A Memoir of Baron Bunsen. Longmans. 2 vols. 1868.

Busch, M. Bismarck. Some Secret Pages of his History. Macmillan. 3 vols. 1898.

Cadogan, E. Before the Deluge. Murray. 1961.

Carey, A. The Empress Eugénie in Exile. Eveleigh Nash. 1922.

Carlton, C. Royal Childhoods. Routledge. 1986.

*Cecil, D. Lord M. Constable. 1954.

Cecil, G. Life of Robert Marquis of Salisbury. Hodder and Stoughton. 4 vols. 1921–1932.

Chadwick, O. The Victorian Church. Black. 2 vols. 1966.

Colson, P. Victorian Portraits. Rich and Cowan. 1932.

Connell, B. Regina v Palmerston. Evans. 1962.

Corti, E. The Downfall of Three Dynasties. Methuen. 1934.

Corti, E. The English Empress. Cassell. 1957.

Cowles, V. The Kaiser. Collins. 1963.

Creston, D. The Youthful Queen Victoria. Macmillan. 1952.

Crewe, Marquess of. Lord Rosebery. Murray. 2 vols. 1931

Cromer, Lord. Modern Egypt. Macmillan. 2 vols. 1908.

Cullen, T. The Empress Brown. Bodley Head. 1969.

Cust, L. King Edward VII and his Court. Murray. 1930.

Dance, E. The Victorian Illusion. Heinemann. 1928.

Dasent, A. John Delane. Murray. 2 vols. 1908.

Douglas, G. (ed) The Panmure Papers. Hodder and Stoughton. 2 vols. 1908.

Drew, M. Catherine Gladstone. Nisbet. 1919.

Duff, D. Albert and Victoria. Muller. 1972.

Duff, D. Hessian Tapestry. Muller. 1967.

Duff, D. The Shy Princess. Evans. 1958.

Duff, D. Victoria in the Highlands. Muller. 1968.

Duff, D. Victoria Travels. Muller. 1970.

Eckardstein, H. Ten Years at the Court of St James'. Butterworth. 1921.

Edel, L. (ed) Henry James Letters. Cambridge University Press. vol 4. 1984.

Eilers, M. Queen Victoria's Descendants. Genealogical Publishing Co. 1987.

Emden, P. Behind the Throne. Hodder and Stoughton. 1934.

Epton, N. Victoria and her Daughters. Weidenfeld and Nicolson. 1971.

Ernest II. Memoirs of Ernest II. Remington. 4 vols. 1888.

Erskine, S. (ed) Twenty Years at Court. Nisbet. 1916.

Esher, Viscount. Cloud-Capped Towers. Murray. 1927.

Esher, Viscount. The Girlhood of Queen Victoria. Murray. 2 vols. 1927.

Esher, Viscount. Journals and Letters. Ivor Nicholson and Watson. 4 vols. 1934–1938.

Esher, Viscount. The Influence of King Edward. Murray. 1915.

Eyck, F. The Prince Consort. Chatto and Windus. 1959.

Farrer, J. The Monarchy in Politics. Fisher Unwin. 1917.

Fawcett, M. Life of Her Majesty Queen Victoria. Allen. 1895.

Feuchtwanger, E. Gladstone. Allen Lane. 1975.

Field, J. Uncensored Recollections. Nash. 1924.

Field, J. More Uncensored Recollections. Nash. 1926.

Fitzmaurice, Lord. The Life of Lord Granville. Longmans. 2 vols. 1905.

Frederick III. The War Diary of Frederick III. Paul. 1927.

Fulford, R. Beloved Mama. Evans. 1981.

*Fulford, R. Darling Child. Evans. 1976.

*Fulford, R. Dearest Child. Evans. 1964.

*Fulford, R. Dearest Mama. Evans. 1968.

*Fulford, R. Hanover to Windsor. Batsford. 1960.

Fulford, R. Queen Victoria. Collins. 1951.

Fulford, R. The Prince Consort. Macmillan. 1949.

Fulford, R. The Royal Dukes. Duckworth. 1933.

*Fulford, R. Your Dear Letter. Evans. 1971.

Gash, N. Sir Robert Peel. Longman. 1972.

Gathorne Hardy, A. Gathorne Hardy. Longmans. 2 vols. 1910.

Gilbert, M. (ed) A Century of Conflict. Hamish Hamilton. 1966.

Gladstone, Visct. After Thirty Years. Macmillan. 1928.

Gladstone, W. Gleanings of Past Years. Murray. 7 vols. 1879.

Gore, J. Creevey's Life and Times. Murray. 1934.

Grey, C. The Early Years of HRH the Prince Consort. Smith Elder. 1867.

Guedalla, P. The Queen and Mr Gladstone. Hodder and Stoughton. 2 vols. 1933.

Guest, J. (ed) Essays by Divers Hands. XXXVIII. Oxford University Press. 1975.

Gwynn, S. The Life of the Rt. Hon. Sir Charles Dilke. Bart. Murray. 1917.

Hamer, F. The Personal Papers of Lord Rendell. Ernest Benn. 1931.

Hanham, J. The Nineteenth Century Constitution. Cambridge University Press. 1969

Hardie, F. The Political Influence of Queen Victoria. Oxford University Press. 1935.

Hardie, F. The Political Influence of the British Monarchy. Oxford University Press. 1970.

Hardinge, A. Life of Henry Fourth Earl of Carnarvon. Oxford University Press. 3 vols. 1925.

Hardy, A. Queen Victoria Was Amused. Murray. 1976.

Havers, M. The Royal Baccarat Scandal. Souvenir Press. 1977.

Helps, A. The Principal Speeches of the Prince Consort. Murray. 1862.

Hewett, O. "And Mr Fortescue". Murray. 1958.

Hibbert, C. The Court at Windsor. Longmans. 1964.

Hobhouse, H. Prince Albert: His Life and Work. Hamish Hamilton. 1983.

Hobhouse, T. Thomas Cubitt. Macmillan. 1971.

Hobley, L. The Monarchy. Batsford. 1972.

Hodder, E. The Life and Work of the Seventh Earl of Shaftesbury. Cassell. 3 vols. 1886.

Holland, S. Personal Studies. Wells Gardner. 1905.

*Hough, R. Advice to a Grand-daughter. Heinemann. 1975.

Hough, R. Louis and Victoria. Hutchinson. 1974.

Jagow, K. (ed) Letters of the Prince Consort. Murray. 1938.

*James, R. Albert, Prince Consort. Hamish Hamilton. 1983.

James, R. Rosebery. Weidenfeld and Nicolson. 1964.

Jenkins, R. Sir Charles Dilke. Collins. 1958.

Jennings, J. (ed) The Correspondence and Diaries of the late J.W. Croker. Murray. 3 vols. 1884.

Jerrold, C. The Married Life of Queen Victoria. Eveleigh Nash. 1913.

*Kennedy, A. My Dear Duchess. Murray. 1956.

Kinloch Cooke, C. A Memoir of H.R.H. Princess Mary Adelaide Duchess of Teck. Murray. 2 vols. 1900.

Kiste, J. Edward VII's Children. Alan Sutton. 1989.

Lang, T. My Darling Daisy. Joseph. 1966.

Lant, J. Insubstantial Pageant. Hamish Hamilton. 1979.

Lecky, W. Democracy and Liberty. Longmans. 2 vols. 1896.

Lecky, W. Historical and Political Essays. Longmans. 1908.

*Lee, A. (ed) The Empress Frederick Writes to Sophie. Faber and Faber. 1955.

Lee, S. King Edward VII. Macmillan. 2 vols. 1925–1927.

Lee, S. Queen Victoria. Smith Elder. 1902.

Lees-Milne, J. The Enigmatic Edwardian. Sidgwick and Jacobson. 1986.

Legge, E. King Edward VII in his True Colours. Nash. 1912.

Leslie, A. Edwardians in Love. Hutchinson. 1972.

Leslie, A. Jennie. Hutchinson. 1969.

Leslie, S. The Film of Memory. Joseph. 1938.

Lever, T. The Letters of Lady Palmerston. Murray. 1957.

Liddel, A. Notes from the Life of an Ordinary Mortal. Murray. 1911.

Lindsay, P. Recollections of a Royal Parish. Murray. 1902.

Lockhart, J. Cosmo Gordon Lang. Hodder and Stoughton. 1949.

Londonderry, Marchioness. Letters from Benjamin Disraeli to F.A. Marchioness of Londonderry. Macmillan. 1938.

Longford, E. Louisa Lady in Waiting. Cape. 1979.

*Longford, E. Victoria. R.I. Weidenfeld and Nicolson. 1964.

Mackenzie, M. The Fatal Illness of Frederick the Noble. Sampson Low. 1888.

Macleod, D. Memoir of Norman Macleod. Worthington. 1876.

Magnus, P. Gladstone. Murray. 1954.

Magnus, P. King Edward VII. Murray. 1964.

*Mallet, V. Life with Queen Victoria. Murray. 1968.

Marie Louise, Princess. My Memories of Six Reigns. Evans. 1956.

Marriott, J. Queen Victoria and her Ministers. Murray. 1933.

Martin, R. Enter Rumour. Faber. 1962.

Martin, T. The Life of HRH the Prince Consort. Smith Elder. 5 vols. 1874–1880.

Martin, T. Queen Victoria as I knew her. Blackwood. 1908.

Masterman, L. Mary Gladstone. Methuen. 1930.

Maxwell, H. Life and Letters of the Fourth Earl of Clarendon. Arnold. 2 vols. 1913.

Maxwell, H. The Creevey Papers. Murray. 1912.

McClintock, M. The Queen thanks Sir Howard. Murray. 1945.

Mersey, Visct. A Picture of Life. Murray. 1941.

Mitford, N. The Stanleys of Alderley. Chapman and Hall. 1939.

Monypenny, W. Buckle, E. Life of Lord Beaconsfield. Murray. 6 vols. 1910–1920.

Montgomery Hyde, H. Their Good Names. Hamish Hamilton. 1970.

Morley, J. Recollections. Macmillan. 2 vols. 1918.

Morley, J. The Life of W.E. Gladstone. Macmillan. 3 vols. 1903.

Mortimer, R. Queen Victoria. Leaves from a Journal. Deutsch. 1961.

Mullen, R. Victoria. Portrait of a Queen. B.B.C. Books. 1987.

Newsome, D. A History of Wellington College. Murray. 1959.

Newsome, D. Edwardian Excursions. Murray. 1981.

Newsome, D. On the Edge of Paradise. Murray. 1980.

Newton, Lord. Lord Lansdowne. Macmillan. 1929.

Nicolson, H. Diaries and Letters. 1945–1962. Collins. 1968.

Nicolson, H. King George the Fifth. Constable. 1952.

Paget, W. Embassies of Other Days. Hutchinson. 2 vols. 1923.

Paget, W. Scenes and Memories. Smith Elder. 1912.

Pakula, H. The Last Romantic. Simon and Schuster. 1984.

Paoli, X. My Royal Clients. Hodder and Stoughton. 1911.

Parker, C. (ed) Sir Robert Peel from his Private Papers. Murray. 3 vols. 1891–1899.

Parry, E. (ed) The Correspondence of Lord Aberdeen and Princess Lieven. Royal Historical Society. 2 vols. 1938–9.

Pearson, H. Labby. Hamish Hamilton. 1936.

Peel, C. A Hundred Wonderful Years. Lane. 1926.

Petrie, C. The Modern British Monarchy. Eyre and Spottiswoode. 1961.

Petrie, C. The Victorians. Eyre and Spottiswoode. 1960.

Pickering, A. Memoirs. Hodder and Stoughton. 1902.

Plowden, A. The Young Victoria. Weidenfeld and Nicolson. 1981.

Pollock. J. Shaftesbury. Hodder and Stoughton. 1985.

*Ponsonby, A. Henry Ponsonby. Macmillan. 1942.

Ponsonby, A. Queen Victoria. Duckworth. 1933.

Ponsonby, F. Letters of the Empress Frederick. Macmillan. 1928.

Ponsonby, F. Recollections of Three Reigns. Eyre and Spottiswoode. 1951.

Ponsonby, F. Sidelights on Queen Victoria. Macmillan. 1930.

Ponsonby, M. Mary Ponsonby. Murray. 1927.

Pope-Hennessy, J. Queen Mary. Allen and Unwin. 1959.

Pope-Hennessy, J. (ed) Queen Victoria at Windsor and Balmoral. Allen and Unwin. 1959.

Pope-Hennessy, U. Agnes Strickland. Chatto and Windus. 1940.

Pound, R. Albert. Joseph. 1973.

Prothero, R. The Life and Correspondence of A.H. Stanley. Murray. 2 vols. 1894.

Quinn, E. Dear Miss Nightingale. Oxford. 1987.

Ramm, A. (ed) Beloved and Darling Child. Sutton. 1991.

Ramm, A. (ed) The Political Correspondence of Mr Gladstone and Lord Granville. 1868–1876. Oxford University Press. 2 vols. 1952.

Ramm, A. (ed) The Political Correspondence of Mr Gladstone and Lord Granville. 1876–1886. Oxford University Press. 2 vols. 1962.

Redesdale, Lord. Memories. Hutchinson. 2 vols. 1915.

*Reid, M. Ask Sir James. Hodder and Stoughton. 1987.

Rhodes James, R. Albert, Prince Consort. Hamish Hamilton. 1983.

Ribblesdale, Lord. Impressions and Memories. Cassell. 1927.

Rich, N. (ed) The Holstein Papers. Cambridge University Press. 4 vols. 1955–1963.

Richardson, J. My Dearest Uncle. Cape. 1961.

Richardson, J. Victoria and Albert. Dent. 1977.

Robertson, J. The Royal Race. Blond and Briggs. 1977.

Rose, K. King George V. Weidenfeld and Nicolson. 1983.

Rose, K. Superior Person. Weidenfeld and Nicolson. 1969.

Rose, K. The Later Cecils. Weidenfeld and Nicolson. 1975.

Roumania, Queen of. The Story of My Life. Cassell. 3 vols. 1934.

Rowell, G. Queen Victoria goes to the Theatre. Elek. 1978.

Russell, B. (ed) The Amberley Papers. Hogarth. 2 vols. 1937.

Russell, G. Collections and Recollections. Smith Elder. 1901.

Sandford, E. (ed) Memoirs of Archbishop Temple. Macmillan. 2 vols. 1906.

Saunders, E. A Distant Summer. Sampson Low. 1946.

Sell, Dr. C. Princess Alice Grand Duchess of Hesse. Murray. 1884.

Sheppard, E. George Duke of Cambridge. Longmans. 2 vols, 1906.

Sinclair, A. The Other Victoria. Weidenfeld and Nicolson. 1981.

Smyth, E. Streaks of Life. Longmans. 1921.

Stamp, R. Royal Rebels. Durdon Press. 1988.

Stanley, A. Life and Correspondence of Thomas Arnold. Murray. 2 vols. 1844.

St Aubyn, G. Edward VII Prince and King. Collins. 1979.

St Aubyn, G. The Royal George. Constable. 1963.

Stevenson, R. Morrel Mackenzie. Heinemann. 1946.

Stockmar, E. Memoirs of Baron Stockmar. Longmans. 2 vols. 1872.

Strachey, L. Queen Victoria. Chatto and Windus. 1921.

Strachey, L. (ed) The Greville Memoirs. Macmillan. 6 vols. 1938.

Stuart, D. The Mother of Victoria. Macmillan. 1941.

Surtees, V. Charlotte Canning. Murray. 1975.

*Tennyson, C. Dear and Honoured Lady. Macmillan. 1969.

Thompson, D. Queen Victoria. Gender and Power. Virago Press. 1990.

Tingsten, H. Victoria and the Victorians. Allen and Unwin. 1972.

Tisdall, E. Queen Victoria's Private Life. Jarrolds. 1961.

Tulloch, W. The Story of the Life of Queen Victoria. Nisbet. 1897.

Varesco, H. Kings and Queens I have known. Harper. 1904.

Victoria, Queen. Leaves from the Journal of our Life in the Highlands. Smith Elder. 1868.

Victoria, Queen. More Leaves from the Journal of a Life in the Highlands. Smith Elder. 1884.

Villiers, G. A Vanished Victorian. Eyre and Spottiswoode. 1938.

*Vincent, J. Disraeli, Derby and the Conservative Party. Harvester. 1978.

Vorres, I. The Last Grand Duchess. Hutchinson. 1964.

Waddington, M. Letters of a Diplomat's Wife. Smith Elder. 1903.

Wake, J. Princess Louise. Collins. 1988.

Walpole, S. The Life of Lord John Russell. Longmans. 2 vols. 1889.

Walsh, W. The Religious Life and Influence of Queen Victoria. Swan Somnenschien. 1902.

Warner, M. Queen Victoria's Sketchbook. Macmillan. 1979.

Watson, V. A Queen at Home. Allen. 1952.

Weintraub, S. Victoria. Biography of a Queen. Unwin Hyman. 1987

Wells, H.G. Experiment in Autobiography. Gollancz. 1934.

Wemyss, R. Memoirs and Letters of Sir Robert Morier. Arnold. 2 vols. 1911.

West, A. The Private Diaries of Sir A. West. Murray. 1922.

Wheeler-Bennett, J. King George VI. Macmillan. 1958.

Whibley, C. Letters of the King of Hanover to Visct Strangford. Williams and Norgate. 1925.

Whibley, C. Lord John Manners and his Friends. Blackwood. 2 vols. 1925.

Whittle, T. Victoria and Albert at Home. Routledge. 1980.

Wilberforce, R. Life of Samuel Wilberforce. Cassell. 2 vols. 1881–1882.

William II. My Early Life. Methuen. 1926.

Wilson, J. C.B. Life of Sir Henry Campbell-Bannerman. Constable. 1973.

Wilson, M. Queen Victoria. Peter Davies. 1933.

Wintle, J. The Story of Victoria R.I. Sunday School Union. 1972

Wood, H. My Life of Music. Victor Gollancz. 1938.

Woodham-Smith, C. Florence Nightingale. Constable. 1949.

*Woodham-Smith, C. Queen Victoria. 1819–1861. Hamish Hamilton. 1972.

Wortham, H. The Delightful Profession. Cape. 1931.

Wyndham, H. (ed) Correspondence of Sarah Spencer Lady Lyttelton. Murray. 1912.

Young, K. Arthur James Balfour. Bell. 1963.

Zetland, Marquis of. The Letters of Disraeli to Lady Bradford and Lady Chesterfield. Benn. 2 vols. 1929.

Ziegler, P. Melbourne. Collins. 1976.

Index